GENDERING GLOBAL CONFLICT

Gendering Global Conflict

Toward a Feminist Theory of War

LAURA SJOBERG

Columbia University Press   *New York*

Columbia University Press
Publishers Since 1893
New York   Chichester, West Sussex
cup.columbia.edu
Copyright © 2013 Columbia University Press
All rights reserved
Library of Congress Cataloging-in-Publication Data

Sjoberg, Laura, 1979-
Gendering global conflict : toward a feminist theory of war /
Laura Sjoberg.
pages cm
Includes bibliographical references and index.
ISBN 978-0-231-14860-3 (cloth : alk. paper) — ISBN 978-0-231-14861-0
(pbk. : alk. paper) — ISBN 978-0-231-52000-3 (e-book)
1. Women and war. 2. Feminist theory. 3. International relations. I. Title.

JZ6405.W66S56 2013
303.6'601—dc23
2012050816

Columbia University Press books are printed on permanent and durable
acid-free paper.
This book is printed on paper with recycled content.
Printed in the United States of America
c 10 9 8 7 6 5 4 3 2 1
p 10 9 8 7 6 5 4 3 2 1

COVER DESIGN: Milenda Nan Ok Lee

References to websites (URLs) were accurate at the time of writing. Neither
the author nor Columbia University Press is responsible for URLs that may have
expired or changed since the manuscript was prepared.

To Ann Tickner

my role model as a scholar and a woman

and

Hayward Alker

who still challenges me

Contents

Acknowledgments

When I initially undertook writing this book, I saw it as the book that I went to graduate school to write—a sort of magnum opus—a statement on how feminism(s) think about war(s). Now that it has been written, I realize (and hope) that it brings up more questions than answers, and lays a foundation for more theoretical and empirical work. The scope of the project ended up far smaller than my initial plans and is perhaps still too ambitious. The final draft inspires reflection, debate, frustration, and rethought in me—and I hope that it will in readers.

It literally took a village to produce this book, and I am indebted to the support of more people than I can ever manage to thank. I appreciate the support and resources of the Department of Political Science at Virginia Tech, where this project began, and the Department of Political Science at the University of Florida, where it was completed. Financial support and research space for parts of this project were provided by a number of great organizations, including the Institute for Society, Culture, and the Environment at Virginia Tech, the Women and Public Policy Program at the Kennedy School of Government at Harvard University, and the Political Science Department at North Carolina State University. Without that support, this book never could have been completed.

Parts of this project were presented and invaluable feedback was received at Harvard University, North Carolina State University, the University of Florida, Wellesley College, the University of

Massachusetts–Boston, Notre Dame, the University of Minnesota, the University of Southern California, and the University of Wisconsin, as well as at annual meetings of the International Studies Association, the American Political Science Association, and those associations' regional conferences. That feedback on early drafts of this project was indispensable in shaping the book that it became. In addition, a number of people have read significant amounts of this book and provided detailed feedback. First and foremost among them is my wonderful editor at Columbia University Press, Anne Routon, who has the patience of a saint to go along with an amazing eye. Ann Tickner was my dissertation adviser a decade ago and remains a treasured mentor and friend, and her careful reading of every page of two drafts of this manuscript matters more to me than she may ever know. Even though he is not here anymore, it was Hayward Alker who gave me the path to deal with diversity, disagreement, incoherence, and argument among the feminisms in International Relations (IR) and the feminisms in my head, and Renee-Marlin Bennett who got me to listen to him. I am also grateful to a great group of feminist IR scholars who read parts of this book, including Brooke Ackerly, Carol Cohn, Catia Confortini, Nikki Detraz, Cynthia Enloe, Caron Gentry, Jen Heeg, Joyce Kaufmann, Helen Kinsella, Jenny Lobasz, Theresa Lund, Megan MacKenzie, Sandra McEvoy, Celeste Montoya, Spike Peterson, Anne Runyan, Christine Sylvester, Jacqui True, Sandy Whitworth, Lauren Wilcox, Kristen Williams, and Susan Wright. My graduate students—particularly Sandra Via, Jessica Peet, Ioannis Ziogas, and Jon Whooley—made invaluable contributions to putting this book together. Other indispensable readings came from Sammy Barkin, Amy Eckert, Harry Gould, Patrick Jackson, Pat James, Chris Marcoux, Sara Mitchell, Dan Nexon, Michael Struett, Cameron Thies, and Brandon Valeriano. Jeff Hamill literally made sense of the footnotes in this book—no small task. Alex Wendt, Duncan Snidal, and anonymous reviewers at *International Theory* helped me figure out chapter 3, after Ken Booth and anonymous reviewers at *International Relations* helped me see the importance of making the argument in IR terms. (An abbreviated version of chapter 3 first was first published as "What Waltz Couldn't See: Gender, Structure, and War," *International Theory* [2012], 4[1]: 1–38.) Also, over countless drafts, a number of anonymous reviewers provided incredibly helpful feedback. Of course, all mistakes remain my own.

This great support community made it possible for me to do a lot of the work for this book in rough times, personally and professionally. Over that (long) time, I have found multiple sources of strength and energy to work: the Study of the United States Institute Participants, the UF Mock Trial LitiGators, the Gainesville Bridge Club, and the sushi (with avocado and mango) from Dragonfly. My three Chihuahuas provided a sense of calm as I worked in tumultuous times. April, my oldest, makes war first and thinks second. Gizmo, the "middle child," continually teaches me about how those who have lost the fight for dominance can still live a happy and fulfilling life. Max, the puppy, shows me daily that even the most aggressive actors have a soft side.

Those who have read my other acknowledgments know that I tend to end them with a story that inspired the work in this book and my research program in feminist international relations. This inspiration came a couple of years ago now, but it was important in getting this book finished. Having submitted an application for employment to a certain (acquaintance) faculty member's university, I ran into him at a conference. He told me that, no offense, his department would not be hiring me. After I did not answer, he volunteered an explanation. It turned out that, while my publication record was "superb," his department would be hiring someone who worked in a credible area of political science. He then asked if I had given any thought to "getting over" my "gender phase." I did not say anything to him, hoping that this book (when it came out) would effectively communicate the message: No.

GENDERING GLOBAL CONFLICT

Introduction

In 1910, Norman Angell instructed political leaders that, in a world of increasing economic interdependence, war could never "avail us anything" and that, therefore, any state that made war would be foolishly casting aside its self-interest.[1] A few years later, World War I resulted in an unprecedented level of human casualties and economic devastation. When the United States joined the war, then-President Woodrow Wilson famously declared World War I the "war to end all wars."[2] In the interwar period, Lewis Mumford explained that "misery, mutilation, destruction, starvation and death characterize the process of war and form a principle part of the product."[3] In 1928, the signing by sixty-two nations of the Kellogg-Briand Pact, in which states forged an agreement "providing for the renunciation of war as an instrument of national policy," cemented this sentiment.[4] A little over a decade later, World War II caused the deaths of almost fifty million people.[5]

Some scholars argue that war is (again) declining in the twenty-first century,[6] but others note that wars remain a consistent and cyclical feature of global politics.[7] Whatever our view of the frequency of war, the scholarly community in international relations (IR) and security studies has been always interested in why, given its terrible consequences, states and other actors in global politics continue to initiate wars. Though the "war puzzle" has attracted much scholarly attention, one leading commentator lamented that "much has been written about the causes of war; little has been learned about the subject."[8]

This commentator did not mean to imply that scholars had failed to produce explanations for wars. Scholarship on the meaning, causes, and consequences of war in political science is, in fact, very diverse, emphasizing different causal factors and different levels of analysis[9] and drawing evidence from different eras in history. The phenomenon of war has been studied through the lenses of a number of theoretical approaches to global politics, including, but not limited to, realism, liberalism, and constructivism.[10]

Still, no single theory of what wars are and why they happen has become dominant. As Hidemi Suganami explains, this may be because "war is a multi-causal phenomenon, not only in the oft-noted sense that a variety of factors contribute to the making of war, but also in the less obvious sense that there are multifarious causal paths to war."[11] Perhaps scholars can agree that war's meaning and causes are complex, and its consequences often brutal. Still, most theoretical approaches to the study of war remain widely divergent and find little common ground.

Despite our collective inability to find a consensus framework to understand or disaggregate war causation, wars continue to plague global politics. It is estimated that war caused more than two hundred million deaths in the twentieth century,[12] and conflicts rage around the world in the early twenty-first century. The financial costs and human casualties of war have been of increasing concern to scholars and policy makers; the war puzzle is both as urgent and as puzzling now as it has ever been.

GENDER AND THE WAR PUZZLE

Several scholars have proposed pieces of, or solutions to, the war puzzle. Scholars from the realist tradition have looked to the influence of international anarchy, shifts of power between states, technological advances that favor either offensive or defensive strategies, and alliances and/or power balancing.[13] Scholars from the liberal tradition have suggested that state regime type, domestic politics, trading interdependence, and bargaining are key predictors of propensities for war.[14] Constructivist scholars (and others) have suggested that cultural differences, state learning, nationalism, or the salience of norms are important variables in the choice and duration of wars.[15] While these theoretical approaches suggest different, and important, pieces of the war puzzle, traditional work on the nature, causes, and consequences of war individually and collectively omits gender analysis.[16] In fact, the great majority of studies seeking constitutive understandings of or causal explanations for war do not consider gender or gender subordination as potential causes or elements of war.[17]

This book argues that this omission is a grave error, because the meanings, causes, and consequences of war cannot be understood without reference to gender. Using gender as a category of analysis transforms the study of war.[18] As scholars fit together pieces of the war puzzle, the missing pieces become more visible, and gender is among them. The feminist tradition in IR[19] has demonstrated that the theory and practice of war have been gendered throughout modern history and that gendered elements are important causal and constitutive factors.[20] Feminists have tried to communicate to the discipline that the gender "neutrality" of its work masks gender subordination rather than magically producing gender equality.[21] Feminist work has redefined core concepts of security, observed new empirical phenomena, and provided important accounts of specific conflicts and security dilemmas.[22] This book aims to extend those critiques and reformulations to argue that war cannot be understood without the use of gender as a primary analytical category—that a specifically feminist approach to the study of war is crucial to learning more about the war puzzle.[23]

While feminists in IR have done important work on gender and security that undoubtedly contributes to this puzzle, epistemological, ontological, and methodological barriers have often prevented this work from attracting a "mainstream" audience in the discipline or the attention of the policy world.[24] Critics of feminist work in the security realm have argued that feminist scholarship has yet to produce a theory of war on par with those of the realist and liberal paradigms in IR, with causal and constitutive elements.[25] They further insist that those who suggest the analytical importance of gender in IR have yet to systematically address the empirical observations that other paradigmatic approaches rely on as data to support their views or to bring new empirical evidence to bear. This criticism is in part a miscommunication, but in part an accurate account of feminist theory's reluctance to engage mainstream accounts of the meanings, causes, and consequences of war.[26]

In answer to that criticism, and in an attempt to reveal and analyze gender as a crucial piece of the war puzzle, this book engages feminist war theorizing.

A FEMINIST APPROACH TO THE STUDY OF WAR

It is important, at the outset, to outline what a specifically feminist approach to war might entail. First, it is necessary to note that there is not one feminist approach to IR theory and therefore not one feminist approach to war.[27] Instead, like other IR theorists, feminists can approach global politics from realist, liberal, constructivist, critical, poststructural, and postcolonial perspectives (among others). These perspectives yield different, and sometimes contradictory, insights about and predictions for global politics. This diversity, however, is a feature of all the major research programs in IR.[28]

Feminist work from a realist perspective is interested in the role of gender in strategy and power politics between states.[29] Liberal feminist work calls attention to the subordinate position of women in global politics but remains committed to investigating the causes of this subordination, using the epistemological, ontological, and methodological assumptions of traditional IR theory.[30] Critical feminism explores the ideational and material manifestations of gendered identity and gendered power in world politics.[31] Feminist constructivism focuses on the ways that ideas about gender shape and are shaped by global politics.[32] Feminist poststructuralism focuses on how gendered linguistic manifestations of meaning, particularly strong/weak, rational/emotional, and public/private dichotomies, serve to empower the masculine and marginalize the feminine.[33] Postcolonial feminists, while sharing many of the epistemological assumptions of poststructural feminists, focus on the ways that colonial relations of domination and subordination established under imperialism are reflected in gender relations, even in relations between feminists.[34]

Many (if not most) feminist studies express epistemological and normative preference for a particular approach. I choose not to do so.[35] Instead of referring to feminism in the singular, I refer to *feminisms* as a plural group, acknowledging "difference, disagreement, and dissonance

among feminisms" but understanding them as "important contribu-
tors to a dialogue mutually interested in gender emancipation."[36] In so
doing, I make the epistemological and methodological choice to present feminisms as an argument productive of a paradigmatic approach to
theorizing wars rather than a singular, coherent whole.[37] Using diverse
feminisms, I propose "a" feminist approach to war, which engages these
feminisms in dialogue with one another and with war analyses that
have omitted gender. This dialogical approach brings multiple feminist
voices to bear on the question of theorizing war, which separately and
together constitute feminist theorizing of war and war(s).[38]

These various feminist approaches to IR share an interest in studying
gender subordination in global politics. Defining gender, however, presents another challenge. Gender is not a box that we check on our taxes
or membership in the traditional biological sex categories, male and
female.[39] While sex categorization is a part of gender analysis, gender
is often described as a social construct,[40] an institutionalized entity or
artifact in a social system invented or constructed by a particular culture
or society that exists because people agree to behave as if it exists or to
follow certain conventional rules.[41] Gender is the socially constructed
expectation that persons perceived to be members of a biological sex
category will have certain characteristics. The social construction of
gender is complex and intersubjective.[42] It is complex because gendering is not static or universal, but relational and changing. Gender can
be constructed differently across time, place, and culture—interacting
with other factors to produce social and political relations while being
produced by them. Gender is, as R.W. Connell explained, both product and producer of history.[43] It is intersubjective because genderings,
while diverse, constitute a shared cognition and consensus essential in
shaping our ideas and relationships, even when we are unaware of their
role in our thoughts, behaviors, and actions.

I point out the intersubjectivity of gendering to note that gender is
not any less "real" because it is a social construction. Genders are lived
in daily lives and global politics. Further, gender is not merely derived
difference, but derived inequality.[44] The perceived differences between
those understood as male and those understood as female create a self-
reinforcing inequality of power both between persons assigned to and
characteristics associated with these groups. In social life and in global

politics, men and characteristics associated with masculinity are valued above women and characteristics associated with femininity. Connell describes this difference in the value of gender-associated characteristics in terms of the dominance of an ideal type of hegemonic masculinity in social and political life, to which all other masculinities should aspire, and of which femininities will, by definition, fall short.[45] This relationship between masculinities and femininities constitutes and is constituted by gender subordination in global politics.

Using this understanding of gender, the feminist approach to war in this book combines the tools of realist (power relations), liberal (looking for women), critical/constructivist (the influence of gender as an idea), poststructuralist (discourses of gender), and postcolonial (the intersection of gender/race/imperialism) feminisms in order to analyze the meanings, causes, and consequences of war. It is easiest here to think of gender as a lens through which the phenomenon of war is studied.[46] All scholarship has a lens, or a focus, that foregrounds some concerns while backgrounding others in order to make the subject matter conceptually viable and empirically limited. A gender lens foregrounds issues of gender, starting with those questions as a way to evaluate the subject matter (here, war) more broadly. Jill Steans describes some of the work that gender lenses do, where "to look at the world through gender lenses is to focus on gender as a particular kind of power relation, or to trace out the ways in which gender is central to understanding international processes."[47] Through gender lenses, then, feminisms' approaches to global politics highlight gendered power, gendered experiences, gendered knowledge, and gendered values. Feminist scholars argue that, though most of everyday global politics lays a self-conscious claim to gender neutrality, in reality, genderings saturate every level of global politics. This book argues that war is constituted by and constitutes gender and that gendering is a key cause of war, as well as a key impact.[48]

FEMINISMS EVALUATE WAR

A quick glance at the stories on war and militarism in the news in early 2012 shows the need to look through gender lenses to understand these phenomena. On 17 December 2011, Private First Class Bradley Manning of the United States Army defended himself from charges of espionage on the basis of his gender identity disorder.[49] His lawyers contended that he could not control his behavior since he thought he might be a (wo)man and implied that inability to determine one's gender identity is a sign of serious disturbance.[50] On 27 December 2011, Lyric Hale argued in a *Huffington Post* editorial that brutal images of women being abused in Egypt and Bahrain are likely to influence Americans' willingness to fight Iran.[51] On 14 January 2012, the *New York Times* featured a story about a political conflict over a woman's immodesty—between ultra-Orthodox Jews and other Israelis—risks Israel's position vis-à-vis its Arab opponents.[52] All of these stories implicate gender in the causes and consequences of conflict.

Looking at war through gendered lenses demonstrates that it is inappropriate to define, analyze, or explain war without reference to gender and gender subordination. Because of their omission of gender, many current theoretical approaches to war have inadequately conceptualized what counts as a war, who actors are in war, and the gendered values reflected in the making and fighting of wars. Gender is conceptually necessary for defining security and war, important in analyzing causes and predicting outcomes, and essential to solutions to violent conflict in global politics.

Gender lenses suggest a group of causal variables in war decision-making that enrich current understandings, including structural gender inequality, a cycle of gendered violence, state masculine posturing, the (often ignored) influence of emotion in political interactions, a gendered understanding of power, and states' mistaken understandings of their own autonomy and unitary nature. Gender lenses also point out that war reaches into places it is rarely if ever evaluated—such as the workplace, the household, and even the bedroom. Gender lenses reapproach, redefine, reevaluate, and reintroduce the war puzzle in IR.

The feminist theoretical approach to war in this book proposes that war is productive of and reflective of gender norms in global politics, gender-based causal variables are required to understand war-making and war-fighting, and the consequences of war can be understood along gender lines. Accordingly, the book includes four major topics: discussions of the causes of war(s), discussions of the practice of war-making, discussions of the experiences of war(s), and discussions of the meaning of war itself.

Chapter 1, "The (Genderless) Study of War in IR," starts this work. This chapter begins the book with a critical review of current approaches to the war puzzle in IR. It points out the systemic omission of gender in "mainstream" security studies, despite the persistent presence of women and gender in war-making and war-fighting. It sets the stage for the categorical approaches to the causes and practices of war(s) that come later in the book's analysis, including systemic, dyadic, state-level, and individual approaches to theorizing wars' causes, and strategic, tactical, and logistical elements of the practice of war(s). It concludes by pointing out the systematic exclusion of gender(s) from these theories and the explanatory, predictive, prescriptive, and normative perils of such an omission.

The critique of current studies of war found in chapter 1 is followed by chapter 2, "Gender Lenses Look at War(s)," which identifies what is "feminist" about feminist theorizing of war. After extending this introduction's discussion of diversity among feminisms and addressing various strategies for dealing with that diversity, chapter 2 discusses in depth the dialogical approach to theorizing war from a feminist perspective employed in this book. The chapter concludes by engaging in a substantive and methodological journey from feminist security studies[53] to feminist war theorizing.

The theoretical foundations from chapter 2 inform the analyses of the causes of war(s) that follow. This book deals with causal mechanisms that may factor into the occurrence (or nonoccurrence) of war(s), including traditionally recognized factors such as relative power, regime type, domestic politics, balancing, state satisfaction, and culture clash, as well as factors that gendered lenses suggest. Organized by "level of analysis,"[54] these chapters engage traditional theories of war(s) through gendered lenses, looking for alternative accounts, questioning traditional boundaries and organization(s), and suggesting critical, reformulative, and transformative contributions of feminist evaluations.

Chapter 3, "Anarchy, Structure, Gender, and War(s)," begins this work with a feminist analysis of structural accounts of the causes of war generally and wars specifically. This chapter focuses on exploring the relevance of gender to understanding the general causes of war, or, in Kenneth Waltz's terms, "third-image"/international system structural analysis.[55] With reference to the work in feminist sociology on gendered organizations and cultures, this chapter sketches an approach to theorizing international system structure through gendered lenses. It is followed by a section that makes an initial plausibility case for the argument that the international system structure is gender hierarchical, focusing on its influence on unit (state) function, the distribution of capabilities among units, and the political processes governing unit interaction. It then outlines the implications of an account of the international system as gender hierarchical for theorizing the causes of war generally and wars specifically, focusing on some places where the Waltzian account of international structure and my own feminist account might predict different outcomes in the making and fighting of wars. The chapter concludes by discussing the potential significance of theorizing gender from a structural perspective and of theorizing structure through gendered lenses.

Chapter 4, "Relations International and War(s),"[56] discusses feminist (actual and potential) engagements with dyadic-level accounts of war that focus both on shared properties of states (like democracy and capitalism) and/or on the process of state interaction (like steps to war, rivalries, and bargaining). It contends that gender lenses demonstrate that these approaches take insufficient account of relations between states and often hold narrow and incomplete understandings of the components of states' relationships. It outlines an approach to studying war at the dyadic level based on viewing "relations international" through gendered lenses, which it argues is normatively profitable and empirically advantageous for war theorizing.

Chapter 5, "Gender, States, and War(s)," moves from engaging with dyadic-level explanations of war(s) to state-level explanations of war, which focus on rivalries,[57] "steps to war,"[58] trading habits,[59] bargaining,[60] class politics,[61] coalitions,[62] diversions,[63] and culture.[64] The first section engages with theories that pair domestic gender equality and the likelihood to go to war, arguing that feminisms have more to contribute to state-level war theorizing than gender essentialism. A second section looks to gendered state identities to explain likelihood of making wars. Engaging with theories of diversion and coalition politics, this chapter argues that gender is often used instrumentally in domestic justificatory discourses of the making and fighting of war(s) and that gendered nationalisms both actually motivate state war choices and are used to manipulate in-state coalitions even when they do not change states' outward war policy choices. Engaging with domestic politics and culture explanations, the chapter discusses states' strategic cultures of hegemonic masculinities as a potential factor accounting for their likelihood to make wars, both generally and in a particular context. The chapter concludes by summarizing potential contributions of feminism(s) to studying state-level causes of war(s).[65]

Chapter 6, "People, Choices, and War(s)," engages individual influence, leadership, and decision-making theories of wars' causes. This chapter argues that gender permeates every level of how "people" impact the causes of and paths to war(s), including, but not limited to, demonstrating the false nature of the "personal/international" dichotomy, interrogating inherited notions of decision-making processes, and reframing how we think about leadership and how it influences war. It begins with a section on gender, leadership, and the causes of war(s), which leads to a section that considers critically feminist empirical research that betrays the oversimplicity and falseness of the personal/international dichotomy. A third section engages approaches to people in war(s) from various critical security approaches. A fourth section, acknowledging the personal as international and the international as personal,[66] considers war decision-making as relationally autonomous. The text draws from feminist political theory approaches to agency and interdependence, arguing that individual-based theories of war(s), as they are currently conceptualized, have an inappropriate understanding of what individuals are, how they make their decisions, and what happens as a result of those decisions, owing to the omission of gender analysis from their characterizations. The chapter concludes by exploring the potential contributions of a feminist "first-image" research program on war.

The book then moves to discuss the potential contributions of gender analysis to theorizing the practices of war(s) by examining warfighting through gendered lenses. According to Clausewitz, strategy, tactics, and logistics are the three major parts of the fighting of a war, or arts of warfare.[67] Strategy is the plan of how to fight a war. Chapter 7, "Gendered Strategy," includes evaluation of the theory and practice of strategy from a gendered perspective. It argues that the strategic choices that belligerents make are guided by their gendered understandings of their society and their opponents, and critiques strategic thought and strategic analysis through gender lenses. It then argues that two strategies—intentional civilian victimization and the deployment of private military and security companies (PMSCs)—cannot be understood causally or constitutionally without reference to gender, and goes on to argue that strategic choice more generally *is* gendered, with each conflict strategy, from economic coercion to infrastructural attacks to aerial bombing, displaying gendered elements and gender-differential impacts, which this chapter explores. It argues that both sex (framed as "biomechanics") and gender (in terms of gendered nationalisms) play a role in strategic choice, and concludes by discussing the potential contributions of a feminist research program on strategy.

Tactics are the methods by which belligerents engage and attempt to defeat their enemies. Chapter 8, "Gendered Tactics," looks at war tactics and logistics through gendered lenses. It starts at the obvious gendered tactics of war-fighting, including wartime rape and forced impregnation. It then moves on to argue that the gendered nature of tactics can be seen across all tactics, not just those tactics obviously aimed at women. A third section discussing *women* as weapons of war on a tactical level leads into a fourth section dealing with feminization as a tactic both between states and at the military level. The chapter then argues that the surface-level gendering of tactics is just that—only the surface level—and that one of the key genderings of war(s) at the tactical level is actually logistical—that gendered political economies and humanitarian consequences are inexorably linked to military movement and the wartime maintenance of fighting forces. The chapter concludes with a discussion of the potential contributions of a feminist research on tactics and logistics.

Chapter 9 moves from the practice of war(s) to the experience of war. Rather than accounting for the impacts of war(s) without acknowledging there are people who experience them, this chapter examines gendered lives in war(s) and the gendered experiences of war(s). It argues that the gendered role expectations for individuals in war are a linchpin in supporting the making and fighting of wars and that the gendered impacts of wars show that gender subordination is alive and well, even in a world that claims to value gender equality and gender mainstreaming, especially in times of war and violence. The first section uses personal narratives to explore the gendered experiences of gendered wars. The chapter then looks at gendered political economies of/in war(s) and the ways that conflicts and gender subordination support and reinforce each other in people's economic and social experiences of everyday life during conflicts and after they have (supposedly) ended. A third section explores the gendered consequences of war(s) and militarism(s) for men, not just women—arguing that wars' subordinating gendered impacts and implications touch more than women's bodies and lives. A fourth section discusses war as sensed/sensual, arguing that an emotional/felt element of war's impacts is missing from war studies literatures, even when they give attention to human rights or civilian casualties. The chapter concludes by theorizing what war would mean if it were theorized as experienced and explores the potential contributions of a feminist research program on war as experienced.

The concluding chapter, "(A) Feminist Theory/ies of War(s)," gathers feminist insights from each chapter and, with their help, proposes a feminist theory of the meaning, causes, fighting, and consequences of war. I argue that, through gender lenses, feminists can provide war theorists a marked increase in the definitional clarity and explanatory value of their theoretical insights. Additionally, and perhaps more valuably, feminist theory provides not only a missing piece to the war puzzle theoretically, but insight into addressing the war problem practically and normatively in global politics. I propose that a feminist theory of war could usefully be considered alongside, and as transformative of, other paradigmatic approaches to the study of armed conflict.

CHAPTER 1

The (Genderless) Study of War in International Relations

The observation quoted in the introduction that "much has been writ-ten about the causes of war; little has been learned about the subject,"[1] tells its readers something important about the study of war; perhaps even something more important than its author meant when he wrote it. In *The War Puzzle*, John Vasquez explored a number of important and previously neglected hypotheses about war.[2] In revisiting *The War Puzzle* more than a decade later, Vasquez notes that recent literature has contributed substantially to addressing these and other crucial variables and has accordingly increased the discipline's explanatory leverage on war.[3] Still, most work in war studies continues to assume the irrele-vance of gender, which has rarely been taken seriously as constitutive or explanatory of the making and fighting of wars.[4]

This may be because, as feminist scholars have observed, gender is often invisible to scholars of global politics, despite its importance in shaping concepts and processes in the global political arena. As Kim-berly Hutchings explains, "a key reason for the ongoing invisibility of women and gender in the theoretical frames through which post–Cold War international politics is grasped is the legitimizing function of mas-culinity discourses within these theories."[5] In contrast to the conven-tional wisdom, this book argues that gender is *essential* to studying war.[6] This is because "the resilience of masculinity as a mode of making sense of global politics reflects the amount of analytics and normative work it accomplishes."[7] Gender, then, is not just *in* war and/or our theories of it, but fundamental to them, legitimating of them, and inseparable from them. Therefore, we have "learned little" about war until we learn about war and gender.[8]

This book makes the case that gender can link together scholarship on the meaning, causes, and consequences of war that emphasizes different causal factors, different levels of analysis, and different eras in history by showing the continuity of gender's influence as a variable, as a constitutive force, and as an analytic category. Seeing gender in war would help us know war better. The first step in making this argument is to discuss the study of war as it currently is. This chapter, therefore, presents a critical review of current approaches to the "war puzzle" in international relations (IR), pointing out the systematic omission of gender in each theoretical perspective, despite its conceptual and empirical relevance to the issues each theory discusses. The theoretical perspectives laid out in this chapter will serve as the basis for the feminist engagements with, as well as critiques, reformulations, rebuttals, and rebuildings of, war studies throughout the rest of this book.

A literature review that demonstrates the omission of gender does only that, however. Critics of feminist work in IR have often argued that is a trivial observation and pressed questions such as—So what do we do now? And why does it matter? Assuming that gender *is omitted* and *does matter*, what transformations of the current orthodoxy on war could be envisioned? After all, the (genderless) study of war in IR often reflects the "real world," which is "primarily engaged by men, and governed by the norms of masculinity," while appearing gender neutral.[9] Rather than demonstrating war theories' omission of gender for its own sake, this book argues that the omission of gender means that these theories, individually and collectively, neglect important parts of the story of the causes, fighting, and experience of war(s).

It is with these goals in mind that this chapter discusses current "mainstream" scholarship in "war studies" defining war, understanding the causes of war, and analyzing the fighting of war(s), as well as the contributions of critical approaches to theorizing war(s). The closing section of this chapter links to the next, by relating the war studies literature's gender blindness to silences and misconceptions in its theoretical and empirical work on the nature of war.

WAR STUDIES[10]

The question of what is in a name is an important one. I call war studies what many (especially in the United States) call security studies. This is not a coincidence. Though war studies is a term more frequently used in the United Kingdom and Europe, in the United States, many scholars equate the study of war and the study of security. While the two are intrinsically interlinked (war impacts security, which in turn impacts war), the narrow study of war is not the same as the broad study of security.[11] I, therefore, use the term *war studies* to signify that, though concerns outside "war" proper (whatever that is) are relevant, the literature addressing (the nature, causes, and consequences of) war specifically will be the main target of engagement in this discussion (and in the book more broadly).[12]

As I mentioned in the introduction, the literature on the nature, causes, and consequences of war is vast, but diverse and without a sense of consensus. In this literature, "scholars disagree not only on the specific causes of war, but also on how to approach the study of war."[13] Evaluations of war are divided on paradigmatic,[14] disciplinary,[15] and geographic[16] lines, and different sorts of wars are often studied differently (e.g., great power wars, interstate wars, intrastate wars, and irregular wars).[17] Recently, Jack Levy and William Thompson tried to find a unified definition of war, seeing it as "sustained, coordinated violence between political organizations,"[18] but that definition is as vague as it is controversial.[19] Still, in Cynthia Enloe's terms, "making feminist sense"[20] of war studies requires *making sense of* war studies, which the remainder of this section tries to do. Following Levy and Thompson,[21] I do so by discussing different broad approaches to the study of war(s) by their commonalities. The rest of this section discusses traditional approaches to defining war, explaining war, and understanding war-fighting.

Defining War

Levy and Thompson discuss the definition of war at length in *The Causes of War*.[22] In their account, there are a number of elements of war definitions common to most of the war studies literature; these elements are a good starting point for thinking about how war has been traditionally defined. First, war is *violent*, where violence is understood as "the use of force to kill and injure people and destroy military and economic resources."[23] Since Carl von Clausewitz noted that this violence had "no logical limit," many scholars have understood war as not only violent, but violent with a magnitude different than what we might consider everyday violence.[24]

It is also commonly understood that wars are between two or more political groups. Levy and Thompson distinguish two important features of this sentence—"between" and "political groups."[25] *Between*, in war studies' understanding, means that there must be two parties fighting—not just one party that attacks and another party that concedes. In these terms, then, invasions that are not militarily resisted are not wars while invasions that are militarily resisted are wars. The second important feature of this part of the definition is that wars are fought by *political groups* (as opposed to individuals). While individuals fight in wars, the actors of those wars are the political groups on whose behalf those individuals fight. Therefore, I (Laura Sjoberg) cannot make a war; but "my" state (the United States) can make a war, which I can participate in (or not) on its behalf.

Most work on war very recently saw war as only between states.[26] Contemporary work, though, has recognized that many wars occur within states or across states rather than between them.[27] This realization has been coupled with historical research demonstrating that the idea of the modern nation-state is very new, and most events we call wars across history were not fought by discretely identifiable nation-states against one another.[28] As a result, there has been a gradual broadening of the political groups capable of fighting wars in the war studies literature.[29] Still, the scope of what actors are included in those capable of fighting wars and what actors fall outside is less than clear.

Inherent in the idea that it is political groups who fight wars is the understanding that war is inherently political. This idea was initially articulated by Clausewitz, who called war "politics by other means."[30] Levy and Thompson quote Frederick the Great arguing that "diplomacy without force is like music without instruments," implying that the use of force is the natural extension of politics and political negotiation—and ever-present even in successful peaceful negotiations.[31] What causes count in this politics, and what causes are primary, however, remain a subject of significant debate. Some talk about the politics of war(s) in terms of interests, others in terms of resources, and still others in terms of relative power.[32]

The final element of the definition that Levy and Thompson supply that bears mention is the idea that war is *sustained*—that is, that it needs to be differentiated from "organized violence that is more limited in magnitude or impact."[33] Both scholarly writing on and data sets operationalizing war usually read "sustained" in terms of a particular number of battle deaths[34] or formal declarations of war.[35] Still, the number of battle deaths and/or the form of declaration remain up for debate.

Defining war is usually associated with identifying wars. By most accounts, wars have been a fairly consistent feature of human history. However consistent the presence of war is, its practice has changed significantly over time and is constantly evolving.[36] Those looking at the trends in war see several: battle-related deaths per war are increasing;[37] the number and frequency of wars between "great powers" is declining, while the number and frequency of wars generally is increasing;[38] the epicenter for war(s) is shifting outside of Europe;[39] and war is increasingly "asymmetric."[40] This has led to a significant literature on "new wars"[41] that attempts to understand what war has become or is becoming.

Understanding the Causes of War(s)

Despite some definitional uncertainty about what war is, many war studies scholars focus on what causes wars to happen. There are number of different approaches to studying what causes war generally and what causes individual wars. This section discusses them briefly, disaggregating them by the level of analysis to look at system-level, dyadic-level, state-level, and individual-level explanations for war and wars. While this organization is not the only one available,[42] I use it because it is a good way to think about a significant amount of material (and links between that material) relatively parsimoniously.

System-Level Theories of War[43]

Much of the system-level theoretical work in war studies falls within the realist paradigm—though there are many realisms to consider. Realist system-level theories attribute their historical development to classical realism, and the work of theorists like Thucydides, Machiavelli, and Hobbes, as well as the (more recent) work of theorists like E. H. Carr and Hans Morgenthau.[44]

Realisms, for the most part, share the ideas that "the key actors in world politics are sovereign states (or other territorially defined groups) that act rationally to advance their security, power, and wealth in an anarchic international system."[45] The consequences of international anarchy are front and center in realist theories, which see this anarchy as inducing "insecurity and a continuous competition for power, which makes the international system inherently conflictual."[46] This can cause war two ways: deliberately and inadvertently. In the deliberate form, "two states have a direct conflict of interests and at least one decides that it is more likely to achieve its interests by military force than by negotiated settlement."[47] Inadvertently, "states that are content with the status quo" and "more interested in maintaining their current positions than in extending their influence" can end up pursuing conflicts "neither side wants or expects" because of the "fear that others might engage in predatory behavior."[48]

Within this broad framework, there are a number of different streams of realist approaches to the study of war(s). Classical realism(s) generally emphasize the role of human nature in the causes of conflicts (in which the world resembles the Hobbesian state of nature, because human nature is intrinsically evil, and that makes life [infamously] "nasty, brutish, and short"[49]). Kenneth Waltz, in developing neorealism(s), was interested in explaining war structurally, rather than by what he saw as the moving target of human nature.[50] Neorealism(s) account[s] for war (not wars)[51] by the competition between actors/states imposed by the unpredictability of others' behaviors in anarchy.[52] The many varieties of neorealisms are the current "state of the art" in system-level theorizing of war.[53]

One variety is known as "defensive" realism. Defensive realists see the anarchic structure of the international system as creating potential security threats, but argue that these potential security threats only materialize when there are states that seek expansion, since states only seeking security and survival have no motivation to start aggressive wars.[54] Defensive realists are often interested, therefore, not only in power generally, but in power as (offensive) military capability. Unlike some realists, though, defensive realists need (and are interested in) domestic-level[55] variables, such as malevolent leaders, hostile regimes, and broken links in decision-making processes.[56]

On the other hand, offensive realists see system-level variables, rather than domestic-level variables, as responsible for the predatory tendencies of states and other actors in the international system.[57] They argue that "the international system is so hostile and unforgiving that uncertainty about the future intentions of the adversary combined with extreme worst-case analysis lead even status quo-oriented states to adopt offensive strategies."[58] Offensive realists contend that aggression is sometimes a good strategy for states and have suggested states seek (regional or global) hegemony to find security.[59] Offensive realism is one of the few strictly structural theories of global politics.[60]

Other realisms, however, are concerned with the lack of construction that the structural realisms pay to both the influence of and the potential to influence variables at the domestic level. Recently, neoclassical realists[61] have maintained structural neorealism's causal focus on the international system's anarchic structure but have given attention to the ways structural constraints and/or opportunities are imperfectly transmitted to and/or manifested in the foreign policy behaviors of states and decisions of state leaders. Neoclassical realists add questions of leaders' perceptions and misperceptions of relative power, bargaining processes, and interest groups to the research interest of structural theory.[62]

Among realisms, a number of other theoretical approaches to war interact and overlap with classical, offensive, defensive, and neoclassical realisms. Balance of power theory is one of the key contributions structural realisms have made to the study of war.[63] While different theorists mean different things by "power" and see it as "balanced" by different criteria,[64] many see power-balancing as a key strategy of states and/or a key feature of a peaceful international system. Early balance of power theorists discussed it as a desirable arrangement, arguing that "the balance of power is an arrangement of affairs such that no State shall be in a position to have absolute mastery and dominate over others."[65] Many balance of power theorists are interested in how states seek balances of power, using concepts such as internal balancing (buildup of domestic military, economic, or industrial power) and external balancing (the formation of counterbalancing alliances against an aggressor or potential aggressor).[66]

Other theoretical approaches are interested in the implications of and desirability of hegemonic international orders in the face of systemic anarchy. Power transition theorists[67] argue that hegemonic (rather than multipolar or balanced) systemic orders are desirable, and that the biggest risk to the stability of the international system comes not in times of hegemony but in times of transition between hegemonies.[68] When the rising hegemon is "satisfied" with the existing international order, the transition between hegemonies is likely to be peaceful; when they are "unsatisfied," the transition between hegemonies is likely to lead to war.[69]

Though most system-level theories of war revolve around realist suppositions about anarchy and relative power, there are several exceptions. David Lake and others classifiable as liberal systems theorists see states as units, each operating as "a firm producing security" that makes decisions about how to relate to other "firms" to best "manufacture security" on the basis of expected costs of opportunism and governance, both (inversely) reliant on relational hierarchy.[70] Such scholars see the system as key to studying war, but contend that changes in what can be described as firm management strategy can lead to changes *of* the system, rather than just changes *in* the system.[71]

Outside of realisms and liberalisms, two other long-standing system-level approaches to war also merit mention: long-cycle theories and world-systems theories. Long-cycle theories of war see global wars as lengthy periods of crisis and conflict (typically spanning two or three decades in a century) that are infrequent, but increasing in intensity,[72] with cycles of global (economic) contraction and regional (economic) emergence responsible for the evolution of large-scale conflicts.[73] World-systems theories are structural Marxist approaches to the way the international system works, focusing on the relationships between the core and the periphery in global politics.[74]

Dyadic-Level Theories of Wars[75]

Some scholars accept the realist assumption that the international system has an anarchical structure, but doubt that it is a determinant of war; others see the international system as something other than anarchical. Both of these theoretical inclinations lead some scholars to be interested in the causes of war that lie between states (called *dyadic* to reference the two primary states in any given war).[76] Dyadic theories of war, mostly (loosely) within liberal approaches IR theory, postulate that the primary causes of war(s) are among the war-fighting parties. There are a number of factors that different dyadic theories of war see as primary in triggering conflict, including rivalry, regime type, and economic interaction.[77]

Scholars who see rivalries as a key cause of war[78] note that "the historical pattern of warfare is such that, at any given point in time, most states are not involved in war . . . there is a relatively small group of states that go to war and often do so repetitively with the same opponents."[79] States also spend their diplomatic capital unevenly—rather than fighting every other state, states focus a disproportionate amount of attention on potential enemies. Rivals, then, are those states that states single out as potential enemies and/or repetitively engage in wars.[80] Scholars who work in this research program point out that between 50 and 75 percent of wars since 1800 have included states that are classified as rivals—a significant percentage, certainly.[81] Different strands of theories about rivalries posit different causes of rivalries—students of enduring rivalries focus on conflict patterns between states,[82] while students of strategic rivalries[83] are more interested in perceived threats.[84] The literature suggests that a single conflict between states predicts future conflicts, because states that have fought are more likely to fight again, and states with histories of conflicts are more likely to escalate disputes into wars.[85]

Other scholars looking at dyadic-level causes of war focus on the idea that war is a process, discussed, for example, in the "steps-to-war" model.[86] This model builds on work discussing different issues that states go to war over,[87] paying attention to territorial disputes, using them to delineate "a set of closely related paths to war that involve a series of steps between states that are roughly equal in power."[88]

The first step is the occurrence of an interstate dispute. Steps-to-war theorists argue that disputes related to territory are more likely to lead to war than other issues.[89] The factors that make territorial disputes most likely to lead to war include the use of coercive threats, military buildups, and alliances.[90] As Levy and Thompson explain,

> Steps-to-war models show that each "step" increases the probability of war, and that the process is cumulative. First, the occurrence of a dispute between two states increases the probability of war, with territorial disputes having the greatest impact. A territorial dispute also increases the probability of another territorial dispute. Crises tend to generate subsequent crises.[91]

Many theorists see the steps-to-war model as empirical, dyadic-level validation of realism's understandings of how the system works, and its applicability to state policy. Still others see it as a theoretical intervention positing the possibility of change within and of the realist-dominated system. If realpolitik behavior is a path to war, path-to-war theorists also suggest that, rather than being endemic to the international anarchy, "those strategies constitute learned behavior that is passed on from one generation to the next and that becomes part of realist strategic culture. Since those strategies are learned, they can be unlearned."[92]

Another rationalist dyadic approach to war is bargaining theory, which draws on game theory and focuses on interactions between actors as agents.[93] Bargaining theories of war are interested in why war(s) happens despite the(ir) cost and therefore focus on why war-fighting parties were unable (or unwilling) to reach a (cheaper) negotiated settlement to their dispute(s).[94] Possible pathologies in negotiations include private information (and/or incentives to misrepresent),[95] commitment problems,[96] indivisible issues,[97] and/or the lack of a "bargaining" space of outcomes that are mutually preferred to war.[98] Bargaining theories of war imply that, even when reaching a negotiated settlement in a dyadic relationship might be preferable to one or both parties, obstacles remain.[99]

Liberal theorists often take a very different message from dyadic analyses of war, arguing that it is not alliances or territory disputes or rivalries that predict whether two states go to war but trade interdependence[100] and/or regime type.[101] The liberal argument about economic interdependence is that states that depend on each other for trade are less likely to go to war. Early liberals like Adam Smith, David Ricardo, and others developed the idea that trade leads to peace in response to the mercantilist view that commerce and war went together.[102] Early liberal ideas about trade and peace formed the basis for Norman Angell's expectation that states would discover war to be outside their interests and would therefore quit fighting.[103] Still, the combination of World War I, the decline of economic interdependence in the interwar period, World War II, and the Cold War made scholars less interested in exploring a potential positive relationship between trade and peace.[104]

Over the last decade, there has been a resurgence of scholarly research exploring whether trade creates peace. Scholars have found a positive correlation between trade interdependence and peace and have posited a number of potential reasons for this correlation.[105] Some scholars argue that war has economic opportunity costs, and that both governments and corporations have an interesting preventing wars with trading partners.[106] Others argue that successful capitalist states combine an interest in a peaceful order and the economic power to enforce that interest, making the "capitalist peace."[107] Still others contend that the cultures of industrial societies (with focuses on productivity and economic equalizing) work against cultures of militarism.[108] Critiques of liberal economic interdependence arguments for peace focus on the negative cases,[109] the times that interdependence might lead to conflict,[110] the tendency of states to turn economic gains into military power,[111] and the problem that neither economic interdependence nor war are often dyadic.[112]

Far more work from a liberal perspective has been done on the dyadic effect of regime type;[113] so much so that many IR scholars have argued that the democratic peace is close to a law in war theory.[114] Democratic peace theory has its roots in Kantian interpretations of international politics and argues that (liberal) democracies are unlikely to fight wars.[115] As Zeev Maoz and Bruce Russett have argued, "recognition of the democratic peace result is probably one of the most significant nontrivial products of the scientific study of world politics."[116] The result to which they refer is that democracies do not fight each other, even when they are not generally more peaceful than nondemocracies.[117]

Democratic peace theorists have a number of explanations of what it is that makes democracies not fight one another, even when they fight as many wars as nondemocracies and the process of democratization is generally violent.[118] Maoz and Russett present two models: the normative model and the structural model.[119] The normative model proposes that the norms of democratic political organization *inside* democracies generalize to democracies' foreign policy practices and external behaviors.[120] The relationships between democracies, then, are dominated by democratic/peaceful values, while "the anarchic nature of international politics implies that a clash between democratic and nondemocratic norms is always dominated by the latter."[121] The structural model accounts for the democratic peace differently, arguing that it is the structure of democratic states that makes them less likely to fight one another. This is because "international challenges require political leaders to mobilize domestic support for their policies. Such support must be mobilized from those groups that provide leadership the kind of legitimacy that is required for international action."[122] In this view, democratic citizens are unlikely to support wars, and even less likely to support wars against like-minded democratic citizens in other countries.[123] While the two arguments are not mutually exclusive, a number of democratic peace theorists are interested in which logic accounts for the democratic peace they observe. Maoz and Russett conclude, as the result of empirical tests, "the relationship between institutional constraints and measures of dispute and war occurrence is not as robust as the relationship between measures of democratic norms and the dependent variables," suggesting the normative model holds more explanatory power.[124]

Some critics of the democratic peace suggest alternative common paths that have little to do with democracy, however. Lars-Erik Cederman suggests that the democratic peace result has more to do with collective security and liberal alliances than democratic governmental structure.[125] Cederman and Rao also provide evidence suggesting the democratic peace is reliant on, and interdependent with, a peace among economic liberals.[126] Eric Gartzke credits the democratic peace to the common interests among existing democracies, such that "democracies fight each other less often because they disagree less often or less intensely and thus have less about which to fight."[127] Others have argued that the democratic peace is "overdetermined,"[128] that it is actually a peace of powerful states (which just happen to be democracies),[129] that the democratic peace can be explained by realist principles,[130] that secure states have the privilege of being democracies (rather than democracy making states more secure),[131] that peace among democracies is a product of American exceptionalism,[132] or that it results from liberal values rather than democracy per se.[133] Doug Gibler argues that both democracy and peace are "symptoms of the removal of territorial issues between neighbors" rather than a relationship in which democracy causes peace.[134] A developing research program focusing on a selectorate model of war-making provides an alternative institutional explanation for the democratic peace, arguing that leaders cater to winning coalitions, and democracies' larger winning coalitions make the distribution of private goods from wars more difficult, disincentivizing war-making among leaders.[135]

Other critics find problems with democratic peace theorists' (narrow) operationalizations of democracy, war, and peace, which (are required to) produce statistically significant results.[136] They point out, particularly, that democratic peace theorists actually study the absence of (severe) conflict, rather than peace and that the two are both conceptually and empirically different.[137] David Spiro notes that large-N democratic peace research "loads" its cases and that the anomalies in which democracies do go to war are more theoretically significant than most of the cases in which they do not.[138] Negative cases discussed in the literature include the War of 1812, the American Civil War, the Spanish-American War, and the 1999 Kargil War between India and Pakistan.[139]

Constructivist approaches wonder if perception of democracy is more important than actual democracy, both in the policy world and among democratic peace theorists.[140] Still other critics express concern that, even if it is empirically accurate, the predictive power of democratic peace theory may be lacking and normatively problematic. Particularly, Steve Chan expresses concern that it "can appear as a smug dogma that dismisses many past instances of aggression committed by democracies" and "fuel[s] a spirit of democratic crusade."[141] This concern is expressed especially in a growing literature that is concerned with the violence involved in democratization and democracy promotion.[142]

Domestic Politics Accounts of War(s)[143]

Other accounts of the causes of wars specifically or war generally focus on what Waltz calls "second-image" or nation-state-level factors.[144] There is certainly a domestic politics element to (especially early) democratic peace theories, which are interested in the political organization of states and its influence on their tendencies to be bellicose.[145] Marxist–Leninist theories of war argue that "modern war arises from the economic imperatives of capitalist societies and the inequitable distribution of wealth between them."[146] Other domestic politics accounts focus on culture, ideology, religion, or nationalism, and are discussed (briefly) below.

Levy and Thompson start with Marxist–Leninist approaches to imperialism and war, which they characterize as "one of the oldest and most comprehensive of all societal-level approaches," when they introduce their readers to state-level theories.[147] In Marxist theory, the capitalist class controls the means of production and operation in the capitalist state, including but not limited to war-making capacity. Like the other tools of the state, the capitalist class uses war and imperialism for the advancement of its class interest.[148] In this explanation, since capitalist systems cannot support themselves, they use war as a tool to further their interests and expansion, either to find external markets to sell goods, to find new places to spend surplus capital,[149] or to gain access to raw materials.[150]

Dominant critiques of Marxist–Leninist approaches to war[151] are skeptical of the causal mechanisms that Marxists propose. Waltz, for example, argues that capitalist states are aggressive not because they are capitalist, but because they are powerful.[152] Liberal theorists argue that commerce can be as effective, if not more effective, than conquest to produce external markets, outlets for surplus capital, or exploitative abilities to obtain raw materials.[153] Liberals also argue that it is the military elite, not the economic elite, that make powerful capitalist states war-prone.[154] Other theorists characterize capitalisms' imperial wars as a "safety valve" against great power conflict and/or a mechanism for the promotion of balances of power.[155]

From these critiques of the dominance of economic coalitions in Marxist–Leninist theories of the relationship between domestic politics and war came a number of theoretical approaches that asked, if not economic coalitions, then what coalitions influence states' decision-making? Accounts that characterize war-making as a two-level game or problem[156] are interested in what factors influence domestic decision-making and how. A subset of these theories are often called *coalitional* models of the causes of war and emphasize the internal distributional consequences of foreign policy decisions.[157] Jack Snyder, theorizing "logrolled coalitions," notes that war can be beneficial to elites if they reap the benefits while spreading the costs to entire societies.[158] These logrolled coalitions maintain foreign policy control and convince the masses of the necessity of expansionism through "strategic myths," according to Snyder, which include exaggeration of enemies' threats, the economic and strategic value of empire, and the likelihood that wars can be easily won.[159] Other coalitional theories focus on potential class conflicts (if not from a Marxist prospective),[160] disagreements on political and budgetary strategies,[161] and interests in gaining or maintaining domestic political power.[162]

One of the approaches that focuses on gaining or maintaining political power is a group of theories that can be understood as diversionary theories of war.[163] Levy and Thompson note that diversionary theories of war have a long history, quoting Bodin as having realized that "the best way of preserving a state, and guaranteeing it against sedition, rebellion, and civil war is. . . . to find an enemy against whom they can make a common cause."[164] While some empirical evidence supports war as scapegoating,[165] empirical tests have generated mixed results.[166] Some argue "diversionary war" is instead intrinsically linked to discussions of regime type[167] or political organization[168] or that the causal relationship goes the other way, with international pressure leading to domestic unrest.[169]

A very different account of the domestic sources of international conflict comes from work on culture and war, which is itself very diverse. Perhaps the most well-known (if least intellectually sophisticated) account of the relationship between culture and war can be found in the "clash of civilizations" thesis advanced by Samuel Huntington.[170] Huntington defined civilizations as "the highest cultural grouping of people and the broadest level of identity people have short of that which distinguishes humans from other species," and identified seven or eight civilizations (depending on whether African civilization is counted).[171] Huntington argued that "the fault lines between civilizations will be the battle lines of the future."[172]

The great majority of scholarly reactions to Huntington's thesis have been negative, arguing that it is oversimple, that it uses "civilization" as a proxy for religion, that conflicts within civilizations are as common as, if not more common than, conflicts among civilizations and that identity is much more complex than just what civilization a state is a part of (should it be "civilized" at all).[173] Most work interested in the role of culture and/or identity in conflicts *between* states takes a more nuanced approach, looking at states' perceptions of one another's civilization or barbarity,[174] conflicts over ideology,[175] religion's influence on war and conflict,[176] cultures of national security,[177] and other similar variables. Significant contributions to this research come from constructivist work in IR, which argues that "social factors shape aspects of national security policy" in which norms "either define (or constitute) identities or prescribe (or regulate) behavior, or they do both."[178] Recently, scholars interested in states' "ontological" security or sense of "self" contend that states act on that interest rather than their physical security because, "while physical security is (obviously) important to states, ontological security is more important because it affirms states' sense of self."[179]

Individual or Decision-Making Theories of War[180]

In 1999, Daniel Byman and Kenneth Pollack called for the (re)inclusion of "great men" in scholarly thinking about how global politics works generally and war works specifically.[181] They argue that the dominance of structural realist and structural and statist liberal theories of global politics have effectively railroaded the individual out of our calculations of causal mechanisms in global politics.[182] Byman and Pollack see this as problematic in light of their claim that it would be hard (if possible) to imagine the twentieth century without *people* like Adolf Hitler, Vladimir Lenin, Mao Zedong, Winston Churchill, Franklin Roosevelt, Joseph Stalin, Ronald Reagan, and Mikhail Gorbachev making decisions and carrying out policies system- and state-level theories sometimes would not anticipate and could not explain.[183]

Of course, Byman and Pollack were not the first or the last to suggest that leaders and decision makers influence when wars are (or are not) made in global politics. As Levy and Thompson explain, "the basic premise of a decision-making approach to war is that an explanation of the foreign policy actions of states requires understanding the processes through which political leaders perceive the external world and make and then implement their decisions."[184] While structural theorists like Waltz[185] (and even Wendt)[186] reject the individual or group level of analysis as essentially unpredictable, except in the context of greater (state or systemic) trends, many theorists think that the crucial causal factors for war are in individuals' and organizations' decision-making processes.[187]

Some decision-making theories of war focus on how decisions *ought* to be made, while others focus on how they *are* made. The former are largely rationalist approaches to decision-making, in which (often game-theoretic) models are proposed to evaluate how leaders would act in their own and their states' interest, were they able to do so perfectly and with complete information. Other theories focus on the ways individual rational decision-making breaks down in practice, including variations in individual beliefs[188] and leadership styles,[189] misperception of empirical facts and/or others' behaviors,[190] cognitive and motivated biases,[191] and risk propensity.[192] Still others are interested in the decision-making habits (and pathologies) of groups rather than the individuals in them, since state policies are often, if not always, made by more than one person, either in voluntary consultation or by mandatory process.[193]

Two models form the foundation for thinking about organizational decision-making in foreign policy: the bureaucratic politics model and the organizational process model.[194] The bureaucratic politics model focuses on politics within the executive branch of government, looking to understand the decision-making processes of inner circles of decision makers and positing that each actor has distinct preferences *both* because they have different perspectives *and* because they represent different parts of (and thus distributional interests within) government.[195] It then predicts that the policy outcome will be the result of "internal political processes of conflict, bargaining, and consensus-building" among the different (rational) actors in the executive branch.[196] The organizational process model focuses on the operating procedures within, rather than the policy preferences of the participating actors in, decision-making bodies. Organizational decision-making is incrementalist,[197] satisficing,[198] and uncoordinated.[199] Some social psychology theories also see "groupthink" as a key problem of executive decision-making, because groups seeking concurrence will make riskier (and often worse) decisions together than any individual within the group would make alone.[200] The result of these issues in organizational process is that organizational decision-making rarely approximates state interests, even were such interests to be easily discoverable. Pathologies and processes of organizational decision-making, theorists argue, impact state strategic thinking,[201] choices of war-fighting tactics,[202] information transmission,[203] and ability to deal with crises.[204]

Analyzing the Fighting of Wars

While a significant amount of scholarship in the field I classify as war studies is about how and why wars are made, there is also significant attention paid to how wars are fought. Once a belligerent has made the decision to enter into a war, it calculates how to achieve its war aims, what its military comparative advantages are compared with its opponents, where a war will be fought, which approaches are likely to be successful, which weapons and formations to use, and how to transport the things that it needs to the battlefield. *During* wars, questions of strategy, tactics, and logistics become paramount. Therefore, in addition to theorizing about the causes of war(s), war studies often evaluates how wars are fought, on both the macro-level (strategy) and the micro-level (tactics), along with how war-fighting is managed practically (logistics). Each is discussed briefly below.

Strategy[205]

This section looks at theoretical and empirical approaches to strategy. During World War II, B. Liddell Hart defined strategy as "the art of distributing and applying military means to fulfill the ends of policy."[206] On the other hand, Williamson Murray and Mark Grimsley suggest that strategy is more difficult to define than a simple "art,"[207] because "strategy is a process, a constant adaptation to shifting conditions and circumstances in a world where chance, uncertainty, and ambiguity dominate."[208] These theorists, however, agree on the shifting and competitive nature of strategy in warfare throughout history, where it acts as "a contest to create mismatches in which our strengths can be directed against the opponent's weaknesses."[209] Given this theme in strategic studies, a leading strategic theorist contends that "strategists may be termed, and should acknowledge that they are, without apologies, neo-realists" and, indeed, neorealism is a dominant theoretical approach in strategic studies.[210]

Looking to understand states' competition through strategy, strategic studies theorists note that states adopt strategies to exploit opponents' weaknesses in a rapidly changing world, in which "strategic problems comprise a moving target and require constant renewal of intellectual attention."[211] This is especially important, because "if the desired ends of any proposed strategy are not clearly understood, realistic, timely, and situated within context, then the executing strategy will be either incomplete or likely to fail."[212]

Most strategic theorists analyze what strategies are available to belligerents and how they choose between them. Reiter and Meek list maneuver, attrition, and punishment as the strategies available to belligerents. They explain that maneuver and attrition are "traditional military strategies that pursue victory through the straightforward defeat of the enemy's military forces."[213] The difference between the two approaches is that "maneuver emphasizes mobility over firepower, whereas attrition emphasizes firepower over mobility."[214] If maneuver is "inserting highly mobile forces deep behind enemy lines," attrition "seeks out the enemy's forces, aiming to destroy or capture them."[215] Reiter and Meek note that punishment strategies are "fundamentally different from maneuver and attrition in that they include important political components, namely, inflicting pain until the adversary relents."[216]

Though many scholars use categories similar to Reiter and Meek's, others argue for either a more simple or a more complex schema. Advocates of a more simple categorization have suggested that strategies are separable into "offensive" and "defensive,"[217] but a number of strategic theorists find this approach theoretically flawed, since many strategies can be used for either offense or defense.[218] Robert Art classifies strategies based on the policy objective they are meant to accomplish, positing four strategies: defense, deterrence, compellence, and "swaggering."[219]

In Art's typology, troops used for defense are used to "ward off an attack and to minimize the damage to oneself if attacked."[220] A strategy of deterrence uses force or the threat of force "to prevent an adversary from doing something that one does not want him to do and that he might otherwise be tempted to do by threatening him with unacceptable punishment if he does it."[221] A state using a strategy of compellence intends "to be able either to stop an adversary from doing something that he has already undertaken or to get him to do something that he has not yet undertaken."[222] The use of military force for "swagger" is "displaying one's military might at military exercises and national demonstrations and buying or building the era's most prestigious weapons" to intimidate enemies into retreat.[223]

Most of these typologies of strategy assume that strategy is employed by large states with large, organized, and professional military forces. Some strategic theorists, however, argue that the changing nature of global politics means that strategists need to cast a broader net, since "at the beginning of the twenty-first century many long-standing strategic beliefs and practices appear to be under serious challenge to the extent that some commentators have even declared the end of strategy"[224] and "the utility of massive conventional force appears to be becoming increasingly questionable."[225] Given this, some scholars urge the consideration of other strategic approaches that have either arisen or been revived in the post–Cold War world, including terrorism and counterterrorism,[226] pre-emption,[227] and/or siege warfare.[228]

Recently, there has been increasing interest in intentional civilian victimization as a strategic choice. This work defines civilian victimization as "military strategy in which civilians are either targeted intentionally or force is used indiscriminately such that tens of thousands of civilians are killed . . . bombardment of urban areas, starvation blockades, sieges, or sanctions, population concentration or relocation, massacres . . . ."[229] Civilian victimization has been of particular interest to scholars studying strategy, because it violates both existing international law and just war theory's platitudes about civilian immunity.[230] Because of the legal and ethical prohibitions on killing civilians, many scholars had previously assumed that states protect civilians intentionally and only kill them accidentally or collaterally. However, despite a consensus that it is both morally wrong and strategically counterproductive to target civilians, many states do so intentionally (rather than merely accidentally or collaterally, which was previously assumed).[231]

The literature looking at the causes of civilian victimization so far builds on a number of research programs in security studies more broadly. Factors like regime type,[232] international law and organizations,[233] ethnicity,[234] culture,[235] and strategic concerns[236] are used to account for belligerents' decisions to intentionally target civilians, following literatures on democratic peace,[237] neoliberal institutionalism,[238] cultural conflict,[239] and strategic studies.[240] Some of the literature sees intentional civilian victimization as decentralized,[241] but most scholars see intentional civilian victimization as a top-down policy choice of leaders and focus on why leaders make that choice.[242]

This is part of a larger debate among strategists on the causes of strategic choice. Even if strategists could agree on what strategies belligerents choose, they propose a number of different explanations for why states choose those strategies. Among the reasons the literature supposes states choose strategies are geography;[243] domestic politics and/or economics;[244] political, military, or cultural experiences of a particular state;[245] technological development;[246] and/or particular war aims.[247] The literature explores how these different potential influences guide war-fighting states and other belligerents to particular strategic choices.

Tactics and Logistics[248]

Often, the study of strategy and the study of tactics are linked, and it is not clear where the macro-level of strategic choices ends and the micro-level of tactical decisions begins. On the one hand, we know it when we see it—attrition, for example, is a strategy; the choice of a grenade rather than a machine gun is a tactical one. Some describe tactics as a smaller part of strategy, in which "the tactical-level actions of particular units of the armed forces on each side are merely subordinated parts of larger actions involving many other units."[249] Others see tactics as largely isolated and independently important, where "a tactical fight can be won by a unit with its own ammunition, fuel, and food even if its resupply has already been cut off."[250] Either way, tactical analysis often has been the business of military historians, whose detailed work on the tactics used in particular wars shed some light on how the wars were fought and/or what tactical choices affected their outcomes.[251]

For example, Grady McWhiney and Perry Jamieson analyze Confederate tactical choices in the U.S. Civil War as initially bold and creative, motivated by certainty and bravado, and later conservative and commonplace, motivated by deflation and fear.[252] Jose Angel Maroni Bracamonte and David Spencer relate the tactics of the Salvadoran Farabundo Marti National Liberation Front (FMLN), which included urban combat, special select forces, and defensive guerilla tactics as part of the FMLN strategy of "prolonged popular war," arguing that strategic vision influences tactical choices.[253] A significant literature on the development of aerial warfare discusses tactics (and ethical evaluations thereof) as evolutionary, proposing that tactical choices might be as much a product of the available weaponry as they are of historical context or strategic purpose.[254] Still others link tactical choices to the personality, skill, experience, and leadership of particular military commanding officers in particular times.[255]

Whatever reason is given for tactical choices, there is no denying that some tactical choices (suicide bombing, kamikaze fighters, cluster bombs, guerilla warfare) are often met with more attention and more shock in scholarly and popular analyses than others (uniformed armies on battlefields). This is because tactical choices are not only selected by and/or judged by military interest, strategic considerations, personality of leaders, and sense of how the war is going. They are also influenced and judged by a long history of literature—in just war theorizing and outside—that provides moral guidelines for the proper *in bello* (warfighting) tactics.[256]

Tactical decision-making in war-fighting is often either made possible by or limited by logistical capacity. In fact, as many stories about the evolution of warfare are about improved logistics (trains, telegraphs, and the like) as are about improved fighting technology.[257] Logistics is the production and maintenance of militaries in times of wars.

From Martin Van Creveld's early work on the question of logistics,[258] scholars of tactical military choices have emphasized that logistics is a key part of the making and fighting of wars and more than a linear science of organization. It is, technically, "moving, supplying, and maintaining military forces."[259] According to Thomas Kane, "every war involves its own story of supply," and while "logistical operations in the military require many of the same skills as management in any other bureaucracy," there is also a military dimension of logistical planning, because military forces doing different things require different supplies, and the art of supplying and moving them is different in (potentially infinite) different locations.[260] The *International Military and Defence Encyclopedia* explains the many dimensions of logistics, including unity of purpose (corporate effort, functional interdependence and integration, mutual understanding and confidence, cooperation and teamwork), preparedness (foresight and military judgment, determination of requirements, coordination of planning and plans, operational readiness), viability (feasibility and credibility, sufficiency, sustainability, dispersion, and protection), economy (elimination of inefficiency and waste, role effectiveness and cost effectiveness, rationalization, standardization and specialization, and integrated support), responsiveness (forward impetus and momentum; local, centralized control of resources; proactive, as well as reactive, support; dedication to duty), and resourcefulness (versatility; improvisation and innovation; self-reliance, self-containment, and self-sufficiency; development of aptitudes and attitudes).[261]

Though all of these technical dimensions are involved, Clausewitz made the argument that logistical decisions were an art, rather than a science, and emphasized the links between logistics and operations.[262] Some see logistics as beyond the control of military leaders, but others argue that "the quartermaster's claim upon history, may, at its root, lie in the effect of logistics on timing."[263] While "logistics does not compete with strategy and tactics," it is not the same, either, since "logistics helps determine which side will have the most options available, [though] not what those options will be or how effectively it will use them."[264] Different states fight different wars at different times, and "different styles of warfare go hand in hand with different styles of logistics."[265]

CRITICAL APPROACHES TO THEORIZING WAR(S)

Outside the (American) mainstream[266] of war studies lie a number of approaches to the study of war that can generally be labeled as "critical."[267] This work is critical of traditional war theorizing, of positivist causal analysis, and even of war itself as a descriptive concept. Particularly, a growing tradition of "critical security studies,"[268] focusing on "the politics of security rather than just its military dimension,"[269] is challenging the narrow scope of the study of war. Generally, the broad array of work understood as critical security studies shares "an 'expansionist' agenda, which, with the end of the Cold War, sought to replace the emphasis on the state and the threat or use of force with a broad array of referent objects and sources of insecurity."[270]

Work in critical security (broadly defined) has begun to ask "how, having adopted a critical approach, the world becomes a different place, whose study must be undertaken with different tools."[271] Within critical security studies, questions about security as representation, as praxis, as a speech act, and as property are commonplace critiques of traditional definitions of security (like Stephen Walt's) that limit it to the "threat or use of military force."[272] These critical understandings of *what security is* mean that critical theorists looking at war are looking for different things. Several approaches focus on broadening the way theorists of war look at security, particularly what they see of the unnatural limiting of security to the realm of war.

Among critical security scholars, it is possible to delineate several major strands of thought. The first is a Marxist-inspired, (modernist) emancipatory strand of critical theory that (self-identifies as, in Ken Booth's terms, Critical Security Studies and) "maintains its faith in the enlightenment project and defends universalism in its ideal of open dialogue not only between fellow-citizens, but, more radically, between all members of the human race."[273] Booth characterizes this strand of critical theorizing as: universalist, inclusive, normative, emancipatory, and progressive.[274] In other words, this form of critical theory shares a sense of the world as in need of change in the form of human emancipation, as changeable generally, and as changeable through the politicization of knowledge.

This work looks at war as one part of a larger framework of violence and insecurity that threatens and oppresses people at the margins of global politics, a concern not out of line with those in feminist theorizing of war and security.[275] Perhaps the most influential book in this strand of theorizing, Ken Booth's *Theory of World Security*, never explicitly theorizes war per se.[276] Booth looks "to understand war in order to eliminate it" and looks to a "war system" understanding of political violence as intrinsically interlinked in order to do that.[277] It is, then, security (in a positive sense) that this strand of critical security is interested in, rather than war, the elimination of which, in their view, is a necessary but insufficient condition to providing people with security in the form of emancipation.

Related but separable is work that critiques traditional security studies, asserting instead a "human security" approach.[278] Human security theorizing is a framework that finds its foundations in Amartya Sen and Martha Nussbaum's capabilities approach,[279] adopted by the United Nations Development Program in its 1994 Human Development Report.[280] Similar to Booth's critical security, human security is more interested in people's security than states' security, and thus argues for a broader approach to security than simple armed conflict between states and a broader approach to looking at who is impacted by wars than most war theorists take. However, rather than looking for emancipation per se, human security theorists look for "freedom from fear and freedom from want," defined by the provision of seven categories of security: community, economic, environmental, food, health, personal, and political.[281]

Yet another critical approach to studying security interested in widening what we see as security is the Copenhagen school.[282] The Copenhagen school has been identified by its emphasis on the social and identity-based elements of security.[283] In contrast to a focus on war as the central concern in studying security, Copenhagen school scholars have identified five sectors of security: military, political, economic, societal, and environmental.[284] These scholars also argue that the key actors, or levels of analysis, in security should be critically reevaluated to include not only states, but also individuals, substate actors, the international subsystem, and the international system.[285]

All of these "widening" approaches to security studies provide important critiques and reformulations of the narrow, statist, war-focused mainstream of the field of inquiry, which disproportionately privileges the military arena. They draw attention to the mass human oppression, insecurity, and death that happens outside the "wars" studied in war studies but leaves people's daily lives constantly embattled. Feminist scholars often share this desire to replace security studies' focus on war with "a broad understanding of what counts as a security issue, and to whom security should be applied," defining it in "multidimensional or multilevel terms" to include not only war and international violence, but also domestic violence, rape, poverty, gender subordination, and ecological destruction."[286] Though appropriate, the commitment to expanding or widening the meaning of security in much critical work on security often becomes a trade-off that focuses attention away from theorizing war *as war*. Because this work normatively rejects war-centric security theorizing, it is often marginalized in war theorizing.[287]

Another force that often marginalizes critical theorizing in war theorizing is epistemological divergences with traditional studies of war. This is because critical security scholars often come to the study of security "with a desire to improve the lot of those who suffer from [not only] military violence [but also] human rights abuses or environmental destruction," again, at odds with traditional theorists, who suggest that scholarship about war and security be fundamentally "disinterested."[288] These explicitly, normatively driven approaches ask different questions than traditional approaches and see different ways of learning the answers, under the assumption that knowledge (about war and more generally) cannot be divorced from its relationship with the knower—it is context-dependent, subjective, and political.[289] As such, a number of critical approaches to theorizing war argue that causal logic, at whatever level of analysis, is an inadequate or even inappropriate way to be thinking about wars, which are often less concrete and less discrete than they are described in the (positivist) literature on the making and fighting of wars. Critical theorists often argue that "language and communication give material conditions meaning for humans," and that such meaning cannot be normatively neutral.[290]

This is especially characteristic of postmodern or poststructural critical approaches to theorizing security. This strand of critical theorizing is skeptical of the modernist project inherent in the Marxist-inspired strand of critical theorizing. It problematizes, in Jim George's words, its dichotomized frames of reference, its "objectivist, linear" view of

Western history, its essentialist reading and writing practices, its universalism, and its "dangerously restrictive" understanding of the detachment of "knowledge" and "reality."[291] A "wariness with metanarratives" has led poststructuralist critical theory to question whether the critical theory project is *the* means to "change the world."[292] As Lene Hansen explains, "the modernist belief in our ability to rationally perceive and theorize the world is in poststructuralism replaced by disbelief in unproblematic notions of modernity, enlightenment, truth, science, and reason."[293] This leads, in Hansen's words, to scholarship by genealogy, which "does not look for a continuous history, but for discontinuity and forgotten meanings; it does not look for an origin, indeed, it is assumed one cannot be found; and it does not, finally, focus on the 'object of genealogy' itself, but on the conditions, discourses, and interpretations surrounding it."[294] In other words, not only can we not *know* objectively, the idea of knowing war at all must be called into question, and the appropriate focus of scholarship on war becomes the conditions, discourses, and interpretations surrounding it, rather than war itself.

Along these lines, critical security theorists have done a significant amount of work on the conditions, discourses, and interpretations surrounding the making and fighting of wars. Perhaps one of the most well-known approaches also comes out of the Copenhagen school, which has developed an understanding of "securitization."[295] In this interpretation, rather than the national security interests for which states are seen to fight wars being naturalized, endogenous, or systemically assigned, they are not fixed and cannot be seen as static. Instead, security issues are constructed by securitizing actors[296] through speech acts of naming issues as national security concerns. Once an issue has been successfully securitized, it merits "extraordinary means" beyond the reach of "normal politics" and can incite war and other political violence.[297] Recognizing particular events as within the realm of security highlights their profile and makes violence around them more likely.

This and other critical approaches to security have led scholars to question what war is, both in terms of its conceptual boundaries and in terms of how it is understood, produced, and made possible. Critical theorists have argued that, rather than being an event, war is a continuum,[298] a practice,[299] and a symbolic politics or performance.[300]

One example, mentioned earlier, is the idea that states' ontological security concerns cause them to act in times of war without regard to, or even in the face of, material or survival interests, because a state's sense of self is a key constitutive factor in statehood.[301] In this understanding, bringing honor to (or keeping shame from) that sense of self can be performed through the making and fighting of wars.[302]

The work of James Der Derian and other poststructuralist theorists of war takes another approach, looking to do work "recognizing and investigating the interrelationship of power and representational practices" that go into our thinking about war.[303] Der Derian coined the term "virtuous war" to describe the "military-industrial-entertainment-media" complex that he sees war as.[304] This virtuous war is fantastic—a performance—unreal.[305] It is "based not only on the capacity to exert extraordinary force, but also on the capacity to keep its actual consequences out of sight lest they undermine the apparent virtues of this kind of warfare."[306] These performances of war appear "ethically, intentionally, and virtuously applied,"[307] legitimating the use of force by seduction[308] and entertainment.

Scholars working in this research program have thus argued that the symbolic politics and performative aspects of war constitute and are constituted by the existence of war(s) and that the two are therefore inseparable. The visceral, corporeal effects of the military-industrial-entertainment-media complex are always felt, but by the "other" in the "war," which leads poststructuralist theorists to ask what is being secured, what constitutes the condition of security, and how ideas about security develop.[309] There is blurring of reality inherent in the virtual/virtuous war world.[310] War is then not only performative,[311] but textual/intertextual,[312] produced and productive.[313]

Poststructuralist security theorists have also explored the discursive violences inherent in limiting war theorizing to questions of the cause and effect of (apparently) objective and observed realities of war(s).[314] For example, Laura Shepherd asks what assumptions are necessary for scholars and policy makers to use terms like "international security" and "national security" as if they were a common language with obvious meaning.[315] Relatedly, much critical theorizing asks war theorists to rethink not only the subject and object of war(s) but also the epistemological assumptions frequently made about the nature and distinctiveness of war(s). These approaches, drawing from different reference points in critical geography, anthropology, postmodern philosophy, and Marxist theory, often critique both the empirical and normative content of traditional war studies.[316] They critically interrogate how much scientific approaches really tell us about the war puzzle in global politics, and whether the puzzle is really framed around appropriate questions.

Some (particularly postmodern) critical approaches argue that theorizing war from a paradigmatic perspective (any paradigmatic perspective) is itself net harmful, arguing instead for a "systematic denaturalization of the real and the given"[317] with a resultant "emphasis on the multiplicity of possible readings or interpretations."[318] Thinking about multiple versions of histories, wars, and theories of war, critical perspectives often note that "the insistence on a singular narrative is itself a form of violence."[319] Accordingly, these perspectives question the scope, methodology, and object of study of most traditional work in war studies.

THE GENDERLESS STUDY OF WAR

Realist approaches to structural theorizing of the permissive cause of war and postmodern skepticism of the parameters of that theorizing, in some sense, could not be more different. Likewise, decision-making theories that emphasize leaders' incentive structures share little either with dyad-level democratic peace theory or critical security approaches focused on the people who need to be emancipated from their decision makers. Theoretical approaches to war are as varied as perhaps they possibly could be—choosing different causal variables, different levels of analysis, different methods, different epistemological approaches, and, in some cases, different ontologies. Yet, the overwhelming majority war theorizing has something in common.

What war theorizing shares is a lack of, and a lack of commitment to, gender analysis. This is, of course, a broad and sweeping generalization that is more accurate and applicable to some theorists and paradigms than others, but is generally fair when applied to war studies.[320] For example, between 1945 and 2006, the five highest-ranked security journals published articles with gender analysis in them in less than one-quarter of 1 percent of their content.[321] Much of the ground-breaking work in critical security studies mentions gender marginally, if at all, and generally fails to adopt gender analysis into its work.[322] In Levy and Thompson's recent (otherwise excellent) book summarizing war theorizing, "gender" makes an appearance twice—in two footnotes.[323] The first one problematizes the "over-aggregation" of human nature in first-image analyses of war, given that they treat "the male and female as indistinguishable and neglect any possible impact of gender on the causes of war."[324] The second discusses "demographic trends" such as "surpluses of men" and "youth bulges" as causes of war.[325] Neither do serious gender analysis in the terms this book intends to engage.

This is not to say that mainstream war studies has never paid any attention to gender, or that gender has been completely absent from critical theorists' work on war and conflict. It is, instead, to make two distinct (and hopefully more modest) claims. The first is that, to the extent that gender has been taken up in war theorizing, it remains peripheral and has not become a central part of research programs outside feminist security studies considering the nature, constitution, causes, and consequences of war(s).[326] The second is that, to the extent that mainstream studies of war have considered gender, they have actually been largely talking about a partial and limited idea of gender that involves women as a biological sex being imbued with characteristics gendered feminine for the purpose of analyzing war.[327] This second claim will be discussed in more detail in chapter 2, when I lay out this book's feminist approaches to studying war ontologically, epistemologically, and methodologically. For now, it is the first claim—that gender theorizing remains absent from (and when not absent from, marginal to) both mainstream and critical war theorizing—that lays the foundation for this book's work. In the remainder of the text, I seek to analyze and problematize "genderless" war studies.

In calling war studies genderless, I am not implying that it is somehow gender neutral or without gender implications. Quite the opposite, I am arguing that it is impossible to think about war *well* without gender analysis and that doing so obscures the empirical operation of and normative consequences of gender in the nature, causes, performances of, and consequences of war(s). Gender is necessary, conceptually, to understanding the nature of war(s); empirically, to understanding wars' causes and consequences; ethically, to understanding its implications; and prescriptively, to understanding how to stop wars. Gender does "analytical and normative work" and serves as a "resource for thought" in almost every aspect of how we fight wars and how we read them.[328] War, wars, and the study of both are fundamentally (if not unalterably) gendered and, therefore, feminist theorizing about war is not only a part of, but a crucial piece of, the war puzzle.[329] Feminist theory "raises the question of what kind of politics and theory would be possible without the work accomplished by gendered logics" in war theorizing.[330]

Also, when I call war studies genderless, I am not arguing that the work I outlined in this chapter does not have a relationship with gender theorizing—I am arguing that its relationship is (normatively and empirically) negative, problematic, and untenable. These relationships between gender theorizing and security or war studies have variously been called "impossible,"[331] "awkward,"[332] "uneasy"[333] "limited,"[334] and akin to "exile."[335] While (many in) IR generally and security studies specifically have conceded that feminist scholarship may exist at the margins, gender analysis "does not simply 'add' gender to an unchanged object of study, but . . . force[s] a more radical rethinking of what properly constitutes I/international R/relations to begin with, transforming the boundaries and conceptual basis."[336] This work starts with the feminist analysis of and deconstruction of war theorizing. It requires showing the gendered nature of that theorizing, of the meaning, causes, and consequences of war(s) at each level of analysis.

The logics, tools, and insights of the approaches to war(s) in this chapter will be used, melded, critiqued, reformulated, called out, and engaged throughout the rest of this book's theorizing of war through feminist lenses. Engaging the genderless study of war is a crucial part of the project of feminist war theorizing, because, as Kimberly Hutchings argues, "one can hope . . . to loosen the hold of *masculinity* on meaning and life only once one has first appreciated how much work is accomplished by masculinity's logical structure."[337] Chapter 2 introduces the feminist theory tools to begin to see, and deconstruct, the influence of masculinity's logical structures on war theorizing.

CHAPTER 2

Gender Lenses Look at War(s)

There are always fresh questions to ask about what it takes to wage wars—all about
the efforts to manipulate disparate ideas about femininity, about the attempts to
mobilize particular groups of women, about the pressures on certain women to
remain loyal and silent. There are more efforts to control women and to squeeze
standards for femininity and manliness into narrow molds than most war wagers
will admit. . . . in the midst of warfare, the politics of marriage, the politics of
femininities, the genderings of racial and ethnic identities, and the working of
misogyny each continue. . . . every war takes place—is waged, is coped with,
and is assessed—at a particular moment in ongoing gendered histories, national
gendered histories, and international gendered history.

—CYNTHIA ENLOE, *NIMO'S WAR, EMMA'S WAR: MAKING FEMINIST SENSE OF THE IRAQ WAR*

Feminist theorists have worked for decades to "make feminist sense" of
war and conflict specifically, and international relations more generally.[1]
This work has shown that looking through gender lenses at wars and
conflicts not only makes us rethink the gendered histories of war(s), but
also consider the 'gendered history' of research about the making and
fighting of wars.[2] This gendered history of research is especially important as we examine the "legitimizing function of masculinity discourses"
within the theories of the causes and consequences of war(s).[3] Feminist
approaches to theorizing war, then, see war as a gendered concept, a gendered event, a gendered logic, and a gendered performance.[4]

This chapter introduces the feminist approaches used to theorize war
throughout the book. It begins with a discussion about what is "feminist" about this book's feminist theorizing, particularly what gender
lenses see that can be distinguished from and seen as contributing to
the work of other approaches to the study of war. It then suggests that

"feminisms" are diverse, rather than monolithic, and discusses some of the methodological, epistemological, and ontological differences that different feminisms bring to engagements with and critiques of war studies. After going over several strategies for dealing with those differences, the chapter suggests a dialectical hermeneutic approach to feminist war theorizing. It argues that a dialogical approach that values difference as the substance of theorizing rather than an obstacle to theorizing is productive. The chapter concludes by introducing feminist security studies[5] dialogically and presenting a method for moving from feminist theorizing of security to feminist theorizing of war and wars.

WHAT IS "FEMINIST" ABOUT FEMINIST THEORIZING?

Perhaps the best place to start thinking about what is feminist about feminist war theorizing is to discuss some common misconceptions about feminist theorizing. One common misconception is that *gender* is synonymous with *women*, and that feminists are interested in promoting women at the expense of men. While some feminists study women, and some people who study women are feminists, they do not map one-to-one. Some feminist scholars do not study women, and some work that studies women does so (sometimes explicitly) without feminisms' political commitments.[6] While feminist scholars are interested in gender equality or gender emancipation, they are (for the most part) not interested in subordinating men or trading women's interests for men's interests. Instead, feminist scholars are studying gender, masculinities and femininities, and looking for what genders and genderings show them about what global politics is and how it works. Another common misconception is that feminists are always thinking that gender is the primary and only explanation for phenomena in global politics. This is not true on two levels—first, feminist scholars are looking at gender to see where it leads; second, feminists often understand gender as power and are therefore looking at the ways that gendered power configures and is configured by events in global politics.

A third common misconception is that, while feminist theory is relevant to global politics, it is relevant to a narrow set of issues that particularly concern women (such as wartime rape) or things that women are (perceived to be) good at (like peace). While, certainly, it is easier to see gender in things that are traditionally understood to concern women, and feminisms are interested in those things, feminist scholarship is as attentive to war as it is to wartime rape, to weapons as to gendered language about them, and to violence as to peace. While feminisms have argued that the traditional concerns of international relations (IR) and the methods with which IR theorists study them are partial, short-sighted, and masculinist, feminist scholars do not ignore those concerns.

So, if feminist war theorizing is not narrowly focused on women, reverse-sexist, and limited to a particular set of marginalized issues, what is it? One of the major commonalities of feminist scholarship is a concern with gender, which Laura Shepherd describes as "a noun, a verb, and a logic that is product/productive of the performances of violences and security."[7] As I discussed in the introduction, feminist work sees gender as an intersubjective social construct in global politics and therefore a necessary analytical category for the study of war (or any other phenomenon in global politics). Gender is a property held by and read onto people, states, and other actors and objects in global politics; gendering is a process between and among those actors; and gendered logics often govern global political interactions. Gender myths serve to naturalize a configuration of gender order particular to a given space and time, which is performed daily though bodily acts of obedience and transgression to those norms. Feminist approaches seek to identify, understand, and deconstruct operative gender hierarchies in global politics by looking through gender lenses at the ways the world works. For feminist war theorizing, this means understanding operative gender hierarchies in the symbolism, making, fighting, and experience of war(s).

Thinking about gender as gender hierarchy means understanding that being male or female is not a (or the) indicator of gender; instead, masculinities and femininities are genders and produce genderings. "Women" can be masculine, and "men" can be feminine; men or women can be masculinized or feminized.[8] Individuals can be gendered, but so can institutions, organizations, and even states. Gendering is about the distribution of power and regard based on *perceived association* with sex-based characteristics, rather than possession of certain sex organs a priori. In these understandings, gender is first, fundamentally social; second, an expression of power; and third, an organizing principle for war specifically and politics and political thought generally.[9]

It is gender as an organizing principle that interests feminists in IR generally, and my feminist war theorizing specifically. As Marysia Zalewski explains, "the driving force of feminism is its attention to gender and not simply women . . . the concept, nature, and practice of gender are key."[10] In this spirit, feminists in IR have argued that the power relations between gendered constructions and institutions significantly impact the ways in which global politics works. Feminist research often understands gender as a "feature of social and political life" that "profoundly shapes our place in, and view of, the world."[11] Feminist scholars characterize gender as "necessary, conceptually, for understanding international relations; important in analyzing causes and predicting outcomes; and essential to thinking about solutions and promoting positive change."[12]

If what makes feminist scholarly inquiry feminist is a concern with gender as an analytic category and gender emancipation as a political aim,[13] how does it relate to other scholarship? What falls outside the boundaries of feminist analysis, and how does feminist analysis relate to whatever falls outside it? I cannot speak as an authorial voice for feminisms on these issues but can outline my perspective, which is employed in the remainder of this book.[14]

In my view, it is important to distinguish gender and sex (even if the two are co-constituted or sociobiological)[15] and correspondingly, to distinguish between thinking about *what men do* and *what women do* and thinking about gendered social structures that select for and value gendered characteristics. Work that is interested in "the empirical realities of women in political life, national or international"[16] is work about women in politics, but may or may not be feminist work, depending on whether or not it analyzes gender as power, and whether or not its work is performed recognizing the normative problems with the current gender order.[17]

For example, work that takes account of sex in war studies often does not pay attention to gendered politics or reflect a normative interest in changing the gendered order. In my view, that work studies sex in global politics, but without a feminist perspective.[18] Some of that work is interested in how fertility rates, the percentage of women in elected legislative bodies, the percentage of women in the labor force, and other indicators of women's equality influence states' likelihood to start or participate in wars, arguing that "the inclusion of women as equal members of society will, therefore, result in fewer and less violent militarized interstate disputes."[19] Other work asks whether men and women see, think about, and act differently in war.[20] This work often focuses on sex dynamics without regard to gender dynamics, and often does not question gendered assumptions about the goals, processes, and results of global politics generally and war specifically.[21]

So what is the difference between theorizing "sex and world peace"[22] and theorizing (gender and) war through feminist lenses? Scholars looking through gender lenses "ask what assumptions about gender (and race, class, nationality, and sexuality) are necessary to make particular statements, policies, and actions meaningful."[23] In other words, gender is not a variable that can be measured as a "yes" or "no" (or male or female question) but a more complicated symbolic and cultural construction.[24] Treating gender as dichotomous and predetermined, and without regard for gender hierarchy, "necessarily presuppose[s] that gender is not already constructed, which leads to problematic empirical results and theoretical conclusions."[25]

In my view, as Brooke Ackerly, Maria Stern, and Jacqui True argue, "what makes scholarship . . . feminist is the research question and the theoretical methodology and not the tool or particular method used."[26] Feminist research questions explore the relationships among gender, genderings, power, and politics.[27] In answer to these research questions, feminist scholars find tools "for moving beyond the knowledge frameworks that construct international relations without attention to gender."[28] These tools are means to "making the invisible visible, bringing women's lives to the center, rendering the trivial important, putting the spotlight on women as competent actors, and understanding women as subjects rather than the objects of men."[29] The feminist approaches I am interested in exploring, then, "transform knowledge in ways that go beyond adding women" to studying gender and pursuing gender emancipation.[30]

In other words, "gender hierarchy *is* a normative problem *and* the failure to recognize it presents an empirical problem" for those interested in how war works.[31] This understanding shapes how I see feminist analysis relating to prefeminist (or nonfeminist) scholarship. Rather than seeing scholarship (discussed in chapter 1) that omits gender analysis as "suspect" or valueless,[32] I argue that it is important but necessarily incomplete.[33] Looking at war without attention to gender hierarchy makes scholarship about war less accurate empirically and problematic normatively. This creates an incentive for feminist engagement of war studies, inspired by the idea that feminist work adds to war studies, which is valuable but (without feminist work) not as valuable as it could be. As such, feminist war theorizing starts "with a different perspective and lead to further rethinking . . . [to] distinguish 'reality' from the world as *men* know it,"[34] which is not to imply that *men as men* have some particular viewpoint, but instead that masculinities bring about a particularized (and often narrow) view of the world and way of analyzing it. I will discuss the strategic approach to engagement taken in this book later in this chapter, but find engagement necessary because "putting gender in" to war analyses produces "new insights, theoretical advances, and conceptual categories."[35]

DIVERSITY AMONG APPROACHES TO FEMINIST THEORIZING

At the same time, the ways that feminist scholars "put gender in" are by no means uniform, even limiting feminism to scholarship that takes note of and critiques not only sex but gender subordination. In the introduction, I noted that there is not one approach to feminist theorizing, but many, including feminist approaches that correspond with different paradigmatic approaches to IR.[36] While many feminist projects share a self-reflexivity about ideas and methods based on observations of gender inequalities not only in the "real world" of global politics but also in the communities that study that world and the methods they use to do so, there remain a number of unresolved ontological and epistemological gaps among feminist theorists potentially predisposed to theorizing wars. These questions are complicated by the fact that multiple feminist approaches mean that feminist insights on global conflict can yield different and sometimes contradictory insights.[37]

This is because "it would be unrepresentative to characterize a 'gendered experience' as if there were something measurable that all men or all women shared in life experience."[38] Consequently, not only are there are several feminist *theoretical* approaches to war(s), there are several feminist *epistemologies* of the study of war(s).[39] The different approaches to gender and war bring up different substantive and research concerns, different methodological choices, different preferences about how to relate to the field as a whole, and even different understandings of the appropriate subjects and objects of war theorizing. Different feminisms have different interests—in power, in equality, in emancipation, in signification, in race and ethnicity, in geography, and in other issues—that focus their gender lenses in different directions.

Some of those differences are just that—differences. Some of them, however, are not only differences but contradictions and critiques. For example, postcolonial feminisms have critiqued liberal feminisms' rights-based approach to thinking about women's needs and gender equality.[40] Poststructuralist feminisms have questioned constructivist feminisms' (perceived) shallow notion of the role of gender in social and political life.[41] Positivist feminisms have looked to provide data about gender subordination, while postpositivist feminisms have seen narrative, biography, and other discursive methodologies as more useful.[42] Feminist security studies scholars have given primacy to the security arena, while feminist global political economy (GPE) scholars have given primacy to the economic arena.[43] Some feminists see knowledge as objective, some see it as perspectival, some see it as experiential, whereas others question the ability to know.[44]

This diversity is significant and often constitutes not only difference but insights that can be seen to conflict with one another. Other examples abound. Some feminists have advocated pornography as sex-liberating, and others have condemned it as a key source of sex subordination.[45] Some feminists have argued that human trafficking can only be prevented by legalizing prostitution, and others have argued that trafficking can only be stopped by enforcing laws against prostitution.[46] Some feminists have supported American military interventions in Afghanistan, Iraq, and elsewhere, while others have argued that those interventions instrumentalized and oppressed women.[47] Some feminists have argued that capitalism is a path to gender emancipation, while others have argued that it is at the root of gender subordination.[48] While some differences among feminisms can be reconciled fairly easily by thinking about feminisms with different research interests going in different directions, others (especially those that appear directly contradictory) may need to be dealt with in thinking about "a" feminist theoretical approach to war theorizing.

STRATEGIES FOR DEALING WITH DIVERSITY AMONG FEMINIST APPROACHES

Feminist scholars have used different strategies for dealing with this diversity (and sometime disagreement) among feminist approaches. Some scholars see feminism as a coherent whole.[49] Many of those scholars see the two sides of a number of key feminist debates as solvable, with one approach being correct and the other incorrect, identifying a single, "true" feminist position on a given issue. To these scholars, feminists who disagree are seen as having taken an incorrect position based on the (singular or reconcilable) goals of feminisms.

Instead of explicitly delineating right and wrong positions, some scholars start their work with something like "feminists see . . .," implying without explicitly claiming that feminisms have uncontroversial agreement on whatever is the predicate of the sentence. While this work does not explicitly endorse a singular notion of feminism, it implies that feminisms, despite their differences, do not disagree on the most important substantive issues.

Others group feminist approaches in service of their theoretical or political interest to downplay or ignore the differences between feminisms. Feminisms then become differentiated by their approaches, whereby one feminism has one perspective and another feminism has another, and the irreconcilability of those positions is irrelevant because the groups or political interests of different feminisms become the unit of analysis.

By contrast, other feminist scholars explicitly deal with potential areas of difference or conflict, looking to either reconcile, navigate, or map potential conflicts. One way of dealing with differences among feminisms is to use a strategy of coexistence, contending, for example, that "multiple feminisms can coexist and contribute to critique and reformulation of research and policy without being considered as a single theory in universal agreement."[50] In this perspective, feminists' disagreements are broad, but the subject of their critique is often singular. Feminisms do not need to agree on the alternative to agree on the critique (usually of gender subordination). In this view, multiple feminist angles aim at the same goal, and the differences among feminisms are less important than their commonalities, such that feminism is a "momentum concept" in which "if feminism is to be coherently defined, . . . it needs to be conceived as one river with numerous currents rather than as a series of rivers."[51]

Others, rather than encouraging coexistence while maintaining difference, look to bridge the divides and reconcile the differences, arguing that feminism *as one* is stronger than feminism *as an aggregate*.[52] Some of this reconciliation is intellectual, looking to compare feminist perspectives, weigh their advantages and disadvantages, and solve the arguments among feminisms through logical reasoning. Other reconciliation attempts look for emotional rather than intellectual or logical paths, "using emotional identification as a bridge for diversity and conflict."[53] Rejecting the masculinism often identified with rational argumentation or Cartesian reason, these feminists look to find *identification* or solidarity rather than agreement across feminisms' differences.

Yet another strategy understands diversity and difference as having additive value, whereby "diverse women ask diverse questions, such as how racial inequality, cultural discrimination, economic subordination, 'North-South' relations, and gendering of political actors relate to gender subordination."[54] From this perspective, "strong" or "dynamic" objectivity is built from different perspectives being compiled, with emphasis on views from the margins of global social and political organization.[55] In this view, different feminisms are distinct pieces of a puzzle, but fit together to be more than a sum of their parts.

Other feminist scholars contend that a particular approach to feminist analysis is more politically appropriate than others. Though, unlike the strategy mentioned above, these scholars do not go so far as to declare that there is a single, "correct" feminism, these feminists talk about preferring particular approaches for their political or instrumental value or even their normative contributions. For example, some postcolonial feminists have argued that American academic feminism essentializes women from the "third world" and constitutes "'feminism' as another form of 'imperialism.'"[56] On the other hand, feminists interested in mainstreaming gender in IR have suggested that more radical feminist approaches to IR are net harmful because they are discipline-alienating in their methodological or epistemological choices.

These various strategies for dealing with the differences among feminisms, I contend, are individually and collectively insufficient.[57] Universalist feminist narratives are in my view in denial of feminisms' real and serious differences, and statements that collectivize feminisms that are at odds are often universalist wolves in sheep's clothing. I find categories limiting, but think that approaches that value their contributions as additive also gloss over the discomfort of conflict. While some disagreements can be reconciled intellectually or emotionally, others cannot. Thinking of unity or ending conflict as a priority for feminisms seems potentially at odds with or at least a distraction from goals associated with ending gender subordination, which may require disunity or conflict. While there are political and intellectual reasons to prefer certain feminist approaches over others, those are themselves subjective and may narrow out some of feminisms' disagreements but not all of them.

These problems are compounded when one realizes each of these strategies can be critiqued by the others. Seeing feminisms as multiple without a particular theoretical understanding of that multiplicity risks perceptions of incoherence and seeing feminisms as unified ignores valuable diversity. Among feminist approaches, urging solidarity, ignoring differences, asserting superiority, bridging conflicts, or valuing diversity for diversity's sake are important tools, but not tools that produce synthesis or a sufficient justification for not seeking synthesis.[58]

Yet the question of feminisms' diversity is key, because it is implicated in how war is understood, what it means to know about war, and the methods that we use to study war through gender lenses. I argue that there is another way to approach the question of difference in feminisms—to see the difference, disagreement, conflict, and argument *as the substance of feminisms* rather than as a substantive problem for feminisms. Such an approach, which I identify as dialogical, is detailed in the remainder of this chapter as a way to approach feminisms' differences and as a method for feminist war theorizing.

A DIALOGICAL APPROACH TO FEMINIST ANALYSIS

A dialogical approach to feminisms' differences looks at them in a new light. Such a perspective sees the substance of feminist analysis not in synthesis or in the additive value of diversity, but in the conflict among feminist approaches and the journey that produces it. Following Hayward Alker and Thomas Biersteker, I argue that "it is the sharing, the interpretation, and the principled opposition of these often antagonistic approaches . . . that truly constitute the global inter-discipline of International Relations."[59] A dialogical approach sees the substance of feminist analysis in its differences, seeing feminist war theorizing as not a result, but a process, and a journey of observation, critique, reformulation, and reflexivity.

Alker saw dialogue as not just the process of IR but its substance, and argued that "there are truths reachable and shareable by a consensually oriented version of the argumentation process."[60] He suggested a questioning, contingent, open approach to argument,[61] one in which there are differences *about* substance, but the difference also *is* the substance. He explains:

> What classical political argumentation can do best, if grounded in a cooperative, uncoerced, moral-political, truth-seeking orientation and used skillfully to ask the right questions—those that critically probe the more fundamental justifications—is to suggest the key determinants of sociopolitical identities, actions, policies, or relationships, and constructively criticize such contingently variable and valuable human things.[62]

I argue that Alker's approach to engaging difference *as substance* can help to navigate the difficult task of theorizing war(s) through feminist lenses. Feminist war theorizing, then, might be seen as a dialectical hermeneutic. While many of the strategies I outlined for dealing with differences among feminists characterize the differences, conflicts, or arguments among feminist theories as a means to the end of determining what *a* feminist theory of war(s) might be, a dialectical-hermeneutic view would find the substance and identity/ies of feminist (war) theorizing in those differences rather than in their resolution. In Alker's terms, focusing on narrative scripts and their underlying plots and associated transformational grammars not only helps reconstitute international relations within the dialectical-hermeneutic tradition as a reconstructive but fallible science of human possibilities.[63]

In this understanding, feminist war theorizing is realist and liberal, rationalist and constructivist, mainstream[64] and critical, Western and postcolonial, structuralist and poststructuralist, positivist and postpositivist, monist and dualist.[65] It looks for gendered power relations, for women's experiences and lives, for the influence of gender as an idea, for the salience of discourses of gender, and for the intersections of gender, race, class, and imperialism. It is interested in meanings and experiences, causes and constitution, consequences and deontological considerations. Those strands of feminist theorizing bridge conflicts, value diversity for diversity's sake, urge solidarity, assert superiority, compete, and ignore differences. It is the sharing, the interpretation, and the principled opposition of antagonistic approaches that *make* feminist theorizing of war (even though they might appear to inhibit it). Seen holistically, "it is a fundamentally and deeply relational journey, full of conflict."[66]

In this view, it is unnecessary to solve or discard the differences among feminist theories, because feminist inquiry is constituted by both contestability and actual contestation. It is not the sum of different strands of feminist theorizing or the victor in a competition between approaches, but "the narrative generated from their engagements, arguments, disagreements, and compromises."[67] Rather than selecting a particular feminist approach, the feminist theorizing about war in this book treats feminisms as plural, finding their substance in the process of theorizing, in the contributions of various different approaches, and in argumentation among those approaches.

Seeing feminist war theorizing as dialectical-hermeneutic changes both the justification for engaging in research and the process of doing research.[68] Such an approach sees the goal of feminist war theorizing as asking questions and raising problems rather than attempting to solve them; as exchanging ideas rather than seeking absolute truths; as drawing attention to a field of inquiry rather than exploring every detail; and as provoking discussion rather than making conclusive statements.

This means feminist war theorizing can have divergent (and sometimes incommensurable) goals.[69] The outline of the conflicts and contestations both among feminists and between feminists and war studies in this book is not a an outline of problems that need to be solved or divides that need to be crossed, healed, or closed. Instead, those debates, along with how they are handled and addressed, constitute a feminist theory of war.[70] It is in this spirit that this book and the feminist war theorizing contained therein is (not only multi-method but) multi-epistemological.[71]

Operating within a positivist epistemological framework, what do gender lenses tell us about war studies? Critiquing a positivist epistemological framework, what do gender lenses tell us about war studies? What does reading gender through both positivist and anti-positivist lenses tell us about what war is, what causes it, and what its consequences are? What do feminisms tell us about different paradigmatic approaches to the study of war? What do different sorts of feminism have to offer? What can we learn from their similarities? From discussions among them? Or from their differences? How might that interact with existing mainstream and critical war theorizing? These are the sort of questions that viewing feminisms' differences dialectically might inspire for feminist war theorizing. The next section talks about setting up feminist war theorizing as a dialogue between multiple feminisms and war studies, seeing the substance in the processes and debates.

DIALOGUING WITH THE WAR STUDIES

It is true that feminist work that might be relevant to war theorizing has often been neglected by nonfeminist war theorists. But it is also true that feminisms, while they have provided important insights about the nature, causes, and consequences of war(s) through early feminist work in IR and the developing subfield of feminist security studies, have rarely addressed the "war question"[72] or the "war puzzle"[73] in the limited terms it is conceived of in traditional war studies and IR directly. This may be because of the difficult and complex nature of such an engagement and/or the fraught politics of studying war on those terms, which has been (in my opinion, correctly) critiqued by feminist scholars as being partial, gendered, biased, epistemologically narrow, and empirically incomplete.[74]

Still, as I argue above, as incomplete as it is, (genderless) war theorizing should be engaged through gender lenses, which should evaluate the war puzzle (or perhaps more aptly, war puzzles), through gendered lenses without losing the epistemological, ontological, and political uniqueness of the contributions of feminist scholarship. Some recent feminist work on war is doing just that in a variety of interesting ways. For example, Christine Sylvester's recent work has been developing a sensory/experiential approach to the war question in (feminist) IR.[75] Cynthia Enloe's recent book on the Iraq War told stories of gender and both macropolitics and micropolitics through narratives about eight women's lives affected in radically different ways by the conflict.[76]

Still, feminist scholars often keep critical distance between their work and study of war "proper,"[77] particularly as understood in the mainstream of war studies/security studies.[78] Some feminists do so because they are concerned with the intellectual and political risks of such engagement. As Sarah Brown warned:

> The danger in attempts to reconcile international relations and feminism is two-fold. Most immediately, the danger lies in the uncritical acceptance by feminists of objects, methods, and concepts which presuppose the subordination of women. More abstrusely, it lies in the uncritical acceptance of the very possibility of "gender equality."[79]

In other words, there are dangers in engaging a field which has the logic of masculinity as a foundational assumption. I agree with Brown that such a danger does exist, no matter how critically engagement is approached. As Marysia Zalewski notes, "while 'moving' feminism transforms it, holding it still or secured by the demands of an established discipline to whom 'we' are to make ourselves understood by only invites critical atrophy."[80] That said, I argue that feminist work can only be transformative of war studies if it convinces war studies to transform. That it is, by definition, a project that requires engagement. This is especially true if Kimberly Hutchings is right that "a key reason for the ongoing invisibility of women and gender" in war studies has to do with the "legitimizing function" of gendered discourses.[81]

As such, I take the position that it is necessary to critically engage both war and war theorizing through gender lenses. Still, the relationship between feminist work and the mainstream of the "discipline" of IR remains a rough spot in the development of feminist theorizing of war and wars.[82] This is because, as J. Ann Tickner describes, there is a "chilly reception" for feminist theorizing, where the mainstream is "asking feminists to do more of the moving" and "give epistemological positions which they believe are better suited to uncovering oppressive gender hierarchies" or risk obscurity.[83] As a result, "all too often, [the mainstream's] claims of gender neutrality mask deeply embedded masculinist assumptions which can naturalize or hide gender differences and gender inequalities."[84] This means that feminist attempts to engage are often greeted with either silence or criticism.[85]

The difficulties with engagement do not only come from the mainstream, but also from some feminist scholars who remain unconvinced that engagement is worthwhile. Some feminist scholars, though they see gender as a crucial analytical category in global politics, choose to write for a feminist audience rather than do the laborious and often unrewarding work of attempting to speak to the discipline as a whole. For some of these scholars, this makes sense because they believe that the mainstream of war studies will never have an interest in making feminist sense of war and conflict, so transformative effort is wasted energy.[86] For others like Sarah Brown, a lack of interest in engaging the mainstream of the discipline comes from a concern with losing the ontological and epistemological uniqueness of feminist scholarship in order to be accepted by or curry favor with the mainstream of the discipline, especially but not only because of a sense that such a mission is likely to fail.[87] As a result, while some feminist scholars look to engage the mainstream of the discipline, others are "now actively reconstructing IR without reference to what the 'mainstream' asserts rightly belongs inside the discipline. In so doing they are showing that it is more effective to refuse to engage in disciplinary navel-gazing inspired by positivist epistemological angst."[88] This approach argues that feminism is freer, better scholarship when it does not get bogged down in the (often irrelevant) politics of disciplinary boundaries.[89]

I am concerned that ignoring the mainstream of the discipline is a luxury that feminist inquiry just does not have, both because there is a serious power inequity between mainstream IR and feminist work[90] and because there is intellectual and policy value in the engagement. I have previously suggested that the engagement strategy is promising for the productivity of mainstream–feminist conversations, and have held J. Ann Tickner's work up as an example of a good engagement strategy:

> Tickner, while maintaining that feminist insights should fundamentally transform the ontological, epistemological, and methodological foundations of IR, consistently engages mainstream scholars' ideas about the factors that make global politics. In her work, Tickner painstakingly demonstrates how IR scholars would benefit from incorporating a feminist perspective in their research and teaching, in terms of issues of import to them, including increased explanatory leverage and more nuanced conceptual operationalization.[91]

A critical engagement that includes critique and rethought could serve to unsettle the discipline's substantive and methodological boundaries.[92] The goals of this rethought include: "to point out the exclusions and biases of 'mainstream' IR[/war theorizing], . . . to make women as visible as social, economic, and political subjects in international politics, . . . to analyze how gender inequalities were embedded in day-to-day practices of international relations, and . . . to empower women as subjects of knowledge."[93]

There are valid arguments that such engagement approaches are risky, and the question of what feminism gives up by talking to the mainstream is an important one. In addition to these issues, questions of how such conversations would occur given the risks are often explored more by trial-and-error than they are by careful theoretical planning and analysis. This may be because of the (personal and intellectual) stakes in engaging with war studies.[94] It may also have to do with the diversity of feminisms addressing the question.

On top of these issues, there also remain specific difficulties inherent in producing what the subtitle of this book promises: feminist theorizing about war. Those difficulties include (but are not limited to): the difficulties of conversations between (largely positivist and largely masculinist) war studies and critical feminist (often postpositivist) theorizing; the multiple feminist perspectives (with some incommensurable elements) that might be incorporated into feminist theorizing about war; the question of how one knows (if one knows) about the meaning, causes, and consequences of war(s); the (intellectual and material) breadth and depth of scholarly material on both "sides" of the divide; and the inaccessibility (either real or contrived) of one discourse to another.[95] This situation seems to amount to an intellectual catch-22, in which embracing engagement with the mainstream seems to risk feminisms' intellectual and political integrity, while failing to engage seems to risk feminisms' political mission within the discipline. Feminist scholars debate whether or not traditional war theorizing and feminist approaches can truly engage, and what the cost is.[96]

I argue that a dialectical-hermeneutic approach to engagements *between* feminisms and war studies similar to the one I have adopted for dealing with differences *among* feminisms is called for in this situation. Such an approach sees feminist war studies as in war studies and marginal to it, in security studies and outside of it, engaged in the methodologies of disciplinary inquiry and critical of their potentially insidious implications. Feminisms relate to the mainstream of the discipline by mimicking war theorizing's theories and methods, confronting and hoping to transform war studies, ignoring either the power or the existence of mainstream war studies, and constructive engagement. Tensions in the relationships between feminist scholarship and work that would study war as if gender were irrelevant to it are as central to the relationship between gender and war theorizing as the commonalities and agreements between the two might be. They make up its substance.

Seeing the relationship between feminist war theorizing and war theorizing more generally as a dialectical hermeneutic suggests interesting questions for feminist war theorizing. Assuming that structural realists are right about the primacy of the international system in causing war(s), what does feminist theorizing tell us about that system? What do feminist critiques of privileging the system level tell us about war? What do reading feminist insights about structure next to feminist critiques of structure tell us about war(s)? Assuming dyadic-level theorists are correct about the primacy of the interstate relations in causing war(s), what can gender lenses tell us about how states relate and their paths to war? What can feminist critiques tell us about privileging interstate relations when thinking about war(s)? How does looking at feminist evaluations of interstate relations next to feminist critiques of statist approaches to war tell us about war(s)? What about comparing these juxtapositions with system-level ones? Substate-level ones? The multi-epistemological framework in this book pairs discussions of particular approaches to war *on their terms* with critical engagements of the terms of the debate(s) on the meanings, causes, and consequences of war(s).

FEMINIST SECURITY STUDIES AS A STARTING POINT FOR FEMINIST WAR THEORIZING

A long tradition of feminist theorizing about gender and security (and an even longer tradition of the presence of gendered tropes in security discourses) can serve as the foundation for such an engagement. Much early work on gender and security emphasized women as war's "others," peaceful themselves and often objecting to the war or conflict.[97] For example, women's peace movements have been a consistent feature of European politics since the mid–nineteenth century.[98] These movements, looking for links between womanhood, motherhood, and peace, remain an important feature in contemporary global politics, both in terms of general global presences (such as the Women's International League for Peace and Freedom [WILPF])[99] and in particular conflict situations.[100]

A significant body of work (by both scholars and practitioners) addressing the warrants for, strategies of, and successes of women's peace movements is an important strand of feminist theorizing about security. If "feminism is the belief that women are of equal social and human value with men, and that the differences between men and women, whether biologically or culturally derived, do not and should not constitute grounds for discrimination against women,"[101] work on women's peace movements falls easily within a feminist analysis of war, broadly defined.[102]

At the same time, a distinct tradition, feminist security studies (FSS), has recently become interested in thinking in depth not only about the relationships between women and security but about gender/genderings and security issues.[103] Rather than "add women and stir,"[104] FSS works on "analysis of *masculinities* and *femininities* in security situations, and how those gender-associated values and characteristics influence (and are influenced by) people understood as men and women, rather than in the study of the (assumed) differences between men and women."[105]

Although this sort of thinking about the relationship between security and gender differs from traditional understandings of women and peace as linked, it does have its roots in some early feminist theorizing. Theorists from Mary Wollstonecraft[106] and Virginia Woolf[107] to feminist philosophers of science[108] and feminist economists[109] have reflected on the nature of gender, the nature of war, and their intersections. In the 1980s, feminist scholars began to explicitly consider the links between gender subordination and war. For example, Betty Reardon characterized the global political arena as functioning as a "war system" dominated by the links between sex and violence.[110] It was Reardon's understanding that stopping violence and stopping gender subordination were necessarily interdependent.

Sara Ruddick also related gender subordination and war, albeit from a different perspective. She understood motherhood as a role that imbued women as an interest in peace in order to protect their children from violence.[111] Brigit Brock-Utne argued that women had an intrinsic interest in peace, but distinguished negative peace (the lack of war) and positive peace (security and freedom from want and need), and saw women's interest as being in the latter.[112] Other feminists, building on Brock-Utne's argument, suggest the idea that "war" and "peace" can be viewed dichotomously is unrepresentative of human experience. Jean Elshtain argued that the war/peace dichotomy is as gender subordinating as the public/private dichotomy, in that it hides the risks to women in the "in between" or "peace" times.[113]

These reflections spurred a significant amount of feminist work on the relationship between gender, nation, and violence. For example, in the late 1980s, Nira Yuval-Davis explained that "a proper understanding of either [gender or nation] cannot afford to ignore the ways that they are informed and constructed by each other."[114] Cynthia Enloe then linked the gendering of war and militarism to society-wide gendered dynamics, demonstrating that militaries depend on the "cheap, often unpaid" labor of women to do recruiting work, logistical work, sexual service, and morale maintenance.[115]

Enloe saw the "ideology of militarism" as gendered, and argued for a strategy of looking for and at women to understand militarism.[116] She contends that "by looking at women we can reveal, not only the spreading institutional encroachment of the military, but also the processes by which that spread becomes publicly legitimized."[117] She sees this as key because we take militarism for granted "without an investigation of how militarism feeds on masculinist values to sustain it,"[118] especially insomuch as "militaries need women—but they need women to behave *as the gender 'women.'*"[119]

Accordingly, much of the scholarship that looks at security from a feminist perspective has focused on understanding how gendered states produce and are produced by gendered militarisms. For example, in 1992, V. Spike Peterson edited *Gendered States*, which focused on "reframing traditional constructs—states, sovereignty, political identity, security"[120] in order to reveal "the role that gendered divisions of labor and power play in the definition and maintenance of the state and its functions."[121] Recognizing that "national security and military might are preeminently masculine activities and have long been dominated by male actors," feminist scholars seek "new understandings of security in the face of systemic gendered violence (war, rape, domestic violence)" in order to bring attention to "the security issue of the relationship between sexual and international violence."[122] This work looks both to broaden the referent of "security" as well as ideas about what makes that referent "secure."[123] In that sense, feminisms share goals with the critical approaches to security discussed in chapter 1.[124] Yet feminisms also intervene in the discourses of critical approaches to security to highlight the roles of gender tropes, gender significations, gender dynamics, and gendered power invisible in but crucial to even critical security stories.

An example is the recognition that secure states contain (and produce) insecure women. This is not incidental but structural, since "the more a government is preoccupied with what it calls national security, the less likely its women are to have the physical safety necessary for sharing their theorizing about the nation and their security within it."[125] It is also not only about women but about gender, where "it is not possible to separate ideas about gender relations from explanations of war, peace, violence, and security."[126] Those observations led Cynthia Enloe to recognize that "'national security' is gendered"[127] and "further entrenching the masculinization of international politics."[128]

It is these foundations on which scholarship self-identified as FSS builds.[129] This research program has analyzed, critiqued, and reformulated traditional concepts and theories in security studies. As I have described before:

> Research in Feminist Security Studies reformulates mainstream approaches to traditional security issues, foregrounds the roles of women and gender in conflict and conflict resolution, and reveals the blindness of security studies to issues that taking gender seriously shows as relevant to thinking about security . . . .[130]

This research has revealed gender bias in dominant conceptualizations of core concepts such as the state, violence, war, peace, and even security itself, and encouraged redefinition of those concepts in gender-emancipatory ways.[131] Accordingly, feminist work has looked to rethink the gendered functioning of the state,[132] violence,[133] war,[134] and peace[135] with the aim of applying new insights to specific security issues. It has applied gendered analysis of security to the crisis in Bosnia,[136] African peacekeeping operations,[137] civil–military relations in South Korea,[138] and the wars in Iraq.[139] Feminists interested in security have also studied specific tools of war and coercive diplomacy, including small arms and light weapons,[140] weapons of mass destruction,[141] nuclear proliferation,[142] military technological advances,[143] and economic sanctions.[144] They have identified gender-based language and assumptions at the foundations of debates about nuclear strategy,[145] the noncombatant immunity principle,[146] peacekeeping,[147] and various aspects of militarization and soldiering.[148] In addition to critiquing concepts traditionally employed in the study of security, "gender-based perspectives have also uncovered new empirical knowledge about sexual violence in war, and gendered participation in armed conflict."[149]

This growing subfield of FSS is not unified by any given ontological, epistemological, or methodological orientation. It has been focused primarily on "a broad understanding of what counts as a security issue,"[150] "an understanding of the gendered nature of the values prized in the realm of international security,"[151] and gender's "broad and diverse role" in the theory and practice of international security, where gender subordination is "epistemologically constitutive for the theory and practice of security."[152] This work has a lot to contribute to theorizing war(s) from a feminist perspective, including substantial engagement with the causes, practices, and experiences of war and wars.[153] At the same time, the commitments of FSS to a broad understanding of security mean that, while FSS can be a foundation for feminist war theorizing, the two are not (and should not be) synonymous. The concluding section of this chapter talks about building a path from FSS to feminist war theorizing, and, in so doing, lays out this book's approach to engaging war studies.

FROM FEMINIST SECURITY STUDIES TO FEMINIST WAR THEORIZING

Thinking about feminist war theorizing inspires the distinction between important feminist critiques of the narrow subject matter and object of traditional security studies[154] and the need for feminists to study the traditional content of security studies (war and militarism) "straight up."[155] As I mentioned in the introduction, looking at war through gendered lenses suggests that using gender as an analytic category is essential to defining, analyzing, and explaining war in causal and constitutive terms. It sees war as productive of and reflective of gender norms in global politics. Theorizing war from a feminist perspective, then, is a significant task.

In my view, seeing gender as a crucial part of war and war studies means characterizing it as both constitutive of and a causal factor in the making and fighting of war(s).[156] In other words, this book does not make the case that gender is useful in rethinking some (constitutive) war narratives and war theories and not other (causal) ones. Instead, it argues that gender analysis is transformative of war theorizing. Some feminists argue that the exclusion of gender concerns from a particular policy decision is a *causal factor* in its failure,[157] or, as this book does, that gender hierarchy is a key *causal factor* in war-making and war-fighting. On the other hand, Birgit Locher and Elisabeth Prugl hold up Cynthia Enloe's work on gender and militarism as an example of constitutive feminist argumentation.[158] According to them, Enloe "claims that relationships between governments depend on the construction and reconstruction of gender and that such relations produce certain notions of femininity and masculinity. Gender in her work emerges as constitutive of international relations and vice versa."[159] Rather than privilege one or the other, this book pays attention to both, arguing that feminist causal claims and feminist constitutive claims combine to give us an idea about how feminism(s) might revision, retheorize, and potentially recreate war(s) and war studies.

Using these tools, feminist theorizing of war needs to account for, and provide evidence for, the claim that "gender matters in what we study, why we study, and how we study global politics."[160] This claim has a number of elements—it suggests that, to know what a feminist theory of war might be, we have to not only rethink the theoretical suppositions of war studies, but its epistemologies, methodologies, and methods. Epistemologically, feminist political theorizing suggests that "whatever knowledge may ostensibly be about, it is always in part about the relationships between the knower and the known."[161] If the relationship between the knower and the known is a central feature of knowledge, then (all) knowledge-building is a political enterprise, and feminist knowledge-building is explicitly engaged a feminist politics of ending gender subordination.[162]

These epistemological understandings have methodological implications for feminist work theorizing war and/or wars, because feminist theorizing of war is/will be looking not only to understand the war-making and war-fighting but also to highlight its injustices, and to change those injustices. For this reason, feminists have led the way in introducing and applying "hermeneutic, historically contingent, sociological, or ethnically based" and "ethnographic, narrative, or cross-cultural methodologies."[163] Even given these methodological innovations, though, it is substance, not methodological commitments, that produces the contents of feminist research journeys in global politics generally and war studies specifically.[164]

The feminist war theorizing in this book grapples with the challenges involved in such a project as a part of a dialogical-theoretical journey. It confronts questions about differences among feminisms, deals with tensions in the relationships between feminist scholarship and non-feminist war theorizing, and suggests an approach to theorizing war from a feminist perspective that might be able to navigate those fault lines. It journeys through exploration, critique, engagement, argument, reconstruction, and reformulation, exploring wars as gendered and gender as fundamental to war(s).

Particularly, using feminist analyses in dialogue, the remainder of this book explores the ways lived experiences of war are fundamentally (although not exclusively) shaped by gender—gendered roles, gendered personality traits, gendered posturing, gendered hierarchies, gendered divisions of labor, and gendered distributions of resources. Gender as a noun, as a verb, and as a performance is constitutive of people's lives before, during, and after wars, and the stories told of those wars. Taking note of the ways that gender(s) and war(s) interact leads one to see war as not only gendered, but as fundamentally more complex, multifaceted, and multilevel than traditionally understood. These understandings of what war is and how it works are different at a very basic level than those in mainstream theoretical approaches, and shape feminisms' engagements with that mainstream in the coming chapters that address the causes, practices, and experiences of war(s).

CHAPTER 3

Anarchy, Structure, Gender, and War(s)

Paying serious attention to women can expose how *much* power it takes to maintain the international political system in its present form.

—CYNTHIA ENLOE, *BANANAS, BEACHES, AND BASES*

What is the nature of the international system? How does that influence whether or not war happens generally? Or whether or not a particular war happens? International relations (IR) theorists have paid significant attention to what the international system structure is—and the great majority of them identify it as anarchical. Decades of theorizing about the causes of war, given international system anarchy, has produced nuanced accounts of balance of power, balance of threat, offensive realism, defensive realism, and cooperation under anarchy, as discussed in some detail in chapter 1.

What these accounts share is a story of states as units in the international system, looking to survive in the state of nature. Because that anarchic state of nature is without an ultimate authority, there is always a risk of conflict among unit-states. This serves as one of IR's foundation narratives about the causes of war. This chapter engages that narrative through gender lenses, asking what if there is more to the international system structure? What if gender hierarchy is structural in the international system? What would it mean to recognize that? How would we understand the system differently? How would we understand war differently?

Inspired by these questions, this chapter focuses on exploring the relevance of gender to understanding the general causes of "war," or, in Kenneth Waltz's terms, "third image"/international system structural analysis.[1] It begins with a brief discussion of the promises and pitfalls of engaging in third-image theorizing of war(s) through feminist lenses.

It then expands on chapter 1's discussion of structural theorizing of war(s), dealing with the relationships among anarchy, structure, and war in traditional war theorizing. The chapter continues, painting a picture of what gender hierarchy would look like as structural—generally and in the international system. It then explores the argument that the international system is gender hierarchical based on expected manifestations of gender in unit identity, unit capability, and unit interaction. It continues to look at what structural gender hierarchy would mean for the causes of war generally and wars specifically, leading up to a conclusion suggesting the productivity of third-image feminist analysis for war theorizing.

ENGAGING THE THIRD IMAGE

The first step to engaging in feminist third-image theorizing is having a sense of which third-image theorizing is the appropriate starting point for feminist analysis. This chapter engages most directly with Kenneth Waltz's understandings of structure in global politics, in part because Waltz's work serves as the foundation for much of IR's history of structural theorizing but also because "structural realism is [a] far richer sociological theory of international politics than its critics and defenders usually recognize."[2] In Waltz's conception of structure, "action is a social and relational category" in which interaction is "the product of discrete and irreducible systems" of component parts.[3] Such an approach emphasizes material and authoritative aspects of international system structure over social or cultural elements but does not reject the influence of the social elements.[4] This approach may be the "hard case" for gender analysis of global politics (which many consider to be exclusively social), but could also serve as foundational for feminist engagements with the core of structural theorizing. This chapter, then, takes a feminist third-image approach to theorizing war, critiquing and building off Waltz's ideas about structure.

It is important to note at the outset of such an engagement, however, that third-image theorizing is not an intuitive step for feminist theorizing and will have feminist critics. Many feminist theorists explicitly express a political commitment to understanding the world from the perspectives of women and/or other marginalized or socially subjugated actors.[5]

Such a commitment seems to be at odds with structural theorizing, and feminists have correspondingly critiqued the neglect of "low politics" in structural war theorizing.[6] Particularly, feminists have read structural realist accounts of anarchy as ignoring questions of the politics of identity, the role of social hierarchy in organizing political life, and the links between militarism and sexism and racism.[7] Feminists have also criticized structural theorizing for disaggregating the three levels of analysis as though they are separable, when in practice they are interdependent.[8]

Perhaps because of these problems, feminist IR scholars rarely use the word "structure" and even more rarely discuss the relationship between gender and structure in the international system.[9] While that reaction is understandable, I argue that failing to engage third-image theorizing directly assumes either that there is no structure in Waltzian terms in global politics or that gender is irrelevant to understanding that structure. This chapter argues that both assumptions are problematic and that there is a structure to the international system—a structure that cannot be fully understood without gender analysis.

STRUCTURAL REALISM AND ITS CRITICS ON STRUCTURE AND WAR

In initially articulating the argument that international system structure is a permissive cause of war(s), Kenneth Waltz was interested in the recurrence of war despite its many, varied, and sometimes contradictory individual or state-level causes.[10] In other words, according to Waltz, the third image was never meant to account for all the variation in war(s) or to be seen in isolation from other causes of wars. Instead, it was a different sort of cause (permissive) with a different role (as a condition of possibility).[11] In this context, Waltz made the argument that there was something inherent in the international structure that was a condition of possibility, or a permissive cause, of war. He defined structure as "the arrangement, or the ordering, of the parts of a system."[12] Structures, in Waltz's understanding, have three properties: the principle by which a system is ordered, the specification of functions of different units, and the distribution of capabilities across units.[13] The effect of structure, according to Waltz, is that "political structures shape political processes" such that "political structure produces a similarity in process and performance so long as a structure endures."[14]

Anarchy is the structural feature of global politics that Waltz sees serving as a permissive cause of war. He argues "the prominent characteristic of international politics . . . seems to be the lack of order and organization" and "in looking for international structure, one is brought face to face with the invisible, an uncomfortable position to be in."[15] Waltz equates the invisibility of structure with its nonexistence and characterizes the international system as "decentralized and anarchic,"[16] which makes war possible.[17] The understanding that the international arena is anarchical has also been adopted by proponents of liberal institutionalism and constructivism, though they often disagree with realists about the consequences of anarchy.[18]

Waltz points to several reasons why structural anarchy explains the recurrence of war, even given wars' multiple causes. First, structural anarchy leaves states without exogenous authority to provide protection or constrain behavior, which leads to the recurrence of war. Waltz explains "there is a constant possibility of war in a world in which there are two or more states seeking to promote a set of interests and having no agency above them upon which they can rely for protection."[19] Second, in a system without any assurances from a higher power, "states seek to ensure their survival," and the international system is one of "self-help."[20] Third, because states in an anarchic system are undifferentiated by function, they "are then distinguished by their greater or lesser capabilities for performing similar tasks," which spurs competitiveness.[21] Neorealism often takes the conception of anarchy as a starting point for analyzing both the causes of war generally and the causes of wars particularly.[22]

The idea that structural anarchy is a permissive cause of war, however, has its critics. Some critics, mostly from the liberal tradition, contend that international anarchy is tempered by the existence of some order and organization. A second set of realists' critics, mainly constructivists, argue that there is nothing essential about anarchy that makes war either possible or probable, because "self-help and power politics do not follow either logically or causally from anarchy."[23] A third approach questions the utility of understanding anarchy as a permissive cause of war. I will discuss these three criticisms, and realisms' answers to them, briefly.

Cooperation Under Anarchy?[24]

A number of IR liberals contend that that international anarchy is somehow modified by some order among states. As Waltz describes, in many of these analyses, "anarchy is taken to mean not just the absence of government but the presence of disorder and chaos. Since world politics, although not reliably peaceful, falls short of unrelieved chaos, students are inclined to see a lessening of anarchy in each outbreak of peace."[25] While this is an oversimplification of the liberal criticism of realist thinking, the key elements are present. This first category of structural realism's critics notes that the lack of government in the international arena is incomplete in two senses: there are some ordering institutions, and those institutions do hold off the sort of chaos Hobbes envisions in the anarchical state of nature.[26]

Realists answer these critics by contending that their argument takes nothing from anarchy as a permissive cause of war: those institutions and the progress they make are process, not structure, and the international system remains fundamentally anarchic.[27] Additionally, John Mearsheimer contends that "institutions have minimal influence on state behavior."[28] Though "pure" anarchy does not exist, "to distinguish realms by their ordering principles is nonetheless proper and important," not least because the theoretical implication of Waltz's work, he insists, remains.[29] Structural realists do not argue that international anarchy is *the only* or even *the main* cause of every war, nor do they argue that it causes constant war. They only argue that anarchy *allows for* the existence of war in the international arena.

Anarchy Is What States Make of It[30]

A second set of structural realism's critics, mainly constructivists, argue that there is nothing essential about international anarchy that makes war possible. For example, Alexander Wendt makes the argument that "self-help and power politics do not follow either logically or causally from anarchy" and therefore "if today, we find ourselves in a self-help world, this is due to process, not structure."[31] Wendt contends that "there is no 'logic' of anarchy apart from the practices that create and instantiate one structure of identities and interests rather than another . . . . Anarchy is what states make of it."[32] The Waltzian definition of anarchy, according to Wendt, "predicts little about states' behavior," omitting important issues such as mutual recognition, dynastic ties, and satisfaction with the status quo.[33] Instead, "the meanings in terms of which action is organized arise out of interaction," and "if self-help is not a constitutive feature of anarchy, it must emerge causally from processes in which anarchy plays only a permissive role."[34] Different constructivist views propose different mechanisms for the evolution of the current form of international anarchy. Wendt suggests, for example, that there are a number of "cultures of anarchy" that can cause anarchy to have different practical implications, accounting for culture as "socially shared knowledge."[35]

Still, Waltz argued in 1979 that "a systems approach is required only if the structure of the system and its interacting units mutually effect each other," implying that a sense of co-constitutive social construction was inherent in his theoretical assumptions.[36] Waltz himself claimed to be arguing *against* theories that paid attention to structure without behavior and omitted function. Instead, he expressed interest in explaining the part of global politics that anarchy shapes. In defending structural realism later, Waltz distinguished between "within-system changes" that "take place all the time, some important, some not" and "changes in the structure of the system" in which "if the system were transformed, international politics would no longer be international politics, and the past would no longer serve as a guide to the future."[37] Waltz argues that "the world, however, has not been transformed" and constructivist theory of the social construction of world politics "does not break the essential continuity of international politics," which can be characterized mainly by the structural realist assumption that the key feature of the system—anarchy—permits and shapes processes of self-help and power politics and, ultimately, conflict.[38]

Anarchy Is the Wrong Question and the Wrong Answer

A third approach, largely presenting arguments as a part of the "agent-structure"[39] debate in IR, argues that the contention that anarchy is a permissive cause of war is either untrue or trivial. This argument was best articulated by Hidemi Suganami, who contends that

> International anarchy can be only *a*—rather, *the* permissive cause (or necessary condition) of war, and it is so only if the term is understood to mean "the absence from the international system of a perfectly effective anti-war device." However, "international anarchy" in this sense accounts for the possibility of war in a trivial manner: war would be impossible in the presence of a perfectively effective anti-war device anywhere. That is what "a perfectly effective anti-war device" *means*. Furthermore, since such a device cannot possibly exist in the international system, . . . what cannot be in principle present cannot very meaningfully be said to be absent. Indeed, the absence from the international system of a perfectly effective anti-war device can hardly be an appropriate definition of international anarchy, nor even a meaningful structural characterization of the international environment: such a device cannot be a part of any social structure.[40]

In other words, Suganami is arguing there is little meaning in calling anarchy a permissive cause of war if anarchy is defined in the strong sense as the absence of a world government—because such a condition is a constant (invariable) feature of the international system, and war is a variable condition in international politics. Therefore, anarchy, in some sense, does not "matter" in determining *when* and *how* war occurs. As a structural feature, it is weakly explanatory, given the lack of variation in anarchy in the strictest sense. The only way to make anarchy a determinant feature in when and how war occurs, according to Suganami, is to define it in a way that trivializes anarchy itself, as the "absence of a perfect anti-war device."[41]

Yet a weaker definition of anarchy does not solve the problems that Suganami identifies. For example, even Waltz acknowledges that there is some order in international politics, and defines anarchy more weakly, as decentralization, disorganization, and/or lack of formal structural differentiation between unit functions. Suganami points out that this definition is insufficient to render anarchy a necessary condition of war. Therefore, Suganami argues, the realist thesis that international anarchy is a permissive cause of war collapses in the face of a dilemma: either it is trivial or it is not verifiable. Suganami argues that anarchy is neither a necessary (permissive) nor sufficient (direct) cause of war, even if it does influence the making of wars. Waltzian analysis might suggest that these differences may be semantic, where realists mean to characterize anarchy as *a*, rather than *the*, permissive cause of war.

Is Anarchy a Permissive Cause of War?

The three groups of critics of the structural realist position together make the important point that international anarchy as a permissive cause of war is fundamentally limited. One concern that many critics share is that anarchy as a permissive cause of war predicts the existence of war, but not individual wars. This is because anarchy is constant; war recurs but is by no means constant. As Waltz originally noted, anarchy is a structural factor that accounts for "the recurrence of war" despite its "various causes."[42] Many, however, find something unsatisfactory about such a structural factor. In Suganami's words, it is "trivial," since it is always there (and thus a permissive cause of war) but never itself sufficient as a cause (of wars individually or variation in them.[43] Beyond that, the constructivist criticism that anarchy does not, either always or inevitably, lead to conflict born of power politics and self-help, resonates.

While some theorists take these problems with a structural realist approach to the third image as a call to move attention from structure to process and/or to radically reconceptualize structure, another route, explored more in Waltz's *Theory of International Politics* than in his critics' work since,[44] looks for a more nuanced understanding of the international system structure that might lend more substance to the international structure as a permissive (and perhaps even sufficient) cause of war. While remaining committed to third-image theorizing, this path of inquiry reopens the question of the content of international structure, if not its meaning.[45] It asks if a structural property of international system *other than* anarchy explain the possibility of (and perhaps occurrence of) war.

A Waltzian understanding of structure as constituting a system's ordering principles, specifying the functions of its units, and distributing capabilities among those units provides space for exploring other potential structural factors in global politics.[46] In this conception, structure is manifested in system order, unit function, unit capabilities, and, perhaps most clearly, in political process, which Waltz contends reflects structural features.[47] These different areas, then, can be looked at for evidence of structural influences other than anarchy.

Waltz himself implies the possibility of such alternatives when he uses the invisibility of structure to determine its nonexistence.[48] If international structure is "the invisible," as Waltz accounts, two possibilities exist: either, as Waltz concludes, international structure is the null set, anarchy; or there is substance to international structure (it exists in some meaningful form) but is invisible (or informal) and thus cannot easily be seen or identified.[49] In other words, one can imagine a structural (or at least structurationist)[50] account of international politics that notes structural features of the international system that are unseen but key ordering principles. It is along those lines that I argue gender hierarchy is structural in the international system, though unseen by most theorists and practitioners of global politics.[51]

SYSTEM STRUCTURE THROUGH GENDER LENSES

Feminist scholars have long been concerned with the enduring nature of gender subordination in social and political life. Feminist political theorists have long argued that all systems of political thought and political interaction have conceptions of gender, and "the conceptions of gender that are implicit and explicit in these systems are not accidental, but necessary" and "are also constitutive."[52] While various feminist theorists have found the source of the enduring nature of gender hierarchy in different sources, such as reproductive capacity, language, performance, sexuality, human nature and/or psychology, human social organization, and evolution, feminist theorizing has emphasized that, though genders and their relationships change over time, place, and culture, gender hierarchies can be found across all of those variations.[53] As such, feminist theorists have provided evidence that "issues of gender are clearly central to any understanding of the political" interpretively, empirically, and/or genealogically.[54]

While gender has not been characterized explicitly in IR as international structure, the groundwork for such an argument has been laid.[55] Feminist theorizing has made the argument that the social and political atmosphere of the international arena is fundamentally gendered. Particularly, J. Ann Tickner has observed that "much of our knowledge about the world has been based on knowledge about men."[56] As such, feminist work in IR has focused on "uncovering previously hidden gender hierarchies" because "they contribute to conflict and injustice in ways that have detrimental effects on the security of both men and women."[57] Feminists have demonstrated the influence of gender in global politics in a number of areas, including but not limited to: "the gendering of nationalist and ethnic identities can exacerbate conflict," "the privileging of characteristics associated with a stereotypical masculinity in states' foreign policies contributes to the legitimization not only of war but of militarization more generally," and "women are disproportionately situated at the bottom of the socioeconomic scale in all societies."[58]

In this view, the relationship between masculinities and femininities constitutes and is constituted by gender subordination in global politics. Seeing gender relations as tied to gender subordination has led theorists like R. W. Connell to characterize gender as constitutive of and constituted by history[59] and Lauren Wilcox to account for gendered social hierarchy as a "structural feature of social and political life" that "profoundly shapes our place in, and view of, the world."[60]

While the existence of gender and gender hierarchies is often characterized as (in various capacities) universal in feminist theorizing, the *genders* in those hierarchies differ. If "gender" is the existence of a set of characteristics associated with (perceived) sex that form a social structure, *a gender* is *a particular* set of social characteristics associated with *a particular* (perceived) sex in a particular sociopolitical context. Masculinities and femininities change over time, and differ by location and cultural context as well as race and social class. In terms familiar to IR, perhaps, the existence of genders and of hierarchies between genders is constant, and the content of those genders varies.

Waltz's distinction between changes *in* the system and changes *of* the system might be useful for understanding this view of gender as structural.[61] Waltz sees "the system" as anarchical, which is the structure so long as there is no world government, which would be a change *of* the system. On the other hand, things *in* the system change regularly—the system of states sometimes contains a couple of stray regional organizations and sometimes contains a robust system of international organizations. In these terms, the constant element of gender is that human social and political organization is authorized, intervened in, legitimated, and organized along gender lines. Changes "in" the system, of changes within the gendered order, are more common and more likely than changes "of" the system (undoing gendered order), since both masculinities and femininities (and the relative power among the multiple ones) change over time, place, and situation.

Regardless, given all of these gendered parts of the international order, feminists have (for the most part) stopped short of characterizing the international structure *as a gender hierarchy*, especially in realist/materialist terms. Feminist concerns with the margins in global politics,[62] as well as feminist wariness of structural realism,[63] may contribute to a reticence to use explicitly structural language. For these reasons, most feminist scholars have avoided explicitly structural analysis in IR. Still, as I argue above, such an avoidance suggests that either there is no Waltzian structure or such structure is gender neutral. Instead, I suggest that there is an international structure, and it is gender hierarchical.

Accordingly, this chapter makes a third-image argument about gender as a factor in the constitution and cause of war(s). This argument is distinct from "second-image" arguments that states are gendered, the level of gender inequality in a state is a predictor of the level of aggressiveness that state will show in interstate relations,[64] or states have gendered relations.[65] That is, if the international system structure is gender hierarchical, its component units (states) are also gendered (particularly in their constitution and relationships), but that is a part and result of structural gender hierarchy rather than confounding evidence for a structural interpretation. In other words, the third-image approach asserts that gender of, within, and among states reflects and reproduces the gendered nature of the international system structure rather than being an incidental property of its units. It is also distinct from "first-image" arguments that gender subordination is a constant part of human nature and therefore a constant part of international interaction or that people's genders or gendered perceptions influence states' likelihood to make wars.[66] Instead, it characterizes gender hierarchy as a sociopolitical ordering principle of the international system rather than an innate property of being human. Finally, it is distinct from the feminist argument that the three levels (the individual, the state, and the system structure) cannot be disaggregated.[67] Though this approach acknowledges connection between the levels, it looks to see if there is something to be gained from an approach that prioritizes a structural approach to thinking about the role of gender.

What Would Structural Gender Hierarchy Look Like?

So what would it mean to see gender hierarchy as structural in global politics? Waltz suggests that a structure in global politics provides an ordering principle, specifications of the functions of the units, and distribution of capabilities among units.[68] Seeing gender hierarchy as structural, then, would mean that gender hierarchy provides an ordering principle for the international system, specifies the functions of units, and distributes capabilities among them. The theoretical groundwork for such an argument can be found in feminist work on gendered organizational structures and cultures in sociology, which explores the idea that gender is a foundational element of organizational structure, where it is "present in processes, practices, images and ideologies, and distributions of power."[69] Joan Acker, talking about organizations more generally, explains that:

> In spite of the feminist recognition that hierarchical organizations are an important location of male dominance, most feminists writing about organizations assume that the organizational structure is gender neutral. . . . on the contrary, assumptions about gender underlie the documents and contracts used to construct organizations and provide the commonsense ground for theorizing them.[70]

Acker is concerned that this dominant feminist approach "implicitly posits gender as standing outside structure" even while critiquing the gender bias in the organizational process.[71] She sees this problem as arising because "the available discourses conceptualize organizations as gender neutral" so "as a relational phenomenon, gender is difficult to see when only the masculine is present," due at least in part to the fact that "men in organizations take their behavior and perspectives to represent the human, organizational structures and processes are theorized as gender neutral."[72] This causes people to think that gender bias and gender discrimination are process-based, rather than structural, in organizations. Therefore, "when it is acknowledged that women and men are affected differently by organizations, it is argued that gendered attitudes and behavior are brought into (and contaminate) essentially gender-neutral structures."[73] Acker suggests that this is a fundamental misreading and instead characterizes gender as a structural feature of organizations:

> To say that an organization, or any other analytic unit, is gendered means that advantage and disadvantage, exploitation and control, action and emotion, meaning and identity, are patterned through and in terms of a distinction between male and female, masculine and feminine. Gender is not an addition of ongoing processes, conceived as gender neutral. Rather, it is an integral part of these processes, which cannot be properly understood without an analysis of gender. . . . Gendering occurs in at least five interacting processes . . . first is the construction of divisions along lines of gender—divisions of labor, of allowed behaviors, of locations in physical space, of power. . . . second is the construction of symbols and images that explain, express, reinforce, or sometimes oppose those divisions. . . . third . . . interactions between women and men, women and women, men and men, including all those patterns that enact dominance and submission. . . . fourth, these processes help to produce gendered components of individual identity. . . . finally, gender is implicated in the fundamental, ongoing processes of creating and conceptualizing social structures . . . a constitutive element in organizational logic.[74]

A gendered structure, in Acker's terms, then, distributes capabilities (defined as advantage and disadvantage, exploitation and control, action and emotion, and meaning and identity) among units on the basis of a unit's place in a gender hierarchy that orders the organization. A gender hierarchical system, then, defines the function of units by dividing labor, constraining allowed behavior, producing gendered components of unit identity, positioning units as dominant and subordinate, and influencing or dictating the ongoing processes of organizational function. Sexes and genders, then, become at least in part differences derived from discrimination in gender-hierarchical organizations.[75]

Tools for Identifying Gender Hierarchy in International Structure

A close look at Acker's understanding of structure in organizations shows that it shares common elements with Waltz's definition of structure in the international system. Both describe structure as a principle that orders systems, specifies the functions of units, distributes capabilities among units, and is productive or constitutive of political processes that shape unit relations. Both also see the structure of the system as shaping unit behavior rather than seeing unit behavior as incidental or as shaping the structure. Mirroring Acker's argument at the international system level might give a sense both of what structural gender hierarchy might look like and of what features might be expected of a gender-hierarchical international system as distinct from a system in which structural gender hierarchy was not a factor. This section lays out what the international system structure might look like were it gender hierarchical, while the next section provides evidence that suggests the feasibility of these propositions.

In spite of the feminist recognition that global politics is an important location of male dominance, most feminist writing about global politics argues that gender hierarchy is socially and politically dominant but does not characterize it as a structural feature of the international system, implying that international structure, if it exists, is gender neutral.[76] On the contrary, assumptions about gender underlie the structure and ordering principles of the international system and provide common-sense ground for theorizing them. Because men in the theory and practice of global politics take their behavior and perspectives to represent the human, international structures and processes are the-. orized as gender neutral. When it is acknowledged that women and men are affected differently in global politics, it is argued that gendered attitudes and behavior are brought into (and contaminate) structures assumed to be gender neutral.[77] When the international system structure is theorized as gender neutral, it is often because of blindness to genderings rather than their absence. Because the available discourses conceptualize international structure as if they constitute gender neutrality, a relational phenomenon, gender is difficult to see when masculinities dominate but are normalized to appear gender neutral. Even feminist theorizing focuses on moving away from structural theory, which implicitly posits gender as standing outside structure. This makes the structural nature of gender hierarchy "invisible" to scholars like Waltz who are not looking for it.

Even if it is invisible, there are ways, following Acker, to tell if gender is a structural feature of global politics. Gender is a key part of international structure if advantage and disadvantage, exploitation and control, action and emotion, meaning and identity, are patterned through masculinities and femininities. If units in the international system have their interactions, competitions, and relationships governed and ordered by perceived associations with gender-based characteristics, the international system can be understood as gender hierarchical. In this understanding, gender is not an addition to ongoing processes that are conceived to be gender neutral. Instead, in a gender-hierarchical international structure, units have their labor, allowed behaviors, locations in physical space, and power distributed on the basis of perceived gender characteristics. This occurs within a system of constructed symbols and images that explain, express, reinforce, and sometimes contest these gendered divisions. Units interact on the basis of these gender distinctions and symbols. Gendered representations help produce gendered components of state and national identity such as notions of honor, shame, chivalry, and protection. Gender is implicated in creating and conceptualizing political processes and social relations between units and is a constitutive element of the international system.[78] One might ask, given these parameters, how would you tell if the system actually *is* these things—and therefore is gender hierarchical?

Combining Waltz's understanding of what an international structure is with Acker's concept of how a gendered structure in manifested in organizational and unit behavior yields a description of what gendered structure might look like. In short, if gender hierarchy were a structural feature of global politics, then, we would expect:

1. State identity having gendered components (unit function);
2. States' positions, allowed behaviors, locations in physical space, and power being distributed on the basis of perceived gender characteristics, and advantage, meaning, control, and action between states to be distributed on the basis of association with masculinity and femininity (unit capability distribution); and
3. Interstate interaction being premised on the gender hierarchy between states (production of political processes for unit interaction).

The next section argues there is evidence for each of these propositions that suggests theorizing the international system as gender hierarchical might be useful for thinking about the causes of war(s).

IS THE INTERNATIONAL SYSTEM GENDER HIERARCHICAL?

This exploration starts by matching work on gender and IR with the general narrative of a hypothesized gendered international system structure that was worked out in the previous section and then goes on to explore the particular predictions outlined above concerning unit function, unit relative capabilities, and political processes.

The first part of the story of the international system as gender hierarchical is that assumptions about gender underlie the ordering principles of the international system and provide commonsense ground for theorizing them. Feminists have characterized the global political arena as a "patriarchal structure of privilege and control."[79] Feminist research has observed times when "the structure of political communities has assumed gendered forms"[80] ordered by "gender relations [which] structure social power," suggesting gender is such an ordering principle.[81] These observations are rooted in empirical feminist work, which shows gender operating in how political leaders are chosen,[82] how state governments work,[83] how militaries function,[84] and how economic benefit is distributed.[85] States have shown their military prowess, judged and asserted their relative power, and demonstrated and adjusted their relative economic status through gendered competition using gendered language.[86] The gender hierarchy in the world "out there" can be read as replicated in the "commonsense ground" or traditional theorizing in IR, which feminist theorists[87] have characterized as partial at best and unrepresentative at worst because it often analyzes the perspectives and lives of only a small, elite, male portion of the global population.

This theme in feminist theorizing in IR lends credibility to the idea that international structures are theorized as gender neutral because men take their perspectives to represent the human. I have noted above that gender is not taken account of either in conventional theories of international structure or conventional theories of war. Feminists have characterized conventional knowledge in IR as problematic because it is constructed only by those in a position of privilege, with resultant distorted views of the world.[88] As such, it has been a crucial part of the feminist project in IR to "not only add women but also ask how gender—a structural feature of social life—has been rendered invisible" by working to disaggregate knowledge from the masculine biases that permeate our perceptions of what it means to know.[89] Often, in disciplinary knowledges, "gender" is seen as a proxy for "women" because women are perceived to have gender while men are not.

Another element of the account above is that, when it is acknowledged that gender plays a role in global politics, it is often discussed as a corruption of a gender-neutral system rather than a product of a gendered system. For example, some work argues that it is states that treat their women poorly that corrupt not only the gender order but the potential for interstate peace.[90] In these accounts, it is not the structure of the international system that is gendered, but the states that are "bad" are gender corrupt an otherwise gender-neutral system. This logic is replicated in many discussions of gender in the policy world. For example, "gender mainstreaming" agendas engage in a process of integrating gender concerns into the structures that already exist in governments and organizations, assuming that the absence of gender is a corruption of a gender-neutral system rather than in line with a gendered structure.[91] The scenario derived from Acker's theorizing suggests that when gender subordination is characterized as the exception, rather than the rule, in international political interactions, gender is difficult to see because the masculine is at once assumed and invisible. The recurrent focus in feminist work on the need to ask war theorizing "where are the women?"[92] and "where is gender?"[93] suggests it is plausible that this is the case in war theorizing specifically and IR more generally. In these terms, it is important to note that the masculine here involves and implicates, but is not reducible to, men.

Waltz "tests" his idea of structure primarily by its predictive power and its indirect manifestations.[94] He argues that because the anarchical nature of the international system is invisible and thus cannot be directly verified or proven; it must be verified by its manifestations and implications.[95] This verification, to Waltz, comes by examining unit function, distribution of capabilities across units, and political processes of unit interaction. Above, we looked at what that would mean if the international system were gender-hierarchical. The remainder of this section considers whether there is evidence in those three observable parts of global politics that the international system may be gender hierarchical.

Unit Function: Does State Identity Have Gendered Components?[96]

In Waltz's account, "a system is composed of a structure and of interacting units" where "the structure is the system-wide component that makes it possible to think about the system as a whole" and "the arrangement of units is a property of the system."[97] Waltz sees the system as an anarchy that by definition specifies that units have the same function. Still, Waltz gives a sense of what would be different if the system were a hierarchy, because "hierarchy entails relations of super- and subordination among a system's parts, and that implies their differentiation."[98] Calling states "like units" in Waltz's terms is "to say that each state is like all other states in being an autonomous political unit."[99] Waltz sees states as performing fundamentally similar tasks in similar ways and argues that the differences between states are in capabilities, not in function.[100]

This section explores two arguments about gender and the function of the units of the international system. First, it argues that gender can be seen as constituting unit "function" in the international system, whether the units are "like" or differentiated. Second, it proposes that gender hierarchy actually differentiates state-unit function.

The argument that gender constitutes the function of units in the international system is supported by the degree to which states define their identities (and therefore the tasks of domestic and foreign policy) in gendered ways. A growing literature on ontological security characterizes state identity in terms of "sense of self," a language that has long been used in feminist accounts of nation and nationalism.[101] Feminists who have worked on nationalism have argued that national identity and gender are inextricably linked and that "all nationalism are gendered, all nationalisms are invented, and all are dangerous."[102] Feminists have shown gendered imagery is salient in the construction of national identities particularly when, often, women are the essence of, the symbols of, and the reproduction of state and/or national identity.[103]

Research in gender and security has demonstrated that state identity has gendered components and interstate interaction is often premised on the gender hierarchy between states, in which gender norms are a crucial part of competition between states. States compete to prove their relative and absolute masculinity, whether or not they are approaching power parity. For example, as J. Ann Tickner explains, "the 1991 Persian Gulf War was frequently depicted as a personal contest between Saddam Hussein and George H. W. Bush and described in appropriate locker-room or football language."[104] In states' competitions, in war, trade, or sport, the winner's masculinity is implicitly and often explicitly affirmed, while the loser's masculinity is subordinated or doubted.[105] Feminist work has provided a number of examples of the relationship between feminization and conflictual interstate relations. Another example can be found in Himani Bannerji's analysis of Canadian national identities. Bannerji has noted that Canadian national identities are constructed through "race," class, gender, and other relations of power causing subordinate classes and races to be feminized in relation to the dominant image of Canadian identity, not only within the Canadian state but also in Canada's external projection of nationalist identity.[106] In a different context, Diana Taylor's analysis of the "dirty war" in Argentina characterizes identity in the conflict as "predicated on the internalization of a rigid hierarchy" of gender and argues that "the struggle, as each group aimed to humiliate, humble, and feminize its other, was about gender."[107] Feminist studies have demonstrated that gender has been essential to defining state identity in Korea,[108] modernizing Malaysia,[109] Bengal,[110] Indonesia,[111] Northern Ireland,[112] South Africa,[113] Lebanon,[114] and Armenia.[115]

A brief look at one example recently used in the literature might further illustrate the point. In his book, *Ontological Security in International Relations*, Brent Steele sees honor and shame as shaping states' self-perception of their identities.[116] Contrary to the realist logic that states prioritize survival over honor, Steele argues that states look for honor even to the point of sacrificing physical integrity.[117] To illustrate this, Steele uses the example of the Belgian choice to fight a losing war against the Germans in 1914 rather than allow Germany access to Belgian territory and avoid the casualties and terror involved in their inevitable defeat. Steele notes that honor was implicated in Belgium's response to Germany's ultimatum, given that most policy statements stressed their need to "fight for the honor of the flag" and "avenge Belgian honor."[118]

Feminist analysis suggests that we cannot understand the role of honor in state self-identity without reference to both masculine and feminine conceptions of honor in the state.[119] Masculine conceptions of honor vary between chivalric and protection-oriented and aggressive and prideful, while feminine conceptions of honor often focus on the purity and innocence of the territory of the state and/or the women and children inside. Through gender lenses, the Belgian discussion of national honor in 1914 was one in which the leaders' (masculine) honor was tied to not giving in to, and even resisting, the would-be violators of the territory's (feminine) honor, which was tied to purity. The honor of the Belgian government was linked to unwillingness to sacrifice the honor of the innocent, neutral, vulnerable, and untouchable identity and position of Belgium vis-à-vis its neighboring Germany. It is no coincidence that the following attack was referred to as the "rape of Belgium."[120] In the rape of Belgium narrative, the German invasion spoiled the feminine elements of Belgian state identity, and emasculated Belgian leaders as protectors of Belgium's feminized territory.

Survival or prudence cannot account for Belgium's actions in 1914; in fact, as Steele pointed out, Belgium acted contrary to both. Honor can explain the behavior, but neither the form nor function of that honor is clear without accounting for the gendered elements of Belgian state identity.[121] An account of state identity as gendered can also be read into Germany (as hypermasculine aggressor) and Britain (as chivalrous protector) in the Belgian narrative.

While some might see the influence of gender on state or national identity as a second-image or unit-level explanation, Waltz explains that a factor is structural if it is not influencing state identity (and therefore state function) in states individually, but instead influencing the identities (and therefore functions) of states generally. Feminist scholars have shown that "nationalism is naturalized, and legitimated, through gender discourses that naturalized the domination of one group over another through the disparagement of the feminine."[122] These gender hierarchies are always present even if specific genders and their orders in hierarchies are fungible. In other words, it is not particular nationalisms that are gendered (and some that are not), it is that gender hierarchy as a structural feature of global politics constitutes constituent units, including their national identities. All nationalisms being gendered does not mean that all nationalisms are the same, however. The mechanism through which gender hierarchy can be seen to influence national identity and state function is through the link between any given state's national identity and the hegemonic masculinity or particular ideal-typical gender that is at the top of the gender hierarchy in which state units are situated.[123]

Feminist theorists have used the term *hegemonic masculinity* as an analytical tool to understand the influence of gender on state identity. According to Charlotte Hooper, "hegemonic masculinity is constructed in relation to a range of subordinated masculinities in opposition to femininity."[124] This work does not suggest that states are masculine because they are (mostly) governed by men. Instead, as R.W. Connell explains, "this is not to imply that the personalities of the top male office-holders somehow seep through and stain the institutions. It is to say something much stronger: the state organizational practices are structured in relation to the reproductive arena."[125] An ideal-typical masculinity establishes cultural hegemony in a given context through social process (moral persuasion and consent), social fact (entrenched ideological ascendancy), and physical process (an ethos of coercion).[126] As a result of these continuing processes, hegemonic masculinity is composed of the masculine attributes that "are most widely subscribed to—and least questioned—in a given social formation: the 'common sense' of gender as subscribed to by all men save those whose masculinity is oppositional or deviant."[127] Each hegemonic masculinity is the set of standards to which men (in a particular society and/or globally) are expected to aspire, and which the society is expected to reflect.

For example, Joshua Goldstein argues that the relationship between the hegemonic masculinity and soldiering becomes closer when shame is required to persuade men to fight wars, and masculinities are less militarized in times of peace.[128] A number of feminist scholars have noted that, sometimes, a state's hegemonic masculinity becomes reactionary or "hypermasculine" in response to feeling threatened or undermined, while other times it is more chivalric or protection oriented.[129] Feminists have identified elements of state hypermasculinity in the United States in the post–9/11 era, as well as in the Spanish-American War and the beginning of the Cold War.[130]

Though the relationship between gender and nationalism generally (and genders and nationalisms specifically) influences the function of units whether they are like units (in anarchy) or not like units (indicative of a hierarchical system), evidence of different gendered nationalisms suggests that gender hierarchy in global politics differentiates between functions of units in the system rather than dictating that all units function similarly. Units in the system (even defined in the narrow realist terms whereby only states count as units) do have many similar functions in terms of governance, education, health care, and the like. But especially in their external relations, states also have a number of differentiated functions, often glossed over in realist theory. Some states were/are colonizers, while some states were colonized and still deal with remaining markers of colonization. Some states are aggressors, while other states are the victims of aggression. Some states are protectors, while other states require protection. Some states provide peacekeeping troops, international humanitarian aid, and other public goods, while other states do not serve those functions.[131] Some states serve to facilitate international cooperation, while others act as cogs in cooperation's wheels. Some states see their masculinity as affirmed in the interstate equivalent of rape and pillage, while other states see it in chivalry, honor, and a sense of the genteel.

While Waltz might classify these differences as merely capabilities gaps, different state functions in the community of states do not map one-to-one onto capabilities. Instead, I propose that they map onto the ways that gender shapes state identities and functions. As V. Spike Peterson notes, "not only subjects but also concepts, desires, tastes, styles, ways of knowing . . . can be [masculinized or] feminized" such that states' ontological security is related to their gendered identities.[132] For example, a number of feminist analyses of the United States during the first Gulf War identify its policy choices and military strategies as consonant with a new, post–Cold War "tough-but-tender" image of American masculinity, which maintained the Cold War–era projection of strength, but added an element of sensitivity and a chivalric conception of protecting the weak.[133] Seemingly inconsistent functions for the U.S. military as at once an attack force and a tool for protection make sense, because the state does *function differently* based on its *self-perception of identity*, which might be seen as a product of structural gender hierarchy in the international arena.

Unit Capability Distribution: Are States and Their Advantages Positioned on the Basis of Gender-Based Characteristics?[134]

Waltz argues that structures dictate the differentiation of capabilities across units, distinguishing this from first- and second-image theorizing by noting that "although capabilities are attributes of units, the distribution of capabilities across units is not."[135] By "distribution of capabilities," Waltz means the organization of states or units, positionally, in relation to each other, on the basis of their relative power.[136] While positionality and power are a part of Acker's understanding of how structures distribute capabilities as well, Acker adds several features (which may be thought of in IR terms as absolute rather than relative differences), including allowed behaviors, meaning, control, and action.[137] In Waltz's relative terms, "structure defines the arrangement, or the ordering, of the parts of a system,"[138] and in Acker's terms, absolute capabilities and constraints as well. While structural gender hierarchy likely has something to contribute to the question of absolute unit capabilities in the international system, this section focuses on the questions of relative capabilities that Waltz identifies as indicative of structure. Along those lines, it contends that states' positions, allowed behaviors, and power are distributed on the basis of perceived gender-associated characteristics.

Changes in hierarchies between masculinities affect both the ordering of the international system and the rigidity of states' placements. As such, different hegemonic masculinities are articulated differently in different contexts, but always involve the subordination of other masculinities and femininities. States position themselves relatively according to the degree to which other states meet their definition of hegemonic masculinity.

Feminists have long argued that differences between hegemonic masculinities and those masculinities they subordinate play a role in the ordering of the international system.[139] This is because "the structural and ideological system that perpetuates the privileging of masculinist" in international relations is "a principle cause for so many of the world's processes [such as] empire-building, globalization, modernization."[140] Enloe explains that "patriarchal systems are notable for marginalizing the feminine" where it is commonplace to trivialize, cast aside, or even scorn those people and organizations associated with femininity.[141] The feminine in these terms is not just women. It is also characteristics associated with femininity wherever they are found. It would follow that a structure in which advantage, meaning, control, and action between states is distributed on the basis of association with masculinity and femininity would be an international system characterized by gender hierarchy in the form of patriarchy.

This section briefly explores two arguments about how a gender-hierarchical international system might distribute unit capabilities: in terms of unit perception of relative position and in terms of unit "actual" relative position. In terms of unit perception of relative position, feminists have argued that states and other political actors position themselves relatively according to the degree to which other states meet their gender expectations or measure up to their ideal-typical masculinity. Feminists have made this argument referencing the United

States, Iraq, and Kuwait; the former Yugoslavia; India and Pakistan; the United States and China; China and Hong Kong; Ireland and Northern Ireland; Russia and Chechnya; apartheid South Africa and its critics; the United States and Egypt; the "Western world" and the "Arab world;" Cyprus, Greece, and Turkey; the Hutus and the Tutsis in the Great Lakes Region in Africa; the major players in international trade and lending; and a number of other conflicts around the world.[142] This is why feminists like Cynthia Enloe have warned that "if we miss patriarchy when it is in fact operating as a major structure of power, then our explanations about how the world works will be unreliable."[143]

A brief contemporary example shows the ways gender tropes influence states' perceptions of relative position and links them to a discussion of "actual" relative position as well. Sikata Banerjee describes this dynamic in the conflict between India and Pakistan over Kashmir particularly, which she calls a "clash of masculinities" where each state amasses troops along the line of control.[144] Banerjee explains that two very different understandings of masculinity, the Indian Hindu ideal-type and the Pakistani Muslim ideal-type are "locked in a struggle defined by the valorization of martial prowess, physical strength, and the unwillingness to compromise" wherein each sees his own ideal-typical understanding of masculinity as superior and uses that as a basis for an understanding of national superiority.[145] Feminists have called this approach a muscular or militarized masculinism, in which states perceive their relative power and position based on their understandings of the most valued masculine characteristics.

At the same time, Banerjee's description of the conflict between India and Pakistan suggests that it is not only states' perceptions of their relative capabilities that are dictated by gender hierarchy but also states' actual relative capabilities and their interests in relative power. At the same time that India and Pakistan are identifying self and other in terms of relative conformity to an ideal-typical masculinity, they are also struggling against each other with means and methods prescribed by those masculinities. It is possible, then, that relative position within the international gender hierarchy helps to define what counts as capability for units. Realists have defined capability in terms of military power and economic resources that can be devoted to the development of military power.[146] Feminists have argued that both the conflation of capabilities and military power and the distribution of military power among states are profoundly gendered.[147]

Relative capability is at least in part *actually constituted by* relative positioning along gender hierarchies. Cynthia Weber gives the example of this in discussing the United States and Cuba:

> A story of conquest, loss, and recovery long played out in U.S. foreign policy but one that reached a critical anticlimax in U.S.–Caribbean relations between 1959 and 1994. During this period, a masculinized United States "lost" its Caribbean reward for hemispheric valor in the Spanish-American War—the feminized Cuba, its symbolic object of desire. Playing a role in the U.S. imaginary as a sort of trophy mistress, Cuba was the near colony and certain feminine complement that the United States relied on to forestall any pending midlife/hegemonic/masculine identity crisis. . . . Misreading Castro and Castro's Cuba, the United States . . . continued to pursue Cuba as an idealized feminine object, even once its mistress had grown a beard. . . . As a result, U.S. policy toward the Caribbean has consisted of a series of displacements of castration or castration anxiety.[148]

In this view, gender can account for the United States' perception of Cuba's relative power as (still inferior but) significantly higher than its military capacity and strategic position might merit, especially outside Cold War politics. Cuba's place as symbolic object of desire can be read as a constitutive part of its relative capability vis-à-vis the United States, and perhaps in global politics more broadly.

In addition to impacting the actual distribution of state relative capability, seeing the international system as a gender hierarchy helps explain why relative power matters so much. Understanding the international system as a gender hierarchy helps to explain the emphasis put on self-help, power politics, action, advantage, and control in distribution of goods and services. If, following Wendt, anarchy is itself inadequate to make the international arena competitive or conflictual, there is an alternative to seeing it as based in variable "cultures of anarchy."[149] There are foundational characteristics of systemic gender hierarchy that could account for state competition and conflict. In patriarchal social structures, equality and coexistence are undesirable, and dominance is a measure of success. As such, international system patriarchy *itself* incentivizes rejection of inequality, competition, and striving for dominance. In a gender-hierarchical international system, we can expect states to find equality undesirable, to see dominance as a goal, and to enforce this dominance on any number of axes. This account has the potential to explain the struggle for relative power among state-units in the international system more compellingly than the logic of survival derived from an understanding that the international system is anarchical. It is this logic that suggests international system patriarchy could be a key explanatory component of conflict in the international arena. Seeing the international system structure as gender-hierarchical could not only help to explain the prevalence of distributional politics and the resultant distributional inequality of goods and power between states in the system, but also variations in distribution on the basis of changing gendered values and changing associations with gender-based characteristics.

Political Processes for Unit Interaction: Are They Produced by Gender?[150]

The third manifestation of international system structure, according to Waltz, is that structure shapes the political processes among units and insures the basic continuity of political processes as long as the structure remains. Though there are a number of political processes between states that could be discussed as related to gender hierarchy, including diplomacy,[151] interstate jurisprudence,[152] and international institutions,[153] this brief exploration will focus on two: competitive power between states generally and militarization specifically.

As mentioned above, a patriarchal social order in the international system would influence unit competition. The international system gender hierarchy is also manifested in the processes by which that competition takes place. Particularly, feminist scholars have argued that the gendered competition between states selects for a particular (masculinized) sort of power (dominance). Amy Allen delineates three sorts of power: power-over (or dominance, the sort of power that is most recognized in the international arena), but also power-to (the ability to act contrary to dominant forces despite their preponderance of power-over) and power-with (the ability of weaker actors to act together for counter-hegemonic purposes).[154]

If power is the driving force behind interstate relations and global politics (an assumption made by much if not most of war theorizing), then seeing power as power-over means that the accumulation of power is necessarily competitive *and* zero-sum, making conflict likely, if not necessary, as power-seeking states race to occupy the coveted position of the hegemon. Viewing power as zero-sum also presumes a stark and delineable distinction between self(state) and other(state) in which accumulated power is a resource whose advantages can be confined to its accumulator. Feminist theorists have noted that "gender is a socially constructed relationship of inequality"[155] in which "gendered power is the victory of certain ideas over others in social [and political] interaction because they are associated with valorized gender."[156] Feminists have long argued that gender not only inspires a reformulation of our understandings of power, but is itself "a particular kind of power relation . . . central to understanding international processes."[157]

States that lack power-over are not necessarily powerless, but alternative, noncompetitive versions of power disappear from states' radar as they compete for masculine dominance. As Amy Allen argues, "to think about power solely in terms of domination neglects . . . empowerment."[158] While "by emphasizing plurality and community . . . [feminist theory] consciously seeks to distance power from domination" and understand power collaboratively, the gender-hierarchical international system is blind both to the potential operation and the theorization of such a concept of power.[159] As such, states' positions in the gendered international hierarchy influence their interactions.

Policy options such as empathy,[160] positive-sum collaboration,[161] unilaterally deconstructing the cycle of violence,[162] care,[163] or empowerment[164] are often missing from states' toolboxes because the gendered system selects for power-over rather than power-to or power-with as a political process among units. The dominance of power-over as how states relate is relatively stable so long as the system remains gender hierarchical. Feminist scholars have seen gender hierarchy inspiring power-over relationships despite other possibilities in human rights discourses in Latin America, international interactions with Saddam Hussein's Iraq,[165] the U.S. "war on terror,"[166] Asia-Pacific relations,[167] state relations in post–Cold War Eastern Europe,[168] and intra–Arab League relations.[169] Countless other examples from realist analyses of foreign policy-making show the dominance of competitive approaches to power among states; feminist work suggests that the source of the dominance of these approaches is in gendered competition as a political process, possibly inspired by structural gender hierarchy in the international system.

If gendered competitions through power-over are one political process that international system gender hierarchy can be seen to shape, a number of related processes can also be discussed in these terms.[170] One example of such a process is militarization. Peterson and Runyan defined militarization as "processes by which characteristically military practices are extended into the civilian arena."[171] Though war is an essential condition of militarism—the apex or climax—militarization is much broader than war, activating an underlying system of institutions, practices, and values. Feminists have pointed out that the militarization pervasive in global politics "occurs through gendered workings of power."[172] In the gendered process of militarization, military–industrial complexes need men to be willing to kill and die on behalf of their states to prove their manhood *and* women to behave as properly subservient to meet the needs of militaries.[173] Militarization is shaped by gender hierarchy in its aims (competitive power-over), its means (the military-industrial complex), its language (of strength and domination), and its impacts (which disproportionately affect women).

While there has been too large a volume of feminist work on militarization to review here, a brief discussion of two recent examples of militarization in the feminist literature might illustrate how I think it fits into Waltz's idea of a process among units. Ronni Alexander has explored the role of militarization in Pacific Island politics, particularly in the Bougainville Crisis.[174] Alexander explains that militarization in the Pacific Islands has progressed in ways uniquely linked to the cultural histories of Pacific Island states but inextricably linked to gender hierarchy, race hierarchy, and cultural governance and "constituted through systemic power relations."[175] In the Bougainville crisis, Alexander describes the conflict, the violence, and the ultimate de-escalation of the violence all in terms of the contestation of gendered ideas of state and nation played out through the process of militarization.

Across the world, Maya Eichler's work shows that the relationship between the gendering of the Russian state's identity and the militarization of Russian soldiers' masculinities in the Chechen wars.[176] By analyzing "notions of masculinity embedded in the stories of Chechen war veterans as well as in the state's and society's view of Chechen war veterans," Eichler demonstrates that "post-Communist transformation and crisis" undermined Russian state masculinity, which rippled through social and political readings of soldiers' performances (and, relatedly, their genders).[177] Eichler's work suggests that these gendered tropes of state and citizen identity are productive of and produced by Russia's post–Cold War position among states and in interstate relations. This and other feminist work suggests that militarization, like the gendered competition it is related to, is one of many political processes among units in the system that may be said to be products of structural gender hierarchy.

This section has demonstrated that there is, in the feminist literature, evidence that gender plays a role in unit function, the distribution of (perceived and material) relative capabilities among units, and the political processes that govern unit interaction. This suggests that, both in Waltz's and in Acker's terms, gender may be a structural feature of the international system. The remainder of this chapter discusses the implications of a system-structural gender hierarchy for war theorizing, as well as potential future research directions.

STRUCTURAL GENDER HIERARCHY AS A/THE CAUSE OF WAR

Gender hierarchy as a structural feature of the international system has a number of implications for understandings of when, how, and why war occurs. First, appropriating a Clausewitzian observation, war is politics by other means. If gender hierarchy is a structural feature of the international system and a key organizing principle in dictating state identity, interactions, and relative position, then conflicts between states can be characterized as conflicts within/about the gendered order of the international structure. Conflict is not, in realist terms, a competition for survival (an explanation that has always been somewhat unsatisfactory given the relative inequality of states and the self-help behavior of states at no risk of failing to survive). Instead, it is a competition for masculinized dominance in which states, as gendered actors in a gendered system, are out to dominate rather than to survive. For example, John Haynes notes that Soviet World War II–era socialist realist films characterize the Nazi breaking of the nonaggression pact in terms of gender, with Nazi Germany's hypermasculinity ultimately being its downfall.[178] Nazi German films of the same period valorize hypermasculinity. This is one example of how states are not looking to continue to exist or to end others' existence but instead to affirm their masculinity (and protect their feminine elements) while feminizing others. When we think of structural gender hierarchy as a key part of explaining state behavior, governments that risk their survival for honor (like the Belgians[179]) do not appear so singular.

Second, gender hierarchy is a/the permissive cause of war, not anarchy, whether or not the international system is structured anarchically. Wendt was correct in arguing that there is nothing inherent about anarchy that makes the international system conflictual, but perhaps too quick in looking for "cultures of" the anarchic structure or, I argue, doing away with a substantive notion of structure altogether. An alternative theoretical path, the one I contend holds the most explanatory potential, is that there is a structural factor *other than* or *in addition to* anarchy in the international system that explains both the conflictual nature of the international system and patterns of conflict within that system, and is neither entirely peaceful nor entirely chaotic. I suggest gender hierarchy is such a structural factor.

Gender hierarchy, though it manifests itself in different ways at different times in different contexts, consistently valorizes characteristics associated with (hegemonic) masculinity over characteristics associated with (subordinated) femininities. As such, regardless of the specific content of the competition, units within the system (states) are in constant competition to prove their masculinity and deny their femininity. Since gender-based characteristics are often measured relatively, this makes the international system inherently competitive (even among states not engaged in conflict) and often conflictual. Still, variations among states' ideal-typical understandings of masculinity can account for variations in the level of competition and bellicosity of states in the gender-hierarchical structure of the international system.

Some scholars might see little theoretical progress in the assertion that gender hierarchy (rather than anarchy) might be a permissive cause of war because it does not predict different state behaviors. I argue that even if this explanation predicted competition the same way that understanding the international system as anarchic does, it would be useful to think about the influence of gender to the extent that it exists. I suggest there is more to it, however.

The third potential implication of system structural gender hierarchy for war theorizing is that it functions differently than anarchy as a permissive cause of war, potentially adding predictive ability and improving explanatory value. This is because variations among states' ideal-typical understandings of genders can account for variations in the levels of competition and bellicosity of states within the gender-hierarchical structure of the international system. Therefore, it is possible that structural gender hierarchy has something to say not only about the causes of war, but also about the causes of *wars* and the variations among them.

Genders in the gender hierarchy among states vary both at the system level (over time) and *within* the system (with context). If gender hierarchy is the structural property of the international system that shapes the system's processes, the particular *gender tropes* along the hierarchy and the relative position thereof both differ among units (states) and change over time despite the immutability of structural gender hierarchy. Put differently, the fundamental problem with anarchy as a structural explanation for war is that it is *only* a structural explanation and *only* a permissive cause. As structural realists insist, anarchy does not go away, and it does not change. Therefore, what Waltz identifies as "other causes" are necessary to explain the occurrence of war when anarchy permits it, given that sometimes war does not occur, while at other times it does. A more parsimonious way to account for the frequent occurrence of wars alongside the frequent nonoccurrence of wars is to look for a structural feature of global politics that is at once structural (constant, ordering) and variable (accounting for when states fight and when they do not). Systemic gender hierarchy provides such a structural explanation.

Therefore, and fourth, it is possible to see that gender hierarchy as a structural feature of the international system predicts state behavior differently (and potentially more precisely) than seeing the international system as an anarchy (alone). While an understanding of gender hierarchy as a structural feature of the international system predicts the system will be to some degree inherently conflictual and always allow for war/conflict (as the realists say anarchy does), one can see other (different) implications of gender hierarchy.

Particularly, a feminist understanding of gender hierarchy as a structural feature of global politics suggests some suppositions about war and about war(s). One hypothesis might be that the content and salience of the hegemonic/ideal-typical masculinity in states would be expected to be a predictor of their relative tendency to go to war. In a gender-hierarchical international system, relative material or symbolic equality between units (or states) would be expected to breed conflict, while conflicts between states with vastly different functions and capabilities would be expected to be less frequent. Still, asymmetric conflicts would be expected to occur when a conflict between states' claims to masculinities conflict and/or state's insults to each others' masculinities intensify.

Put differently, (state) gender relations would be expected to be an intervening variable in how power parity influences aggression. The more competitive a state's hegemonic masculinity, the more likely that state is to make war; this risk is compounded by high salience. States with elements of hypermasculinity[180] in their nationalist discourses would be expected to be more aggressive, while states with elements of gender equity in their nationalist discourses (state feminists) would be less likely to be aggressive.[181] This is not because of any inherent property of the state but instead because of where the (perceived or actual) properties of the state place it on a gender hierarchy among states. The relative frequency of wars would be expected to vary with the relative intensity of gendered competition between states, which would be expected to vary with the relative aggressiveness of the ideal-typical masculinity in the international system. Gendered elements of state identities (honor, protection, chivalry, aggression) would be expected to determine "centers of gravity"[182] that will be direct causes of war, while gender hierarchy among states is a permissive cause of war.

A dominant hypermasculinity in the international system structure would lead states to approximate hypermasculinity in their functions, search for capabilities, and interaction with one another. Such an international arena would be expected to be conflictual and competitive. A dominant chivalric masculinity would produce different results, emphasizing values such as "the responsibility to protect" and incentivizing states to function and relate in ways that maintain toughness and tenderness. This can be expected to be manifested across states, not only in individual ones, using Waltzian logic. This feminist hypothesis places primary emphasis on states' jockeying for position in a hierarchical system. Because jockeying for position can occur without military conflict, the feminist hypothesis expects gendered competition between great powers even when they do not go to war.[183]

Anecdotal evidence for such a supposition can be found in Carol Cohn's analysis of the Cold War, in which she reports that a "well-known academic security adviser was quoted as saying that 'under Jimmy Carter the United States is spreading its legs for the Soviet Union'"[184] or in John F. Kennedy's campaigns for office "promising to halt America's decline into flabbiness and impotence against the threat of a 'ruthless' and expanding Soviet empire."[185] Cynthia Enloe links this competition not to immediate dissatisfaction[186] with the international system, but instead to "the inherent nature of states. . . . [and] the masculine character of the state elite" competing in a patriarchal international system.[187]

An example of such a scenario can be found in the genesis of World War I, which has been described as an accidental war resulting from competitive national pride and (individual and state) jockeying for position in a hierarchy defined by hegemonic masculinity.[188] Feminist scholars have also noted the relationship between the competition in the Spanish-American War and "US and European male codes of honour" including state "competitiveness, independence, and persistence."[189] Chivalry has been credited as a motivation for interventionary wars in Iraq, Libya, Afghanistan, and East Timor.[190] Masculine competition has been linked to great powers' arms races, asymmetric attacks by great powers, and terrorist attacks.[191] These examples suggest the plausibility of the feminist supposition that the patriarchal atmosphere of the international system could have something to do with why states fight wars when they reach relative power parity.

These potential hypotheses provide an opportunity to examine whether or not structural gender hierarchy is present in the international system, whether or not it influences the likelihood of actors in the international system to make and fight wars, whether or not it provides more explanatory leverage than the realist theoretical understanding of anarchy as a permissive cause of war, and the degree to which it accounts for variation in the making and fighting of wars.

THE POTENTIAL CONTRIBUTIONS OF A THIRD-IMAGE FEMINIST RESEARCH PROGRAM ON WAR

Certainly, it is not possible in one chapter to offer proof for the thesis that the international system structure is gender hierarchical, a characteristics that serves as both a permissive cause of war and a direct cause of wars. Still, this discussion has attempted to make an initial plausibility case for such a proposition with the dual aims of considering the potential implications for war theorizing and encouraging further research to explore, understand, and/or test the propositions and expectations it suggests might be manifested in the global political arena.

The argument that gender hierarchy is a key part of the structure of the international system as laid out here is not meant to imply that gender hierarchy is prior to other hierarchies in global social or political life. It is instead meant to argue that hierarchies in global politics (of gender, race, religion, culture, ethnicity, etc.) are also fraught with gendering, wherein devalorizing the "other" in hierarchies often takes place through feminization.[192] This approach may beg the question: If gender is in all hierarchies, why would it be useful to talk about gender as a system-structural cause of war when it could be hierarchy more generally? First, were gender in all hierarchies, then it would be useful to talk of gender as a constitutive feature of hierarchies. Second, the argument is not that all hierarchies are *about gender* instead, I postulate that even hierarchies that are (first-order) "about" something else are often performed in gender terms as well. This discussion, then, has been interested in gender as manifested in the international system structure as a cause of war.

Accordingly, this chapter has asserted that seeing gender hierarchy as (a part of) the international system structure is consonant with decades of feminist work across disciplines on the nature of gender (both generally and specifically in global politics) and fills a gap in the understanding of the international system that currently dominates war theorizing. From feminist perspectives, seeing gender as structural pushes feminists to understand the ordering logics of gender hierarchies. From the perspective of war theorizing, seeing gender as system structural might account for (as structural realism claims to) war's existence (in a permissive sense) but also (as structural realism cannot) variation in the occurrence of specific wars.

Gender as system structural in global politics generally and the causes of war specifically could be explored in a number of different ways. Case studies (like the many mentioned here) might flesh out the relationship between gender as a system-ordering principle and unit function, the distribution of unit capabilities, and the political processes that govern unit interaction. Coding state press releases for claims about gender in belligerents' (and potential belligerents') sense of "self"[193] and statements about opponents (and potential opponents) for the purpose of comparison with existing data sets[194] that contain information about actors' likelihood to make wars might give some insight into how relative position along a gender hierarchy among units in the international system impacts the probability for those units to engage in disputes, conflicts, and/or wars. The supposition that systematic patriarchy discourages peace among equals could be explored by comparing existing collected data on the frequency of symmetric and asymmetric conflicts[195] with a narrativized timeline of dominant hegemonic masculinities among states in the international system.

Moving away from hypothesis-testing approaches, much of the evidence for seeing gender as international system structural can be found in the ethnographic, discourse analysis, interview, and theoretical work that is common in existing feminist IR work generally and FSS work specifically. From Laura Shepherd's understanding of the normalized gender signification in the ideas of national and international security to Lene Hansen's recognition that (gendered) insecurity is often invisible and unhearable to Annick Wibben's understanding of gendered narratives of security as "a primary way by which we make sense of the world around us," critical feminist work has been demonstrating that gender is not only structural but naturalized and invisible as structure not only in IR but in global social and political life more broadly.[196]

As a dialogue among feminisms, feminist third-image theorizing of war and wars brings trepidation, controversy, hesitance, and enthusiasm, and takes both theoretical foundations and evidence from a wide variety of feminist work across perspectives, across disciplines, and across the world. As a dialogue between feminisms and war studies, feminist third image theorizing of war and wars brings with it both critique of and desire to build on existing war theories. It asks—Is gender hierarchy a structural feature of global politics? Of politics between states? If so, what are the implications for the making and fighting of wars?

This chapter has argued that it is possible to see gender as international system structural in a Waltzian sense—as an ordering principle of the international system reflected in unit function, relative distribution of capacity among units, and the political processes that govern their interactions. If these propositions bear out, than the implications for structural theorizing of war(s) are significant.

For structural realism, it means seeing the international system as an anarchy may be (at best) incomplete, and other forces that are (in Waltz's terms) "invisible" may influence not only system structure, but relative power, balancing, deterrence, and alliance formation. It means that permissive and other causes of war may be more closely linked than Waltz supposed, since this approach suggests a gendered order is structural (and therefore a permissive cause of war), but there is a fungibility among genders within that ever-present gendered order that might account for when and why individual wars do (or do not) occur. For constructivist theorizing, it suggests that those interested in the social dynamics of the international system may have been too quick to abandon Waltz's idea of structure as an ordering principle rather than looking to other potential ordering principles in addition to or as replacements for the Waltzian idea of anarchy.

Engaging structural realist theory challenges feminisms to think seriously about *how* gender manifests in global politics among and between states, as well as in their identities, functions, and relative capabilities. Engaging structural constructivist theorizing shows feminisms a number of key similarities (like a rejection of the idea that anarchy necessarily shapes global politics) as well as, in my opinion, key differences (about the nature and changeability of other potential influences). For feminist war theorizing, the potential of a feminist third-image research program, in my view, cannot be overlooked. Feminists have consistently pointed out the invisibility of gender to mainstream theorists of war(s). This blindness is partly a blindness to gender but partly a blindness to gender *at the locations those theorists study*. In other words, feminist critique of the system- and state-centric nature of war and security theorizing is valuable, not least because mainstream war theorizing fundamentally fails to see individuals (particularly women) in wars and at their margins. While that is, in the eyes of many feminist theorists, myself included, one of the biggest failings of war theorizing, feminist third-image war theorizing helps to demonstrate the relevance of gender to war (even) where war theorists usually look and do not see it.

In addition to the intellectual and political advantage in dialogue, I contend that there is definitional, operational, explanatory, and predictive value in researching the role of gendered structure(s) in/of the international system as permissive and/or direct causes of war. If gender is an ordering principle of the international system, it specifies (in whole or in part), the war function of states, the distribution of (military and other) capacity between them, and the (gendered) political processes of competition among them. Gender as system structural alone might be enough to theorize (the causes of) war(s) from a feminist perspective, but the chapters that follow explore the influence of gender hierarchy (either as system structural or more generally) on the dyadic-, "domestic"-, and individual-level accounts of the making of war(s).

CHAPTER 4

Relations International and War(s)

> Relationships are central to our individuality; they do not contradict it . . . . Humans are relational beings . . . they are born into and develop through society, that is to say, through relationships. The uniqueness of the individual derives precisely from the particular and specific character of the relationships into which individuals enter . . . an element of mutuality necessarily arises.
>
> —JOHN HOFFMAN, *GENDER AND SOVEREIGNTY: FEMINISM, THE STATE, AND INTERNATIONAL RELATIONS*

A significant amount of feminist research in international relations (IR) has emphasized the importance of relationships. Through gender lenses, feminist research has become accustomed to looking at autonomy as relational,[1] seeing sovereignty as relational,[2] paying attention to the relationships between citizens and states,[3] and exploring the relationships between the personal and the international in theorizing global politics.[4] This attention to relationships analyzes not only *who relates* but *how they relate*—the structure of relationships and the process by which they are built and evolve.

This is in contrast to war studies, wherein much of the work on dyadic-level interactions has focused on the properties that both states bring to their interaction that influence the likelihood that their interaction is peaceful or leads to (violent) conflict.[5] This is particularly true about research on regime type and war(s), including both the normative and structural models of democratic peace theory.[6] Theorists who do pay attention to interactions[7] often assume those interactions are largely material, focusing either on material "issues" between states[8] or trade relations.[9] Even the theoretical approaches that do analyze nonmaterial interactions between states do not look at relationships with the same depth and complexity as much feminist theorizing does.[10] Feminist attention to relationships (and, relatedly, interdependence and intersubjectivity) has something valuable to contribute to war studies' analyses of the "dyadic" causes of war.[11]

This is particularly true because feminists have suggested rethinking both the international and relations in IR, characterizing the prevailing discourses in the field as neither particularly international nor particularly about relations.[12] The argument that IR is not particularly international is a criticism that the discipline both selectively includes (privileged) voices and (as a result) focuses on substantive concerns about "global" politics that are partial rather than global. The argument that IR is not particularly about relations (which is perhaps more relevant for the purposes of this chapter) sees feminist theory as serving to highlight the (normative and empirical) importance of *relating* as a substance of global politics, something that is missing from most accounts of the "war puzzle"[13] that the discipline produces.

This chapter is interested in accounting for dyadic-level (or between-states) causes of war through gender lenses as both international and relational. It argues that whether or not gender is a structural feature of the international system (and therefore a permissive cause of war), it is a key feature of the relationships between states and a key dyadic-level factor in the making of war(s). It begins by discussing feminist engagements with dyadic-level accounts of war that focus on particular properties of states (for example, theories of democratic peace and capitalist peace). It contends that trait-based accounts of dyadic relationships among states identify problematic traits, do so in a way that takes insufficient account of relations between states, and do discursive violence in their silences. A second section addresses dyadic-level theories of war(s) that take account of and/or focus more on how states interact, contending that the assumptions of progressive interaction, unitary states, and rational actors are limiting and incomplete. It suggests that the interactions these approaches observe are gendered and observed in gendered ways. A third section outlines an approach to studying the dyadic-level causes of war in "relations international" through gender lenses, suggesting such an approach might be both empirically advantageous and normatively preferable. The chapter concludes with a discussion of the implications of such a move for dyadic-level war theorizing specifically and war theorizing more generally.

STATE TRAITS, RELATIONS, AND WARS

Liberal peace accounts often make the argument that certain traits states have in common make them more likely to interact harmoniously. Many of these "common trait" theories (whether they emphasize democracy, economics, gender equality,[14] or territorial security) are less about the relations between the states than they are about the traits states bring to relationships. Feminist engagements with these theoretical approaches have argued that they identify a narrow set of traits, take insufficient account of relations between states, and often have problematic discursive and material impacts for people whose lives are lived at the margins of global politics. The question of which traits of states are significant in predicting the likelihood of conflict between them will be addressed in more detail in chapter 5; this section will deal with the idea that the properties of states constitute their relationships, as well as with some of the empirical and normative problems with current trait-based dyadic accounts of war through gender lenses.

Dyads and Relations

A number of different feminist theorists have criticized trait-based work on the dyadic causes of war for its neglect of *relations* between states. For example, while recognizing the empirical robustness of the democratic peace result, Juliann Emmons Allison finds the accompanying causal story uncompelling.[15] She contends that the problem with democratic peace accounts is that both the normative and structural models rely on rights-based theorizing,[16] while feminist theorizing suggests that the substance is to be found not in an instrumental, individualistic conception but instead in a conception that pays attention to "emotional connectedness and social interdependence."[17] Building on Carol Gilligan's work, Juliann Allison suggests "an alternative, feminist ethic of care" based on "relationships and responsibilities, as opposed to rules and rights" and highlighting care in the work of policy-making.[18] She distinguishes care epistemologically (based on experience rather than reason) and practically (based in responsiveness rather than reaction) from instrumentalized liberal accounts of interstate relations.[19]

In this view, the (simplistic) assumption that similar states with similar values relate more effectively needs to be questioned, critiqued, and reformulated through gender lenses. Analysis of "relating" should be more than a game of identifying like traits. Certainly, states "relate" (perhaps in a shallow sense) to traits, structures, and ideas that they recognize and identify in other states. At the same time, those relationships are symbolic, emotional, and communicative as much as they are material; multidimensional, complex, and fraught with risk more than they are stable and fixed; and reliant on a variety of factors of *relating* as much as they are based on the "fit" of a relationship. If that is true, then emphasizing traits, as accounts of liberal, democratic, territorial, or even "feminist" peaces often do, has insidious implications, both in gendered terms and more generally. The next part of this section discusses some of those implications.

The Victims of Liberal Peace(s)

In addition to having a narrow conception of what states' *relationships* are, the literature on dyadic causes of war often focuses on a narrow subset of states that *have* relationships. While much of the quantitative work on dyadic causes of war includes either all dyads or all politically relevant dyads,[20] many of the case studies look at great powers, and most of them do not dig significantly deeper than the (assumed rational, unitary) governments of those great states.

By contrast, feminist analyses have come to see individual welfare rather than great power stability or even how governments interact as a central factor in global politics. The security of the least powerful women in the least powerful states in the world is not only a key security issue for feminists but also a key unit of analysis, given that many feminists see the margins as a crucial and inseparable part of local, global, and international politics.

Feminist research shows how those at the political margins can be made insecure even while states are being made more secure. Women's bodies have been considered the means to an end in debates over the U.S. security force in South Korea, the prevalence of and possible solutions to AIDS, and debates about refugee camp composition and makeup, to name a few, at the state and system level.[21] Research into women's lives in war and conflict has shown that they are often made insecure when military operations cut off households' access to food, water, or electricity; when soldiers rape them; when crime and "domestic" violence increases as a result of war; and when severe economic deprivation leaves them vulnerable to disease.[22] These threats are often, both statistically and existentially, more vicious than the threat of great power war.[23]

Feminist work has demonstrated a link between what happens to women in wars and the gendered dynamics of the making and fighting of wars.[24] Because feminists often see individual security as a central issue in global politics, their work has critiqued the hierarchy that many liberal approaches to war(s) identify and espouse in global politics. Feminists have recognized that the least fortunate and the least free in global politics are often the people whose needs are neglected by policy decision makers and policy analysts.[25] Additionally, "feminist scholars have repeatedly shown that gender operates at various levels at which it intersects with class, ethnicity, race, nationality, and sexuality to produce and reproduce an intricate web of inequalities between and among men and women."[26] Feminist theory, then, is critical of social and political hierarchy for the pressure that it puts on the "bottom" of that hierarchy.[27]

Many dyadic theories of war, like many system-level theories of war, do not share feminist theorists' interests in identifying, critiquing, and deconstructing hierarchies in and among states.[28] Instead, I argue that dyad-trait accounts of war value hierarchy by valuing the domestic organization of states (and how that organization affects peoples' lives) as a means to the end of interstate peacefulness without particular regard for how what happens inside the state affects the people inside the state. Some "mainstream" war theorists concede that those left out of the planning of the international system "consider the system to be unfair, corrupt, biased, skewed, and dominated by hostile forces" but often do not give significant attention to the possibility that such a perception is true and normatively problematic.[29]

Feminist work has provided critiques both of the narrow definition of power (as domination)[30] and the narrow view of whose power and security matters in these accounts. Arguing that it is possible to recognize through gender lenses the normative value and empirical impact of lives on the margins of international security, much feminist work looks for alternative ways to analyze war. This is important because, as Fiona Robinson notes, "those who care for others, and those who are most in need of care, are among the world's most marginalized people."[31]

While some characterize small powers as irrelevant because they "pose no threat to the dominant nation's leadership in the international system,"[32] many feminist perspectives express concern that this view justifies political and social oppression for the good of peace among great powers. Likewise, while some would ignore the concerns of the weak within states, because they do not make decisions or change policies directly, many feminist scholars have seen such a move as not only empirically problematic but also discriminatory:

> A concept of national security which gives priority to military threat rather than to dangers in the economic and social sectors of society can be bought only at the cost of poverty and misery and the violation of human rights—a cost borne by all poor people but especially by women and future generations.[33]

As referenced above and discussed in more detail in chapter 9, wars tend to have a number of gendered and sex-differential impacts in a number of areas, including direct material destruction, the implications of infrastructural damage, interactions with patriarchal militaries, the fallout of economic downturn, and the problems associated with environmental destruction.[34] These harms are often distributed disproportionately on the basis of not only sex but also race and class to the margins of societies,[35] and those people's suffering is often ignored in dyadic and state-level war theorizing. Feminist theorizing, on the other hand, often looks for what happens at the margins.

Looking at the margins, one finds not only marginalized people but also marginalized states. Instead, there is a whole class of states that looking for what happens the margins in global politics might identify as the victims not only of liberal war(s) but also of liberal peace(s). For example, the "long peace"[36] of the Cold War was fought on the back of satellite wars, many of which either would not have happened or would not have been as brutal without great power intervention.[37] The "democratic peace" has inspired many war(s) of democratization through the combination of external political pressure, increasing mass political participation, and weak political institutions.[38] The "capitalist peace" can be seen as being bought at the expense of proletariat(s) who deal with the increasing income inequality produced by trade global-ization, as well as poor working conditions and limitations on upward mobility.[39] "hegemonic peace" is often beneficial to empires and other hegemons but is bought at the expense of the peripheral states that the hegemon subordinates.[40]

Feminist scholars have also argued that there are potentially problem-atic implications of the "sex equality peace" as discussed in sex-based dyadic accounts of war.[41] As discussed briefly in chapter 1, sex-based dyadic accounts of war argue that the level of sex equality, rather than the level of democracy or the level of trade, is the property of a state most likely to predict the state's decisions to make wars.[42] Feminist theorists have wondered if this is the appropriate lens and level of analysis through which to view the interaction of gender equality and peace. Particularly, Anna Karamanou takes a different look at the dyadic cause(s) of peace and war through gender lenses, arguing that it is not (as authors of the sex equality peace suggest[43]) a question of sex equality *within states* projected outside but of relative sex equality *among* states that influences how they relate.[44] Karamanou contends that "the balancing of the dis-tribution of power between the sexes may lessen the tensions created by hegemonic masculinity and may lead to the resolution of crises through dialogue and peaceful coexistence of human beings."[45] In this under-standing, in addition to there being *sex differentiation* between people, there is *sex differentiation* between states based on their readings and reproductions of that sex differentiation between people. Looking only at sex differentiation between people and groups *within* a state, then, is an incomplete account that inappropriately focuses scrutiny on "men," "women," and material distribution among them within the state, not to improve sex inequality for its own sake but as an (ultimately ineffective) means to peace, given that gendered power relations *among and within* states are important but crucially neglected in these approaches.[46]

Feminist analyst Katherine Allison sees even broader implications for gender relations and state relations, with particular concern for the ways that women's rights are being enmeshed with a "feminised liberal democratic peace."[47] Noting that conflict resolution and peacebuilding initiatives in the policy world have come to recognize women's agency in ways that were not previously the case, Katherine Allison is interested in how relating women to femininity has come to be reified in employing them as the makers and builders of peace in the policy world—traditional women in untraditional roles.[48] She is critical of the way this agential role in *producing* dyadic democratic peace(s) assigned to women is harmful both *to women* and ultimately *to peace*. Arguing that the idea that women are the makers and maintainers of peace obscures women's (broad array of) experience in and of conflict, and saddles women with a responsibility to *mother* states while still denying them broad access to policy options and tools. In Katherine Allison's understanding, this at once obscures the complexity of women/gender and potential alternatives to liberal democratic models of making and keeping peace(s), especially given a "conceptual sliding between women, women's rights, and liberal democracy."[49]

In these ways, feminist perspectives on dyadic approaches to warfighting suggest both that trait-based approaches have problematic empirical and normative implications and that their understandings of how states relate are incomplete. I have argued that they focus inadequately on the process of relating among states in theorizing war and conflict among them. This forms the basis for the reformulation at the end of this chapter that focuses on how states relate as a dyadic-level account of war. Before getting there, however, it is important to note that some dyadic-level approaches do explicitly acknowledge and deal with state interaction as a cause of war. While those approaches, I argue, inadequately conceptualize what it means to relate and how relations may be an indicator of the likelihood of war, it is important to discuss and critique their insights en route to a feminist alternative.

(GENDERED) INTERNATIONAL INTERACTIONS

Some dyadic accounts of war are interested in how states' interactions lead to (or help prevent) conflict between them in the sense of signaling, rather than in the sense of relating. "Steps-to-war" models lay out "a set of closely related paths to war that involve a series of steps between states that are roughly equal in power."[50] As Levy and Thompson explain, "they show each 'step' increases the probability of war, and that the process is cumulative."[51] Relatedly, rivalry theories of war see specific interstate relationships as more likely to lead to war than others. They suggest that because states "focus selectively on the states that appear to represent the greatest threat," the act of singling out antagonists is key in predicting interstate wars, suggesting that "repetitive war behavior" points to conflict probability.[52] In this view, states' interactions are cumulative in causing conflict and war(s), and some states' rivalries account for the majority of wars.

Another theoretical approach to war that takes account of interaction focuses on bargaining. Bargaining theories of war are interested in why war(s) happen(s) despite the(ir) cost, and therefore focus on why war-fighting parties were unable (or unwilling) to reach a (cheaper) negotiated settlement to their dispute(s),[53] with emphasis on possible pathologies in negotiations, including commitment problems,[54] private information (and/or incentives to misrepresent),[55] the lack of a "bargaining" space of outcomes that are mutually preferred to war,[56] and/or indivisible issues.[57] This work implies that it is difficult to reach a negotiated settlement even when such a deal would be optimal for all parties involved.[58]

All three of these models assume that states interact with some linear action and reaction, in which "the primary factors in determining war and peace are the foreign policy strategies adopted by states to deal with their disputes."[59] All three models also assume an internal coherence, or unitary nature, of the actors interacting, whereby each is making decisions for an internally united whole. The bargaining models add the assumption that the unitary actors interacting progressively do so rationally and calculate cost–benefit analysis in conflict decision-making. Feminist research has questioned each of these assumptions, arguing that states interact more relationally than reactively; suggesting that states are, rather than unitary, diverse and full of internal conflict that should not be neglected when defining (or critiquing the idea of) "interest"; and that states are not the rational actors that bargaining theorists assume them to be.[60]

Action and Reaction

As I mentioned above, a number of dyadic-level theories of the causes of war either do not theorize how states interact explicitly,[61] or, in the case of bargaining, rivalry, and steps-to-war models, assume states' interactions are individuated and progressive. By individuated and progressive, I mean that one state acts, the other (or others) respond, and then the first actor acts again in a sequence of interaction that can be understood chronologically[62] and told as a coherent story.

Feminist theorists' understandings of the incomplete independence of decision makers and their decisions[63] frequently suggest that this picture needs to be complicated significantly. For our purposes now, the idea of state interaction in these theoretical approaches takes account of (as discussed in chapter 3) Allen's ideas of power-over (as domination) and power-to (as resistance of domination)[64] but takes inadequate account of power-with, both directly (as states can act together) and in its implications for interpreting state interactions (as neither necessarily individuated or progressive).

Power-with, or the ability to act in concert, pooling (symbolic or material) power, resources, and/or knowledge, suggests that a model of state behavior in which we understand actions and responses to actions dichotomously does not tell the whole story. Discussing methods such as participatory planning,[65] multisited feminist social criticism,[66] and empowerment,[67] feminist theorists have suggested both that actors are interdependent and that they can act together, simultaneously, and in role-similar and role-differentiated ways.[68] In this view, instead of seeing policy as (always) assertion and/or response, it can be seen as responsiveness, more complicated constitutively (in terms of who the actor is) and directionally (in terms of where policies are going).[69] For process-based dyadic war theorizing, this suggests that there may be different, more empirically nuanced, ways of looking at the nature of relationships between states to understand how it is that they end up in conflict, particularly in terms of their (gendered) war narratives and (gendered) cycles of violence. Before sketching out what that might look like, this section continues to think about the problems with assumptions of state unity, state rationality, and the gender neutrality of the process to war in process-based theories.

Unitary Units

Feminist scholars have also interrogated the unitary nature of the state, pointing out that efforts to maximize the state's security interests often threaten the security of people *inside* the state. Specifically, as I discussed in the previous section, the state's most marginalized citizens are often made insecure by state security-seeking, making it clear that a state does not have a single interest in interstate interaction but many that conflict. J. Ann Tickner contends that "an explanation of the historical development of state sovereignty and state identities as they have evolved over time does indeed suggest deeply gendered constructions that have not included women on the same terms as men."[70] This is because, according to Tickner:

> From the time of their foundation, states have sought to control the right to define political identity. Since their legitimacy has constantly been threatened by the undermining power of sub-national and transnational loyalties, states' survival and success have depended on the creation and maintenance of legitimating national identities; often these identities have depended on the manipulation of gendered representation. . . . Drawing on metaphors that evoke matrimonial and familial relations, the nation has been portrayed as both male and female. . . . The sense of community implicit in these family metaphors is deeply gendered in ways that not only legitimate foreign policy practices but also reinforce inequalities between men and women.[71]

Using these gendered metaphors, the state can, while shoring up its "national interest," both threaten the interest of marginalized citizens inside it and reinforce power inequalities among its groups. Catherine MacKinnon has explained that the "state's structures and actions are driven by and institutionalize strategy based on an epistemic angle of vision" that can "distinguish public from private, naturalize dominance as difference, hide coercion beyond consent, and conceal politics beyond morality."[72] These structures require a certain standard of behavior from some members of the state,[73] while suppressing the voices of others altogether.[74]

With these tools, the state can appear unitary by suppressing its diversity and presenting *one* concept of national interest, autonomous of and not necessarily representative of its citizens. In this understanding, the sovereign state can be "an extension of the separation-minded realist man, also autonomous to various degrees from the diverse 'domestic' interests he-it allegedly exists to protect."[75] Additionally, states are complicit with gender subordination when they fail to intervene in domestic violence, perpetuate a heterosexist bias in education, exercise discrimination in welfare policies, and operate on patriarchal laws.[76]

In this conception, the unitary state is a misleading and malignant construction. Two implications for the process of state interaction follow: states that interact often promote unrepresentative interests, and those unrepresentative interests exclude gender, racial, and cultural minorities. In this sense, states' elites often make wars (or fail to) "representing" a limited group or groups among their populations, while claiming full representativeness, effectively rendering a significant portion of their supposed "constituency" invisible in the process of interacting with other states. Empirically, this means that there are a number of levels of interstate interaction, many of which are omitted from process-based notions of dyadic war theorizing. Normatively, it suggests that our conceptions of *how* states interact (and the content of those interactions) are problematically skewed.

Rationality in Interaction

This skew is particularly evident in the assumption of rationality.[77] The rationality assumption implies that the knower/actor can separate himself/herself from the "other" in interactions with that other. Feminists have argued that knowledge is always perspectival and political; therefore, states and their leaders' decisions about how to interact with others are not rational, but informed by their situational and political biases. In this view, the rationality assumption may be seen as at once itself a political bias and obscuring other political biases. As Naomi Scheman argues, perceived rational cost–benefit analysis about war-making and war-fighting should "always be seen as especially problematical when . . . constructed only by those in positions of privilege . . .

[which provide] only distorted views about the world."[78] In this view, rational calculation is not an objective, attainable, and desirable end, but a partial representation of both interest and actors' representation of those interests. In this way, through gender lenses, rationality has been seen as importantly incomplete, leaving out significant (if not the most significant) factors that go into decision-making.[79]

In addition to understanding the rationality assumption as partial (and therefore unrepresentative), feminist research has pointed out links between rationality and masculinism.[80] As Karen Jones notes, advocates of rationality as a guide for interstate interactions[81] assume:

1. Available . . . conceptions of rationality and reason represent genuinely human norms and ideals;
2. The list of norms and ideals contained within available conceptions of rationality and reason are sufficiently complete; and
3. The external normative functions assigned to reason and rationality are unproblematic.[82]

Looking through gender lenses shows problems with each of these assumptions. Feminists have argued that "the identity of the modern subject—in models of human nature, citizenship, the rational actor, the knowing subject, economic man, and political agency—is not gender-neutral but masculine (and typically European and heterosexual)."[83] This impacts not only how we see the rational subject, but how we predict and understand *his* decisions, at the state level as well as at the individual level. According to Margaret Atherton, the possibility of rationality has "been used in a disturbing fashion to mark a gender distinction. We have, for example, on the one hand, the man of reason, and, on the other, the woman of passion."[84] In rationality assumptions, traits associated with masculinity are normalized and traits associated with femininity are excluded. The impact is compounded because (masculinized) rationality and its (feminized) alternatives are not on equal playing fields. As a result, Karen Jones notes that "women's assumed deficiency in rationality" has been used to exclude both women and knowledge associated with femininity from accepted views of the world.[85] The alleged gender neutrality of rationality, then, "is often a covert form of privileging maleness"[86] and omission of "what has traditionally counted as 'feminine.'"[87]

Still, adding women and values associated with femininity to current concepts of rationality is unlikely to create a gender-neutral concept of rationality.[88] This is because, epistemologically, the sovereign rational subject constructs artificial gendered boundaries between rationality and emotion, male and female, and knower and known.[89] Among states, those boundaries are not benign. Instead, they breed competition and domination that inspire and foster war(s) and conflict(s).[90] This competition frequently relies on contrasting the state's own masculinity to the enemy's (actual or perceived) femininity. This cycle of genderings is not a series of events but a social continuum. In these gendered relationships, as Zillah Eisenstein argues, "gender differentiation will be mobilized for war and peace," especially moving forward into the age of an American empire focused on manliness.[91] Feminists have long argued that competitions between hegemonic masculinities and subordinate masculinities play a role in causing war(s).[92]

Hidden beneath the assumed independence, rationality, and unity of state interaction leading to war are gendered interstate interactions that cause, constitute, and relate to war and wars. Feminist scholars have recognized the extent to which the preeminence of masculine values dominates (particularly conflictual) accounts of interstate interactions, wherein "rational" interactions often become "a self-reproducing discourse of fear, suspicion, anticipated violence, and violence" in which "force is used to checkmate force."[93] Interstate interactions leading to wars often show the gendered nature of war narratives, war logics, and war languages, which produce (and reproduce) gendered cycles of violence.

Gendered War Narratives, Logics, and Languages

War narratives are the stories of war that are told, both during the wars to the citizens of the participant states (and the world) and in history books that tell of wars in retrospect. One of the gendered ways states interact is in gendered war narratives. Plots of war narratives include the "good guys" fighting the "bad guys" for valorous reasons and after overcoming extreme hardship and suffering, winning "the good fight."[94] These stories motivate and sustain war efforts on individual and national levels, where "war imitates war narrative imitates war," which means that stories of wars are conditions of possibilities for and models of war, and wars create fodder for war stories.[95] War stories climax with victories in which "the actual number of victims—and *a fortiori* their innocence and guilt, are secondary considerations; what counts is the capacity to kill the triumphal narrative of the enemy."[96] Physical violence and war narratives are need to be understood as distinct *parts of the war* instead of as "the war" and "the story about the war" as if they were separable.[97]

But no war has just one story. Instead, belligerents use war stories to compete with each other.[98] The question of which (war) stories are heard is important, especially because gender matters in these discursive contests.[99] For the purposes of thinking about the dyadic causes of war, gendered narratives of conflicts held by different belligerents compete, and competing potential belligerents are competing be the one whose narrative of their masculinity (and by definition others' femininities or subordinated masculinities) wins. This plays out in communication between (and performances of) potential belligerents and in their competitions to prove their masculinities.[100] The scholarly study of these competitions often replicates competing states' prioritization of the masculine.[101]

These competitions valorize the masculinity of the victors and subordinate the masculinity of the vanquished.[102] Whether it is in "penetrating the inner sanctum" of the enemy or using "deep penetrating" missiles that "shove it up theirs" or some other phraseology, the language of war and the language of sex go hand-in-hand.[103] This has been well-documented in the feminist literature, most pointedly by Carol Cohn.

The sexualized aggressive masculinity of offensive maneuvers in wars, Cohn explains, is paired with a discourse of femininity that makes war seem humane and masterable despite sexualized aggression.[104] As such, "the language of missile construction and invention is a language of male birth and creation."[105] The "feminine" counterpart to *war sex* discourse is a discourse of *war cleanliness* that "cleans up" sexual(ized) violence and pretends that the abuse [rape] did not happen.[106] In these terms, "one basic task of a state at war is to portray the enemy in terms as absolute and abstract as possible in order to distinguish as sharply as possible the act of killing from the act of murder."[107]

The gendered sanitization of war discourses at once depersonalizes and shrinks the impacts of war to the speaker, allowing abstract thought about warfare to make invisible personal fear, either of destruction or of monstrousness.[109] Cohn explains, "the fire-breathing dragon under the bed, the one who threatens to incinerate your family, your town, your planet, becomes a pet you can pat."[110] These discourses can be contagious,[111] marginalizing to outsiders,[112] and discursively exclusive of critical perspectives.[113]

Gendered Cycles of Violence

Gendered war narratives also justify not only states' (individual) decisions to go war, but also states' (increasingly brutal) competitions with opponents. As such, they make war not only possible but likely at the interstate level, as well as increasing the likelihood of that two states that have fought a war fight another one.

As mentioned in chapter 2, Betty Reardon has used the phrase "war system" to talk about the continuous cycle of violence brought about by gendered competition among states.[114] She explains the war system as "our competitive social order, which is based on authoritarian principles, [which] assumes unequal value among and between human beings, and is held in place by coercive force."[115] She defines "coercive force" as "threat, intimidation, and when necessary, violent coercion."[116] This coercive force is assumed to be "the ultimate and most effective mechanism for obtaining and maintaining desired conditions."[117] In this reading, war is a state of existence as opposed to an event.[118]

Reardon's interpretation is one of a number of feminist approaches that link gender narratives, gendered behaviors and war-making. These feminist approaches suggest that seeing war as a continuum or a state of existence reveals cycles of violence that come from posturing about gendered positionality among states. A state, a group of states, or a group of actors in global politics, concerned with its relative position along a gendered hierarchy between states in the international arena, can perpetuate conflict and create relationships that are conflictual, either by nature or in their dominant manifestations.

This dynamic would predict that states behave differently than assumed in many of the trait-based and process-based notions of the dyadic causes of war(s). This is a small part of the potential contribution to dyadic theorizing of war coming from thinking about global politics generally and war specifically in terms of relations, the focus of the next section.

RELATIONS INTERNATIONAL

Feminist work on trait-based dyadic theories of war has suggested that it is important to pay attention to the interactive part of interstate interactions. Engagement through gender lenses with process-based dyadic approaches to war that do give attention to interaction suggests there is more to how states relate than current theories explore. Taking both of those observations into account, this section argues that idea that states *relate*, materially, symbolically, and emotionally, as a fundamental part of being states, should be key to theorizing the dyadic causes of war through gender lenses.[119]

As I mentioned above, many dyadic approaches to thinking about the cause(s) of war(s) are actually focused more on the properties of the two states involved in the dyad, or their material interchanges, than on their relationships. Steps-to-war, rivalry, and bargaining models of war implicate relations among states, but they do so in a partial, unrepresentative way. The feminist analysis in the remainder of this chapter looks to complete the picture by asking what the relations part of IR really describes. On the one hand, it seems trivial to invert the word combination "international relations" to "relations international" and call that a contribution to war theorizing, particularly as the discipline is interested in what war(s) is/are and what causes it/them. On the other hand, very little attention has been paid to the relational dimension of war-making, even among dyadic theories, and I argue such attention can have significant payoffs for causal war therapy.

For the most part, in IR as a discipline, the term *relations* seems to simply complement a narrow interpretation of *international*—we study what the international (by which we mean elite states) does, and whatever the international does is characterized as relating. Security studies, war studies, and strategic studies omit the term *relations* altogether, and the scholarship therein often reflects a narrow, materialistic understanding of relating that does not account for either discursive/symbolic, interactionist, or emotional content inherent in *relationships as relationships*. While feminist work has long been critical of gendered dichotomies both in war-making and in war theorizing,[120] this section suggests there is another dichotomy to be broken down in dyadic-level war theorizing: the distinction between the (properties and) *actions of actors* rather than the *relations within and among them*.

In order to break down that dichotomy, it is important to think seriously about the work that relating does in interstate interactions. Thinking about relations requires defining the concept. While I will provide definitions and theoretical explanations from within the feminist literature shortly, it is important to me to show that common usage actually differs significantly from the (term-of-art, narrow) usage in scholarly work on the causes of war(s) and peace(s). Among common definitions of the word "relate" are "associate or connect,"[121] "have relation,"[122] "social or sympathetic relationship with person or thing,"[123] "to show or establish logical or causal connection between,"[124] and "to find or show a connection."[125] In this spirit, a "relationship" is a "connection, association, or involvement,"[126] "an emotional or other connection,"[127] "having dealings with each other,"[128] and "the mutual dealings, connections, or feelings that exist between two parties, countries, people, etc."[129] A few of the properties of relating and having relationships recur: bi-directional, interdependent/mutual, connected, having an emotional dimension, and among individuals *or other entities*.

State Personhood and Ontological Security as a Way into Relating

In chapter 3, we discussed a growing literature that characterizes states as having a sense of self (or a sense of ontological security) that is fundamental to how states behave, even trumping material interests (as traditionally understood) when the two come into conflict.[130] This subsection explores that work in more depth, arguing that it could serve as a foundation to understanding both how states relate (through gender lenses) and how states' relationships influence the likelihood that those states make wars.

The central argument of ontological security perspectives is that "states pursue social actions to serve self-identity needs, even when those actions compromise their physical existence."[131] These self-identities are based on what states consider central to *who they are*, much like human self-identity needs. Brent Steele argues that "while physical security is (obviously) important to states, ontological security is more important because its fulfillment affirms a state's self-identity," which allows states to "maintain *consistent self-concepts*" wherein "the 'Self' of states is constituted and maintained through a narrative which gives life to routinized foreign policy actions."[132] The consequence of ignoring its ontological security needs to a state is high, as "consistently ignored threats to ontological security produce . . . 'shame' for nation-state agents . . . used as a metaphor to understand how identity disconnects can compel states to purse social actions which sacrifice physical security interests but strengthen ontological security."[133] Steele and other ontological security theorists describe ontological security-seeking behavior (even when it damages physical security) as "self-help"[134] in traditional, realist terms, contra the realist literature that suggests that social behavior is by nature other-regarding instead of self-regarding.[135] In terms of the causes of war, this perspective means that states are likely to make wars for and about issues related to their ontological security, even when ontological security interests conflict with physical security interests. Because ontological security interests are by necessity relational, it is important to pay attention to the ways in which relationships construct or inhibit a state's ontological security in order to understand that state's likelihood to make war and the states with which it is likely to fight.[136]

Such an analysis has the potential to include a number of the dimensions of *relating* that are absent from traditional approaches to dyadic-level war theorizing. If neorealist and neoliberal approaches to the study of causes of war(s) ignore and/or trivialize their own and/or war actors' social components, constructivist-theoretical approaches pay attention to states as social actors who shape the international system.[137] If constructivist work on the causes of war acknowledges the social component of international "relations" only to the extent that the sum total of social interactions between states influence the shape of the international system in a way subordinate or complementary to (but always distinct from) material interests, work in ontological security notes that states' interests are sometimes not only material, but tied to the emotions produced by having, and having a stake in, identities.[138]

That said, the ontological security literature focuses on state-as-self in how states interact with and react to other states, entrenching another gendered dichotomy that feminists have problematized—the self/other dichotomy. Feminists have been critical of the self/other divide both because it (falsely) classifies self as ontologically and operationally separate from the other[139] and because it defines others' experiences of global politics as nonpolitical problems.[140] The division of the international arena into self and other by definition marginalizes the interests, ideas, and self-identities[141] of those considered to be the other.[142]

Yet the self is always related to the other to the extent that self-esteem[143] or ontological security[144] not only projects onto but is also constantly reevaluated within and redefined by relations with the projected other(s).[145] The classification of self as entirely separate from other is insidious, because the self/other distinction means that (without understanding relationality) self state has no (material or moral) obligations to treat other state fairly or humanely. Instead, in many feminisms, the self is inherently connected to the other, both empirically (because self/other are relationally, rather than reactively, autonomous)[146] and normatively.[147]

Even this comparison between self and other assumes that self is a unitary, internally coherent actor—an assumption that feminist theorizing has critiqued in traditional war studies. As mentioned above, feminist theorists have suggested that states have citizens who are left out of the process of determining their "interests" in interacting with other states, and citizens whose interests are actually contrary to the interests that the state acts to further. People at the margins of states are often the victims of state action, and even powerful minorities or repressed majorities within states often have a very different vision of what the state is or should be than the government of that state. The state "self," then, is itself socially constituted through contestation and dialogue both *within* and *outside* it, making the self/other dichotomy all the more untenable.

If these observations are accurate, then ontological security makes the mistake of placing self before relationship even as it takes a broader view of what relating is in analyzing the way(s) that state(s) relate socially, emotionally, and (therefore) politically. In my view, it is crucial that a feminist approach to dyadic-level analysis maintain some of the strengths of the ontological security framework, including but not limited to that framework's understanding that there are emotional dynamics to international "relations," that those emotional dynamics can and do trump material dynamics, and that understanding state interactions must include not just one dimension of the ways that states interact, but many. At the same time, a feminist approach to *relations* international would be fundamentally based in *relating* as primary (seeing relationships as the primary unit of analysis among dyads), situating it within a broad idea of the international. The next subsection of this chapter discusses what that might look like.

Gendering Relations International

Through gender lenses, the first element of relations is the interdependence of self and other, whereby how self and other relate is not only a characteristic of their relationship but a fundamental part of defining each. In Naeem Inayatullah and David Blaney's words, "identity always owes a debt to alterity."[148] This debt that identity owes to alterity, though, is not linear or reactive, but interdependent and liminal. As Christine Sylvester sees it, "liminality suggests borderlands that defy fixed homeplaces in feminist epistemology, places of mobility around policed boundaries, places where one's bag disappears and reappears before moving on."[149] We can then think of human interactions in terms of "different subjectivities, different travelling experiences, which we can think of as mobile, rather than fixed, criss-crossing borderlands rather than staying at home."[150]

The second element of relating is that it is both interdependent and multilayered. Relationships are not only often power unequal, those inequalities constrain how actors are able or unable to communicate and relate. Feminist work in IR began paying careful attention to the "voices" of people, particularly women, at the margins of global politics.[151] Gayatri Spivak, however, made the controversial argument that the subaltern in global politics cannot speak or be heard in the halls of power.[152] A similar conversation took place between Copenhagen school securitization theorists, who argue that the utterance of security produces it,[153] and Lene Hansen,[154] who expresses concern that such an approach to security excludes those in the international arena whose silence is not voluntary. Feminist theorists in IR have looked to make the invisible visible, asking, after Cynthia Enloe, "where are the women?" in global politics, a question that implies finding people who were previously unseen and revealing them to change our ideas of the world "out there."[155] When actors relate, they interact in ways that are frequently (if not always) laced with genderings, class dynamics, race dynamics, power differentials, and communication pathologies. Those fraught relationships do not disappear when states make war policies; instead, understanding their nuances is key to understanding the causes of war(s).

This brings us to a third important dynamic of how actors relate: their relatings are as likely to be negative as positive; aggressive as bonding; disidentifying as identifying. The concept of disidentification is important both to understanding how states come to make wars and as a potential strategy for decreasing the frequency of war-making. *Disidentification*[156] is the act of disassociation with (presumed or actual) "natural" affinities or characteristics. It is used in transgender theorizing in reference to trans- people's disidentification with the biological sex assigned to the at birth, suggesting that the question of whether identity is primordial and fixed[157] is not a yes/no question and can be answered with hybridity.[158] This disidentification can be purposive or incidental and results in a change of (or change in perception of) sense of self.

For war theorizing, it may be useful to inquire when and how people *disidentify* with ethnic groups, organizations, nations, and states to which they are assigned at birth or with which their association is assumed to be primordial. Such a path of inquiry may provide explanatory leverage about the causes of intransigent conflicts specifically and wars generally above and beyond the leverage provided by asking when and how people identify with their assigned or primordial identities. In addition to disidentifying, people can be *disidentified with* identities they are assigned or see as primordial. In trans- theorizing, disidentification can also be something that *happens to* trans- people when they are rejected as members of the biological sex to which they perceive themselves as belonging. For war theorizing, it might be productive to ask when primordial groups *disidentify* people, either by rejecting them outright or by "the experience of misrecognition, this uneasy sense of standing under a sign to which one does and does not belong."[159] Such an approach might shed light on the causes of conflict, particularly individualized violence and cultural conflict.[160]

In practice, "to disidentify is to read oneself and one's own life narrative in a moment, object, or subject that is not cultural coded to 'connect' with the disidentifying subject."[161] To disdentify, then, is to separate one's self-perception from inclusive *and* exclusive narratives of belonging and identification, "what would I be were I not situated in a particular context?"[162] This could as easily be performed by or inflicted on states as on people. In this process, "disidentificatory performances . . . circulate in subcultural circuits and strive to envision and activate new social relations . . . [that] would be the blueprint for minoritarian counterpublic spheres."[163]

Because that "counterpublic" sphere does not mirror the hegemonic public sphere, the idea of disidentification can bring up more general questions about the representativeness of traditional notions of action and reaction, unitary units, and rationality among them. But it does more than that—it suggests that the positive and negative coexist in relationships, rather than particular relationships being all good or all bad. Extrapolated from this, *relations* are not just positive or negative, public or private, empowered or disempowered, but often all of those at once.

As a result, understanding disidentification the ways that one might interpret social relations between states. This does not mean disregarding the built-up contexts of relationships between states. Instead, it means making sure that context is not fully determinative of political interaction, such that "disidentification is . . . the survival strategies that [the] minority subject practices in order to negotiate a phobic majoritarian public sphere that continuously elides or punishes the existence of subjects who do not conform."[164] Seeing the political and contingent nature of knowledge allows feminists to use the tools of dialogue and empathetic cooperation with the other as a way of relating to that other by looking to see or feel their perspectives.[165] Such a strategy can also be extended to engaging in disidentification with one's own assigned or primordial identities intentionally, looking for the alterity in self as a bridge across the self/other divide.

A *relationship* between states therefore includes not only their relative or absolute economic strength, their regime types, or their state self-identities. It is not only one side *relating to* the other, which in turn *relates to* the first state; instead, it is states *relating with* each other, in context of other relationships, and constituting each others' identities. It is not a result, but a process, in which dialogue is constituted by sharing, interpretation, and oppositions.[166]

Relationships include not just interactions, but arguments. Contending that it is dialogue that constitutes interstate relations, Hayward Alker understood that truth is to be found through the process of argumentation rather than as the result of resolving arguments.[167] As I discussed in chapter 2, Alker suggests a "controversy-based path of knowledge cumulation"[168] using argument and constructive criticism to find truth.[169] Particularly, he emphasizes that "dispute *description* is not completely separable from the cognitive practices or *procedures* that produced it."[170] In Alker's understanding, relations international are a "performable repertoire or grammar of arguments and counter-arguments."[171]

This dialogical approach to understanding dyadic war theorizing would allow for analysis of actor differences as process, rather than only as result, allowing for the potential for deeper analyses of the fundamental concepts underlying the different approaches. While many dyadic theories of war look for meaning and significance in interstate relations in material interaction and regime type(s), feminist theory suggests that often the discourse *is* the meaning and significance—the discourse is the content rather than representing it. Seeing relations international as a dialectical-hermeneutic argument has implications for both the process and product of scholarship about the causes of war(s).

While dyadic democracy may correlate both with peace (defined as the absence of war) and some properties of relations international, I argue that looking at those relations directly and in all of their complexity will provide more accurate understanding of what is really going on between peaceful and bellicose dyads. Those dyads are not two independent entities that relate based on their properties of governance or the volume of trade they exchange. They instead relate within a complicated number of dimensions, including social, economic, reputational, political, and communicative, and they do that relating not as simple, unitary actors but as complex sites of dissonance. These interactions rely on intersubjective communicative norms, co-constitutive identities of actors, emotional interactions, empathy, identification, disidentification, and the like.

As such, states can be "relationally rather than reactively autonomous with those we have defined as unmistakably other, with those who are not inside 'our' community, our value system."[172] If this is true, *relationships* constitute not only states but their relationships with other states; the nature of states' relationships are a key factor in how they interact. If states' relationships are gendered, and the gendered nature of those relationships influences their propensity to go to war(s), feminist analysis poses empirical questions for dyadic accounts of the making and fighting of wars.

For example, we would expect a cycle of increasingly intense gendered competition would cause war, and gendered narratives would reflect that competition. We would expect the abstraction and sexualization of war discourse to increase with the brutality of violent confrontations, and the brutality of violent confrontations to increase both with the abstraction and sexualization of war discourses and the intensity of gendered competitions between states. We would expect rivalries to be driven at least in part by the gendered nature of the relationships between states, and those gendered relationships to drive and be driven by the intersubjectivity of not only state identity but state violent behavior. These empirical expectations suggest a world that looks significantly different than many dyadic theories of war currently understand it, yet perhaps significantly more representative of the world's contingencies and complexities.

POTENTIAL CONTRIBUTIONS OF A FEMINIST DYADIC-LEVEL RESEARCH PROGRAM ON WAR

Feminisms looking at the dyadic causes of war not only see different boundaries and issues than many traditional theories, but also different causal factors. Traditional IR's boundaries for dyadic-level war theorizing include looking for the causes of war and peace in the traits states have (or do not have) in common and in pathologies in the actions and reactions of (presumably unitary and rational) independent states. Gender lenses engaging with these approaches suggest the boundaries be expanded to focus not only on the properties of each state but on relations international, broadly interpreted, and a broader understanding of who is *in* and *impacted* by wars, whereas traditional dyadic approaches normally focus not only on states but "great states."

The current war studies literature takes account of trait-based causal factors such as regime type, levels of trade, and levels of sex equality as well as process-based causal factors such as rivalries, bargaining, and steps-to-war. Gender lenses have suggested that this list of causal factors is too narrow in important ways. Trait-based accounts (whether intentionally or not) portray the health of a relationship as reducible to what the interacting parties have (or do not have) in common, suggesting that similar states have positive relationships and states with serious differences are likely to have negative relationships. Process-based causal theories of the dyadic-level causes of war make assumptions about war-making actors that are partially representative (if they are representative at all) of what states are, what interests they have, and what interests they pursue. Therefore, "a" feminist approach to the dyadic-level causes of war suggests that fuller accounting for relations is necessary, including the relational autonomy (and therefore relational dependency) of war-making actors and gendered pathologies of interstate interactions.[173]

If feminist theorizing recognizes different boundaries and causal mechanisms for dyadic-level war theorizing, it also has different normative prescriptions. Perhaps unique in war theorizing, dyadic-level war theorizing has spurred normative policy endorsements of the traits and processes it finds lead to peace. Policy makers have endorsed trade, gender equality, and democracy specifically for the purpose of increasing the likelihood of peace among states.[174] They have also urged rationality and other communicative strategies understood to decrease the likelihood that states' interactions will "go bad" and lead to war(s).[175] Still others suggest the fruitfulness of a "pax Americana" whereby the overwhelming power of the hegemon among states makes those states averse to fighting when the hegemon would disapprove.

Feminist dyadic-level war theorizing also has the potential for normative policy guidance. Rather than endorse a position that the strong should dominate the weak for continued control, feminist work has suggested normative endorsement not of a particular regime type or traits associated with masculinity in interstate interactions, but instead a guiding ethos of empathy for states relating to other states. In Christine Sylvester's words, "empathy rests on the ability and willingness to enter into the feeling or spirit of something and appreciate it fully. It is to hear . . . and be transformed in part by our appreciation."[176] Such an approach "enables respectful negotiations with contentious others because we can recognize involuntary similarities across difference as well as differences that mark independent identity."[177] As such, "there is no arrogance of uniqueness" and "precious little committed defensiveness."[178]

A feminist normative approach to dyadic relationships between states, then, might emphasize empathy and by extension, care. In Fiona Robinson's recent book, she argued that "care is a *global* political issue and that decisions regarding the provision and distribution of care are of profound moral significance, insofar as they are central to the survival and security of people around the world."[179] Robinson argues that "by foregrounding and prioritizing the consideration of a politics of care, we can recover the potential of human security."[180] If an ethic of care (as an emotion and as labor) were envisioned as a possible transgressive alternative to relations international based on an ethos of masculinity, war narratives specifically and interstate relations generally might be reconceived in a manner cognizant of both relations and relational identities. Such an approach might encourage "the broadening of security beyond its conventional military focus" and the broadening of states relationships beyond posturing, competition, and violence.

In sum, whether or not the international system is a gender hierarchy, states often interact in gendered ways—competing, posturing, and telling gendered stories of wars and conflicts, and those interacting states are not either fully unitary or fully independent. Analyzing dyadic causes of war through gender lenses not only reveals these often invisible parts of the processes leading to wars, but calls for re-evaluation of how scholars studying the dyadic-level causes of war think not only about the international but also about *relations* among actors in the international arena. Particularly, feminists think of *relations* among states as multidimensional, intersubjective, interdependent, and co-constitutive—whereby relationships shape and are shaped by state identity, and state behavior iteratively shapes and is shaped by those relationships. In dialogue with traditional war theorizing, feminist work suggests engaging the dyadic level is importantly fruitful, but the gaze of that theorizing needs to be expanded significantly. This view suggests the normative value not of particular traits or processes, but of approaches to *relating* based on empathy and care, and constitutes a radical reformulation of not only the normative implications of dyadic-level war theorizing, but also the scope and hypotheses. This reformulation is impacted by and reverberates onto the discussion of the gendered international system in chapter 3 and the upcoming discussion of gendered states and substate actors in chapters 5 and 6.

CHAPTER 5

Gender, States, and War(s)

Each Hutu man must know that the Tutsi woman, no matter whom, works in solidarity with her Tutsi ethnicity. In consequence, every Hutu man is a traitor
    Who marries a Tutsi woman
    Who makes a Tutsi woman his concubine
    Who makes a Tutsi woman his secretary or protégé . . . .
    Every Hutu man must know that our Hutu girls are more dignified and more conscientious in their roles as woman, wife, and mother. Aren't they pretty, good secretaries, and more honest? . . .
Hutu women, be vigilant, bring our husbands, brothers, and sons to reason. . . .
            —"HUTU TEN COMMANDMENTS," PUBLISHED IN *KANGURA*, A RWANDAN NEWSPAPER

This account of Hutu identity, published by Hutu extremists in Rwanda before the genocide and often referenced during the perpetration of the genocide in the summer of 1994, ties a sense of nation and ethnicity to strict gender roles and gendered rules.[1] In the "Hutu Ten Commandments," what it means to be a Hutu is intimately tied to (sexual) relationships between Hutu men and Hutu women, and corrupting the Hutu nation/ethnicity involves corrupting those sexual relationships. This story of state/nation/ethnicity constitutes and is constituted by gender tropes. The gendered nature of Hutu identity influenced not only *that* the conflict in Rwanda happened (as the purity of Hutu identity was a major motivator for the *Interahamwe,* or fighters) but also *how* (particularly the level of wartime rape and the gendered nature of many of the attacks) it happened.[2]

Chapter 4 argued that states' relationships are gendered, and that gendered lenses provide a unique perspective on the complexities of these relationships. This chapter looks at the gendered dimensions of state and organizational identities, particularly as they contribute to the state-level causes of war(s). In the war studies literature, state-level theories of war address a variety of factors, including trading habits,[3] class politics,[4] coalitions,[5] diversions,[6] and culture.[7] These theories share the idea that the major causes of states making wars can be found not among or between states, but within their borders. In this view, states make wars because of their economic organizations or governing processes, to appease or reconcile interest groups, to serve the needs of their collectivized identities as states, or to divert attention from serious "domestic" problems. As such, it is crucial to see what happens inside states to understand what happens between them.

Feminist work has consistently argued that it is necessary to see the (gendered) insides of states to understand interstate interactions.[8] This chapter argues that feminisms' critical analyses of the state can make significant contributions to theorizing the "domestic" sources of war. It begins with perhaps the best-known work on addressing gender, states, and war—research that argues that domestic gender equality or women's leadership stems the quantity and severity of war(s). While the question of women's leadership will be addressed in more detail in chapter 6, the first section of this chapter explores whether domestic gender equality is a major factor in when and/or how states make wars. It argues that this hypothesis is important, but oversimplified, relying on an assumed (but inaccurate) correlation between indicators of "gender equality"[9] rising and a shifting balance between the values associated with masculinities and the values associated with femininities in the security sphere. While the former is important for a variety of reasons, this chapter contends that only the latter (and the necessarily accompanying deconstruction of the discursive/performative structure of gender subordination) substantively impacts the ways in which states make wars.

Using this argument as a starting point, the remainder of the chapter contends that feminisms have much more to contribute to state-level war theorizing than just work that relates women, gender equality, and peacefulness. Building on the arguments of chapters 3 and 4 that states are situated in a gendered international system structure and have gendered relationships, this chapter looks at the state itself through gendered lenses. It recognizes that states have relationally autonomous identities, which are gendered. Gendered state identities play a part in states' war decision-making, because state identity, militarism, nationalism, and war-making are all linked and gendered, which accounts for the gendered nature of state identity and nationalism and the role of gender in state-level causes of war. Accordingly, this chapter engages with domestic politics explanations for war and war(s) generally by thinking about the ways in which state identities are gendered and the ways in which the gendering of state identities can serve as both a cause of war and an instrumental excuse for the making and fighting of wars. The chapter looks at the concept and operation of strategic culture through gendered lenses, contending that states' gendered strategic cultures help to understand when and how states make wars. It then argues that gendered state identities and gendered strategic cultures serve not only as causes of states making wars but also as justifications for state war-making. The chapter concludes by summarizing potential contributions of feminism(s) to studying state-level causes of war(s).

"DOMESTIC" GENDER EQUALITY AND WAR(S)

Often, when war theorists consider gender, they think about it as a variable influencing states' likelihood to make wars. Particularly, thinking of gender as synonymous with or mapping onto sex, they explore questions of whether women really are less likely to make war than men, or whether domestic gender equality at home makes states less likely to be violent abroad. These or similar empirical findings would add fuel to more general feminist claims for women's rights and the inclusion of women in politics and would provide justification for studying women and war(s). They would also provide a security-based mandate for sex equality because, if sex inequality domestically is a cause of violence internationally, it becomes important to stop sex inequality domestically for the purpose of stopping war internationally.

As I discussed briefly in chapters 1, 2, and 4, there is a self-identified liberal feminist research program interested in the relationship between the status of women domestically and the likelihood of making war(s) internationally.[10] This research program contends that the inequality between the sexes is foundational to societal, state, and international violence, and that women's security is essential to "national security."[11] Therefore, low levels of gender inequality, measured by bodily security, sex equality in family law, and representation in political decision-making, make a state more likely to be secure.[12] For those reasons, some researchers contend that sex inequality is a significant explanatory variable in violence between states.[13] Theoretically, these authors explain the link between sex inequality and violence as caused by the translation of the hierarchical socialization of sexual difference to the treatment of all "others."[14]

These claims are supported with empirical findings from statistical work, coming most recently from the WomanStats Database.[15] The researchers find, in a variety of studies, that states with higher levels of sex equality are less likely to fight one another and less likely to make war(s) more generally.[16] As a result of this empirical research and theoretical analysis, the authors advocate that a "fundamental reordering of human collectives" is necessary not just to make women's lives better, but for national security, and propose both top-down and bottom-up steps to reach such a reordering.[17] Though there are, in my view, some methodological critiques to be made of this conclusion (particularly in attempts to fit a universalized notion of sex equality across cultures, geographies, and states), it builds on long-held understandings of gender roles and has a broad "mainstream" appeal.[18]

This work builds on long-held notions about gender by appropriating and exploring the idea that there is a relationship between women and peace. As I discussed in chapter 2, early work on gender and war focused on women's absence from and opposition to war-making, often arguing that there was some essential relationship between femininity (and therefore women) and incapacity for violence.[19] Research on the relationship between sex equality and peace calls upon familiar notions of women as outside of war and violence or as forces of moderation or passivity.

Theorizations that link indicators of sex equality to propensity for peace also have appeal to the mainstream of war studies. Because this work conceptualizes gender bias as an operationalizable (countable) causal variable (rather than as a power relation and a constitutive force), it can be performed using the conceptual structures and methodological tools that the mainstream of the field use to evaluate other variables' influence on states' likelihood to make wars.[20] As such, this work often appears to demonstrate the possibility of methodologically sophisticated, data-based, positivist, quantitative analysis of the relationship between sex (and by extension gender) and war.

Certainly, whether for its affinity with popular notions of femininities, its appeal to the mainstream of war studies, or its own intellectual merits, the question of whether states with more sex equality are more peaceful is worth exploring. This is especially true given empirical findings demonstrating a correlation between the variables.[21] Still, other feminist analysis suggests that there are a number of potential roadblocks to the theoretical conclusion that states that are more humane to their women are generally less violent. Some of these roadblocks are critiques of the ways that the argument has been presented in the literature so far,[22] while others are conceptual in nature.

Conceptually, it could be seen as an oversimplification to assume a linear mapping between women's material "equality" and the prioritizaiton of values associated with femininity, especially given feminist legal scholars' work on the continuing gaps between legal equality and substantive equality[23] and feminist IR work on the persistence of the discursive structures of gender subordination even when women are permitted to participate in masculine (and masculinized) institutions of state decision-making.[24] Much of this work (perhaps unreflectively) assumes that inclusion is linear, benign, and productive, and that women's inclusion in the political and economic processes, material benefits, and military activities of statehood is straightforward.[25]

Some feminist work has come to the opposite conclusion, arguing that approaches that just "add women and stir" are potentially counterproductive.[26] This is because the masculine structures of governments (and governmentality[27]), militaries, and other organizations are often maintained, and women are permitted to participate so long as they meet the already-existent standards of personality and practice masculinities.[28] I agree with those critiques and therefore find the "sex-equality peace" argument incomplete and potentially conceptually flawed. While I do not want to argue against promoting diversity generally or promoting sex equality specifically on their own merits, I contend that there is both intellectual and normative danger in appropriating them in the service of peace.

On normative grounds, promoting sex equality for peace might detract from the (crucially important) argument that sexism (with heterosexism and cissexism[29]) are on their own merits worthy of critique and deconstruction.[30] There is also a normative risk that work associating sex equality and peace will (intentionally or not) entrench existing gender-subordinating notions that link women, passivity, and nonviolence.[31] While promoting women's rights to promote femininity to promote peace appears to help women by promoting their rights, it is in fact complicit in the dichotomization of the sexes, the conceptual linking of sexes and genders, and the perpetuation of inequalities between masculinities and femininities.

Even were the sex-equality peace argument not normatively problematic, some feminist theoretical work has suggested that the correlation does not necessarily suggest the causal relationship that relative sex inequality predicts relative likelihood to make war.[32] Theoretical accounts of a gendered international system and gendered relations among states, as well as gendered sovereignty, gendered nationalisms, gendered strategic cultures, and the instrumental use of gendered narratives in the making and fighting of wars, suggest that there may be, in positivist terms, a common causal variable for sex equality and peace, as well as potential intervening variables.[33]

The common causal influence on sex equality and peacefulness may be the discursive deconstruction of gendered political and social structures of gender subordination—where gender emancipation loosens the association between masculinities and politics and femininity and women while denaturalizing hierarchies between masculinities and femininities. There is evidence that the correlation between sex equality and peace is stronger where characteristics associated with femininity (rather than [just] women) have been integrated into the political arena and/or assigned material, economic, and/or symbolic value.[34] At the same time, there is evidence that states with high levels of women's material equality but low levels of integration of and respect for values associated with femininity remain fairly bellicose.[35] Therefore, it is possible that the sex-equality peace, rather than showing a causal relationship between improvements of women's status and decreases in state violence, shows the two variables as collinear or commonly caused.[36] Even were sex equality and peace not commonly caused, feminist work has suggested a number of intervening variables in any potential causal relationship between them.

For example, if gender is a key component of state identity and state nationalism, and play a reproductive role in (biologically, socially, and culturally) reproducing state and nation (symbolically, actually, or both),[37] then the reorganization of domestic gender roles cannot be read independently of the reorganization of nationalist identities and war narratives— and nationalist identities and war narratives serve as inertial forces for the maintenance of domestic gender inequities. Feminist analyses have shown that, in times of war and conflict or as an excuse for war and conflict, states often return to and find refuge in traditionalist gender narratives.[38] More than that, though, different (and even equality-promoting) narratives of gendered state identities can inspire the making and fighting of wars or be used instrumentally to serve their purposes.

For example, as Annick Wibben explains, in November of 2001 United States First Lady Laura Bush suggested that the "war on terror" was a war for the rights of women, arguing that:

> The fight against terrorism is also a fight for the rights and dignity of women . . . Afghan women know, through hard experience, what the rest of the world is discovering: The brutal oppression of women is the central goal of terrorists. Long before the current war began, the Taliban and its terrorist allies were making the lives of children and women in Afghanistan miserable.[39]

This narrative links the United States' identity as gender equality-promoting to its responsibility to pursue military intervention in Afghanistan.

Given these potential normative implications and theoretical problems for the argument that domestic sex equality is a predictor of the likelihood for war, the remainder of this chapter argues that feminist theory has more to contribute to state-level war theorizing than linking, women, peace, and gender equality.[40] Making the break from sex analysis (what happens to women and why it matters) to gender analysis (how gendered identities and constructions, of people but also of states, function), the rest of this chapter asks questions about and explores the way that gender tropes interact with, constitute, justify, and even serve as direct or indirect causes of war(s) in gendered narratives of state identities, in structural gender inequality, and in sites of operation of gendered expectations from bedrooms and workplaces to state governments to international organizations.

GENDERED STATE IDENTITIES[41]

Instead of basing arguments on the relationship between gender equality and states' likelihood to make and fight wars, many feminist scholars look to the gendered nature of states' identities to understand how they come to make war(s). Feminists have analyzed the gendered constitution of the Westphalian state and its sovereignty;[42] the role of gender in constructing and perpetuating nationalism;[43] and how these gendered identities influence when, where, why, and how states make war(s), and serve as conditions of the possibility of war-making.[44]

Drawing on the work in chapter 4 on states as entities with (not only material, but social, psychological, and emotional) relationships (and relatedly, identities), this section builds on previous feminist work to argue that gendered states make and are made by gendered strategic cultures that lead both to gendered war decision-making and gendered war-justificatory narratives.

The argument that states are gendered is not new in (feminist) IR. Instead, feminism in IR began by arguing that both the state as state and IR theory's readings of the state are gendered.[45] Feminist theorists have accounted for the state as gendered, particularly in that states adopt, use, and reproduce traits associated with (their perceptions of) dominant masculinities. This argument is distinct from the observation that most states are led mostly by men. While that observation is accurate, I am not arguing that male leaders make states masculine—quite the opposite, in fact. As I will discuss in more detail in chapter 6, I argue, with R. W. Connell, that masculine states select for (perceived) masculinities in male leaders, making male leadership a circular result of institutional and behavioral state masculinity.[46] While women are capable of (and exhibit) traits associated with masculinities, masculine institutions often assume men's masculinity while women must prove theirs. This is because the organizational behaviors of states are structured in relation to masculine values and use an assumed relationship between identifiable men and masculinity as shorthand for identifying desirable traits in leaders and/or decision makers.[47]

Feminist theorists have demonstrated that the tendency of the state generally and states specifically to value masculinity in (particularly war) decision-making is related to gender tropes serving as the basis for states' notions of human nature, citizenship, political agency, rationality, and subjectivity.[48] In Connell's words, within states "there is a gendered configuring of recruitment and promotion, a gender configuring of the internal division of labor and systems of control, a gender configuring of policymaking, of practical routines, and ways of mobilizing pleasure and consent."[49] Connell contends that these below-the-surface genderings presuppose and reify the subordination of women while creating the appearance that the state is institutionally gender neutral.[50] Certainly, at the very least, Connell's description of the prevalence of genders in the everyday practices of statehood recalls Acker's description of a gendered organization—where location, relative ability, and process are distributed in whole or in part by relative position along gender hierarchies.[51]

Recalling Acker's description of a gendered organization might lead a feminist theorist of the gendered nature of the state to ask how (if at all) the visibility of the masculine and the invisibility of the feminine affect (even feminist) readings of the gendered state. After all, seeing the dominant discourse of state (war) policy-making as masculinized begs the question of where the feminized other on whom masculinized discourses rely can be located and what the role of that other is. This section argues that the "womenandchildren"[52] that constitute the nation serve as the feminized other that justifies and selects for the state as a masculinized (apparent) protector. It also contends that variations in the relationship between the masculinized state and its feminized other nation can account for some of the variation in state war decision-making.

To understand this, it is important to see state patriarchy both in the omission of women in traditional accounts of statehood and the overrepresentation of women in traditional accounts of the state's protective functions.[53] The omission of women is evidence of a gendered skew in state politics and governance, while the overrepresentation of women in states' protection narratives serves as a justification for states' monopolies on the means of violence domestically.[54] This pairing functions to solidify women's "place" in the contemporary nation-state generally. Still, it is important to note both that gender functions differently in different states and that this argument characterizes the state institutionally and states functionally as currently, though not necessarily and fundamentally, gender subordinating.[55] Gendered states are built by (and perpetuate) gendered militarisms and gendered nationalism, which support gendered strategic cultures.[56]

Gendered Militarisms and Gendered Nationalisms

Feminists have described militarism as essentially masculine and have argued that seeing gendered militarism in the theory and practice of statehood is key to understanding war-making.[57] Particularly, they have traced gendered militarism to gendered notions of sovereignty.

In this account, states' sovereignty licenses them to hold military forces, and states' employment of military forces is permissive of conflictual security ethics and strategic cultures. States' militaries inspire and are supported by militarism—or the militarization of everyday life. This is because feminist work on militarism has argued that military violence is not a rare or delineable event but a presence, wherein militarism affects people, particularly marginalized people, not only during wars but always.[58] Military support, military needs, and military violence form a "constant undertone, white noise in the background of social existence."[59] Militarism affects lives within a state as well as across state borders. Cynthia Enloe discusses the effects of militarization on the gendering of individuals' (especially women's) lives.[60] This militarization privileges the masculine idea of male heroes as good soldiers and links heroism, soldiering, military service, and leadership, which in turn overdetermines reification of women's perceived proper position as homemakers. As Enloe observes, "the militarism of the United States and other countries needs us all to behave *as women*" in order for it to function properly.[61]

Enloe cites, among others, the life of Kim Gorski as an example.[62] Kim was a real estate agent married to a banker who was a member of the California National Guard. Mike was deployed in service of the war on terror, and Kim suddenly became a "military wife," a process which involved intense socialization and brought with it high expectations which "simultaneously supported the military's mission."[63] In service to that cause, "each woman needed to be persuaded that she was most helpful and loyal to her husband if she organized her labor and emotions in a way that enhanced the military *as a whole*."[64] For Kim, this meant that she was expected to play a support role for other military wives, plan meetings, provide economic support and advice, and lead a "family readiness group."[65] All of these (unpaid, feminized) duties were *assumed done* by the United States military, and a condition of possibility of the war effort as it was structured. That effort relied on and produced *women as women* to function.

In this way, the militaristic state is both gendered and gender constitutive. Maleness, statism, and capitalism contribute to the gendered process of militarization.[66] Sovereignty also contributes to the gendering of power in international politics. States need power to protect and strengthen their "sovereign" control. State power is normally interpreted as the ability to wield some kind of coercive force over other international actors, or "power-over."[67] Such a coercive notion of power is gendered and incentivizes dominance as the currency of successful political interaction, which in turn increases the appeal of military force as a mode of relating. In these terms, the "powerful" possess coercive force to which the weak must submit. This dynamic often informs states' hegemonic or ideal-typical masculinities, whereby militarism encourages masculinity which encourages militarism. This is because, as feminist scholars have argued, "some men fight wars while other men *could* fight wars; war-fighting is always tied to the image of masculinity."[68] Judith Gardam has explained that often "the social construct of what it is to be male . . . is represented by the male warrior, the defender of the security of the state."[69] In these models, "masculinity, virility, and violence have been linked together."[70]

These links have consequences not only for masculinities and femininities but for state social organization more generally. These consequences can best be understood with reference to Charlotte Hooper's notion of the hegemonic masculinity within a given social or political organization.[71] According to Hooper, "hegemonic masculinity is constructed in relation to a range of subordinated masculinities in opposition to femininity."[72] An ideal-typical masculinity establishes cultural hegemony through moral persuasion and consent, entrenched ideological ascendency, and an ethos of coercion.[73] Hegemonic masculinity consists of the attributes that are most frequently performed in any given social organization, opposition to which or deviance from is rare and often punished.[74] Each state's assumed hegemonic masculinity is the set of standards to which war decision makers[75] are expected to aspire. I argue that states' hegemonic masculinities are often based in the links between militarism and virility, whose standards of being a good "man" (regardless of sex) and thereby a good war decision maker map onto the standards of militarized masculinity, including the austerity and heroism of soldiering, the toughness of military action, and the responsibility for protection that comes from the just-warrior role.

In order to understand those elements of militarized masculinities, though, it is essential to analyze the gendered nature of nationalism(s). Feminist work has analyzed the reliance of nationalisms on gender tropes, particularly during wartime, arguing that "war as an institution depends on gendered images of combatants and civilians,"[76] which Jean Elshtain has identified as (male) 'just warriors' and (female) 'beautiful souls.'"[77] Just warriors' duty is protection of civilians and defense of good and/or righteous causes, while beautiful souls' role is to need protection and defense.[78] Feminist scholarship has demonstrated both the complications that come with these tropes evolving and their continued salience in war decisions and war justifications.[79]

The gendered nature and operation of nationalisms create and perpetuate these gender tropes. Feminists have argued that in nationalist discourses, gender roles are a foundational element. This is because, as Jan Jindy Pettman points out, a nations' constitution relies on "construction of women as mothers of nation, responsible for its physical, cultural, and social reproduction."[80] Because of the relationship between femininity and nationalism, "gendered bodies and sexuality play pivotal roles as territories, markers, and reproducers of narratives of nations, and other collectives,"[81] including biological reproduction of national collectives, transmission and production of national culture, symbolic signification of national distinction and difference, and participation in nationalist struggles.[82]

It is here that the ugly underside of nationalism as a marker of gender difference becomes clear[83] and feminists find a warrant for exploring the ways that gendered nationalisms both impact national identities and the ways that they are deployed in war decision-making. In exploring this question, Anne McClintock contends that "all nationalisms are gendered, all are invented, and all are dangerous."[84] The danger that McClintock is talking about is twofold. The immediate danger is to women, causing personal vulnerability, given that, "women's bodies, relations, and roles become the battleground for different idealized versions of the past and constructions of nationalist projects for the future."[85] As discussed in more depth in chapter 7, women's bodies also become a battleground for the fighting of wars.

The second danger is violence committed for the purpose of (or using the excuse of) providing protection to the state's feminized others, either in the nation generally or in women specifically. This violence logically follows from the feminization of nation because women's bodies become the symbol of national identity and pride, where "the personification of nature-as-female transmutes easily to nature-as-woman, where the Motherland is a woman's body and as such is ever in danger of violation by foreign males/sperm."[86] This creates an incentive for two behaviors: control over "our" women[87] and violence toward "their" women and nation.[88] In both of these ways, there is "a complex relationship between actual women's bodies and nationalist discourse using representations of women's bodies to mark national or communal boundaries,"[89] fundamentally because "gender roles are at the heart of cultural constructions of social identities and collectives."[90]

These accounts of gender tropes as key to the identity of state and/or nation create a narrative of *that which states defend*—femininity, purity, their capacities as masculine protectors; and *that which states must be to defend* —masculine, tough, protecting, militaristic, and nationalistic. These delineations serve as direct and indirect causes of bellicose war choice and to build state strategic cultures based on (aggressive) hegemonic masculinities.

Gendered Militarisms, Gendered Nationalisms, and State Strategic Cultures

Looking at strategic culture through gender lenses reveals important and otherwise unseen dimensions. Strategic culture refers to "a nation's traditions, values, attitudes, patterns of behavior, habits, symbols, achievements, and particular ways of adapting to the environment and solving problems with respect of the threat or use of force."[91] Strategic culture and/or cultures of national security have been the subject of several state-level analyses of war.[92]

Colin Gray has argued that "the subject of strategic culture matters deeply because it raises core questions about the roots of, and the influences on, strategic behavior, defined as state behavior relevant to the threat or use of force for political purposes."[93] Strategic culture has been characterized as "a shaping context for behavior" as well as "a constituent of that behavior."[94] While scholars of strategic culture have different opinions on its content and operation,[95] they agree that the term "culture" is important to describe states' differing, sticky but potentially fungible, unique sets of "ideals . . . evidence of ideals, and behavior."[96]

More precisely, strategic culture has been described as the cultural and ideational influences on states' decisions about how and when to make conflicts with other states.[97] Jack Snyder noted that strategic cultures are "the body of attitudes and beliefs that guides and circumscribes thought on strategic questions, influences the way strategic issues are formulated, and sets the vocabulary and the perceptual parameters of strategic debate."[98] Others have defined it as related to war policy navigation and/or the fundamental assumptions behind the composition and use of military force, which influences states' "body language (operational doctrine and behavior)."[99] Rather than being a constant,[100] it varies both between states and over time, and those variations can be observed in states' behavior.[101] The literature on strategic culture has taken account of a number of variables, including history, military organization, political structure, and religious values[102] but has yet to account for the ways that gender shapes states' strategic cultures.[103]

In these terms, strategic culture is not something identifiable, countable, falsifiable, or distinguishable from other variables[104] but rather "the traffic between ideals and behavior."[105] In this view, "the unity of cultural influence and policy action denies the existence of the boundaries needed for cause and effect,"[106] but crucially forms the context for strategic policy-making. This subsection contends that understanding strategic culture as context is crucial to seeing how states fight wars and that states' strategic cultures[107] or "national styles of strategy"[108] are gendered, but often differently. The relationship between gender and strategic culture has been borne out by feminist work on state communication, militarism, and state identity.[109]

I argue that state strategic cultures are shaped by hegemonic masculinity in a given state at a given time and that the relationship between gendered nationalisms and gendered militarisms constitute and are constituted by gendered strategic cultures. Because militarized masculinities of states and their soldiers rely on the existence and symbolic protection of nation and woman as constitutive others, strategic cultures are shaped around seeking masculinization and eschewing (but claiming) feminized others.

This is because they interact in gendered performances of masculinisms and feminizations. *Masculinism* is the social preference for masculinity and social exclusion of femininity. *Feminization,* on the other hand, is subordinating people, political entities, or ideas by associating them with values perceived as feminine.[110] V. Spike Peterson accounts for feminization *as* devalorization:

> Not only subjects (women and marginalized men), but also concepts, desires, tastes, styles, "ways of knowing" . . . can be feminized—with the effect of reducing their legitimacy, status and value. Importantly, this devalorization is simultaneously ideological (discursive, cultural) *and* material (structural, economic). . . . This devalorization normalizes—with the effect of "legitimating"—the marginalization, subordination, and exploitation of feminized practices and persons . . . the "naturalness" of sex difference is generalized to the "naturalness" of masculine (not necessarily *male*) privilege, so that both aspects come to be taken-for-granted "givens" of social life.[111]

Along these lines, feminists have long argued that hegemonic masculinities and subordinate masculinities play a role in shaping global politics and shaping conflict among states.[112] This influence, though, is not static (where wars happen in a pattern, regularly, or only in particular states). Variations in the characteristics and salience of a state's hegemonic masculinity over time influences state behavior. The more competitive a state's hegemonic masculinity, the more likely that state is to make war; this risk is compounded by high salience.

States' hegemonic masculinities, then, shape their strategic cultures, which shape strategic decisions, which are "inescapably cultural."[113] The world of war decision-making "mind, feeling, and *habit*" has gendered dimensions.[114] An example is Jane Parpart's recent discussion of masculinity/ies, gender, and violence in the nationalist struggles in Zimbabwe.[115] Seeing Cynthia Enloe's argument that "no person, no community, no national movement can be militarized without changing the ways in which femininity and masculinity are brought to bear on daily life,"[116] Parpart points out that "gendered assumptions and practices framed, explained, and legitimized the struggle."[117] Rival claims to the nation, according to Parpart, were manifested in and reflected in rival claims to masculinity, supported by strategic cultures in contending groups that, when studied, reveal "the very masculinist rhetoric and practice required of converts to the nationalist cause."[118] While "participants on both sides celebrated war as a means for making 'real' men,"[119] "sexualized, masculinized language among soldiers differentiated those who knew how to fight and had been hardened by the war and those who had not."[120] Parpart explains that, "in the end, the war turned out to be a triumph for masculinist authority and long-established gender hierarchies" since "the militant masculinist imaginary that framed so much of the war fostered a vision of masculinity that prized physical toughness, the ability and willingness to use violence, and loyalty to the cause."[121]

In the same edited volume, Dibeysh Anand talks about a different sort of hegemonic masculinity that begets a different sort of violence.[122] Arguing that hegemonic masculinities (and thus strategic cultures) are sometimes highly sexualized, Anand coins the term "porno-nationalism" and illustrates how it might be applied to Hindutva nationalism in India, especially in its recent conflicts with Pakistan.[123] While Hindu nationalism explicitly and consciously frames Hindu men as asexual, it engages in "the framing of the hyper-sexed Muslim as a grave threat to India."[124] This goes hand-in-hand with a strategic culture that emphasizes potency as a feature of a successful nationalist movement, in which "what makes these men potent is not their ability to perform sexually as an individual body, but their willingness to sacrifice their individual desires to serve the higher cause of the collective Hindu body."[125] Chastity is associated with masculinity in Hindutva, and untrustworthiness, lust, and sexual craze are imputed characteristics of the Muslim other in this nationalist narrative.[126] This narrative serves a double function: "it assures the Hindu nationalist self of its moral superiority; yet, at the same time, it instills anxiety about the threatening masculine other."[127] Violence, then, "is reactive, justified, and demanded," but it is violence characterized as defending the purity of Hindu masculinity and Hindu femininity rather than a raw, aggressive justification for violence.[128]

Sandra Whitworth's discussion of Canadian militarized masculinity shows yet another manifestation of masculinity in the ways that states make and fight wars.[129] Whitworth notes that the image of Canada as (peaceful) peacekeeper is one of the "core myths"[130] of Canada's "imagined community"[131] with the punch line that it "locates Canada as an altruistic and benign middle-power, acting with a kind of moral purity not normally exhibited by contemporary states."[132] Whitworth notes that, while war is unpopular in Canada, peacekeeping has always been "extremely popular," owing in part to the impression it creates that "Canada is a good global citizen, projecting beyond our borders our values of generosity, tolerance, and an unswerving commitment to peace and democracy."[133] In the Canadian attachment to peacekeeping, "the Canadian soldier as peacekeeper is not a warrior but a protector."[134] The Canadian protector-masculinity is often contrasted in Canadian politics with an American warrior-masculinity: "Americans fought wars, but Canadians made peace."[135]

All three of these cases show a link between culturally dominant hegemonic masculinities (an aggressive masculinity based on reclaiming territory/identity in Zimbabwe, a chaste but violent Hindutva masculinity, and a protection-based Canadian masculinity), but those culturally dominant hegemonic masculinities create and constitute different strategic cultures, which make war more (or less) likely and also influence how wars are made and how they are fought. While together these cases demonstrate how a hegemonic masculinity mediated the relationship between gendered militarisms and gendered nationalisms to constitute gendered strategic cultures, they also show that gendered strategic cultures can vary and, particularly, can be variably bellicose. This is because strategic cultures are essentially prescriptive and "the prescriptive character of strategic culture flows inexorably from the nature of strategy."[136]

Gender lenses then suggest that gendered strategic cultures influence when, where, how, and against whom states fight war(s), and therefore have both descriptive and predictive value. In this account, hegemonic masculinities are a part of the constitution of state identities and state strategic cultures, which co-constitute each other. The next section engages the possibility that state masculinist-nationalist narratives serve not only to directly cause and influence states' engagement in and making of wars, but also serve as instrumental justificatory narratives, both when states (and/or their leaders) choose violent foreign policies for other reasons, and when states have an interest in maintaining gender-unequal power balances in state domestic politics.

GENDERED NATIONALISM AND STATE IDENTITY AS A WAR-JUSTIFICATORY NARRATIVE

> Targeting innocent civilians for murder is always and everywhere wrong. Brutality against women is always and everywhere wrong. There can be no neutrality between justice and cruelty, between the innocent and the guilty. We are in a conflict between good and evil, and America will call evil by its name. . . . And we will lead the world in opposing it.
>
> GEORGE W. BUSH, 2002[137]

This section argues that, while political decision makers do not necessarily always base their choices about war on considerations of gender, they often claim gender as a part of their motivations for wars and humanitarian interventions, referring to the moral principles inherent in just war theories.[138]

In these justificatory stories, states-as-men protect their homeland-as-women and masculinized soldiers protect feminized innocents.[139] The women in these stories, as Elshtain notes, are "beautiful souls," not involved in war-making but reliant on war to survive.[140] Women's vulnerability justifies fighting wars. As such, militarism often relies on control of femininity generally and women specifically.[141] This chapter up to this point has characterized this as a part of the state narrative of self and a crucial factor in motivating and shaping gendered nationalisms. This section, though, deals with the possibility that states *sometimes* tell gendered narratives of war(s) disingenuously (as with the discussion of George W. Bush and the war in Iraq that starts this section). This section, then, asks: When states intentionally militarize femininity, to what ends? Do they mean it? How is gender an instrument of state policies in war(s)?

The state feminism literature provides a foundation for the argument that gender is a key factor in state decision-making about war(s).[142] "State feminism" is a term used to describe when states adopt (domestic) policies that are or appear to be feminist (supporting the goal of gender emancipation).[143] Scholars studying state feminism have repeatedly recognized that gender-emancipatory policies are sometimes adopted for reasons not directly related to women's rights.[144] Legal scholarship on women's rights has recognized that the piecemeal deconstruction of particular oppressions does not take apart the gendered system of state power that feminists have critiqued. As Catherine MacKinnon observed:

> Perhaps the failure to consider gender as a determinant of state behavior has made the state's behavior appear indeterminate . . . it is not autonomous of sex. Male power is systemic. Coercive, legitimated, and epistemic, it *is* the regime.[145]

MacKinnon continues to observe that "inequality because of sex defines and situates women as women"[146] even in a world that appears increasingly sex-equal, such that:

> In life, "woman" and "man" are widely experienced as features of being. . . . Gender, in other words, is lived as ontology, not epistemology. . . . In male supremacist societies, the male standpoint dominates civil society in the form of an objective standard—the standpoint which, because it dominates the world, does not appear to function as a standpoint at all.[147]

Scholars looking at state politics through gendered lenses have responded with some skepticism about state feminist policies. State policies proclaiming feminist motives have been referred to as "stealth misogyny" and states' motives have been questioned in policies that appear to be interested in gender emancipation.[148] For example, in interrogating the U.S. government's interest in women's rights in

Afghanistan (which was a claimed motive for the U.S. invasion), "the concern is that the Bush Administration is not actually committed to women's equality and rights, but has cynically used this rhetoric to increase support for its foreign policy and to win reelection by appealing to women voters."[141]

Another example might be found in Saddam Hussein's Iraq. Under Saddam Hussein, women acquired the right to work; the right to buy, own, and inherit property; the right to divorce their husbands; protection from execution for adultery; the right to dress as they pleased; and the right to attend institutions of higher education.[142] The interesting question is why Saddam Hussein and his party, by all accounts a brutal dictatorship with little regard for human rights, much less progressive, feminist politics, made these gender-emancipatory changes within the Iraqi state. Certainly, Saddam Hussein could not be characterized as a women's advocate. The traditionally accepted explanation for this policy innovation on the part of the Ba'ath Party is that in a multi-ethnic and unstable Iraqi state, the government found that coalition in women: it gave them rights in order to secure their support and therefore the government's hold on power.[143]

In reality, often even "liberal" countries implement (apparently) gender-emancipatory policies for the appearance of progressiveness, the service of national security, or the service of some economic goal.[144] These "progressive" state feminist policies can appear motivated by concerns for equality when other motivations play a dominant role in states' decision-making. While it is easy to assume that states' claims to fight war(s) for women are genuine, this conclusion might be short-sighted in some cases.[145]

Another possibility exists: existing (masculinist) power structures use gender equality instrumentally. In other words, on-face emancipatory policies are implemented and enforced for strategic reasons, and their enforcement betrays those motivations.[146] This argument is that states adopt (apparently) gender-emancipatory justifications for war(s) for reasons other than a direct interest in gender emancipation. Because these other reasons, rather than gender emancipation, constitute the primary purpose of these policies, when the gender-emancipatory ends are pursued at all, it is in a partial and haphazard way that fails to seriously challenge male or masculine dominance in global politics.[147]

If it is possible that states (as they justify wars using gender) may be motivated by other driving goals than gender emancipation, identifying what those goals are and if (and why) they matter must be seen as a primary task. In other words, if (apparently) gender-emancipatory policies really are the product of coinciding interests, with which interests do they coincide?[156] This section argues that states justify war(s) in terms of women's rights or talk about strategy in terms of gendered protection *instrumentally*, in pursuit of their (perceived) interests and relative power. It contends that interest and gains logic is sometimes more important in determining the adoption, content, and enforcement of gender-emancipatory war policies than is the actual suffering of women in global politics or women's advocacy to redress that suffering, except insomuch as those interest coincide. The use of gender as an instrumental justification for war(s) works, however, because of how deeply engrained gendered narratives of state identity (and even human nature) are in those to whom gendered reasons for the making and fighting of wars are packaged and sold.

In this sense, the instrumental use of femininity as a justification for war(s) on the part of "feminist" states can be seen as symbolic politics. Keck and Sikkink describe symbolic politics as "the ability to call upon symbols, actions, or stories that make sense of a situation for an audience that is frequently far away."[157] As Stuart Kaufman notes: "the central argument of symbolic politics is that emotional symbols, such as flag, national anthem, history of the group, myths of motherland and fatherland, can become tools in politics to influence the masses' decisions in the elite's quest for power.[158] Appropriating this logic to talk about (apparently) gender-emancipatory motivations for war(s), it is possible to see that states have an interest in their citizens' perception of their position on gender emancipation. In international political competition and conflict, women serve "symbolically and literally as that which requires protection."[159] Women being literally that which requires protection allows gendered notions of states' sense of self and strategic culture to influence the making and fighting of wars; women being symbolically that which requires protection allows states and their leaders/dominant groups to use gendered justificatory rhetoric in war-making even when it is not the primary (or even a secondary) goal of the policy being pursued.

The uncritical acceptance of the assumption that states' gendered war stories are what they appear can be materially dangerous. Genderings beneath the surface presuppose and reify the subordination of women while creating the appearance that there is no gender problem.[160] This promotes complacency and perpetuates gender subordination. States, through symbolic politics, *use* (apparently) gender-emancipatory policies as (misleading) *symbols* of having eliminated gender subordination.[161] This means that the gendered nature of states' identities, particularly as they influence the making and fighting of war(s), have several layers: gendered nationalist narratives that beget gendered strategic cultures, and enterprising political entrepreneurs who take advantage of those gendered nationalist narratives to appropriate them in service of other political goals and/or the maintenance of gendered power structures in domestic political organizations.

POTENTIAL CONTRIBUTIONS OF A STATE-LEVEL FEMINIST RESEARCH PROGRAM ON WAR

This chapter has made the argument that doing state-level war theorizing without attention to gender is less descriptively accurate and predictively valuable than taking account of gender as it influences states' likelihood to make war(s). While some people see the main potential contribution of feminist theorizing to state-level war theorizing as an analysis of the relationship between domestic gender equality and states' likelihood to make war, this chapter has both problematized that assumption and delved deeper into the ways that gender tropes influence states' likelihood to make war(s).

Particularly, this chapter has asserted that the sex-equality peace thesis is normatively problematic and empirically suspect. It is normatively problematic because it universalizes and instrumentalizes gender equality, essentializes women and femininity, and misses what feminisms really have to offer to normative analysis of states' likelihood to go to war. Empirically, this chapter questioned whether sex equality accounts for war between states and built the case that it might be instrumentally used by states in claiming feminisms. Contending that feminists have more to say about the state-level causes of war and gender than "women are peaceful" and "gender equality causes peace," this chapter has focused on the ways in which states, identities, militarisms, nationalisms, strategic cultures, and war-justifying narratives are also gendered.

Building on chapter 4's discussion of states as entities with (not only material but social, psychological, and emotional) senses of self, this chapter has argued that gender tropes generally and hegemonic masculinities specifically are key to a state's sense of self. It has presented gendered militarisms and gendered nationalisms, contending that states' militarized masculinities are dependent on relationships with feminized nations as constitutive others. This chapter has argued that it is the gendered relationship between the (masculinized) state and the (feminized) nation that is constitutive of gendered strategic culture. Having identified strategic culture as a key context for states' likelihood to make wars, the argument has made here that it is possible that differences between and shifts in (the hegemonic masculinities inspiring) states' strategic cultures produce differences in states' propensity to make war(s).

Chapter 3 argued that gender is system-structural in the international system, and structural gender hierarchy serves both as a permissive and direct cause of war(s). Chapter 4 contended that states *relate* in gendered ways, and that feminist analysis is key to understanding dyadic-level causes of war(s). Without these analyses, this chapter argued that states *work* in gendered ways and that gender tropes help to explain and predict state war-making. Building on the work in previous chapters, I argued here that gendered states constitute and are constituted by gendered interstate relations and the gendered international system.

Situated in (other) domestic politic accounts of the causes of war, this feminist analysis suggests rethinking those traditional accounts. It suggests that economic models of predicting states' likelihood to make wars are limited by their failure to recognize both the interdependence of the economic and political spheres and the gendered nature of the state. Feminist work might see tactical war decision-making, like that suggested by diversionary theories of war-making, to be a part of a larger context of war decision-making to be located in (gendered) strategic cultures. Building on culture-based accounts of war, feminist analysis suggests that gendered state identities are constitutive of gendered (strategic and other) cultures.

As a dialogue among feminisms, second-image feminist theorizing brings gendered lenses to viewing not only state war behavior but the state itself. Arguing that the war-making institutions and cultures of states are gendered provides insight into how gender constitutes and is constituted by states and their interactions. This gender analysis plays an important role in theorizing the role of gender in substate, or individual, war decision-making, the task of chapter 6.

People, Choices, and War(s)

As Prime Minister in 1971, Indira Gandhi led India in a war against neighbouring Pakistan which resulted in the creation of Bangladesh . . .

Her role in the war was only one of her controversial actions.

She is remembered most for her campaign against Sikh separatists . . .

The June 1984 attack killed an estimated 450 people, and left a legacy of bitterness.

Five months later, Indira Gandhi was shot dead by her Sikh bodyguards in revenge . . .

Khalid Ahmed said: "She was a true feminist to the core, a woman of substance who . . . possessed all the virtues of a woman and fought valiantly for women's rights in a man's world."

—BBC NEWS, "INDIRA GANDHI 'GREATEST WOMAN'" (YEAR?)

Women are underrepresented in political leadership in every country in the world, and have been underrepresented at every point in modern history.[1] The number of women in legislative bodies has increased more than twofold over the last two decades, but the average still remains below twenty percent.[2] Though women constitute the majority of the population of 132 countries around the world, there is only one country in the world where there is a woman-majority parliament.[3] Analysis of political leadership often neglects both women who do lead and the potential contributions of characteristics associated with femininity, especially in the security realm. Women who lead or look to lead are treated differently than their male colleagues on the basis of assumptions about their sex and its relation to the gendered charac- teristics leaders are expected to portray.[4] Much scholarship on the roles of people and/or their choices in war(s) treats a "leader" as masculine but sexless or necessarily male, and "great men" are often the heroes of modern war stories.[5] These gendered traits form the *"ideal-typical* leader: male in appearance and gender, and masculine in character traits."[6] Discussions of leaders' roles in war-making often emphasize the advantages of characteristics associated with masculinity (particularly bravery, chivalry, rationality, and strength) over characteristics associated with femininity (particularly restraint, emotional identification, cooperation, and passivity).[7]

Even when the literature in war studies recognizes that individuals and groups matter in the decisions to make war(s) and the causes of war(s), gender is largely absent from researchers' analyses. As discussed in chapter 1, some approaches to studying war at the individual level ask us to pay attention to leadership generally and leaders specifically,[8] while others focus on decision-making processes, problems, and pathologies.[9] Decision-making theories often focus either on agency (bureaucratic politics model) or structure (organizational process model) in organizational/group decision-making.[10]

Much of this literature includes people in accounting for global politics generally and war specifically, but looks only at the individual with elite power for influence, and even then, only at the male individual with elite power.[11] While work that includes people's roles in war decision-making widens the spectrum of relevant actors in war(s), the narrowness of the individuals it includes limits its effectiveness as an interpretive framework and reproduces the gender, class, and race biases often present in system-level and state-level international relations (IR) scholarship. Further, most individual-level work in war theorizing characterizes people as discrete, so their interdependence and their relationships do not matter as much. In this research, individuals appear to act alone, without reliance on one another, and with a complete set of choices; when they work together, it is in reaction to other discrete individuals. They also appear to 'matter' insomuch as they are related to and consonant with state policy-making, without attention to their roles contra state policy or as (a part of) nonstate actors. This independent, discrete, state-compliant, elite individual is unlike most people in the "real world"—who act in a world of relational, rather than reactive, autonomy.

This chapter argues that gender permeates every level of how people impact the causes of and paths to war(s). First, it engages "great man" theories of historical development and war-making, arguing that states select for characteristics associated with masculinity in security decision makers and in the decisions that states require them to make and that challenges to (male and female) leaders' masculinity often provoke aggressive decision-making and policy behavior. Second, arguing that "mainstream" war theories are short-sighted and ultimately incorrect when they look only to elite individuals, organizations, and movements to account for the role of people in war, I present a feminist argument linking the personal and the international in the making of war (war is personal, and the personal is war). I read the personal in war(s) through exploring the impact of militarized masculinities and femininities on people. Third, engaging with critical theoretical approaches that also integrate the personal into thinking about security, I contend that there are benefits to an explicitly feminist approach that directly engages war. Finally, this chapter argues that gender is not only integral to who we think about as actors in the making of war and how those actors influence war-making, but also how we understand decision-making in war—both in terms of actor capacity and process. The chapter concludes by arguing that not only can war decision-making be seen as gendered at the international system level (chapter 3), the dyadic level (chapter 4), and the state level (chapter 5), but in its relationships with (and constitution of) people and their everyday lives.

GENDER, LEADERSHIP, AND THE CAUSES OF WAR(S)

Feminist approaches to political leadership have argued there is more to the gendered nature of leadership than the fact that men are the majority of leaders or the observation that studies of leadership often either neglect or essentialize women leaders.[12] Both of those problems are rooted in expectations of maleness and masculinity as requirements of good leadership, even when those doing the leading are women.[13] As Tickner explains, "stories [which privilege masculinity in leadership] reinforce the belief, widely held . . . throughout the world by both men and women, that military and foreign policy are arenas of policy-making least appropriate for women."[14] That belief, and its manifestation in the sex composition and gender composition of world leaders, shows that the selection of political decision makers and their processes of decision-making are gendered. When evaluating leaders and their war decisions, "strength, power, autonomy, independence, and rationality, all typically associated with men and masculinity" are often valued, which results in an ethos of war decision-making where women are perceived as being too emotional or too weak for the tough life-and-death decisions" required of a leader.[15]

In order to understand possible engagements between individual-level or decision-making theories of war and gender analysis, it is important to see gender in approaches to and theories of political leadership, especially given the diversity of the literature on leadership generally and individual-level causes of war specifically. Opinions on what makes "good" decision makers or leaders are as diverse as the world's leaders.[16] What many theoretical accounts of (particularly wartime) leadership share is association of decision-making capacity and masculinity. The subject of good leadership often excludes people of the female sex by virtue of their (perceived) femininity. In this chapter, the study of gender and war decision-making is not meant to conflate male leaders and masculine traits, but instead to demonstrate that those who select leaders often use "masculinity" as a proxy for good leadership and men as a proxy for masculinity, mapping "femininity" (and therefore poor decision-making) onto women, regardless of the inaccuracy of that mapping.

Because of these proxies, characteristics identified as traits of good leaders are generally associated with masculinity, even when leaders are not male.[17] Technicality, abstraction, strategic thought, and result-oriented behavior are all psychological traits traditionally associated with masculinity, as opposed to women's instrumentality, personalization, emotion, and process-driven behavior.[18] Selectorates and voters prize traits representing *instrumentality* (assertiveness, coarseness, toughness, aggressiveness, sternness, masculinity, activeness, rationality, and confidence) and are critical of traits representing *warmth* and *expressiveness* (gentleness, sensitivity, emotiveness, talkativeness, and cautiousness).[19] The prized instrumental values are traditional markers of masculinity while the devalued warm values are traditional markers of femininity. The instrumental traits have been associated not only with masculinities generally but with militarized masculinities specifically and that has translated into instrumental traits being especially prized in military and war leadership.[20]

Understanding those traits as traditionally associated with masculinity does not mean either that the characteristics are ones that women cannot have or that they are necessarily negative characteristics. On the contrary, many women have been "masculine" in leadership positions, and successfully so.[21] However, women continue to be underrepresented in political leadership because "the *definition* of what it means to be a good leader is couched in masculine terms."[22] Therefore, D'Amico and Beckman make the argument that women who become elite political leaders often succeed by drawing attention to their masculine traits (often more dramatically than their male opponents) in order to fit into stereotypical assumptions about able decision-making.[23] Because women adopt masculinized personas to succeed in politics (and/or masculinized women succeed in politics), women's integration into decision-making positions in the making and fighting of wars is not necessarily a signifier of disappearing gender stereotypes or rising gender equality in conceptions of leadership. Instead, "though the numerical exclusion of women from public life is (if slowly) subsiding, gender integration is leaving in place the discursive and performative elements of gender subordination."[24]

The continued presence of gender subordination in dominant ideas of political leaders and their war decision-making is particularly visible in two areas. First, women neither obtain those positions nor fulfill their duties in the absence of traditional gender expectations and ideal-types about femininity. Instead, women often lead either when selectors express an interest in characteristics traditionally associated with femininity *or* when a woman leader can adequately prove her masculinity over assumptions of her incapability. Second, because of the salience of gendered values and the limits they place on war decision-making, women's opportunities to lead and the integration of feminine values into war decision-making will remain limited until our understandings of war decision-making come to see and deconstruct gendered assumptions about leaders and their decisions.

To this end, feminists have been critical of trait-based theories of leadership as prizing masculine traits[25] and of rational actor models of leadership as privileging a masculine notion of leadership processes.[26] They have also been critical of work that uses the sex of leaders as a dependent variable—looking at what women do differently than men as if there were something innate about biological femaleness that changes leadership propensities.[27] These biases, as R. W. Connell argues, make male leadership self-perpetuating.[28] Most leaders are men because of the gendered structure of divisions of labor, systems of control, and political routines within states.[29] Connell expresses concern that this gender configuration will perpetuate and maintain a close relationship between ideal-typical leaders and ideal-typical masculinities.

This means that understanding the relationship between gender and war decision-making is significantly more complicated than identifying how women leaders behave or why women are often excluded from decision-making in war(s). Instead, feminist theorizing about war decision-making "pushes us to consider how the epistemological and ontological bases of conceptual frameworks may misrepresent the experiences of women as leaders, thereby distorting our specific knowledge of such experiences and our general knowledge of the phenomenon of leadership as gender-encompassing."[30]

Such a consideration reveals systematic gender bias in individual-level theorizing of wars. Many conventional theories of how and why leaders matter in the making of wars focus on how systemic, state-level, or government-organization structures weaken or have flexibility to permit individual personalities to influence state war policies. In these theoretical stories, the mechanism through which individual leaders have influence seems to largely be through their personalities, and personalities are analyzed through political psychology.[31] Much of this research, when it identifies gender as influential, reduces it to traits associated with sex (women do this, men do that).[32]

This section proposes that not only sex but also gender influences war decision-making. As I argued above, constituencies expect not only maleness, but (more importantly) masculinity from our leaders—and they challenge their leaders' masculinity/ies when their policies fall short of characteristics associated with the states' masculinized strategic culture or state identity. As such, gendered expectations for leaders influence not only which leaders are chosen but also what decisions those leaders make. Particularly, leaders are expected to serve as protectors when the state's hegemonic masculinity is bound up in protection are pressured to protect. Leaders are expected to serve a cause of vengeance when the state's hegemonic masculinity is bound up in retributive justice are pressured to act retributively. A feminist approach to war decision-making demonstrates that conventional theoretical views of how individuals influence war(s) rely on a (false and masculinized) dichotomy between structure and agent, the privileging of masculine concepts and traits, and an assumption of people's homogeneity when they are really both diverse and unequal.

Jennifer Heeg Maruska's work on the hypermasculinity of American foreign policy after 11 September 2001 demonstrates the potential impacts of such an error.[33] Particularly, she analyzes the gendered discourses in the 2004 presidential election surrounding the question of the war(s) in Iraq and Afghanistan. While incumbent President George W. Bush's statements about foreign policy could be characterized as "hypermasculine" in their emphasis on the need to extract revenge on the dangerous, terrorist "other,"[34] John Kerry's statements suggested a "multinational, law-enforcement-like approach"[35] that the media characterized as a "French and feminine" position.[36] Heeg Maruska argues that dominant expectations of hypermasculinity in American foreign policy culture selected for a leader pursuing hypermasculine policies, rather than a more subdued approach that might be gender-balanced and/or value subordinated masculinities and femininities. This selection for hypermasculine characteristics then increases the state's likelihood of making war(s).

Along with the gendered nature of the international system, the gendered nature of interstate relationships, and the gendered identities and nationalist stories of states, the gendered expectations of people-as-leaders tend to overdetermine particular policy paths "chosen" by individual leaders. As the remainder of this chapter will demonstrate, feminist reinterpretations of decision-making and war re-evaluate both autonomy and power, showing that war decision makers' "choices" may be more constrained than much traditional war theorizing acknowledges, and a broader range of choices (and lives) may matter to (and be constitutive of) war(s).

THE PERSONAL AND THE INTERNATIONAL: THINKING ABOUT THE LEVELS OF ANALYSIS AND WAR(S)

> Read forward, "the personal is international" insofar as ideas about what it means to be a "respectable" woman or an "honorable" man have been shaped by colonizing policies, trading strategies, and military doctrines. . . . the implications of a feminist understanding of international politics are thrown into sharper relieve when one reads "the personal is international" the other way round: *the international is personal.* This calls for a radical new imagining of what it takes for governments to ally with each other, compete with, and wage war with each other.[37]

A central theme in feminist scholarship engaged with IR has been critique of the discipline's tendencies either to ignore the role of people in global politics or to notice people's roles selectively with bias toward elite individuals in positions traditionally seen as powerful. Feminists have instead understood people to be the key substance of global politics, arguing that international politics impacts people's daily lives and that people's daily lives are international politics. This is why Cynthia Enloe edited the popular feminist phrase "the personal is political" to read "the personal is international," and added that "the international is personal.[38] Enloe is arguing that the personal sphere and the international sphere overlap and constitute each other, rather than being neatly separate forces that interact.[39] Gendered lenses see "people as actors, the system as multiple hierarchies, and as characterized by multiple relations."[40] With this perspective, feminists have been able to identify individuals outside the halls of elite power as important to politics generally and war decision-making specifically. Rather than understanding war decision-making as the purview of great men,[41] feminist work has demonstrated the relevance of people at global politics' margins, including but not limited to Korean prostitutes,[42] immigrant domestic servants,[43] and Sierra Leonean women soldiers.[44] Further, the individuals who make war(s) do not do their decision-making (or living or working) isolated from other decision makers. Instead, they exist in their relationships with others, "maintaining a sense of individualized identity while being inseparable from political and social context."[45]

War Is Personal[46]

A number of scholars have drawn attention to people at the margins of global politics as the "subjects" of international security generally and war(s) specifically.[47] As Katharine Moon notes, "we have a tendency to understand foreign relations as sets of policies that are formulated and executed by an elite group of men in dark suits, as abstracted from individual lives, especially the lowest reaches of society."[48] To rebut this tendency, Moon shows how Korean camptown prostitutes played a crucial role in military negotiations and decisions between the United States and South Korea in the 1970s, despite their invisibility in mainstream politics and theorizing thereof.[49] Despite the fact that the military policies of the time *could not be explained without* reference to those women's bodies, both their bodies and their lives were omitted from the policy narratives of the very policies they were indispensable to shaping. The role that *their* personal played in *the* international was *invisibilized*, because "to question their role in U.S. camptown life would have been to raise questions about the need for and the role of U.S. troops and bases in the two countries' bilateral relations."[50] In this view, the lives of prostitutes serving militaries not only collectively but *individually* are "not simply a women's issue, sociological problem, or target of disease control" but "a matter of international politics and national security" that here influenced states' decision-making about war(s).[51] The international became personal when state military decision makers came to care (and make decisions based on) who Korean prostitutes slept with and how they were (or were not) tested for venereal diseases. Moon demonstrates that camptown women are not only a part of security policy but *"personify and define*, not only underlie, relations between governments."[52]

It is therefore possible to understand that serious attention to people's lives at the margins of global politics not only interrogates the traditional scope of war studies but also changes traditional views of war(s). This is because the international is mapped onto almost every dimension of personal life. The relationship between particular states restricts people's ability to move between them. Tariff relationships help to dictate where jobs are and therefore who works and for how much money. A crisis in the banks or in the currency of one state influences the ability of people in another financially or trade-dependent state to support their families. How one state deals with a particular natural disaster or health crisis influences the environmental or health security of people in another state. This is all the more true in the area of war, where war(s) change many of the very basic ways that daily life works.

One poignant account of war as personal is that of Alicia Appleman-Jurman, who was a nine-year-old girl in Buczacz, Poland, during the *blitzkrieg* in September of 1939.[53] With the town initially under Russian occupation, Alicia's brother Moshe was sent to Moscow to be re-educated and was captured, imprisoned, and worked to death after an escape attempt.[54] Her father was executed by a German firing squad to "leave the Jews leaderless," and her family was "resettled" in a slum.[55] Alicia lost two more brothers, one to slavery and one to public hanging, before she was imprisoned herself.[56] After her mother was killed, Alicia spent the last year of the war hiding in the woods avoiding both Russian and German troops as the Soviet Army pushed the Nazi Germans back through Europe.[57] Promised a better life after World War II, Alicia moved to Israel, where she found herself in the middle of another war, this time for Israeli independence and this time as a soldier.[58] Alicia finally escaped conflict when she met an American in Israel, married him, and moved to California.[59] Alicia's life was shaped by war. The violence done to her and her family during her childhood, her emigration from Poland, and her life in Israel were all unimaginable without taking account of the interstate wars of which they were an essential part.

Alicia's story and countless others demonstrate that no international is more pervasively personal than war. War impacts people's livelihoods, physical security, locations, bodies, risk for domestic violence, and political interests. War affects people's family structure, personal relationships, economic security, jobs, and modes of transportation. War matters to what (if any) state people live in, what nationalist stories they tell, what form of government they have, and how safe they are as they live their daily lives. Wars cause and contribute to diseases, infrastructure damage, and environmental insecurities. The international *matters* in people's lives, especially in war. But the other half of Enloe's phrase—that the personal is international—suggests that the impact of war on ordinary (often marginalized or subaltern) people is not one-directional—that people influence war(s) as well.

The Personal Is War[60]

The other half of Enloe's phrase—the personal is international—argues that people, even (and especially) at the margins of global politics, matter to the making and fighting of wars. A number of historic tales feature marginal women's lives as key variables in major wars. One of the largest wars in ancient Greek history was allegedly fought over the love and honor of Helen of Troy.[61] Henry VIII's dissatisfaction with his wife is credited with the beginning of the Anglican church.[62] The Indian *Ramayana* tells of a war fought between the Hindu preserver-God Vishnu and the demon king of Lanka, Ravana, over Vishnu's wife, Sita.[63] A close look at these and many other stories shows that "these women's lives were not only *affected by* international politics, they *were* international politics."[64]

Understanding people's lives as global politics from a feminist perspective starts with "viewing even the most dispossessed women as 'players' in world politics," a viewpoint that demands an analytic framework where "without jumping back from two opposite poles of self-agency and victim-hood, a middle ground must be found."[65] Some women who "matter" in war do so in a traditional, power-politics sense. For example, leaders like Golda Meir,[66] Indira Gandhi,[67] Hillary Clinton,[68] and Ellen Johnson Sirleaf[69] have made traditional, state-level decisions about war(s).

Other women that feminists see as important in war(s), however, are not political leaders, but that does not make their lives less consequential for global politics, either in their living or in the stylized narratives told of their lives. The genderings inherent in scholarship on people in war(s) means that scholarship often has a limited understanding of the type of people whose lives should be accounted for in war studies. Looking for women in war(s) shows not only women but others (feminized and then) excluded from traditional studies of wars. Normal people not only live in but constitute the militarization of the international arena.

A feminist understanding of women's lives *as* war(s), then, has several dimensions. First, women's choices matter in global politics.[70] For example, the choice that Wafa Idris made to become the first Palestinian woman suicide bomber had ramifications not only for the relative status of organizations within the Palestinian territories but also for gender roles within Palestinian society, for the relationship between Israel and the armed Palestinian resistance, and for the roles that women had in resistance and terrorist organizations more generally.[71] Second, how these women's decisions are portrayed matters not only to/for their lives, but also in the constitution of the war(s) or conflict(s) in which they participate. For example, the portrayal of the 2011 U.S. military intervention in Libya as a decision that U.S. President Barack Obama made because he was "henpecked" by female members of his cabinet had an important impact on the ways that the military policy was received in the United States and abroad.[72] These gendered framings of women in wars come to constitute both femininity and war. Finally, if women's lives and the stylized narratives thereof *are* war, we need to understand them to understand war. As Moon argues, the "key is to pinpoint which women at what time in what gendered way are identified with the politics of a foreign policy issue."[73] Cynthia Enloe recently talked about this in terms of relating war histories to gender histories.[74]

Actors in the making of wars are not limited to the international system or even to states, and sometimes actors in international politics need to be sought and found in locations not traditionally considered bastions of power. Instead, it is important to deconstruct the ideal-typical "actor" we see influencing war(s). If people's lives constitute war, so do stylized narratives about those people's lives, which are often produced without their consent and contrary to their self-understandings.[75] People can be actors in world politics with or without directly influencing the ultimate or secondary intentions of the state.[76] People can also matter in war (whether or not they affect state policy) without the specific intent to do so. Given that, feminist work has recognized that "seemingly private conduct, such as sexual relations between men and women, are intimately related to international politics through their organization and institutionalization by public authorities."[77]

While constructivist theoretical approaches to thinking about war also see individuals as significant, some of them (particularly Alexander Wendt) limit individuals' influence to causal rather than constitutive roles, contending that "individuals must be constitutionally independent."[78] In this view, independent individuals' actions can sometimes reverberate in the international arena, but the *individual* is not internationalized. Therefore, "[in] any would-be individualist theory of how agents are constructed, individuals, and thus culture (which is carried by them), can play only a causal but not constitutive role."[79] I argue that such an approach does not adequately account for people's contexts, especially their interdependence, and is therefore partial at best. This is because gender as a social force influences not only (or even mainly) behavior, but instead (also) identity, constitution, epistemology, and even ontology. In Nancy Hirschmann's words, "this construction of social behaviors and rules comes to constitute not only what women are allowed to do, however, but also what they are allowed to *be*."[80]

In this view, not only do people play both constitutive and causal roles in war-making, their roles are mediated by gender tropes and gendered expectations of them, their social groups, their political coalitions, and even their states and nations. Still, all people do not exert equal influence on war, and war does not impact all people equally. Instead, where people are positioned (socially, politically, economically, and geographically, among others) is important in determining how they interact with (and/or constitute) war-making. One of the key elements of people's positions for their relationships with war and wars is power. As V. Spike Peterson and Anne Sisson Runyan explain, in war narratives, "ideologies are reconfigured to suit the changing interests of those in power, not those whose lives are controlled by them."[81] Accordingly, feminist research has pointed out that people's actions and relationships influence whether and how war(s) are made and fought; this influence is causal, constitutive, and/or symbolic; the modes and processes by which individuals interact with and influence war(s) is gendered; the degree and type of people's influence on war(s) will rely heavily on their place in the gendered structures of political systems; and the symbolic appropriation of people(s) and their behavior(s) is key to understanding how the personal is international and the international is personal.[82]

First, people's actions matter in when, how, and why wars are fought. Sometimes people are *causal* in wars—a person's (or persons') behavior(s) are violent themselves[83] and responded to violently by others.[84] Alternatively, people's actions can be causal in preventing war—people play a role in diffusing tensions or stopping cycles of violence.[85] People can also be constitutive of war and conflict—their political choices change the meaning of, or even *are*, war generally or a particular conflict specifically.[86] People's constitution of war can be direct (in them being, living, or experiencing wars) or indirect (when their behavior is appropriated in stylized war narratives by belligerents looking to serve political interests that may or may not have been consonant with the individuals' original interests or intents). Symbolic influence occurs when a stylized appropriation of individuals' behavior is used by other political actors in the furtherance of their political interest or goals.

Second, the modes and processes by which people impact wars are gendered. People understood to be men and people understood to be women have different opportunity structures in the making and fighting of wars and are called upon to serve different functions. This means that the constitutive and symbolic dimensions of people's roles in wars demonstrate that people make (both in decision-making and constitutive senses) wars in a gendered political context. As such, if people make wars, then, the level and direction of their impact cannot be understood without reference to people's (multiple) positionings along gender hierarchies in their (local, global, and even "glocal"[87]) sociopolitical environments. This is because the very availability of war as an option for decision makers[88] depends on the assumed presence of an innocent, interior, feminized other generally and women's needs for the protection provided by states specifically.[89]

As such, elite individuals or leaders (in Byman and Pollack's terms, "Great Men"[90]) are indeed more likely to have direct, causal influence over war policy-making, given their preponderance of "power-over,"[91] in the forms of money, influence, or political access. People who live their lives outside of or at the margins of the traditional spheres of influence of war policy-making, with less access to political power as traditionally conceived, are more likely to have constitutive or symbolic influence and "less likely to be able to control either how their story is related or who they are in it."[92] Given this, marginal individuals are often either entirely omitted from or instead appropriated by traditional accounts of war-making (often as "voters" and "civilians"), while elite leaders often tell the stories of their own influence.[93] These appropriations and omissions invisibilize nonelite individuals while sustaining race, gender, and class subordinations in traditional accounts of war-making.[94]

Militarized Masculinities and Femininities

Militarization of gender roles is one way in which the personal is war and war is personal. Building on the discussion of the ways that the making and fighting of wars relies on gendered nationalisms and gendered militarization, this section argues that gendered militarisms impact societies from the traditional halls of power in political leadership and military command to the traditional private sphere in the home and in the workplace.[95] Militarized masculinity is a phrase referring to wars' reliance on militarism and militarism's reliance on commanding and transforming masculinity/ies in times of war. This militarized masculinity is not only a national phenomena (as discussed in chapter 5) but also an individualized one. In times of war, men (all men, whether potentially or actually) are expected to be able to be transformed into people willing to go through the torture and terror of soldiering, war-fighting, and killing. The practice of war-fighting requires, then, the military control of masculinity/ies (and by extension, men) asking them to behave *as men*—as soldiers, protectors, and providers—not only for their family or their city or their town but for state and nation, at the risk of all else, including death.[96] In these terms, "militaries have historically been associated with masculinity, but what constitutes military masculinity changes with time and context, with new military roles and advances in technology, and with major political, economic, and social changes."[97]

Idealized militarized masculinities are necessarily complemented by idealized militarized femininities. As Cynthia Enloe has argued, the working of state militaries and military–industrial complexes relies on the behavior of women *as women*—filling traditional gender roles of care, social reproduction, innocence and the need for protection, and, often, sexual service to soldiers.[98] Militarized femininity, then, is the development of militarization being reliant on the control of femininity (and by extension, women) for the purposes of extending and succeeding in a war effort. Melissa Brown notes that militaries "have historically depended on female labor for a wide range of necessary support work," which has been contrasted to soldierly masculinity."[99] Even as women come to be included in militaries, idealized gender roles remain entrenched, as with "nostalgia for a time when masculinity was supposedly more secure and men's prerogatives less endangered by women's demands."[100]

In addition to being military-wide, these gender roles are sometimes individualized and sometimes talked about in terms of family structure. Denise Horn discusses military "family readiness" policies like the one Kim Gorski was involved with in these terms.[101] Looking at the U.S. military's preparations for the wars in Iraq and Afghanistan, Horn notes that idealized military family structures included a "community of spouses within the military," including idealized roles for wives, children, and extended families of troops.[102] Viewing the homefront as a gendered organization, Horn discusses gendered roles such as key volunteers, Family Readiness Officers, and officers' wives as key to war effort mobilization.[103]

War, then, requires militarization, which relies on and reinforces the regulation of gender roles variously but consistently. These militarized gender roles and the militarization they constitute and are constituted by remain in times of "peace" (or preparation for war) around military bases, in military recruiting, and in veteran's affairs politics.[104] In these ways, war is personal (it shapes personal gender roles) and the personal is war (militarized masculinities and femininities are a condition of possibility for the making and fighting of wars).

CRITICAL APPROACHES TO PEOPLE IN GLOBAL POLITICS

Some scholars have argued that critical approaches to security and war are adequate to address the presence of individuals in the making and fighting of wars. As discussed in chapter 1, various critical approaches analyze war with a priority on security, people's emancipation, and/or people's agency in security and/or war.[105] In other words, it is possible to ask why it is necessary to use gender lenses to evaluate individuals in wars if approaches like human security, critical security, or securitization draw attention to similar factors in similar ways with similar normative concerns.

In order to understand these questions, the context of the feminist intervention in the discipline should be explored. Explicitly feminist work entered IR and war studies in the late 1980s and early 1990s, and has generally been associated with the "third debate" in the discipline.[106]

This debate in IR coincided with the end of the Cold War and is generally understood to include critical approaches, such as those discussed in chapter 1, challenging the positivist orientation of the discipline. In the historical sociology of the discipline, at the beginning of the third debate, "certain scholars began to question both the epistemological and ontological foundations of a field which, in the United States especially, had been dominated by positivist, rationalist, and materialist theories."[107] Critical approaches and feminist work (often if not always) "share the postpositivist commitment to examining the relationship between knowledge and power."[108] Because of these commonalities, it is fair to see feminist work as closer to a number of postpositivist approaches than the disciplinary orthodoxy as such. As I discussed in chapter 1, critical approaches broaden what security is, look for emancipation and human security, critique the epistemological narrowness of mainstream war theorizing, and pay attention to war discourses, priorities many feminisms share.[109] While recognizing these commonalities as important, feminist theorizing of war generally and of substate actors in war specifically can be empirically and normatively differentiated from other critical approaches and has added value to that work.

One of the major dividing lines between other critical approaches and feminist analysis is that, in feminist theory, gender subordination is seen to constitute the relationship between people, gender, and wars. Feminists have recognized that "IR postpositivists have been as slow as positivists to introduce gender into their research."[110] In fact, postmodern work on war and/or security has often underplayed gender tropes' roles in war narratives.[111] Critical work has often failed to take account of the need for gender emancipation.[112] Constructivist work has often stopped short of analyzing the social construction of gender.[113] I argue that many approaches to war(s) that take individuals into account continue to neglect gender analysis. Still, other approaches' neglect of gender analysis is not a prima facie case that feminisms make a substantive contribution to the study of people and wars. The remainder of this section discusses feminist contributions by contrast with three other approaches that account for people in wars: human security, critical security, and the Copenhagen school critical security approach.

Feminist concerns with people in war(s) have often been understood as related to or subsumed by human security accounts. As discussed in chapter 1, human security is an approach that theorizes security from the individual level and is concerned with people's economic, food, health, environmental, personal, and community security. Human security accounts, while they can be used to analyze war, reject a myopic focus on wars as security threats. Human security approaches, especially as they are concerned with wars' impacts on people at the political margins, define human (in)security as significantly broader than war and have a significant amount in common with feminist approaches.[114] In fact, a number of feminists analyzing security have incorporated insights from human security into their analyses of security.[115]

Still, in J. Ann Tickner's words, "feminist approaches differ in that they adopt gender as a central category of analysis for understanding how unequal social structures, particularly gender hierarchies, negatively impact the security of individuals and groups."[116] Without the recognition that the people who need to be secured are gendered and live in gendered worlds, human security loses both explanatory power and normative justification. Scholars who have gendered human security analyses have often noted the need to pay attention to the security needs of individuals *as they identify themselves with particular groups,* arguing that there is "a feminist standpoint which takes as its point of departure the conception of security as the human experience in everyday life mediated by a variety of social structures."[117] The "person" in feminist analyses of people and war is social, interdependent, and relationally autonomous.[118] In this way, feminist research "highlights the need to link a normative approach to human security with an interpretive approach that "recognizes the complexity of the operation of power within and across categories of gender, ethnicity, and generation."[119]

Rather than being subsumed by human security, feminist approaches offer a paradigmatic alternative to human security that avoids many of human security's problems while replicating many of its advantages. While human security analysis has been critiqued for being indeterminate[120] and atheoretical,[121] as well as for relying on top-down thinking to prioritize among human insecurities,[122] feminist theory offers a theoretical justification for including people in war analysis inspired by a concern for gender subordination and political marginality. Feminist theory also "suggests a counter-hierarchical foundation for developing policy priorities within a broadened notion of security."[123] Human security is an important framework for seeing people's needs in security generally and war specifically, but feminist analysis adds empirical complexity, analytical clarity, and normative direction.

Another approach with which feminisms have been associated is the brand of critical security concerned with human emancipation.[124] Often, feminists, like critical security theorists, are interested in emancipation, and see war theorizing as a(n often oppressive) political process. Some feminist theorists have therefore argued that there is a natural affinity between critical security and feminist theory when it comes to thinking about people and war(s), particularly when emancipatory security praxis can be applied to the margins of global politics, gender lenses can help deconstruct traditional notions of power in wars, and feminist theory can be used as a tool to combat insecurity.[125]

That said, while critical security work often takes a liberal individualist approach to security analysis, a number of feminist theorists have suggested that such a view needs to be complicated by co-constitution, interdependence, and attention to relationships.[126] Critical security's interest in emancipation requires categorizing people by particularized identities that may be unrepresentative of how people self-identify. Feminists have expressed concern that "the 'we' see emancipation for 'them' (however those categories are understood)" in a way that "could be categorized as inherently patriarchal."[127] Further, while emancipation is an admirable goal, some feminist theorists have expressed concern that uncritically accepting the possibility of (gender or other) emancipation is dangerous,[128] such that the cost of a feminist–critical theory alliance may be greater than the benefits.[129] In my view, identification with the status-quo-changing political goals of security as emancipation is important for feminist war theorizing, but critical security approaches to war that take gender analysis seriously are stronger than those which universalize the potential for emancipation.

Feminist approaches have also been conflated with the Copenhagen school, particularly with its view of security as squarely within the social realm.[130] As discussed in chapter 1, the Copenhagen school has looked to broaden the (statist) referent of traditional approaches to security and widen the (war-based) scope of security that is customarily used in the field[131] while looking critically at the speech acts that convince people of "security issues" and their primacy.[132]

Feminist work on people in wars shares with the Copenhagen school both broadening what counts as security and paying attention to the production of security,[133] but feminists have expressed concern with the Copenhagen school's omission of gender analysis[134] and its neglect of power dynamics among the forces of securitization.[135] For example, Lene Hansen has argued that the Copenhagen school's understanding of security as speech is gendered, because it "presupposes the existence of a situation where speech is indeed possible," which leaves out those who "are constrained in their ability to speak security and are therefore prevented from being subjects worthy of consideration and protection."[136] Though it is important to see the Copenhagen school's contribution to understanding security as a process, most scholarship in this vein fails to ask the critical questions that inspired feminist IR's critique of the way we see the relationship between people and wars. These include questions regarding who does the securitizing, who is securitized, who is marginalized by securitizing processes, and what gendered power relations are involved in securitization.

There is, then, unique value to feminist theorizing of people's making wars. Feminist theorizing not only offers a unique referent (gender subordination and gender tropes, in addition to people at the margins of global politics) but a unique way of analyzing (through relational autonomy, complexity, contingency, and intersubjectivity as theorized when looking for gender subordination and gender tropes). Additionally, while many critical security theoretical approaches do a fair amount of work toward thinking about people's security (and by extension how the international may be personal and/or personalized), no other approaches analyze either that the personal as war or war as personal.[137] Feminist theorizing characterizes war as personal *and* the personal as war, which, as I discuss in the next section, influences the ways we understand war decision-making. Finally, many critical approaches (and even many explicitly feminist approaches) do not engage the individual with "war proper" (and specifically) rather than security generally. While there are a number of (excellent) normative and empirical justifications for broadening a scholarly focus from the narrow idea of war to a wider idea of (human) security, there are also a number of benefits to engaging intellectually the relationships among gender, people, and the specific world(s) of war(s).

GENDER AND (WAR) DECISION-MAKING

As has been discussed, feminist analysis offers a different way of think-ing not only of who makes war decisions and what decisions should be considered as "war decisions," but it also offers an alternative account of *how* war decisions are made and should be explained. This section analyzes current theoretical approaches to how war decisions are made for their gender biases and gendered omissions and then explores a feminist theory of war decision-making.

Theories of War(s) Decision-Making and Their Genderings

One of the major biases in war decision-making theories is that they are often not applied to the less than 20 percent of world political leaders who are women. Instead, women's war decision-making is often analyzed first as decision-making *by women* and second as war decision-making, producing sex-specific accounts of women's political behavior.[138] The practice of failing to use existing theories to analyze women's war decision-making, I argue, is not a coincidence. Instead, we generally do not apply individual-level theories of war-making to women because most of those theories either implicitly or explicitly exclude not only women but the femininities they are seen to rep-resent. Even approaches that envision the possibility of women as decision makers often maintain a masculine notion of leaders, their knowledges, their values, and their actions. These approaches take into account masculine values, but neglect feminine ones, resulting in the use of traditional notions of leadership to analyze women actors when those notions were shaped by all-male understandings of decisions and decision makers. This misapplication shows not only that traditional notions of war decision-making cannot inadequately understand the less than 20 percent of the world's leaders that are women, but also that they are not up to the task of fully accounting for war decision-making generally. The genderings in traditional approaches to war decision-making render them inadequate to explain *both* men's and women's decisions and the paths that those decisions take to influence war(s). This is because values and traits associated with femininity, neglected in traditional theoretical approaches, are not absent from real-world decision-making processes.

For example, rational-choice accounts of war decision-making assume individuals have "goals, wants, tastes, or utilities"[139] and make their decisions looking for "outcomes that bring the greatest expected benefits."[140] In this view, people make war(s) because they are looking to achieve political ends.[141] While this approach treats men and women "equally," seeing them both as rational calculators, the rational calculation they do is often based both on values and processes associated with traits that signify masculinities. In addition, rational decision-maker accounts often neglect emotion and interdependence in decision-making[142] and therefore are "based on a partial representation of human behavior" that "tends to privilege certain [masculinized] types of behaviors over others," which places "limits on what can be said with the language of strategic discourse constrains our ability to think fully and well about . . . security."[143]

The flip side of the coin is theories that pay attention to emotion and impulse at the expense of understanding the intellectual and political content of war decision-making. These theories are no more appropriate and no more inclusive. For example, although its intellectual roots are very different, psychoanalytic theory makes many of same gendered assumptions that we find in rational choice theory. Psychoanalytic theories of people's (especially violent) decision-making focuses on presumed differences between biological men and biological women.[144] Analyzing individual violence, Freud concluded that "besides the instinct to preserve living substance and to join it into ever larger units," there is a contradictory instinct to "dissolve those units and to bring them back to the primeval, inorganic state" because men are instinctively violent and women are instinctively nonviolent.[145] As a result, feminist critiques of psychoanalytic theory express concern for its "normative masculinity, masculine bias, [and] devaluation of women."[146]

A similar theme can be seen in learning approaches to individual decision-making.[147] Many learning theories, like many other theories of how *people* make *war decisions*, have "either ignored women or ignored gender" by presenting a theoretical account of male decision-making that does not account for women's agency.[148] Some argue that social learning theory *still explains* men's decisions but fails to explain women's, but others argue that because it cannot account for femininity in decision-making, social learning theory is an inappropriate tool for analyzing war decision-making.[149]

Because theories of decision-making often (explicitly or implicitly) assign motivations and responsibility for people's choices on the basis of gender expectations, they do not account adequately for the behavior of either sex: "these theories often use maleness and the male experience to measure their understandings of individual psychology and politics, causing their explanatory power to be partial at best, even when explaining the violence of the men that they are analyzing."[150] Women are either included in approaches that define individuals' roles in reference to masculine standards of individual conduct or included in *gender-differentiated* ways. Femininities (of men and of women) are often excluded.

Rethinking People's Decisions in Wars

The question of people's agency in their decisions, while it appears unproblematic (or at the very least an easily defined problem) in the literature,[151] is one that feminist understandings of social and political life have something to say about, both in terms of the nature of agency and the terms of the agent-structure debate. Feminists have argued that notions of autonomy in decision-making theories of war are problematic and need to be interrogated.[152]

Particularly, feminist theory has explored the level of choice people (especially women) have in their decision-making. Most theories of people's war decision-making assume that people, through explicit consent or social contract, have traded full control of their decision-making in order to obtain the protection and support provided by political organization.[153] As such, people have voluntarily ceded a portion of their autonomy but maintain full command of their decision-making. This understanding of how people consent to limits on decision-making, however, has two key shortcomings. First, sometimes responsibilities are assigned without fully voluntary consent. Second, even when it is fully voluntary, consent is complicated.

Feminist political theorists have explored the idea that responsibility can be assumed involuntarily because there are obligations that "people do not choose, actively or passively."[154] Feminist understandings of responsibilities that are unrelated to people's choices come from analyses of gendered experiences like pregnancy resulting from rape, which women to not agree to either implicitly or explicitly, and which shows gender bias in political agency in theory and practice.[155]

This is especially true because nonvoluntary obligation is often allocated on gendered lines.[156] Nancy Hirschmann explains that through "oppressive socialization," "powers and freedoms are inevitably intertwined with, and even defined by limitations and structures."[157] The gendered relationship between obliger and obliged means that "even acts of dissent are interpreted as acts of consent, and unfair bargaining positions belie the freedom implicit in free choice."[158]

Even obligations assumed "freely" are not as straightforward as they seem. That is because people who decide do so with unequal power and therefore with differentiated capacities to choose. They also decide among choices limited by social context that shapes discursive terrains.[159] Decision makers are thus not only constrained by relative power and a restricted set of choices, but also by the fluid and flexible boundary between self and other, where "'internal' factors of will and desire . . . and factors 'outside' the 'self'"[160] have a complex relationship. Still, even in the face of these limits, decision makers make decisions.[161] Though all choices are not fully free, responsibility exists and is intersubjective. Rather than being discrete and fully individuated, obligation is relational and people are relationally autonomous.[162]

My feminist theorizing of *how* people choose *wars*, then, starts with the recognition that freedom of action is defined and limited by social relationships.[163] Political choice is a question of both position and degree.[164] The "lived experiences of women . . . demonstrate that existing theories of freedom fail to challenge the duality of internal and external dimensions of freedom."[165] Decisions can be made within limits or with others whose decisions are also limited, but they are never completely limited and never without any limits. As such, "decisions are not made without others, but instead either with or around them."[166] Actors can use their limited autonomy to breed conflict with others, to evade others, or to cooperate with them. War decisions, then, are not, as they are characterized in the literature, progressive, reactive chains of events. Instead, war decisions are context-dependent, reliant on allies and opponents' behavior, and, while they are "decided," these decisions are relational and cannot be understood without references to the relationships that inform them.

Within these relationships, conflictual decisions are often characterized in feminist analyses as the use of power-over,[167] wherein power is often conflated with "the crude instrumentalism of violence."[168] In this sense, power-over is the an actor's ability to constrain the choices of another actor or set of actors meaningfully.[169] War decisions reached by seeing power narrowly defined as power-over "privilege an androcentric definition of power" for decision makers.[170] Alternatively, relationally autonomous decision makers can look to act around others, in spite of others, or in reaction to others' actions.[171] They can oppose, rebel against, or attempt to circumvent power-over. Decision makers can also choose to act with others "by emphasizing plurality and community."[172] In all of these scenarios, available choices are "simultaneously restraining and producing new realities."[173]

The options to act against, around, or with others highlight potential *processes* of war decision-making for relationally autonomous actors. In this view, identities of self and other are interlocked and co-constitutive. In other words, all people—from the most to the least powerful—make war(s) and war decisions. Those decisions are constrained by relational autonomy, which can be accommodated by acting against, around, or with others.

The hegemony of values traditionally associated with masculinity[174] in war theorizing naturalizes the gendered identities in the performance and practice of conflict in the global political arena.[175] Therefore, gender lenses look for masculine gender norms even where masculinity does not readily reveal itself.[176] One instance of this is the tendency of war decision-making actors to seek power-over at the expense of other understandings of power, desire, or gain. Feminists in IR have long been using a curiosity about the role of gender norms in international politics to deconstruct purportedly gender-neutral theories.[177] Feminists also engage the project of adding women's knowledge to institutions in which masculine values are privileged.[178] The exclusion of women's knowledge from security institutions is manifested in silences about gender. Charlesworth explains that "all systems of knowledge depend on deeming certain issues irrelevant, therefore silences are as important as positive rules."[179] As a result, the absence of gender in analyses of wars cannot be simply read as blind omission but as (intentional or unintentional) skew.

Knowing that the most deeply gendered facets of the international political arena are those that do not acknowledge gender difference but present their theories and evidence within predominantly or exclusively masculine ontology, epistemology, and method, feminists in IR have learned to look for gender where gender is claimed as absent. It is with this methodological disposition that I approach questions of the individual-level causes of war. According to a feminist understanding of relational autonomy, human choice is never entirely free, but it is also never entirely constrained. As such, it is epistemologically and methodologically important to see war decisions *as decisions*, but to analyze those decisions in more nuanced ways than much of the war decision-making literature does. In this view, the radical denial of agency that omits women and gender from war narratives is both gendered and unwarranted, but the (masculine) rational choice (or psychoanalytic or social learning) theory at the other end of the spectrum is also an incomplete explanation. Including previously hidden gender inequalities in the analysis of the individual's role in war decision-making "allows us to see how many of the insecurities affecting us all, women and men alike, are gendered in their historical origins, their conventional definitions, and their contemporary manifestations."[180]

THE POTENTIAL CONTRIBUTIONS OF A FIRST-IMAGE FEMINIST RESEARCH PROGRAM ON WAR

In these ways, feminist theory is uniquely poised to add to international relations' understanding of the scope of the role of *people* (and stories told about them) in war. Feminists have asked, repeatedly and in a variety of contexts: (1) Where are the women?[181]; and (2) What is their agency?[182] If those same questions are applied to the question of actor(s) in war-making, some insights can be derived. When women are there, they are often described as incapable of decision-making or made singular in discourses that isolate their decisions from others' decisions. By contrast, men's war decisions are often characterized as rationally chosen or approximating rationality, as if men and women were different and rationality is gender neutral. Neither is accurate—there is nothing inherent making women different than men, and our readings of both decision-making processes are gendered. Looking at agency in war(s) from a gender-critical perspective, the "whys" and "hows" are the next questions to be answered in relation to the gendering of each person and her participation in her context. Feminists look for *women* (female bodies), *gender* (characterizations of traits assigned on the basis of perceived membership in sex groups), and *genderings* (application of perceived gender tropes to social and political analyses) in stories about the genesis and practice(s) of war(s).

These realizations critique and necessitate the reformulation of some models of how individuals make war decisions (e.g., rational actor, psychoanalytic, and social learning models). Understanding these models as neglecting characteristics associated with femininity in favor of characteristics associated with masculinity reveals that they are (at best) incomplete accounts of the war decision-making of men and women.

Looking through gender lenses not only at theories of leadership and decision-making but also at its practice in global politics shows the underrepresentation, not only of women but also of the femininity women are often assumed to represent. In the arena of security and war, women are generally more underrepresented in leadership positions than they are generally in the political arena, reinforcing the traditional separation of femininity and war, in which women are wars' constitutive others and therefore not its perpetrators.[183] Still, pressure remains on women decision makers to prove their excellence as relates to traits associated with masculinity, which has created incentives for women to make bellicose foreign policy decisions.

The 20 percent of state leaders that are women and the 80 percent of state leaders that are men both act in a gendered world, constituted, constrained, and enabled by relational autonomy. Understanding these contexts is important, because it shows a key component of what it means to make war decisions, but also because it has implications for existing models of how people cause and/or make wars.

Feminist insights demonstrate that it is necessary to understand the dominance of masculinity and the absence of women in "great man" approaches to theorizing war, especially insomuch as those theories assume separability of the person and the international. Gender lenses suggest that models of war decision-making that emphasize people's interactions, such as bureaucratic politics and organizational process models, inadequately account for both decision-maker relational autonomy and gendered social context. Relational autonomy means the influence of group members on one anothers' decisions is fundamental (at the identity level) rather than solely interactive or social. Gendered social contexts mean that organizational structure, role behavior expectations, and interactions among actors are influenced by gendered ideas of how people should behave.

Rather than asking whether war would be different if women ruled the world,[184] this chapter has explored the importance of asking how both war and individual-level war theorizing would be different if femininity were not excluded from or marginalized in their arenas. Through gender lenses, war is personal and the personal is constitutive of war. War decision-making processes at the individual level, as well as how peoples' choices influence war(s), must be seen differently if war theorizing's gaze expands from (only) masculinities (among men and women) to a broader understanding, including (women and) femininities.

Like system-level, dyadic-level, and state-level analyses, individual-level analyses of the causes of war(s) are fundamentally incomplete without attention to gender in three senses: empirically (i.e., we do not understand which roles women play), in terms of process (i.e., we do not understand how individuals play their roles), and normatively (i.e., we do not have the ethical tools to understand that participation fully). The boundaries of theorizing the causes of war were set before war studies took account of the existence of women and were not adjusted to understand either women or gender once they were recognized as members of the international community and forces in how global politics function. Reversing this blindness is not only normatively important but can help us see the causes of war(s) differently *and better*. Theoretical approaches to war-making, like war-making itself, are often gendered and often gender-blind. The next two chapters of this book show a similar pattern in the theory and practice of war-fighting, where gender is everywhere in strategy and tactics and yet insidiously absent from work theorizing how wars are fought.

CHAPTER 7

Gendered Strategy

The most persistent sound which reverberates through men's history is the beating of war drums.

—ARTHUR KOESTLER, *JANUS: A SUMMING UP*

All wars are civil wars, because all men are brothers.

—FRANÇOIS FÉNELON

Many of the stories of how wars were fought throughout history are the stories of great or brave men's heroic feats. Stoic men outlast wars of attrition, great generals creatively maneuver troops, and strong men get vengeance on their enemies through punishment strategies. In all of these stories, men are either the explicit or assumed subject—strategists and the soldiers who implement strategies are male in sex and masculine in personality.

For example, the United States Marines hold 1st Lieutenant Brian Chontosh as an example of the ideal soldier on the ground.[1] Chontosh's biography on a U.S. military website honoring heroes begins with the observation that "in the face of danger, the mark of a great warrior is he who values his country above his own safety."[2] Chontosh is credited with having done exactly that when he was "caught in a kill-zone with no clear exist or relief" and "chose to meet numerous threats head-on" despite "enemy fire raining down on their position."[3] When the battle was going poorly, "he continued advancing, even when his ammunition began to run low" and "used anything he could find—enemy rifles, RPG launchers, grenades—to continue his ferocious attack."[4] Chontosh, by having "cleared more than 200 meters of enemy trench, killing some 20 insurgents and wounding several others" was among great warriors, "he who values his country."[5] As a result, he was awarded the Navy Cross on 6 May 2004.[6] Chontosh is one of thousands of war fighters honored because of a heroism that is indistinguishable from dominant notions of masculinity. This chapter, along with chapter 8, suggests that the practices of war-fighting are usefully analyzed through gender lenses.

This chapter addresses the question of military strategy from a feminist perspective. It has been argued that "the exhaustive study of warfare must include the study of military strategy," which is key to understanding how wars are fought once they have begun.[7] Still, feminists and other postpositivist scholars have critiqued strategic studies for "privileging the state and military sector" in its focus on military strategy and for the gendered assumptions of theories and histories of military strategy.[8] This chapter looks at the process of strategizing, available strategic choices, how states and other actors choose between them, and the impacts of strategic choices through gender lenses. Accordingly, contrary to Colin Gray's supposition,[9] I argue that not only can strategy be analyzed outside the neorealist paradigm, such analysis is crucial for a complete conceptual and empirical understanding of strategy.

This chapter begins by arguing that the theory and practice of strategy are gendered. It critiques the concept of strategic thought through gender lenses, demonstrating that it rests on gendered and inaccurate assumptions about the international arena. Given the conceptual and practical limitations of strategizing, the remainder of the chapter turns to the gendered elements of actors' strategic choices. It suggests that gender is a key part of the causal story of two particular strategic choices—intentional civilian victimization and the employment of private military security corporations (PMSCs). It also argues that gendered lenses can help us to understand how belligerents choose particular strategies by exploring relationships between androcentrism, biomechanics, and strategic selection, as well as between gendered nationalisms and strategic selection. The chapter concludes that gender lenses increase the conceptual complexity and explanatory value of strategic studies because feminist theory has fruitful alternative suggestions both for strategizing and for analyzing strategic decisions.

GENDERING STRATEGIC THOUGHT

Strategic studies looks at both the particular strategies that are adopted by particular militaries in particular wars, and the process of strategizing that leads to those strategic choices. In describing strategic thought, Richard Betts explains that:

> If effective military strategy is to be real rather than illusory, one must be able to devise a rational scheme to achieve an objective through combat or the threat of it; . . . rational strategic behavior should be value maximizing, choosing appropriate means through economistic calculations of cost and benefit.[10]

In this conception, the strategic thinking and acting is done by a unitary state, strategizing is rational, and its rationality is based on a cost–benefit analysis. Strategies are made and carried out by a state furthering a set of political objectives. This assumes that the state can and does have a coherent political objective shared by its members—that the "national interest" is unitary, rather than diverse and/or conflicting. Indeed, Alan Stephens and Nicola Baker explain that whatever interest a strategy is pursued in favor of should be one "towards which all resources—human, diplomatic, economic, scientific, informational, social, industrial, military, perhaps even artistic, and so on—are directed."[11] Without a particular national interest to serve, strategic thought becomes significantly fuzzier, given the wide variety of available strategies. For strategic scholars, the puzzle of strategy is, therefore, which means are best to reach the goal that was preset by the unitary state.

The second assumption is that a strategy is the result of rational calculation of the unitary state.[12] As Stephens and Baker note, in order to strategize rationally, there are several criteria states must meet, including understanding what they mean by winning, ensuring their ends are realistic, and ascertaining that the ways chosen to pursue the means are suitable and feasible.[13] These criteria for rational strategizing are meant to ensure that strategizing is, and to analyze strategizing as, goal-oriented behavior, whereby a rationally produced plan is implemented to achieve the goal of victory.

The third assumption concerns the goal of strategy as maximizing expected utility of a unitary state in cost–benefit terms. This is, for the most part, about winning the war and achieving its political objective. Still, strategists are careful to note that states' expected utility has a "domestic" political component as well.[14] Thus, strategy refers to a singular (largely material) utility function that includes both domestic and international components. This utility function can be wielded in calculating that losses must be taken to achieve the goals of rational, unitary belligerents. Cost–benefit analyses weigh the different factors in strategic choice, including the level of violence used, the level of casualty averseness, the choices between offense and defense, and the level of commitment to the use of military force. Feminist work has questioned each of these assumptions, both generally and as they apply to strategizing.

Feminist Critiques of the Assumptions of Strategic Thought

Generally, as we discussed in chapter 4, feminist concern for people inside a state victimized by the state's security-seeking behavior inspires work on the different and often-neglected security interests of states' marginalized citizens. Feminists interested in the ways that militarism reinforces gender hierarchy also express concerns that the pursuit of states' interests as if they were unitary (and therefore as if the interests of the elite coincide with the interests of those at the margins) actively reinforce differential effects on different parts of populations.

This effect is clear when one looks at gendered dimensions of labor in militaries, both generally and in service of particular strategic decisions. Generally, as discussed in more detail in chapter 9, military action relies on the service of a number of unpaid or undercompensated feminized others playing a variety of support roles essential to but rarely acknowledged in the planning and execution of combat maneuvers. Often, labor is distributed unevenly across race, gender, class, and other axes of difference. For example, militaries deploy frontline troops in which minorities and the underclass are overrepresented but women are underrepresented, but deploy elite, college-educated, largely majority troops to less dangerous missions and destinations.

Different strategies often affect people differently as well. Strategies of attrition often require poor living conditions for troops for long periods of time, whereas the recently more popular strategic choice of long-distance warfare poses almost no physical danger for those doing the war-fighting. Offensive strategies often require a reshuffling of "domestic" economic capacities to produce the weapons, vehicles, and technologies essential to advancing successfully, while defensive strategies often require a reconfiguring of the defended territory that displaces its residents. These differential impacts of different strategies are only exacerbated when their effect on their targets is taken into account. For example, aerial bombing affects different parts of target populations (usually in urban areas) than ground warfare (usually outside of urban areas), and siege warfare affects whole populations while maneuver or other targeted strategies impact certain parts of the population more than others.

When strategies have different impacts on different parts of domestic or international populations, these impacts are often not accounted for in strategic calculation or studies of strategic choice. The unitary state that strategists understand as an analytical unit is, through gender lenses, a snapshot of the what happens to elite portions of populations rather than a comprehensive view of the consequences for states' diverse citizens. I argue that this unrepresenativeness is gendered and have seen that gendering as a key part of strategic thought, I am therefore concerned that the appearance of state unity results in the marginalization of states' most disposed citizens in both choosing and executing strategies.

In "questioning the role of states as adequate security providers," feminist scholarship has "pointed to the masculinity of strategic discourse and how this may impact on understanding of and prescriptions for security."[15] Feminists have also been critical of the idea that war-fighting parties can (or should) strategize rationally. As we discussed in chapter 4, the rationality assumption implies both that the knower and the known are separable and that such a separation is desirable. Feminist theorizing, on the other hand, has suggested that both implications are deeply problematic. Arguing that the alleged gender-neutral "objectivity" of rationality is frequently if not always a covert form of privileging maleness, feminists understand knowledge as perspectival and political. The dichotomies between the rational and the emotional, the knower and the known, and male and female have been linked in feminist critiques of assumed rationality.[16] These critiques are often sharpened in the area of military strategizing, given that strategists' rational calculation happens within a limited and constructed world with specialized rules and knowledges. For example, Carol Cohn suggested that nuclear strategists spend a significant amount of time justifying why it is rational to possess weapons of a quantity and quality it would never be rational to use.[17] Cohn sees this puzzle as explainable in terms of the extraordinarily high level of abstraction that has to go into war strategizing to plan extreme human destruction.[18] That is why feminists have questioned the applicability of cost–benefit analysis as it relates to war strategic decisions.

In fact, feminists have suggested that economistic cost–benefit analysis has "hidden symbolic and structural agendas" on gender lines.[19] This is important because cost and benefit are associated with value, and value is subjectively determined. While military strategists usually calculate costs either in terms of deaths of troops or civilians and/or the monetary expenditure necessary to achieve the strategy, those are only a couple of the many ways to calculate costs and benefits. Something that might not "cost" at all (e.g., housework performed by a wife) is essential to the function of a given institution (here, the nuclear family), but does not figure prominently in materialist cost–benefit analyses. These different sorts of cost are almost never taken into account in strategic choice, and there are many. There are many costs that are rarely tallied in the cost column, including environmental damage,[20] the suffering of children born of war rape,[21] and the care labor necessary to sustain seriously injured soldiers over the course of a lifetime.[22] These costs (and many others) are omitted because cost–benefit analysis in strategizing is not only state-centric but elite-centric in gendered ways.

Feminists have also interrogated how rational cost–benefit analysis works in different arenas (from microeconomics to grand strategy), arguing that it assumes actors have full and free choices among costs and benefits.[23] This assessment, too, takes place from a position of privilege, rather than from the standpoints of those who are, in Julie Nelson's terms, "provisioned" their position.[24] Actors who do have such freedom (assuming potentially erroneously that such actors exist) are certainly the exception and not the norm. Most strategic cost–benefit analyses are done in constrained military choice environments where all available choices are suboptimal, and actors' freedom is often to react to, interact with, act in concert with, or act constrained by both material and relational limits.

Rethinking Analysis of Strategizing Through Gender Lenses

The very postulation that the sort of strategic thought envisioned by strategists is possible rests on a number of gendered assumptions about the world and how it works, including rationality, state unity, and economic cost–benefit analysis. Given how fundamental these assumptions are to both strategizing and the scholarly analysis of military strategy; and how at once strategic studies fetishizes militarism and ignores gender, it is hard to envision strategic studies changing significantly. Still, feminist theorizing provides some potential ways forward for thinking about strategizing.

Particularly, it suggests "strategizing" about issues traditionally excluded from the realm of war-making and war-fighting, such as gender subordination, economic inequality, and environmental degradation might be fruitful. In addition to expanding what is strategized about, I suggested expanding the content of strategizing, focusing also on care, compassion, and other values that gender lenses highlight. This approach suggests both that strategizing is actually more complicated than its neorealist students recognize, and that it is normatively important to change strategic studies' substantive foci and methodological choices. Along those lines, feminist theorizing provides tools to apply in reformulating strategy—including emotion, empathy, and "strong" or "dynamic" objectivity as a way to understand strategy perspectivally.

In my view, the first conceptual tool that feminist theory provides is emotion. Hanne Marlene Dahl urges us to recognize that emotion already does and should continue play a critical role in policy decision-making.[25] She explains that "the role of emotions does not have to be idiosyncratic and dangerous" as it is portrayed by many proponents of rationality.[26] Instead, decision-making can "combine respect and concern."[27] Concern here is for the other, "an attention towards the other which is not a feeling but a general being-in-the-world-with-others."[28] This approach is also called empathy, which Christine Sylvester describes as "the ability or willingness to enter into the feeling or spirit of something and appreciate it full . . . to hear what . . . [they] say and be transformed in part by our appreciation of their stories."[29]

Kathleen Jones suggests that empathy, translated to the realm of strategizing, can inspire compassionate authority, a second tool to deconstruct the apparent unity of "state interests."[30] If the current (masculine) view of authority that inspires the assumption of state unity is understood as "indivisible, unambiguous, and hierarchical," compassionate authority is "more horizontal" and is about "equality, heterogeneity . . . speech, communication and common understanding."[31] Compassionate authority includes diversity, considers equity in participation and empowerment, acknowledges and accommodates subjectivity and value differences, and encourages the involvement of women and other marginalized groups.[32] Feminist theorists have argued that "care can be both moral principle and practice in global politics," a worldview that holds transformative potential.[33] Applying compassionate authority would diversify both the people that are included in the concept of the state interest and the quantity and quality of concerns recognized by governments and leaders, in turn transforming the cost–benefit analysis that goes into strategic choice.

Such a transformation goes hand in hand with *dynamic* or *strong* objectivity—a third tool feminist theory provides.[34] As Evelyn Fox Keller describes it, dynamic objectivity "relies on our connectivity," producing "a form of knowledge of other persons that draws explicitly on the commonality of feelings and experience in order to enrich one's understanding of another in his or her own right."[35] Sandra Harding describes strong objectivity as recognizing that "different cultures' knowledge systems have different resources and limitations for producing knowledge" and as such, conceptualizing neutrality as the problem, not the solution.[36] What these two visions share is a method for including more voices in states' decision-making about what the national interest(s) are and how to pursue them. This could be read not only as a guide for strategizing but also as a way of strategizing. States employing diversity *as* their strategic thought could more accurately reflect the needs and interests of all of their members, not only the elite/male/rationally minded ones usually included.

In this approach, seeing the perspectives of those normally marginalized in state and global politics betrays the incompleteness of traditional cost–benefit analyses. The costs and benefits that concern most people in the world are not measured in terms of territorial expansion or military weaponry, but instead about the provisioning of scarce resources for health and survival.[37] If strategic thought paid attention to those people's concerns, it would still be appropriate to theorize national interests in territory, economic benefit, and state security. But it would be equally appropriate to theorize national interests in terms of solving urban poverty, preventing deaths from starvation and curable disease, decreasing rape rates, solving race and gender subordination, and any number of other concerns that uniquely affect those currently left out of a decision-making process that, according to Harding, is based on a weak and exclusive approach to objectivity.[38]

If a feminist approach to strategic thinking alters how actors think about the composition, needs, and pursuits of their own states, it may have a similar effect on deconstructing the us/them dichotomy between a state and its perceived enemy. Currently, the "anarchy outside/order inside" dichotomy of realist IR theory implies, and in fact necessitates, a radical separation between states.[39] If the principles of strong objectivity, concern, and empathy were applied not only to *who* makes state decisions but also to *how* a state views its potential opponent(s), it is possible that states could understand their strategic interests as sometimes complementary rather than always at odds. As Christine Sylvester explains, "one appreciates the similarities that are echoes of one's independent experience . . . empathy enables respectful negotiations with contentious others because we can recognize involuntary similarities across difference as well as differences that mark independent identity."[40] This could lead states to see each other less individually and therefore treat each other less acrimoniously.

These different understandings of the assumptions of unity, rationality, and cost–benefit analysis are potentially transformative both of the theory and practice of strategizing. In practice, strategizing is based on perspectival knowledges of elite actors taking into account a narrow spectrum of costs and benefits, rather than the singular, broad-brush, goal-oriented process it appears to be in neorealist analyses of strategic thought. The study of that theorizing, then, could and should take into account its (gendered) biases and the inequities they both create and perpetuate.

This analysis suggests that the (gendered) assumptions of strategists and scholars who study them both need to change radically to make strategizing more just and more representative. In practice, strategists should broaden who they consider in strategizing, what issues are strategized about, and how strategizing is done in order to account for diversity generally and the lives, concerns, and knowledges of people at the margins of global politics specifically. The study of strategizing then could look at the processes and results of strategizing with an eye toward being productive of dynamic objectivity and social justice.

At the same time, it is important to look through gender lenses to see that none of these transformations have happened in the current realms of the theory and practice of strategy, strategic choices, and the strategies they result in, which remain highly gendered. The remainder of this chapter explores both the ways that gender is deployed in the selection of strategies and the ways that war-fighting strategies can be read as gendered.

ATTACKING WOMEN AS STRATEGY[41]

A woman in Misrata, Libya testified "she was raped in front of her four children after Qaddafi fighters burned down her home."[42] In fact, "259 women said they had been raped," including Iman al-Obeidi, who "burst into a hotel housing foreign journalists in Tripoli in March and accused pro-Qaddafi militiamen of gang-raping her."[43] Early evidence shows that these rapes may have been strategically planned rather than isolated or incidental, since there have been "reports of condoms and Viagra found in the pockets of dead Qaddafi soldiers."[44] An interviewer who has talked to many of the rape victims explained:

> They are using rape not just to hurt women but to terrorize entire families and communities. . . . The women I spoke to believed they were raped because their husbands and brothers were fighting Gadhafi. I think it is also to put shame on the tribes or the villages, to scare people into fleeing, and to say: "We have raped your women."[45]

Feminists have studied the frequent occurrence and terrible effects of wartime rape (which will be discussed in more detail in chapter 8), but have only recently begun characterizing it as a part of a larger military strategy of (gendered) intentional civilian victimization.[46] This section contends that intentional civilian victimization is deployed strategically by belligerents in a way that can only be understood fully by recognizing the gendered logics of war-fighting. Particularly, I argue that intentional civilian victimization as strategy is a direct logical consequence of the deployment of the (gendered) noncombatant immunity principle as a justification for war(s).[47] I explain that *civilian* is a fundamentally gendered concept, and that its genderings can account for the use of intentional civilian victimization (of men and women) as a strategy. This section will show that, far from being a gendered aberration in ungendered strategic decision-making, experiences like Iman al-Obeidi's in Libya are the core of "intentional civilian victimization" as a strategy—one aimed at women (not as women per se but) as "centers of gravity" of opponents in war(s) and conflict(s).[48]

As I discussed in chapter 1, the recent focus on intentional civilian victimization in research on strategy has identified it as a strategy in which civilians are targeted either intentionally or indiscriminately.[49] Existing accounts operationalize intentional civilian victimization strategies as carried out through tactics such as urban bombing, blockading, sieging, sanctioning, relocating, and massacring.[50] Scholars who study intentional civilian victimization suggest a variety of causes for the strategic choice, including levels of regard (or disregard) for international law,[51] the constraints of democratic governance,[52] the cultural traits of belligerents employing the strategy,[53] and factors about the particular conflict (such as whether or not ethnicity plays a role,[54] whether or not territory is at stake,[55] and level of desperation[56]).

Both the definition of intentional civilian victimization and the causal analysis of this strategy in the mainstream literature omits gender, and I argue that gender is crucial both to knowing what intentional civilian victimization is and how it is chosen strategically. First, in terms of defining intentional civilian victimization, the existing literature omits war rape and other sex-specific tactics from its understanding of what constitutes intentional civilian victimization.[57] In other words, Iman al-Obeidi's experience would not be accounted for in descriptions of (or calculations of) intentional civilian victimization in the conflict in Libya in most mainstream models.

Scholars defending the omission of sex-specific and sexual violence from intentional civilian victimization argue that rape is not murder and that intentional civilian victimization is concerned with the killing of civilians, rather than the abuse of civilians.[58] This response, though, has two major problems. First, the literature's operationalization includes cases in which civilian deaths are indirect (as often the case with war rape), such as concentration, relocation, siege, and blockade. Wartime rape is also often fatal itself and a part of a strategy not only to kill the victim but to corrupt and/or end the purity of the victim's racial or ethnic group.[59] Second, it allows for a discursive but not actual separation of intentional civilian victimization and sex-specific violence, one in which it appears that the two can be analyzed separately, because war rape is by definition *not* "intentional civilian victimization" but something else that happens within and coincidentally to it. At the same time, however, scholars who study intentional civilian victimization reject work demonstrating correlations between sex-specific violence and intentional civilian victimization as tautological, since it seeks to provide a correlation between two things that are essentially the same.[60] In this way, conventional definitions of intentional civilian victimization both assume away and make invisible sex-specific and sexual violence, despite their prevalence and symbolic importance in seeing and accounting for intentional civilian victimization.

Understanding Intentional Civilian Victimization as Gendered

My claim that sex-specific and sexual violence is a key part of what constitutes intentional civilian victimization is straightforward. If the mystery of intentional civilian victimization both violates the civilian immunity taboo and is strategically inefficient, sex-specific and sexual violence would seem to be a special and includable case if for no other reason than it meets these criteria and also violates a taboo on violence against women. More than that, though, sex-specific and sexual violence simply *are* intentional civilian victimization—perpetrated intentionally at the strategic level, targeting (largely if not exclusively) those understood to be civilians,[61] and causing death both directly and indirectly.[62]

The argument that recognizing sex-specific and sexual violence as a part of the strategy of intentional civilian victimization is key to explaining why intentional civilian victimization is chosen as a strategy is less straightforward but still important. This section contends that the purpose of employment of intentional civilian victimization is linked to the gender (and therefore secondarily the sex) of its victims. Without discounting some of the important work done to date on the cause of intentional civilian victimization, I argue that accounts of its employment are incomplete without reference to sex and gender.

Particularly, recent accounts have isolated territorial war, belligerent desperation, and organizational culture as key predictors of intentional civilian victimization.[63] This section builds the argument that women's bodies are the territory being contested, that emasculation is a key element of the desperation that incentivizes attacking civilians, and that intentional civilian victimization relies on organizational cultures constituted by and constitutive of the gendered civilian immunity principle. It accounts for civilian victimization as the assertion of one belligerent's (masculine) virility and dominance and the revealing of another's (feminized) inadequacy, often inscribed on women's bodies.[64] This argument suggests that intentional civilian victimization is actually intentional victimization of the feminine, wherein war-fighting parties that choose to target civilians are actually aiming at women specifically, not *as women per se* but as the symbolic centers of states, nations, and war efforts that gendered war justification narratives frame them to be.[65]

This argument builds on the feminist literature on nationalism, militarization, and war discussed in more detail in chapter 5. Specifically, this work has argued that the strategic discourses belligerents use in referencing civilians are inherently gendered and scholarship that ignores those genderings is necessarily incomplete. Particularly, feminist work has drawn attention to the interdependence of war as an institution and gendered images of combatants and civilians,[66] particularly the tropes in which male "just warriors" play the role of "defenders of righteous causes," while female "beautiful souls" are treated as "delicate" and in need of just warriors' protection in the civilian immunity principle.[67]

These norms, salient because of their relationship with gendered nationalisms, have functions other than supporting war-justifying narratives, as discussed in chapter 5. Gendered war narratives are salient in strategic decision-making, at least in part because sexed bodies play different roles in nationalist discourses. These tropes' domestic impacts have been well-documented in the feminist literature on gender and war, as a creator and perpetuator of gender inequalities; in their tendencies to link protector-ability, masculinity, military service, and full citizenship; and in their key role in war-justifying narratives. This work has led to understanding that the logical structure of the civilian immunity principle is gendered.

This gendered logical structure results in an immunity principle that creates the appearance of providing women protection while actually producing both gender subordination and threats to women's lives.[68] Because of the immunity principle's gendered foundations (in chivalry, religious law, and state sovereignty),[69] feminists have argued that its gender bias is structural in, rather than incidental to or separable from, its provisions for the protection of civilians. The key logical result of the gendered immunity principle, in this view, is a link between the nobility and honor gained from fighting a war and providing protection to feminized others.[70] Because of this link, war-fighters' reward (of validation of their masculinity) is to be found in the honor gained from their (apparent) provision of protection, which is rendered at once necessary and apolitical. The presumption of the civilian immunity narrative is that women (as wars' feminized others) are presumed innocent of wars (regardless of their actual innocence)[71] and presumed protected by just warriors (often with little regard for whether any protection results).[72]

This phenomenon has been identified as the "protection racket," in which the protection of vulnerable citizens is used to justify violence that puts those citizens at more risk.[73] In these terms, the gendered stories of the immunity principle create and reify illusions of protection.[74] States then use protection discourses and self-identify as just warriors as a way to shield their threatening behavior from scrutiny, which allows them to threaten their own (particularly female) citizens even as one of the very basic properties of statehood is protection of the innocent. This internally contradictory narrative means that the protection racket can be wielded domestically in justification of violence, even when women's protection is unrelated to the actual goals of the war.[75] In these terms, "the gendered protection racket can even be characterized as a creating condition of possibility for war, since innocent, defenseless women (and their love and virtue) *to fight for* motivate men to fight, even absent other motivation."[76]

The source of this motivation is that just warriors' raison d'etre, throughout the history of war-fighting, has been closely tied to the defense of "their" women and children, defined either personally or nationally.[77] This has the function of motivating men to fight, creating a notion of soldierly masculinity that functions to "glue the army together and keep the men in line or at least enough in line for the organization to produce its violent effects."[78] Masculinity becomes that which defends the nation, while femininity holds it together, and women's need for protection *and* men's obligation to protect combine to justify *both* wars and individuals fighting in them.[79]

While these negative effects "at home" have been explored in the feminist literature, less attention has been paid to the question of what if any impact the importance of the protection racket at home has on relations among states, nations, or other belligerent groups. What attention has been paid has largely focused on states looking to serve as state-level just warriors to other states' helpless beautiful souldom for apparently noble state-level (e.g., the claim to protect a feminized Kuwait from a hypermasculine Iraq in the first Gulf War) or individual-level (e.g., saving Afghan women from Afghan men by invading Afghanistan) goals.[80] The remainder of this section argues that there is a less-explored but potentially even more insidious implication when one recognizes states' reactions to other states' symbolic valuing of feminized others in war-justifying narratives. The (domestic) embeddedness of the protection racket serves as the underlying logic to incentivize the strategic choice of intentional civilian victimization.

The gendered protection racket serves as a justification for (gendered) civilian victimization in wars because the roles of women as beautiful souls and men as just warriors also reproduce and are reproduced in gendered conceptions of state and/or nation. As we discussed in chapter 5, nationalism is gendered, and gender is militarized. These genderings of militarism and nationalism construct and are constructed by the gendered civilian immunity principle, whereby women serve as symbolically protected in state-justifying and war-justifying narratives. This role of symbolic protection is a key part of how and why individual soldiers fight.[81]

Jessica Peet and I have characterized gender tropes, therefore, as key to understanding civilian women as a 'center of gravity' in Carl von Clausewitz's strategic terms.[82] A *center of gravity* is "neither a strength nor a source of strength, per se, but rather a *focal point* where physical and psychological forces come together."[83] It is necessarily effects-based, rather than capabilities-based, which makes it both more difficult to identify and for an opponent, more important to target.[84] Clausewitz theorized centers of gravity because he saw them as "the pivots against which decisive force should be applied, or, in the case of our own centres, be resolutely defended."[85] This incentivizes belligerents to look to decimate others' centers of gravity while protecting their own in order to ensure victory. An approach that takes centers of gravity into account recognizes that an attack that has a large impact symbolically or psychologically can lead to moral surrender, which can cause physical surrender.[86] To obtain such an end, "in order to generate a strategic outcome, it is imperative that strategists define both their own and their enemy's centre/s of gravity."[87]

There is evidence that states often (consciously or unconsciously) see their own centers of gravity in women as the symbolic and material centers of their collectives. The roles women play as beautiful souls, biological reproducers, cultural reproducers, and wars' feminized others make them both materially valuable (in a sex-disaggregated way) and symbolically valuable to states as belligerents. If women are (some) states' centers of gravity, Clausewitz's strategic logic implies that the protection racket would have not only the domestic result of (performed) protection but also the international result of attack. In other words, "if belligerents fight for *their* women, it follows that a belligerent wins an absolute victory by exterminating the women understood as 'belonging' to the opponent."[88] In this view, the same logic that justifies one state's protecting particular women justifies another state's violence toward those same women. As Jessica Peet and I have explained, "if 'beautiful souls' motivate fighting because they represent the good worth defending . . . destroying 'beautiful souls' could play a role in destroying both the opponent's will to fight and (symbolically and sometimes physically) the nation itself."[89]

The choice to target women also assaults the opponents' will to fight by emasculating the opponents' men. This emasculation happens through depriving men of their ability to protect and with it, one of the central ways to indicate, perform, and prove masculine prowess. In order to emasculate "enemy" men, "enemy Woman's real and imagined body becomes a tool through which the nation can project its own desires and deficiencies on another" and belligerents will attack the "enemy Woman" as a method of humiliating the Other, as a means of conquering their soul."[90]

Understood this way, if women (as feminine) are belligerents' centers of gravity, then the "civilian" in civilian victimization can be read as a proxy for "women," not *as women* but in their role as the (gendered feminine) symbolic center of state and/or nation. This suggests gender as an alternative explanation for intentional civilian victimization as a strategy, in contrast with explanations prominent in the current literature. Intentional civilian victimization can be seen as the intentional violation of the feminine other as an assault on the masculinity of the opponent. In this reading, belligerents victimize (women) civilians seen as the property of the enemy under the same logic that motivates them to provide protection to the (women) civilians that they see as their own property—because the protection racket justifies not only wars but the political institutions that make and fight them.

Of course, women are not the only victims of intentional civilian victimization, and each strategic use of intentional civilian victimization is not necessarily explicitly or only aimed at female bodies. To make such a claim would both be oversimplified and contradictory to currently existing empirical evidence. Instead, though it is true that a number of tactical manifestations of intentional civilian victimization are sex-specific, others are not, either explicitly or implicitly. Instead, "some have little sex-differential impact or target civilian men."[91] The argument that gender tropes are a key incentive for the strategic choice of intentional civilian victimization does not rely on all the victims being women or all the perpetrators actively looking to harm and/or kill women. Instead, it suggests that intentional civilian victimization is, consciously or not, an attack on the masculinity (and therefore will to fight) if the enemy, carried out by the destruction of the feminine and often inscribed on women's bodies. The enactment of intentional civilian victimization sometimes leaves civilian men unscathed and sometimes harms them, but these effects (like the effects on actual civilian women) are secondary, because the target is the enemy's sense of masculinity and the strategy to target that masculinity is destruction of the feminine. This account of the incentives for choosing intentional civilian victimization, I argue, could potentially provide more leverage for understanding instances of civilian massacre than more conventional effect. The next subsection explores empirical evidence in line with this theoretical framing.

Seeing Gendered Intentional Civilian Victimization in War(s)

Existing work provides evidence that gender influences states' choices to engage in intentional civilian victimization. Particularly, Jessica Peet and I tested two indicators of gender's influence across existing models in the literature on civilian victimization to inquire into whether or not they had influence on states' choice of this particular strategy.[92]

The first indicator that has influence in predicting intentional civilian victimization is the sex ratio of civilian deaths in war.[93] The sex ratio indicator is an indirect measure of whether more women die when civilian victimization is intentional. If states are really trying to attack women as a center of gravity, of course they will not *only* kill women, but they are likely to kill more women than when civilian deaths in war are incidental or collateral.[94] Therefore, one would expect a smaller percentage of "accidental" civilian casualties would be women than "intentional" civilian casualties if civilian victimization is really an attack on civilians-as-women. These expectations are borne out in large-N analysis, in which the sex ratio of civilian casualties is a statistically significant predictor of intentional civilian victimization with high marginal effects.[95] A model including the sex ratio of civilian deaths has better explanatory power and more robustness than models that omit gender in accounting for intentional civilian victimization.

The second indicator, levels of sexual violence in the conflict, also has high predictive value for intentional civilian victimization.[96] The levels of sexual violence indicator is a measure of whether sex-specific tactics are correlated with intentional civilian victimization. If intentional civilian victimization is really a proxy for the victimization of women (as nation), then it is reasonable to expect the form and demographic results of violence toward civilians to differ in cases of intentional civilian victimization (in which sex-specific violence would be highly prevalent) from cases of incidental or collateral civilian victimization (in which sex-specific violence would be less prevalent, because incidental or collateral civilian damage will not include systemic violence against *women specifically*). Statistical analysis also supports these expectations, since the level of sexual violence in war is a significant predictor of intentional civilian victimization at the 95 percent level and increases the overall explanatory value of models of intentional civilian victimization.[97] It also has a high marginal effect, accounting for almost one-third of all change in the strategic choice of intentional civilian victimization.[98]

A few twentieth-century conflicts also demonstrate the plausibility of a gender-based account of intentional civilian victimization. For example, many of the elements of the discussion of intentional civilian victimization above can be found in the conflict in Bosnia-Herzegovina in the 1990s.[99] The conflict, which has been characterized as a war *of* civilian victimization,[100] disproportionately affected women. The Bosnian ambassador to the United Nations characterized Bosnia-Herzegovina as being "gang-raped"[101]—which he meant both literally and symbolically.[102] Lene Hansen argued that the sort of rape in the Bosnian conflict "happens not as a consequence of thoughtless, provocative, or unfortunate behavior but as a question of national warfare"[103] wherein rape "works to install a disempowered masculinity as constitutive of the identities of the nation's men."[104] The gendered dimensions of this war *of intentional civilian victimization* included rape of women (as a proxy for state and nation), killing of men (as heads of reproductive households), forcing men to watch women and children be raped and killed (as emasculation), and forced impregnation (as an assault on ethnic purity).[105] These tactics used in combination suggest that a strategy of victimization of the feminine as an assault on enemy masculinity was in place and perceived by its victims.

At the same time, skeptics might suggest that the war in Bosnia-Herzegovina is an easy case for gendered analysis given the high prevalence of war rape. It seems reasonable to ask, then, if this logic has any salience in more "normal" wars. The evidence shows a very similar pattern in a very different case—intentional civilian victimization perpetrated by the Soviet Union in Germany (particularly Berlin) in 1945. As the Soviets pushed the Germans back into Germany and ultimately took control of Berlin, the Soviet use of sexual violence and sex-specific tactics went from sporadic to routine.[106] Soviet images of the planned defeat of Germany were full of sexuality and emasculation.[107] One of the most recognizable results of this association between conquering and destroying masculinity was the campaign of mass rape that "degraded German men, labeling them as impotent for their inability to protect German women."[108] The Soviet attack "functioned, then, to establish masculine domination . . . [and] symbolized the defeat of the entire Nazi Nation."[109]

These mass rapes are well-documented historically[110] and had an estimated victim list between 100,000 and 200,000.[111] The Soviet targeting of German women was not limited to rape but also included intentional direct killing of women.[112] The rape and killing of women was an object of state policy: "Stalin explicitly condoned it as a method of . . . terrorizing German civilians."[113] World War II historian Chris Bellamy suggests that "the hideous spectre of mass rape was not only condoned, but, we can be pretty sure, legally sanctioned by the political officers speaking for the Soviet Union."[114] If the Soviet government intentionally victimized women in Berlin, there is evidence that victimization was related to women's symbolic significance as markers of state and/or nation.[115] Soviets saw attacking German women as an assault on the virility of German men in which "values that are connected to the idea of virility play a decisive role in the formation of soldierly self-image" and conquering German men could happen through the exploitation and destruction of German women's bodies.[116] The Soviets used attacking German women as a strategy because "violence against their [German] women is but one way to destroy their national pride, manhood, and honor."

If the Soviets meant attacks on German women as a message of emasculation, it was a message that Nazi Germany heard loud and clear. As Grossman recounts, "the mass rapes of civilian women signaled the defeat of Nazi Germany"[117] to the extent that Hitler[118] saw Soviet destruction of

German women and children as the symbolic and material destruction of German civilization. As Grossman points out, "the very last newsreel released [by the Nazi Government] in 1945 showed a white fence with a desperate message scrawled on it 'protect our women and children from the Red Beast.'"[119] This account of the final weeks of World War II contains many of the same elements of gender as an exploration, as well as a vehicle, for the manifestation of intentional civilian victimization.

Gendered accounts of intentional civilian victimization can be found in many conflicts at many different times in history and different places in the world.[120] These accounts demonstrate that belligerents may well be intentionally victimizing civilians not indiscriminately or gender neutrally but instead in a way that makes gender a key element of the causal story. Gender tropes that specify protecting women as a key justification for nationalism and for war incentivize opponents' decisions to target those very (women) civilians. Rather than being coincidental, then, the near-perfect correlations between intentional civilian victimization, levels of sexual violence in war, and sex ratios of civilian victims in war can be explained by seeing the strategic choice of intentional civilian victimization as a choice to assault the masculinity of the enemy through gendered attacks on (women) civilians' bodies.

GENDER AND THE STRATEGIC USE OF PRIVATE MILITARY AND SECURITY CORPORATIONS

The strategic deployment of intentional civilian victimization is one of many strategies that can be seen as gendered. Another is the deployment of private military and security corporations (PMSCs). While "the terms of the public/private divide differ from 'domestic' to international society," it functions similarly, suggesting focus on the public sphere and maintaining the invisibility of the private sphere.[121] Though the "private sphere" in strategizing terms is not singular but has many layers, all of those layers are often invisible in the selection and implementation of war strategies. In strategizing, then, the "public sphere" of states and their soldiers has been visible (perhaps even hyper-visible) while the private sphere in its various iterations has been overlooked. Yet the distinction between expectations in the public and private spheres in war(s) remains, and the private sphere (from the kitchen to PMSCs) plays a significant role in wars. Looking at the role of the private sphere in strategizing through gender lenses suggests denaturalizing the public/private dichotomy that puts states on the inside in strategic analysis and nonstate actors on the outside, whether that outside is marginalized (in the case of kitchens) or a privileged space (in the case of PMSCs).[122]

To this end, feminist theory interrogates and deconstructs the dichotomized thinking that strictly separates state and nonstate actors in strategic theorizing. Feminist studies of international conflict have demonstrated how the security of individuals is related to national and international politics, as well as how international politics impacts the security of individuals at the local level. This leads to a general questioning of the public sphere as the place where security happens, in contrast to a private sphere that remains unseen. Chapter 6 of this book discussed in detail the argument that the private sphere inside families, homes, and social networks both constitutes and is constituted by war(s), and chapter 9 will talk about war as experienced in the private sphere of the margins of global politics as much, if not more, than in the traditional locations taken seriously by war studies.

This section looks at a different deployment of the private sphere in war—the use of PMSCs as a strategic choice.[123] "Penetrating" the "virgin" market of "private," clandestine military service,[124] PMSCs come to fulfill some functions that previously were filled by state militaries in conflict zones. Dominant accounts of the strategic deployment of PMSCs contend that these companies are chosen largely because state militaries have found cost-efficiency in subcontracting military work to private corporations that can do the "work" of war-fighting faster and more efficiently than traditional militaries.[125] Because of the cost savings, the story goes, states have become increasingly reliant on the strategic use of PMSCs, such as Academi (once Blackwater and Xe), DynCorp, and Triple Canopy. As a bonus, dominant accounts defending PMSCs talk about them as ways to head off the necessity of drafts while increasing the overall prowess of fighting personnel.[126] These PMSCs, in turn, find the business extremely profitable, both for individual (usually former state) soldiers and as a corporate enterprise.[127]

Looking at PMSCs through gender lenses shows that there is more to the story than "private" companies coming to fill "public" duties more efficiently than the "public" sphere could provide the services itself. Interrogating the gendered public/private divide allows feminist scholars to ask questions about what strategic utility the "unseen" nature of the private sphere has when militaries are privatized, and what assumptions about gender (and class and sex and race) are necessary to make the strategic choice to employ private military corporations rather than using state militaries to fulfill the traditional functions of war-fighting. Searching for these silences demonstrates that the strategy of employing PMSCs may also be a (gendered) strategic deployment of the private sphere.

Looking at how they are deployed, one sees that PMSCs inhabit a private sphere in some ways similar to the private sphere of those whose lives are marginalized in global politics.[128] Both private spheres are invisible in traditional strategic discourses pairing state militaries against each other, and both live behind an imagined veil of secrecy, where what happens in the private sphere is somehow unmentionable or unknowable to the public sphere of war-fighting.[129] At the same time, what happens behind the veil in the marginalized private sphere is domestic violence, sex inequality, starvation, deprivation, fear, and uncounted danger.[130] What happens behind the veil of PMSCs privileged private sphere is a militaristic exceptionalism in which militaristic cultures, routine behaviors, and abuses that would never be tolerated in the 'public' sphere are often the norm rather than the exception.[131]

Some scholars see this as a regulatory problem, whereby PMSCs are deployed for reasons of cost-efficiency and military capacity and regulation of and proper punishment for their human rights abuses and war crimes are a legal puzzle.[132] Still others more skeptically argue that PMSCs are being employed strategically at least in part because of the murkiness of the laws that govern their conduct in war zones.[133] Through gender lenses, it is possible to see this not as the intentional deployment of PMSCs for their ability to go undetected, but as the deployment of PMSCs as an instance of the strategic use of the (gendered) private sphere for the purpose of capitalizing on the private sphere's invisibility.[134] The very same veil over the private sphere that makes invisible the domestic abuse of women also makes invisible the abuses of PMSCs, which, when "discovered" can then be discussed as incidental rather than as a systematic result of military cultures prone to proscribed violence.

The private sphere can then be strategically deployed for the purpose of hiding, making clandestine, or making appear anomalous, the abuses state militaries desire to commit but for which they desire to avoid ownership or accountability. An example of the recent use of PMSCs is as "interrogation support" in Iraq, Afghanistan, and Cuba by the U.S. military, in which the PMSCs engaged in "interrogation methods" that the military-member soldiers with whom they worked were constrained not to use, given both domestic and international law.[135] In this and other cases, the gendered public/private divide is not being incidentally engaged in a strategic deployment interested in efficiency but is itself being deployed with strategic intent interested in the "privacy" of the private sphere.

While others have noted the strategic advantage of the secrecy and apolitical nature of PMSCs for states interested in hiding and depoliticizing their military actions,[136] viewing the use of PMSCs (through gender lenses) as the strategic deployment of the private sphere has several advantages. First, it adds depth to the analysis of the operational cultures of PMSCs as hypermasculine, since the very possibility of that hypermasculinity exists because of its invisibility to the public sphere, where a more moderated military masculinity reigns.[137] Second, it draws links between the invisibility of private destruction in the (feminized) traditional private sphere and the invisibility of private abuse in the (masculinized) new private sphere. Third (and perhaps most importantly), it shows the possibility of wielding privacy as a (weaponized) military strategy for the purpose of the pursuit of war goals that would be unattainable through the use of normally accepted, public sphere strategies. These implications, in my view, make it worth pursuing gender analysis not only of the strategic choice to deploy PMSCs, but of strategic choice more generally.

GENDERING STRATEGIC CHOICES

In addition to the gendered nature of strategic thought and the failure of strategic studies to recognize the gendered nature of either intentional civilian victimization or the employment of PMSCs, I argue that there are a number of ways in which genderings play a role in states' decisions to choose one strategy over another as they fight in wars. As I discussed in chapter 1, in thinking about which strategies states choose to use to fight their wars, theorists of strategy developed different schemes to delineate strategies available to states, including offense and defense; maneuver, attrition, and punishment; continental, maritime, and aerial; pre-emption, terrorism, and siege; and, most recently, intentional civilian victimization. In looking at how states choose among this myriad of strategies, strategic theorists suggest that a number of factors, from culture to technology and war aims to economics, can be used to account for strategic selection.

This section suggests a number of ways in which gender is present in strategic discourses and is an influence on belligerents' choices among strategies. First, it suggests that biological sex plays a role in strategic selection, as it discusses the intersection of androcentrism, biomechanics, and choice of strategies. Second, it suggests that not just sex but gender influences how states choose strategies, as they are guided by the gender tropes that constitute their nationalisms and senses of self.

Androcentrism, Biomechanics, and Strategic Selection

In discussing the potential contributions of gender theorizing to security studies at a recent conference, one mainstream security scholar started a discussion of the relevance of gender to security studies by observing that he liked sex, but was not a big fan of gender.[138] While he was mainly looking to get a metaphorical rise out of his (mostly feminist) audience, he went on to give a talk about the utility of studying sexed bodies for military strategic purposes—the "biomechanics" of certain military strategies.

This scholar's argument was that sexed bodies are interesting to the extent (and only to the extent) that differently sexed bodies are differently shaped and differently equipped and, therefore, need to be taken into account when designing military technology. This has certainly been a question evaluated in strategic work on biomechanics both inside militaries and by scholars who analyze the military.[139] The example that the speaker at the recent conference used was the (lack of) suitability of women's bodies to sit in fighter plane cockpits, a "fact"

that meant women should not serve as fighter pilots, given the suboptimal size and shape of their bodies for the task. Certainly, strategists
have been concerned with the size and shape of bodies for military
aircraft since the advent of aerial warfare,[140] and this work has often
focused on the question of the suitability of women's bodies for fighter
plane cockpits.[141] Some have gone so far as to characterize the presence
of women's bodies in military equipment that was *not made for them* as
a risk to the success of military operations.[142]

At the same time, military equipment was "not made for" women
(to the extent that it was actually *not* made for women) because of a
prevailing assumption that soldiering is the business of men and not
women. As Rachel Weber observed, "both defense and civilian cockpits have traditionally been built to engineering specifications based on
male anthropometry and tend to embody a physical bias against women
and smaller-statured men."[143] It is not, then, that women "don't fit"
cockpits, it is that cockpits are made not to fit women. This and other
choices to utilize biomechanical arguments to exclude women's bodies have led some feminist scholars to characterize militaries as using
androcentric strategies to maintain sex divisions in militaries even as
civilian populations insist on military sex integration.[144]

These observations open the door to the possible argument that strategies are chosen along the lines of particular notions of sex inclusion and
exclusions, which means military strategies are designed around the sort
of bodies that strategists prefer to include. Usually, these choices take on
an androcentric tone, with technologies that select for and advantage
bodies sexed male.[145] Male bodies are selected for in strategic decisions
because it is men who, in keeping with traditional gender tropes, have
the bravery, prowess, and responsibility to execute military missions.

Still, perhaps nowhere is strategic change more evident than in the
increasing, twenty-first-century tendency to select neither for male nor
female bodies but instead drone, robotic, and other "unmanned" elec-
tronic soldiers.[146] In a lecture at the U.S. Naval Academy, Peter W. Singer
described the loss of a soldier on an explosive ordnance disposal team
hunting for an improvised explosive device (IED) in Iraq in 2006.[147]
Singer let the audience know that "this particular bomb call did not end
well," since "by the time the soldier got close enough to see the telltale
wires coming out from that IED, it exploded" and the soldier was closer

than the fifty yards away that it would have taken to escape injury and almost certain death.[148] As a result, Singer explained:

> That night, the unit's commander sat down to do his duty, writing a letter back to the United States that described how hard the loss had been on that unit, how they all felt they had lost their greatest soldier, a soldier who had saved others' lives time and again. The commander apologized for not being able to bring that soldier home, back to the United States.[149]

This sounds like a "normal" story of the loss of a soldier in a military at war, and Singer intends it to, until he concludes, explaining that "then the commander talked about the silver lining in this loss. This is what the officer wrote: 'At least when a robot dies, you don't have to write a letter to its mother.'"[150] This account shows a U.S. military moving away from selecting for strategies that potentially sacrifice men's bodies to embrace stereotypes about men's masculinity and bravery (and correspondingly women's need for protection) to selecting for strategies that potentially sacrifice asexual, nonhuman bodies. Still, in Singer's account, the reason for selecting the strategy that "kills" the drone rather than a person has its roots in traditional sex roles—one does not have to write a letter home to the robot's *mother* when the robot dies. This implies that the gendered reasons why women were excluded from combat positions in traditional strategic choices are maintained, rather than deconstructed, in the strategic choice of drone warfare.[151]

This is not to say that strategies are selected purely (or even mainly) for the sexed bodies that they include or the sexed bodies that they exclude, but instead to suggest that sexed bodies are not irrelevant to strategic choice. Still, the relationship between sexed bodies and strategic choice that some traditional theorists of strategy suggest (wherein some sexed bodies are appropriate for some tasks, while others are not) obscures androcentric sex selection in militaries as they make strategic choices. However, while the strategic choice of aerial warfare (and concomitant cockpits designed for men) has (or at least had) a relationship with choosing male bodies to participate, the strategic choice of drone warfare (and concomitant lack of a need to write letters to dead soldiers' mothers) has a (gendered) relationship with disembodying fighting.

Gender, Nationalism, and Strategic Selection

Choices of what bodies to make killable and what bodies to spare are not the only ways that gender tropes can and do influence strategic selection, but they are not the only ways gender can be seen to interact with how state militaries select their war strategies. Instead, as this subsection argues, the same gendered nationalisms that often contribute to states' war-making decisions (see discussion in chapter 5) play a role in the strategies those states select to fight in those wars. Feminists have argued that the legitimation of nationalism relies on gender hierarchies that prioritize masculinity and devalue femininity, naturalizing male dominance.[152] If gendered nationalism were a constant, however, it could not influence strategic choice, because strategic choices are not constant for any state over time. The presence of gendered nationalism in state structures is constant, but its form and content change over time.

Particularly, feminist research has documented that gendered nationalism mirrors the idealized, or hegemonic, version of masculinity dominant in culture.[153] While some scholars have treated that hegemonic masculinity as a constant, recent feminist research has discovered that a state's ideal, or hegemonic, masculinity changes over time.[154] Jennifer Heeg Maruska explains that, at times, a state's nationalistic hegemonic masculinity can become *hypermasculine*, as opposed to other times, when idealized masculinity reflects other, less aggressive characteristics.[155] If the characteristics of the hegemonic masculinity change over time, and the content of gendered nationalism changes with them, then it is possible to envision a state's (changing) strategic choices being guided by its (changing) understanding of idealized masculinity.

In such an understanding, states choose more aggressive strategies when their idealized masculinity resembles hypermasculinity. As Meghana Nayak explains, "hypermasculinity is the sensationalistic endorsement of elements of masculinity, such as rigid gender roles, vengeful and militarized reactions, and obsession with order, power, and control."[156] This hypermasculinity is reactionary, and can be characterized as "extreme behavior within gender roles, brought about by some internal or external threat."[157] When the hegemonic masculinity in a state is hypermasculine, the state's objectives may be ambitious and the strategies it employs to achieve them bold and aggressive. In these terms, one would expect hypermasculine states to pursue strategies classified as "offensive," "punishment," "swagger," and "compellence," If, on the other hand, the hegemonic masculinity in a state moves further from hypermasculinity and closer to, for example, the just warrior stereotype, the state would be more likely to employ strategies that are less bold and less aggressive. Instead, those states would pursue strategies less useful for projection and more useful for protection, such as those characterizable as "defensive," "deterrence," and "attrition."

The influence of gender on strategic choice may also range outside the state's sense of its own masculinity and onto its sense of the gender(s) of its enemies. Cynthia Weber suggests that states' gendered perceptions of their enemies also impact strategic decision-making.[158] Comparing U.S. movie representations of strategic choices against Japan in World War II and against al Qaeda/Afghanistan after 9/11, Weber suggests that "the rhetoric of Pearl Harbor abides by the gendered and sexualized Second World War formula for understanding and rehabilitating an enemy—a hypermasculine/hypersexual enemy requires emasculation" while "attack on America's moral grammar locates no clear enemies, no clear homefronts, and no clear traditional codes."[159] Al Qaeda becomes "gender doubled" where it "is neither masculine nor feminine, straight not gay. Instead, it is both," a very different perception than that of hypermasculine, World War II Japan.[160] This difference in gendered perception of the enemy, Weber argues, leads to different strategic goals. Where in World War II against Japan, the United States looked for security, in the "global war on terror":

> What America wants is a moral grammar that will promise it not security, but a U.S.-led discourse of securitization; not closure, but the possibility of enclosure of its enemy and its rescued domestic space; not a baseless, premature fatherhood for this war-torn world, but a domestically grounded, proper fatherly role in a post-war world.[161]

Weber suggests, as have other feminist researchers, that states' gendered perceptions of "self" and gendered notions of the "enemy" impact not only when states go to war but how, in the form of choices of strategy. Strategies that are more aggressive are chosen when states are hypermasculine, while strategies that are more subdued are chosen when states' masculinities focus on more subdued traits. Likewise, states treat a defined, clear, hypermasculine enemy with more harshness (perhaps competition between masculinities) and a (potentially genderqueer) undefined enemy with caution, mixed strategies, and mixed messages.[162] While this work does not suggest that states' gendered perceptions of self and other are the only factors in strategic choice, it does suggest that theorists looking to understand why militaries choose particular strategies would do well to look at gender as they also look at other potential influences.

THE POTENTIAL CONTRIBUTIONS OF A FEMINIST RESEARCH PROGRAM ON STRATEGY

Certainly, a single book chapter cannot rewrite strategic theorizing as if it were from its inception viewed through gender lenses with awareness of the gendered influences on and gendered implications of military strategizing. Still, this chapter has attempted to explore the ways in which it is possible to see gender as both constitutive of strategic thought, strategizing, and strategic analysis and causal in states' choices of strategies. It has been argued that not only is gender a factor in whether states *make* wars, it is also a factor in how they *fight* wars. It has done so with the dual aims of understanding strategic thought as gendered and understanding the gender considerations that go into choosing among strategies.

This chapter has asserted that looking at traditional scholarly accounts of strategizing through gender lenses leads to a feminist critique of the assumptions of strategic thought and to rethinking strategizing and the analysis thereof in order to take account of that feminist critique. Particularly, it has contended that feminisms question the idea that strategizing is the rational product of a unitary actor using material, cost–benefit analysis in order to make choices of how to fight wars. This leads to critical reflection on the rational/emotional dichotomy, engagement with the possibility that states are diverse rather than unitary, and a broader interpretation of cost–benefit analysis. To this end, this chapter has offered normative alternatives as guides for strategic choice, including care, empathy, and strong or dynamic objectivity.

Even without a radical reformulation of how strategies are made and studied, however, the chapter argued that strategic choice is currently gendered. It discussed both intentional civilian victimization and the employment of PMSCs as gendered strategies, in which the former is motivated by women as a center of gravity in gendered nationalist justificatory stories for war, and the latter constitutes the strategic deployment of the gendered private sphere. This led to the argument that strategic choice more generally rests on both sexed and gendered assumptions about the relationships between states and the relationships between strategies. I framed the relationships of sex, biomechanics, and strategic selection to understand the ways that states often use biomechanics to select strategies on the basis of the sexed bodies that they include or exclude in an androcentric or gender-hierarchical way. It then turned to the relationships among gender, nationalism, and strategic selection to argue that the character of the hegemonic masculinity in a state and the state's gendered perceptions of its opponents in a particular war influence its choices among strategies for that war. While these propositions were explored briefly in this chapter, one could imagine comparative case study evidence for the relationships among sex, gender, and strategic choice generally and the gendered elements of intentional civilian victimization and the deployment of PMSCs specifically.

As a dialogue among feminisms, feminist strategic theorizing puts gender analysis into the (sometimes uncomfortable) discussion of how and why states make (normally masculinized) choices between military strategies. While some feminisms critique *all* war violence and others suggest that the current operation of the making and fighting of war is gendered, engaging the question of whether gender influences *what strategy is* and *how states strategize* can bring about important realizations both for feminisms and for strategic thought. Feminist theorizing of strategy then brings with it the simultaneous desire to engage with and interject in strategic theorizing and to radically reformulate the ways that strategy is defined and considered, both for theorists and for practitioners.

If this chapter is correct both that feminist theorizing poses a challenge to how strategy is conceptualized and that gender is a significant causal factor in how states choose strategies, the implications for strategic theorizing are significant. As a dialogue with, engagement of, and critique of strategic theorizing, this analysis means that the narrow situation of strategic studies in contemporary neorealism gives an incomplete picture of what strategy is *and* which strategies are chosen by war-fighting actors for what reasons. Particularly, it means that strategizing is significantly more complicated than the (gendered masculine) conceptions put forward by both its practitioners and its theorists. It also means that gender needs to be considered as a factor in how strategies are chosen and how they are practiced.

Engaging strategic theory challenges feminisms to think seriously about *how* gender interplays with other factors in strategic choice and how to simultaneously think of strategizing as gendered, gender as a factor in strategic choice, and the enactment of strategies as gendered. Feminist engagement challenges strategic theorizing to understand that gender is not something just incrementally relevant when one sees women's bodies in war, but across strategic theorizing. In addition to the intellectual advantages of these engagements, I contend that there is explanatory, operational, and definitional value in understanding the gendered dimensions of strategy for accounts of how wars are fought. This chapter made that argument, while the next chapter argues that gender is also key to understanding tactical and logistical decisions and actions.

CHAPTER 8

Gendered Tactics

When they were about to kill me, one of them said I resembled his sister and that I would become his wife instead. They killed another woman. We were beaten many times. . . . My sister-in-law was killed during a dispute between two men who wanted to have her as a wife. They decided to solve the problem by killing her. Another woman was impregnated. She tried to abort the baby, but she bled too much and died due to lack of access to medical treatment.

—LUCIENNE M'MAROYI'S STORY, *STORIES FROM WOMEN: DEMOCRATIC REPUBLIC OF CONGO*[1]

In discussing strategy in chapter 7, I argued that states employ strategies in gendered ways, but also that states employ gendered strategies—particularly, strategies that target women not as women per se but as feminine markers or centers of gravity of the "enemy." If protecting women and/or states' feminine others can serve as a war justification (as argued in chapter 5), attacking women targets opponents' justifications for those wars directly and their will to fight indirectly (as argued in chapter 7). Strategies of attacking the gendered foundations of state and/or nation are accomplished through traditional tactics of war-fighting, like the use of tanks, bombs, ships, and airplanes. Whether it is the British blockade of Germany (1914–1919) or the mass killing at Srebrenica (1995), traditional war tactics can communicate gendered messages.[2]

Still, as this chapter explores, reading war tactics through gender lenses is revealing about the ways that the day-to-day fighting of wars happens, as well as about the practice and signification of war-fighting. In chapter 1, I discussed the scholarly literature on tactics, which has largely been the purview of military historians. This literature analyzes tactical selection, technological change, the normative impacts of particular tactics, and the ways that norms influence tactical choice. It is related to and derivative of a literature on logistics, interested in how particular tactical choices are made possible by the support, transportation, munitions, rations, backup, and medical care available, or constrained by problems in the provision of any of these key factors. Here, I contend that gender-blind analysis of the tactical and logistical levels of war-fighting misses important dimensions of how war works in practice and what war means to its practitioners, most of whom experience war primarily at the tactical and logistical levels.

This chapter starts with the argument that the gendered strategy of intentional civilian victimization that targets women as a center of gravity for states is often carried out using explicitly gendered tactics, particularly wartime rape. In contrast to many analyses of wartime rape which separate it, in theory and in practice, from other "conventional" tactics of war, I argue that wartime rape is a key war tactic because of the symbolic function it serves of attacking (and corrupting the purity of) women as a way to communicate dominance over the enemy state and/or nation. After suggesting that these gendered tactics serve gendered strategic goals, a second section contends that reading tactical choices through gendered lenses reveals there is a strong link between gender tropes and the tactics that constitute war-fighting practices. In a third section, I make the case that it *is* a tactical choice when and how belligerent forces choose (or not) to include women among their ranks. Particularly, I look at when women are weapons of war, both in "terrorist" organizations and traditional wars. Taking first an embodied approach to theorizing gendered weaponry, I contend that the material and symbolic content of women *as women* can be weaponized. I then argue that the weaponization of women paves the path for the weaponization of the feminine in the form of feminization—a tactic that I suggest is commonplace at both the macro- and micro-levels of war-fighting. A final section explores logistics of war-fighting through gender lenses, contending that logistical practice cannot be understood but as a part of the gendered political economies of war. The chapter concludes by discussion of the potential contributions of a feminist research program on tactics and logistics.

(GENDERED) TARGETING OF WOMEN IN WAR(S): WARTIME RAPE AND FORCED IMPREGNATION

Some accounts suggest that the Rwandan genocide had the highest frequency of conflict rapes in the history of wartime.[3] Countless rape victims were killed, yet more than a quarter of a million rape survivors are estimated to still be living in Rwandan society as it tries to recover from that and other traumas related to the genocide.[4] Stories like this are not as rare as it might be comfortable to think they are.

Sexual violence, whether it is a part of a strategy of victimization of women as a proxy for the symbolic center of state and/or nation or employed to serve some other ends, is a common occurrence in war(s). While some scholars characterize it as incidental or collateral to warmaking, this section argues that wartime rape is used purposively, both at the command level and among individual soldiers and civilians, to send a message of emasculation of individual opponents, as well as to opposing states and nations.[5]

There are those who ask whether wartime rape is as prevalent as women's rights advocates[6] and human rights advocates[7] would have us believe. Certainly, there are varying rates of wartime sexual violence, with low levels attributed to the behavior of individual soldiers and high levels likely to be seen as either tactical or collateral.[8] In some conflicts, rape is pervasive, while in others, it occurs in short, intense bursts.[9] In still other conflicts, war rape is more likely to be perpetrated among soldiers than to be committed against civilians.[10]

All those caveats considered, some level of sexual violence is identifiable in most wars, from ancient times to contemporary conflicts.[11] From the wars of ancient mythology to the wars of the second decade of the twenty-first century, wartime rape is frequent, horrifying, and a source of outrage, but at the same time commonplace and frequently ignored. High levels of the use of rape as a tactic of war have been reported in a number of conflicts, including but not limited to post–Cold War conflicts like the one in Bosnia,[12] twenty-first-century intrastate conflicts like the one in Darfur,[13] and twentieth-century great power campaigns like the Japanese invasion of China[14] and the Eastern front of World War II in Europe.[15] Recent news stories have covered wartime sexual violence in Egypt,[16] the Democratic Republic of Congo,[17] Libya,[18] the Cote d'Ivoire,[19] Chechnya,[20] and Kashmir,[21] and they are only the latest in what seems like a constant stream of war rape stories.[22]

In the twenty-first century, sexual violence in war and conflict seems to be, if anything, increasing in both regularity and severity.[23] If rape has been a weapon of war throughout history, it is only recently that it has been explicitly recognized as such.[24] This recognition has been due largely to the proliferation of a variant of wartime rape called genocidal rape.[25] While recent conflicts were not the first in which rape has been an instrument of genocide (and likely will not be the last), they have brought visibility to rape in war.[26] Genocidal rape has been condemned in the international arena, and a jurisprudential strategy to deal with it is forming.[27] Advocacy against and jurisprudence condemning war rape has emphasized its links with gender subordination.[28] As Frances Pilch describes, "the revolutionary changes that have taken place in this area of the law in large part reflect the growing mobilization and influence of non-governmental organizations articulating the importance of the rights of women."[29] As jurisprudence changes, militaries have been putting together formal rule sets discouraging or outlawing wartime sexual violence.[30] At the same time, in a number of resolutions, the United Nations Security Council has recognized international peace and security as crucially linked to women's security and has called for an end to sexual violence in war.[31]

All of these policy, legal, and advocacy strategies against wartime rape, I argue, constitute progress, but fail to see that wartime rape is not just an incidental occurrence in all conflicts and a weapon of the extreme parties in intransigent conflicts or ethnic wars. Instead, as the title of this section suggests, wartime rape is a tactic of war, both on a one-on-one level and as a part of the gendered strategy of the victimization of the feminine discussed in chapter 7. Some wartime sexual violence is centrally planned, while other cases of rape are either planned at the unit level or the product of individual soldiers or groups of soldiers. In all of these cases, it is useful to see rape as tactical.

This section discusses what rape as a tactic means, as well as what it communicates to belligerents' audiences and their opponents. In order to be considered tactical, war rape must be either intentional or the product of some other intentional acts performed to serve particular ends. I argue that war rape is often used intentionally as a tactic on its own and at other times is a part of a schema of gendered civilian victimization that indirectly encourages it through the logic of femininity as a center of gravity.

This approach frames wartime sexual violence as experienced by individuals and often experienced and suffered both at the time of the rape and for the rest of the victim's life singularly, but as still never truly an individual phenomenon. Instead, it is important to contextualize the act of war rape in terms of understandings of gender roles, gender histories,[32] and the social dynamics of the community at large. Though wartime sexual violence, the (mostly) women it hurts, and the messages it communicates are as old as war itself, it is committed, suffered, and punished (or, more likely, not punished) in the context of particular belligerents in particular conflicts.

Across those conflicts, though, feminists have found common purposes, meanings, and messages of wartime sexual violence, since it happens largely to people identified as female and expresses feminization when perpetrated against men.[33] This gendering of rape victims is systematic, not incidental;, during wars, rape "becomes a metaphor for national humiliation . . . . as well as a tactic of war used to symbolically prove the superiority of one's national group."[34] Raping women is a symbolic attack on men's virility and their ability to protect their women, as well as a material attack on the sustainability of the state, nation, or ethnic group.[35]

Cindy Snyder and her coauthors recognize this as an act of communication, wherein the belligerent is using rape tactically (either at the command level or at the level of individual soldiers) and attacks and injures women and/or the feminine (or sexually feminizes men and/or the masculine) as a way to emasculate the opponent.[36] They explain:

> The mass war rapes can be understood as an element of communication—the symbolic humiliation of the male opponent. By dishonoring a woman's body, which symbolizes her lineage, a man can symbolically dishonor the whole lineage. . . . Thus, sexual violence against women became a tool of genocide for destroying the enemy's honor, lineage, and *nation*.[37]

The gendered nationalisms that incentivize the strategic victimization of women (as wars' feminized others) as a proxy for civilians also incentivize war rape as a tactic. As a result, "rape in war, ethnic-national war in particular, becomes a powerful symbolic weapon against the 'enemy.'"[38] Because "women are seen as precious property of 'the enemy,'" women and their bodies become territories to be seized and conquered.[39] Women's (raped) bodies in these interactions are not violated humans or injured people but tablets for sending messages to the men who witness and cannot prevent the violation and injury. War rape as a tactic then subordinates the material existence of women and/or the feminine to the symbolic communication of men and/or the masculine.

In this dynamic, raping women perceived as belonging to an enemy asserts dominance over that enemy. Inger Skjelsbaek notes that this feminizes "both the sex and the ethnic/religious/political identity group to which the victim belongs."[40] As a result, Jeanne Vickers has characterized wars as battles in cradles (biological reproduction) and nurseries (social reproduction) as much as they are contests between armies, navies, and air forces.[41] Raping women functions tactically in two important ways. First, it "functions as a strategy to deliver a blow against a collective enemy by striking at a group with high symbolic value."[42] Second, when rape is a centrally or unit-level organized tactic, forced impregnation is often an explicit reason for rape and the intent of the (individual and collective) rapist. When forced impregnation results from wartime sexual violence, it functions to injure not only the particular woman against whom the rape is perpetrated and the man or men who are seen to be responsible for her protection, but also to "disrupt—by planting alien seed or destroying reproductive viability—the maintenance of the community through time."[43] Forced impregnation, or "occupation of the womb,"[44] is "committed systematically" in many wars and conflicts, where the twofold purpose is the physical destruction of (both feminine and racial/ethnic) purity and the emotional generation of "mass terror, panic, and destruction."[45] It is, in this way, a material attack on the sustainability of an ethnic group, state, or nation looking to corrupt its ability to reproduce, biologically and socially.

These impacts mean that wars are not only fought "for" women[46] but also through them, on their (actual and represented) bodies. This is why several feminist scholars have identified the tactic of wartime rape as a key threat to gender equality, even when the message is not "aimed at" the women raped.[47] There is a level of dehumanization of women that is necessary not only to commit that sort of violence but to use the butchering of women's bodies instrumentally. This practice signals a deep inequality lingering in societal images of masculinities and femininities despite increasing gender equity legislation around the world.[48] For these reasons, scholars have seen war rape as a barrier to women's being secure, either from the direct threat of wartime rape or more generally in social and political life.[49] Women and the feminine are at risk, both materially (for bodily harm) and conceptually (as something against which weapons of corruption and destruction should be used in order to communicate messages of dominance). Judith Gardam explains that, therefore, war rape is "an integral part of the system ensuring the maintenance of the subordination of women."[50]

The fact that the message of war rape is addressed to someone other than the victims (or to the victims and other people)[51] does not mean that women (or feminized male victims) are less harmed by rape, individually or as a class.[52] Instead, it means that these harms are done to feminized bodies often without regard to their personhood. It is therefore not only that war rape is frequently normalized in conflict but also that, concurrently, the dehumanization of the feminine is also normalized. Together, then, belligerents destroy and disregard the feminine in the act of war rape for the purpose of communicating gendered nationalist messages to opponents. Women's bodies are the markers and notepads of the destruction of others' masculinity, abstracted as they suffer, bleed, and die.

A message was inscribed on Le My Hanh's dead body in 1977, after the 17-year-old New Yorker of Vietnamese descent had been "bound, gagged with her own scarf, punched in the jaw, beaten 'over and over,' raped, sodomized, and finally, strangled."[53] Her attacker, when confessing to the crime, said that he "just knew she was Vietnamese," and he had been trained to kill Vietnamese women *in Vietnam*, where inscribing sexual force on them (as he did on Le My Hanh) was a message of emasculation to the Vietnamese enemy.[54] Had the attacker killed his victim in Vietnam, it would have been a part of the regular war-fighting tactics used by soldiers to mark the defeat of the enemy on women's bodies. The soldier, however, made the mistake of not understanding that the "war" was different in Vietnam than it was in New York, and was ultimately held not guilty by reason of insanity (since he was incapable of understanding the wrongness of his actions).[55]

Rape as a tactic, then, targets men's masculinity, particularly the ability to protect women, and leaves raped (men and) women as collateral damage in the tactical communication of the message that states' feminized others are not only destructible but destroyed. If intentional civilian victimization at the strategic level aims at women (as the feminine) as a proxy for civilians for the purpose of emasculating the opponent and destroying his will, reason, and/or justification for fighting, war rape as a tactic can be seen as a key performance of these strategic goals. Command-level, planned tactical rape can be seen as a belligerent's attempt to systematically destroy an enemy through and on the bodies of "its" women. Individual or unit-level rapes, even when not centrally planned, can often be read as individualized or group disdain for the masculinity of the enemy and a sense of dominance over the victimized group.

The very normalization of rape as a weapon of emasculation and the sexual violence in war that accompanies it suggests that sex, sexuality, and violence are more closely linked than traditional analyses of tactics suggest. The next section suggests that the terrible combination of sexual abuse, abstraction, and dehumanization found in war rape can be found across a wide variety of war tactics, all of which are gendered.

GENDERING TACTICAL CHOICES: GENDER TROPES, WEAPONS, AND WAR(S)

Much of "mainstream" IR and security work acknowledges a gendered dimension to wartime rape, even if it does not explore that gendering as deeply as some feminist analysis does.[56] Feminist analysis of the gendering of war tactics often (though not always) focuses gender lenses exclusively or mainly on war rape.[57] Together, this work implies that, as a gendered tactic of war-fighting, war rape is the exception and not the norm—and other war tactics can be seen as gender neutral or less in need of critical analysis through gendered lenses. This section argues that, though wartime rape is one of the most easily visible gendered weapons of war, other tactical choices are also entrenched in gendered norms of war-fighting. Particularly, this section links technological development, weapons choices, and gender tropes, arguing that even seemingly mundane tactical decisions like the use of particular planes or drones are productively viewed through gender lenses.

In order to make the case that wartime weapons choices (as traditionally understood) are gendered (in their evolution and implementation), it is important first to understand the vast number of available tactical choices over the history of war, and the resulting variety of tactical conversations to be had. Tactical choices change frequently with time, place, strategic needs, and the evolution of wartime technology. Historical war tactics have included a number of weapons that current war-fighters are unlikely to even consider, and war tactics that we have yet to imagine may be used in the future. While some scholars argue that the fundamentals of war-fighting do not change over time despite changes in available weapons choices,[58] others contend that revolutions in military affairs mean that radical changes in available war technologies translate into fundamental changes in the ways that wars are fought and even made.[59]

Whichever approach more accurately reflects the development of tactical choices over time, both the evolution of wartime tactical choices and the making of those choices on the ground level can be seen as filtered through and contested with prevalent gender tropes. Almost thirty years ago, Carol Cohn, looking through gender lenses at nuclear technostrategic discourses, identified an "astounding chasm between image and reality" in which "sanitized abstraction" functioned "to deny the uncontrolled messiness" of the fighting of wars.[60] Cohn referenced discussions of atomic weapons as surgical tools, which she argued "is unspeakably ludicrous when the surgical tool is not a delicately controlled scalpel but a nuclear warhead."[61] She observed that the sanitized abstraction and sexual imagery she had seen "even if disturbing, seemed to fit easily into the masculine world of nuclear war planning."[62] In this planning, "the reference point is not human beings but the weapons themselves."[63] Cohn wrestled, then, with keeping human concerns in mind in tactical and technical discussions, given that "if humans are not the reference point, then it is not only impossible to talk about humans in this language, it becomes in some sense illegitimate to ask the paradigm to reflect human concerns."[64] Cohn tasks feminists with creating an alternative space to these gendered technostrategic discourses by interrogating the relationship between masculinity, science, rationality, and the fighting of war(s), arguing that "deconstructing strategic discourse's claims to rationality is, then, in and of itself, an important way to challenge its hegemony as the sole legitimate language for public debate."[65]

At the same time, these links are deep, and challenging them is complicated. Not only, as Cohn noted, are the discourses of abstraction in the fighting of wars self-referential, seductive, and solvent for individuals as coping mechanisms, they reflect a continuing relationship between the search for and selection of (especially technological) tactical choices and gender tropes that favor values associated with masculinity.[66] In military realms, discussions of tactical innovations and tactical decisions are often framed in terms of advances in, and dictation by, the principles of science.[67] These discussions appear gender-neutral and even objective, but deeper inquiry reveals substantive gendering.

In these discussions of science and military technology, science provides the control over nature that military decision makers need to maintain languages (and appearances) of abstraction and cleanliness in terms of the weapons used and the impacts of those weapons.[68] Scientific advances in military technology are often associated with the very characteristics of militarized masculinity most valued in military leadership, especially objective calculation and control.[69] In Lauren Wilcox's words, "scientific ideology can be seen as based on masculine projects of control over nature and built upon the gendered Western dichotomies of mind/body, culture/nature, rationality/emotionality, control/dependence, and objectivity/subjectivity."[70] In those dichotomies, each of the first terms are associated with masculinity, and (therefore) given priority over their feminine opposites.

While the masculinization and concurrent abstraction of technostrategic discourses have served at once to make palatable brutal war tactics and abstract away their victims, not all military tactics are positioned equally along gender hierarchies. Instead, while gendered discourses serve as a condition of possibility for the commission of brutality by "normal" people, they also mediate, limit, and select among usable technologies for war-fighting parties. Tactical choices have been filtered by the fact that, even within the masculinity of science, some "technologies have been considered feminine while some have been considered masculine at different points in history."[71]

For example, often, offensive developments in military technology have been celebrated for their link with masculinity. In 2009, the Obama administration endorsed the U.S. Air Force's development of the "Massive Ordnance Penetrator (MOP)," a "bunker buster" bomb called "Big BLU," because of an "urgent operational need (UON) for the capability to strike hard and deeply buried targets." Big BLU has been called the "mother of all bombs" and all focus has been on "how deeply" the Defense Threat Reduction Agency "wants MOP to penetrate."[72]

What the MOP is supposed to "penetrate" is Iran's suspected/alleged underground nuclear arsenal.[73] Though nuclear policy talks have changed significantly since Carol Cohn's Cold War–era observations, those discourses also remain fundamentally couched in the language and aspirations of masculine sexuality. For example, in discussions of nuclear proliferation in the Middle East, established nuclear states like the United States (and Israel) have been compared with mature men, while the (attempted or assumed) proliferation of states like Iran, Iraq, and Syria has been characterized as the "missile envy" of immature men.[74] The possession of and potential to use (paired with restraint from actually using) a particular class of weapon puts a belligerent firmly within a technological and tactical idealized masculinity. This idealized masculinity, though, is secondary to the one where a state has the ability to destroy others' possession of and potential to use such weapons of mass destruction. On the other hand, as Lauren Wilcox points out, "many defensive developments in military technology have been seen as emasculating since they lessen the importance of traditional warrior values of personal courage, physical strength, and honor in warfighting."[75] Generally, these defensive developments are the ones that decrease the level of physical confrontation among war-fighters and/or protect defenders without requiring their bravery or personal risk. While it is important to note that gender-based associations of weapons choices with manliness and emasculation can change over time and place,[76] it is equally important to pay attention to the impact of these associations on the choices of tactics militaries make, as well as on the public perceptions of those choices.

One recent example of the salience of gendered discourses about a weapon choice is general discontent expressed by the United States' opponents about its dramatic increase in the use of drones for intelligence purposes and as weapons of tactical-level warfare.[77] Particularly, as Peter W. Singer describes, U.S. military use of robots and drones is interpreted as a decline of the U.S. masculinity (and, relatedly, its capacity for global dominance), because it is cowardly to kill with a machine rather than looking an opponent in the eyes, and "real men" would not use drones and robots.[78] These discourses simultaneously challenge U.S. state masculinity and U.S. military prowess, suggesting that there is something inherent about warfare that requires the bravery of face-to-face combat usually associated with the masculine citizen-warrior, and anything less just will not do.

In fact, discourses of emasculation are used to describe not only the use of new technologies but also other tactical choices (or mistakes) seen as weakening the chooser's position and/or eschewing traits understood to be masculine and (therefore) good for military confrontation. The *Washington Post's* description of Stanley McChrystal's interview with *Rolling Stone* provides such an example:

> While General Stanley McChrystal opened his inner sanctum to a *Rolling Stone* reporter, he violated more than just the military chain of command . . . . in a White House full of message mavens, in an administration where access to decision-makers is fiercely defended, this was an enemy conquest . . . .and he's talking like he's in ninth-grade at an all boys' school.[79]

The remainder of the article references McChrystal's errant discussions of sex and sexuality, suggesting that his exposure of himself was just that, and that compliance with the values befitting a military decision maker worthy of making U.S. strategic and tactical decisions in Afghanistan was expected of but not delivered by McChrystal.

But how to reconcile the shame of McChrystal's revealing his inner sanctum with the seduction of the potential to penetrate Iran's? What is the relationship between the discourses of masculinity of the possession of nuclear weapons and the discourses of femininity in the employment of drones? These discourses' foundations can be all found, I argue, in gendered perceptions of chivalry influencing how certain tactics are seen (and thus whether, and how, they are used) in wars.[80]

Lauren Wilcox uses these gender tropes to account for a World War I–era belief that the use of airplanes to drop projectiles in wars was unchivalrous[81]—resulting in the use of planes "mostly for reconnaissance, support of ground troops, and more prominently, attacks on enemy planes"[82] and creating controversy over the use of planes for bombing.[83] This is because it had long been "held as an article of faith that honorable combat was personal—specifically, that the warrior could not strike without himself being at risk"—a holdover from the Middle Ages.[84] As such, "technologies which make it strategically advantageous for soldiers to lie in wait, hold back, and defend" have been feminized in tactical discourses.[85]

By contrast, hand-to-hand combat remains romanticized in tactical discourses, despite its increasing infrequency, because many "facets of chivalry have a strong resonance with us today."[86] This resonance can be seen in the popularity of martial arts training, the prevalence of hand-to-hand combat in movies and television shows, and the valorization of soldiers who fight on battlefields as traditionally conceived. Idealized militarized masculinity, then, centers around the idea of bravery—and how a tactic relates to bravery is a key part of its evaluation and potential use in war. This phenomenon is manifested in the sexualized images and discourses that Carol Cohn has recognized as key to war-fighting generally and the use of technology specifically,[87] especially insomuch as masculinized/sexualized discourses of weapons as male birth/creation[88] are accompanied by feminized discourses of *war cleanliness*.[89]

The implication is that, while not determinative necessarily, discourses of masculine chivalry are still very influential in the selection, practice, and reading of military tactics. As such, the selection of wartime rape as a tactic is not the only gendered tactical choice that belligerents make. Instead, tactical choice itself is based at least in part on gendered tropes that rely on the association of a particular sort of militarized masculinity and war-fighting. In this way, looking at tactical decision-making through gender lenses shows not only that gender considerations weigh heavily in tactical decision-making, but also that there are important and fundamental links between gender-based expectations and the tactical decision-making constitutive of war-fighting practices. It is this intrinsic link that provides an explanatory logic for the discussions in the next two sections about gender itself as a tactic of war-fighting, both in the weaponization of women and the weaponization of femininity.

THE WEAPONIZATION OF WOMEN IN WAR(S)

When I argue that gender is not only constitutive of tactical war decisions but is itself a tactical war decision, I mean that claim in several senses. As I discussed in the first section of this chapter, rape is often used to target men's and states' masculinities, using gendered assumptions as a weapon of war and marking the preservation of traditional ideas about gender as an indicator of of the preservation of the traditional state. In this section and the next, I explore gender as tactical in a different sense—the sense of the explicit use of gender tropes as weapons, either through women's bodies as weapons of war or through feminization as a tactic. This section discusses women as war weapons.

The very idea that women can be weapons of war seems counterintuitive. After all, even putting aside the fact that weapons are usually inanimate[90] and women are generally understood to be human,[91] traditional images of femininity as nonviolent make *women as weapons* difficult to grasp.[92] Traditional feminine images put emphasis on women's innate peacefulness, related to experiences with mothering and care work. Such emphasis means that the idea of women as weapons of war is incommensurable with many (if not most) cultures' prevailing notions of femininity. Women's violence or even the deployment of women for violent ends, then, "falls outside of these ideal-typical understandings of what it means to be a woman"[93] and seems to contradict "protection racket" narratives of women as the state's feminized others who must be protected in war(s). That is because

> Violent women, whether terrorists, suicide bombers, war criminals, or perpetrators of genocide, interrupt gender stereotypes about women, their role in war, and their role in society more

generally: women who commit proscribed violence are not the peaceful, war-resistant, conservative, virtuous, and restrained women that just warriors protect from enemies . . . Instead, these women are a security threat themselves.[94]

As discussed in detail in chapters 5 and 7, the ideal-typical woman in many wars and conflicts is the biological and cultural reproducer of family, state, and nation; the backbone of family structure; the defender of faith; and the source of life. A woman who engages in wartime violence, then, seems to be interrupting traditional notions of femininity as pure, innocent, and nonviolent. Yet, "in almost every culture and every period of history," women emerge as warriors and war weapons, often framed as "far deadlier than the male" whose fighting is normal.[95] In three subsections, this section explores that paradox by looking at two of the major violent roles women play in wars briefly (as terrorists and as soldiers) and then discussing theoretically how women came to be weaponized and the implications of that weaponization for tactics specifically and war generally.

Women as Terrorists

Though terrorism is frequently framed as the exclusive domain of men and masculinity, women's involvement in terrorist[96] acts and/or insurgent groups is neither particularly rare nor particularly new. In fact, though women's engagement in terrorism has only recently gained scholarly and media attention,[97] women have been a prominent part of a number of twentieth- and twenty-first-century insurgent and terrorist groups, including the Iraqi insurgency, Abu Sayyaf (Philippines), the Zapatistas (Mexico), the FARC (Colombia), the Taliban (Afghanistan), the Kurdistan Workers' Party (Turkey), the Sendero Luminoso (Shining Path, Peru), al Qaeda (globally), Hamas (Palestine), the Liberation Tamil Tigers of Elam (LTTE, Sri Lanka), Republican and Loyalist groups in Northern Ireland, and the Symbionese Liberation Army (the United States).[98] In addition to general participation, women have played leadership roles in a number of terrorist and insurgent groups, including the Red Brigades (Italy), the Weather Underground (the United States), the Baader-Meinhof Gang (Germany), Prima Linea (Italy), the People's Liberation Front for Palestine (PFLP, Palestine), and the ETA (Spain and France).[99] Women have engaged in high-profile attacks as well, including airplane hijacking[100] and the killing of Indian Prime Minister Rajiv Gandhi.[101] Women frequently engage in terrorist activity, sometimes for organizations that include in their missions an explicit commitment to gender equality, but more often than not for organizations that could be characterized as conservative on gender issues.[102]

Many if not most of these women are left out of scholarly analyses of terrorism. Even when women's terrorism is analyzed, violent women are rarely characterized as having chosen their violent actions and even more rarely portrayed as having made a reasoned choice.[103] Ironically, when the mainstream literature recognizes women as weapons, it is often in an abstract and dehumanized sense that makes women's violence seem so counterintuitive. For example, in many discussions of women suicide terrorists, the woman martryr is not a person who chose the self-martyrdom for some (personal or political) reason, but instead a part of the technology of the bomb apparatus—a literal weapon.

This section argues that the weaponization of women terrorists is not reducible to women as inanimate conduits for bombs. Instead, "this voiceless picture of women terrorists, however, shows a lack of knowledge and understanding," particularly as "sensationalized media coverage of female terrorists follows a storyline that portrays women as only capable of becoming bombers if they are dominated by men."[104] This is a problematic view because it frames women as less capable of agency in their actions and less political than men, reifying women as separable from and less than men. At the same time, it is possible to simultaneously critique the negative implications of the account of women terrorists as without agency in their violence and recognize its salience in the tactical practice of conflict, especially as it influences decisions such as when to weaponize women.

Even assuming (I believe correctly) that women (like men) have limited but existent agency in their decisions (generally and to engage in terrorism) and that women (like men) choose terrorism for a variety of personal, social, and political reasons,[105] those commonalities alone do not make women's terrorism *like* men's terrorism. Even when women commit similar acts for similar reasons as men, those behaviors are read differently, making women's terrorism distinguishable if by its reception alone. Many policy makers perceive terrorist organizations "use" or inclusion of women as an ominous sign, both because violent women are more likely to fool victims who assume women's peacefulness and because fighters' "use" of traditionally nonviolent women shows a level of desperation indicative of the abandonment of "rational," "civilized" thought and/or behavior.[106] It is for these reasons that women terrorists are frequently perceived as more dangerous than men, given the shock value of their acts along with access to more sensitive areas than men may be able to penetrate.[107]

Women terrorists, then, are not weapons in the traditional sense of a nuclear warhead or a MOP bomb. But they are, nonetheless, weaponized, both by their actions and by the significations of the groups that weaponize them and the victims of their violence. At the same time, as I will discuss below, the very presence of a female body in the places that it is assumed that only male bodies ought to be is a tactical choice with important reverberations. Before discussing this theoretically in more detail, however, I will briefly introduce another violent role that women play in war(s): soldiers.

Women as Soldiers

Just as women have been involved in terrorist organizations with significantly more frequency and prevalence than many have noticed, women's presence as soldiers and fighters in most of the major conflicts in world history has had limited visibility. Still, across the history of warfare, women have been military leaders, soldiers, and support staff in military organizations. While some accounts of women fighting in (or even leading) battles are well-known (the Amazons in Greek mythology or Jeanne d'Arc in France), others have received little if any notice in historical accounts of their battles and wars.[108]

In ancient times, there is evidence that women had key roles in conflicts across the world, including the battles to eject the Chinese from Vietnam, the (alleged) Korean defense against the Japanese invasion, several battles for control of the Roman Empire, the siege of

234 • GENDERED TACTICS

Lacedaemon, several biblical campaigns, and the Peloponnesian War.[109] In the Middle Ages, Priestess Hind al-Hunnud commanded troops in a battle against Muhammed[110] around the same time that Saint Genevieve allegedly diverted Attila from Paris.[111] From Kahina in the Berber resistance in North Africa[112] to Akkadevi in the Indian siege at Gokage,[113] tales of women's bravery in are often erased from historical accounts of war(s). Women fought as Vikings,[114] as knights,[115] and as generals[116] from Sweden to China. Women's participation in war-fighting as soldiers and commanders has become more frequent and more frequently recognized since the advent of the Westphalian state system. Substantial involvement of women soldiers has been recorded in the American Revolution, the American Civil War, the Mexican Revolution, the Russian Civil War, the Spanish Civil War, World War II, the Korean War, the Vietnam War, the Iran–Iraq War, and the civil war in Sierra Leone, among others.[117]

These women's fighting happens often but is rarely (and often only recently) visible. When women's fighting, like women's terrorism, is recognized, it is often as something fundamentally different than men's fighting, even when women are doing the same things as men for the same reasons. Women's soldiering is often talked about as *women's* soldiering, rather than simply as soldiering that women do. Rather than being accounted for as normalized in war (like men's soldering violence is), women's soldiering violence is often explained in terms of extremes in or flaws of their femininity, their maternity, their physiology, or their sexuality.[118]

This is in part because giving women the same jobs as men in militaries does not transform those militaries into gender equal or gender neutral institutions.[119] While several militaries have developed policies specifically aimed at the integration of women into their ranks,[120] those policies have not generally reached the level of "mainstreaming" gender.[121] Instead, these women are allowed to participate in a military force still dominated by masculinities. In addition to formal restrictions on which military roles women can fill[122] and a perceived glass ceiling on women's advancement in militaries,[123] women enter militaries that have transformed their "gender balance" while paying "little attention to the discursive and performative elements of gender dichotomies."[124] A woman soldier, then, is a woman who can demonstrate her masculinity without losing her femininity. She is included in wars not because militaries have questioned or changed their privileging of masculine values, but instead because she is willing and able to adopt those masculine values in her participation in these militaries.

Militarized masculinity remains a standard—it just becomes a standard that women can approximate, if not meet. Still, what women must do is be *masculine enough* without losing femininity. Therefore, though women increasingly fight in wars, they often get caught in a gender-stereotype catch-22: they take all of the risks that men do, while missing both the reward and the elusive status of equality. The result has been "the preservation of the discursive structures of gender-subordination even in gender-integrated militaries."[125]

At the same time, the deployment of women *as women* has become much more pervasive in recent years. For example, the U.S. military has recently begun the deployment of "FETs," or female engagement teams, in Afghanistan.[126] The effort to start "building connections with the local population" aims at getting "that information that a woman is willing to share with another woman."[127] The job of FETs is to "develop trust-based and enduring relationships with the Afghan women they encounter on patrols" using the commonalities of womanhood.[128] Examples like this demonstrate that women's participation in militaries can be both read and deployed sex-specifically even when it is intended and enacted similarly to men's participation in those same conflicts in those same roles. The next subsection discusses how to read women as weapons and suggests some theoretical and empirical implications of understanding the weaponization of women's bodies.

Women Weapons

While the association between (expectedly peaceful) women and (by definition violent) weapons is hard to make, women's bodies have been wielded in service of war aims in a number of contexts, both symbolically and materially. This is not only true when women are terrorists or soldiers, but more generally. For example, a number of people have used the rhetoric of women's rights and women's liberation as a cultural challenge (as well as as justification for military challenges) to Islamic countries, governments, and cultures.[129] Additionally, there is a sense that a woman in the same position in the same military in the same war as a man is a different thing, and, potentially a more powerful weapon. This comes, as Caron Gentry and I once argued, with perceptions of women's violence as a monstrous outgrowth of the extremes of (still fundamentally peaceful) "real" or "normal" femininity.[130]

Perhaps this is why news media repeatedly describe women soldiers as weapons. In Kelly Oliver's words, "women warriors are not referred to as women with weapons or women carrying bombs, but their very bodies are imagined as dangerous."[131] For example, Kelly Oliver described "an example of the most astounding modern weapon in the Western arsenal" as "named Claire, with a machine gun in her arms and a flower in her helmet."[132] Claire was apparently not just holding a weapon, but a weapon herself, because the element of surprise and horror coming from a *woman* soldier prepared to fight to kill would be a military advantage. Likewise, gendered characterizations of women interrogators have shown that women soldiers not only carry weapons but are weapons themselves. There was media fascination with the United States "using" women as interrogators at the prison at Guantanamo Bay.[133] Particularly, a *Time* magazine headline read "female sexuality used as a weapon," as if the fact that the interrogators were women was an extra tool in the military arsenal—one that was irregular and somehow especially scary and dangerous.[134] The sex of interrogators was especially isolated as a weapon in itself when accusations of prisoner abuse became rampant—*women interrogators' womanhood was a tool of abuse*. According to the *Washington Post*:

> Female interrogators repeatedly used sexually suggestive tactics to try to humiliate and pry information from devout Muslim men held at the U.S. military prison at Guantanamo Bay, Cuba, according to a military investigation . . . The prisoners have told their lawyers, who compiled the accounts, that female interrogators regularly violated Muslim taboos about sex and contact with women. . . . The inquiry uncovered numerous instances in which female interrogators, using dye, pretended to spread menstrual blood on Muslim men.[135]

In this account, there are women who are accused of committing war crimes in their interrogation tactics, but there is more to the story. The fact that the interrogator is a woman is in this account a weapon in itself—her femininity, as it interacts with a masculine realm, is itself dangerous, taboo, and therefore to be leveraged. Underlying the conflict between the U.S. government and its detainees are two key *agreements*—first, that the realm of militarism is a realm of masculinity to which women do not belong (where the United States has added them as a tool of aggression and shame, which has affected its detainees), and second, that women's femininity (and particularly their sexuality) is an effective weapon against traditional masculinities.

Similar stories can be told of accounts of women as terrorists—women terrorists are not only weapons the way male terrorists are—where a person literally becomes a bomb in a suicide mission. Instead, women suicide terrorists are a modern-day, double-edged sword; they are a different sort of weapon *because they are women*. As Kelly Oliver reports, "the *London Times* described Palestinian women suicide bombers as "secret weapons" and "human precision bombs . . . more deadly than the male."[136] This is because women terrorists' femininity is a special weapon—in terms of access to secure areas[137] and signification of desperation,[138] both related to the shock value of the gender transgression involved in women's violence.

It is not only in the twenty-first century that women's femininity has been seen as a dangerous actual or potential weapon in wars. Before women like Claire were featured in *Time* magazine with a machine gun in their hand and a flower on their helmets, women were bombs in the jungles of the Vietnam war(s).[139] Before women were themselves frequently suicide terrorists, they served Palestinian militant organizations as support personnel who crossed Israeli checkpoints with the materials for suicide bombs.[140] Before women were tank commanders in the Iraqi desert, Jeanne d'Arc led troops into battle against the British.[141]

In these accounts, women *are* bombs, they *hide* bombs, and they *build* bombs.[142] Women *as weapons* happens in two important ways: women are the physical weapons and *as the physical weapons*, they have some (actual or symbolic) value assigned to them on the basis of their (perceived) gender and their performances can play on gender stereotypes to interrupt or disrupt sex-based interpretations of how wars are fought to gain a tactical advantage.

At the same time, some see it as difficult to reconcile the weaponization of women *as women* and the "beautiful soul" narrative that constructs women as states' feminized others in need of protection from the very horrors of war that (states and nonstate actors) ask some women (to) commit.[143] After all, if women are (necessarily innocent) civilians in war-justificatory narratives and traditional notions of femininity paint women as necessarily peaceful, women's engagement in violence and the use of women as weapons seems to interrupt both key stories. I argue that a closer look at understandings of the weaponization of women, however, maintains a clear narrative of appropriate femininity, from which violent femininities are to be distinguished.

Elements of the old "beautiful soul" narrative are evident in the account of (helpless) weaponized women terrorists, characterized as nothing more than conduits for bombs and victims of their own violence.[144] Characterizations of femininity as necessarily innocent or nonviolent are also evident in accounts of women soldiers, from concerns about physical and sexual violation during Jessica Lynch's captivity in Iraq to the deployment of FETs to penetrate the private sphere in Afghanistan.[145] Even accounts that blame violence on the flaws in violent women's femininity are careful to distinguish those women's (problematic) femininity from the ideal-typical womanhood, which remains peaceful, calm, and removed from violence (and therefore in need of protection).[146] Idealized militarized femininities retain traits associated with the inherited beautiful soul narrative, despite women's increasing likelihood of sharing both the responsibility for and the costs of wars. The weaponization of women's bodies and the increasing attention to that weaponization is altering the traditional gendered narrative of war-fighting, but seems to be reifying many of its essential elements.

FEMINIZATION AS A TACTIC

It is the persistence of those essential elements of gendered war narratives that makes feminization an effective and frequently employed war tactic. Earlier in this chapter, we discussed wartime rape as a tactic that emasculates the men of the enemy by violating women when such a violation shows men's incapacity to fulfill the fundamental masculine function of protection. This section argues that this phenomenon, termed *feminization*, is used more broadly as a tactic of war-fighting.[147]

Feminization is intentional subordination, because things that are feminized can be seen as falling lower along social hierarchies of gendered power than things that are understood to be gender neutral or associated with masculinities. R. W. Connell has talked about feminization in war and conflict as the subordination of nonhegemonic masculinities to hegemonic masculinities by the (discursive and material) assertion of power and control.[148] As I mentioned above, the example in which it is easiest to see feminization as a tactic of war is in war rape. Particularly, a male victim of war rape is feminized. This does *not* mean "he" is *made female* in the process of being raped. Instead, it means that the signification of the act feminizes "him" by treating him in ways that show the dominance of "the masculine" over "the feminine." This is not to say that femininities or masculinities are either singular or dichotomous in the process of feminization. Quite the opposite—it is possible to feminize masculinities, and there are not one but many paths to feminization.

While war rape and sexual abuse can be expressions of feminization, so can other tactical choices, including bombings, declarations of war, battle plans, and a number of other options. Though patriarchy requires the subordination of women to men, feminization renders those who are feminized (regardless of biological sex) subservient to dominant discourses and performances of hegemonic masculinities. In Tim Kaufman-Osborn's words, feminization constitutes "a strategy of power" implicating "scripted practices of subordination designed to create helplessness and dependence" by association with the feminine.[149] As Mary Hawkesworth accounts,

Underlying the logic of feminization in each of these instances is a vindictive construction of femininity. Those who are produced as "feminine" are weak, violated, silenced, docile, obedient, humiliated, and craven. The solution to their existential situation is invariably a masculine assertion of power for which the appropriate feminine response is gratitude. This is the discursive gender regime produced and reproduced.[150]

In this way, "feminizing processes simultaneously produce and justify profound inequalities" by "trading on forms of gender symbolism that naturalize hierarchies of dominance and subordination."[151]

In previous work, I have used the example of U.S. military conflicts with Saddam Hussein's Iraq as a demonstration of the use of feminization as a tactic by both sides of a conflict.[152] Similar discourses took place between U.S. President George W. Bush and former North Korean dictator Kim Jong-Il, who Bush called an "evil little pygmy" and compared him with a "spoiled child at dinner time."[153] Kim Jong-Il's aides responded in kind, labeling Bush a "philistine" and a "hooligan" and questioning his ability to run a stable government with a predicable foreign policy.[154] Characterizing George W. Bush as "undistinguished" and "hostile" and comparing him to Hitler, Kim Jong-Il attempted to paint himself as the model of restrained masculinity in contrast to Bush's impulsiveness.[155] Bush, in turn, characterized the North Korean leader as a tyrant who was a danger to "his women and children," evoking a moral imperative of protector masculinity against the hypermasculine other.[156]

These feminizing discourses can be seen in a number of other international conflicts as well. Feminist work on the phenomenon of feminization has demonstrated that this tactic does not remain at the level of the exchange of quips between leaders in a conflict, however.[157] It is often evidenced at the traditional tactical level of war-fighting as well, where the feminization of soldiers, prisoners, and civilians expresses a message of domination from one belligerent to another. An example of such tactical feminization can be seen in the prison abuse at Abu Ghraib committed early in the American invasion of Iraq.

The public image of this prisoner abuse was American soldier Lynndie England standing over the sexually abused body of an Iraqi prisoner of war, though more than a dozen American soldiers and private military contractors were implicated in the abuse that took place at the prison.[158] Still, the question of why the images of American women (and men) (sexually) abusing Iraqi prisoners that dominated the coverage of and public reaction to the scandal did so—why they were so salient—is an important one. Feminists have suggested that a sense of superiority of American (militarized) masculinity may have created social space to allow the occurrence of the torture, which feminized the inferior masculinity.[159] The images of the prisoner abuse at Abu Ghraib silently tell a story of the ultimate humiliation of Iraqi masculinity because Iraqi men were deprived of their manliness by American women.[160] The result of this social dynamic is pictures of American men and women raping Iraqi men.[161]

As first, it seems doubtful that feminist observations about the community effects of sexual abuse can be translated to the situation at Abu Ghraib. If sexual abuse is directed toward those identified as men, it is not an attack on women. When rape is directed toward men, it is a masculinity or a group of masculinities that is being attacked and subordinated. The masculinity being attacked here is that of Iraqi men. Male prison guards attacked Iraqi men's masculinities not only by subjecting them to the torture of (often homosexual) rape but by allowing them to be subjected to torture at the hands of women—feminized by the feminine. Sexual abuse of Iraqi men by American women communicates (whether it was intended to or not) a disdain for Iraqi masculinities so strong that subordinated American femininities are the appropriate tool for their humiliation. Sexual torture is certainly about power, but were it only about power, there are plenty of nonsexual ways to express power over people. Sexual torture is about comparative *sexual power*; here, the sexual power of American masculinities and militarized/masculinized femininities over their reading of Iraqi masculinities. The story of the prison abuse at Abu Ghraib is about power and sexual power—but the currency of gaining both of those forms of power as well as of inflicting it on the enemy is feminization as a war tactic.

Feminization as a war tactic, however, is hardly the product of twenty-first-century conflicts. Instead, other feminist scholars have documented feminization as a war tactic in a number of contexts. As Elisabeth Prugl documents, "feminization of enemies was widespread throughout the ancient world" and included "the execution of men" as well as "the castration of prisoners, anal rape of enemy soldiers, and insults that intonated homosexuality or effeminateness."[162] Jack Cheng and Marian Feldman find that, as King of Assyria more than three millennia ago, Tukulti-Ninutara used to call on the gods to change the enemy from a man to a woman by dwindling his manhood away.[163] Sidney Donnell finds feminization of the enemy, particularly through involuntary transvestism, to have been a common theme in both the practice and dramatization of militarism in sixteenth- and seventeenth-century Spanish imperialism.[164] Nalia Ceribasic finds the feminization of the enemy in Serbian practice and musical representations thereof in 1991–1992, in which "the process of feminization of the enemy is also achieved . . . by the use of the diminutive . . . the representation of the enemy on the rum . . . [and] mocking the female" on the battlefield and off.[165]

These and a multitude of other examples across time, place, and conflict show the use of feminization to subordinate enemies, to communicate messages of subordination to enemies, and to communicate messages of dominance and superiority to domestic audiences. If it is a sense of masculinity that inspires men to fight and gives them pride in themselves and the cause that they are fighting for, it is essential to construct the enemy as something other than the masculine ideal that brings pride to the good men who fight wars.

It follows, then, that states will always feminize their enemies if the valorization of their masculinity is key to their will to fight. As Joshua Goldstein explains, "they assume a masculine and dominant position relative to a feminine and subordinate enemy."[166] Still, like gendered nationalism, the feminization of enemies is not a constant. Goldstein implies that the feminization of enemies depends on the absence of actual women in the conflict, which "frees up the gender category to encode domination."[167] Others have suggested that the feminization of the enemy depends on the racial/cultural dynamics between (presumed autonomous) self and other, with hyperfeminization being applied to those seen as culturally or racially inferior.[168] Still others have suggested that the feminization of a state's enemy is based on its size and perceived virility in the international arena.[169]

If feminized images of the other state are rare, and rely on subordinate masculinities rather than outright association with feminine characteristics, then we might expect a state to choose tactics of restraint, interpreting the low level of feminizing rhetoric as proxy for respect and perceived membership in some sort of peer class. If feminized images of the other state are constant and vicious in the period leading up to the fighting of the war, then we might expect bolder tactical choices reflecting a relationship wherein the state does not take the enemy seriously as a competitor or adversary. In other words, we might expect the boldness of a state's chosen tactics to vary positively with the degree and frequency of feminizing rhetoric toward its opponent as the conflict that leads to war develops. In these ways, feminization is weaponized *as a tactic* and becomes another discursive, symbolic, and physical tool to attack the gendered foundations of an opponent's (collective) motivations for war-fighting and (individual) dignity.

LOGISTICS, GENDER, AND THE POLITICAL ECONOMIES OF TACTICS

If it is important to look at the gendered nature of war rape as a tactic, gender in tactical decision-making more generally, and the weaponization of both women and femininity, this section contends that it is also essential to look at the logistical operations in war(s) through gendered lenses. Often, logistics are assumed to be purely process-based and (therefore) gender neutral, but this section argues that war's most banal processes are the location of many of its most serious genderings. In fact, embedded in many historical descriptions of logistical troop movement, we find descriptions of assumptive violation of the feminine and violence against women. One description accounts for soldiers passing through a town to "thoroughly trash the place, abuse the women, [and] steal everything portable."[170]

These offenses are often explained away by the difficulties of moving troops. This is because the movement of troops in medieval wars can be seen both as a key feature of the civilian experience of war and as an element of war with gendered elements and gendered impacts. Medieval forces had difficulty moving food for the fighters and even more difficulty moving food for animals that they moved with or on. They stole what they could not carry, and slept wherever they found themselves, with or without permission. Also, medieval generals had significant amounts of trouble with what we might now call disciplinary issues—their troops wanted to (and sometimes joined militaries for the privileges of) rape and pillage—and very little could be done to stop it.[171] The literature often characterizes these issues as the logistical challenges of pre–Industrial Age warfare.

If these issues are logistical challenges, they are also (gendered) impacts on peoples' lives. The wartime maintenance of fighting forces, like the other dimensions of the fighting of war(s), is more than it appears on the surface and has a number of gendered dimensions and gendered impacts. These impacts include, but are not limited to, the exploitation of women's labor and increases in rape, prostitution, and disease.[172] From the early modern military days when moving troops occupied homes from which they required the production of food and provision of shelter[173] to the current use of prostitution-based camptowns to service soldiers stationed far from home,[174] the movement of military troops has always been reliant on the (gendered) interaction with the people that are being moved on, through, and about.

It is therefore important to note that gender can be seen at every level of logistics, and not just in pre–Industrial Age warfare. In the wars of the twentieth and twenty-first centuries, states rely on women to motivate recruitment, encouraging men to show bravery and shaming them into protection.[175] Women are often asked to serve their countries by taking over the jobs that men leave to fight wars and giving up those jobs when men return.[176] They are asked to entertain men (at USOs),[177] to write letters to them as they fight wars,[178] to provide militaries with support (nursing, cooking) labor,[179] and to serve militaries in a variety of sexual capacities.[180] Women are expected to give troops when they are asked and are forced when they are not asked.[181] Logistical support systems commandeer the resources normally available to manage households, and often commandeer households.[182] Base economies interfere with local economies, and troops moving through or stationed in particular locales increase the level of sexual and domestic violence, both by committing that violence and by creating atmospheres of violence. [183]

Widespread "gender violence by 'friendly' forces against their own" is just the tip of the iceberg, as "military men have come to expect sexual servicing not just as a perk but as a right and even a necessity."[184] Troops sexually exploit (and rape) the "locals" not only at home but wherever they are, creating tiers of (sexual) economies.[185] Those sexual economies include prostitution, bush "wifehood," forced sexual encounters, unwanted children born out of wartime sexual abuse, breakouts of sexually transmitted diseases, trafficking and migration crises, and other difficulties.[186]

Looking at logistics through gender lenses reveals not only that women are often differently situated as compared with men in wartime logistics and that logistical processes are deeply sexed and gendered, but that there are gender implications in almost all facets of logistics, such as the production and transportation of weapons; the shaping, support, and movement of soldiers; and the maintenance of troops. This is because, as noted in chapter 5, the contemporary practice of war relies on the existence of women behaving *as women* to fill war's support functions.[187] As such, the simple processes of logistics are not gender neutral but have gendered impacts, and the differences among them are not trivial but may have differential impacts on the margins of societies in (and on) which wars are fought.

Gendered impacts of logistics are wide-ranging and diverse. For example, the feminized experience of logistics for South Korean women of the (continuing, cease-fire held) Korean War, includes the establishment of class-stratified camptowns for prostitution, the separation of proper Korean femininity and the women servicing those camps, an uneasy link between prostitution and patriotism, and a developed fetishization of Asian femininity by white, Western (militarized) masculinities.[188] By contrast, the feminized experience of logistics in Sierra Leone's twenty-first-century conflict featured abductions of teenage girls as bush wives and soldiers, woman-headed households looking for available refugee camps and other migratory spaces, social stigmas attached to both abducted women and war babies, household food rations stolen by troops passing through, and general confusion about the identity of neighbors and friends as well as their side(s) of the conflict.[189] Though they are very different, both experiences (and countless others not recounted here) show an intrinsic link between gender expectations, sexed bodies, and logistical operations and support.

THE POTENTIAL CONTRIBUTIONS OF A FEMINIST RESEARCH PROGRAM ON TACTICS AND LOGISTICS

When we think about the ways tactics are gendered, some are obvious—like wartime rape as a gendered tactic or the gendered implications of forced impregnation. Others, such as the gendered nature of the development of and decisions to use military technologies and/or the use of feminization as a tactic of war-fighting, sometimes easily slip under the radar of discussions about gender and war-fighting as theorists tell stories that plausibly account for those things as gender neutral. As this chapter has shown, though, these "gender neutral" accounts of the fighting of war(s), the choice of weapons, the progression of military technologies, and the symbolic wars waged along with the material ones, leave out gender as a crucial factor of not only interstate but intermilitary and battlefield interactions.

If traditional scholarship about tactics asks how tactical choices are made, gender lenses suggest that gendered tactics can be employed both generally and in the service of gendered strategic ends. If traditional scholarship on tactics suggests that technological development and rational strategic thought combine to produce available tactical options for belligerents, feminist inquiries suggest that technological development genders and abstracts tactical options and tactical choices. Gender lenses also expand the list of tactics that should be seen as available to and used by belligerents, particularly looking to belligerents' tendency to fight wars on women's bodies through wartime rape; to weaponize women as soldiers, insurgents, and terrorists; and to weaponize femininity at both the strategic and tactical levels. Finally, while traditional scholarship either downplays logistics or sees logistics as gender neutral, gender lenses show the gendered nature of logistical practices and their sex-differential impacts.

As a dialogue with traditional scholarship on tactics, then, this chapter has suggested that it is important both to broaden the view of how tactics are chosen and to pay specific attention not only to the ways that tactics are gendered but the ways that gendering itself can be seen as *tactical* when deployed as a weapon against enemies. This chapter has argued that, like strategic choices, the tactical and logistical parts of the practice and performance of warfare are fundamentally gendered, and these genderings impact why they happen and how they happen.

As a dialogue among feminisms, feminist theorizing of tactics and logistics pushes the traditional gender analysis of wartime rape as a gendered tactic to see the operation of gender in tactics more generally. It also suggests that gendered tactics are multiple and operate at multiple levels, where women's bodies are weaponized in gendered ways but feminization does not always rely on the presence of women or their bodies. It asks feminists looking at what happens to women's bodies during war to, while maintaining attention toward that crucial factor, broaden their gaze to see gendered tactics used as communication among men and among states.

Engaging theoretical approaches to tactics and logistics challenges feminisms and the mainstream theories that they criticize to conceptualize the (bi-directional) relationships between strategy and tactics, seeing gendered tactics as manifesting gendered strategies, and gendered strategies as selecting for gendered tactics. Understanding these complex relationships can provide a more accurate picture of how tactics are chosen and how they are performed.

These linkages, however, not only aid the study of tactics specifically, but the study of war more generally. As chapter 9 will explore, gendered tactics and logistics are a part of the gendered nature of the practice of war(s), and the gendered practice of war(s), paired with the gendered nature of the causes of war(s) discussed in chapters 3 through 6, make the experience of war gendered as well.

Living Gendered War(s)

International relations theory generally and the work that I have classified as war studies specifically talk about the causes of war and the fighting of wars with frequency and ease. The chapters in this text have engaged the questions that war studies traditionally asks both on their own terms and critically, but this chapter argues that traditional accounts of wars as made and fought are importantly partial. Instead, as critical security theorists have noted, there are a number of dimensions of war(s) that traditional theorizing does not analyze.

As discussed in chapter 2, feminist theorizing often includes a political commitment to understanding the world from the perspective of those most socially subjugated in it, and it is in that context that it looks to transgress and redress gender subordination.[1] This chapter contends that looking at war(s) from the perspective of people marginalized in global politics reveals war(s) as lived, experienced, and felt, rather than just made or fought. In it, I explore what is to be gained by understanding experiences of wars through gender lenses.

Accordingly, this chapter deals with the question of how wars are lived. The first section explores the idea of "living" wars both through narratives of (gendered) lives who live (gendered) wars and through theorizing experience in wars through gender lenses. The remainder of the chapter leverages this work to understand particular ways in which war is experienced. The second section analyzes the gendered political economies of wars by looking at where women are (as actors, as victims, as participants, and as all of the above) in war economies and how women navigate the gendered political economies of war(s) to see how women survive in, adapt to, feel, and understand the gendered experience of war(s). A third section recognizes that it is not just women who live through the gendered experience of gendered wars and gives attention the ways men live wars. A fourth section theorizes both men's and women's gendered experiences of war together as a part of war as a sensed experience. This chapter concludes by analyzing what the lived, gendered experiences of war might mean for defining war through gender lenses.

GENDERED EXPERIENCES OF GENDERED WARS

Hedy Epstein escaped from Nazi persecution via the Kindertransport to England when she was 14, in 1938. Since arriving in the United States in 1948, she has been a strong advocate of the rights of Palestinians, protesting Israeli aggression in the Free Gaza movement, founding the St. Louis chapter of Women in Black, and traveling to the Gaza Freedom March with Code Pink. During nonviolent protests, Epstein has been assaulted, labeled a terrorist, and lost her hearing to an Israeli sound bomb meant to break up a protest. Still, she explains, "I'm an inveterate optimist, so someday, there will be peace," and, in her eighties, marches with women's peace organizations all over the Middle East and North Africa in pursuit of that elusive goal.[2]

Fifty-one-year-old Samira Ahmed Jassim was arrested in January of 2009, under allegations that as a member of Ansar al-Sunna, "she directly supervised training of more than 80 female terrorists in Baghdad and Diyala."[3] Nicknamed Um al-Mumenin (mother of believers), she confessed to running a training camp that provided expertise, supplies, targets, and support for twenty-eight woman suicide bombers. Some reports, however, allege an even darker side to her work, claiming "she was a part of a plot in which young women were raped and then sent to her for advice" and "she would try and persuade the victims to become suicide bombers as their only escape from shame."[4] Though these reports were "not supported by subsequent investigations," they portray a certain idea of a monstrous, violent woman.[5]

Suhail Najim Abdullah Al Shimari was arrested at his Baghdad home and taken to a prison called Abu Ghraib on November 7, 2003, where he was held by the U.S. military and private contractors for four years "without ever having been charged with any crime or having received judicial process."[6] Suhail was not only deprived of food and sleep, subject to sensory deprivation and extreme temperatures, threatened with dogs, and threatened with death; he was subject to sexual abuse. He was kept naked, forcibly shaved, and was forced to engage in sexual activity with other prisoners. He also watched another prisoner be choked to death. After being released, Suhail returned to his family land and began to farm for a living. He has filed a lawsuit against several private military contractors for torture and other war crimes.[7]

Kate Bartholomae was trained as a nurse by a convent in the early twentieth century in Germany. Her early career was spent working in a hospital related to her convent, but the advent of the World War I changed that. When the *Chicago Tribune* reported on her life in November of 1914, reporter James O'Donnell Bennett characterized her as a "fitting example of the 'sisters' who mother Kaiser's men," as she worked at a hospital for wounded soldiers near a dismal railway station at Maubeuge.[8] Kate, working long hours with few resources, was responsible for helping soldiers heal physically and emotionally. While it was expected that she return the soldiers to the battlefield as quickly as they were physically able to engage in combat, she was also charged with making sure that the soldiers were *geistesvorbereitung*—emotionally prepared—to do battle for their country, despite having being seriously injured once.

In December of 2009, the U.S. military announced a policy designed to punish with criminal charges or court-martials women who "fall pregnant" and men who impregnate female soldiers while stationed in Iraq. Major General Anthony Cucolo, commander of U.S. forces in northern Iraq, "defended his decision as a means to help guard against the loss of valuable female soldiers" who return to the United States upon becoming pregnant.[9] Though the policy was revoked several days later without ever going into force, "the Army has struggled with balancing parenthood and soldier readiness ever since it added a significant number of women to its ranks."[10] Susan Struck was one of the first soldiers to experience this, as the first Air Force officer in history to give birth while on active duty, in 1971. Her involuntary discharge was upheld by the U.S. Supreme Court on the grounds that the Air Force had "a compelling public interest in not having pregnant female soldiers in the military establishment."[11]

A Sudanese woman, "Beth," recounts being the victim of war crimes committed by the Ugandan Lord's Resistance Army as it kidnapped people in Sudan and Congo between September 2008 and June 2009. She remembers that, "at night the fighters used to tie the abducted men to one another, make them lie on the ground, and cover them with a plastic sheet . . . they would then take all the women to the bush and rape us. They barely gave us any food and would beat us on a regular basis with sticks, the butts of guns, and their fists."[12] "Beth" reported that, six months after having been freed, she remained haunted not only by the torture she experienced, but also by the terrors she watched others endure, including the chopping off of limbs, removing of teeth, and death by machete.

Leath Chumbory is the leader of Cambodia's first all-woman de-mining team, looking for land mines in one of the most heavily mined areas of the world. She argues that what her team lacks in speed and strength, they make up for in patience and effort. She contends that they are "a real example of what women in Cambodia can achieve," and thinks that the effort will provide a model for Cambodian society, "empowering the women and encouraging strong bonds between them."[13] Working to end war is important to Leath Chumbory, who was once enslaved by the Khmer Rouge. After walking 400 kilometers, she built dams for fifteen hours a day under the constant threat of abuse and death. During her enslavement, she witnessed the deaths of her father and two brothers at the hands of her captors. Chumbory now works do de-mine Cambodia, so that those living there, particularly her daughter, "are able to live their lives free from the threat of landmines."[14]

Hedy, Samira, Suhail, Kate, Susan, "Beth," and Leath experienced different conflicts at different times in different parts of the world, and played different roles in the conflicts that they experienced. Many are women, one is a man. Some looked for peace, like the well-known Women in Black,[15] Women's International League for Peace and Freedom,[16] Code Pink,[17] and Greenham Common.[18] Others played a supporting role from home, like the American icon Rosie the Riveter in

World War II[19] or the soldiers' wives that Cynthia Enloe finds crucial to the possibility of the 2003 war in Iraq.[20] Others served in the capacity of providing logistical, moral, or health care support in the field, similar to Joan Cote in USO[21] and Clara Barton with the Red Cross.[22] Still others soldiered,[23] were members of rebel groups,[24] or engaged in terrorist activity.[25]

What these seven people have in common, despite all their differences, is that they lived, sensed, felt, and experienced war(s) and conflicts in gendered ways, as countless people have and will across the history of war. While war and conflict are constantly changing, as are gender relations, war-making and war-fighting remain gendered, and not only at the causal and operational levels that get attention in "mainstream" war theorizing. While war has gendered causes, gendered practices, and gendered consequences, it is also lived and experienced in gendered ways. The (gendered) experience of war(s) gets little attention in the war studies literature, but gender lenses reveal it as an important aspect of theorizing war(s). Gender is a key factor in the causes/choices of going to war (and what war is), in the practices/performances of war (how wars are made), but also in how war is received/experienced. Sex differences and gendered expectations pervade how people *live* wars.

This is why it is important to understand war through gender lenses and see it as not only caused and practiced, but lived and experienced. The neglect of theorizing war as experienced or lived in contemporary war theorizing is related to the neglect of the feminine in those approaches. In Cristina Masters' words, the "feminine has been historically constituted as outside of politics and a problem that contemporary war theorizing continues to reproduce."[26] That feminine has also been associated with personal feelings about and/or reactions to war(s). Citing Ronit Lentin, Masters sees dire impacts to the related omissions of the feminine and lived experience in war theorizing:

> Woman, due to her function as a vehicle of ethnic cleansing and to her sexual vulnerability, arguably becomes femina sacra at the mercy of male sovereign power: she who can be killed, but also impregnated, yet who cannot be sacrificed due to her impurity.[27]

In other words, the gendered formulations of war-making and war-fighting discussed in previous chapters are reliant on a narrow understanding of what is to be seen and understood about war. Expanding war theorizing to include how wars are experienced, lived, and felt could be a rich contribution not only to seeing what happens to women and/or how gender is deployed, but also what war is, how it comes to be, and how it is practiced.

Feminist theorizing provides an important framework for understanding war as experience and experienced. First, feminists have cast war as an experience in (and not separable from) everyday life[28] and a "repetitive politics of violence that crosses human history."[29] In this framing, war as an experience is to be conceptualized both as normalized and as pervasive. Starting with the lives of people, Christine Sylvester contends, give us not just a different method of studying war but a different view of war, one which

> draws our attention away from strategic and national interest politics of war to the prospect of theorizing war from a starting point of individuals, the ones who experience war in the myriad of wars possible—as combatants, casualties, voyeurs, opponents, artists, healers, grave diggers, and so many other identities. What unites them all is the human body, a physical sensing entity that can touch war, and an emotional thinking body is touched by it in innumerable ways.[30]

Understanding that "we all touch war or are touched by it"[31] makes questions of "what people see, feel, hear, smell, and even taste when they are confronted with violence in international relations" of both substantive and methodological interest.[32]

In Judith Butler's understanding, such an exploration is not only of interest but essential both to conceptualizing war (as discussed above) and to understanding gender as a condition of possibility of war, given that casting "enemy" populations as (already lost) existential threats whose experiences of war are irrelevant to making and fighting those wars is essential to war-justifying narratives, war-making policies, and war-fighting strategies.[33] In this view, it is crucial to see wars as lived, because a blindness to the living of wars both limits the scope of war analyses and is a constitutive feature of contemporary war-making.

Theorizing war as lived, then, is a key part of theorizing war(s) from a feminist perspective. While the project of understanding all of the ways that war is seen, felt, heard, smelled, and tasted is perhaps impossible and certainly beyond the scope of this chapter, it is both possible and necessary to explore some of the major dimensions of the ways in which gender is interwoven with the ways in which war is lived. That is the task of the remainder of this chapter.

LIVING WARS' GENDERED POLITICAL ECONOMIES

One of the ways to understand how wars are lived is to see how they impact the daily lives of people who live through them. This section looks at both first-order and second-order impacts of war on daily lives through an attempt to understand how wars affect people. It uses political economy lenses for two primary reasons. First, war is rarely seen *as a political economy*, yet most of its first-order affects on people at the margins of global politics are political-economic in nature. Second, looking at war *as a political economy* illuminates many of the gendered aspects of how it is experienced.

A number of first-order impacts of war on people's lives are well-documented, often (misleadingly) as though they were gender neutral. For example, in times of conflict, families are often separated by forced migration, economic migration, war-fighting, or war casualties. Within families, each member assumes additional burdens as regular divisions of labor are overturned[34] and household systems that have developed over time to deal with crisis situations are lost.[35] Economic resources such as land, farming resources, and animal herds are often either looted or destroyed.[36] Health also deteriorates as individuals lose access to health care due to poor supply chains and the need to treat soldiers. Health challenges are often even more severe for refugees, whose camps often lack basic necessities such as clean water,[37] which makes hygiene difficult and increases risks for infectious disease.[38] The lack of access to water also compromises families' access to nutritious food, setting off a cycle of poor health and malnutrition.[39]

Once society's normal institutions have been debilitated or destroyed by war, then politics, culture, production, and protection come to be defined by militarization. In Cynthia Enloe's words, militarization is "a step by step process by which a person or thing gradually comes to be controlled by the military or comes to depend for its well being on militaristic ideas."[40] As Ronni Alexander reminds us, people come to see, hear, feel, touch, and taste war.[41] Militarization comes be a condition of daily life. Most obviously it influences troops and rebels participating in the conflicts, even if they are participating in a peacekeeping operation or an act of humanitarian intervention, but it also bears on civilians who are not formally part of the conflict. Militarization at a global level can spawn economic, military, and political processes that infest social and everyday life at the local level. The damage created by these processes also has sex-specific effects.

One of these is based on relative vulnerability. Studies show that the first to feel the health, economic, and social effects of wars are women and children, who find themselves on the margins of wars and war economies.[42] Pre-existing social organizations and sex-based expectations often compound these effects. For example, in many societies, the household or "domestic" economy is characterized by a division of labor that is based on sex.[43] These sexual divisions of labor dictate how households manage resources. In times of crisis, sexual divisions of labor are also part of the way in which family units confront crisis.[44] In times of war and conflict, these roles shift. When men become participants in the armed conflict or are forced to migrate because of the conflict, the roles of other family members shift. Women must assume the household responsibilities that were previously performed by men.[45] In economic terms, families who are forced to separate suffer from the lost income provided by the missing family member. Women who must flee or who are left behind are often left without the main source of family income. Children also assume new roles as a result of the departure of male family members.[46] If male members of households are killed or leave permanently, then the women left behind struggle to provide for the family despite restrictive gender roles in their societies. They may lack access to credit or financial institutions and are restricted in the ability to obtain employment or administer farms. In this respect, the sexual division of labor not only constrains the freedom of individuals in the household, it literally threatens households' chances of survival during times of conflict. The obstacles that women would normally face in terms of gender roles become compounded in light of destruction of infrastructure.

The resulting social upheaval also compounds the obstacles that women face in trying to provide for their families. War and forced displacement disrupt "social insurance" and other coping mechanisms on which women would normally rely, and these disruptions happen in gendered ways. Under conditions of war and conflict, family and friends who would often be a source of support most likely face the same obstacles themselves. The social networks themselves suffer, as it is women and their social interactions that often contribute to their creation and maintenance.[47] During wartime, these interactions are more likely to be constrained by other family members—particularly men and older women—because they may pose a danger in the climate of suspicion that war and conflict generate.

These transformations within household economies have a variety of different effects on the broader economy, and these effects manifest themselves in sex-specific ways. One of the most significant effects is the growth of illicit economies.[48] These illicit economies range from trade in resources and commodities such as timber, rubies, diamonds, and gold to drugs or even to trade in human beings.[49] The collapse of formal economies in war zones often pushes those trying to survive into these illicit economies.[50] Women are particularly vulnerable to survival work in the sex industry.[51] Beyond the effects on their personal physical autonomy and family life, prostitution exposes these women to the dangers of sexual violence and disease, including exposure to HIV/AIDS.[52] Sex industries during wartime tend to increase in volume and include more violence and force.[53]

The presence of soldiers, peacekeeping troops, and humanitarian aid agencies sometimes alleviates these dangers, but sometimes makes them worse and/or creates other threats. Many outsiders expect that women and girls will exchange sex for money, and peacekeepers, soldiers, and aid workers have all been involved in patronizing and sustaining prostitution.[54] Many participants in the illicit economy—drug and human traffickers keen to sell their wares—are drawn to (presumably wealthier) outsiders as well. The frequent coincidence of prostitution and human trafficking on one hand and the presence of soldiers, peacekeepers, and aid workers on the other hand leads many to view prostitution and human trafficking as natural by-products of war.[55] This view serves to solidify the links between sex subordination, gender stereotypes, and war-fighting. Through gender lenses, it is possible to see that the selling of sex and people is neither natural nor a necessary part of war— instead, this process is a key link in the chain of the gendered political economy that produces war and conflict and is in turn produced by it.[56] Feminist work reveals these links between gender subordination and the organization of wartime political economies.[57]

"Wedad's" experience in Iraq is a real-life example of this.[58] When her husband died in sectarian violence, Wedad lacked economic opportunity. She had three young daughters, and tried to get a job to support them, but found that the men interviewing her for jobs were less interested in her résumé than in her body. Though prostitution is illegal in Iraq, the militarized violence over the last decade has increased the demand exponentially. "Wedad" cannot get out of the cycle of prostitution because she has no support system and no other way to make a living, but she lives in constant fear of being found out, either by her daughters or by the law. Prostitution in Iraq increasingly caters to U.S. soldiers and private military corporations, and "the war has created an enormous number of homeless girls and boys who are most vulnerable to the sex trade."[59] An American army reservist reported that "for one dollar, you can get a prostitute for one hour," which is a key expectation of soldiers' "R&R."[60] Cynthia Enloe has recognized that these practices are not just incidental to the war, but constitute it.[61]

The risks of prostitution and sexual violence are not the only ways in which wars are often lived sex-differentially by women. War is lived in many areas of women's lives, including access to health care.[62] Several factors add up to make health care more difficult for women to get during war: conflicts destroy health care facilities, militaries consume health care resources, displaced people disrupt services, and general economic downturn makes services more expensive.[63] These dynamics have grave, and often gendered, negative outcomes on war-affected communities. Infectious diseases alone can exact a heavy toll, especially among the most vulnerable: babies, children, and women who are either pregnant or lactating,[64] exacerbating their vulnerability to a whole host of other conflict-related deprivations. If women are raped or forced into prostitution, their risk of sexually transmitted diseases and HIV/AIDS will be compounded.[65] Women's risks are increased when they are often the first to be turned away from health care facilities as resources become scarce. Even within families, household resources are often allocated away from women when food and other resources are inadequate to meet everyone's needs. Taken together, these dynamics mean that in times of conflict, women find themselves with more health and nutritional problems and less access to health care, both absolutely and compared with men. Even something as routine as menstrual cycles become difficult to manage due to the lack of materials, privacy, and sanitation.[66]

Women who are displaced as a result of conflict experience their own particular set of sex-specific threats.[67] In addition to the struggles that they face in keeping their families together, including coping with new economic circumstances and continuous physical threats, women also face difficulties in performing the functions associated with their traditional gender roles.[68] Something as simple as cooking, even when food is available, becomes more difficult by virtue of the lack of technology, particularly electricity. When they become displaced, women's ability to satisfy their specific nutritional needs, especially when pregnant, becomes compromised. When displaced women are pushed into refugee camps, they need to be constantly vigilant because of the increased threat of sexual violence to themselves as well as the possibility that their children will be subsumed into the conflict.[69] Militarization trickles down into the smallest details of women's daily lives.[70]

The tightening of regulation of traditional gender norms that tends to accompany war violence can exacerbate these impacts, because social and political limitations on women's activities both deny them equal access to resources and limit the availability of solutions to (relative and absolute) deprivation. All of these ways that war is written onto women's bodies are on top of the risk of "gender-based violence" or sex-specific targeting that can be omnipresent even in times of peace but increases in frequency and brutality during times of conflict. For women, sex-specific violence includes direct targeting, domestic violence, kidnapping, sex slavery, rape, and forced impregnation. This sex-specific violence has a performative, symbolic dimension that exists alongside the physical aspects of the brutality. Specific acts of brutality such as amputation (of arms, lips, and ears), kidnappings, torture, rape, and degrading humiliation have an undeniable physical component, but they are also seen as significant performance acts because they have many significations for both perpetrator and victim.[71] Communities create and respond to violence through mechanisms that include vital mechanisms for the performance, representation, witnessing, and retelling of gendered violence.

An example of this is Honorata's story. In 2002, Honorata was abducted by fighters in the Democratic Republic of Congo and taken away from her husband and five children.[72] She describes having been subject to torture, gang rape, sexual abuse, and constant humiliation for months until she was able to escape.[73] She walked 150 miles to be reunited with her children, only to be abducted into sexual slavery again.[74] When Honorata finally escaped yet again, members of her community rejected her both because she was a rape victim and because she was seen as cursed.[75] Honorata never saw her husband again, never received medical care, and was never compensated for her pain and suffering.[76] No one was ever prosecuted for the rape and sexual slavery she endured, and Honorata and her family continue to live among the perpetrators of such crimes.[77]

Honorata's story is far too commonplace in times of war, when women are the victims of extreme, sadistic, consistent sexual violence in atmospheres where there is little hope of medical care, prosecution, or justice and a significant risk of social stigma, pregnancy, disease, and repeated violence. This is not either incidental or coincidental, but a result of the reshaping of gendered identities (particularly masculinities) in times of conflict in ways that select for and encourage violence.

While Honorata did not become pregnant as a result of the multiple rapes she endured, many women do. Pregnancy adds a dimension to women's experiences of war and to how they are signified in war stories.[78] Pregnancy without adequate access to health care, perhaps even while enduring abuse, compounds the "common" hardships of pregnancy born of rape.[79] In wartime, pregnancy has a number of meanings that are inscribed on women's bodies. This is because one of the roles women play during conflicts is as the collective "womb" to be used for the perpetuation of the group itself and to create more warriors. These new identities rest on the view of women as "biological reproducers of group members needed for defense, signifiers of group identities, agents in political identity struggles, and members of sexist and heterosexist national groups."[80] When impregnated by their husbands or "friendly" soldiers, women experience pressure to carry the pregnancies in order to support the nation; when they are impregnated by soldiers from the other side, the women (and their children) bear a social stigma and experience isolation.[81]

All of these ways in which women experience war(s) are violent, sex-specific, and importantly reliant on gendered conceptions of people, states, and wars inscribed onto women's bodies. In some sense, these accounts are stories of women's victimization in wars through gender lenses. While they could be read to deprive women of agency in war(s), that is not the intent of this analysis. Instead, in my view, it is important to transgress the stereotypical assumption that women are either wars' victims or their agents but cannot be both. Important accounts of women's disproportionate (and different) suffering in wars point out the ways in which biological sex continues to evoke gendered treatment in the making and fighting of wars, which continues to gender war as a lived experience. At the same time, war as a gendered experience is not only received but also practiced and inhabited by women.

Therefore, it is important to pay attention to the fact that women are not limited to being victims of wars and their aftermaths. Instead, when women (personally or as a class) are victimized by wars, they endure wars, but they do not *only* endure wars. They are not, as the "beautiful soul" trope might have us believe, just innocent and helpless, without choices or contributions to making, fighting, or living wars.[82] Even though they often deal not only with pre-existing gender discrimination but also with the ways war exacerbates it, women often make choices about how to cope with, engage with, and react to war(s).

Women often choose to be a part of illicit economies. They make decisions about how to allocate scarce resources both among families in communities and within families. Women often make decisions about whether to stay in their homes despite the dangers of war or to risk the dangers of fleeing and looking to become refugees. They also choose where to place their political loyalties in order to get the best chance for survival and the survival of their loved ones in times of war.

Many of these choices are among bad alternatives and severely constrained. For example, the choice about loyalties sometimes takes the form of women becoming "bush wives" to insurgent groups to avoid brutal wartime sexual violence or death. In Sierra Leone, one such bush wife was Fatu Kamara.[83] Fatu was captured by rebels when they launched a raid on her village, and offered survival in exchange for being a bush wife. As a part of her "deal," "four men used her as a wife."[84] Fatu was also forced to cook and clean for her "husbands." She was made to fight in the conflict. She was, in some sense, one of the "lucky" bush wives, because she was able to escape by feigning illness and sneaking away, whereas most bush wives who tried to leave were killed. Still, when Fatu escaped, she was pregnant and had no access to food or shelter and no protection from other male fighters. Fatu's child was stillborn, and Fatu developed fistula (which caused her to constantly leak urine) as a result of the delivery.[85] Both because of her illness and the stigma of being a bush wife, "it was hard for her to rejoin her community."[86] Because of stories like Fatu's, the Special Court for Sierra Leone ruled that forced marriage is itself a war crime above and beyond the wartime rape that takes place within forced marriage. Because forced marriage included not only sex but other services, it encompassed not only wartime rape but also a form of indentured servitude. At the same time, many women are stigmatized for their "choice" of a bush wife lifestyle over either running from captors, dying for the cause, or fighting back.

This is one of many severely constrained choices that women make in navigating gendered wartime political economies. As I mentioned above, some women choose to participate in wartime prostitution. These choices are well-documented in conflicts like the Korean War, World War II, the Iraq War, and other modern conflicts. Wartime prostitution also occurs the places it is least expected, from historical conflicts such as the U.S. Civil War to contemporary conflicts in which sexual violence is almost invisible, such as the Afghan War or the Israel–Palestine conflict.[87]

It is problematic to discuss prostitution as a choice in traditional terms for a number of reasons. It is often a choice between bad options, wherein the alternative is almost always poverty, and often starvation, death, or wartime violence. It is also often semi-voluntary at best; women receive partial information about what they will be asked to do and partial (if any) compensation for what they have done. Many prostitutes who join the industry voluntarily are then not allowed to leave if they change their mind. Wartime prostitution often comes with physical and sexual abuse and almost always comes with gender subordination.

Despite all of these abuses, traps, and victimizations in wartime prostitution, it is important to see that it is not something just done to women but that women do. Making choices among suboptimal options is one of many ways women deal with the sex-differential impacts of war(s). These choices are (as discussed in chapters 4 and 6) are constrained and relationally autonomous, but it is important to see women's bodies as actors in war(s) rather than simply tablets with war(s) inscribed on them.

Another way women act in war(s) is by becoming fighters (as discussed briefly in chapter 8). Some women participate in state militaries. Like men, women have a variety of motives for military service, including the economic stability that comes from the military as a career, the feeling of personal safety that comes with having a weapon and belonging to the state's military, the collective identity that comes from being one of the "good guys" in a divisive intrastate conflict, an ideological sympathy with the cause for which the state is fighting, or a careerist desire to be a soldier. Women also join rebel movements during times of conflict, either as fighters or in a support capacity. Being part of an insurgent group may provide women with a community to replace the family or community group that has been broken up by the conflict. They also acquire steady access to income and/or food and a level of protection by the group that they would not have if they remained neutral in the conflict. Beyond this, women may also be drawn to the political causes of these groups, particularly when their agendas include a formal call for gender equality.[88] During times of conflict, both state and rebel militaries become more willing to include women.[89]

Women who do not participate on one side or the other as fighters or join illicit economies may look to capitalize on the war economies, which can be more fragile and open than peacetime economies and have heavily gendered structures. Women enter workplaces to replace men who have left to fight wars. Even positions in factories, medical fields, and other industries that were previously off limits to women may become available to them when men vacate their positions in favor of military service. They also often provide goods and services during wartime and look to make inroads into commerce, industry, and production, taking advantage of wartime economic "softness." Changes in the previous divisions of labor can result in women finding opportunities in their new situations. While some women benefit economically from wars, more often, women's role in war remains marginal. Most often, women are making sets of subsistence choices looking to survive in the face of war and gender subordination as they intersect.

While some women respond to war(s) by participating militarily or economically, others choose to reject war by participating in peace protests and peace movements, arguing that wars should be ended. This choice seems to reject many of the insidiously gendered properties of war, but often, even women who choose to deal with war through anti-war movements cannot escape the gender-differential impacts of fighting. These peace movements often entail significant costs to the women who participate in them. As such, even this opposition to war often exacerbates the gendered effects of war on women.

Particular women participate in the politics, economics, fighting, and even ending of wars, and all women serve a crucial symbolic function in the stories about why wars are made and fought. Still, it is important to note that, while women live (gendered) war(s) often largely as victims, it is also sometimes as their participants, manipulators, and even leaders.

IT IS NOT JUST WOMEN WHO SEE THE GENDERED IMPACTS OF WAR(S)

When we talk about the gendered impacts of wars, it is easy to talk about the sex-specific ways that women experience war(s) and how those war(s) impact women's lives. It is easy because women's oppression is both so primary and so invisible and because feminisms are fundamentally concerned with the question of where the women are in global politics generally and war(s) specifically.

That said, feminist scholarship looks not only for women, but for gender; and not only for women's oppression, but for the ways that gender hierarchies shape people's lived experiences and interactions, both generally and in terms of global politics specifically. This has led feminists to expand their understanding of what happens *to* women, seeing it as a crucial part (but only part) of the implications of gender hierarchy in social and political life. When we talk about gender and lived experiences in war(s), then, women's experiences *as women* are only a part of the story. Men's lived experiences *as men* are also important, as are the masculinities and femininities that constitute both men's and women's lived experiences.[90] It takes this focus to emphasize the importance of realizing that not only women, but also men, experience war(s) in gendered ways, and feel the negative impacts of the co-constitutive relationships between gender and the war system.

While some "good" things for "men" result from wars—heroism, chivalry, and the like—many men's relationships with war(s) are not as straightforward as (hegemonic) militarized masculinities might suggest.[91] As Raewyn Connell notes, "the costs to men and boys from the existing gender order have increasingly been publicized."[92] While patriarchal power and masculinized gender hierarchies remain dominant in global politics, the "benefits" to such a system are often distributed unequally. As such, "the sexed bodies of men and the injuries of masculinity emerged as significant sites of enquiry in our investigations into relationships between power, gender and violence."[93] It is, then, a key part of the feminist scholarly mission in war studies is "to keep open and reopen debates about how sex, gender, masculinity, and femininity are implicated in one another."[94]

Both in this chapter and before, this book has done a lot of work on how gender-essentialist notions of what "women" and "femininity" are impact women, and how those expectations are foils of, and dependent variables against, hegemonic and/or ideal-typical masculinities in global politics. Similarly, though, and despite a difference in power in which masculinities dominate the debate, the things that we expect of *men* (since we associate them with masculinity/ies) are dependent on, and related to, their contrast with femininities and their place in gender(ed) hierarchies.[95] Much as individual women's choices and experiences are colored by the expectations of what women as (assumedly feminine) women can and/or should do, individual men's choices and experiences (of war and more generally) are influenced by expectations of what men as (assumedly masculine) men should and/or can do. This is particularly true for masculinities because, in Charlotte Hooper's explanation:

> Masculinity appears to have no stable ingredients and therefore its power depends entirely on certain qualities constantly being associated with men. Masculine spaces are precisely the places where such associations are cemented and naturalized. Therefore, even the marginal appearance of women . . . . together with feminist ideas, and/or other self-conscious references to gender issues, may sufficiently alter the overall ambivalence of such spaces that their masculine associations become weakened.[96]

Therefore, when confronted with questions of femininities/feminisms, hegemonically/hypermasculine spaces like the making and fighting of wars potentially react in two ways (either simultaneously or in conflict): by shoring up masculinities and/or protecting the masculine heritage of the concept, idea, or practice; or by fundamentally changing. Both responses have impacts not only on the theoretical, conceptual, and symbolic gender hierarchies in war, but also on how people's (including men's) lives are lived.

Along these lines, men experience war(s) in a number of gendered ways. Cynthia Enloe explains that "militarized forms of manliness" not only pervade the militaries of modern states, but shape both military and state identity.[97] The ideal-type in a given society is used by soldiers and citizens to "construct hierarchies of militarized masculinity among themselves."[98] Enloe is not arguing that *the same* gender norms dominate and define citizenship in every state around the world. Instead, she explains that "variations in militarized masculinity may deserve more of our attention," especially because "particular variations do not only spring from diverse cultural groundings; they may also be dictated by historically significant militarisms."[99]

As Joshua Goldstein notes, one of the major gendered effects of war(s) on men is that men are expected, trained, and often required (by conscription or otherwise) to be soldiers in service of war causes.[100]

Male soldiering remains a norm even when women are included in militaries, both because "gender-inclusive" militaries largely still exclude women from (elite) combat positions and also because the ideal-typical soldier remains gendered masculine if not embodied male.

While many narratives about soldiering read a desire to fight onto individual men, a number of analysts have argued that stereotypical notions of masculinity are relied upon to do a fair amount of the work to convince men both to risk their lives and to commit acts of brutality. This is because stereotypical notions of masculinity in war(s) at once demand brutality (to demonstrate bravery) and obscures the same brutality (as heroism).[101] This means that ideal men are not either killers or afraid to die, but given the common knowledge that idealized masculinity is linked to an image of the male warrior, and refusal or inability to fight is characterized as feminine.[102] Traditionally, maleness is associated with war-fighting and femaleness is associated with the need for protection that necessitates the war.

If women are expected to play the role of beautiful souls, innocent others, mothers, biological and social reproducers of nations and fighting forces, and supporters of war efforts, men are expected to be good soldiers, military sons, good comrades, and civilian strategists.[103] In each of these roles, the concept of heroism is dependent on "masculinity, virility, and violence" and their intersections.[104] In this way, masculinized just warriors occupy a privileged position in state gender discourses, because their monopoly on taking up arms in defense of the state makes them more valuable than those who hold characteristics associated with femininities or even other (subordinated) masculinities.[105]

The masculine warrior-hero image impacts men who fight wars, but it also impacts men who do not fight. It does so in two ways. First, while some men do serve as soldier-protectors, masculinized warrior-hero narratives imply that all men could or should fight. In this way, masculinity remains necessarily staked on war-fighting. As Judith Stiehm explains, "some men have become actual protectors; the rest remain potential protectors" and the ability to serve as a protector is a key part of validating manliness.[106] The gendered role assignments in just war are crucial to producing an army that will fight. The second impact, then, is that men who are either unwilling or unable to fight are on the defensive about their masculinity—which falls into question.

That is why, as we discussed in chapter 6, standards of masculinity play a large role in procuring men's willingness to fight wars.[107] Because *men* are produced rather than born, and *manhood* is an achievement rather than a pre-existing status, war heroism becomes a way to make men and achieve manhood.[108] Unwillingness to protect or fight becomes a signifier of femininity, while successful fighting becomes a signifier of masculinity. Heroic masculinities become a goal of manhood and are enforced (often violently) by both men and women on men.[109] As Joshua Goldstein notes, "women are often active participants in shaming men to try to goad them into fighting wars."[110] This is because sex-based expectations of men based on gender stereotypes often constrain the ways in which men live and experience wars.[111]

Gender tropes in war mean that men are pressured to meet expectations of masculinities—as actual or potential protectors (and therefore as actual or potential soldiers).[112] As such, men are expected to go through the brutalities of war and to do so bravely and without complication.[113] The reality/ies, of course, are not that simple—many if not most men are afraid to fight wars, and war is hell.[114] Men have to be prodded, encouraged, and shamed into performing war(s) and often suffer both during and afterwards, though that suffering is often required to be silent, because it does not fit in with idealized images of (heroic) militarized masculinities.[115] As Barbara Ehrenreich has explained, "the difference between an ordinary man or boy and a reliable killer, as any drill sergeant could attest, is profound. A transformation is required."[116] The process of military indoctrination is often a process of deconstructing and rebuilding soldiers into idealized images of militarized masculinities.[117]

This indoctrination deeply impacts how men live and experience wars in a number of ways. First, men often fight in wars that they may not have otherwise fought in because of the incentive structures of militarized masculinities.[118] They experience brutal war-fighting during the conflict. Those who survive are subject to a long list of physical and psychological effects of war over the course of their lives, including, but not limited to, a high instance rate of post-traumatic stress disorder (PTSD).[119] Indoctrinated militarized masculinities have also been shown to increase both the length and brutality of wars and conflicts, because the motivation to fight and kill does not automatically disappear when a political solution to the conflict is found (especially given that the motivation to fight is often not located in the political conflict [which ends] but in aspirations to idealized manliness [which continues]).[120]

SENSING WAR(S)

Wars do not just "impact" people (men and women) in countable (if gendered) ways, wars are embodied, felt, and sensed. Part of experiencing war certainly is the content of this chapter so far—what happens to people, the choices they have, and the constraints placed on them are important parts of how those people see, feel, and experience wars. Still, it is important to understand that the experience of war cannot be reduced to what happens *to* people combined with the choices they make. If we are really to read war(s) as experience(s) rather than just event(s), it is important to see more depth, particularly in terms of feeling and sense. This is because things like wartime rape, PTSD, homelessness, and migration happen *to* bodies and are *felt*, both physically and emotionally. War's impacts, then, and the experience of war(s), are often explored in a one-dimensional way that looks at what happens to people during war in the aggregate or along particular axes related to health, economics, or the like. This is why feminists, in contrast with traditional war theorists, have long been interested in a wider variety of experiences *as political*—looking not only into parliaments and militaries but households and brothels and churches and beauty salons.[121]

The location of war changes but so do the senses that are necessary to understanding war. As such, feminist scholarship has begun to ask how wars are lived, felt, and sensed as emotional and physical.[122] Studying how war is felt is a tricky enterprise, fraught with potential methodological and conceptual stumbling blocks. Still, the feminist literature provides a number of tools to help work toward an understanding of war and feeling. The first tool, patience, can be found in Cynthia Enloe's discussion of the gendered phases of war(s):

> Gendered wartime phases marked the Iraq War as well. For instance, Iraqi women's beauty salons did not become the target of bomb-throwing militiamen at the outset of the Iraq War. They were set afire in its second gendered phase, when some men organized into militarized groups had convinced themselves that a certain practice of feminized beauty was subverting the country's wartime civic order . . . this is not to argue that all wars proceed lockstep through identical gendered phases . . . . [yet] paying attention to these eight particular women over the time throughout this one war has taught me to cultivate a long attention span.[123]

The second tool can be found in how that long attention span needs to operate with an ethic of care in order to see and collect how war is felt. Such care is by definition contingent and interdependent,[124] as well as both normative and practical.[125] It is the practice of care that makes feminist theorizing particularly interested in exploring *feeling* wars and that is key to the study of how wars are felt. I argue that we should look at how wars are felt with an ethic of care, caring both for the subjects of the research and the feelings that they have.[126] Such an ethic of care is cognizant of equity, subjectivity, relationality, diversity, value differences, and gender subordination.[127] Operationally, such an ethic of care suggests researching wars' senses empathetically.

In these terms, as discussed in chapter 7, empathy is engaging with the feeling, spirit, or essence of something outside the self for the purpose of seeing or experiencing it fully, not only hearing but feeling others' stories and being changed by that experience.[128] Empathizing, therefore, is neither having others' experiences nor pitying them when you cannot. Instead, it is, on some meaningful level, feeling others' pain[129] and thereby establishing a sense of solidarity.[130] In feminist war theorizing, empathetic research is performed with eyes and ears focused toward political and social subordination.[131] It is for this reason that the question of how war is *felt*, even when such feeling is not visible or obvious or in the locations where we traditionally look for the impacts of war(s), is not an experience that feminists see as individual or apolitical, *even when it is unique*. Feminisms recognize that war takes place on the individual, state, and global levels, and therefore must be considered at all of those levels simultaneously, without privileging the state over the needs of individuals.[132]

War is not something that people can participate in without being affected by it; relational autonomy means that people are in part defined by their experiences. Moreover, war is not something that occurs solely between states with body counts for their casualties. Men and women with names die in combat, lose their families and homes in collateral damage, and fire the weapons that cause other men and women with names to suffer. Empathetic cooperation with others *personalizes* the suffering of the enemy and makes war an emotional experience for participants. Empathetic cooperation makes war both a *personal prosecution* and a *personal experience*.

That personal experience cannot be relived, but it can be heard and empathized with. It is not possible to relive Hedy Epstein's loss of her parents, the torture that Suhail Najim Abdullah Al Shimari went through while he was a prisoner of war, or the pain that "Beth" felt as she was raped and imprisoned. It is not possible to *feel* Samira Ahmed Jassim's motivation for recruiting and training suicide terrorists. It is not possible to endure Leath Chumbory's enslavement, or watch injured soldiers suffer with Kate Bartholomae. While it is clear that there is no reliving, re-experiencing, or re-feeling these lived experiences of war, it is equally clear that they were once lived and felt. To suggest otherwise, or to ignore the lived and felt dimensions of those people's wars, seems on-face ridiculous as one reads and hears their stories through gender lenses.

Recognizing war as meaningful on the personal level requires any definition of war to address attacks on the quantity and quality of individual life, both materially and emotionally. War is traditionally defined as the use of military force to protect and bolster the security of the state in terms of safety from attack and safety of state interests. Feminists revision war theorizing which is concerned with how war is felt, sensed, endured, experienced, tasted, and smelled. A feminist understanding of security includes the diminution of all forms of violence—physical, structural, and ecological.[133] People's experiences of wars, then, are both personally and macrotheoretically significant when those experiences are abstract and when they are embodied; when they are physical and when they are emotional; when they are public and/ or publicized and when they are private and/or privatized. Thinking of war as something *people* feel is a whole different realm of thinking than considering war as something that is between states or involves people only insomuch as it impacts them.

EXPERIENCING WAR THROUGH GENDER LENSES

Much of this book, for the purposes of engagement, takes common definitions of *war* as given for the purposes of engaging theorists who interpret *wars* that way. I often accept the interpretation of wars as time-limited but sustained violent encounters between two or more political groups over some political dispute.[134] Still, even as this book engages those interpretations of war/wars, it does so critically and mindful of the contributions of feminist theorizing to rethinking not only the causes and consequences of war(s) and its/their logics, but what constitutes war and how it is defined. Seeing how wars are *lived* and *felt* through gender lenses helps inform a feminist re-reading of war and wars.

Some feminist scholars have argued that understandings of oppression that come from analyzing gender subordination lead naturally to questioning traditional understandings of the state, violence, and war on which war theorizing premises its assumptions. For example, as mentioned in chapter 2, feminist security studies shares understandings of security as broad and multidimensional.[135] This interpretation of security leads many feminist scholars to see that the impacts of war at the margins of global politics neither start when a war starts nor end when a war ends, and that the trauma(s) of war(s) sometimes continue from one war to another. Often, looking at security through gender lenses inspires scholars to talk about security in embodied terms, including focusing on "inequality, structural violence, militarism, maldevelopment, and human rights abuses [that] are not only relevant to our understanding of the multiple insecurities which people face, but profoundly affect the process of conceptualization and theorization too."[136] By prioritizing not only order but justice, emancipation, and deconstructing gender hierarchies, feminist theory provides ground to question when *war* ends and *peace* begins.[137] A number of conditions that do not initially appear to be within the definition of *wars* become clearly important, including, but not limited to, domestic violence,[138] structural violence,[139] economic instability, unemployment, poverty, poor working conditions, the impending threat of war, and/or infrastructural damage.[140] A war happens when state militaries clash, but it also happens when public housing units kick residents out of their homes;[141] when soldiers rape prostitutes;[142] when a state "takes out" a "key target" in another state, "incidentally" killing the night janitorial staff[143]; as well as in a myriad of other situations that traditional war theorists do not consider.

Seeing these wars *as wars* requires understanding war not as a clear and finite event but instead as a process or continuum without a clear start or end point.[144] The security concerns discussed above are features of life before, during, and after the event that *war* usually describes. The problem with not classifying these processes as war and security is that they are then accorded less weight in political discourse.[145] It is important to recognize that war as traditionally defined has impacts that are rarely seen and even more rarely understood at the margins of global politics, in human security impacts of traditional wars, and in other forms of political violence.

I argue that failing to see this violence as essentially not only related to but part of war neglects much of how war is lived and experienced outside the halls of power of great states and therefore misses many of the gendered dimensions of the making, fighting, and living of war(s). Crisis-based definitions of war obscure the suffering that leads up to and follows wars and distract attention from the accompanying everyday violence. Such interpretations, however common they are in traditional war studies, are necessarily partial.[146] In other words, "crisis-based ethics and politics are problematic because they distract attention from the need for sustained resistance to the enmeshed, omnipresent systems of domination and oppression that so often function as givens in most people's lives."[147] Chris Cuomo suggests that "the spatial metaphors used to refer to war as a separate, bounded sphere indicate assumptions that war is a realm of human activity vastly removed from normal life."[148] Instead, war is a process and a presence that affects and is affected by daily political life.

This reading changes both the content of the term *war* and its conceptual shape. Seeing war as a process of political life rather than a singular or discrete event allows for a broader umbrella of what counts as war to include many of the situations presented across this chapter. War happens when a leader is killed in an intelligence operation and/or a terrorist attack,[149] when a college student opens fire on campus,[150] and when one state military uses force to deny basic needs goods to the population of another state.[151] These events are not really events at all—they are parts of continual politically violent processes. They use violence to produce (and reproduce) insecurity at the individual level as well as at the international level. Reading this as a continuum, Betty Reardon called the international system a "war system," characterizing it as a continuum of structural and physical violence produced by and reproducing the masculine nature of the international political arena.[152]

Through gender lenses, the argument that war should not be seen as an isolated event is a powerful critique of war theorizing's traditional definitions of war. Most theories of war assume as foundational that war is a discrete event. Very few theorists of war analyze physical or structural violence before or after a war when they make determinations concerning the nature, causes, consequences, or ethics of a war. Even fewer deal with war as felt rather than purely material. Therefore, war theorizing often has no means to account for the suffering of a family that ate contaminated food during a food shortage in a war, went to a hospital lacking electricity and doctors, and/or had chronic stomach problems for the next twenty years.

War theorizing is generally similarly ill-equipped to deal with a child who grows up malnourished and, therefore, developmentally disabled because his mother did not have enough vitamins to enrich her breast milk for her child born during wartime. Traditionally, war theorizing has no tools to accommodate the woman who loses her life because she takes to the streets after having lost her job or the man who commits suicide, overwhelmed with care labor after the war injures his family. Confined, limited notions of war are inadequate to identify and analyze the institutional and structural violence that is an important part of the impact of international conflicts. Frequently, theories of war are isolated from the everyday life impacts, experiences, and feelings of such inter- and intrastate conflicts.[153]

Looking to rewrite and therefore re-understand the concept of war, feminisms have looked to analyze its gendered dimensions. But, as we have been discussing, when looking at war from the perspective of women's lives, it becomes apparent that the category *war* itself is problematic. The idea of war as a discrete event with an identifiable beginning and end and a clear location does not stand up to scrutiny when we examine women's experiences before, during, and after war or when we think about what is required to wage war.

Instead of taking account of militarism and structural violence, war theories often draw lines between war and horrific violence that is "not war," creating an illusion of neatness not present in the world they analyze. In fact, theories of war often only attempt to account for a fraction of the coercive force in the world today—that which occurs in organized combat between recognized and recognizable combatants sponsored by political organizations.[154] Gender lenses looking at war(s) look beyond national militaries' engagements on battlefields to find wars' genderings.

Still, Betty Reardon's understanding of all violence as sexist and all sexism as inherently violent is difficult to appropriate as a basis for defining war from a feminist perspective.[155] While it may represent what really happens in the world in important ways,[156] it contributes little leverage to many of the most important questions about how wars are made, fought, and felt, including, but not limited to, questions of variation in the causes, practices, and experiences of war(s).

Instead, I suggest that feminist war theorizing read the continuity of war(s) through the gendered implications and significations of various violences. If gendered violence is a particular sort of violence that needs gender stereotypes and gendered assumptions as raw condition of possibility, certainly both war as traditionally understood and many things that fall outside of what is traditionally understood as war count as gendered violence. I propose that it is not useful to characterize all violence or even all gendered violence as war, yet war is more than declared military conflicts between states that recognize each other's legitimacy.

It is coercive violence used in service of competition and domination.[157] Such coercive violence usually (though not always) relies on the *masculinization* of self and the *feminization* of the enemy.[158] This cycle of genderings is not a series of events but a social continuum.

While the distinction may not appear to be immediately meaningful, feminisms attach substantial importance to seeing violence as a continuum instead of as a delineated and separate event in personal interactions of international politics. This understanding has the benefit of linking individual experiences to international policy[159] and making connections between violence against women in the home and violence between states in traditional notions of war. In fact, seeing war as an isolated event can actually be counterproductive for feminisms' goals of opposing gendered militarism. Cuomo explains that "crisis-driven attention to the declarations of war might actually keep resisters complacent about and complicitous in the general presence of global militarism."[160]

A modified understanding of a war system reflects feminisms' insight that violences are continua that run through different levels of interpersonal and political interaction. This analysis problematizes not only what war is constitutionally but also how wars are made causally. If war is a continuum, the idea of a decision to make a war suddenly becomes more complicated. Read as infinitely regressive, a continuum understanding of war deprives deciding to make war of having any meaning at all. That is not the intent of the deployment of a continuum approach to war in this chapter. Instead, this redefinition of war is meant to complement, build on, critique, and complicate, rather than render invalid, the work engaging with war as traditionally defined in the rest of this book. Recognizing war as a continuum can be seen as compatible with the idea that wars have separable identities and practices if we think about war as a continuum and personal wars as parts of that continuum.

Such a continuum interpretation of war has several implications. First, wars start earlier and go on longer than traditional interpretations identify; second, wars reach deeper into societies than conventional reports would portray; finally, wars can be fought with a wider variety of means by a wider variety of actors than previously imagined. This interpretation relies on intellectual and emotional connections with those who are affected by war; given this interpretation, feminist empathy analyzes levels of violence and war generally neglected by reactive approaches.

Seen this way, not only is war a continuum, war is a *gendered* continuum. Carol Cohn and Sara Ruddick provide a particularly useful understanding of war as a gendered institution.[161] They argue that war is dominated by men and masculinities, that the masculinities that perpetuate war are socially constructed as dominant, and that the words and meanings that shape our thinking about war and provide metaphors for the assignment of hierarchical value come out of those masculinities.[162] As such,

> State militaries, armed insurgent groups, multilateral security institutions, development assistance agencies, international financial institutions, humanitarian relief organizations, local and international nongovernmental organizations, parliaments and transitional governments, foreign ministries and defense ministries, courts and police forces—all of these shape the conditions within which women experience war and try to build peace, and all of them are gendered organizations.[163]

This expansion of the definition of war(s) is inclusive of the central theme in many feminist accounts of war as bound neither by space nor by time, but instead culturally or materially pervasive.[164] As Carol Cohn explains, "there is a continuum of violence running from bedroom, to boardroom, factory, stadium, classroom and battlefield, 'traversing our bodies and our sense of self.'"[165] Weapons of violence, and representations of those weapons, travel through interlocking institutions—economic, political, familial, technological, and ideological.[166]

When the fighters put down their guns, the social fabrics of war-torn societies are not automatically healed or restored; instead, infrastructures remain destroyed, families remain devastated and grieving, combatants remain traumatized, weapons and violence remain available, and environmental markings of war will be a constant feature for years, if not decades. Thinking about war as a continuum does not mean that it is impossible or useless to think of a difference or a line between war and peace or that there is not point in distinguishing between the intensity and frequency of violences. Such a definition recognizes that there is more to war and peace than a dichotomous reading of surface-level, interstate violence.

THE POTENTIAL CONTRIBUTIONS OF A FEMINIST RESEARCH PROGRAM ON WAR AS EXPERIENCED

This chapter has looked to understand war as lived, experienced, and felt. It began by discussing the different ways that war's experiences can be gendered, both by relating personal war experience narratives and theorizing the ways that gender maps onto how war is lived. That theorizing continued into a discussion of the gendered political economies of war, and the ways that women feel, experience, and navigate them, even when their choices are severely constrained. Arguing that the gendered nature of both wars and the societies they take place in means that women live and experience war in sex-specific ways, this chapter looked to trace those sex-specific ways in households, workplaces, economies, social relationships, health care provision, and other areas. Still, remembering the feminist lesson that *gender* and *women* are not synonymous, I also explored the gendered ways men live and experience war. Taking all these experiences into account, it proposed that war is not just caused and practiced or performed but also sensed and experienced and that understanding war as sensed and experienced changes not only how it is to be evaluated but also how it is to be defined and understood.

As a dialogue with war studies, this argument is a critique and a reformulation of traditional analysis of war perhaps in a more radical way than the engagements of previous chapters, because there is no easy "fit" for feminist analysis of war as a felt, experienced continuum either in the levels of analysis traditionally used to disaggregate the causes of war or the categories traditionally used to understand how wars are planned and fought. At the same time, it is as crucial an intervention in war studies as any of the feminist engagements that fit more easily, not least because the insights of an approach that sees war as both continuous and experienced is, through gender lenses, not only enriching to war theorizing but essential to even approximating a comprehensive understanding of war, conceptually, causally, or in practice.

This chapter has argued that feminist theorizing challenges the traditional scope of war theorizing in two key ways: seeing war as experienced and seeing it as continued. Seeing war as experienced renders situations and feelings traditionally deemed irrelevant to the study of war central to understanding it, while seeing war as continued extends the gaze of war theorizing not only substantively but temporally. As such, the material covered here suggested the productivity of a radically reformulated notion of war theorizing: thinking about how war is experienced.

While such a suggestion is a challenge to war studies, it is also a challenge to feminisms, as they look for tools to understand and theorize the lived experiences of war. This chapter explored some of those tools, beginning by analyzing war experiences materially and sex-differentially, looking at what happens to women and men during wars as a result of the gendered expectations of them and the gender stereotypes inscribed on them. It found that women are often victimized in wars both as a result of the gendered tropes that are inflicted on them specific to wars (and discussed in depth in previous chapters) and as a result of general second-class citizenship. It also found that expectations of what men are and how they should behave also shape men's experiences of war, arguing that war also relies on stereotypes of masculinity, influencing how men live wars in order to marshal men's willingness to fight, their capacity for brutality, their fortitude in continuing to fight, and their silence about the suffering as they do so and after.

Still, it highlighted the importance of theorizing women's experience in war (however disempowered) as not only happening to and written on women but lived by women as relationally autonomous actors. The joint task of theorizing victimization and agency in the same political situation is one with which feminisms struggle and one requiring a complex approach to analyzing war as experienced and sensed, such that seeing war as sensed does not get reduced to thinking about it as inscribed on bodies that do not feel and respond to those inscriptions.

Both as it suggests the reformulation of traditional definitions and analyses of war(s) and as it challenges feminisms to further explore war as experienced and felt, the idea of war as not only caused and practiced but *lived* has important implications. It argues that cause, effect, and performance are only part of the story—that war cannot be told without feeling. It asserts that material accounts of war's impacts are inadequate—they must be supplemented by social and emotional accounts. As such, this chapter has suggested that it is not only productive but essential to fill the void in war studies where it should account for war as sensed and sensory, and has tried to make a preliminary sketch of what that might look like.

Conclusion

(A) Feminist Theory/ies of War(s)

The different discussions, interventions, engagements, critiques, and reformulations in this book have looked to demonstrate both the broad potential for feminist war theorizing and its variety in providing pieces of the "war puzzle" both within the traditional landscape of what war studies finds relevant and as it pushes the epistemological, methodological, and even ontological boundaries of the study of war and conflict in global politics.

While a wide variety of feminists in international relations (IR) have done important work to reveal the gendered dimensions of war, security, and global politics more generally,[1] the mission of this project has looked to engage both feminisms and war studies differently. First, as I mentioned in the introduction, this book's primary purpose has been to demonstrate that not only does gender analysis enhance war studies, "using gender as a category of analysis transforms the study of war" because "the meanings, causes, and consequences of war cannot be understood without reference to gender."[2] Second, in demonstrating the importance of gender to war studies, this book looked to avoid a one-sided approach of critiquing war studies for its inadequacies or privileging the contributions of a particular feminist approach. Instead, using a dialogical method, it has looked for the contributions of various feminisms to conversations with various traditional approaches.

This concluding chapter looks to extend that dialogical approach to understand war(s) as productive of gender norms and gender norms as productive of war(s). It does so by first positioning this book in the broader debate in the field about the productivity (or lack thereof) of engagement with the "mainstream" of the field as it informs feminist work theorizing, engaging, looking to understand, and representing war(s). I discuss the importance of a dialogical approach not only in analysis but also in analyzing the results of that analysis. The chapter then engages feminist contributions to the meanings, causes, and practices of war(s) as they have been dealt with over the course of this book. The book ends (hopefully only to begin again) with a discussion of the feminist politics of war theorizing and suggestions for building a research program in feminist war theorizing.[3]

SITUATION, DIALOGUE, AND FEMINIST THEORY/IES OF WAR(S)

As I discussed in chapter 2, there is significant controversy among feminists about the value of the project of engaging mainstream and/or traditional work in IR, a debate that is perhaps more intense when the traditional work being discussed is work in international security, possibly the narrowest of IR's subfields.[4] Recently, several scholars interested in questions of gender and war have revived that debate, positioning feminist security studies very differently vis-à-vis the mainstream field. After briefly discussing this debate, this section will situate this book's dialogical approach to engagement as a "third way" and lay the methodological and theoretical groundwork to conceptualize its contributions to theorizing war from a feminist perspective.

The first perspective in this recent discussion is Mary Caprioli's, published in *International Studies Review* in 2004 as a part of a discussion on quantitative methods and feminist theory.[5] Caprioli takes what I see as a somewhat radical position of situating gender analysis firmly within the traditional boundaries of the field. She contends that feminism should sit among paradigmatic, theoretical, and empirical approaches to the study of war rather than outside, critical of, and encouraging transformation of those approaches. Citing Fred Halliday's argument that "gender is not the core of international relations or the key to understanding it,"[6] Caprioli sees gender as a variable that war theorists can pay attention to when they believe it is relevant and ignore when they believe it is irrelevant. In this view, "it is not as if consideration of gender will alter the teaching and research of international relations as a whole," and people who think it should "overstate the case" for gender-based approaches.[7] As such, incorporation of feminist perspectives "would not necessarily require a revolutionary recasting of the field."[8] This perspective sees gender as (sometimes) a part of war theorizing, sometimes not.

By contrast, there are those who argue that Caprioli's framing of the positioning issue is very problematic. For example, as I discussed in chapter 2, Sarah Brown argued that the "danger" in "uncritical acceptance by feminists" of gender-subordinating methods, ideas, and frameworks warranted a presumption against engagement.[9] Such "uncritical acceptance" might cause feminisms to lose their identity trying to fit into the masculine world of mainstream approaches to war and security, in Brown's terms.[10] Along these same lines, Christine Sylvester has expressed concern that IR is a place where "the bodies, assigned places, and evocations of 'women' are unproblematically marginalized," which creates problems for attempts to engage war theorizing through gender lenses.[11] While feminisms destabilize the boundaries of IR,[12] feminists are also concerned that engagement with war studies can destabilize the mission of feminism(s). As Emily Rosenburg tells us, "efforts to integrate women into existing theories and consider them equally with men can only lead to a theoretical cul-de-sac which further reinforces gender hierarchy."[13]

Recently, Annick Wibben has extended that argument to serve as a warning about the potential pitfalls of engaging the mainstream of the field in security and war theorizing. Taking what I see as a somewhat radical position of rejecting engaging the mainstream as such, she puts forth "a plea to recognize the dangers involved in establishing FSS [feminist security studies] as a subfield of security studies when feminist aims and the scope of their concerns explode its confines at every turn."[14] She urges feminists to "move far beyond a broadening and deepening of security studies toward an opening."[15] Wibben sees the scope of security studies as inadequate for, and caging of, the breadth, depth, and creativity of feminist scholarship about conflict, war, and security. Therefore, a level of disengagement, Wibben argues, is necessary such that "feminist security scholarship remains true to feminist methodological and political commitments, and to continual, radical, and deliberate critique."[16]

Particularly, contra Mary Caprioli's claims, Wibben argues that "it is, above all, feminists' methodological commitments that distinguish FSS from other approaches."[17] Working methodologically within, or methodologically engaging, (positivist) security studies is, in Wibben's view, not only limiting to but destructive of feminist thinking about war(s). This is, in Wibben's terms, because asking feminist research questions and answering them using feminist methods necessarily looks different than traditional war studies. Doing work within the confines of the mainstream therefore takes a significant amount of what is unique about feminist analysis away. Consequently, Wibben argues, "feminist security scholars cannot let traditionalists have the uncontested say about what the concept of security refers to, especially because security is so powerful when evoked."[18]

A feminist theory of war based on either of those perspectives would be radically different than the one put forth in this book. A feminist theory of war based on the idea that gender is not key to understanding how international politics works, and a part of, rather than transformational of, traditional war studies, would accept the existing ontological, epistemological, and methodological boundaries of the field. It would shy away from the argument that gender is not only relevant to but crucial to theorizing about the meanings, causes, and consequences of war(s) at every level of analysis. It would uncritically accept the epistemological, methodological, and even possibly ontological boundaries of the field which de facto exclude a level of depth in gendered analyses of war. An approach that finds the methods traditionally used in the discipline sufficient would not stray outside them and, therefore, might not be able to recognize many of the unique ways one needs to look to see how gender influences the making and fighting of war(s). Such an approach mainstreams gender in the field, but a diluted concept of gender that is neither intellectually robust nor field transformative.

On the other hand, a feminist theory of war that sees feminist engagement with the traditional concerns and structures of war studies as a priori dangerous would not engage with, and respond to, existing takes on the war puzzle within the preconceived boundaries of the discipline. An approach that sees the traditional confines of the discipline as not only problematically constraining but irreversibly intellectually restrictive would see engagement with mainstream theories (and possibly even mainstream theorists) as counterproductive. A feminist theory of war that rejects on face the traditional methods of the discipline as fundamentally gendered and/or anti-feminist would not use them at all. Such an approach transforms the discipline intellectually, but often has little impact on it politically, since the work is not read or engaged by the mainstream.

Carol Cohn framed this debate in less stark terms, and perhaps her framing is useful in attempts to identify a third path for feminist war theorizing.[19] Cohn noted that it was important to decide whether we are doing *feminist security* studies or feminist *security studies* when referencing the content and mission of the growing subfield called feminist security studies.[20] Presumably, the *feminist security* studies foregrounds feminist concerns about security, interrogating the discipline's traditional foci, whereas feminist *security studies* leaves the boundaries of the discipline intact and analyzes what is inside through gender lenses. Certainly, in these terms, it is reasonable to ask whether a feminist theory of war is first feminist or first situated in war studies and to express concerns about the potential trade-offs involved in both.

This project has looked for ways to avoid those trade-offs, which might be thought of as between intellectual rigor (in feminist terms) and (field macro-)political impact. It has looked to maintain the epistemological, methodological, and ontological commitments of (multiple) feminisms while politically intervening in, engaging, and perhaps even occupying[21] the mainstream of the field. Consonant with that goal, this book has looked to take neither extreme, employing a dialogical approach to find a third way.

Accordingly, the argument I make is that feminist war theorizing can be both first feminist and first war studies, and it should be. It *can* be both because gendered lenses can look at any phenomenon—whether it be regression models of democratic peace hypotheses or the lives of women prostitutes in South Korea. Different feminisms offer different tools differently suited to different situational and empirical analyses, but gender lenses include, encompass, and see many tools that, taken together, are broadly applicable to analysis in the field. As a collective, they are also multidimensional, conflicting, diverse, and confusing.

This is because looking through gendered lenses at any phenomenon in global politics does not just tell us one thing. Instead, substantively and methodologically, it has a wide gaze with many explorations and observations. While, taken together, feminist perspectives unsettle, rewrite, destroy, and transform traditional theory, taken separately, they can dialogue with it, and reform it, potentially from the inside. These potential interventions come from many angles, many methods, and many levels of engagement and analysis. Start at structural realism? There is a feminist engagement with the gendered nature of the international system structure and its impacts on the conditions of possibility of war and the likelihood that wars are made. Start at poststructuralism? There is a feminist engagement of war as performed, felt, and experienced.

These may be reconcilable, they may not be. I argue that, reconcilable or not, feminist war theorizing is not and should not be about constructing a coherent narrative of what war is, what feminism is, and how precisely they are co-constituted. Instead, this book has argued that thinking of feminist theorizing of war(s) as needing to be one thing and/or address one subject is fundamentally limiting, and underestimates the potential of feminist theorizing as debate/dialogue, and as a momentum concept. Taking a dialogical approach both among feminisms and between feminisms and war studies, this book has looked to find a feminist theory of war in the argument, in the conflicts, in the differences, and in the debates. It has argued that feminisms can at once protest, intervene in, engage, critique, and reformulate war theorizing. Not only is such an internally diverse approach available, I argue it is in fact only by simultaneously using those multiple strategies that feminist war theorizing can be produced. Accordingly, this project has looked to engage in productive dialogues about the subject, causes, and practices of war using those multiple strategies through gender lenses.

GENDER AND THE SUBJECT OF WAR(S)

Since the outset of feminist theorizing explicitly about war, war narratives have taken a front seat in feminist thinking about what war(s) is/ are and how they can be read, interpreted, and experienced. Wibben argues that "entering into the processes of framing security in narrative allows for a fundamentally different approach to issues of security" that "pays attention to how subjects and meanings are constructed through security narratives and how those processes are gendered."[22] Feminist security narratives, in Wibben's terms, "suggest that traditional conceptions of violence as an identifiable *thing* or *given* limit our imagination" and recommend "a rethinking of security and violence as *made*" and made in gendered ways.[23]

This sort of rethinking leads feminists to see war differently than traditional theorists do. If traditional theories see war(s) as time-delimited violent conflicts between two or more individually identifiable actors, extending politics by other means, feminisms see it differently. Gender lenses see war(s) as a continuum or a war system, wherein war(s) do not neatly start and end in a way that causes them to be conveniently fileable in neat history books. Instead, as chapter 9 discussed, wars begin before the first shot is fired and end days, weeks, months, years, and even decades after the cease-fire is signed. War is cyclical, but it is also enduring, and it not only looks different in time but also in space. War impacts people and is impacted by people traditionally invisible to war theorizing. There are a lot of ways to understand war as a "war system,"[24] including the tools that make war(s) possible, the political-economic systems of production that support and are supported by war(s), the making and fighting of war(s), the perpetuation of conflicts, the infrastructure damage they cause, their recurrence, their long-reaching impacts, and the politics around conflicts. Gendered lenses reveal these complexities and show the places and ways that war(s) are more complex than, more than, and more pervasive than they appear generally.

Gendered lenses also show gender and war(s) as co-constituted. Traditional or traditionalized gender roles are essential for the justificatory stories of, as well as the production, practice, and performance of, war(s). Without the relationships between gender and nationalism, protection racket logic and women and children back home, just citizen-warriors and military service, and the like, war as we know it would be unthinkable. So, as much as war relies on gender stereotypes, gender stereotypes rely on war(s). Even as they change in the quickly changing twenty-first century, (nationalized) gender roles (and the competitions between them) are pinned to idealized militarized masculinities and femininities. Everything about war—what it is, why it is made, how it is fought, and how it is read, can be related to the operation of gender tropes in global politics. Gender, too, is intrinsically tied to and defined by how we think about and operate in war(s) and conflicts.[25] Wars are *lived* and *felt* as gendered, and therefore gender should be a central element of how we think about and define war(s).

Seeing war as lived leads one to look for the gendered experiences of war(s), the subject of most of chapter 9. One of these gendered experiences is that effects of war as various as law enforcement gaps, decreased availability of household goods, lower quality and availability of health care, electricity shortages, corruption of water supplies, and economic downturns have sex-differential impacts often felt more severely by women than by men.[26] These sex-differential material impacts of war(s) reflect previously existing gender hierarchies in war-torn communities, but also produce them. This means that gender hierarchy *does* make war gender unequal, but the causal arrow is not unidirectional. Instead, "it is gender inequality that *makes war* that makes gender inequality."[27]

That is why (and how) feminists have come to conceptualize war as sensed and experienced and experiences of war as gendered, as chapter 9 in this book posits and outlines. Looking at the lives of people such as Hedy, Samira, Suhail, Kate, "Beth," Joan, Leath, "Wedad," Catherine, Fatu, and the countless men and women whose experiences produced the evidence used in chapter 9 without being mentioned there, it is easy to see that war is lived and experienced through gendered lenses. Gender shapes political economies of war, and how people live, experience, and interact with them—both men and women. This "lived" experience of war is not only material, but also emotional, mental, personal, and sensual; gendered lenses demonstrate the productivity of thinking of war as felt and sensed, both for understanding what wars are and for seeing how people live them. This is a key part of feminist retheorizing of war-making and war-fighting.

Seeing war as lived, felt, and continued, as I argue in chapter 9 can be done through gender lenses, is a significant departure from the instrumentalized, event-based understanding of war often used in mainstream war discourses. That means that, at its core, feminist war theorizing is necessarily transformative of the traditional project of war theorizing even as it engages that theorizing, particularly as it broadens notions of when and where and how war happens, as well as how it is experienced.

It may then be difficult to understand engaging causal and practice theories that assume a priori an overly narrow interpretation of what war is and where to look for its practices and impacts. That was precisely the project of this book, however—looking to engage the terms and assumptions of war theories fundamentally incompatible with what I propose is a necessarily transformative feminist approach to studying war(s). This is because the utility of a dialectical-hermeneutic approach to (feminist war) theorizing is not in its ability to engage with those who share the same assumptions in order to produce substantive consensus. Instead, its strength is in constructing the theory *with* and *in* the argument, and theorizing at multiple levels. It is with that interest in mind that this book has engaged traditional theorizing of the making and fighting of war(s) without deferring to the hegemony of mainstream interpretations.

GENDER AND WAR-MAKING

This book has argued that gender should be a key part of how war studies analyzes the causes of war, not only (and perhaps even not at all) in asking whether individual men and women are more or less likely to make wars. Instead, it has argued that understanding gender as complex, multifaceted, social, performative, and powerful in global politics requires a critical rethought of systemic-level, dyadic-level, state-level, and substate-level theories of war. This section briefly reviews and contextualizes those potentially transformational movements.

The System

This book put forth a feminist approach to system-level theorizing of wars, building on both prior feminist theorizing and previous feminist critiques of structural neorealist approaches to theorizing war. Feminist scholars like J. Ann Tickner have previously expressed their skepticism about realist readings of the international system as anarchic, concerned that "realists have applied [Hobbes'] description of individuals' behavior in a hypothetical precontractual state of nature, which

Hobbes termed the war of everyman against everyman, to the behavior of states in the international system,"[28] an unrealistic approach. Tickner explains:

> Feminists have argued that such behavior could be applicable only to adult males, for if life was to go on for more than one generation in the state of nature, women must have been involved in activities such as reproduction and child rearing rather than in warfare.[29]

The "state of nature" can only be a war of all against all, as Hobbes contends, if it is time-limited, decontextualized, and inhabited only by individuals with masculine physical and social identities.[30] Following Hobbes, neorealists draw a distinction between the anarchy that exists among states and order within states, but as Tickner has noted, the anarchy outside/order inside dichotomy is itself problematic because it constructs a "boundary between a public domestic place protected, at least theoretically, by the rule of law, and the private space . . . where, in many cases, no such legal protection exists."[31] Christine Sylvester likewise contends that this selectivity in drawing boundaries between anarchy/order and outside/inside hides some patterns of patriarchy and reveals others.[32] In fact, as Jacqui True suggests, the very idea of the separability of the third image is problematic, because gender lenses see that "relationships between domestic and international, masculine and feminine agents are mystified by the levels-of-analysis schema that separates the individual, the state, and the international system."[33] Feminist theorists, then, have suggested that the Waltzian account of the third image is fundamentally gendered.[34]

By contrast, gendered lenses see that the levels of analysis are not separate but related and that delineating the levels as separable only further entrenches gender hierarchy. In response, "feminist alternatives . . . do not promote more universal abstractions, but demand greater context in order to map more adequately the complexity and indeterminacy between agent and structure."[35] This book has attempted to develop a feminist engagement with third-image theorizing that takes account of the careful nature of feminist critiques of system-structural analysis while demonstrating the relevance of gender to those who might take system structure as a given and appropriate level of analysis.

It began with the foundational work of number of feminists IR scholars who have defined gender as a structural feature of social and political life. In this context, gender is "a particular kind of power relation . . . central to understanding international processes,"[36] and "a socially constructed relationship of inequality" that is pervasive within global politics.[37] Building on this work, the structural approach in chapter 3 focused on the elements feminist theory and structural neorealism have in common, such as understandings of what organizational or system structure might look like and traits selected for by the system. For example, Waltz has argued that the anarchy within the international system "selects for" or rewards certain traits at the state level such as power and survival instincts/skills. Similarly, Cynthia Enloe has argued patriarchy privileges traits associated with masculinity in its units (states) and subunits (substate actors).[38] If this approach is correct, with gender being a structural factor (or perhaps even *the* structural factor) in global politics, then accounts of the third image that do not acknowledge the role of gender contain an explanatory deficit.

In this vein, chapter 3 suggested that the (Waltzian) structure of the system is itself gender hierarchical. Waltz observed that "in looking for international structure, one is brought face to face with the invisible, an uncomfortable position to be in."[39] Feminist insights from the sociology of organizations suggest ways in which we might understand gender as (in Waltz's terms) "invisible" but also structural, by thinking about the ways in which "advantage and disadvantage, exploitation and control, action and emotion, meaning and identity, are patterned through and in terms of a distinction between male and female, masculine and feminine."[40] Applying this framework, the international system would include gender hierarchy if perceived association with gender identity (masculinity and femininity) were used to distribute advantage, disadvantage, exploitation, control, action, emotion, meaning, and identity *among states*.

This insight has the potential to reshape how IR views the third image and systemic accounts of war. There are three key, interconnected ways in which gender hierarchy transforms third image theorizing and its role in explaining war(s). First, if the structure of the international system incorporates gender hierarchy, and this gender hierarchy is a key organizing principle in dictating state identity, interaction, and relative position, then conflicts between states are not exclusively about relative power and survival, but instead take place within or about the gendered order of international structure. Second, we can appropriately view gender hierarchy as a/the permissive cause of war in global politics, in place of or perhaps alongside anarchy, which Waltz identified as a permissive cause of war. Third, the gendered international structure may also be a direct cause of war. On one level, gender hierarchy is structural and in this sense constant, but at the same time the masculinities and femininities that are a part of that hierarchy are variable and they change across time, context, and culture. Because of this duality, gender hierarchy as a structural feature of the international system has the potential to predict state behavior differently (and potentially more precisely) than anarchy.

There are two comparative advantages that this understanding of gender hierarchy as structure holds over the Waltzian conception of anarchy as structure. One advantage is that gender hierarchy at the structural level can account for both *war* generally (a permissive cause that explains why war breaks out at all) and *wars* specifically (a direct cause of particular conflicts). The other advantage is that gender hierarchy accounts for changes in the intensity and frequency of war in different time periods, whereas anarchy cannot. Even if the argument that the international system *is* gender hierarchical does not grow into a valuable line of feminist inquiry and research, the insights of the international system as gender hierarchy established the gendered nature of war, as well as the gaps in the neorealist conception of the international system.

States and Interstate Relations

As I discussed in chapter 5, some scholars studying gender and global politics have looked at the correlations between domestic gender equality and states' likelihood to go to war. In these analyses, scholars have shown domestic gender equality to be a statistically significant indicator of a state's propensity for war-making, even when controlling for other variables that the literature on the causes of war sees as important, like democracy, cultural similarity, or trade.[41] While this suggests that states that treat women fairly are somehow overall less violent, many feminists are interested in probing deeper into state-level war theorizing, objecting both to reading gender as reducible to sex and to dichotomizing states' likelihoods to act violently.

Rather than look for correlations between international violence and domestic gender equality, most feminists study the properties of states that cannot be understood adequately without gender lenses, including a "gendered configuring of recruitment and promotion, a gendered configuring of the internal division of labor, a gendered configuring of policymaking, of practical routines, and of ways of mobilizing pleasure and consent" in the workings of states.[42] This work sees the state as an inherently gendered construction, shaped by the masculinities of those who run it and those who study it.[43] Feminist scholars have queried the philosophical and political justifications for the existence of states to find the roots of their gendered identities, cultures, and strategic cultures.[44]

Particularly, feminists like Carole Pateman have argued that states rely on gendered social contract theory for their warrant to determine that citizens consent to their governance.[45] Social contract accounts of consent often omit the responsibilities imposed on women without their (implicit or explicit) consent, gendering the political community from its formation.[46] Feminist work has argued that these gendered foundations bleed into gendered state identities, behaviors, and practices, including, but not limited to, gendered militarism, gendered nationalisms, and gendered relationships that influence when and how states make wars, as discussed in chapters 4 and 5.

The gendered and gender-constitutive nature of the state manifests in gendered militarisms, as discussed in some detail in chapters 5 and 8. If militarism is the extension of war-related practices, activities, and meanings into the broader sphere of political life,[47] feminists have argued that it requires sex- and gender-differentiated roles as it calls for men's bravery to fight by highlighting women's innocence.[48] As discussed in chapter 6 and chapter 9, this creates a link between violence, virility, and masculinity at the individual and state levels through gender indoctrination and misogynist training.[49] Those links are neither coincidental nor natural, but instead gendered and fundamental to the justificatory logic of states making wars.[50] Many feminist scholars of war see such state militarism as incomprehensible without understanding the genderings of militarism, conceptually and in practice.[51]

Chapter 5 linked this gendered militarism to gendered nationalisms as manifestations of gendered state identities, in which "national chauvinism" and other gendered nationalist identities simultaneously "constitute the identity of the nation" and "reproduce traditional gender roles."[52] Within gendered nationalism, "gender difference . . . seems to symbolically define the limits of national difference."[53] This gender differentiation among states can be seen as a key cause of state competition, conflict, and even war, as well as a key expression of these phenomena. Feminist theorists have found elements of gendered nationalisms in a number of war-justifying narratives, including, but not limited to, the "war on terror" in Afghanistan,[54] the conflict between Russia and Chechnya,[55] the conflict in the former Yugoslavia,[56] the first Gulf War,[57] the Cold War,[58] and World War I.[59]

Gendered nationalisms cast women as states' biological and cultural reproducers for the purpose of state identity and feminize others for the purpose of the protection racket.[60] In these narrations, women's contributions to nationalist causes depends on fulfilling their roles *as women*, and war-justifying narratives rely on women's gender-stereotypical compliance.[61] For these reasons, "feminists have suggested that war cannot be understood without the gendered notion of protection used to inspire male soldiers to fight wars."[62] This gendered nationalism establishes connections between state identity and gendered identity and inscribes gender onto states' competitive relationships.

It is the way that gender shapes those relationships that was the subject of chapter 4, which looked through gender lenses both at traditional assumptions about how states interact and the meaning of a relationship between states. While traditional war theorizing sees interaction states as "abstract unitary actors" guided by a "higher rationality,"[63] feminists have argued that these approaches "privilege characteristics associated . . . with masculinity,"[64] which reify the "inside/outside" dichotomy in global politics.[65] Chapter 4 argued that the assumption that states relate as rational, unitary, fully distinguishable actors rather than as "compilation[s] of agents" comes both with a human cost and an analytical cost.[66]

The human cost is that some theorists use this model of the state to assume away the insecure people within secure states either by internal order or by resource distributions that benefit some at the expense of others. By contrast, some feminists object to the manner in which this approach instrumentalizes individuals, particularly those who are already marginalized within the international system.[67] If feminists are right that war is at least sometimes advantageous to states, but usually disadvantageous to women, then the "unitary" interests of the state differ from the interest of the women living within the state.[68] Feminists contend that the state has many interests that are diverse and sometimes at odds with one another. The powerful can reconcile these conflicts for purpose of creating an illusory unity, but they do so by ignoring the gendered nature of the state. In reality, the state is more complicated, less unified, and less representative than neorealists assume, and it is only with reference to the gendered identities involved in casting state behavior as rational and unified that we can truly understand this behavior.[69]

This messier picture of the state as decision maker comes to the table when states relate to other states. While traditional scholarship on war often understands states' relationships as unidimensional and largely material, chapter 4 looked to read content into the idea of "relations" between states. Obscuring both the depth and complexity of states' relationships is the analytical cost of many traditional, overly simple notions of how states relate. This is why chapter 4 explores states' relationships as interdependent, intersubjective, emotional, political, and co-constitutive, and contends that the nature of states' relationships is an important factor in understanding when and how those relationships break down into war and conflict.

This is also why chapter 4 looked through gendered lenses at the complexity of states' relationships, and the priority that relating states put on their relative position on a gender hierarchy among states. Thinking about *identity* and *relationships* is itself a distinct ontological approach to state- and dyadic-level war theorizing, and this book shows that, through gendered lenses, it is not only key to take that theoretical orientation, but to understand how states' *identities* and *relationships* are gendered. If both states and how they relate have gendered elements, than dyadic- and state-level analyses of the causes of war(s) are incomplete without attention to gender and therefore need gender analysis to be able to more completely account for when and how states make war(s).

People

Feminists have always emphasized the ways in which gender lenses offer a unique understanding the role of the individual in global politics generally and war theorizing specifically.[70] Engaging individual-level or human-level theories of war, feminists have argued that the accounts of human nature in many traditional first-image theories ignore gender and are therefore incomplete in important ways.[71] As a result, feminists argue that the "man" or "individual" that war studies scholars study when they look to the "first image" is gendered.[72] Including the feminine in the first-image *man* demonstrates that *people* are connected with the (third-image) *system* such that there is an interdependence of the international system with the its most vulnerable inhabitants.[73]

Feminists have long critiqued war theorizing's understandings of human nature, arguing, for example, that classical realism's pessimistic view of human nature makes assumptions that "in modern Western culture, are associated with masculinity"[74] in opposition to and excluding "devalued femininity."[75] Still, feminist critiques of realism's ideas about human nature have not led to embracing a liberal individualistic notion of *man* for first-image war theorizing. Instead, feminists have argued that the liberal *man* privileges reason over emotion and roots political agency in autonomy, demonstrative of *his* gendered masculine nature.[76]

Chapter 6 read these masculinized interpretations into "great men" theories of the individual-level causes of war, arguing that these foundations make first-image theories of war partial at best.[77] This creates two problems: states' likelihood to behave in ways that emphasize character traits associated with (hegemonic) masculinities and the exclusion of femininity (and, by extension, women) from control over states' resources. Therefore, feminist theorists have suggested an alternative image of the individual in global politics,[78] looking beyond and away from the (masculine) "individual with elite power"[79] to explain war, starting at the margins of global politics and using women's lives as a starting point.[80]

Because of this, the institutional structures of the state themselves manifest gender between "man, the state, and war." The third and second images have effects on the first image, personal lives. At the same time, people also exert influence over the state and the system. The linkages among the images of international politics are both empirical and ontological.[81] As feminists have argued, we cannot make sense of any of these images in the absence of the others. Instead, as we discussed in chapter 6, the personal is international and the international is personal.[82] By extension, for war theorizing, the personal is war and war is personal.[83]

The implications of this for thinking about *who* is relevant to war theorizing and how to conceptualize their relevance is, as this book has argued, transformative. Gender lenses broaden the relevant actors to theorizing the causes and consequences of war (even as traditionally understood), and, perhaps more importantly, suggest new ways of thinking about *how* people matter in war-making and in the war narratives that support it. If the personal is war and war is personal, then a breakdown of the (gendered) public/private and rational/emotional dichotomies would be fruitful for helping not only theorizing, but perhaps providing policy responses to, international conflict.

GENDER AND WAR-FIGHTING

This book has argued that gender is not only a causal factor in the making of war, but a key to understanding how wars are fought, once made. Chapter 7 analyzed strategy through the lenses of gender in global politics. It argued that the theory and practice of strategy are gendered, conceptually and operationally. First, it looked at the gendered assumptions inherent not only in analyses of strategic thought from scholarly perspectives, but also in the performance of strategizing in military and policy communities. It then pointed out the ways in which states' (and other actors') strategic choices are both gendered themselves and influenced by gender-based considerations. Particularly, it suggested that two particular strategies—intentional civilian victimization and the strategic deployment of private military and security companies—are often told and understood without reference to gender, but cannot be understood without accounting for gender as a condition of possibility of the deployment of the strategy. The chapter also looked at the ways in which gendered perceptions influence how belligerents choose particular strategies, because strategic choice is influenced by the character of a state's gendered nationalism at the time the conflict begins, and the frequency and degree of a state's feminizing rhetoric toward its potential opponent leading up to the conflict.

Gendered strategies are mirrored and reified in gendered tactics, as chapter 8 discussed. When we think about the ways tactics are gendered, some come to mind more quickly than others—wartime rape as a gendered tactic or the gendered implications of forced impregnation. After all, a number of wartime atrocities specifically affect women, including sexual violence, wartime rape, and genocidal rape. This book discussed and accounted for those tactics, but also explored others, such as the gendered nature of the development of and decisions to use military technologies and/or the use of feminization as a tactic of war-fighting. The genderings of those tactics (and the choice to employ them) sometimes easily slip under the radar of discussions about gender and war-fighting as theorists tell stories that plausibly account for those things as gender neutral. This chapter also talked about the tactical use of women as weapons of war (as soldiers, as revolutionaries, and as terrorists), and the tactical deployment of femininity as a weapon in itself. The chapter then turned to account for one of the key (but often unseen) locations of the genderings of war(s) at a tactical level—logistics. It accounted for the ways in which gendered political economies and humanitarian consequences are inexorably linked to military movement and the wartime maintenance of fighting forces.

This section of the book simultaneously engaged with and challenged strategic studies' accounts of strategy, tactics, and logistics, arguing that gender lenses increase the conceptual complexity and explanatory value of strategic studies, and that feminist theory has fruitful alternative suggestions both for strategizing and for analyzing strategic, tactical, and logistical decisions and their impacts on people, states, and the practice/performance of war(s).

(THE POLITICS OF) A FEMINIST THEORY OF WAR

Feminism and war are not often thought of in the same plane of academic analysis or political action. After all, women and feminism are perceived to be peaceful. Often, feminisms have been excluded from that conversation because they did not provide specific and concrete descriptions, explanations, predictions, and prescriptions for making and fighting wars. Certainly, there is *no such thing* as a single feminist theory of war(s).

Instead, multiple feminist theories of war(s) come from different feminist perspectives, engage different theoretical approaches to war(s), deal with different levels of analysis, and address the making, fighting, or experiences of war(s) separately or together. In this book, these multiple perspectives have been brought into dialogue to produce feminist war theorizing.

Much of this work has explicit normative content—looking to understand the world from the points of view of marginalized people, seeking gender emancipation, seeking to recognize *felt* violence, and seeking to decrease violence in the global political arena. This normative content is a regular feature of feminist analysis, which often recognizes knowledge to be perspectival, political, and purposive.[84] In this sense, the feminist theory/ies of war throughout this book are explicitly political, and expose their (feminist) politics. But at the same time, it seems appropriate to conclude this book's feminist war theorizing by (in Annick Wibben's terms), looking to "tackle the politics of security directly."[85]

Particularly, it can appear when feminisms engage war theorizing that the politics of feminisms can sometimes be subverted to the apparent apolitical nature of much of the scholarship it engages (in positivist theory) or the politics of the scholarship that it engages with (in critical theorizing). This is in part because the politics of feminist theorizing often does its work beneath the surface level of the analysis, but also in part because feminist research ethics apply to the work at multiple levels.[86] This chapter (and this book) concludes by engaging the politics of feminist war theorizing on two levels. First, the politics of feminist theorizing certainly touches how to make and fight wars, and, just as certainly, touches how to theorize wars. The dialogical approach to feminist theorizing in this book is more than a method, it is an ethic—of communicative, perspectival, and contingent ways of knowing brought into argument where the argument *is* the substance.[87]

That substance becomes a "weak ontology,"[88] known but not *knowledge*; learned but always with more to learn; developed but susceptible;

concrete but always open. Such a project is importantly complete, but capable of being altered by the inclusion of voices it has neglected, political events that shake its assumptions, and/or the intervention of ideas it has forgotten. While a weak ontology includes "cognitive focusing" and "affective attachment" to and with the tenets it has developed (here, feminist war theorizing as outlined in this book), it is also flexible, and never fully fixed.[89]

Such an approach allows us to recognize relationality to, contingency on, and an emotional element of political thought and action. Feminist war theorizing as a weak ontology provides a framework for political action as well as a way to see the world without decisively concluding what the world is. A feminist weak ontology for war theorizing can question the assumptions of the status quo, deconstruct the meanings of national and international politics, and maintain uncertainty about the exact meanings of gender and war while *acting in the world* toward feminisms' political goals of ending gender subordination.

The second part of a politics of feminist war theorizing, then, is imagining what acting in the world toward feminisms' political goals would look like in the practice of war, or war-making and war-fighting. A feminist theory of war(s) is itself a feminist ethic of war(s), but ethics itself must be addressed directly. A feminist ethic of war-making pays attention to gender dynamics in war decision-making at the structural, dyadic, state, and individual levels, as well as how those gender dynamics affect the likelihood, shape, content, duration, and impact of those wars, not only as scholars analyze them but as policy makers make them.

Along these lines, a feminist ethic generally moves away from abstracting human suffering in war, therefore, and toward assigning culpability for all of the effects of war-fighting—immediate or long-term, traditionally considered or invisible. It therefore pays attention to the impacts of strategic and tactical decision-making "real" people's lives, particularly at the margins of global politics, making a special effort to take note of those impacts least likely to be taken into account in traditional war theorizing. These include, but are not limited to, the health effects on the state's poorest citizens, effects on family structure, problems with literacy, and reactive gender conservativism.

In so doing, a feminist ethic of war-fighting abandons the gender essentialism of the protection racket, but pays attention to the real gendered dimensions of war-fighting and the gendered experiences people have of war(s).[90] A feminist ethic of seeing experiences in war(s) understands wars as felt, experienced, and sensed, not only materially, but socially, psychologically, and emotionally. A feminist approach is normatively invested not only in seeing experiences of war in this broad sense, but in bringing to the forefront war experiences normally silenced in narrow media coverage and partial scholarly analysis, such that it is committed to the visibility of wars' least visible dimensions.

It can strive towards that normative investment by an extension of the dialogical epistemology used to theorize war from a feminist perspective in this book. Following Robin May Schott, I suggest that this is best carried out by giving "weight to the role of witness during wartime."[91] As Schott explains, "an ethical discourse of war that gives weight to witness . . . generates a discourse of war based on their experience of war, not abstracted from experience."[92] This is because witnesses, whether they are survivors of, perpetrators of, or bystanders during war violence, pierce the veil of the abstraction of the injured other by highlighting the pain of war, the powerlessness of war, and the hopelessness of war, which are constitutive of rather than incidental to war(s).

As Schott explains, "the discourse of witness also makes evident that there are many more complex positions in war than the position of warrior or the victim" and "gives *weight* to the pain of individuals and communities." This weight is not just symbolic but operative—operative in countering the abstraction of the 'other,' operative in inserting self into the suffering of the 'other,' and operative in invoking individual and collective emotion in conflict decision-making.

Such an approach can be seen to build off of Christine Sylvester's analysis of sense and war. Sylvester encourages us to think about "what security feels like and does not feel like" as a way to understand war experiences and their consequences. She suggests that there is a "war sense" and a "security sense" that people experience as they make, fight, engage with, and respond to war(s). This suggests that feminist war theorizing need not only take place in the confines of the mainstream of IR theorizing, IR theorizing more generally, or even in the confines of traditional research narratives and monographs. Instead, feminist war theorizing can start in those places and manifest in war practices.

One way that feminist war theorizing can be practiced is through Schott's suggestion that people can *testify to* their 'war sense' by highlighting the *felt* experiences of war. Such testimony from witnesses in a multiplicity of of positions (individually and collectively)—'soldiers,' 'civilians,' 'politicians,' and 'people'—could be collected and leveraged not to create new rules of war but to serve as themselves rules of war. In this sense, rather than "reinstall the identity of subjects as either warriors or victims," hearing alternative narratives of war based on the testimony of those who live it "can respond to evil in terms of collective harm done to human beings and human freedom through the war systems."[93] Such an approach might lay the foundation for the dialogical space for translating feminist reimaginings of war theorizing to practical reimaginings of war.

Notes

INTRODUCTION

1. Norman Angell, *The Great Illusion* (New York: Putnam, 1910).

2. Cited and extensively discussed in Thomas J. Knock, *Woodrow Wilson and the Quest for a New World Order* (Princeton: Princeton University Press, 1995).

3. Lewis Mumford, *Technics and Civilization* (New York: Harcourt Brace, 1934).

4. "Kellogg-Briand Pact 1928," found in *United States Statutes at Large* vol. 46, part 2, 2343. Discussed extensively in Robert H. Ferrell, *Peace in Their Time: The Origins of the Kellogg-Briand Pact* (New Haven: Yale University Press, 1952).

5. See http://www.historyplace.com/worldwar2/timeline/statistics.htm.

6. John Mueller, *Retreat from Doomsday* (New York: Basic, 1989); John Mueller, *Remnants of War* (Ithaca, NY: Cornell University Press, 2004); Steven Pinker, *The Better Angels of Our Nature: Why Violence Has Declined* (New York: Penguin, 2011). Joshua Goldstein adapted the argument for International Relations in *The Decline of Armed Conflict Worldwide* (New York: Penguin, 2011).

7. For a detailed explanation of the idea of war cycles, see Joshua Goldstein, *Long Cycles: Prosperity and War in the Modern Age* (New Haven: Yale, 1988); for an updated analysis, see T. C. Devezas, ed., *Kondratieff Waves, Warfare and World Security* (New York: IOS, 2006).

8. John Vasquez, *The War Puzzle* (Cambridge: Cambridge University Press, 1993), 3. An updated version of this book was published as John Vasquez, *The War Puzzle Revisited* (Cambridge: Cambridge University Press, 2009). Like the first iteration of the book, *The War Puzzle Revisited* focuses on aggregating "scientific" evidence about war and wars and "examining the patterns of behavior delineated by existing research" (7). While this book's goals are different, its interest in the puzzle of war is not.

9. A "level of analysis" describes the "level" of global politics being studied. In *Man, the State, and War* (New York: Columbia University Press, 1959), Kenneth Waltz identified three levels of analysis—man, the state, and war. A similar schema was echoed by J. David Singer, "The Levels-of-Analysis Problem in International Relations," *World Politics* (1961), 14(1): 77–92. Barry Buzan (*People, States, and Fear: An Agenda for International Security in the Post-Cold War Era* [Boulder: Lynne Rienner, 1991]) expanded this list to include fourth and fifth levels—superstate and substate actors. While several scholars (e.g., Jacqui True, "Feminism," in *Theories of International Relations*, ed. Scott Burchill and Andrew Linklater [London: Macmillian, 1996]; R. W. Cox, "Social Forces, States, and World Orders: Beyond International Relations Theory," in *Neorealism and Its Critics*, ed. Robert Keohane [New York: Columbia University Press, 1986]) have correctly critiqued the construction of false boundaries in between these levels. This book employs them as an analytic t ool to map to work that classifies itself along those lines.

10. This list of paradigmatic approaches is not meant to ignore the existence of others (such as poststructuralism, critical theory, postcolonialism, etc.) but to recognize disciplinary politics that privileges certain approaches over others. For recent discussions of the intellectual and political problems with the paradigmatic mapping of the field, see Patrick Thaddeus Jackson and Daniel Nexon, "Paradigmatic Faults in International-Relations Theory," *International Studies Quarterly* (2009), 53(4): 907–930; Brian Schmidt, "IR Theory: Hegemony of Pluralism," *Millennium: Journal of International Studies* (2008), 36(2): 295.

11. Hidemi Suganami, "Stories of War Origins: A Narrativist Theory of the Causes of War," *Review of International Studies* (1997), 23: 401–418, 401. John Vasquez and Brandon Valeriano (in "Classification of Interstate Wars," *Journal of Politics* [2010], 72[2]: 292–399) argue that multicausality is a reason to call for a typology of wars. Suganami's argument (and mine) instead means to characterize wars as individually and commonly multicausal such that causation cannot per se be distinguished even if, on face, it exists.

12. Taken largely from Andre Corvisier, *A Dictionary of Military History* (London: Blackwell, 1994), and cross-referenced on a number of online databases. The estimate is not meant to be precise, only to give some sense of the magnitude of the problem of war.

13. Waltz, in *Man, the State, and War*, gives a good explanation of anarchy as a permissive cause of war. Power shifts, power transitions, and power balancing have been featured in the work of Ronald L. Tammen et al., *Power Transitions: Strategies for the 21st Century* (New York: Chatham House, 2000); A. F. K. Organski, *World Politics* (New York: Knopf, 1958); Jack Levy, *War in the Modern Great Power System, 1495–1975* (Louisville: University Press of Kentucky, 1983). Richard Ned Lebow and Benjamin Valentino critique power transition theory in "Lost in Transition: A Critical Analysis," *International Relations* (2009), 23(3): 389–410. Offense/defense theory is explained well in Stephen Van Evera, "Offense, Defense, and the Causes of War," *International Security* (1998), 22(4): 5–43 and tested/questioned in Yoav Gortzak, Yoram Haftel,

and Kevin Sweeney, "Offense-Defense Theory: An Empirical Assessment," *Journal of Conflict Resolution* (2005), 49(1): 67–89. Alliance theory is detailed in Thomas J. Christensen, "Perceptions and Misperceptions of Alliances in Europe, 1865–1940," *International Organization* (1997), 51(4): 65–98; Thomas J. Christensen and Jack Snyder, "Progressive Research on Degenerate Alliance," *American Political Science Review* (1997), 91(4): 919–922. See, recently, Jack Levy and William Thompson, "Balancing on Land and at Sea: Do States Balance against the Leading Global Power?" *International Security* (2010), 35(1): 7–43. The dynamics are discussed in more detail in chapter 1.

14. The democratic peace research program (e.g., Michael Doyle, "Kant, Liberal Legacies, and Foreign Affairs," *Philosophy and Public Affairs* (1983), 12(4): 323–353; Bruce Russett, *Grasping the Democratic Peace* [New Haven: Yale University Press, 1993]) has done the most work on regime type/war. For recent work, see, e.g., Bruce Russett, "Democracy, War, and Expansion Through Historical Lenses," *European Journal of International Relations* (2009), 15(1): 9–36. Domestic politics is referenced in work of Robert D. Putnam, "Diplomacy and Domestic Politics: The Logic of Two-Level Games," in *Theory and Structure in International Political Economy*, ed. Charles Lipson and Benjamin Cohen (Cambridge, MA: MIT Press, 1999); Harvey Starr, "Revolution and War: Rethinking the Linkage Between Internal and External Conflict," *Political Research Quarterly* (1994), 47(2): 481–507; Bruce Bueno de Mesquita, James D. Morrow, Randolph M. Siverson, and Alastair Smith, "Testing Novel Implications from the Selectorate Theory of War," *World Politics* (2004), 56(3): 363–390. For recent work, see, e.g., Scott Sigman Gartner, "Reopening the Black Box of War: War and Domestic Politics," *Conflict Management and Peace Science* (2008), 2(2): 95–97. Economic interdependence is emphasized in the work of John R. Oneal, Francis H. Oneal, Zeev Maoz, and Bruce Russett, "The Liberal Peace: Interdependence, Democracy, and International Conflict, 1950–1985," *Journal of Peace Research* (1996), 33(1): 11–28; Lars-Erik Cederman and Mohan Penubarti Rao, "Exploring the Dynamic of the Democratic Peace," *Journal of Conflict Resolution* (2001), 45(6): 818–833; John R. Oneal and Bruce Russett, "The Classical Liberals Were Right," *International Studies Quarterly* (1997), 41(2): 267–293. Dan Reiter's "Exploring the Bargaining Model of War," (*Perspectives on Politics* [2003], 1[1]: 27–43) and Darren Filson and Suzanne Werner's "A Bargaining Model of War and Peace: Anticipating the Onset, Duration, and Outcome of War" (*American Journal of Political Science* [2002], 46[4]: 819–838) are good examples of work on a bargaining approach to war. These dynamics are discussed in more detail in chapter 1.

15. It is important to note that not all work on culture and war takes a constructivist approach, e.g., perhaps the most well-known work on culture and war is Samuel Huntington's *The Clash of Civilizations and the Remaking of World Order* (London: Simon & Schuster, 1997), but a significant amount of it does, e.g., Peter J. Katzenstein, ed., *The Culture of National Security: Norms and Identities in World Politics* (New York: Columbia University Press, 1996). Learning theories include the work of Robert Powell, "Bargaining and Learning while Fighting," *American Journal of Political Science* (2004), 48(2): 344–361; Robert Jervis, *Perception and Misperception in International*

Politics (Princeton: Princeton University Press, 1976). Ernest Gellner's *Nations and Nationalism* (London: Blackwell, 1993) and Edward Mansfield and Jack Snyder's *Electing to Fight: Why Emerging Democracies Go to War* (Cambridge, MA: MIT Press, 2005) emphasize nationalism as an explanation for armed conflict. For work on norms, see Theo Farrell, *The Norms of War: Cultural Beliefs and Modern Conflict* (Boulder: Lynne Rienner, 2005); Robert D. English, *Russia and the Idea of the West: Gorbachev, Intellectuals, and the End of the Cold War* (New York: Columbia University Press, 2000). These dynamics are discussed in more detail in chapter 1.

16. See discussion of the exclusion of feminist work from mainstream security journals in Laura Sjoberg, "Introduction to Security Studies: Feminist Contributions," *Security Studies* (2009), 18(2): 183–213.

17. There are exceptions (though they do not, for the most part, mean the same thing by gender that this book does). These include: Joshua Goldstein, *War and Gender* (Cambridge: Cambridge University Press, 2001); Andrea Den Boer and Valerie Hudson, "A Surplus of Men, A Deficit of Peace: Security and Sex Ratios in Asia's Largest States," *International Security* (2002), 26(4): 5–23; Mary Caprioli, "Gendered Conflict," *Journal of Peace Research* (2000), 37(1): 51–68; Valerie M. Hudson, Mary Caprioli, Bonnie Ballif-Spanvill, Rose McDermott, and Chad Emmett, "The Heart of the Matter: The Security of Women and the Security of States," *International Security* (2009), 33(3): 7–45; Mary Caprioli, Valerie M. Hudson, Rose McDermott, Bonnie Ballif-Spanvill, Chad Chad Emmett, and S. Matthew Stearmer, "The WomanStats Database: Advancing an Empirical Research Agenda," *Journal of Political Research* (2010), 46(6): 839–857; Valerie M. Hudson, Bonnie Ballif-Spanvill, Mary Caprioli, and Chad Emmett, *Sex and World Peace* (New York: Columbia University Press, 2012); Mary Caprioli, "Primed for Violence: The Role of Gender Inequality in Predicting Internal Conflict," *International Studies Quarterly* (2005), 49(2): 161–178; Rose McDermott and Peter K. Hatemi, "Distinguishing Sex and Gender," *PS: Political Science and Politics* (2011), 44(1): 89–92. These will be discussed in more detail throughout the book, particularly in chapters 1 and 5.

18. There is a debate, which will be dealt with in more detail in the chapter 2 presentation of feminist foundations for thinking about war-making and war-fighting, concerning the difference between using gender as a variable to analyze international conflict ("gender and security," e.g., R. Charli Carpenter, "Gender Theory in World Politics: Contributions of a Non-Feminist Standpoint" *International Studies Review* [2003], 4[3]: 153–165) and using gender subordination as a lens through which to understand international conflict ("feminist security," e.g., Helen Kinsella, "For Careful Reading: The Conservativism of Gender Constructivism," *International Studies Review* [2003], 5[2]: 287–302; Laura Sjoberg, "The Gendered Realities of the Immunity Principle: Why Gender Analysis Needs Feminism," *International Studies Quarterly* [2006], 50[4]: 889–910).

19. Not to claim unity of ontology, epistemology, method, or theory in the feminist tradition in IR, as discussed in more detail in chapter 2.

20. For the gendering of war, see Laura Sjoberg, *Gender, Justice, and the Wars in Iraq* (New York: Lexington, 2006). For gender as a causal and constitutive factor, see, e.g., J. Ann Tickner, *Gendering World Politics: Issues and Approaches in a Post-Cold War Era* (New York: Columbia University Press, 2001); Jill Steans, *Gender and International Relations: An Introduction* (New Brunswick, NJ: Rutgers University Press, 1998); J. Ann Tickner, "Hans Morgenthau's Principles of Political Realism: A Feminist Reformulation," in ed. Rebecca Grant and Kathleen Newland, *Gender and International Relations* (Bloomington: Indiana University Press, 1991); V. Spike Peterson and Anne Sisson Runyan, *Global Gender Issues* (Boulder: Westview, 1991): Brooke Ackerly, Maria Stern, and Jacqui True, *Feminist Methodologies for International Relations* (Cambridge: Cambridge University Press, 2006).

21. See, for example, J. Ann Tickner, *Gender in International Relations* (New York: Columbia University Press, 1992).

22. These dynamics are discussed in more detail in chapter 2.

23. See Laura Sjoberg, "The Gendered Realities of the Immunity Principle," for an empirical discussion of the distinction, arguing that understanding gender as power helps you see more empirically.

24. The reasons for this are discussed in J. Ann Tickner, "You Just Don't Understand: Troubled Engagements Between Feminists and IR Theorists," *International Studies Quarterly* (1997), 41(4): 611–632; J. Ann Tickner, "Continuing the Conversation . . .," *International Studies Quarterly* (1998), 42(1): 205–210; Marianne H. Marchand, "Different Communities/Different Realities/Different Encounters: A Reply to J. Ann Tickner," *International Studies Quarterly* (1998), 42(1): 199–204; Cynthia Weber, "Good Girls, Little Girls, and Bad Girls: Male Paranoia in Robert Keohane's Critique of Feminist International Relations," *Millennium: Journal of International Studies* (1994), 23(2): 337–349, among other places.

25. See Robert Keohane, "Beyond Dichotomy: Conversations Between International Relations and Feminist Theory," *International Studies Quarterly* (1998), 42: 193–198; Robert Keohane, "International Relations Theory: Contributions of a Feminist Standpoint," *Millennium: Journal of International Studies* (1989), 18(2): 245–253; Fred Halliday, "Hidden from International Relations: Women and the International Arena," *Millennium: Journal of International Studies* (1988), 17(3): 419–428. Most of this work equates "gender" with "sex" and "sex" with thinking about women.

26. See, for example, Sarah Brown, "Feminism, International Theory, and the International Relations of Gender Inequality," *Millennium: Journal of International Studies* (1988), 17(3): 461–475; Marysia Zalewski, "Do We Understand Each Other Yet? Troubling Feminist Encounters With(in) International Relations," *British Journal of Politics and International Relations* (2007), 9(2): 302–312.

27. A good description of typologies of feminist theories can be found in J. Ann Tickner and Laura Sjoberg, "Feminism," in *International Relations Theories*, 3rd ed., ed. Tim Dunne, Milja Kurki, and Steve Smith (Oxford: Oxford University Press, 2013), 195–221.

28. See, for discussion, Colin Elman and Miriam Fendius Elman, "Lessons from Lakatos," in *Progress in International Relations Theory: Appraising the Field*, ed. Colin Elman and Miriam Fendius Elman (Cambridge, MA: MIT Press, 2003).

29. Most typologies leave out a feminist/realist approach from their list of types of feminist theories. Still, feminists have suggested that the research programs have potentially fruitful commonalities—e.g., Sandra Whitworth, "Gender and the Inter-paradigm Debate," *Millennium: Journal of International Studies* (1989), 18(2): 265–272; Laura Sjoberg, "What Waltz Couldn't See: Gender, Structure, and War," *International Theory* (2012), 4(1): 1–38.

30. For example, they have investigated the particular problems of refugee women, income inequalities between women and men, and human rights violations incurred disproportionately by women, such as trafficking and rape in war. See Mary Caprioli and Mark Boyer, "Gender, Violence, and International Crisis," *Journal of Conflict Resolution* (2001), 45(4): 503–518; Caprioli, "Gendered Conflict."

31. Critical feminism builds on the work of Robert Cox, studying the interacting forces of material conditions, ideas, and institutions, and committed to understanding the world in order to change it. See Sandra Whitworth, *Feminism and International Relations* (London: MacMillan, 1994); Christine Chin, *In Service and Servitude: Foreign Female Domestic Workers and the Malaysian Modernity Project* (New York: Columbia University Press, 1998).

32. See Elisabeth Prugl, *The Global Construction of Gender* (New York: Columbia University Press, 1999); Catia Confortini, *Imaginative Identification: Feminist Methodology in the Women's International League for Peace and Freedom, 1945–1975* (New York: Oxford University Press, 2012).

33. See Charlotte Hooper, *Manly States: Masculinities, International Relations, and Gender Politics* (New York: Columbia University Press, 2001); Annick T. R. Wibben, *Feminist Security Studies: A Narrative Approach* (New York: Routledge, 2011); Laura Shepherd, *Gender, Violence, and Security: Discourse as Practice* (London: Zed, 2008); Laura J. Shepherd, "Victims, Perpetrators, and Actors Revisited: Exploring the Potential for a Feminist Reconceptualisation of (International) Security and Gender (Violence)," *British Journal of Politics and International Relations* (2007), 9(2): 239–256.

34. See Chandra Mohanty, "Under Western Eyes," in *Third World Women and the Politics of Feminism*, ed. Chandra Mohanty, Anne Russo, and Lourdes Torres (Indianapolis: Indiana University Press, 1991); Marianne Marchand, "The Future of Gender and Development after 9/11: Insights from Postcolonial Feminism and Transnationalism," *Third World Quarterly* (2009), 30(4): 921–935; Jawad Sayad and Faiza Ali, "The White Woman's Burden: From Colonial Civilisation to Third World 'Development'" *Third World Quarterly* (2011), 32(2): 349–365; Sung-Ju Park-Kang, "Utmost Listening: Feminist IR as a Foreign Language," *Millennium: Journal of International Studies* (2011), 39(2): 861–877; Anna M. Agathangelou and L. H. M. Ling. *Transforming World Politics: From Empire to Multiple Worlds* (New York: Routledge, 2009).

35. I also made this choice explicitly in *Gender, Justice, and the Wars in Iraq*. Here, as discussed in more detail in chapter 2, it is less an empirical move (to get the most information) and a more principled one (embracing difference as substance).

36. Sjoberg, *Gender, Justice, and the Wars in Iraq*, 42.

37. Hayward Alker, *Rediscoveries and Reformulations* (Cambridge: Cambridge University Press, 1996); Laura Sjoberg, "Arguing Gender and International Relations," in *Alker and IR: Global Studies in an Interconnected World*, ed. Renee Marlin-Bennett (New York: Routledge, 2011), pp.55–68.

38. Ibid., 32. That makes the product "a" feminist theory of war, but in the sense that it is one among many feminist theorizings of war(s).

39. Biological sex classes, in addition to not representing natural social characteristics of persons in sexed bodies, are unrepresentative in themselves—there are persons born neither biological male nor female, but intersexed (for a full discussion of the issues this implicates, see Laura Sjoberg and Caron Gentry, *Mothers, Monsters, Whores: Women's Violence in Global Politics* [London: Zed, 2007]). Also, there are those who have suggested that sex "differences" are themselves socially constructed (Anne Fausto-Sterling, "The Bare Bones of Sex: Part I—Sex and Gender," *Signs: Journal of Women in Culture and Society* [2005] 30[2]: 1491–1527), discrimination that is only derivatively different and/or performative, suggesting sex categories themselves are a false dichotomy. For a detailed discussion of the complications of sex classes, see, e.g., Talia Mae Bettcher, "Evil Deceivers and Make-Believers: On Transphobic Violence and the Politics of Illusion." *Hypatia* (2007), 22(3): 43–65; Cressida J. Heyes, "Feminist Solidarity after Queer Theory: The Case of Transgender," *Signs: Journal of Women in Culture and Society* (2003), 28(4): 1093–1120.

40. This claim is common, and can be traced back to Kate Millet's discussion of gender socialization (in *Sexual Politics* [London: Granada, 1971]). For a discussion in IR, see V. Spike Peterson, "Feminist Theories Within, Invisible to, and Beyond IR," *Brown Journal of World Affairs* (2004), X(2): 35–46; Tickner, *Gender in International Relations*.

41. Taken from Peter L. Berger and Thomas Luckmann's *The Social Construction of Reality* (Garden City, NY: Anchor, 1966).

42. Selya Benhabib, *Situating the Self: Gender, Community, and Postmodernism in Contemporary Ethics* (New York: Routledge, 1992); Judith Butler, *Precarious Life: The Powers of Mourning and Violence* (New York: Routledge, 2006).

43. R. W. Connell, *Masculinities* (Berkeley, CA: University of California Press, 1995); this relates to discussions of the performativity of gender (e.g., Judith Butler, *Gender Trouble: Feminism and the Subversion of Identity* [New York: Routledge, 1990]; Judith Butler, *Undoing Gender* [New York: Routledge, 2004]). For application to IR, see Cynthia Weber, "Performative States," *Millennium: Journal of International Studies* (1998), 27(1): 77–95.

44. In fact, some feminists have characterized sex as a difference that comes from inequality.

45. Connell, *Masculinities*.

46. This concept, as far as I can tell, comes from Peterson and Runyan, *Global Gender Issues*, 2; it is also discussed in depth in Steans, *Gender and International Relations*, 5.

47. Steans, *Gender and International Relations*, 5.

48. Using causal language here is neither an implicit nor an explicit endorsement of positivist epistemological privileging of an idea of cause, especially a linear one. See, e.g., Kimberly Hutchings, "Cognitive Short Cuts," in *Rethinking the Man Question: Sex, Gender, and Violence in International Relations*, ed. Marysia Zalewski and Jane Parpart (London: Zed, 2008), 27.

49. Larry Shaughnessy, "Bradley Manning's Gender Identity Disorder Comes Up in Testimony," CNN, 17 December 2011; http://articles.cnn.com/2011–12–17/us/us_bradlley-manning-hearing_1_bradley-manning-manning-s-article-gender-identity?_s=PM:US (accessed 4 May 2012).

50. Ibid.

51. Lyric Hughes Hale, "The Accidental Coming War with Iran," *Huffington Post* 27 December 2011; http://www.huffingtonpost.com/lyric-hughes-hale/the-coming-accidental-war_b_1170574.html (accessed 4 May 2012).

52. Ethan Bronner and Isabel Kershner, "Israel Facing a Seismic Rift Over Role of Women," *New York Times* 14 January 2012; http://www.nytimes.com/2012/01/15/world/middleeast/israel-faces-crisis-over-role-of-ultra-orthodox-in-society.html?pagewanted=all (accessed 4 May 2012).

53. See Laura Sjoberg and Jillian Martin, "Feminist Security Theorizing," in *International Studies Compendium*, ed. Robert Denemark (London: Wiley-Blackwell, 2010); Laura Shepherd, "Feminist Security Studies," in *International Studies Compendium*, ed. Robert Denemark (London: Wiley-Blackwell, 2010); Sjoberg, "Introduction to *Security Studies:* Feminist Contributions;" Laura Sjoberg, ed. *Gender and International Security: Feminist Perspectives* (London: Routledge, 2010); Annick Wibben, *Feminist Security Studies: A Narrative Approach* (London: Routledge, 2011); Lene Hansen, "The Little Mermaid's Silent Security Dilemma and the Absence of Gender in the Copenhagen School," *Millennium: Journal of International Studies* (2000), 29(2): 285–306; Christine Sylvester, "Tensions in Feminist Security Studies," *Security Dialogue* (2010), 41(6): 607–614; Megan MacKenzie, "Securitizing Sex?," *International Feminist Journal of Politics* (2010), 12(2): 202–221; Annick T. R. Wibben, "Feminist Security Studies," in *Routledge Handbook of Security Studies*, ed. Victor Mauer and Mariam Dun Cavelty (London: Routledge, 2010). For a discussion of progress, see Elisabeth Prugl, "Feminist International Relations," *Politics and Gender* (2011), 7(1): 111–116.

54. See note 9.

55. Kenneth Waltz (and others) theorized the "third image" or international system from a realist perspective, but Christian Reus-Smit, "Reading History Through Constructivist Eyes," *Millennium: Journal of International Studies* (2008), 37(2): 395–414, sees systemic theorizing in constructivism, particularly in the work of Alexander Wendt, for example, Alexander Wendt, "Anarchy Is What States Make of It: The Social Construction of Power Politics," *International Organization* (1992), 46(2): 391–425.

56. The term "relations international" comes from Christine Sylvester, *Feminist International Relations: An Unfinished Journey* (Cambridge: Cambridge University Press, 2002), 10.

57. Paul Diehl and Gary Goertz, *War and Peace in International Rivalry* (Ann Arbor, MI: University of Michigan Press, 2000); James Klein, Gary Goertz, and Paul Diehl, "The New Rivalry Dataset: Procedures and Patterns," *Journal of Peace Research* (2006), 43: 331–348; William Thompson, "Identifying Rivals and Rivalries in World Politics," *International Studies Quarterly* (2001), 45: 557–586; Michael Colaresi, Karen Rasler, and William Thompson, *Strategic Rivalry: Space, Position, and Conflict Escalation in World Politics* (Cambridge: Cambridge University Press, 2007).

58. Paul Huth, "Territory: Why Are Territorial Disputes Between States a Central Cause of International Conflict?," in *What Do We Know About War?*, ed. John Vasquez (Lanham, MD: Rowman & Littlefield, 2000); Richard Mansbach and John Vasquez, *In Search of Theory* (New York: Columbia University Press, 1981); Paul Hensel, "Theory and Evidence on Geography and Conflict," in *What Do We Know About War?*, ed. John Vasquez (Lantham, MA: Rowman & Littlefield, 2000); John Vasquez, *The War Puzzle*.

59. Charles de Montesquieu, *The Spirit of Laws*, ed. and trans. Anne Cohler, Basia Miller, and Harold Stone (New York: Cambridge University Press, [1748] 1989).; Thomas Paine, *Rights of Man*, ed. H. Collins (Baltimore, MD, [1791/2] 1969).

60. See, for example, James Fearon, "Rationalist Explanations for War," *International Organization* (1995), 49(3): 379–414.

61. As explained in Jack Levy and William Thompson, *Causes of War* (Oxford: Blackwell Publishing, 2010), 83; citing V. I. Lenin, *Imperialism* (New York: International Publishers, [1916] 1939).

62. For example, Graham Allison, "Conceptual Models and the Cuban Missile Crisis," *American Political Science Review* (1969), 63(3):689–718; Robert Putnam, "Diplomacy and Domestic Politics: The Logic of Two-Level Games," *International Organization* (1988), 42(3): 427–460; Jack Snyder, *Myths of Empire: Domestic Politics and International Ambitions* (Ithaca, NY: Cornell University Press, 1991); Benjamin Fordham, *Building the Cold War Consensus: The Political Economy of U.S. National Security Policy, 1949–1951* (Ann Arbor, MI: University of Michigan Press, 1998); Steven Lobell, "The Political Economy of War Mobilization: From Britain's Limited Liability to a Continental Commitment," *International Politics* (2006), 43: 283–304; Kevin Narizny, *The Political Economy of Grand Strategy* (Ithaca, NY: Cornell University Press, 2007); Ronald Rogowski, *Commerce and Coalitions: How Trade Affects Domestic Political Alignments* (Princeton: Princeton University Press, 1989).

63. Jean Bodin, *Six Books of the Commonwealth*, trans. Michael Tooley (Oxford: Basil Blackwell, [1576] 1955), 168–169, cited in Levy and Thompson, *Causes of War*, 99. More recently, Jaroslav Tir has articulated a diversionary theory of war, e.g., "Territorial Diversion: A Diversionary Theory of War and Territorial Conflict," *Journal of Politics* (2010), 72(2): 213–225; Jaroslav Tir and Michael Jasinski, "A Domestic-Level Diversionary Theory of War," *Journal of Conflict Resolution* (2010), 52(5): 641–664.

64. Samuel Huntington, "The Clash of Civilizations?" *Foreign Affairs* (1993), 72(3): 22–29; Samuel Huntington, *The Clash of Civilizations and the Remaking of World Order* (New York: Simon & Schuster, 1996). Critics include: Bruce Russett, J. R. Oneal, and Michaelene Cox, "The Clash of Civilizations, or Realism and Liberalism Déjà vu? Some Evidence," *Journal of Peace Research* (2000), 37(5): 583–608; Edward Said, "The Clash of Definitions," in *Identities: Race, Class, Gender, and Nationality*, ed. Linda Alcoff (London: Wiley, 2003), 330–359; Daniel Chirot, "A Clash of Civilizations or of Paradigms? Theorizing Progress and Social Change," *International Sociology* (2001), 16(3): 341–360.

65. This is not meant to say that war is exclusively the domain of states. Quite the opposite, state-to-state war(s) are decreasing while wars between entities that are not states are increasing. For a theoretical treatment, see Mary Kaldor, *New and Old Wars: Organized Violence in Global Politics*, 2nd ed. (London: Polity, 2006).

66. In the words of Cynthia Enloe, in *Bananas, Beaches, and Bases* (London: Pandora, 1989).

67. Carl von Clausewitz, *On War*, ed. and trans. Michael Howard and Peter Paret (Princeton: Princeton University Press, [1832] 1976).

68. See, e.g., Christine Sylvester, ed. *Experiencing War* (London: Routledge, 2011).

1. THE GENDERLESS STUDY OF WAR IN INTERNATIONAL RELATIONS

1. John Vasquez, *The War Puzzle Revisited* (Cambridge: Cambridge University Press, 2009) 3. I interpret Vasquez as meaning the accumulation of knowledge about war(s) has so many divergent empirical findings and theoretical suppositions it is hard to parse them, and crucially important areas have been neglected.

2. John Vasquez, *The War Puzzle* (Cambridge: Cambridge University Press, 1993).

3. Vasquez, *The War Puzzle Revisited*.

4. Here, I'm explicitly not making a methodological choice between seeing gender as contributing to causal or constitutive theorizing. To do so would be to render gender (if silently) irrelevant to the other sort of theorizing. While I think that causal analysis is (and I think feminist theorizing demonstrates it to be) oversimplified, I think that feminist work can engage it on its (partial, flawed) terms, as engaging imperfection is a practice that is often done/not usually discussed either in scholarly work or in daily life.

5. Kimberly Hutchings, "Cognitive Short Cuts," in *Rethinking the Man Question: Sex, Gender, and Violence in International Politics*, ed. Marysia Zalewski and Jane Parpart, (London: Zed, 2008), 23.

6. Laura Sjoberg, "Introduction to *Security Studies*: Feminist Contributions." *Security Studies* (2009), 18(2): 184–214.

7. Hutchings, "Cognitive Short Cuts," 31.

8. Vasquez, *The War Puzzle Revisited*.

9. Carol Cohn and Sara Ruddick, "A Feminist Ethical Perspective on Weapons of Mass Destruction," in *Ethics and Weapons of Mass Destruction*, ed. S. Lee and S. Hashmi (Princeton: Princeton University Press, 2002), 3.

10. "War studies" has been used (especially in the United Kingdom) to describe the multidisciplinary study of war (see, e.g., the King's College Department of War Studies, the University of Birmingham Centre for War Studies; the Trinity College Dublin Centre for War Studies, etc.), whereas "security studies" has generally been understood as the subfield of international relations (as a subfield of political science) interested in militarized conflict, or, in Stephen Walt's words, the "threat or use of military force" (Walt, "The Renaissance of Security Studies," *International Studies Quarterly* [1991], 35[3]: 211–239).

11. While some see the study of security and the study of war as the same (since security is seen as military security), those interested in "widening" the subject of security (especially discussed in the section on critical theorizing) have (appropriately) begun to distinguish between the study of security and the study of war.

12. None of this is meant to privilege war as an activity more interesting than, more important than, or to be valued over things that are "not war" (if that distinction even makes sense), only to analytically narrow the topic at hand.

13. Jack Levy and William Thompson, *Causes of War* (Oxford: Blackwell Publishing, 2010), 2.

14. For example, realist, liberal, constructivist, critical, etc.

15. For example, political science (and within political science, IR/comparative politics), international studies, etc.

16. For example, the war studies orthodoxy in the United Kingdom is different than in the United States (most importantly for the analyses in this book), and there are other geographic variations. See note 266 in this chapter for more discussion.

17. Concerning great power wars, see, e.g., Jack Levy, *War in the Modern Great Power System: 1495–1975* (Lexington, KY: 1983); interstate wars, see, e.g., J. David Singer, "The Etiology of Interstate War," *Polemos* (2002), 5(1–2): 13–31; intrastate wars, see, e.g., Nicholas Sambanis, "What Is Civil War: Conceptual and Empirical Complexity of an Operational Definition," *Journal of Conflict Resolution* (2004), 42(6): 814–858; irregular wars, see, e.g., Mary Kaldor and others' works on new wars (discussed in detail in note 36).

18. Levy and Thompson, *Causes of War*, 5; citing a longer discussion of definitions of wars in Levy, *War in the Modern Great Power System*, and Vasquez, *War Puzzle*.

19. For an alternative from mainstream security/strategic studies, see Steven Metz and Philip R. Cuccia, *Defining War for the 21st Century* (Carlisle, PA: Army War College Strategic Studies Institute, 2010).

20. Cynthia Enloe, *Nimo's War, Emma's War: Making Feminist Sense of the Iraq War* (Berkeley: University of California Press, 2010).

21. Levy and Thompson, *Causes of War*.

22. Ibid., 4–5.

23. Ibid., 5. Levy and Thompson spend time making sure that we know that it is violence that distinguishes war from other interstate conflicts, such as "the long peace" (John Lewis Gaddis, *The Long Peace* [New York: Oxford University Press, 1987]) of the Cold War.

24. Carl von Clausewitz, *On War*, ed. and trans. Michael Howard and Peter Paret (Princeton: Princeton University Press, [1832] 1976). Much of the feminist literature critiques the separation of war and everyday violence. See, e.g., Chris J. Cuomo, "War Is Not Just an Event: Reflections on the Significance of Everyday Violence," *Hypatia* (1996), 11(4): 30–45; Catia Confortini, "Galtung, Violence, and Gender: The Case for a Peace Studies/Feminism Alliance," *Peace and Change* (2005), 31(3): 333–367.

25. Levy and Thompson, *Causes of War*.

26. Feminist critiques of the statist nature of war theorizing (discussed in more detail in chapter 5) were some of the first work to point out that a focus on "states" is inadequate to see where (even interstate) wars take place. See, e.g., J. Ann Tickner, *Gender in International Relations: Feminist Perspectives on Achieving Global Security* (New York: Columbia University Press, 1992).

27. Including a developing literature that crosses the comparative politics/ IR boundary on interstate war(s). See, e.g., John Kurt Jacobson, "Are All Politics Domestic? Perspectives on the Integration of Comparative Politics and International Relations Theories," *Comparative Politics* (1996), 29(1): 93–115 (general discussion); and Cameron Thies and David Sobek, "War, Economic Development, and Political Development in the Contemporary International System," *International Studies Quarterly* (2010), 54(1): 267–287.

28. This is true, not least because the advent of the nation-state system is generally agreed to have begun after the Peace of Westphalia (1648); see, e.g., Leo Gross, "The Peace of Westphalia, 1648–1948," *American Journal of International Law* (1948), 41(1): 20–41. While most data sets about war and conflict start then (or after), that portion of the timeline of wars in history is relatively short in perspective.

29. It is still unclear if "terrorists" or other sub- or trans-state advocacy groups are included in the actors who fight war(s), however.

30. Clausewitz, *On War*.

31. Levy and Thompson, *Causes of War*, 8.

32. In terms of interest, see, e.g., Karen A. Rasler and William Thompson, *War and State Making: The Shaping of the Global Powers* (Boston: Unwin Hyman, 1989); in terms of resources, see, e.g., John A. C. Conybeare, *Trade Wars: The Theory and Practice of International Commercial Rivalry* (New York: Columbia University Press, 1987); in terms of great power politics, see, e.g., William R. Thompson, *Great Power Rivalries* (Charleston: University of South Carolina Press, 1999).

33. Levy and Thompson, *Causes of War*, 10.

34. A logic that does not particularly make sense when disaggregated, considering that the base populations of embattled groups vary significantly, and, for example, 1,000 battle deaths in the Seychelles signifies a significantly larger conflict than 1,000 battle deaths in China, India, or the United States.

35. Though those have become less common, and/or basically disappeared, in part due to the United Nations Charter prohibition on member-states making war(s). For a discussion of declaring war in a postdeclaration era, see J. Gregory Sidak, "To Declare War," *Duke Law Journal* (1991) 41(1): 27–121; Harold H. Koh, "The Coase Theorem and War Power: A Response," *Duke Law Journal* (1991), 41(1): 122–132; J. Gregory Sidak, "The Inverse Coase Theorem and Declarations of War," *Duke Law Journal* (1991–1992), 41(2): 325–328.

36. For work on the changing nature of war(s), see Mary Kaldor, *New and Old Wars: Organized Violence in Global Politics*, 2nd ed. (London: Polity, 2006). For empirical/popular/practitioner accounts, see Chris Hables Gray, *Postmodern War: The New Politics of Conflict* (New York: Guilford Press, 1997); Ralph Peters, *Beyond Baghdad: Postmodern War and Peace* (New York: Stackpole, 2003).

37. Jack Levy and William Thompson, *The Arc of War* (University of Chicago Press, 2011).

38. Levy, *War in the Modern Great Power System*, 124. Steven Pinker (in *The Better Angels of Our Nature: Why Violence Has Declined* [New York: Penguin, 2011]) and Joshua Goldstein (in *Winning the War on War: The Decline of Armed Conflict Worldwide* [New York: Penguin, 2011]) argue that war is actually declining in the twenty-first century. Others have situated that within long-cycle analysis and/or suggested that war violence is changing rather than declining.

39. Levy and Thompson, *Causes of War*; see, for a critical analysis, Stanley Aronowitz and Heather Gautnet, *Implicating Empire: Globalization and Resistance in the 21st Century World* (New York: Basic Books, 2003).

40. Levy and Thompson, *Causes of War*. For recent theoretical discussions of asymmetric war, see T. V. Paul, *Asymmetric Conflicts: War Initiation by Weaker Powers* (Cambridge: Cambridge University Press, 1994); Michael Horowitz and Dan Shalmon, "The Future of War and American Military Strategy," *Orbis* (2009), 53(2): 300–318.

41. In addition to work cited in note 36, see Martin van Creveld, *The Transformation of War* (New York: Free Press, 1991); Stathis Kalyvas, "'New' and 'Old' Civil Wars: A Valid Distinction?" *World Politics* (2001), 54(1): 99–118; Herfried Munkler, *The New Wars* (Oxford: Oxford University Press, 2004); Sinisa Malesevic, "The Sociology of New Wars? Assessing the Causes and Objectives of Contemporary Violent Conflicts," *International Political Sociology* (2008), 2(2): 521–550.

42. Other ways to disaggregate include by the type of war (international, interstate, intrastate, and irregular or substate), by the issues related to the war (trade, security, resources, and the like), by the historical period in which the war was fought, and by the type of strategies or weapons used in the war.

43. See discussion in chapter 3 of feminist approaches to these issues.

44. Thucydides, *The History of the Peloponnesian War* (431 B.C.E.), accessible as translated by Richard Crawley in its entirety at: http://classics.mit.edu/Thucydides/pelopwar.html; Thomas Hobbes, *Leviathan* (London: Andrew Crooke, 1651); Niccolo Machiavelli, *The Prince* (1515), available in its entirety as translated by W. K. Marriott (1908) at: http://www.constitution.org/mac/prince00.htm; E. H. Carr, *The Twenty Years'*

Crisis: 1919–1939 ([1939], [1945], New York: Palgrave, 2001), citations refer to the 2001 edition; Hans Morgenthau, *Politics among Nations: The Struggle for Power and Peace* (New York: Knopf, 1948).

45. Levy and Thompson, *Causes of War*, 28; See also Patrick James, "Structural Realism and the Causes of War," *Mershon International Studies Review* (1995), 39: 181–208; Robert Gilpin, "The Richness of Tradition of Political Realism," in *Neorealism and Its Critics* ed. Robert Keohane (New York: Columbia University Press, 1986) 301–321; Stephen Van Evera, *Causes of War* (Ithaca, NY: Cornell University Press, 1999); Stephen Walt, "The Enduring Relevance of the Realist Tradition," in *Political Science: State of the Discipline*, ed. Ira Katznelson and Helen Milner (New York: Norton, 2002), 197–220.

46. Levy and Thompson, *Causes of War*, 29.

47. Ibid., 29. In the negotiations literature, this is discussed as the "best alternative to negotiated agreement" as understood by the parties negotiating; while most of this literature addresses economic negotiations, it is relevant thinking about when war is a strategic calculation as well (see, e.g., John S. Odell, *Negotiating the World Economy* [Ithaca, NY: Cornell University Press, 2000]).

48. Levy and Thompson, *Causes of War*, 29.

49. Morgenthau, *Politics among Nations*; see also Hobbes, *Leviathan*.

50. Kenneth Waltz, *Theory of International Politics* (New York: Columbia University Press, 1979).

51. War, as in the existence of the phenomena of war (in other words, permissive causes or underlying conditions of possibility of), as opposed to wars, as in each war when it happens. Some war theories talk about how and why war exists among states at all; others talk about how particular wars came to occur. In this book, theorizing of war and theorizing of wars are understood as separable but related and are discussed either separately or together as the theorizing of war(s).

52. See John Mearsheimer, *The Tragedy of Great Power Politics* (New York: Norton, 2001).

53. In Levy and Thompson's account, this is why realisms are subject to so much criticism in IR/security studies/war studies today.

54. Stephen Walt, *The Origins of Alliances* (Ithaca, NY: Cornell University Press, 1987); Van Evera, *Causes of War*; Charles Glaser, "The Security Dilemma Revisited," *World Politics* (1997), 50(1): 171–201; Andrew Kydd, "Sheep in Sheep's Clothing: Why Security Seekers Do Not Fight One Another," *Security Studies* (1997), 7(1): 114–154.

55. The double entendre of the "domestic" as the gendered feminine private sphere here is, in my view, important to note and substantive in war studies' understandings of the abstraction of the "system" out there and the domestic in here. See discussion in note 143 of this chapter.

56. Jack Snyder, *Myths of Empire: Domestic Politics and International Ambitions* (Ithaca, NY: Cornell University Press, 1991); Glaser, "The Security Dilemma Revisited."

57. See, e.g., the discussion of the system-level variables in Christopher Layne's critical engagement, "The 'Poster Child for Offensive Realism': America as a Global Hegemon," *Security Studies* (2002), 12(2): 120–164.

58. Fareed Zakaria, "Realism and Domestic Politics," *International Security* (1992), 17(1): 177–198; Mearsheimer, *Tragedy of Great Power Politics*; Colin Elman, "Extending Offensive Realism: The Louisiana Purchase and America's Rise to Regional Hegemony," *America Political Science Review* (2004), 98(4): 563–576.

59. Mearsheimer, *Tragedy of Great Power Politics*; Elman, "Extending Offensive Realism."

60. I point this out because a discussion of what structure is becomes key to thinking about/understanding the analysis in chapter 3 of this book, which discusses what feminist system-level theorizing of war might/should look like.

61. Gideon Rose, "Neoclassical Realism and Theories of Foreign Policy," *World Politics* (1998), 51(1): 144–172; Randall Schweller, *Unanswered Threats: Political Restraints on the Balance of Power* (Ithaca, NY: Cornell University Press, 2006); Steven Lobell, Norrin Ripsman, and Jeffrey Taliaferro, eds., *Neoclassical Realism, the State, and Foreign Policy* (New York: Cambridge University Press, 2009).

62. Lobell et al, *Neoclassical Realism.*

63. For justification, see Stephen Walt, "The Progressive Power of Realism," *American Political Science Review* 91(4), (1997): 931–935.

64. For example, Inis Claude, *Power & International Relations* (New York: Random House, 1962). See discussion in John Vasquez, *The Power of Power Politics: From Classical Realism to Neotraditionalism* (Cambridge: Cambridge University Press, 1998).

65. Emmerich Vattel, *The Law of Nations*, trans. Charles Fenwick (Washington, DC: Carnegie Institute, [1758] 1916).

66. Kenneth Waltz, *Theory of International Politics* (Reading, MA: Addison-Wesley, 1979); Edward Gullick, *Europe's Classical Balance of Power* (Ithaca, NY: Cornell University Press, 1955).

67. A. F. K. Organski, *World Politics* (New York: Knopf, 1958); Jacek Kugler and Douglas Lemke, eds., *Parity and War* (Ann Arbor: University of Michigan Press, 1996); Ronald Tammen, Jacek Kugler, Douglas Lemke, Carole Alsharabati, Brian Efird, and A. F. K. Organski, *Power Transitions: Strategies for the 21st Century* (New York: Chatham House, 2000). Recently, Alex Braithwaite and Douglas Lemke (in "Unpacking Escalation," *Conflict Management and Peace Science* (2011), 28(2): 111–123) have explored implications for the level of conflict, while Okon Eminue and Henry Ufomba have used power transition theory to account for terrorist target selection (in "Modeling Terrorist Target Selection: Organski's Power Transition Theory," *Defense and Security Analysis* [2011], 27[3]: 375–382).

68. A related debate about the stability (see Barry Posen, "Command of the Commons: The Military Foundation of U.S. Hegemony," *International Security* [2003], 17[1]: 5–46; Stephen Brooks and William Wohlforth, *World Out of Balance: International Relations and the Challenge of American Primacy* [Princeton: Princeton University Press, 2008]) or lack thereof (Christopher Layne, *The Peace Illusion: American Grand Strategy from 1940 to Present* [Ithaca, NY: Cornell University Press, 2006]) of American hegemony interplays with this discussion.

69. Tammen et al., *Power Transitions.*

70. David Lake, "Anarchy, Hierarchy, and Variety in International Relations," *International Organization* (1996), 50(1): 1–33, expanded on in David Lake, *Hierarchy in International Relations* (Ithaca, NY: Cornell University Press, 2009).

71. See, for a discussion, David Lake, "The New Sovereignty in International Relations," *International Studies Review* (2003), 5(3): 303–323, contra Kenneth Waltz, "Structural Realism after the Cold War," *International Security* (2000), 25(1): 5–41.

72. Karen Rasler and William Thompson, *The Great Powers and Global Struggle, 1490–1990* (Lexington, KY: University of Kentucky Press, 1994); Karen Rasler and William Thompson, "Explaining Escalation to War: Contiguity, Space, and Position in the Major Power Subsystem," *International Studies Quarterly* (2000), 44: 503–530; Joshua Goldstein, *Long Cycles: Prosperity and War in the Modern Age* (New Haven: Yale University Press, 1988).

73. See Rasler and Thompson, *Great Powers and Global Struggle*.

74. See Immanuel Wallerstein, "Three Instances of Hegemony and the History of the World Economy," *International Journal of Comparative Sociology* (1984), 24: 100–108; Christopher Chase-Dunn and Bruce Podobnik, "The Next World War: World-Systems Cycles and Trends," *Journal of World-Systems Research* (1995), 1(6); available at jswr.ucr.edu/archive/vol1/v1-n6.php.

75. Discussed in chapter 4 from a feminist perspective.

76. Multi-party wars are then talked about as a number of different dyadic wars occurring simultaneously. Paul Poast's notion of *k*-adic rather than dyadic analysis (see, e.g., "(Mis)using Dyadic Data to Analyze Multilateral Events," *Political Analysis* [2010], 18[4]: 403–425) seems to have transformative potential for this literature. Poast's argument is that, rather than considering the relationships between states, theorists should consider multilateral interactions (particularly conflicts) as such.

77. In this book, I treat some war approaches traditionally understood to be dyadic as state-level for the purposes of feminist analysis. This is as a part of a project to disaggregate work that pays attention to and focuses on relationships as complex rather than assuming that traits are relationships. For more discussion see note 106.

78. Paul Diehl and Gary Goertz, *War and Peace in International Rivalry* (Ann Arbor: University of Michigan Press, 2000); James Klein, Gary Goertz, and Paul Diehl, "The New Rivalry Dataset: Procedures and Patterns," *Journal of Peace Research* (2006), 43: 331–348.; William Thompson, "Identifying Rivals and Rivalries in World Politics," *International Studies Quarterly* (2001), 45: 557–586; Michael Colaresi, Karen Rasler, and William Thompson, *Strategic Rivalry: Space, Position, and Conflict Escalation in World Politics* (Cambridge: Cambridge University Press, 2007).

79. Thompson and Levy, *Causes of War*, 56.

80. Paul Diehl and Gary Goertz, "The Rivalry Process: How Rivalries Are Sustained and Terminated," in *What Do We Know About War?*, ed. John Vasquez (Lanham, MD: Rowman & Littlefield, 2000), 83–110, 84, citing Klein et al., "The New Rivalry Dataset"; and Diehl and Goertz, *War and Peace in International Rivalry*. In that same book,

Brandon Valeriano ("Becoming Rivals: The Process of Rivalry Development," 63–82) traces the evolution of rivalries.

81. Paul Diehl, *The Dynamics of Enduring Rivalries* (Urbana, IL: University of Illinois Press, 1998).

82. Diehl and Goertz, *War and Peace in International Rivalry*; Klein et al., "The New Rivalry Dataset."

83. Thompson, "Identifying Rivals and Rivalries in World Politics"; Colaresi et al., "Strategic Rivalry."

84. The debate goes both ways: "enduring" conflict patterns might not show rivalry, because one state might actually not see the other as a threat (Levy and Thompson use the United States and Haiti as an example of an enduring conflict pattern that is not a rivalry), but "strategic" threat consideration may be a rivalry but may also be a performance of rivalry with no intent to act on it. Another significant difference is in data collection, in which those who study enduring rivalries use data on militarized interstate disputes, and those who study strategic rivalries contend that such data brings attention to irrelevant rivalries and leaves out important regions.

85. See Russell Leng, "When Will They Ever Learn? Coercive Bargaining in Recurrent Crises," *Journal of Conflict Resolution* (1983), 27: 379–419; Paul Hensel, "One Thing Leads to Another: Recurrent Militarized Disputes in Latin America, 1816–1986," *Journal of Peace Research* (1994), 31: 281–298; Michael Colaresi and William Thompson, "Hot Spots or Hot Hands? Series Crises Behavior, Escalating Risks and Rivalry," *Journal of Politics* (2002), 64: 1175–1198.

86. John Vasquez, "The Steps to War: Towards a Scientific Explanation of the Correlates of War Findings," *World Politics* (1987), 40(1): 108–135; Michael Colaresi and William R. Thompson, "Alliances, Arms Build-ups, and Recurrent Conflict: Testing a Steps-to-War Model," *Journal of Politics* (2005), 67(2): 345–364.

87. Paul Huth, "Territory: Why Are Territorial Disputes Between States a Central Cause of International Conflict?", in Vasquez, *What Do We Know About War?* From the same book, see also Paul Hensel, "Territory: Geography, Contentious Issues, and World Politics," 3–24; Douglas M. Gibler, "The Implications of the Territorial Peace," 211–236.

88. Levy and Thompson, *Causes of War*, 60.

89. Paul Senese and John Vasquez, *The Steps to War: An Empirical Study* (Princeton: Princeton University Press, 2008); building on Stuart Bremer, "Dangerous Dyads: Conditions Affecting the Likelihood of Interstate War, 1816–1965," *Journal of Conflict Resolution* (1992), 36(2): 309–341.

90. Colaresi and Thompson, "Alliances, Arms Build-ups, and Recurrent Conflicts."

91. Levy and Thompson, *Causes of War*, 61.

92. Ibid., 63.

93. See, e.g., Thomas Schelling, *The Strategy of Conflict* (Cambridge: Harvard University Press, 1960).

94. For example, James Fearon, "Rationalist Explanations for War," *International Organization* (1995), 49(3): 379–414.

95. An easy example, used in Levy and Thompson, *Causes of War*, 66, is that states that are actually weaker than their opponents perceive have an incentive to misrepresent their weakness in order not to undercut their negotiating position.

96. Commitment problems take place when shifts in relative power are underway, such that states agree to a bargain that is in their best interest *now*, with the knowledge that they will be interested in changing that agreement in the near future, or do not agree now, because they anticipate a shift in their power making circumstances more desirable in the near future (see Fearon, "Rationalist Explanations for War"; Robert Powell, "War as a Commitment Problem," *International Organization* [2006], 60[1]: 169–204).

97. Indivisible issues are issues on which a compromise cannot be reached. See Fearon, "Rationalist Explanations for War."

98. Ibid. This is often talked about in terms of the possibility of violent alternatives to negotiation, e.g., John Odell and Larry Crump, "Analyzing Complex U.S. Trade Negotiations," *Negotiation Journal* (2007) 24(3):355–369.

99. See special issue of *International Interactions* on "A Capitalist Peace?" (2010), 36(2), including articles by Gerald Schneider and Nils Petter Gleditsch, "The Capitalist Peace: The Origins and Prospects of the Liberal Idea," 107–114; Erik Gartzke and J. Joseph Hewitt, "International Crises and the Capitalist Peace," 115–145.

100. See introduction, note 14.

101. Adam Smith, *An Inquiry into the Nature and Causes of the Wealth of Nations*, ed. Edwin Cannan (London: Methuen, [1776] 1904).; David Ricardo, *Principles of Political Economy and Taxation* (London: John Murray [1817] 1821).; Charles de Montesquieu, *The Spirit of Laws*, trans. and ed. Anne Cohler, Basia Miller, and Harold Stone (New York: Cambridge University Press, [1748] 1989).; Thomas Paine, *Rights of Man*, ed. H. Collins (Baltimore, MD, [1791/2] 1969); Immanuel Kant, *Perpetual Peace* (Berlin: n.p., 1795).

102. Norman Angell, *The Great Illusion* (New York: Putnam, 1910).

103. Though Charles Kindleberger, *The World in Depression, 1929–1939* (Berkeley: University of California Press, 1973) argued that the decline of interdependence in the 1930s contributed significantly to the outbreak of World War II.

104. For example, John R. Oneal and Bruce Russett, "Assessing the Liberal Peace with Alternative Specifications: Trade Still Reduces Conflict," *Journal of Peace Research* (1999), 36(4): 423–442.

105. Soloman Polachek, "Conflict and Trade," *Journal of Conflict Resolution* (1980), 24(1): 55–78; Etel Solingen, *Regional Orders at Century's Dawn: Global and Domestic Influences on Grand Strategy* (Princeton: Princeton University Press, 1998); Patrick McDonald, *The Invisible Hand of Peace: Capitalism, the War Machine, and International Relations Theory* (New York: Cambridge University Press, 2009).

106. For example, Erik Gartzke, "The Capitalist Peace," *American Journal of Political Science* (2007), 51(1): 161–191. Michael Mousseau (in "A Market-Capitalist or Democratic Peace," in Vasquez, *What Do We Know About War?* 189–210, 191–192) explains several models: the trade model (in which trade promotes democracy,

peace, and development, citing Russett and Oneal, *Triangulating Peace: Democracy, Interdependence, and International Organizations* [New York: Norton, 2001]), the capital openness model (citing Erik Gartzke, Quan Li, and Charles Boehmer, "Investing in Peace: Economic Interdependence and International Conflict," *International Organization* [2001], 55[2]: 391–438), the public sector model (citing McDonald, *The Invisible Hand of Peace*), and the social-market model (in which contract-richness and contract-poverty is actually the line of distinction on which the capitalist peace is drawn (citing Michael Mousseau, "Market Civilization and Its Clash with Terror," *International Security* [2002–3], 27[1]: 5–29).

107. George Blainey, *The Causes of War*, 3rd ed. (New York: Free Press, 1988), citing work by Schumpeter and Veblen (for a comparison, see Jan Toporowski, "Debt, Innovations, and Deflation: The Theories of Veblen, Fisher, Schumpeter, and Minsky," *History of Political Economy* [2010], 42[2]: 395–397).

108. For example, Barry Buzan, "Economic Structure and International Security: The Limits of the Liberal Case," *International Organization* (1984), 38: 597–624; Jack Levy, "The Diversionary Theory of War: A Critique," in *Handbook of War Studies*, ed. Manus Midlarsky (Boston, MA: Unwin Hymen, 1989).

109. For example, Katherine Barbieri, *The Liberal Illusion: Does Trade Promote Peace?* (Ann Arbor: University of Michigan Press, 2002).

110. Samuel Huntington, "Why International Primacy Matters," *International Security* (1993), 17(4): 68–83; Joanne Gowa, *Allies, Adversaries, and International Trade* (Princeton: Princeton University Press, 1994).

111. Levy and Thompson, *Causes of War*, 76.

112. There is a question whether this is a dyadic effect or a monadic/domestic politics effect; some (e.g., Levy and Thompson, *Causes of War*; Poast, "The (Mis)Use of Dyadic Data"; David Rousseau, Christopher Gelpi, Dan Reiter, and Paul Huth, "Assessing the Dyadic Nature of the Democratic Peace, 1918–1988," *American Political Science Review* [1996], 90[3]: 512–533). Some characterize it as monadic, but it is covered here in dyadic explanations, because the majority of democratic peace theorists characterize it that way. That said, in this book, I analyze it in two different places—as a trait-based dyadic theory (in Chapter 4), and as a "property of state" theory (in Chapter 5).

113. The statement was made initially by Jack Levy, "Domestic Politics and War," *Journal of Interdisciplinary History* (1988), 18: 653–673.

114. Kant, *Perpetual Peace*; a discussion of the Kantian roots of democratic peace can be found in Sara McLauglin Mitchell's "Norms and the Democratic Peace," in Vasquez, *What Do We Know About War?*, 167–188.

115. Zeev Maoz and Bruce Russett, "Normative and Structural Causes of Democratic Peace, 1946–1986," *American Political Science Review* (1993), 87(3): 624–638, 624; building on Michael Doyle, "Kant, Liberal Legacies, and Foreign Affairs," *Parts I & II, Philosophy & Public Affairs* (1983), 12: 205–235, 323–353; Bruce Russett, *Grasping the Democratic Peace* (Princeton: Princeton University Press, 1993).

116. Maoz and Russett, "Normative and Structural Causes of the Democratic Peace," 624. Some (though few) democratic peace theorists argue that democracies

are more peaceful not only with other democracies but more generally; see John MacMillan, "Beyond the Separate Democratic Peace," *Journal of Peace Research* (2003), 40(2): 233–243; and R. J. Rummel, "Democracies ARE Less Warlike Than Other Regimes," *European Journal of International Relations* (1996), 1(4): 457–479.

117. Edward Mansfield and Jack Snyder, "Democratization and the Danger of War," *International Security* (Summer 1995), 20(1): 5–38.

118. Maoz and Russett, "Normative and Structural Causes."

119. Ibid., building on Wilson, Kant, and Doyle.

120. Ibid., 625.

121. Ibid., 626.

122. Bueno de Mesquita (cited in Christopher Gelpi and Michael Griesdorf, "Winners or Losers? Democracies in International Crisis, 1918–1994," *American Political Science Review* [2001] 95[3]: 633–647, 634) suggests that the structural impact is actually a cost on democratic leaders who choose to use force in international disputes. Fearon (cited in Gelphi and Griesdorf, "Winners or Losers?", 634) conceptualizes this in terms of audience cost. An interesting related literature (e.g., Alex Mintz and Nehemia Geva, "Why Don't Democracies Fight Each Other? An Experimental Study," *Journal of Conflict Resolution* [1993], 37[3]: 484–503) looks not only at the constraints on democratic leaders in making wars against other democracies, but the incentive for democratic leaders to make (diversionary) wars against nondemocracies.

123. Maoz and Russett, "Normative and Structural Causes," 636.

124. Lars-Erik Cederman, "Modeling the Democratic Peace as a Kantian Selection Process," *Journal of Conflict Resolution* (2001), 45(4): 470–502, 470; see also Errol Henderson, "Neoidealism and the Democratic Peace," *Journal of Peace Research* (1999), 36(2): 203–231.

125. Lars-Erik Cederman and Mohan Rao, "Exploring the Dynamic of the Democratic Peace," *Journal of Conflict Resolution* (2001), 45(6): 818–833, 829; this work is a time-series analysis based on a methodological critique of the "static assumptions" in the statistical methods of leading democratic peace theorists, particularly insomuch as they cannot account for change over time (818).

126. Both the normative and structural models (and, to some extent, Cederman's work) suggest an unmitigatable value to democratization, whereas this model "yields different predictions about the global consequences of democratization" (Erik Gartzke, "Preferences and the Democratic Peace," *International Studies Quarterly* [2000], 44[2]: 191–212, 193).

127. Gelpi and Griesdorf, "Winners or Losers?"

128. David Lake (in "Powerful Pacifists: Democratic States and War," *American Political Science Review* [1992], 86[1]: 24–38), cited in Gelpi and Griesdorf, "Winners or Losers?", 624, argues "democratic peace is the result of the power of democratic states."

129. Sebastian Rosato, "The Flawed Logic of Democratic Peace Theory," *American Political Science Review* (2003), 97(4): 585–602; Christopher Layne, "Kant or Can't: The Myth of the Democratic Peace," *International Security* (1994), 19(2): 5–49.

130. Layne, "Kant or Can't,"45.

131. Rosato, "The Flawed Logic of Democratic Peace Theory."

132. John Owen, "How Liberalism Produces Democratic Peace," *International Security* (1994), 19(2): 87–125.

133. Douglas M. Gibler, "Bordering on Peace: Democracy, Territorial Issues, and Conflict," *International Studies Quarterly* (2007), 51(3): 509–532.

134. Bruce Bueno de Mesquita, Alastair Smith, Randolph Silverson, and James Morrow, *The Logic of Political Survival* (Cambridge: MIT Press, 2005). A key contention of selectorate theory is that all leaders (democratic or autocratic) are looking to maintain and/or advance their political power, and that the smaller the ratio of the size of the winning coalition to the size of the selectorate, the more sensitive leaders are to wars. This means that "an unsuccessful war involves greater political costs for a democratic leader than an autocratic leader" (Levy and Thompson, *Causes of War*, 112).

135. Steve Chan, "In Search of the Democratic Peace: Problems and Promise," *Mershon International Studies Review* (1997), 41(1): 59–91, 65, goes so far as to say that the definition of democracy is a product of desire for the democratic peace.

136. Ibid., 66.

137. This is because they test what some call "irrelevant dyads" that would never go to war; the possibility of any dyad going to war is really, really small; and not all dyads are created equal. He notes that wars between democracies are "big exceptions in a small-n" world. David Spiro, "The Insignificance of the Liberal Peace," *International Security* (1994), 19(2): 50–86, contends that the result of the democratic peace is (therefore) statistically and theoretically insignificant.

138. For a discussion of the War of 1812, see John Owen, *Liberal Peace Liberal War: American Politics and International Security* (Ithaca, NY: Cornell University Press, 1997). For a discussion of the Kargil War, see Reeta Tremblay and Julian Schofield, "Institutional Causes of the India-Pakistan Rivalry," in *The India-Pakistan Conflict: An Enduring Rivalry*, ed. T. V. Paul (Cambridge: Cambridge University Press, 2005), 225–248, 231. Some suggest that most, if not all, of these cases are negative cases for the democratic peace, but the Kargil War is the one that most theorists agree on.

139. Mark Peceny, "A Constructivist Interpretation of the Liberal Peace: The Ambiguous Case of the Spanish-American War," *Journal of Peace Research* (1997), 34(4): 415–430.

140. Chan, "In Search of the Democratic Peace," 59; see also Layne, "Kant or Can't."

141. See Edward Mansfield and Jack Snyder, "Democratic Transitions, Institutional Strength, and War," *International Organization* (2002), 56(2): 297–337; Edward Mansfield and Jack Snyder, *Electing to Fight: Why Emerging Democracies Go to War* (Cambridge, MA: MIT Press, 2005); Jack Snyder, *From Voting to Violence: Democratization and Nationalist Conflict* (New York: Norton, 2000).

142. Jack Levy, "Declining Power and the Preventive Motivation for War," *World Politics* (1987), 40(1): 82–107.

143. Discussed in chapter 5 from a feminist perspective. The use of the term domestic in international relations/security studies/war studies often implies that

what happens inside a state's borders is either inconsequential or in the private sphere—the domestic is that which is under the control of, and inside, the house/family/unit, and thus (however horrific) questionably of concern to the international. Feminist IR scholars have consistently argued that, not only should war theorists consider the domestic in the sense it has been used/appropriated by IR theorists, but also in its common usage—at the margins, inside the household, and in/at the personal (see Cynthia Enloe, *Does Khaki Become You?* [London: Pluto, 1983]), as well as a discussion in Laura Sjoberg and Caron Gentry, *Mothers, Monsters, Whores: Women's Violence in Global Politics* (London: Zed, 2007), chap. 7.

144. Waltz, *Man, the State, and War* (New York: Columbia University Press, 1959, 2001 [rev. ed.]).

145. For example, Immanuel Kant, "Eternal Peace," in *The Philosophy of Kant*, ed. C. J. Frederich (New York: Modern Library, [1795] 1949), 430–476.

146. As explained in Levy and Thompson, *Causes of War*, 83; citing V. I. Lenin, *Imperialism* (New York: International Publishers, [1916] 1939).

147. Levy and Thompson, *Causes of War*, 85.

148. Marx was not so much an IR theorist, but Lenin, *Imperialism*; Rudolf Hilferding, *Finance Capital: A Study of the Latest Phase of Capitalist Development*, trans. Morris Watnick and Same Gordon, ed. Tom Bottomore (London: Routledge, [1910] 1981); and Rosa Luxemberg, *The Accumulation of Capital* (New York: Monthly Review Press [1913] 1964) discussed this explicitly.

149. The surplus capital model, emphasized by Lenin, *Imperialism*; and Hilferding, *Finance Capital*.

150. Emphasized in Harry Magdoff, *The Age of Imperialism: The Economics of U.S. Foreign Policy* (New York: Modern Reader, 1969).

151. For example, Raymond Aron, "War and Industrial Society," in *War*, ed. Leon Bramson and George Goethals (New York: Basic Books, 1968); Anthony Brewer, *Marist Theories of Imperialism* (London: Routledge, 1980).

152. Waltz, *Theory of International Politics*.

153. For example, Richard Rosencrance, *The Rise of the Trading State: Commerce and Conquest in the Modern World* (New York: Basic Books, 1986); Karen Rasler and William Thompson, *War and State Making* (Boston, MA: Unwin Hyman, 1989).

154. Joseph Schumpeter, *Imperialism and Social Classes* (Oxford: Oxford University Press, [1919] 1951) argues that military coalitions and warrior elites are able to make states fight wars that would otherwise not be in their interest. Levy and Thompson, in *Causes of War*, argue that Schumpeter overestimated the influence of militaries and underestimated the real conflicts between states, but note that his ideas have been influential in many theories of the military-industrial complex.

155. For example, Morgenthau, *Politics Among Nations*.

156. For example, Graham Allison, "Conceptual Models and the Cuban Missile Crisis." *American Political Science Review* (1969), 63(3): 689–718.

157. Snyder, *Myths of Empire*; see also introduction, note 62.

158. See Snyder, *Myths of Empire*. Mancur Olson, *The Logic of Collective Action* (Cambridge: Harvard University Press, 1971) discusses something similar in terms of collective action theory.

159. Snyder, *Myths of Empire*. Note this runs contrary to "learning models," which argue that people genuinely learn from history (e.g., Robert Jervis, *Perception and Misperception in International Politics* [Princeton: Princeton University Press, 1976]; Yuen Foong Khong, *Analogies at War* [Princeton: Princeton University Press, 1992]), since it argues people "learn" the (false) things their elites tell them.

160. See, for example, Kevin Narizny, *The Political Economy of Grand Strategy* (Ithaca, NY: Cornell University Press, 2007).

161. See, for example, Steven Lobell, "The Political Economy of War Mobilization: Metaphors, Myths, and Models," *International Politics* (2006), 43: 283–304.

162. See, for example, Bruce Russett, "Economic Decline, Electoral Pressure, and the Initiation of International Conflict," in *The Prisoners of War*, Charles Gochman and Alan Sabrosky (Lexington, MA: Heath, 1990), 123–140.

163. Recently, see, e.g., Jaroslav Tir, "Territorial Diversion: Diversionary Theory of War and Territorial Conflict," *Journal of Politics* (2010), 72: 413–425; Jaroslav Tir and Michael Jasinski, "Domestic-Level Diversionary Theory of War," *Journal of Conflict Resolution* (2008), 52(5): 641–664.

164. Jean Bodin, *Six Books of the Commonwealth*, 168–169, cited in Levy and Thompson, *Causes of War*, 99.

165. See, e.g., Richard Ned Lebow, *Between Peace and War* (Baltimore, MD: Johns Hopkins University Press, 1981); Jack Levy and Lily Vakili, "External Scapegoating in Authoritarian Regimes: Argentina in the Falklands/Malvinas Case," in *The Internationalization of Communal Strife*, ed. Manus Midlarsky (London: Routledge, 1992), 118–146.

166. Russett, "Economic Decline"; James Meernick, *The Political Use of Military Force in US Foreign Policy* (Burlington, VT: Ashgate, 2004).

167. Christopher Gelpi, "Democratic Diversions: Governmental Structure and the Externalization of Domestic Conflict," *Journal of Conflict Resolution* (1997), 41(2): 255–282; Barbara Geddes, *Paradigms and Sandcastles: Theory Building and Research Design in Comparative Politics* (Ann Arbor: University of Michigan Press, 2003).

168. Miriam Elman, "Unpacking Democracy: Presidentialism, Parliamentarianism, and Theories of Democratic Peace," *Security Studies* (2000), 9(4): 91–126.

169. Jack Snyder, *From Voting to Violence*, makes this argument about the Rwandan genocide; others argue that domestic scapegoating happens even in the absence of external threats (e.g., Gagnon's discussion of the former Yugoslavia [V. P. Gagnon, *The Myth of Ethnic War: Serbia and Croatia in the 1990's* (Ithaca, NY: Cornell University Press, 2004)]).

170. Huntington, "The Clash of Civilizations?"

171. Huntington, "The Clash of Civilizations?", 24; the seven certain civilizations are: Western, Confucian, Japanese, Islamic, Hindu, Slavic-Orthodox, and Latin American.

172. Ibid., 25.

173. I was particularly influenced by Hayward Alker's critical perspectives on this approach in conversation with him. See also introduction, note 64.

174. Mark Salter, *Barbarians and Civilizations in International Relations* (New York: Pluto, 2002).

175. See Robert English, *Russia and the Idea of the West: Gorbachev, Intellectuals, and the End of the Cold War* (New York: Columbia University Press, 2000) on the end of the Cold War; also John Ruggie, *Constructing the World Polity: Essays on International Institutionalism* (New York: Routledge, 1998); Alexander Wendt, *Social Theory of International Politics* (Cambridge: Cambridge University Press, 1999); Richard Ned Lebow, *A Cultural Theory of International Relations* (New York: Cambridge University Press, 2008).

176. Richard Little, "Religious Militancy," in *Managing Global Chaos*, ed. Chester Crocker and Fen Hampson, with Pamela Aall (Washington, DC: United States Institute of Peace Press, 1996).

177. Peter Katzenstein, ed., *The Culture of National Security: Norms and Identity in World Politics* (New York: Columbia University Press, 1996); Jef Huysmans, "Defining Social Constructivism in Security Studies," *Alternatives* (2002), 27(1): 41–62; Maja Zehfuss, "Constructivism and Identity: A Dangerous Liaison," *European Journal of International Relations* (2001), 7(3): 315–348.

178. Peter Katzenstein, "Introduction," in Katzenstein, *Culture of National Security*, 5.

179. Jennifer Mitzen, "Ontological Security in World Politics: State Identity and the Security Dilemma," *European Journal of International Relations* (2006), 12(3): 341–370; Brent Steele, *Ontological Security in International Relations: Self-Identity and the IR State* (New York: Routledge, 2008).

180. Discussed from a feminist perspective in chapter 6.

181. Daniel Byman and Kenneth Pollack, "Let Us Now Praise Great Men: Bringing the Statesman Back In," *International Security* (2001), 25(4): 107–146.

182. Ibid.

183. Ibid.

184. Levy and Thompson, *Causes of War*, 128.

185. Waltz, *Theory of International Politics*.

186. Wendt, *Social Theory of International Politics*. Wendt considers himself a structural theorist, but I (in chapter 3) disagree.

187. For example, Richard Snyder, H. W. Bruck, and Burton Sapin, eds., *Decision-Making as an Approach to the Study of International Politics* (New York: Free Press of Glencoe, 1962); James Rosenau, *The Scientific Study of Foreign Policy* (London: Francis Pinter, 1980).

188. Ole Holsti, "Cognitive Dynamics and Images of the Enemy," in *Image and Reality in World Politics*, ed. John Farrell and Asa Smith (New York: Columbia University Press, 1967); Jervis, *Perception and Misperception*.

189. Margaret Hermann, "How Decision Units Shape Foreign Policy: A Theoretical Framework," *International Studies Review* (2001), 3(2): 47–81.

190. Robert Jervis, "War and Misperception," *Journal of Interdisciplinary History* (1988), 18(4): 675–700; Jack Levy, "Misperception and the Causes of War: Theoretical Linkages and Analytical Problems," *World Politics* (1983), 36(1): 76–99. Though Levy and Thompson, in *Causes of War*, note that this is complicated by the theoretical problem that misperception could as easily lead to peace as it could to war.

191. Amos Tversky and Daniel Kahneman, "Judgment Under Uncertainty: Heuristics and Biases," *Science, New Series*, (1974), 185(4157): 1124–1131; Robert Jervis, "Perceiving and Coping with Threat," in *Psychology and Deterrence*, Robert Jervis, Richard Lebow, and Janice Stein, (Baltimore, MD: John Hopkins University Press, 1985).

192. Perhaps the most popular of these is prospect theory, which (with its roots in economic theories of wealth) suggests that people are loss averse: that we value things already in our possession more than comparable things that we forego, creating an endowment effect, and encouraging risk-averse behavior with respect to gains and risk-acceptant behavior with respect to losses. See, e.g., Jack Levy, "Prospect Theory and International Relations: Theoretical Applications and Analytical Problems," *Political Psychology* (1992), 13(2): 283–310; Rose McDermott, *Risk-Taking and International Politics: Prospect Theory in American Foreign Policy* (Ann Arbor: University of Michigan Press, 2001).

193. See Morton Halperin and Arnold Kanter, *Readings in American Foreign Policy* (Boston, MA: Little Brown, 1973).

194. These are in Graham Allison, *Essence of Decision* (New York: Longman, 1971).

195. Ibid. Allison describes this as "where you stand is where you sit" in organizational interests.

196. Levy and Thompson, *Causes of War*, 165.

197. That is, the best predictor of an organization's behavior "now" is how it behaved the last time it had a decision to make.

198. Where, as Levy and Thompson in *Causes of War* describe, "instead of considering all options, they consider options sequentially until they find one that is good enough, that meets some pre-determined target level" (167), citing Herbert Simon, *Administrative Behavior: A Study of Decision Making Processes in Administrative Organization* (New York: Free Press, 1949); and John Steinbrunner, *The Cybernetic Theory of Decision* (Princeton: Princeton University Press, 1974).

199. The literature describes these as "factored problems," whereby organizations routinely deal with part of but not all of a problem.

200. For example, Irving Janis, *Groupthink: Psychological Studies of Policy Decisions and Fiascos*, 2nd ed. (Boston, MA: Houghton Mifflin, 1982).

201. For example, Joseph Schumpeter, *Imperialism and Social Classes* (Oxford: Oxford University Press, [1919] 1951); Stephen Van Evera, "Primed for Peace," *International Security* (1990), 15(3): 7–57; Richard Betts, *Soldiers, Statesmen, and Cold War Crises* (New York: Columbia University Press, 1977).

202. Van Evera, *Causes of War*; Jack Snyder, "Civil-Military Relations and the Cult of the Offensive, 1914 and 1984," *International Security* (1984), 9(1): 108–146;

Barry Posen, *The Sources of Military Doctrine: France, Britain, and Germany Between the World Wars* (Ithaca, NY: Cornell University Press, 1984).

203. See, for example, Richard Betts, *Enemies of Intelligence: Knowledge and Power in American National Security* (New York: Columbia University Press, 2007).

204. Which is often discussed in the literature as "policy rigidity," based in A. J. P. Taylor's work (A. J. P. Taylor, *War by Time-Table* [London: Macdonald, 1969]).

205. Discussed from a feminist perspective in chapter 7.

206. B. Liddell Hart, *The Way to Win Wars* (New York: Faber and Faber, 1942). Colin Gray, a contemporary theorist of strategy, characterizes strategy similarly, as "the art of employing or threatening to employ military force for political ends." (Colin Gray, *Strategic Studies and Public Policy* [Lexington: University Press of Kentucky, 1982], 5).

207. Williamson Murray and Mark Grimsley, "On Strategy," in *The Making of Strategy: Rulers, States, and War*, ed. Williamson Murray, Macgregor Knox, and Alvin Bernstein (Cambridge: Cambridge University Press, 1994), 1–24, 1. This is because an "art" implies that strategy is linear, can be mastered, and can be implemented with predictability.

208. Murray and Grimsley, "On Strategy," 1.

209. Alan Stephens and Nicola Baker, *Making Sense of War: Strategy for the 21st Century* (Cambridge: Cambridge University Press, 2006), 87.

210. Gray, *Strategic Studies and Public Policy*, 188.

211. Ibid., 1; Colin Gray, *War, Peace, and Victory: Strategy and Statecraft for the Next Century* (New York: Simon and Schuster, 1991), 12.

212. Stephens and Baker, *Making Sense of War*, 11. In other words, miscalculation, misperception, and misinterpretation all threaten the success of strategies, and thus the survival and welfare of states.

213. Dan Reiter and Curtis Meek, "Determinants of Military Strategy: A Quantitative Empirical Test," *International Studies Quarterly* (1999), 43(2):362–87, 365.

214. Ibid., 365.

215. Ibid., 366.

216. Ibid., 365. Though different scholars' interpretations of what counts as a punishment strategy differ, Allan Stam's interpretation is generally accepted (Allan C. Stam, *Win, Lose, or Draw: Domestic Politics and the Crucible of War* [Ann Arbor: University of Michigan Press, 1996]).

217. For example, Elizabeth Kier, *Imagining War: French and British Military Doctrine Between the Wars* (Princeton: Princeton University Press, 1997); Barry Posen, "Nationalism, the Mass Army, and Military Power," *International Security* (1993), 18(3): 80–124; Jack Snyder, *The Ideology of the Offensive: Military Decision-Making and the Disasters of 1914* (Ithaca, NY: Cornell University Press, 1984). Reiter and Meek contend that this is problematic because "the distinction between offensive and defensive strategies is theoretically flawed, and that the whole notion of a balance favoring the offense or defense is nebulous and indeterminate" (Reiter and Meek, "Determinants of Military Strategy," 367).

218. Reiter and Meek, "Determinants of Military Strategy," 367.

219. Robert Art, "To What Ends Military Power," *International Security* (1980), 4(1): 4–35.

220. Ibid.

221. Ibid. See also Elli Lieberman, "The Rational Deterrence Debate: Is the Dependent Variable Elusive?" *Security Studies* (1996), 3(3): 384–427.

222. Ant, "To What Ends Military Power"? See also Peter Viggo Jakobson, "Reinterpreting Western Use of Coercion in Bosnia-Herzegovina," *Journal of Strategic Studies* (2000), 23(2): 1–22.

223. Ibid. For gender analysis, see discussion in Laura Doan, "Topsy-Turvydom: Gender Inversion, Sapphism, and the Great War," *GLQ: A Journal of Lesbian and Gay Studies* (2006), 12(4): 517–542.

224. Stephens and Baker, *Making Sense of War*, ix.

225. Ibid., x.

226. For example, Ariel Merari, "Terrorism as a Strategy of Insurgency," in *History of Terrorism: From Antiquity to Al Qaeda*, ed. Gerard Chailand and Amaud Blin (Berkeley: University of California Press, 2007); Robert W. Orttung and A. S. Makarychev, *National Counter-Terrorism* (New York: IOS Press, 2006); Robert Pape, *Dying to Win: The Strategic Logic of Suicide Terrorism* (New York: Random House, 2006).

227. For example, John Gaddis, "A Grand Strategy of Transformation," *Foreign Policy* (2002), 133: 50–57; M. E. O'Hanlon, S. E. Rice, and J. Steinberg, *The New National Security Strategy and Preemption* (Washington, DC: Brookings Institution, 2002); Joseph S. Nye, Jr., "U.S. Power and Strategy after Iraq," *Foreign Affairs* (2003), 82(4): 60–73.

228. See, for example, S. Graham, "Vertical Geopolitics: Baghdad and After," *Antipode* (2004), 36(1): 12–23; Neil Arya, "Economic Sanctions: The Kinder, Gentler Alternative?" *Medicine, Conflict, and Survival* (2008), 24(1): 25–41; Joy Gordon, "A Peaceful, Silent, Deadly Remedy: The Ethics of Economic Sanctions," *Ethics and International Affairs* (1999), 13(1): 123–142.

229. Alexander Downes, *Targeting Civilians in War* (Ithaca, NY: Cornell University Press, 2008), 44.

230. See Michael Walzer, *Just and Unjust Wars* (New York: Basic Books, 1977).

231. Alexander Downes, "Desperate Times, Desperate Measures: The Causes of Civilian Victimization in War," *International Security* (2006), 30(4): 152–195, 152–153.

232. R. J. Rummel, "Democracy, Power, Genocide, and Mass Murder," *Journal of Conflict Resolution* (1996), 39(1): 3–26; Dan Reiter and Alan Stam, *Democracies at War* (Princeton: Princeton University Press, 2002). Some scholars see democratic regimes as more likely to target civilians as they attempt to secure quick victories and (therefore) avoid the audience costs associated with protracted conflicts (Reiter and Stam, *Democracies at War*). Others see democratic states as less likely to target civilians, arguing that the real audience cost to democratic governments comes in having to account for inhumane behavior toward civilians (Rummel, "Democracy, Power, Genocide, and Mass Murder").

233. Benjamin Valentino, Paul Huth, and Sarah Croco, "Covenants without the Sword: International Law and the Protections of Civilians in War," *World Politics* (2006), 58(3): 339–377.

234. Stathis Kalyvas, "Wanton and Senseless: The Logic of Massacres in Algeria," *Rationality and Society* (1999), 11(3); Stathis Kalyvas, "Ethnic Defection in Civil War," *Comparative Political Studies* (2008), 41(8): 1043–1068.

235. Salter, *Barbarians and Civilizations in International Relations*.

236. Benjamin Valentino, *Final Solutions: Mass Killing and Genocide in the 21st Century* (Ithaca, NY: Cornell University Press, 2004). Downes argues that civilian victimization can be explained by a combination of desperation (intensity of the need to win the war) and war aims (particularly the aim of territorial annexation) (Downes, "Desperate Times, Desperate Measures: The Causes of Civilian Victimization of War"; Downes, *Targeting Civilians in War*).

237. Bruce Russett, *Grasping the Democratic Peace* (New Haven: Yale University Press, 1993).

238. Robert Keohane and Lisa Martin, "The Promise of Institutionalist Theory," *International Security* (1995). 20(1): 39–51.

239. Huntington, "The Clash of Civilizations?"

240. Stephens and Baker, *Making Sense of War*.

241. For example, McCartan Humphreys and Jeremy Weinstein, "Handling and Mishandling Civilians in Civil War," *American Political Science Review* (2006), 100(3): 429–447.

242. See, for example, Michael Boyle, "Bargaining, Fear, and Denial: Explaining Violence Against Civilians in Iraq 2004–2007," *Terrorism and Political Violence* (2009), 21(2): 261–287.

243. For example, Reiter and Meek suggest a geography-based hypothesis for states' choice between maneuver and attrition strategies, but do not find any support for it (Reiter and Meek, "Determinants of Military Strategy," 369). Murray and Grimsley, however, argue that "the size and location of a nation are crucial determinants of the way its policy-makers think about strategy" (Murray and Grimsley, "On Strategy," 7; also advocated by Colin Gray, *War, Peace, and Victory* [New York: Simon and Schuster, 1990], 14).

244. Reiter and Meek suggest that the level of industrialization of a state correlates with the likelihood that it will choose a maneuver strategy (Reiter and Meek, "Determinants of Military Strategy," 370).

245. Ibid., 370.

246. MacGregor Knox, "Conclusion: Continuity and Revolution in the Making of Strategy," 615; Gray, *Strategic Studies and Public Policy*, 11; Gray, *War, Peace, and Victory*, 14. In fact, they argue that the question of whether technological developments favor offense or defense influences not only how but whether wars are fought (e.g., Jack Levy, "The Offensive/Defensive Balance of Military Technology: A Theoretical and Historical Analysis," *International Studies Quarterly* [June 1984], 28[2]: 219–38; Stephen Van Evera, "Offense, Defense, and the Cause of War," *International Security* [1998], 22[4]: 5–43).

247. Richard Betts, "Is Strategy an Illusion?" 15. These strategists suggest that states' cost/benefit calculation make is based on the benefit, or value, of the objective that will be achieved by the implementation of the strategy.

248. See discussion from a feminist perspective in chapter 8.

249. Edward Luttwak, *Strategy: The Logic of War and Peace* (Cambridge: Harvard University Press, 2001), 88.

250. Ibid., 89.

251. See, for example, Paddy Griffith, *Battle Tactics of the Western Front: The British Army's Attack of 1916–1918* (New Haven: Yale University Press, 1996); Raoul Naroll, Vern Bullough, and Frada Naroll, *Military Deterrence in History: A Pilot Cross-Historical Study* (Albany: State University of New York Press, 1974).

252. Grady McWhiney and Perry D. Jamieson, *Attack and Die: Civil War Military Tactics and the Southern Heritage* (Birmingham: University of Alabama Press, 1982). See also Griffith, *Battle Tactics of the Civil War*; Herman Hattaway and Archer Jones, *How the North Won: A Military History of the Civil War* (Urbana-Champaign, IL: University of Illinois Press, 1991).

253. Jose Angel Moroni Bracamonte and David E. Spencer, *Strategy and Tactics of the Salvadoran FMLN Guerillas* (New York: Greenwood Publishing, 1995).

254. See, e.g., Robert Pape's work, *Dying to Win: Air Power and Coercion in War*, as well as Derek Wood and Derek Dempster, *The Narrow Margin: The Battle of Britain and the Rise of Air Power, 1930–1940* (London: Hutchinson, 1961); Robin Hingham, *Air Power: A Concise History* (New York: St. Martin's, 1972).

255. For example, Bevin Alexander, *How Great Generals Win* (New York: Norton, 2002); Eliot Cohen and John Gooch, *Military Misfortunes: The Anatomy of Failure in War* (New York: Simon and Schuster, 2005).

256. See, e.g., Walzer, *Just and Unjust Wars*.

257. See, e.g., the discussion of the evolution of war technologies in Eliot Cohen, "Technology and Warfare" in John Baylis, James Wirtz, and Colin Gray, eds. *Strategy in a Contemporary World* (Oxford: Oxford University Press, 3rd ed. [2012]), 141–60, as well as the discussion in Michael Sheehan's chapter in the same book ("The Evolution of Modern Warfare," 43–66). While Sheehan and Cohen come at the discussion of how wars are fought very differently, the logistical issues play a large part in each account.

258. Martin Van Creveld, *Supplying War: Logistics from Wallenstein to Patton*, 2nd ed. (Cambridge: Cambridge University Press, 2004).

259. Thomas Kane, *Military Logistics and Strategic Performance* (London: Cass, 2001), 2.

260. Ibid., 4.

261. Ibid., 4.

262. Ibid., 6.

263. Ibid., 8.

264. Ibid., 9.

265. Ibid., 9.

266. While my hope is that readers from a wide variety of intellectual traditions (including those outside feminist IR and what I have identified as mainstream, American war studies) will find significant intellectual and practical benefit in this book, it explicitly engages what I (for lack of a better term) call the "(American) mainstream" of inquiry into the causes of war(s), the fighting of war(s), and the consequences of war(s). It might appear contradictory, then, for me to argue that such a mainstream does not, strictly speaking, exist—that is, there are not clear contours of what is "in" and what is "out" in terms of acceptable ways to theorize wars. This is especially true given that there are conventions in terms of the construction of textbooks, the construction of course syllabi, and the construction of field conversations that cannot be ignored, especially given their relative power in streamlining conventional thought in the discipline. Those conventions change over time, are different in the United States than in the United Kingdom, and in those places, as compared with the rest of the world, vary across subfields of IR and (though less so) from scholar to scholar. To essentialize the boundaries of the mainstream would, in my view, do significant violence; at the same time, to ignore the existence of orthodoxies with a disciplining effect on war theorizing would do similar violence. As such, I choose to use the words "mainstream" and "traditional" not as ideas with clear boundaries, but instead in terms of regulating representations among scholars. Feminist work in IR has identified a "malestream" in the discipline (e.g., Gillian Youngs, "Feminist International Relations: A Contradiction in Terms? Or, Why Women and Gender Are Essential to Understanding the World 'We' Live In," *International Affairs* [2004], 80[1]: 75–87; Marysia Zalewski, "Feminist Standpoint Theory Meets International Relations Theory: A Feminist Version of David and Goliath," *Fletcher Journal of World Affairs* [1993], 17[1]: 13–31). I think that this is an important identification (by Kimberly Hutchings ["Cognitive Short Cuts"]), that the discipline of IR is structured by masculinist logic. At the same time, I choose the words "traditional" and "mainstream" over "malestream" both to signify that women have engaged in and been complicit with a masculine (but not entirely male) mainstream and to engage traditional or mainstream war studies less confrontationally than the consistent use of malestream would communicate.

267. Critical theory is used in two (very distinct) senses in IR/security theorizing. The first is a Marxist-inspired, [modernist] emancipatory strand of critical theory. By contrast, the poststructural or postmodern brand of critical theorizing is skeptical of the modernist project inherent in the Marxist-inspired strand of critical theorizing. Since both self-identify as "critical," as do a number of different schools of thought that do not, strictly speaking, fall in either camp, I use the term broadly in this chapter and in this book.

268. Sometimes abbreviated as CSS. Some people who identified themselves with critical security studies (e.g., Ken Booth, *Theory of World Security* [Cambridge: Cambridge University Press, 2007]) associated with the Frankfurt school, while others (e.g., Keith Krause and Michael C. Williams, *Critical Security Studies: Concepts and*

Cases [New York: Psychology Press, 1997]) use the term more broadly to capture non-mainstream approaches critical of the scope and methodology of the mainstream.

269. Karen Fierke, *Critical Approaches to Security* (London: Polity, 2007), 1.

270. Fierke, *Critical Approaches to Security,* 2, citing Krause and Williams, *Critical Security Studies.*

271. Ibid., 3.

272. Walt, "The Renaissance of Security Studies."

273. Andrew Linklater, "Critical Theory," in *International Relations: Discipline and Diversity,* ed. Milja Kurki, Steve Smith, and Tim Dunne (Oxford: Oxford University Press, 2nd Edition, 2010).

274. Booth, *Theory of World Security,* 38.

275. Discussed in more detail in chapter 2.

276. Booth, *Theory of World Security,* which talks about war as among violences that oppress people, but not as a sort of violence itself, or even as a variant in violences that merits either explanatory or analytic attention. Booth would certainly argue that war is theorized among security issues in the book; while I do not doubt that, his goals and mine are different in that respect.

277. Ibid., 65. This sounds a lot like, but does not reference, Betty Reardon's ideas (see Reardon, *Sexism and the War System* [New York: Teachers' College Press, 1985]).

278. See, e.g., Lloyd Axworthy, "Human Security and Global Governance: Putting People First," *Global Governance* (2001) 7(1): 19–25; Astri Suhrke, "Human Security and the Interests of States," *Security Dialogue* (1999), 20(2): 265–276; Nicholas Thomas and William T. Tow, "The Utility of Human Security: Sovereignty and Humanitarian Intervention," *Security Dialogue* (2002), 33(2): 177–192; Gary King and Christopher J. L. Murray, "Rethinking Human Security," *Political Science Quarterly* (2001–2002), 116(4): 585–610.

279. Amartya Sen and Martha Nussbaum, eds. *Quality of Life* (Oxford: Clarendon, 1993).

280. United Nations Development Program, *Human Development Report: New Dimensions of Human Security* (New York: United Nations, 1994); http://hdr.undp.org/en/reports/global/hdr1994 (accessed 19 October 2008).

281. Ibid. Feminists have critiqued this approach because it remains top-down and does not have a mechanism for recognizing differences in relative power among people who are to be secured, and have offered alternative ways of thinking about it. See, e.g., Heidi Hudson, "'Doing' Security as though Humans Matter: A Feminist Perspective on Gender and the Politics of Human Security," *Security Dialogue* (2005), 36(2): 155–174; Gunhild Hoogenson and Kirsti Stuvoy, "Gender, Resistance, and Human Security," *Security Dialogue* (2006), 37(2): 207–228.

282. See Bill McSweeney, "Identity and Security: Barry Buzan and the Copenhagen School," *Review of International Studies* (1996), 22(1): 86–93.

283. Barry Buzan, *People, States, and Fear: The National Security Problem in International Relations* (New York: Wheatsheaf, 1983).

284. Ibid., 2, where the military sector is traditionally concerned with war, economic security is about a stable economy with access to needs, political security is about a stable and responsive government, societal is about a stability of culture and social norms, and environmental is in the sense of local health hazards, as well as global environmental risks and threats.

285. Barry Buzan, Ole Waever, and Jaap de Wilde, *Security: A New Framework for Analysis* (Boulder: Lynne Rienner, 1998), 5.

286. Sjoberg, "Introduction to Security Studies: Feminist Perspectives," *Security Studies* (2009), 18(2):183–213, 198, citing Tickner, *Gender in International Relations*.

287. Often, even if inappropriately, marginalized.

288. Fierke, *Critical Approaches to Security*, 9; contra Walt, "Renaissance of Security Studies."

289. For a discussion of human rights, see Fierke, *Critical Approaches to Security*; for a discussion of emancipation, see Booth, *Theory of World Security*; for a discussion of basic needs, see Axworthy, "Human Security and Global Governance."

290. Richard Shapcott, "Critical Theory," in *Oxford Handbook of International Relations*, ed. Christian Reus-Smit and Duncan Snidal (Oxford: Oxford University Press, 2009), 332.

291. Jim George, *Discourses of Global Politics: A Critical Introduction to International Relations* (Boulder: Lynne Rienner, 1994), x.

292. Raymond Duvall and Latha Varadarajan, "On the Practical Significance of Critical International Relations Theory," *Asian Journal of Political Science* (2003), 11: 82.

293. Lene Hansen, "A Case for Seduction? Evaluating the Poststructuralist Conceptualization of Security," *Cooperation and Conflict—Nordic Journal of International Studies* (1997), 32(4): 372.

294. Ibid, citing Jef Huysmans, "Security! What Do You Mean? From Concept to Thick Signifier," *European Journal of International Relations* (1998), 4(2): 226–255.

295. See Buzan, Waever, and de Wilde, *Security*, for an early articulation. For recent discussions, see Rita Taureck, "Securitization Theory and Securitization Studies," *Journal of International Relations and Development* (2006), 9(1): 53–61; Thierry Balzacq, ed., *Securitization Theory: How Security Problems Emerge and Dissolve* (London: Routledge, 2011); Holger Stritzel, "Towards a Theory of Securitization: Copenhagen and Beyond," *European Journal of International Relations* (2007), 13(3): 357–383.

296. For a critical discussion, see Thierry Balzacq, "The Three Faces of Securitization: Political Agency, Audience, and Context," *European Journal of International Relations* (2005), 11(2): 171–205.

297. Barry Buzan and Ole Waever, *Regions and Powers: The Structure of Security* (Cambridge: Cambridge University Press, 2003).

298. Cuomo, "War Is Not Just an Event."

299. Lene Hansen, *Security as Practice: Discourse Analysis and the Bosnian War* (New York: Routledge, 2006).

300. Michael C. Williams, *Culture and Security: Symbolic Power and the Politics of International Security* (New York: Psychology Press, 2007). See also Laura Shepherd,

Gender, Violence, and Security (London: Zed, 2008); Judith Butler, *Precarious Life* (London and New York: Routledge, 2006) for feminist readings.

301. Mitzen, "Ontological Security in World Politics"; Steele, *Ontological Security in Internatonal Relations.*

302. Steele, *Ontological Security in International Relations.*

303. James Der Derian, *Antidiplomacy: Spies, Terror, Speed, and War* (London: Blackwell, 1992).

304. James Der Derian, *Virtuous War: Mapping the Military-Industrial-Media-Entertainment Network,* 2nd ed. (London: Routledge, 2009).

305. Ibid., relying on Baudrillard's idea of unreality and simulacra. See, e.g., Jean Baudrillard, *Simulacra and Simulation,* trans. Sheila Faria Glaser (Ann Arbor: University of Michigan Press, 1994).

306. Nick Vaughn-Williams and Colomba Peoples, *Critical Security Studies: An Introduction* (London: Taylor and Francis, 2010).

307. Der Derian, *Virtuous War,* 39.

308. Jean Baudrillard, *Seduction* (London: Macmillan Education, 1990).

309. Ronnie Lipschutz, "On Security," in *On Security,* ed. Ronnie Lipschutz (New York: Columbia University Press, 1995), 2.

310. James Der Derian, "The Value of Security," in Lipschutz, *On Security,* 38.

311. See, e.g., Lauren Wilcox, *The Practices of Violence: Theorizing Embodied Subjects in International Relations* (yet-unpublished book manuscript).

312. See, e.g., Hansen, *Security as Practice.*

313. Jean Baudrillard, *The Gulf War Did Not Take Place* (Bloomington: Indiana University Press, 1995).

314. See, for example, Krause and Williams, *Critical Security Studies;* Ido Oren, *Our Enemies and US: America's Rivalries and the Making of Political Science* (Ithaca, NY: Cornell University Press, 2003); David Campbell, *Writing Security: United States Foreign Policy and the Politics of Identity* (Minneapolis: University of Minnesota Press, 1998); Booth, *Theory of World Security;* C.A.S.E. Collective, "Critical Approaches to Security in Europe: A Networked Manifesto," *Security Dialogue* (2006), 37(4): 443–487.

315. Shepherd, *Gender, Violence, and Security.*

316. Robin Eckersley, "The Ethics of Critical Theory," in Reus-Smit and Snidal, *Oxford Handbook of International Relations* (Oxford: Oxford University Press, 2009), 348.

317. Anthony Burke, "Postmodernism," in Christian Reus-Smit and Duncan Snidal, *Oxford Handbook of International Relations* (Oxford: Oxford University Press, 2009), 359.

318. Peter Lawler, "The Ethics of Postmodernism," in Reus-Smit and Snidal, *Oxford Handbook of International Relations* (Oxford: Oxford University Press, 2009), 384.

319. Annick Wibben, *Feminist Security Studies: A Narrative Approach* (London: Routledge, 2011), 2, "the choice to privilege one perspective over another is never innocent or obvious but always intensely political."

320. However the boundaries are drawn.

321. See discussion in Sjoberg, "Introduction to *Security Studies.*"

322. Which one might think, because of its relatively leftist theoretical content, would have more affinity to gender work, but not so much. For a discussion, see Christine Sylvester, "Anatomy of a Footnote," *Security Dialogue* (2007), 38(4): 547–558.

323. Levy and Thompson, *Causes of War.*

324. Ibid., 27n38.

325. Ibid., citing Ronald Krebs and Jack Levy, "Demographic Change and the Sources of International Conflict," in *Demography and National Security*, ed. Myron Weiner and Sharon Stanton Russell (New York: Berghahn, 2001), 62–105; and Valerie Hudson and Andrea Den Boer, *Bare Branches: The Security Implications of Asia's Surplus Male Population* (Cambridge, MA: MIT Press, 2005), 126n65.

326. See note 53 in the introduction for discussion of some of the work in this area.

327. For example, in February of 2010 in a conference discussion on gender and security studies, when asked to identify work in gender and security, mainstream security scholars almost universally could identify only work on whether women (or places with sex equality) were more or less peaceful than men (or places with significant disparities between the sexes).

328. Hutchings, "Cognitive Short Cuts," 31.

329. Vasquez, *War Puzzle.*

330. Hutchings, "Cognitive Short Cuts," 31.

331. Laura Sjoberg, "The Impossible Relationship Between Feminisms and IR." Paper Presented at the 2008 Annual Meeting of the International Studies Association, 26–29 March 2008, in San Francisco, CA.

332. J. Ann Tickner, "You Just Don't Understand: Troubled Engagements Between Feminists and IR Theorists," *International Studies Quarterly* (1997), 41(4): 611–632; J. Ann Tickner, *Gendering World Politics* (New York: Columbia University Press, 2001).

333. Marysia Zalewski, "Women's Troubles Again in IR," *International Studies Review* (2003), 5(2): 287–302.

334. Jill Steans, "Engaging from the Margins: Feminist Encounters with the Mainstream of International Relations," *British Journal of Political Science* (2003), 5(3): 428–454, 436.

335. Marysia Zalewski, "Do We Understand Each Other Yet? Troubling Feminist Encounters With(in) International Relations," *British Journal of Political Science* (2007), 9: 302–312, 302.

336. Judith Squires and Jutta Weldes, "Beyond Being Marginal: Gender and International Relations in Britain," *British Journal of Politics and International Relations* (2007), 9: 185–203, 189.

337. Hutchings, "Cognitive Short Cuts," 23, citing Kathy Ferguson, *The Man Question: Visions of Subjectivity in Feminist Theory* (Berkeley: University of California Press, 1993), 29.

2. GENDER LENSES LOOK AT WAR(S)

1. This is a phrase Cynthia Enloe has used often, including in *Nimo's War, Emma's War: Making Feminist Sense of the Iraq War* (Berkeley: University of California Press, 2010). See also Cynthia Enloe, *Bananas, Beaches, and Bases: Making Feminist Sense of International Politics* (Berkeley: University of California Press, 1990); Amy Lind, "Making Feminist Sense of Neoliberalism: The Institutionalization of Women's Struggles for Survival in Ecuador and Bolivia," *Journal of Developing Societies* (2002), 18(2–3): 220–258.

2. Enloe, *Nimo's War, Emma's War*, 5.

3. Kimberly Hutchings, "Cognitive Short Cuts," in *Rethinking the Man Question: Sex, Violence, and International Politics,* ed. Marysia Zalewski and Jane Parpart (London: Zed, 2008), 23.

4. This is not meant to dictate or summarize what all feminist perspectives contain or a way that all feminist approaches work. Instead, I acknowledge there is diversity among feminisms and position my work generally and this book specifically among them later in the chapter.

5. See introduction, note 53. For a recent discussion, see the December 2011 "Critical Perspectives" section of *Politics and Gender* ([2012], 7[4]); "The State of Feminist Security Studies," ed. Laura Sjoberg and Jennifer Lobasz, 573–604.

6. For example, R. Charli Carpenter, "Gender Theory in World Politics: Contributions of a Non-Feminist Standpoint," *International Studies Review* (2002), 4(3): 153–165.

7. Laura Shepherd, *Gender, Violence, and Security: Discourse as Practice* (London: Zed, 2008).

8. "Men" and "women" are in quotes in this sentence because there are people who are either/or or neither/both. See introduction, note 39.

9. In this view, gender symbolism describes the way in which masculine/feminine are assigned to various dichotomies that organized Western thought where "both men and women tend to place a higher value on the term which is associated with masculinity" (Lauren Wilcox, "Gendering the Cult of the Offensive," *Security Studies* [2009], 18[2]: 214–240).

10. Marysia Zalewski, "Well, What Is the Feminist Perspective on Bosnia?", *International Affairs* (April 1995), 71(2): 339–356.

11. Wilcox, "Gendering the Cult of the Offensive."

12. Laura Sjoberg, "Introduction to *Security Studies:* Feminist Contributions," *Security Studies* (2009), 18(2): 183–213.

13. In my view, both elements are essential, as is solidarity with critiques of racism, imperialism, classism, heterosexism, and cissexism in global politics. At the same time, I do not want to draw boundaries of what "feminist inquiry" "is" for others as I choose ethical, intellectual, and practical priorities. As I discuss later in this chapter, I draw boundaries for my theorizing and for this book as a part of constituting feminist (war) theorizing by argument.

14. Not to take away from anyone's right to self-identify as feminist, of course.

15. See discussion in the introduction, note 41.

16. Jean Elshtain, "Women, the State, and War," *International Relations* (2009), 23(2): 289–303, 289.

17. For an extended discussion, see Laura Sjoberg, "Gender, the State, and War Redux: Feminisms Across the 'Levels of Analysis,'" *International Relations* (2011), 25(1): 108–134.

18. There are those who disagree, including a number of authors of some of that work. While some scholars acknowledge studying gender without feminism explicitly (e.g., R. Charli Carpenter, "Gender Theory in World Politics: Contributions of a Non-Feminist Standpoint," *International Studies Review* [2002] 4[3]: 153–165), others see feminist IR as "inclusive" of work that uses gender as a variable but not an analytical category (e.g., Valerie Hudson, "But Now Can See: One Academic's Journey to Feminist Security Studies," *Politics and Gender* [2011], 7[4]: 586–590), a broader interpretation than my usage.

19. For example, Ronald Inglehart and Pippa Norris, *Rising Tide: Gender Equality and Cultural Change Around the World* (Cambridge: Cambridge University Press, 2003); Valerie Hudson and Andrea M. Den Boer, *Bare Branches: The Security Implications of Asia's Surplus Male Population* (Cambridge: MIT Press); Valerie Hudson, Bonnie Ballif-Spanvill, Mary Caprioli, and Chad F. Emmett, *Sex and World Peace* (New York: Columbia University Press, 2012).

20. For example, Joshua Goldstein, *War and Gender* (Cambridge: Cambridge University Press, 2001).

21. There is an extent to which this work is included in, and recognized by, war studies; my claim that war studies ignores gender (or at least sex) seems not to be borne out. When I call war studies "genderless," though, I do not mean to neglect this work. Instead, I mean to critique it—arguing that it reifies the public/private divide, includes epistemological and methodological problems in gender analysis, and reflects a serious misunderstanding of what gender is and how it functions in (feminist theories of) global politics. These dynamics are discussed more in chapter 5.

22. Hudson et al., *Sex and World Peace*.

23. Wilcox, "Gendering the Cult of the Offensive."

24. Feminists have argued that Carpenter's approach (in "Gender Theory in World Politics") to studying "gender from a non-feminist perspective" relies on failing to interrogate the naturalness of sex, making it fundamentally at odds with feminist approaches whose work is built on a critique of the assumed immutability of the male/female dichotomy. (Lauren Wilcox makes this argument most articulately in a yet-unpublished manuscript, "What Difference Gender Makes: Ontologies of Gender and Dualism in IR.")

25. Helen Kinsella, "For a Careful Reading: The Conservativism of Gender Constructivism," *International Studies Review* (2003), 5(2): 294–307; Terrell Carver, "Gender/Feminism/IR," *International Studies Review* (2003), 5(2): 288–290.

26. Brooke Ackerly, Maria Stern, and Jacqui True, "Feminist Methodologies for International Relations," in *Feminist Methodologies for International Relations*, ed. Brooke Ackerly, Maria Stern, and Jacqui True, (Cambridge: Cambridge University Press, 2006), 1–17, 5.

27. For example, Sandra Harding and Merrill B. Hintikka, eds., *Discovering Reality: Perspectives on Epistemology, Metaphysics, Methodology, and Science*, 2nd ed. (New York: Springer, 2003); Helen Longino, "Can There Be a Feminist Science?" *Hypatia* (1987), 2(3): 51–64; Liz Stanley and Sue Wise, *Breaking Out Again: Feminist Ontology and Epistemology* (New York: Psychology Press, 2003).

28. J. Ann Tickner, "You Just Don't Understand: Troubled Engagements Between Feminists and International Relations Theorists," *International Studies Quarterly* (1997), 41(4): 611–632, 621.

29. S. Reinharz, *Feminist Methods in Social Research* (Oxford: Oxford University Press, 1992), 248.

30. Tickner, "You Just Don't Understand," 621.

31. See Laura Sjoberg and Jillian Martin, "Feminist Security Theorizing," in *International Studies Compendium*, ed. Robert Denemark (London: Wiley-Blackwell, 2010); Laura Sjoberg, "Introduction to *Security Studies*"; Laura Sjoberg, ed. *Gender and International Security: Feminist Perspectives* (London: Routledge, 2010).

32. As Jean Elshtain misinterprets in "A Reply," *International Relations* (2011), 25(1), 135–141, 138.

33. I mean "necessarily incomplete" in two senses: empirically (since it either does not tell us something about the world that we need to know or obscures information about the world that would be useful in our analysis) and normatively (since those things it ignores and/or obscures have moral value).

34. V. Spike Peterson and Jacqui True, "New Times and New Conversations," in *The Man Question in International Relations*, ed. Marysia Zalewski and Jane Parpart (Boulder: Westview, 1998). Many feminists critique the implicit naturalness of the categories of male and female that are often used to label both sex and gender. See, for example, V. Spike Peterson, "Sexing Political Identities/Nationalism as Heterosexism," *International Feminist Journal of Politics* (1999), 1(1): 34–65, 38.

35. Sjoberg, "Gender, the State, and War Redux."

36. Including realism, liberalism, constructivism, critical theory, postcolonialism, and poststructuralism. J. Ann Tickner and I discuss these in some depth in "Feminism," in *International Relations Theories: Discipline and Diversity*, 3rd ed., ed. Tim Dunne, Milja Kurki, and Steve Smith (Oxford: Oxford University Press, 2010), 193.

37. See discussion in Laura Sjoberg and Caron Gentry, *Mothers, Monsters, Whores: Women's Violence in Global Politics* (London: Zed, 2007), 16.

38. Sjoberg and Gentry, *Mothers, Monsters, Whores*, 16. Because women's "perspectives provide varied, and sometimes conflicting, insights about problems" one might come to question if it is meaningful that "they share gender subordination as common inspiration" (Sjoberg, *Gender, Justice, and the Wars in Iraq* [New York: Lexington, 2006], 37), but some even consider that assumption problematic.

39. Sjoberg, "Introduction to *Security Studies*," 196.

40. See, e.g., Ratna Kapur, "The Tragedy of Victimization Rhetoric: Resurrecting the 'Native' Subject in International/Postcolonial Feminist Legal Studies," *Harvard Human Rights Journal* (2005), 15(1): 1–39.

41. See, e.g., discussion by Christine Sylvester, "The Contributions of Feminist Theory to International Relations," in *International Relations Theory: Positivism and Beyond*, ed. Steve Smith, Ken Booth, and Marysia Zalewski (Cambridge: Cambridge University Press, 2006).

42. See discussion between Laura Parisi, "The Numbers Don't Always Add Up: Dilemmas in Using Quantitative Research Methods for Feminist IR Scholarship," *Politics and Gender* (2009), 5(4): 410–419; and Clair Apodaca, "Overcoming Obstacles in Quantitative Feminist Research," *Politics and Gender* (2009), 5(4): 419–426.

43. For a discussion of feminist global political economy (GPE), see V. Spike Peterson, "International/Global Political Economy," in *Gender Matters in Global Politics*, ed. Laura J. Shepherd (London: Routledge, 2010). See reconsideration of this political economy/security distinction in the conclusion, note 1.

44. For a discussion, see, e.g., J. K. Gibson-Graham, "'Stuffed If I Know!' Reflections on Postmodern Feminist Research," *Gender, Place, and Culture* (1994), 1(2): 201–224.

45. For a discussion, see Karen Ciclitira, "Pornography, Women, and Feminism: Between Pleasure and Politics," *Sexualities* (2004), 7(3): 281–301.

46. For a discussion, see Jennifer Lobasz, "Beyond Border Security: Feminist Approaches to Human Trafficking," *Security Studies* (2009), 18(2): 319–344.

47. See discussion in Robin Riley, Chandra Talpade Mohanty, and Minnie Bruce Pratt, eds., *Feminism and War: Confronting US Imperialism* (London: Zed, 2008).

48. For example, pro-capitalism: Victoria Bernal, "Gender, Culture, and Capitalism: Women and the Remaking of Islamic 'Tradition' in a Sudanese Village," *Comparative Studies in Society and History* (1994), 36(1): 36–67; anti-capitalism, which is a significantly larger group of feminists, including the strand of feminism known as Marxist feminism: J. K. Gibson-Graham, *The End of Capitalism (As We Knew It): A Feminist Critique of Global Political Economy* (Minneapolis: University of Minnesota Press, 2006); Nancy Hartsock, "The Feminist Standpoint: Developing the Ground for a Specifically Feminist Historical Materialism," in *Discovering Reality*, ed. Harding and Hintakka.

49. See, e.g., Catherine MacKinnon, *Are Women Human?* (Cambridge: Harvard University Press, 2006).

50. John Hoffman, *Gender and Sovereignty: Feminism, the State, and International Relations* (London: Palgrave, 2001), 48.

51. Ibid., 48.

52. Along these lines, some approaches to diversity among feminists have (explicitly or implicitly) used an understanding comparable to Stephen White's understanding of weak ontologies, in which one asserts ones own position as contestable, signaling is own limits. (Stephen White, *Sustaining Affirmation: The Strength of Weak Ontology in Political Theory* [Princeton: Princeton University Press, 2000], 8). This is

2. GENDER LENSES LOOK AT WAR(S) • 339

53. See Laura Sjoberg, "Arguing Gender and International Relations," in *Alker and International Relations: Global Studies in an Interconnected World*, ed. Renee Marlin-Bennett (New York: Routledge, 2011), 55–68, citing, on empathy, Christine Sylvester, "Empathic Cooperation: A Feminist Method for IR," *Millennium: Journal of International Studies* (1994), 23(2): 315–334.

54. Sjoberg, *Gender, Justice, and the Wars in Iraq*, 37.

55. Evelyn Fox Keller, *Reflections of Gender and Science* (New Haven: Yale University Press, 1985); Sandra Harding, *Is Science Multicultural?* (Bloomington: Indiana University Press, 1998).

56. Anna Agathangelou and L. H. M. Ling, *Transforming World Politics: From Empire to Multiple Worlds* (New York: Routledge, 2009). On the other hand, some have been critical of the lack of diversity in many feminist approaches to theorizing global politics, e.g., Marianne Marchand, "Different Communities/Different Realities/Different Encounters: A Reply to J. Ann Tickner," *International Studies Quarterly* (1998), 42(2): 199–204.

57. Which does not mean I have not used each of them. Along with other feminist theorists, my work has taken a number of different approaches to (alternatively) bridging, ignoring, minimizing, or valorizing these divides.

58. While progress has been made in relating different feminist approaches to one another, much of the "relating" has been done in the production of scholarship and the justification thereof, rather than in the process of thinking about gender and IR (as a discipline) and gender and international relations (as a subject). See Sjoberg, "Arguing Gender and International Relations."

59. Hayward Alker and Thomas Biersteker, "The Dialectics of World Order: Notes for a Future Archeologist of International Savoir Faire," *International Studies Quarterly* (1984), 28: 121–142, 123.

60. Hayward Alker, *Rediscoveries and Reformulations: Humanistic Methodologies for International Studies* (Cambridge: Cambridge University Press, 1996), 209, 79. An advocate of classical political argumentation, Alker suggests a "controversy-based path of knowledge cumulation" (53).

61. Ibid.

62. Ibid., 61.

63. Ibid., 273. Certainly, feminisms have used the reading of narrative scripts *as method* to do feminist substantive research (most recently and effectively in Annick Wibben's *Feminist Security Studies: A Narrative Approach* (London: Routledge, 2011). This approach looks to capitalize on the advantages of those employments of narrative analysis and takes two steps further: applying the method to constituting feminist approaches and looking for and valuing differences within the narrative scripts being analyzed.

64. See chapter 1, note 266 for a more in-depth discussion.

65. For a discussion of monism and dualism, see Patrick Thaddeus Jackson, *The Conduct of Inquiry in International Relations* (New York: Routledge, 2010).

66. Sjoberg, "Arguing Gender and International Relations."

67. Ibid. In Hoffman's terms, a "momentum concept" provides a way forward for feminist security studies because it is "constantly changing in both size and shape to accommodate new interpretations, internal disagreement, and change over time" (Hoffman, *Gender and Sovereignty*, 8, 25).

68. By "changes," I mean gives it different priorities than those generally understood to belong to or assigned to it.

69. See Laura Sjoberg, "Looking Forward: Conceptualizing Feminist Security Studies," *Politics and Gender* (2011), 7(4): 600–604. Particularly, I think it is important to speak to the policy world, to engage in reflexivity, to be inclusive, to maintain a distinct feminist politics, and to push feminisms beyond the materials, and I do not have a problem with the feminist pursuit of those goals, even when they conflict.

70. If a narrative is a story about an event or set of events that frames complicated things to fit into discrete categories, this approach sees feminist IR as a narrative generated by argument and conflict among feminists and with the discipline called IR. Knowledge about gender and global politics and about the epistemological and methodological choices in the study of gender and global politics, can be generated argumentatively, both in the results of arguments and in the arguments themselves. Such an approach can see feminism in IR (in Marysia Zalewski's terms, in "Do We Understand Each Other Yet? Troubling Feminist Encounters With(in) International Relations," *British Journal of Politics and International Relations* [2007], 9[2]: 302–312) "undoing itself" and "undoing IR" while simultaneously building itself, its identity, and its research program from the fruits of those (argumentative) undoings (see Sjoberg, "Arguing Gender and International Relations.")

71. While "epistemologically pluralist" would indicate a preference for a particular set of epistemological assumptions with tolerance for others or modesty about the potential to universalize that set of assumptions, in these (experimental) "multi-epistemological" signifies analysis within different, and across, epistemological frameworks.

72. This is also Christine Sylvester's phrasing, in "The Art of War/The War Question in (Feminist) IR," *Millennium: Journal of International Studies* (2005), 33(3): 855–878.

73. In John Vasquez's words in *The War Puzzle Revisited* (Cambridge: Cambridge University Press, 2009).

74. As I recently tried to explain to/in response to Jean Elshtain in "Gender, the State, and War Redux."

75. Christine Sylvester, ed. *Experiencing War* (London: Routledge, 2011); Christine Sylvester, "War, Sense, and Security," in *Gender and International Security*, ed. Laura Sjoberg (London: Routledge, 2010); 24–37; Sylvester, "The Art of War/the War Question in Feminist IR."

76. Enloe, *Nimo's War, Emma's War.*

77. By "war proper" I mean studying war as the work I identify as war studies sees it, rather than (or more appropriately in addition to) critiquing the narrowness of that work.

78. For example, Wibben, *Feminist Security Studies*; Annick Wibben, "Feminist·Politics of Feminist Security Studies" *Politics and Gender* (2011), 7(4): 589–595. Wibben argues that engaging the mainstream can be counterproductive because of the borders that it sets for theorizing.

79. Sarah Brown, "Feminism, International Theory, and International Relations of Gender Inequality," *Millennium: Journal of International Studies* (1988), 17(3): 461–475, 472.

80. Zalewski, "Do We Understand Each Other Yet?," 310.

81. Hutchings, "Cognitive Short Cuts," 30.

82. J. Ann Tickner, "You Just Don't Understand: Troubled Engagements Between Feminisms and IR Theorists," *International Studies Quarterly* (1997), 41(4): 611, 612.

83. J. Ann Tickner, "Continuing the Conversation," *International Studies Quarterly* (1998), 42(1): 205–210, 209.

84. Tickner, "You Just Don't Understand," 614.

85. Cynthia Weber, "Good Girls, Little Girls, and Bad Girls: Male Paranoia in Robert Keohane's Critique of Feminist International Relations," *Millennium: Journal of International Studies* (1994), 23(2): 337–349.

86. As Tickner laments, "feminist theorists have rarely achieved the serious engagement with other IR scholars for which they have frequently called. When they have occurred, conversations have often led to misunderstandings and other kinds of miscommunication" ("You Just Don't Understand," 628).

87. Marysia Zalewski, "Do We Understand Each Other Yet?"; Brown, "Feminism, International Theory, and International Relations of Gender Inequality."

88. Judith Squires and Jutta Weldes, "Beyond Being Marginal: Gender and International Relations in Britain," *British Journal of Politics and International Relations* (2007), 9(2): 185–203, 185.

89. Other (interactive) strategies include studying gender with the methods that those who study war without gender use (which I call mimicry), looking for a dramatic punch line to attract the attention of the mainstream (which I call attention-seeking), and being confrontational toward the mainstream's gendered assumptions (which I call battle mode). I do not mean any of those as insulting—I have used all of them (probably in this book)—but I think it is important to have a sense of the coping mechanisms that scholars use to deal with difficult communications and (scholarly) relationships.

90. Tickner, "You Just Don't Understand," 629.

91. Sjoberg, "Introduction to *Security Studies*: Feminist Contributions."

92. Jill Steans, "Engaging from the Margins: Feminist Encounter with the 'Mainstream' of International Relations," *British Journal of Politics and International Relations* (2003), 5(3): 445.

93. Steans, "Engaging from the Margins," 435.

94. For my discussion of the personal stakes, see Laura Sjoberg, "Emotion, Risk, and Feminist Research in IR," *International Studies Review* (2011), 13(4): 699–703. The piece was a part of a forum on emotion and the feminist IR researcher, edited by Christine Sylvester and with contributions by Sandra Marshall, Megan MacKenzie,

Shirin Saeidi and Heather Turcotte, and Swati Parashar, which also discuss the personal risks and investments of feminist research in different scenarios.

95. See ongoing conversation between Tickner (in "You Just Don't Understand"; "Continuing the Conversation"; and "You May Never Understand: Prospects for Feminist Futures in International Relations," *Australian Feminist Law Journal* (2010), 32: 9–20), Robert Keohane (most directly in "Beyond Dichotomy: Conversations Between International Relations and Feminist Theory," *International Studies Quarterly* [1998], 42[2]: 193–198), and others (including Weber, "Good Girls, Little Girls, Bad Girls"; and Steans, "Engaging from the Margins." These discussions bring up communication and language issues along with epistemological and ontological ones.

96. For a positive opinion, see Mary Caprioli, "Feminist IR Theory and Quantitative Methodology: A Critical Analysis," *International Studies Review* (2004), 6(2): 253–269. For more skepticism, see Tickner, "You Just Don't Understand." For a discussion about the costs, see Carol Cohn, "'Feminist Security Studies': Towards a Reflexive Practice," *Politics and Gender* (2011), 7(4): 581–586.

97. The "founding mothers" of the feminist movement were often vocal about the link between feminism and pacifism. See Jane Addams, *The Spirit of Youth and the City Streets* (Ubana-Champaign: University of Illinois Press, 1909); Elizabeth Cady Stanton, Susan B. Anthony, and M. J. Gage, *History of Women's Suffrage, 1848–1861* (Rochester, NY: Charles Mann, 1887); Birgit Brock-Utne, *Educating for Peace: A Feminist Perspective* (London: Pergamon, 1985).

98. Harriet H. Alonso, *Peace as a Women's Issue: A History of the US Movement for World Peace and Women's Rights* (Syracuse, NY: Syracuse University Press, 1993). See also Adrienne Harris and Yneistra King, *Rocking the Ship of the State: Towards a Feminist Peace Politics* (Boulder: Westview, 1989); Karen Warren and Duane Cady, "Feminism and Peace: Seeing the Connections," *Hypatia* (1994), 9(2): 4–19; Catia Confortini, "Links Between Women, Peace, and Disarmament: Snapshots from the WILPF," in *Gender, War, and Militarism: Feminist Perspectives*, ed. Laura Sjoberg and Sandra Via (Santa Barbara, CA: Praeger Security International, 2010), 157–168.

99. See www.wilpf.org; see also Catia Confortini, *Intelligent Compassion: Feminist Critical Methodologies in the Women's International League for Peace and Freedom*, (Oxford: Oxford University Press, 2012).

100. Paula Banerjee, *Women in Peace Politics* (London: Sage, 2008); E. Romanova, *Women's Civil-Societal Actions in Chechnya and Russia* (London: Paradigm, 2009); Laura Toussaint, *The Contemporary US Peace Movement* (New York: Taylor and Francis, 2008).

101. Betty Reardon, *Sexism and the War System* (New York: Teacher's College Press, 1985), 20.

102. See also Sara Ruddick, *Maternal Thinking: Towards a Politics of Peace* (New York: Houghton-Mifflin, 1989); Nancy Chodorow, "Gender as a Personal and Cultural Construction," *Signs: Journal of Women in Culture and Society* (1995), 20(3): 516–544.

103. J. Ann Tickner, "Hans Morgenthau's Principles of Political Realism: A Feminist Reformulation," *Millennium: Journal of International Studies* (1988), 17(3): 429–440; Tickner, *Gender in International Relations*; Jane Flax, "Postmodernism and Gender

Relations in Feminist Theory," *Signs: Journal of Women in Culture and Society* (1987), 12(4): 621–643; Charlotte Hooper, *Manly States: Masculinities, International Relations, and Gender Politics* (New York: Columbia University Press, 2001).

104. Sandra Harding, *The Science Question in Feminism* (Indianapolis: Indiana University Press, 1986). Italics in original.

105. Sjoberg and Martin, "Feminist Security Theorizing," citing Elisabeth Prugl, *The Global Construction of Gender: Home-Based Work in the Political Economy of the 21st Century* (New York: Columbia University Press, 1999); R. W. Connell, *Masculinities* (Berkeley: University of California Press, 1995), 156; Gibson-Graham, "'Stuffed If I Know!'"

106. Mary Wollstonecraft, *A Vindication of the Rights of Woman* (New York: Penguin, [1792] 1985).

107. Virginia Woolf, *Three Guineas* (New York: Harcourt, Brace, and World, [1938] 1967). Barbara Andrew has argued that Virginia Woolf's theorizing about gender and security is derived from Wollstonecraft's ideas (see, e.g., Barbara Andrew, "The Psychology of Tyranny: Wollstonecraft and Woolf on the Gendered Dimensions of War," *Hypatia* [1994], 9[2]: 85–101).

108. Keller, *Reflections on Gender and Science*; Sandra Harding and Merrill Hintikka, *Discovering Reality: Feminist Perspectives on Epistemology, Metaphysics, Methodology, and the Philosophy of Science* (Dordrecht: D. Reidel, 1983); Sandra Harding, *Feminism and Methodology* (Bloomington: Indiana University Press, 1987).

109. June Nash, ed., *Women and Men in the International Division of Labor* (Albany: State University of New York Press, 1983); Kate Young, Carol Wolkowitz, and Roslyn McCullagh, eds., *Of Marriage and the Market: Women's Subordination in International Perspective* (London: CSE Books, 1978).

110. Reardon, *Sexism and the War System*.

111. Ruddick, *Maternal Thinking*. Ruddick also argued that mothers tend to see potential enemies as the children of others and therefore object to war more generally. See also Judith Stiehm (*Women and Men's Wars* [Oxford: Pergamon, 1983]; Judith Stiehm, "The Protected, the Protector, the Defender," *Women's Studies International Forum* [1982], 5[3/4]: 367–376).

112. Brigit Brock-Utne, *Feminist Perspectives on Peace and Peace Education* (New York: Teachers' College Press, 1989). For further discussion of the relationship between positive peace and negative peace, see Johan Galtung, *The True Worlds: A Transnational Perspective* (New York: Free Press, 1980).

113. Jean Elshtain, "The Problem with Peace," *Millennium: Journal of International Studies* (1988), 17(3): 441–449.

114. Nira Yuval-Davis, *Gender and Nation* (London: Sage, 1997).

115. Cynthia Enloe, *Does Khaki Become You? The Militarization of Women's Lives* (London: Pandora, 1983), 5.

116. Ibid., 7.

117. Ibid., 10.

118. Enloe, *Bananas, Beaches, and Bases*, 133.

119. Ibid., 212 (emphasis in original).

120. V. Spike Peterson, ed. *Gendered States: Feminist (Re)Visions of International Security* (Boulder: Lynne Rienner, 1992), 1.

121. Tickner, *Gender in International Relations*, ix.

122. V. Spike Peterson and Anne Sisson Runyan, "The Radical Future of Realism: Feminist Subversions of IR Theory," *Alternatives* (1991), 16: 67–106; V. Spike Peterson and Anne Sisson Runyan, *Global Gender Issues* (Boulder: Westview, 1991): 70, 11, 28.

123. Tickner, in *Gender in International Relations*, included a chapter focusing on "gendered perspectives on national security," developing the feminist critique of state security (27).

124. Feminists like J. Ann Tickner (*Gendering World Politics* [New York: Columbia University Press, 2001]), Annick Wibben (*Feminist Security Studies*), Maria Stern ("'We' the Subject: The Power and Failure of (In)Security," *Security Dialogue* [2006], 37[2]: 187–205), and Lena Hansen, "The Little Mermaid's Silent Security Dilemma and the Absence of Gender in the Copenhagen School," *Millennium: Journal of International Studies* [2000], 29[2]: 285–306), have engaged with critical security studies directly and pointed out the similarities between their interpretations and the views through gender lenses.

125. Cynthia Enloe, *The Morning After: Sexual Politics at the End of the Cold War* (Berkeley: University of California Press, 1993), 38.

126. Ibid., 115.

127. Ibid., 123.

128. Enloe, *Bananas, Beaches, and Bases*, 168.

129. See the introduction, note 53, discussing major works in feminist security studies.

130. Sjoberg, "Introduction to *Security Studies*," 184.

131. Tickner, *Gendering World Politics*; Peterson, ed., *Gendered States*; Jan Jindy Pettman, *Worlding Women: A Feminist International Politics* (London: Routledge, 1996). See discussion in chapter 5.

132. Jean Elshtain and Shelia Tobias, eds., *Women, Militarism, and War* (Lanham, MD: Rowman and Littlefield, 1990).

133. Tickner, *Gendering World Politics*; Pettman, *Worlding Women*.

134. Elshtain, "The Problem with Peace"; Reardon, *Sexism and the War System*; Chris Cuomo, "War Is Not Just an Event: Reflections on the Significance of Everyday Violence" *Hypatia* (1996), 11(4): 30–45.

135. Peterson and Runyan, "The Radical Future of Realism," 86.

136. Zalewski, "Well, What Is the Feminist Perspective on Bosnia?"

137. Charlotte Hooper, "Masculinities in Transition," in *Gender and Global Restructuring: Sightings, Sites, and Resistances*, ed. Marianne Marchand and Anne Sisson Runyan, (New York: Routledge, 2000).

138. Katharine Moon, *Sex Among Allies: Militarized Prostitution in U.S.-South Korean Relations* (New York: Columbia University Press, 1997).

139. Sjoberg, *Gender, Justice, and the Wars in Iraq*.

140. Carol Cohn, Felicity Hill, and Sara Ruddick, "Relevance of Gender for Eliminating Weapons of Mass Destruction," *Disarmament Diplomacy* (2005), 80: 39–48.

141. Carol Cohn and Sara Ruddick, "A Feminist Ethical Perspective on Weapons of Mass Destruction," in *Ethics and Weapons of Mass Destruction*, ed. Steven Lee and Sohail Hashmi (Princeton: Princeton University Press, 2004).

142. Runa Das, "How Strategic Culture Matters for Gender and (In)Security: Indian Women, Anti-Nuclear/Peace Activism, Civil Society, and Visions of a Sustainable Future—Connecting the Local to the Global." Paper Presented at the 2005 Annual Meeting of the International Studies Association, 26–29 March 2005, in Honolulu, HI.

143. Wilcox, "Gendering the Cult of the Offensive"; Cristina Masters, "Bodies of Technology: Cyborg Soldiers and Militarized Masculinities," *International Feminist Journal of Politics* (2005), 7(1): 112–132.

144. Sjoberg, *Gender, Justice, and the Wars in Iraq*

145. Carol Cohn, "Sex and Death in the World of Rational Defense Intellectuals," *Signs: Journal of Women in Culture and Society* (1987), 12(4): 687–718.

146. Sjoberg, *Gender, Justice, and the Wars in Iraq*.

147. Sandra Whitworth, *Men, Militarism, and Peacekeeping* (Boulder: Lynne Rienner, 2004).

148. Cynthia Enloe, *Maneuvers: The International Politics of Militarizing Women's Lives* (Berkeley: University of California Press, 2000). For another example, Galia Golan's work on the gendered nature of Israeli militarization demonstrates the crucial role that gender plays in security politics and policy (Galia Golan, "Militarization and Gender: The Israeli Experience," *Women's Studies International Forum* (September–December 1997): 20[5/6]: 581–586, 581). For in-depth coverage of the gendered dimensions of the Israel/Palestine conflict, see Simona Sharoni, *Gender and the Israeli-Palestinian Conflict: The Politics of Women's Resistance* (Syracuse, NY: Syracuse University Press, 1994).

149. See, e.g., Sjoberg, "Introduction to *Security Studies*."

150. Tickner, *Gender in International Relations*. Though there is no single unifying ontology, epistemology, or method behind feminist security studies that could clearly be translated into theorizing war through gender lenses, much of the work so far addressing security has several common themes, including a broad understanding of what security is.

151. If "masculinism is the ideology that justifies and naturalizes gender hierarchy by not questioning the elevation of ways of being and knowing associated with men and masculinity over those associated with women and femininity," (Charlotte Hooper, "Masculinist Practices and Gender Politics: The Operation of Multiple Masculinities in International Relations," in Zalewski and Parpart, eds. *The Man Question*, 31), then the values socially associated with femininity and masculinity are awarded unequal weight, perpetuating inequality in perceived gender difference. This means that "from a feminist point of view, masculinity poses a problem in two different ways. It is a problem insofar as masculine identities have concrete effects . . . [and] because it incorporates a hierarchical logic of exclusion of women and the feminine" (Hutchings, "Cognitive Shortcuts," 30).

152. Sjoberg and Martin, "Feminist Security Theorizing," citing Peterson, "Sexing Political Identities"; Hooper, *Manly States*.

153. About the causes of war, see, e.g., Cynthia Cockburn, "Gender Relations as Causal of Militarization and War: A Feminist Standpoint," *International Feminist Journal of Politics* (2010), 12(2): 139–157; Elisabeth Prugl, "Gender and War: Causes, Constructions, and Critique," *PS: Political Science and Politics* (2003), 1(2): 335–342. About the practices of war, see, e.g., Dubravka Zarkov, *The Body of War: Media, Ethnicity, and Gender in the Break-up of Yugoslavia* (Durham, NC: Duke University Press, 2007); Annica Kronsell, *Gender, Sex, and Post-National Defense* (Oxford: Oxford University Press, 2012). About experiences of war, see, e.g., Cynthia Cockburn, *From Where We Stand: War, Women's Activism, and Feminist Analysis* (London: Zed, 2007); Sylvester, ed. *Experiencing War*.

154. Tickner, *Gender in International Relations*; Tickner, *Gendering World Politics*; Reardon, *Sexism and the War System*.

155. A description I first heard from Christine Sylvester at the 2004 Annual Meeting of the International Studies Association.

156. Alexander Wendt, "On Constitution and Causation in International Relations," *Review of International Studies* (January 1998), 24(1): 101–122.

157. Megan MacKenzie, "Securitization and Desecuritization: Female Soldiers and the Reconstruction of Women in Post-Conflict Sierra Leone," *Security Studies* (2009), 18(2): 241–261; Sandra McEvoy, "Loyalist Women Paramilitaries in Northern Ireland: Beginning a Feminist Conversation About Conflict Resolution," *Security Studies* (2009), 18(2): 262–286.

158. Birgit Locher and Elisabeth Prugl, "Feminism and Constructivism: Worlds Apart or Sharing the Middle Ground?" *International Studies Quarterly* (March 2001), 45(1): 111–129.

159. Ibid., 116.

160. Ackerly et al., "Feminist Methodologies for International Relations," 5.

161. Naomi Scheman, *Engenderings: Constructions of Knowledge, Authority, and Privilege.* (New York: Routledge, 1993); Sandra Harding, *Is Science Multicultural?*; Sandra Harding, *Postcolonialisms, Feminisms, and Epistemologies* (Bloomington, IN: Indiana University Press, 1998); Mary Hawkesworth, "Knowers, Knowing, Known: Feminist Theory and Claims of Truth," *Signs: Journal of Women in Culture and Society* (Spring 1989), 14(3): 533–557. Instead, "objective" knowledge is only the "subjective" knowledge of privileged voices disguised as neutral by culturally assumed objectivity, "where the privileged are licensed to think *for* everyone, so long as they do so 'objectively.'" (e.g., Mary Maynard and June Purvis, eds., *Researching Women's Lives from a Feminist Perspective* [London: Taylor and Francis, 1994]; Anne Marie Goetz, "Feminism and the Claim to Know: Contradictions in Feminist Approaches to Women in Development," in *Gender and International Relations*, ed. Rebecca Grant and Kathleen Newland (Bloomington: Indiana University Press, 1991); Keller, *Reflections on Gender and Science*.

162. Christine Sylvester, *Feminist International Relations: An Unfinished Journey* (Cambridge: Cambridge University Press, 2002), 275; Tickner, *Gendering World Politics*. Feminist scholars have argued that all IR scholarship has political commitments, even though most of the discipline hides its politics behind claimed objectivity (Jill Steans, *Gender and International Relations*, 29). Many feminist scholars explicitly

express a political commitment to understanding the world from the points of view of marginalized peoples and actors (e.g., Tickner, *Gender in International Relations*).

163. Tickner, "Continuing the Conversation"; Tickner, "Feminism Meets International Relations."

164. Different feminists hold different perspectives on the degree to which feminism is *necessarily* a methodological and epistemological critique of mainstream war studies. For example, Mary Caprioli argues that it is possible to "build a bridge among feminist and traditional worldviews" by providing a rationale for the incorporation of feminism into conventional IR using a quantitative approach. (Mary Caprioli, "Feminist IR Theory and Quantitative Methodology: A Critical Analysis," *International Studies Review* [June 2004], 6[2]: 253–269). On the other hand, others argue that "reason itself is more deeply implicated in our oppression; [therefore] the problem is not one that can be solved by a shift in emphasis . . . the core idea is that a rational stance is itself a stance of oppression or domination, and accepted ideals of reason both reflect and reinforce power relations that advantage white privileged men." (Sally Haslanger, "On Being Objective and Objectified," in *A Mind of One's Own: Feminist Articles in Reason and Objectivity*, ed. Louis M. Anthony and Charlotte Witt [Boulder: Westview, 2002]). It should also be noted that even this dialogical understanding of feminism's diversities is importantly limited by language, location, and the debates being engaged. As an American whose primary language is English, interested (for this project) in engaging the American mainstream of the discipline, I will inevitably (if not intentionally) focus substantive discussion and citational practice in that direction.

3. ANARCHY, STRUCTURE, GENDER, AND WAR(S)

An abbreviated version of this chapter was published as "What Waltz Couldn't See: Gender, Structure, and War," *International Theory* (2012), 4(1): 1–38.

1. Kenneth Waltz, *Man, the State, and War* (New York: Columbia University Press, 1959). See also J. David Singer, "The Levels-of-Analysis Problem in International Relations," *World Politics* (1961), 14(1): 77–92. Waltz (and others) theorize the "third image" or international system from a realist perspective, but Christian Reus-Smit sees systemic theorizing in constructivism, particularly in the work of Alexander Wendt. Reus-Smit characterizes this as systemic because "everything that exists or occurs within the domestic political realm is ignored, and an account of world politics is derived simply from theorizing how states relate to one another" (Christian Reus-Smit, "Constructivism," in Scott Burchill, Andrew Linklater, Richard Devetak, Jack Donnelly, Terry Nardin, Matthew Paterson, Christian Reus-Smit, and Jacqui True, *Theories of International Relations* [4th ed. New York: Palgrave Macmillan, 2009], 223). In Waltz's terms, this is a *systemic*, but not *structural* account.

2. Stacie E. Goddard and Daniel H. Nexon, "Paradigm Lost? Structural Realism and Structural Functionalism," *European Journal of International Relations* (2005), 9(1): 9–61, 10.

3. Ibid., 15, 16.

4. This should not be taken as arguing that exploring the relationship between gender and the social and cultural elements of the international system is not a fruitful avenue of exploration; quite the opposite, a feminist exploration of the "cultures of anarchy" (Alexander Wendt, *Social Theory of International Politics* [Cambridge: Cambridge University Press, 1999]) would be an important contribution to the literature, if a different one than this chapter's project.

5. J. Ann Tickner, *Gender in International Relations* (New York: Columbia University Press, 1992); Sarah Brown, "Feminism, International Theory, and the International Relations of Gender Inequality," *Millennium: Journal of International Studies* (1988), 17(3): 461–475.

6. V. Spike Peterson, "Transgressing Boundaries: Theories of Knowledge, Gender, and International Relations," *Millennium: Journal of International Studies* (1992), 21(2): 183–206.

7. Tickner, *Gender in International Relations*, 56; Charlotte Hooper, *Manly States* (New York: Columbia University Press, 2001).

8. Jacqui True, "Feminism," in *Theories of International Relations*, ed. Scott Burchill and Andrew Linklater (London: MacMillan, 1998).

9. As discussed below, the literature on patriarchy in global politics (though mostly outside IR) that characterizes gender hierarchy as structural (if not in Waltzian terms) is a notable exception.

10. Kenneth Waltz, *Theory of International Politics* (Boston, MA: Addison Wesley, 1979), 67.

11. Nexon and Goddard (in "Paradigm Lost?") go so far as to characterize Waltz's third image as a thought experiment that was to him analytical, rather than, strictly speaking, real. While that is debatable, that Waltz saw anarchy as a cause of *war* among other causes of *wars* is not.

12. Waltz, *Theory of International Politics*, 81.

13. Ibid., 100–101.

14. Ibid., 82, 87.

15. Ibid., 89.

16. Ibid., 88.

17. Kenneth Waltz, *Man, the State, and War: A Theoretical Analysis* (New York: Columbia University Press, 1959), 233.

18. For liberal institutionalists, see, e.g., Robert Axelrod and Robert Keohane, "Achieving Cooperation Under Anarchy? Strategies and Institutions," *World Politics* (1985), 38(1): 228–254; Duncan Snidal, "Coordination versus Prisoner's Dilemma: Implications for International Coordination and Regimes," *American Political Science Review* (1985), 79(4): 932–942. For constructivists, see, e.g., Alexander Wendt, "Anarchy Is What States Make of It: The Social Construction of Power Politics" *International Organization* (1992), 46(2): 391–425; Ted Hopf, "The Promise of Constructivism in International Relations Theory," *International Security* (1998), 23(1): 171–200.

19. Waltz, *Man, the State, and War*, 227.

20. Waltz, *Theory of International Politics*, 91, 104.

21. Ibid., 94, 97. John Mearsheimer agrees in *The Tragedy of Great Power Politics* (New York: Norton, 2001), 29.

22. See, e.g., Mearsheimer, *The Tragedy of Great Power Politics*; Joseph Grieco, "Anarchy and the Limits of Cooperation: A Realist Critique of the Newest Liberal Institutionalism," *International Organization* (1988), 42(4): 485–507; Stephen Walt, "Testing Theories of Alliance Formation: The Case of Southwest Asia, *International Organization* (1988), 42(2): 275–316.

23. Wendt, "Anarchy Is What States Make of It," 304.

24. Axelrod and Keohane, "Achieving Cooperation Under Anarchy."

25. Waltz, *Theory of International Politics*, 114.

26. See, e.g., Michael Doyle, "Kant, Liberal Legacies, and Foreign Affairs," *Philosophy and Public Affairs* (1983), 12(4): 323–353; Bruce Russett, *Grasping the Democratic Peace* (Princeton: Princeton University Press, 1994).

27. John Mearsheimer, "A Realist Reply," *International Security* (1995), 20(1): 82–93; Robert Keohane, "Realism, Neorealism, and the Study of World Politics," in *Neorealism and Its Critics*, ed. Robert Keohane (New York: Columbia University Press, 1986).

28. Mearsheimer, "A Realist Reply," 7.

29. Waltz, *Theory of International Politics*, 114.

30. Wendt, "Anarchy Is What States Make of It."

31. Ibid.

32. Ibid., 394, 395.

33. Ibid., 396.

34. Ibid., 403; Alexander Wendt, "The Agent-Structure Problem in International Relations Theory," *International Organization* (1986), 41(3): 335–370, 362–365.

35. Wendt, *Social Theory of International Politics*, 142.

36. Waltz, *Theory of International Politics*, 31.

37. Waltz, "Structural Realism After the Cold War," *International Security* (2000), 25(1): 5–41, 5–6.

38. Ibid., 39–41.

39. For example, Colin Wight, *Agents, Structures, and International Relations: Politics as Ontology* (Cambridge: Cambridge University Press, 2006).

40. Hidemi Suganami, *On the Causes of War* (Oxford: Clarendon Press, 1996), 62, 201.

41. Ibid.

42. Waltz, *Theory of International Politics*, 1.

43. Suganami, *On the Causes of War*, 201.

44. See, e.g., some of the alternatives Waltz cites, like Paul Baran and Paul Sweeny, *Monopoly Capital: An Essay on American Economic and Social Order* (New York: Monthly Review Press, 1966); Warren Weaver, "Science and Complexity," in *The Scientists Speak*, ed. Weaver (New York: Bonir Gaer, 1942).

45. There has been some discussion of this in the constructivist literature, (e.g., Wendt, "Anarchy Is What States Make of It"; Wendt, *Social Theory of International Politics*; Goddard and Nexon, "Paradigm Lost?")

46. Waltz, *Theory of International Politics*, 81.

47. Ibid., 100–101.

48. Ibid., 82, 87.

49. Ibid., 89.

50. There is a significant literature on informal structures of organizations—unspoken, unwritten, and unrecorded rules that nonetheless all members know (consciously or unconsciously) and follow. See, e.g., M. Aoki, *A Cooperative Game Theory of the Firm* (Oxford: Clarendon, 1988); Diane Reyniers, "Cooperation in Contests: A Model of Mixed Organizational Culture," *Rationality and Society* (1996), 8(4): 413–432; J. S. Ott, *The Organizational Culture Perspective* (Pacific Grove, CA: Brooks/Cole, 1989). This pairs with feminist work on looking for silences (e.g., Hilary Charlesworth, "Feminist Methods in International Law," *American Journal of International Law* [1999], 93[2]: 379–394) or looking at the gendered assumptions of organizational discourses (e.g., Laura J. Shepherd, "Sex, Security, and Superheroines: From 1325 to 1820 and Beyond," *International Feminist Journal of Politics* [2011], 13[4]: 504–521) to suggest that gender can be both structural and invisible as structure.

51. See Anthony Giddens, *New Rules of Sociological Method* (Stanford, CA: Stanford University Press, 1976) in which structuration attempts to take account of both structure and agency and contextual rules influence behavior.

52. Elizabeth Frazer, "Feminist Political Theory" in *Contemporary Feminist Theories*, ed. Jackie Jones and Stevi Jackson (Edinburgh: Edinburgh University Press, 1998), 54.

53. Feminist theorizing has emphasized that, though genders and their relationships change over time, place, and culture, gender hierarchies can be found across all of those variations. For specific discussions of: reproductive capacity (see Joan Scott "Gender: A Useful Category of Historical Analysis," *American Historical Review* [December 1986], 91[5]: 1053–1075), language (Deborah Tannen, *You Just Don't Understand: Women and Men in Conversation* [New York: Morrow, 1990]), performance (Judith Butler, *Gender Trouble: Feminism and the Subversion of Identity* [New York: Routledge, 1990]), sexuality (Catherine MacKinnon, *Towards a Feminist Theory of the State* [Cambridge: Harvard University Press, 1993]), human nature and/or psychology (Nancy Hirschmann, *The Subject of Liberty: Toward A Feminist Theory of Freedom* [Princeton: Princeton University Press, 2003]), human social organization (Wendy Brown, *States of Injury: Power and Freedom in Late Modernity* [Princeton: Princeton University Press, 1995]), and evolution (Barbara D. Miller, *Sex and Gender Hierarchies* [Cambridge: Cambridge University Press, 1993]).

54. Judith Squires, *Gender in Political Theory* (London: Wiley Blackwell, 2000).

55. The closest feminist theorizing has come to such an argument is in discussions about patriarchy (largely in sociology and women's studies). Sylvia Walby (in "Theorizing Patriarchy," *Sociology* [1989], 23[3]: 213–234) defines patriarchy as "a system of social structures, and practices, in which men dominate, oppress, and exploit women" making sure to eschew both biological determinism and assigning individual guilt to individual men. She finds patriarchy in modes of production, in relations of paid work, within the state, in male violence, in sexuality, and in cultural institutions (214).

A number of feminists in the 1980s believed that patriarchy as a concept was the most appropriate way to account for gender hierarchy in social and political life, given that it included a structural element. Still others were concerned that it neglected ethnic difference (e.g., bell hooks, *Ain't I a Woman?* [London: Pluto, 1982]), that it was gender essentialist (e.g., Lynne Segal, *Is the Future Female? Troubled Thoughts on Contemporary Feminism* [London: Virago, 1987]), that it was ahistorical (e.g., Michele Barrett, *Women's Oppression Today: The Marxist/Feminist Encounter* [London: Pluto, 1980]), or that it mandated heterosexuality (Adrienne Rich, "Compulsory Heterosexuality and the Lesbian Existence," *Signs: Journal of Women in Culture and Society* [1987], 5[4]: 631–660). At the founding moments of feminist IR in the late 1980s and early 1990s, most feminist IR scholars chose terms such as *gender inequality* and *gender hierarchy* over *patriarchy* both to avoid these problems and to demonstrate the complexity of gender relations (e.g., Rebecca Grant and Kathleen Newland, eds. *Gender and International Relations* [Bloomington: Indiana University Press, 1991]). With that move, though, feminist IR theorists lost the structural element of the study of patriarchy, in my view.

56. J. Ann Tickner, *Gendering World Politics* (New York: Columbia University Press, 2001), 4.

57. Ibid., 5.

58. Ibid., 6–7.

59. R. W. Connell, *Masculinities* (Berkeley: University of California Press, 1995).

60. Lauren Wilcox, "Gendering the 'Cult of the Offensive,'" *Security Studies* (2009), 18(2): 214–240.

61. Waltz, "Structural Realism After the Cold War."

62. Brown, "Feminism, International Theory, and International Relations of Gender Inequality," 472.

63. Feminists critique structural realists for the gendered nature of their microeconomic analysis, exclusive politics, rationalist logic, and/or privileging system-level explanations at the expense of analyzing the margins of global politics. I argue that these flaws of structural realism are not essential to structural theorizing.

64. See chapter 6 for a discussion of the arguments that states are gendered or that the level of gender inequality in states is predictive of the level of violence.

65. See chapter 5 for a discussion of states' gendered relations.

66. See chapter 7 for a discussion of gender and war in first-image analysis (in which I also do not argue that human nature is gendered, but point out the ways that gendered individual interactions can be causal in and constitutive of war[s]).

67. See discussions of issues of cross-fertilization and inseparability of levels of analysis in chapter 9 and the conclusion.

68. Waltz, *Man, the State, and War.*

69. Dana Britton, "The Epistemology of the Gendered Organization," *Gender and Society* (2000), 14(3): 418–434. The material element of this understanding of gender as structural is key, much as it is to Waltz's understanding.

70. Joan Acker, "Hierarchies, Jobs, Bodies: A Theory of Gendered Organizations," *Gender and Society* (1990), 4(2): 139–158, 139. See also Patricia Martin and

David Collinson, "Over the Pond and Across the Water: Developing a Field of Gendered Organizations," *Gender, Work, and Organization* (2002), 9(3): 244–265; Dana M. Britton and Laura Logan, "Gendered Organizations: Progress and Prospects," *Sociology Compass* (2008), 2(1): 107–121; Joan Acker, "Theorizing Gender, Race, and Class in Organizations," in *Handbook of Gender, Work, and Organization*, ed. Emma Jeanes, David Knights, and Patricia Yancey Martin (London: Wiley, 2011); Mats Alvesson and Yvonne Due Billing, *Understanding Gender and Organizations* (London: Sage, 2009).

71. Acker, "Hierarchies, Jobs, Bodies: A Theory of Gendered Organizations."

72. Ibid., 142.

73. Ibid.

74. Ibid., 146–147.

75. Catherine MacKinnon, *Only Words* (Cambridge: Harvard University Press, 1993).

76. For example, Tickner, *Gender in International Relations*; Jan Jindy Pettman, *Worlding Women: A Feminist International Politics* (New York: Psychology Press, 1996).

77. Tickner, *Gender in International Relations*.

78. A reviewer for the article version of this chapter contended that this is a catch-22: if the unit can escape this structure, units matter more, and this is fundamentally second-image analysis; if it cannot, this is a pessimistic view of global politics. Instead, I think that units operate in a system that uses gender codes to organize units, but the gender codes it uses are fungible and could be more humane, giving the unit hope, despite the inflexibility of the overall system.

79. Cynthia Enloe, *The Morning After: Sexual Politics at the End of the Cold War* (Berkeley: University of California Press, 1993), 73.

80. Jill Steans, "Engaging from the Margins: Feminist Encounter with the 'Mainstream' of International Relations," *British Journal of Politics and International Relations* (2003), 5(3): 428–454, 443.

81. Pettman, *Worlding Women*, 43.

82. Tickner, *Gender in International Relations*.

83. Peterson, *Gendered States*.

84. Cynthia Enloe, *Bananas, Beaches, and Bases: Making Feminist Sense of International Politics* (Berkeley: University of California Press, 1989).

85. Pettman, *Worlding Women*.

86. Carol Cohn, "Sex and Death in the World of Rational Defense Intellectuals," *Signs: Journal of Women in Culture and Society* (Summer 1987), 12(4): 687–718.

87. For example, J. Ann Tickner in "Hans Morgenthau's Principles of Political Realism: A Feminist Reformulation," *Millennium: Journal of International Studies* (1988), 17(3): 429–440.

88. There is a sociology to what is understood as central to the discipline, where the scholarship that counts as "IR" matches what men do more than it matches what women do, at least in part because the perspectives of male scholars have defined the boundaries of the discipline. See Laura Sjoberg, "The Norm of Tradition," *Politics and Gender* (2008), 4(1): 173–180 for further discussion, analyzing the results of the

TRIP (Teaching and Research in International Politics) survey, as published in Daniel Maliniak, Amy Oakes, Susan Peterson, and Michael J. Tierney, "Women in International Relations," *Politics and Gender* (2008), 4(1): 122-44.

89. V. Spike Peterson and Jacqui True, "'New Times' and New Conversations," in *The Man Question in International Relations*, ed. Marysia Zalewski and Jane Parpart (Boulder: Westview, 1998), 23.

90. Ronald Inglehart and Pippa Norris's work ("Gender Equality and Democracy," *Comparative Sociology* [2002], 1[3/4]: 321–345) is based on a survey of values, while Valerie Hudson, Mary Caprioli, Bonnie Ballif-Spanvill, Rose McDermott, and Chad Emmett ("The Heart of the Matter: The Security of Women and the Security of States," *International Security* [2009], 33[3]: 7–45; and *Sex and World Peace* [New York: Columbia University Press, 2012]) base their work on their collected empirical data about indicators of women's rights.

91. For discussions of gender mainstreaming, see Jacqui True and Michael Mintrom, "Transnational Networks and Policy Diffusion: The Case of Gender Mainstreaming," *International Studies Quarterly* (2001), 45(1): 27–57; Laura Shepherd, "Power and Authority in the Production of United Nations Security Council Resolution 1325," *International Studies Quarterly* (2008), 52(2): 384–404.

92. Cynthia Enloe, *Does Khaki Become You? The Militarization of Women's Lives* (London: Pandora, 1983).

93. Christine Bell and Catherine O'Rourke, "Does Feminism Need a Theory of Transitional Justice? An Introductory Essay," *International Journal of Transitional Justice* (2007), 1(1): 23–44.

94. Kenneth Waltz, "Reflections on Theory of International Politics: A Response to My Critics," in *Neorealism and Its Critics*, ed. Robert Keohane, (New York: Columbia University Press, 1986), 72.

95. Ibid., 73.

96. Discussed briefly in chapter 4 on interstate relationships, then in more detail in chapter 5 on state identities and properties.

97. Waltz, "Reflections on Theory of International Politics," 70, 71.

98. Ibid., 87.

99. Ibid., 89.

100. Ibid., 91.

101. For example, Brent Steele, *Ontological Security in International Relations: Self-Identity and the IR State* (New York and London: Routledge, 2008). The relationship between gender and ontological security is discussed more in chapters 4 and 6 concerning states' identities and how states relate.

102. Anne McClintock, "Family Feuds: Gender, Nationalism, and the Family," *Feminist Review* (1993), 44(2): 61–80. These discussions are not meant to conflate state and nation, an area where feminists have done a lot of work on the differences and nuances (e.g., Nira Yuval-Davis, *Gender and Nation* [London: Sage, 1997]), but instead to focus on addressing the state, the "unit" in third-image theorizing in IR, despite broader applicability.

103. Yuval-Davis, *Gender and Nation*; Wilcox, "Gendering the Cult of the Offensive."

104. Tickner, *Gender in International Relations*, 9.

105. For example, discussion of the United States in the first Gulf War in Steve Niva, "Tough and Tender: New World Order Masculinity and the Gulf War," in Zalewski and Parpart, eds. *The Man Question*, 109–128. See, for a similar argument, Laura Shepherd, "Veiled References: Constructions of Gender in the Bush Administration Discourse on the Attacks on Afghanistan Post-9/11," *International Feminist Journal of Politics* (2006), 8(1): 19–41.

106. Himani Bannerji, *The Dark Side of the Nation: Essays on Multiculturalism, Nationalism, and Gender* (Toronto: Canadian Scholars' Press, 2000), 173.

107. Diana Taylor, *Disappearing Acts: Spectacles of Gender and Nationalism in Argentina's "Dirty War"* (Durham, NC: Duke University Press, 1997), 92, 34.

108. Katherine Moon, *Sex Among Allies: Militarized Prostitution in US-South Korea Relations* (New York: Columbia University Press, 1997).

109. Christine Chin, *In Service and Servitude: Foreign Female Domestic Workers and the Malaysian "Modernity" Project* (New York: Columbia University Press, 1998).

110. Samita Sen, "Motherhood and Mothercraft: Gender and Nationalism in Bengal," *Gender and History* (1993), 5(2): 231–243.

111. Saraswati Sunindyo, "When the Earth Is Female and the Nation is Mother: Gender, the Armed Forces, and Nationalism in Indonesia," *Feminist Review* (1998), 58: 1–21.

112. Elisabeth Porter, "Identity, Location, Plurality: Women, Nationalism and Northern Ireland," in *Women, Ethnicity, and Nationalism*, ed. Rick Wilford and Robert Miller (London: Routledge, 1998).

113. Sheila Meintjes, "Gender, Nationalism, and Transformation: Difference and Commonality in South Africa's Past and Present," in Wilford and Miller, eds., *Women, Ethnicity, and Nationalism*.

114. Kirsten Schulze, "Communal Violence, Civil War, and Foreign Occupation: Women in Lebanon," in Wilford and Miller, eds., *Women, Ethnicity, and Nationalism*.

115. Vahe Tachjian, "Gender, Nationalism, Exclusion: The Reintegration Process of Female Survivors of the Armenian Genocide," *Nations and Nationalism* (2009), 15(1): 60–80.

116. Steele, *Ontological Security in International Relations*.

117. Ibid.

118. Ibid., 112.

119. Forouz Jowkar, "Honor and Shame: A Feminist View from Within," *Gender Issues* (1986), 6(1): 45–65.

120. Catherine Niachros, "Women, War, and Rape: Challenges Facing the International Tribunal for the Former Yugoslavia," *Human Rights Quarterly* (1995), 17(4): 649–690.

121. The story about gendered state identity can also be read onto Germany (as a hypermasculine aggressor) and Britain (as chivalrous protector).

122. V. Spike Peterson, "Sexing Political Identities/Nationalism as Heterosexism," *International Feminist Journal of Politics* (1999), 1(1): 34–65.

123. Charlotte Hooper, "Masculinist Practices and Gender Politics: The Operation of Multiple Identities in IR," in Zalewski and Parpart, eds. *The Man Question,* 28–53, 34.

124. Ibid.

125. Connell, *Masculinities,* 73.

126. Hooper, "Masculinist Practices and Gender Politics," 34.

127. John Tosh, "Hegemonic Masculinity and Gender History," in *Masculinities in Politics and War: Gendering Modern History,* ed. Stefan Dudink, Karen Hagemann, and John Tosh (Manchester: Manchester University Press, 2004), 55.

128. Joshua Goldstein, *War and Gender: How Gender Shapes the War System and Vice Versa* (Cambridge: Cambridge University Press, 2001), 261.

129. Jennifer Heeg's work on state hypermasculinity has been key to my understanding of this concept; see, e.g., Jennifer Heeg Maruska, "When Are States Hypermasculine?" in *Gender and International Security: Feminist Perspectives,* ed. Laura Sjoberg (New York: Routledge, 2009), 235–255.

130. Heeg Maruska, "When Are States Hypermasculine?"; Hooper, *Manly States,* 66, 72.

131. For example, Lynn Savery, *Engendering the State: The International Diffusion of Women's Human Rights* (London: Routledge, 2007).

132. V. Spike Peterson, "Informalization, Inequalities, and Global Insecurities," *International Studies Review* (2010), 12(2): 244–270.

133. Niva, "Tough but Tender"; Laura Sjoberg, *Gender, Justice, and the Wars in Iraq* (New York: Lexington, 2006).

134. Discussed more in chapter 4 on interstate relationships.

135. Waltz, "Reflections on Theory of International Politics: A Response to My Critics," 93.

136. Ibid.

137. Acker, "Hierarchies, Jobs, Bodies."

138. Waltz, "Theory of International Politics Revisited: A Response to My Critics," 93.

139. Charlotte Hooper, "Masculinities in Transition: The Case of Globalization," in Marianne Marchand and Anne Sisson Runyan, eds. *Gender and Global Restructuring* (London: Routledge, 2000), 59–73, 70.

140. Cynthia Enloe, *The Curious Feminist: Searching for Women in a New Age of Empire* (Berkeley: University of California Press, 2004), 4, 6.

141. Ibid., 5.

142. Referencing the United States, Iraq, and Kuwait (Laura Sjoberg, *Gender, Justice, and the Wars in Iraq*); the former Yugoslavia (Marysia Zalewski, "Well, What Is a Feminist Perspective on Bosnia?" *International Affairs* [1995], 71[2]: 339–356), India and Pakistan (Sikata Banerjee, *Muscular Nationalism: Gender, Violence, and Empire in India and Ireland, 1914–2004* [New York: New York University Press, 2012];

Runa Das, "Engendering Post-Colonial Nuclear Policies Through the Lens of Hindutva: Rethinking the Security Paradigm of India," *Comparative Studies of South Asia, Africa and the Middle East* (2001), 22(1–2): 76–89), the United States and China (Laura Sjoberg, "Gendering Power Transition Theory," in *Gender in International Security*, ed. Laura Sjoberg [London: Routledge, 2010]; V. Spike Peterson and Anne Sisson Runyan, *Global Gender Issues*, 3rd ed. [Boulder: Westview, 2010]), China and Hong Kong (Sarah Swider, "Working Women of the World Unite? Labor Organizing and Transnational Gender Solidarity Among Domestic Workers in Hong Kong," in *Global Feminism: Women's Transnational Activism, Organizing, and Human Rights*, ed. Myra Marx Ferree and Aili Mari Tripp [New York: New York University Press, 2006], 110–140), Ireland and Northern Ireland (Banerjee, *Muscular Nationalism*), Russia and Chechnya (Maya Eichler, "Russian Veterans of Chechen Wars: A Feminist Analysis of Militarized Masculinities," in *Feminism and International Relations: Conversations about the Past, Present, and Future*, ed. J. Ann Tickner and Laura Sjoberg [London: Routledge, 2011], 123–140), apartheid South Africa and its critics (Daniel Conway, "Masculinities and Narrating the Past: Experiences of Researching White Men Who Refused to Serve in the Apartheid Army," *Qualitative Research* [2008], 8[3]: 347–354), the United States and Egypt (Kelly MacFarland, *All About the Wordplay: Gendered and Orientalist Language in U.S.-Egyptian Foreign Relations, 1952–1961*, unpublished doctoral dissertation in history at Kent State University, 2010), the "Western world" and the "Arab world" (Peterson and Runyan, *Global Gender Issues*), Cyprus, Greece, and Turkey (Anna M. Agathangelou, "'Sexing' Globalization in International Relations: Migrant Sex and Domestic Workers in Cyprus, Greece, and Turkey," in *Power, Postcolonialism, and International Relations: Reading Race, Gender, and Class*, ed. Geeta Chowdhry and Sheila Nair, [London: Routledge, 2002], 142–170), the Hutus and the Tutsis in the Great Lakes Region (Alison Desforges, *Leave None to Tell the Story: Genocide in Rwanda* [New York: Human Rights Watch, 1999]), among the major players in international trade and lending (Juanita Elias and Christine Beasley, "Hegemonic Masculinity and Globalization: 'Transnational Business Masculinities' and Beyond," *Globalizations* [2009], 6[2]: 281–296; Chandra Mohanty, "'Under Western Eyes' Revisited: Feminist Solidarity Through Anticapitalist Struggles," *Signs* [2003], 28[2]: 499–535).

143. Enloe, *The Curious Feminist*, 4.

144. Sikata Banerjee, *Make Me a Man! Masculinity, Hinduism, and Nationalism in India* (Albany, NY: State University of New York Press, 2005), 12.

145. Ibid., 12–13.

146. For example, Waltz, *Theory of International Politics*; Mearsheimer, *Tragedy of Great Power Politics*.

147. Enloe, *Does Khaki Become You?*; Enloe, *The Morning After*; Enloe, *Bananas, Beaches, and Bases*; Enloe, *Nimo's War, Emma's War*.

148. Cynthia Weber, *Faking It: U.S. Hegemony in a Post-Phallic Era* (Minneapolis: University of Minnesota Press, 1999), 1–3.

149. Wendt, "Anarchy Is What States Make of It"; Wendt, *Social Theory of International Politics*.

150. Discussed more in chapter 4 on interstate relationships.

151. Cynthia Enloe, *Maneuvers: The International Politics of Militarizing Women's Lives* (Berkeley: University of California Press, 2000).

152. Hilary Charlesworth, Christine Chinkin, and Shelley Wright, "Feminist Approaches to International Law," *American Journal of International Law* (1991), 85(2): 613–650.

153. Caroline Moser and Annalise Moser, "Gender Mainstreaming since Beijing: A Review of the Successes and Limitations of International Institutions," *Gender and Development* (2005), 13(2): 11–22.

154. Amy Allen, *The Power of Feminist Theory* (Boulder: Westview, 2000).

155. Francine D'Amico and Peter Beckman, eds., *Women Gender and World Politics: Perspectives, Policies, and Prospects* (Westport, CT: Greenwood, 1994), 5.

156. Sjoberg, *Gender, Justice, and the Wars in Iraq*, 33.

157. Steans, *Gender and International Relations: An Introduction*, 5.

158. Allen, *The Power of Feminist Theory*, 122.

159. Ibid., 121.

160. Christine Sylvester, *Feminist Theory and International Relations in a Postmodern Era* (Cambridge: Cambridge University Press, 1994).

161. June Lennie, "Deconstructing Gendered Power Relations in Participatory Planning: Towards an Empowering Feminist Framework of Participation and Action," *Women's Studies International Forum* (1999), 1(2): 97–122.

162. Jean Elshtain, ed. *Just War Theory* (New York: New York University Press, 1992).

163. Fiona Robinson, *The Ethics of Care: A Feminist Approach to Human Security* (Philadelphia: Temple University Press, 2011).

164. Patricia Hill Collins, *Black Feminist Thought: Knowledge, Consciousness, and the Politics of Empowerment* (New York: Routledge, 2000).

165. Laura Sjoberg, "Gendered Realities of the Immunity Principle: Why Gender Analysis Needs Feminism," *International Studies Quarterly* (2006), 50(4): 889–910.

166. Catherine MacKinnon, *Are Women Human?* (Cambridge: Harvard University Press, 2006).

167. Bina D'Costa and Katrina Lee-Koo, eds., *Gender and Global Politics in the Asia-Pacific* (New York: Palgrave Macmillan, 2008).

168. Georgina Waylen, "Women and Democratization: Conceptualizing Gender Relations in Transition Politics," *World Politics* (1994), 46(3): 327–354.

169. Mark Tessler and Ina Warriner, "Gender, Feminism, and Attitudes Toward International Conflict: Exploring Relationships with Survey Data from the Middle East," *World Politics* (1997), 49(2): 250–281.

170. Like capitalism, governance, globalization, and governmentality, which have been discussed extensively in the feminist literature before. About capitalism, see, e.g.,

J. K. Gibson-Graham, *The End of Capitalism (As We Knew It): A Feminist Critique of Political Economy* (Minneapolis: University of Minnesota Press, 2006). About governance, see e.g., Mary Meyer and Elisabeth Prugl, *Gender Politics in Global Governance* (Lanham, MD: Rowman and Littlefield, 1999); Marianne Marchand and Anne Sisson Runyan, *Gender and Global Restructuring: Sightings, Sites, and Resistances*, 2nd ed. (New York: Routledge, 2011). About globalization, see Tine Davids and Francien van Driel, *The Gender Question in Globalization* (Aldershot, UK: Ashgate, 2005). About governmentality, see Rahel Kunz, *The Political Economy of Remittances: Gender and Governmentality* (London: Routledge, 2011); Vivienne Jabri, "Michel Foucault's Analytics of War: The Social, the International, and the Racial," *International Political Sociology* (2007), 1(1): 67–81.

171. V. Spike Peterson and Anne Sisson Runyan, *Global Gender Issues*, 2nd ed. (Boulder: Westview, 1999), 258.

172. Cynthia Enloe, *The Morning After*, 246.

173. Peterson and Runyan, *Global Gender Issues*, 118; Enloe, *Does Khaki Become You?*, 212.

174. Ronni Alexander, "Confronting Militarization: Intersections of Gender(ed) Violence, Militarization, and Resistance in the Pacific," in *Gender, War, and Militarism*, ed. Laura Sjoberg and Sandra Via (Santa Barbara, CA: Praeger Security International, 2010), 69–79.

175. Ibid., 71.

176. Eichler, "Russian Veterans of Chechen Wars," 124.

177. Ibid., 138.

178. Or the Melians in Thucydides' *The Peloponnesian War* (trans. Richard Crawley, original publication date 431 BC, accessed 1 December 2012 at classics.mit.edu/Thucydides/pelowar.html).

179. John Haynes, *New Soviet Man: Gender and Masculinity in Stalinist Soviet Cinema* (Manchester, UK: Manchester University Press, 2003), 7.

180. Meghana Nayak, "Orientalism and Saving the US Identity Post-9/11"; Heeg Maruska, "When Are States Hypermasculine?"

181. Amy Mazur and Deborah Stetson, eds., *Comparative State Feminism* (Thousand Oaks, CA: Sage, 1995); Amy Mazur, *State Feminism, Women's Movements, and Job Training: Making Democracies Work in the Global Economy* (London: Routledge, 2001); Joni Lovenduski and Claudie Baudino, eds., *State Feminism and Political Representation* (Cambridge: Cambridge University Press, 2005).

182. Carl von Clausewitz, *On War*, ed. and trans. Michael Howard and Peter Paret (Princeton: Princeton University Press, [1832] 1976).

183. For example, arms races, taunting, propaganda wars, and brinksmanship.

184. Carol Cohn, "Wars, Wimps, and Women: Talking Gender and Thinking War," in *Gendering War Talk* ed. Miriam Cooke and Angela Wollacott (Princeton: Princeton University Press, 1993), 236.

185. Robert D. Dean, "Masculinity as Ideology: John F. Kennedy and the Domestic Politics of Foreign Policy," *Diplomatic History* (1998), 22(1): 29–53, 30, citing

John F. Kennedy, "Are We Up to the Task?" in *The Strategy of Peace* (New York: Harper Brothers, 1960).

186. In power transition theorists' terminology (see Ronald Tannen and Jacek Kugler, "Power Transition and China-US Conflicts," *Chinese Journal of International Politics* (2006), 1(1): 35–55).

187. Enloe, *The Morning After*, 46.

188. For the historical example of World War I Germany, see, e.g., Michael C. C. Adams, *The Great Adventure: Male Desire and the Coming of World War I* (Indianapolis: Indiana University Press, 1990); Paul F. Lerner, *Hysterical Men: War, Psychiatry, and the Politics of Trauma in Germany, 1890–1930* (Ithaca, NY: Cornell University Press, 2003).

189. See, e.g., Joane Nagel, "Masculinity and Nationalism—Gender and Sexuality in the Making of Nations," in *Nations and Nationalism: A Reader*, ed. Philip Spencer and Howard Wollman (New Brunswick, NJ: Rutgers University Press), 113.

190. For example, Claire Duncanson, "Forces for Good? Narratives of Military Masculinity in Peacekeeping," *International Feminist Journal of Politics* (2009), 11(1): 63–80; Cynthia Cockburn, "Gender Relations as Causal in Militarization and War," *International Feminist Journal of Politics* 12(2) (2010): 139–157.

191. See, e.g., Weber, *Faking It*; Cohn, "Wars, Wimps, and Women"; Cohn, "Sex and Death in the World of Rational Defense Intellectuals."

192. V. Spike Peterson, "Gendered Identities, Ideologies, and Practices in the Context of War and Militarism," in Sjoberg and Via, eds., *Gender, War, and Militarism: Feminist Perspectives*, (Santa Barbara: Praeger Security International, 2010), 17–30; Peterson and Runyan, *Global Gender Issues*, 3rd ed.; MacKinnon, *Only Words*.

193. Steele, *Ontological Security in International Relations*; Will K. Delahunty and Brent J. Steele, "Engaging the Narrative of Ontological (In)Security Theory: Insights from Feminist IR," *Cambridge Review of International Affairs* (2009), 22(3): 523–540.

194. For example, the Correlates of War Datasets (www.correlatesofwar.com/datasets.htm), the PRIO Data on Armed Conflict (http://www.prio.no/CSCW/Datasets/Armed-Conflict/), the Militarized Interstate Disputes Data (http://www.correlatesofwar.org/), the Dyadic Militarized Interstate Disputes Dataset (DYDMID2.0, http://psfaculty.ucdavis.edu/zmaoz/dyadmid.html), the ICB Crisis Data (http://www.cidcm.umd.edu/icb/), and Fearon/Laitin's Ethnicity, Insurgency, and Civil War Data (http://www.stanford.edu/group/ethnic/).

195. For example, the Worldwide Incidents Tracking System (https://wits.nctc.gov/FederalDiscoverWITS/index.do?N=0).

196. Laura Shepherd, *Gender, Violence, and Security* (London: Zed, 2008); Lene Hansen, "The Little Mermaid's Silent Security Dilemma and the Absence of Gender in the Copenhagen School," *Millennium: Journal of International Studies* (2000), 29(2): 285–306; Annick Wibben, *Feminist Security Studies: A Narrative Approach* (London: Routledge, 2011).

4. RELATIONS INTERNATIONAL AND WAR(S)

1. Nancy Hirschmann, "Freedom, Recognition, and Obligation: A Feminist Approach to Political Theory," *American Political Science Review* (December 1989), 83(4): 1227–1244; Nancy Hirschmann, *The Subject of Liberty: Towards a Feminist Theory of Freedom* (Princeton: Princeton University Press, 2003).

2. See, e.g., Cynthia Weber, *Simulating Sovereignty: Intervention, the State, and Symbolic Exchange* (Cambridge: Cambridge University Press, 1995).

3. See, e.g., the chapters in V. Spike Peterson, ed., *Gendered States* (Boulder: Lynne Rienner, 1992).

4. See, e.g., Cynthia Enloe, *Bananas, Beaches, and Bases: Making Feminist Sense of International Politics* (Berkeley: University of California Press, 2000).

5. This chapter (like other chapters in the book) deals with international war theorizing with the state as the main actor despite feminist recognition that states are an (often insidious) social construction for the purposes of engaging with theorizing that is state-centric. While there most certainly is some violence in doing so, there is also, I argue, productivity in understanding the multiple levels at which feminist critique can be applied. I also make a point to reinterpret the state as existent but not unitary through gender lenses, looking to avoid some of the more dangerous implications of the reification of the state.

6. Zeev Maoz and Bruce Russett, "Normative and Structural Causes of Democratic Peace, 1946–1986," *American Political Science Review* (1993), 87(3): 624–638; Sebastian Rosato, "The Flawed Logic of Democratic Peace Theory," *American Political Science Review* (2003), 97(4): 585–602; See chapter 1, notes 108–134.

7. For example, rivalry theories (chapter 1, notes 78–85); steps-to-war theories (chapter 1, notes 86–92).

8. J. David Singer and Melvin Small, The *Wages of War, 1816–1965: A Statistical Handbook* (New York: John Wiley, 1972); J. David Singer and Melvin Small, *A Resort to Arms: International and Civil Wars, 1816–1980* (Beverly Hills, CA: Sage, 1982); Merideth Sarkees and Phil Schafer, "The Correlates of War Data on War," *Conflict Management and Peace Science* (2000), 18(1): 123–144.

9. See chapter 1, notes 100–101.

10. Several "mainstream" scholars focus on state interaction (including, as discussed later in this chapter, the rivalry and steps-to-war models), but very few talk about relationships, either implicitly or explicitly. A reviewer for this book suggested that Stuart Bremer's work was in practice about relationships (e.g., "Dangerous Dyads: Conditions Affecting the Likelihood of Interstate War, 1816–1965," *Journal of Conflict Resolution* [1992], 36[2]: 309–341). While Bremer's multivariate analyses do provide nuanced results, they stop short of analyzing *relationships* as such. Brandon Valeriano's work on rivalries ("Becoming Rivals: The Process of Rivalry Development," in *What Do We Know About War?*, 2nd ed., ed. John A. Vasquez [New York: Rowman and Littlefield, 2012], 63–82, 74) calls rivalries "relationships" but does not analyze them as such. Still, Valeriano (65)

talks about states as if they can relate, using the term "distrust," which has frequently occurred in bargaining models of war in the past. Likewise, in a discussion of territory as a cause of war, Paul Hensel considers state "reputation" (certainly a relational property) as an intervening variable (in, "Territory: Geography, Contentious Issues, and World Politics," in Vasquez, *What Do We Know About War?*, 3–27, 11). Still, much of the literature (e.g., Susan Sample, "Arms Races: A Cause or a Symptom?" in Vasquez, *What Do We Know About War?*, 111–138) decontextualizes clearly relational and related variables (in Sample, "mutual military buildup" is discussed as though it could be exogenous).

11. See chapter 1, note 76 discussion about k-adic relations rather than dyadic relations.

12. J. Ann Tickner related to me that this was Peggy McIntosh's observation (when she was the Director of the Wellesley Centers for Women) at one of the initial conferences with discussions between feminists and IR scholars, held at Wellesley College in 1990. It resonates with feminist critiques and reformulations of IR theory and practice.

13. John Vasquez, *The War Puzzle* (New York: Cambridge University Press, 1993).

14. For example, Mary Caprioli, "Gendered Conflict," *Journal of Peace Research* (2000), 37(1): 51–68; Mary Caprioli and Mark Boyer, "Gender, Violence, and International Crisis," *Journal of Conflict Resolution* 45(4): 503–518; Mary Caprioli, "Primed for Violence: The Role of Gender Inequality in Predicting Internal Conflict," *International Studies Quarterly* 49(2): 161–178. See discussion of this work in chapter 5. This work frequently uses the word *gender* where many feminists would use "sex" (see discussion in chapter 2).

15. Juliann Emmons Allison, "Peace Among Friends: A Feminist Interpretation of the 'Democratic Peace.'" *Peace and Change* (2001), 26(2): 204–222.

16. Ibid., 207.

17. To the extent that this is an empirical argument, I think it is normatively skewed; to the extent that it is a normative argument, it suffers as an empirical argument. The intent, however, I am on board with, especially as it lends support to considering dyads *relationally*.

18. Allison, "Peace Among Friends," 209, citing Carol Gilligan, *In a Different Voice* (Cambridge: Harvard University Press, 1982).

19. Ibid., 210.

20. See, e.g., Doug Lemke and William Reed, "The Relevance of Politically Relevant Dyads," *Journal of Conflict Resolution* (2001), 45(1): 126–144; Michelle A. Benson, "The Relevance of Politically Relevant Dyads in the Study of Interdependence and Dyadic Disputes," *Conflict Management and Peace Science* (2005), 22(2): 113–133; Stephen L. Quackenbush, "Identifying Opportunity for Conflict: Politically Active Dyads," *Conflict Management and Peace Science* (2006), 23(1): 37–51.

21. On military-related prostitution, see Katharine Moon, *Sex Among Allies* (New York: Columbia University Press, 1997). On AIDS, see H. Amaro, "Love, Sex, and Power: Considering Women's Realities in HIV Prevention," *American Journal of Psychology* (1995), 50(6): 437–447. On refugee camps (and Disarmament, Demobilization, and Reintegration, or DDR Processes) see M. J. Toole and R. J. Waldman, "The Public

Health Aspects of Complex Emergencies and Refugee Situations," *Annual Review of Public Health* (1997), 18: 283–312. For the general argument that "women's lives are international relations, international relations are women's lives," see Cynthia Enloe, *Bananas, Beaches, and Bases*; Laura Sjoberg and Caron Gentry, *Mothers, Monsters, and Whores: Women's Violence in Global Politics* (London: Zed, 2007), chap. 7. For a general overview, see Carol Cohn, ed. *Women and Wars* (London: Polity, 2012).

22. See discussion of these issues in chapter 9.

23. See, e.g., Cynthia Cockburn, *From Where We Stand: War, Women's Activism, and Feminist Analysis* (London: Zed, 2007). This should not be taken as a conflating of women and gender or feminism and gender. Instead, it is the research process of *looking for gender* that showed the *sex-differential impacts* of security policies, which in turn drew empirical and normative attention to the unequal ways in which states' citizens experience state war-making and war-fighting.

24. Cohn, *Women and Wars*.

25. Sarah Brown, "Feminism, International Theory, and International Relations of Gender Inequality," *Millennium: Journal of International Studies* (1988), 17(3): 461–475, 472.

26. Marianne H. Marchand and Anne Sisson Runyan, eds., *Gender and Global Restructuring: Sightings, Sites, and Resistances* (London: Routledge, 2000), 8.

27. See discussion in Laura Sjoberg, "Gendering Power Transition Theory," in *Gender and International Security: Feminist Perspectives*, ed. Laura Sjoberg (London: Routledge, 2010), 83–102.

28. I do not think that this is intentional—that is, I do not think the normative choice to instrumentalize people's lives for the purpose of producing states less likely to go to war is thought of in those terms. At the same time, the real risks and costs of some of these transformations, and the absence of a cost–benefit analysis in the literature advocating them, shows that such a normative choice has often been made. For example those who advocate the democratic peace rarely talk about the dangers of democratization, *domestically* or *internationally*, despite the recognition of such dangers in the literature more broadly (see, e.g., Edward Mansfield and Jack Snyder, "Democratization and the Danger of War," *International Security* [1995], 20[1]: 5–38).

29. Ronald L. Tammen, Jacek Kugler, Douglas Lemke, Carole Alsharabati, Brian Efird, and A. F. K. Organski, eds., *Power Transitions: Strategies for the 21st Century* (New York: Chatham House, 2000), 11.

30. Tickner explains that power-as-domination "has always been associated with masculinity since the exercise of that power has always been a masculine activity" (J. Ann Tickner, *Gender and International Relations: Feminist Perspective on Achieving Global Security* [New York: Columbia University Press, 1992], 33).

31. Fiona Robinson, *The Ethics of Care: A Feminist Approach to Human Security* (Philadelphia: Temple University Press, 2011), 8.

32. Tammen et al, *Power Transitions*, 6.

33. Jean Vickers, *Women and War* (London: Zed, 1993), 68.

34. Ibid.; see also Cohn, *Women and Wars*.

35. For a discussion of gender-differential impacts, see the material cited in notes 23–27 of this chapter. For a discussion of the broader socially differentiated impacts of war, see John Modell and Timothy Haggerty, "The Social Impact of War," *Annual Review of Sociology* (1991), 17(2): 205–224.

36. John L. Gaddis, *The Long Peace: Inquiries into the History of the Cold War* (Oxford: Oxford University Press, 1987).

37. As explained in, e.g., Yaacov Bar-Siman-Tov, "The Strategy of War by Proxy," *Cooperation and Conflict* (1984), 19(4): 263–273 (about the Middle East); and Bhabani Sen Gupta, "The Soviet Union and Vietnam," *International Studies* (1973), 12(4): 559–567 (about Vietnam).

38. See, e.g., Edward Mansfield and Jack Snyder, *Electing to Fight: Why Emerging Democracies Go To War* (Cambridge: MIT Press, 2005); Mansfield and Snyder, "Pathways to War in Democratic Transitions," *International Organization* (2009), 63(2): 381–390. These pieces of research argue that democratizing states are more likely to make war.

39. For a discussion of the "capitalist peace," see chapter 1, notes 93 and 95. For a critique of the impacts of capitalism in global politics, see, e.g., the work of Immanuel Wallerstein, *The Capitalist World-Economy: Essays* (Cambridge: Cambridge University Press, 1979), or, from a feminist perspective, Zillah R. Eisenstein, *Capitalist Patriarchy and the Case for Socialist Feminism* (New York: Monthly Review, 1978); J. K. Gibson-Graham, *The End of Capitalism (As We Knew It): A Feminist Critique of Political Economy* (Minneapolis: University of Minnesota Press, 2006).

40. The idea of a relationship between hegemony and peace is discussed extensively in Robert O. Keohane, *After Hegemony* (Princeton: Princeton University Press, 1984).

41. For example, the work cited below and in the remainder of this chapter. My original discussion of this can be found in "Introduction to *Security Studies:* Feminist Contributions," *Security Studies* (2009), 18(2): 183–213. The actual impact of domestic sex equality on a state's likelihood to make peace is discussed in detail in chapter 5. This section just discusses it in its framing as a dyadic-level account for states' likelihood to make war(s); e.g., Mary Caprioli, "Gendered Conflict," *Journal of Peace Research* 371: 51–68.

42. See the introduction, note 19 (with the exception of Joshua Goldstein's work) for citations to this work.

43. For example, Caprioli, "Gendered Conflict."

44. Anna Karamanou, "The Gender Dimension in International Politics," *International and European Politics* (2007), 5.

45. Ibid., 1.

46. At the same time, a number of feminist alternatives to dyadic, trait-based theories such as the sex-equality peace or even the democratic peace are implicated in their own critiques and/or other feminist critiques. For example, Juliann Allison's feminist reformulation of democratic peace theories (in "Peace Among Friends," discussed above), relies on an essentialist notion of women as more

peaceful than men and therefore ties women and femininity to the need to rethink the democratic peace, rather than engaging the research program in all its complexities through gender(ed) lenses. Such approaches are problematic, not least because they reify some of the very (hidden) sex essentialisms in current dyadic-level war theorizing.

47. Katherine L. Allison, "Feminising a Democratic Peace and the New Agential Woman," draft paper posted at: www.ecprnet.eu/sg/ecpg/documents/papers/A-K/AllisonK.doc, 1. Permission to cite was obtained.

48. In my view, this is certainly an important dimension of a feminist critique of traditional theoretical approaches to dyadic explanations for war(s) and peace(s), especially insomuch as it cautions against potentially oversimple attempts to relate sex equality and peace between nations.

49. Allison, "Feminising the Democratic Peace," 21, noting that this "ignores the ways that women's rights and democracy have not had an uncontested relationship" as well as other forms women's rights could take.

50. Jack Levy and William Thompson, *Causes of War* (Malden, MA: Wiley-Blackwell, 2010), 60.

51. Ibid., 61.

52. Ibid., citing Paul Diehl and Gary Goertz, *War and Peace in International Rivalry* (Ann Arbor, MI: University of Michigan Press, 2000). See also chapter 1, note 76.

53. For example, James Fearon, "Rationalist Explanations for War," *International Organization* (1995), 49(3): 379–414.

54. See chapter 1, note 139.

55. See chapter 1, note 138.

56. See chapter 1, note 141.

57. See chapter 1, note 140.

58. For example, Jack S. Levy, "Declining Power and the Preventive Motivation for War," *World Politics* (1987), 40(1): 82–107.

59. Levy and Thompson, *Causes of War*, 60.

60. In fact, some feminist theorists have argued that the very delineation of a concept of rationality has gendered implications. For an applied discussion, see, e.g., Paula England, "A Feminist Critique of Rational-Choice Theories: Implications for Sociology," *American Sociologist* (1989), 20(1): 14–28.

61. One example is democratic peace research, which privileges the single-state level of interaction even when looking at how dyads come to go to war or to keep peace.

62. Historically speaking, of course—the idea being that a particular sequence of actions and reactions can be traced, each is responsive to the other, and independent decision makers act freely as opposed to related decision makers acting under constraints.

63. Discussed in more detail in chapter 7.

64. Amy Allen, "Rethinking Power," *Hypatia* (1998), 13(1): 21–40.

65. June Lennie, "Deconstructing Gendered Power Relations in Participatory Planning: Towards an Empowering Feminist Framework of Participation and Action," *Women's Studies International Forum* (1999), 22(1): 97–112.

66. Brooke Ackerly, *Political Theory and Feminist Social Criticism* (Cambridge: Cambridge University Press, 2000).

67. For example, Lauren Bennett Cattaneo and Alyia R. Chapment, "The Process of Empowerment: A Model for Use in Research and Practice," *American Psychologist* (2010), 65(7): 646–659; Brian D. Christens, "Toward Relational Empowerment," *American Journal of Community Psychology* (2012), 50(1–2): 114–128. Applied to global politics more critically, see Rosalind Euben and Rebecca Napier-Moore, "Choosing Words with Care? Shifting Meanings of Women's Empowerment in International Development," *Third World Quarterly* (2009), 30(2): 285–300; Brooke Ackerly and Katy Attoanasi, "Global Feminisms: Theory and Ethics for Studying Gendered Injustices," *New Political Science* (2009), 31(4): 543–555.

68. Which, for the purposes of chapter 3's analysis, interrogates further Waltz's notion of unit similarity.

69. For example, Selma Sevenhuijsen, "The Place of Care: The Relevance of a Feminist Ethic of Care for Social Policy," *Feminist Theory* (2003), 4(2): 179–197; building on work like Margaret Urban Walker's "Moral Understandings: Alternative Epistemology for Feminist Ethics," *Hypatia* (1989), 4(2): 15–28; Denis K. Mumby and Linda Putnam, "The Politics of Emotion: A Feminist Reading of Bounded Rationalist," *Academy of Management Review* (1992), 17(3): 465–486; Seyla Benhabib and Drucila Cornell, *Feminism as Critique: On the Politics of Gender* (Minneapolis: University of Minnesota Press, 1991).

70. J. Ann Tickner, *Gendering World Politics: Issues and Approaches in the Post-Cold War World* (New York: Columbia University Press, 2001), 54.

71. Ibid.

72. Catherine MacKinnon. Talk at the Institute for Women and Gender, Columbia University, 14 November 2006.

73. For example, Cynthia Enloe explains that "the militarism of the United States and other countries needs us all to behave *as women*" in order for it to function properly (*Bananas, Beaches, and Bases*, 204).

74. For example, the internment camps that the United States set up on the West Coast for Japanese Americans have been defended as in the "national interest" of the United States at the highest levels of government (see, e.g., *Korematsu v. United States* [323 U.S. 214, 1944]), but were certainly not in the interest of Japanese Americans.

75. Christine Sylvester, "Feminists and Realists on Autonomy and Obligation in International Relations," in *Gendered States: Feminist (Re)Visions of International Relations Theory* ed. V. Spike Peterson (Boulder: Lynne Rienner, 1992), 155–178.

76. Jacqui True, "Feminism," in *Theories of International Relations*, ed. Scott Burchill and Andrew Linklater (New York: St. Martin's, 1995), 213–235.

77. See discussion in chapter 4.

78. Naomi Scheman, *Engenderings: Constructions of Knowledge, Authority, and Privilege* (New York: Routledge, 1993), 211–212. Also, "gender ideology can make a difference in what problems are selected for research, how research is operationalized, and how findings are interpreted" (Marianne Ferber and Julie Nelson, eds., *Beyond Economic MAN: Feminist Theory and Economics* [Chicago: University of Chicago Press, 1993], 7).

79. Especially to the extent that those who employ rational-actor understandings hold "the mistaken notion that the mind-body dualism in Cartesian rationality is a universal rather than cultural construction" (Drucila Barker, "Dualisms, Discourses, and Development," in *Decentering the Center: Philosophy for a Multicultural, Postcolonial, and Feminist World*, ed. Uma Narayan and Sandra Harding [Bloomington: Indiana University Press, 2000]).

80. "In which *man* is the author of *his* thoughts and speech" and "women have never fully been included by this discourse," (Chris Weedon, *Feminist Practice and Poststructuralist Theory* [New York: Wiley, 1997], 168).

81. Some people actually know that states are not rational, unitary actors but make the assumption anyway. See discussion in Miles Kahler, "Rationality in International Relations," *International Organization* (1998), 52(4): 919–941.

82. Karen Jones, "Gender and Rationality," In *Oxford Handbook on Rationality*, ed. Alfred R. Mele and Piers Rawling (Oxford: Oxford University Press, 2004), 301–321, 303.

83. V. Spike Peterson, "Sexing Political Identities/Nationalism as Heterosexism," *International Feminist Journal of Politics* (1999), 1(1): 34–65, 38.

84. Margaret Atherton, "Cartesian Reason and Gendered Reason," in *A Mind of One's Own: Feminist Essays on Reason and Objectivity*, ed. Louise M. Antony and Charlotte Witt (Boulder: Westview, 1993), 19–34, 19; Sara Ruddick, "Pacifying the Forces: Drafting Women in the Interest of Peace," *Signs: Journal of Women in Culture and Society* (1983), 8(3): 471–489, 474.

85. Jones, "Gender and Rationality," 301.

86. Genevieve Lloyd, "Maleness, Metaphor, and the 'Crisis' of Reason," in Antony and Witt, eds., *A Mind of One's Own*, 69–83, 77.

87. Sally Haslanger, "On Being Objective and Objectified," in Antony and Witt, eds., *A Mind of One's Own*, 85–125, 85.

88. Ibid.

89. V. Spike Peterson, "Transgressing Boundaries: Theories of Knowledge, Gender, and International Relations" *Millennium: Journal of International Studies* (1992), 21(2): 183–206, 197; Scheman, *Engenderings*, 211.

90. Charlotte Hooper, "Masculinist Practices and Gender Politics: The Operation of Multiple Masculinities in International Relations," in *The Man Question in International Relations*, ed. Marysia Zalewski and Jane Parpart (New York: Westview, 1998).

91. Zillah Eisenstein, *Against Empire: Feminisms, Racism, and the West* (London: Zed, 2004).

92. Charlotte Hooper, "Masculinities in Transition: The Case of Globalization," in Marchand and Runyan, eds., *Gender and Global Restructuring*, 70.

93. Jean Elshtain, ed. *Just War Theory* (New York: New York University Press, 1992), 263.

94. Nancy Huston, "Tales of War and Tears of Women," in *Women's and Men's Wars*, ed. Judith Steihm (Oxford: Pergamon Press, 1983), 271.

95. Ibid., 273.

96. Ibid., 273.

97. Ibid., 271.

98. These belligerents are often, though not always, states, and it is becoming increasingly important to pay attention to nonstate actors not just in their wars but in their war narratives.

99. Deleuze and Guattari point out the circularity of social license, explaining that, "linguistics is nothing without a pragmatics (semiotic or political) to define the effectuation of the *condition of possibility* of language and the *usage* of linguistic elements" (Gilles Deleuze and Felix Guattari, *A Thousand Plateaus: Capitalism and Schizophrenia*, trans. Brian Massumi [Minneapolis: University of Minnesota Press, 1987], 85). Discursive contest is circular: it bestows social license, which is required to participate in that contest.

100. See, for a similar argument, Laura J. Shepherd, "Veiled References: Constructions of Gender in the Bush Administration Discourse on the Attacks on Afghanistan Post-9/11," *International Feminist Journal of Politics* (2006), 8(1): 19–41.

101. Ashworth and Swatuk claim that liberalism and realism can be seen as an all-masculine debate, in which realism is based on violence and liberalism is based on domination. Lucian Ashworth and Larry Swatuk, "Masculinity and the Fear of Emasculation in International Relations Theory," in Zalewski and Parpart, eds., *The Man Question*, 86. Whether or not this is true, a politics of domination does permeate the study and practice of international relations.

102. Tickner, *Gender in International Relations*, 9.

103. As I discussed in *Gender, Justice, and the Wars in Iraq* (New York: Lexington, 2006), sexual intercourse is used as an analogy for fighting in many accounts of the Gulf Wars.

104. Carol Cohn, "Sex and Death in the World of Rational Defense Intellectuals," *Signs: Journal of Women in Culture and Society* (1987), 12(4): 687–718, 700.

105. Ibid.

106. Ibid.

107. Jean Baudrillard, *The Gulf War Did Not Take Place* (Bloomington: University of Indiana Press, 1995).

108. Judith Butler talks about this in terms of making space inhabitable, e.g., Butler, *Precarious Life* (London and New York: Routledge, 2006).

109. Jean Elshtain, "Reflections on War and Political Discourse: Realism, Just War, and Feminism in a Nuclear Age," *Political Theory* (1985), 13(1): 39–57, 50; Lucinda Peach, "An Alternative to Pacifism? Feminism and Just-War Theory," *Hypatia* (1994), 9(2): 152–171; Sara Ruddick, *Maternal Thinking: Towards a Politics of Peace* (New York: Houghton-Mifflin, 1989). These references to *cleanliness*, though, risk both unrepresentativeness and harmful abstraction.

110. Cohn, "Sex and Death in the World of Rational Defense Intellectuals," 698. See also Annick Wibben, *Feminist Security Studies: A Narrative Approach* (New York and London: Routledge, 2011).

111. Cohn, "Wars, Wimps, and Women."

112. Cohn, "Sex and Death in the World of Rational Defense Intellectuals," 707.

113. Ibid., 693.

114. Betty Reardon, *Sexism and the War System* (New York: Teacher's College Press, 1985).

115. Ibid., 10.

116. Ibid., 11.

117. Ibid., 13.

118. For a similar reading in the scholarly literature, see Chris Cuomo, "War is Not Just an Event: Reflections on the Significance of Everyday Violence," *Hypatia* (1996), 11(4): 30–45.

119. Feminists have thought about this before (e.g., Christine Sylvester, *Feminist International Relations: An Unfinished Journey* [Cambridge: Cambridge University Press, 2002]), though often not directly in terms of dyadic war theorizing. By characterizing it as a "fundamental part of being states," I do not mean to imply that states are unitary or fully independent/distinguishable, only to understand relating as a property of diverse, interdependent states as constituted in the current organization of global politics.

120. In these policies, values associated with masculinities (such as "hard" security, public life, strength, aggression, autonomy, and protection, to name a few relevant ones) are often prized over values associated with femininities (such as "soft" peace, private lives, passivity, interdependence, and weakness, to name a few relevant ones). See, e.g., Julian Lindley-French, "The Revolution in Security Affairs: Hard and Soft Security Dynamics in the 21st Century," *European Security* (2004), 13(1-2): 1–15, for a perspective on the impending collapse of this dichotomy.

121. Dictionary.com

122. Ibid.

123. Ibid.

124. See http://www.merriam-webster.com/dictionary/relate.

125. See http://dictionary.cambridge.org/dictionary/british/relate_1.

126. See http://dictionary.reference.com/browse/relationship.

127. See http://dictionary.reference.com/browse/relationship.

128. See http://www.thefreedictionary.com/relationship.

129. See http://www.thefreedictionary.com/relationship.

130. See discussion in chapter 3, pages 86–87, citing Brent Steele, *Ontological Security in International Relations: Self-Identity and the IR State* (New York: Routledge, 2008).

131. Ibid., 2.

132. Ibid., 2, 3 (emphasis in original).

133. Ibid., 3.

134. Ibid., 4.

135. Colin Elman, "Horses for Courses: Why Not Neorealist Theories of Foreign Policy?" *International Security* (1996), 6: 7–53, 24, as cited in Steele, *Ontological Security in International Relations*, 4.

136. This dovetails with the constructivist assumption of "state personhood" (Alexander Wendt, "The State as Person in International Theory," *Review of International Studies* [2004], 30[2]: 289–316) but takes it deeper, seeing relationships as social but also seeing identity as social, shaped by honor and shame (Steele, *Ontological Security in International Relations*) or fear and hate (e.g., Neta Crawford, "The Passion of World Politics: Propositions on Emotion and Emotional Relationships," *International Security* [2000], 24[4]: 116–156; Neta Crawford, *Argument and Change in World Politics* [Cambridge: Cambridge University Press, 2002]). While feminists have problematized the uniformity assumption in taking the state-as-person, they have urged scholars to think more seriously about the range of motivations for state behaviors (e.g., Peterson, ed., *Gendered States*; John Hoffman, *Gender and Sovereignty: Feminism, the State, and International Relations* [London: Palgrave, 2001]; Weedon, *Feminist Practice and Poststructuralist Theory*; Ruth Lister, *Citizenship: Feminist Perspectives* [New York: New York University Press, 2003]). This chapter takes Steele's middle ground theoretically, where "states are not people, but considers it necessary for both ontological and methodological reasons to consider states 'as if' they are people" (*Ontological Security in International Relations*, 18). At the same time, the assumption of "state personhood" used here is a little different, because it does not assume the unitary nature of state-as-person, but instead understands state-as-person as internal dissonance, identity struggles, and change.

137. Alexander Wendt, *Social Theory of International Politics* (New York: Cambridge University Press, 1999); Peter Katzenstein, ed., *The Culture of National Security* (New York: Columbia University Press, 1996).

138. That is not to say that a state has *one* identity representative of all of its members, but instead to say that the state has competing identities, where dominant identities are resolved and presented.

139. See discussion of relational autonomy in chapter 6; Hirschmann, *The Subject of Liberty*.

140. Jean Elshtain, *Women and War* (Brighton, MA: Harvester, 1987).

141. In Steele's terms (in *Ontological Security in International Relations*)

142. See discussion in Sjoberg, *Gender, Justice, and the Wars in Iraq*.

143. In V. Spike Peterson's terms in "Sexing Political Identities/Nationalism as Heterosexism."

144. Jennifer Mitzen, "Ontological Security in World Politics: State Identity and the Security Dilemma," *European Journal of International Relations* (2006), 12(3): 341–370; Steele, *Ontological Security in International Relations*.

145. Mitzen, "Ontological Security in World Politics."

146. See discussion in Sylvester, "Feminists and Realists Look at Autonomy and Obligations in International Relations."

147. As a transgression of gendered social hierarchy/ies (see Laura Sjoberg, "Gendered Realities of the Immunity Principle: Why Gender Analysis Needs Feminism," *International Studies Quarterly* (2006), 50(4): 889–910; Scheman, *Engenderings*).

148. Naeem Inayatullah and David Blaney, *International Relations and the Problem of Difference* (New York: Routledge, 2004), 219. Still, "instead of recognizing the possibility of the overlap of self and other, boundaries are [often] rigidly drawn, carefully policed, and mapped onto the difference between good and evil" (Ibid., 11).

149. Sylvester, *Feminist International Relations*, 255. It is also important to remember that "home" might be as dangerous as the "liminal" and that there might be empowerment (as bell hooks' *Feminist Theory: From Margin to Center* [London: Pluto Press, 1990]) suggests about marginality) in embracing liminality.

150. Sylvester, *Feminist International Relations*, 255.

151. For example, J. Ann Tickner, "Hans Morgenthau's Principles of Political Realism: A Feminist Reformulation," *Millennium: Journal of International Studies* (1988), 17(3): 429–440.

152. Gayatri Spivak, "Can the Subaltern Speak?" in *Marxism and the Interpretation of Culture*, ed. Cary Nelson and Larry Grossberg (Urbana, IL: University of Illinois Press, 1988).

153. For example, Barry Buzan, Ole Waever, and Jaap de Wilde, *Security: A New Framework for Analysis* (Boulder: Lynne Rienner, 1998).

154. Lene Hansen, "Gender, Nation, Rape: Bosnia and the Construction of Security," *International Feminist Journal of Politics* (2001), 3(1): 55–75.

155. Critical theorists have argued that mainstream IR sometimes "sees" with "blinders" (Jim George, *Discourses of Global Politics: A Critical (Re)Introduction to International Relations* [Boulder: Lynne Rienner, 1994]). On one hand, some of these references to visibility are meant as metaphors. On the other hand, the discussions bring up very real issues that are important in formulating both ontological and epistemological approaches to global politics.

156. Derived from but separate from the psychological use of the term in the 1960s and 1970s, a concept popular in trans theorizing.

157. Kathryn Woodward, *Identity and Difference* (Thousand Oaks, CA: Sage, 1997).

158. Homi Bhabha, *The Location of Culture* (New York: Routledge, 1994).

159. Jose Munoz, *Disidentifications: Queers of Color and the Performance of Politics* (Minneapolis: University of Minnesota Press, 1999), 12, citing Judith Butler, *Bodies That Matter: On the Discursive Limits of Sex* (New York: Routledge, 1993).

160. See Laura Sjoberg, "Towards Trans- Gendering International Relations," *International Political Sociology* (2012), 6(4): 337–54.

161. Munoz, *Disidentifications*, 12.

162. Sjoberg, "Towards Trans- Gendering International Relations," 349.

163. Ibid., 5.

164. Ibid., 4.

165. For example, Sylvester, *Feminist International Relations*: Sjoberg, *Gender, Justice, and the Wars in Iraq*.

166. Hayward Alker and Thomas Biersteker, "The Dialectics of World Order: Notes for a Future Archeologist of International Savoir Faire," *International Studies Quarterly* (1984), 28(2): 121–142, 123.

167. Hayward Alker, *Rediscoveries and Reformulations: Humanistic Methodologies for International Studies* (Cambridge: Cambridge University Press, 1996), 209, 79.

168. Ibid., 53. In Alker's understanding, "practical reasoning is argumentation which: contains goals, is knowledge-based, ends or concludes in actions, is dynamic and global/local, fits into various types of dialogue, and takes side effects into account" (402).

169. Ibid., 61.

170. Ibid., 343. Emphasis in original.

171. Ibid., 52. Alker formalizes this in a number of different ways, including Rescher's understanding of moves and countermoves (Nicholas Rescher, *Dialectics: A Controversy-Oriented Approach to a Theory of Knowledge* [Albany, NY: State University of New York Press, 1977]), Toynbee's interpretive readings (A. Toynbee, *A Study of History* [Oxford: Oxford University Press, 1946]), Havel's humanism (Vaclav Havel, "The End of the Modern Era," *New York Times*, March 1, 1992), and Leibnizian internal relations (referencing Leibniz's *Philosophical Papers and Letters* (trans. Leroy E. Loemker, London: Springer, 1976), to name a few.

172. Sylvester, *Feminist International Relations*, 119.

173. A recurring theme in chapters 5 and 6, which explore state- and substate-level theoretical approaches to the causes of war(s).

174. Then-U.S. President Bill Clinton endorsed democratization for the purpose of peace in the 1994 State of the Union Address; United Nations Security Council Resolution 1325 endorsed the inclusion of women for the purpose of peace (S/Res/1325/2000); in the 2003 State of the Union Address, then-U.S. President George W. Bush suggested that a "US-Middle East Trade Zone" would bring peace to the region.

175. See discussion in Fearon, "Rationalist Explanations for War."

176. Christine Sylvester, *Feminist Theory and International Relations in a Postmodern Era* (Cambridge: Cambridge University Press, 1994), 96; Jill Bystudzienski, *Women Transforming Politics: Worldwide Strategies for Empowerment* (Bloomington: Indiana University Press, 1992); Ruddick, *Maternal Thinking*.

177. Sylvester, *Feminist International Relations*, 119.

178. Ibid., 120.

179. Robinson, *The Ethics of Care*, 3.

180. Ibid.

5. GENDER, STATES, AND WAR(S)

1. Originally published in *Kangura* (December 1990), no. 6; full text available at http://www.trumanwebdesign.com/~catalina/commandments.htm (accessed 1 May 2012). For a gender analysis, see Christopher C. Taylor, "A Gendered Genocide: Tutsi Women and Hutu Extremists in the 1994 Rwandan Genocide," *PoLAR: Political and Legal Anthropology Review* (1999), 22(1): 42–54.

2. This is an example of an intrastate conflict, and much of the analysis in this chapter is state-based. This chapter, and this book generally, focuses on state(s) and war(s), not because they constitute all wars, or even the majority of wars, but because it needed to be limited in scope somehow, and this limit functioned to make the book's contents coherent. A project that focuses on nonstate actors through gender lenses would be a complement to this project and is indeed necessary to make it in any sense complete.

3. See chapter 1, note 95. For more recent analysis, see Phillipe Martin, Thierry Mayer, and Mathais Thoening, "Make Trade Not War," *Review of Economic Studies* (2008), 75(3): 865–900; Edward D. Mansfield, *Power, Trade, and War* (Princeton: Princeton University Press, 1995); James D. Morrow, "How Could Trade Effect Conflict?" *Journal of Political Research* (1999), 36(4): 481–489.

4. As explained in Jack Levy and William Thompson, *Causes of War* (Oxford: Blackwell Publishing, 2010), 83; citing V. I. Lenin, *Imperialism* (New York: International Publishers, [1916] 1939).

5. See Introduction, note 62, for references.

6. See, e.g., chapter 1, notes 163, 164.

7. As discussed in chapter 1, the most notorious of these is Huntington's "The Clash of Civilizations," but the majority of work on culture and conflict has been from a constructivist point of view, arguing that socially constructed cultures within and among states impact states' likelihood to make war(s). See chapter 1, notes 175 and 177, for a discussion of constructivist work on culture and conflict.

8. This point is made, for example, in J. Ann Tickner, *Gender and International Relations* (New York: Columbia University Press, 1992); V. Spike Peterson, ed., *Gendered States: Feminist (Re)Visions of International Relations Theory* (Boulder: Lynne Rienner, 1992).

9. The research program often uses the term *gender equality*, although that phrase is usually deployed to mean what feminists would call *sex equality*. The difference is that "sex equality" is the "equality" of those understood to be biological men and those understood to be biological women (which is what this literature refers to) and "gender equality" is about the social construction of masculinities and femininities. Though this research program uses the phrase "gender equality," I choose to call it *sex equality* to acknowledge the diversity of genders and genderings not taken into account when gender is reduced to (material) men and women.

10. For example, Mary Caprioli and Mark Boyer, "Gender, Violence, and International Crisis," *Journal of Conflict Resolution* (2001), 45(4): 503–518; Ronald Inglehart

and Pippa Norris, *Rising Tide: Gender Equality and Cultural Change Around the World* (Cambridge: Cambridge University Press, 2003). Postcolonial feminists (e.g., Geeta Chowdhry and Sheila Nair, *Power, Postcolonialism, and International Relations: Reading Race, Gender, and Class* [London: Routledge, 2002]) argue that this is not only a narrow and problematic way of understanding gender subordination, but one that ultimately does violence to women outside the West, on whom western values are often imposed without dialogue and discussion.

11. Valerie M. Hudson, Bonnie Ballif-Spanvill, Mary Caprioli, and Chad F. Emmett, *Sex and World Peace* (New York: Columbia University Press, 2012).

12. Hudson et al., *Sex and World Peace*; Valerie M. Hudson, Mary Caprioli, Bonnie Ballif-Spanvill, Rose McDermott, and Chad F. Emmett, "The Heart of the Matter: The Security of Women and the Security of States," *International Security* (2008/9), 33(3): 7–45; Mary Caprioli, "Gender Equality and State Aggression: The Impact of Domestic Gender Equality on State First Use of Force," *International Interactions* (2003), 29(3): 195–214; Mary Caprioli, "Gendered Conflict," *Journal of Peace Research* (2000), 371(1): 51–68; Mary Caprioli, "Primed for Violence: The Role of Gender Inequality in Predicting Internal Conflict," *International Studies Quarterly* (2005), 49(2): 161–178.

13. Valerie Hudson and Bradley Thayer ("Sex and the Shaheed: Insights from the Life Science on Islamic Suicide Terrorism," *International Security* [2010], 34[4]: 37–62) extend it to nonstate actors, arguing that (men's) sex and sex drive cause violence. For an explicitly feminist treatment of nonstate actors, ethics, and war, see Laura Sjoberg, "Gender, Just War Theory, and Non-State Actors," in *Ethics, Authority, and War: Non-State Actors and the Just War Tradition*, ed. Brent J. Steele and Eric Heinze (New York: Palgrave, 2009), 151–176.

14. Or in the case of Inglehart and Norris (*Rising Tide*), that backwards cultures abuse their women, which signifies the propensity to commit other violent acts.

15. See www.womanstats.org, accessed December 14, 2012, cited in Hudson et al., *Sex and World Peace*.

16. See work cited in note 12.

17. Hudson et al., *Sex and World Peace*.

18. I find this "mainstream" appeal somewhat ironic, though, given that, in order to get a statistically significant result, the authors use non-traditional measures of state aggression and limited gender equality measure [where the dominant measures of conflict initiation in the MID (militarized interstate dispute] and COW [correlates of war] databases are bypassed in favor of the less-used Global Peace Index), bypass traditionally used measures of gender equality (The United Nations' Gender Development Index, Gender Equality Measure, and Gender Inequality Index, Social Watch's Gender Gap Index, and World Economic Forum's Gender Equality Index) in favor of the WomanStats indicators, and use a measure for "islamic civilization" as if the clash of civilizations hypothesis might have value, contrary to dominant trends in the field. It is my argument that, were this work not about "gender" it would find itself open to a number of critiques of the methodological shortcomings that it has,

including these indicators, but not only that. Another shortcoming is that the data tested only represents that which was collected from 2006 to the writing of the book—there is no testing to see if the relationship between sex equality and peace holds up over time. My preliminary tests (using more traditional indicators over time) suggest that it does not.

19. Helen Kinsella (in *The Image Before the Weapon: A Critical History of the Distinction between Combatant and Civilian* [Ithaca, NY: Cornell University Press, 2001]; and "Gendering Grotius: Sex and Sex Difference in the Laws of War," *Political Theory* [2006], 32[4]: 61–91) traces this association between women and incapacity to fight through historical discussions of the immunity principle.

20. This is an engagement strategy I characterize as mimicry in chapter 2 (see note 89).

21. See work cited in note 12.

22. I am particularly concerned that current explorations of the relationship between sex equality and peace have a tendency to conflate sex and gender in ways that undercut potential theoretical sophistication in the literature (see discussion in note 9). Also, as it is currently presented, the sex-equality peace argument often includes racisms (e.g., the derogatory reference to "traditional cultures" as sexist in Hudson et al., *Sex and World Peace*, 2, 11), oversimplified and biased notions of the relationships between religions and sex inequality (like the treatment of Islam in Hudson and Thayer, "Sex and the Shaheed"), a heteronormative approach to (sex and) gender relations (e.g., the hundred-plus separate references to heterosexual marriage in Hudson et al., *Sex and World Peace*) and cultural conflation (such as the references in *Sex and World Peace* to "sub-Saharan African culture" in the singular or sweeping statements about Islamic culture in a number of these sources, e.g., Hudson et al., *Sex and World Peace*, 34, 110, 111, 112). These and related issues are why, for me, not only is this work not to be a part of my feminist theorizing of war, it is actually at cross-purposes with it. Still, as discussed in chapter 2, this book is meant to represent only *a* feminist theory of war, rather than *the* or *a definitive* feminist approach to war to the exclusion of others; and, even in its pluralist approach, it cannot (and would not) embrace all approaches that claim to do gender analysis, at the risk of a normatively indefensible position.

23. For example, Catherine MacKinnon, *Sex Equality* (New York: Thomson West, 2001); Catherine MacKinnon, *Are Women Human?* (Cambridge: Harvard University Press, 2006).

24. For example, Melissa Brown, *Enlisting Masculinity: The Construction of Gender in US Military Recruiting Advertising During the All-Volunteer Force* (New York: Oxford University Press, 2012).

25. For example, Swanee Hunt and Cristina Posa, "Women Waging Peace," *Foreign Policy* (May–June 2001), 124: 38–47; Swanee Hunt, "Women's Vital Voices: The Costs of Exclusion in Eastern Europe," *Foreign Affairs* (1997), 76(4): 2–7; Swanee Hunt, *This Was Not Our War: Bosnian Women Reclaiming the Peace* (Durham, NC: Duke University Press, 2004). Recent and forthcoming gender-based work has talked about the

violences of inclusion, e.g., the *International Feminist Journal of Politics* special issue (2013), 15(4) on "Murderous Inclusions," edited by Adi Kuntsman, Jin Haritaworn, and Silvia Posocco.

26. For an extensive discussion, see Marysia Zalewski, "Well, What Is the Feminist Perspective on Bosnia," *International Affairs* (1995), 71(2): 339–356.

27. Michel Foucault, "Governmentality," in *The Foucault Effect: Studies in Governmentality*, ed. Graham Burchell, Colin Gordon, and Peter Miller (Hemel Hempstead: Harvester Wheatsheaf, 1991), 87–104.

28. Cynthia Enloe, *Globalization and Militarism: Feminists Make the Link* (New York: Rowman and Littlefield, 2007).

29. "Cissexism" is the belief that trans- identifications are inferior to or less authentic than those of cis- persons (Julia Serano, *Whipping Girl: A Transsexual Woman on Sexism and the Scapegoating of Femininity* [Emeryville, CA: Seal, 2007]). The terms *cisgender, cissexual,* and *cissexism* are used to critically interrogate the trans/normal dichotomy.

30. In other words, it is a good and productive idea on its own terms to value women in states' memberships, their positions of service, their positions of power, and in indicators of opportunity, success, and staying power in global politics, but this thinking does not have a complex enough notion of diversity and should not be instrumentalized.

31. Feminists have often pointed out that it is problematic to make "essentialist" statements about gender—to assume that women are *naturally* something while men are *naturally* something else, not least because the practical impact of such statements is usually to disempower women. For a discussion of the problems with gender essentialism, see V. Spike Peterson and Anne Sisson Runyan, *Global Gender Issues in the New Millennium*, 3rd ed. (New York: Routledge, 2010).

32. Empirical work that my students and I have been doing supports the supposition that there is no statistically significant relationship between sex equality and peacefulness long-term, but that work is in too early stages to be conclusive.

33. I discuss this in some detail in "Gender, the State, and War Redux: Feminist International Relations across the 'Levels of Analysis,'" *International Relations* (2011), 25(1): 108–134.

34. See discussion in Cynthia Cockburn, "Gender Relations as Causal in Militarization and War," *International Feminist Journal of Politics* (2010), 12(2): 139–157.

35. Ibid.

36. A traditional example of common causality is the correlation that "as ice cream sales increase, so do deaths by drowning" when really summer is the common cause.

37. See, e.g., Nira Yuval-Davis, *Gender and Nation* (London: Sage, 1997), and discussion of gender and nationalism later in this chapter.

38. For example, the United States' use of "life back home" and the "American way of life" to justify the "war on terror," even as that war became significantly more expansive than any plausible threat to the U.S. homeland or homeland security. See,

e.g., discussions in Cynthia Weber, *I Am an American* (Chicago: University of Chicago Press, 2011); David L. Altheide, "Consuming Terrorism," *Symbolic Interaction* (2004), 27(3): 289–308.

39. Annick Wibben, *Feminist Security Studies: A Narrative Approach* (New York: Routledge, 2011), 10, citing Laura Bush, "Radio Address by Laura Bush to the nation, 830pm" White House. Online. Available at http://www.whitehouse.gove/news/releases/2001/09/20010911-16.html, accessed December 1, 2012. For more information, see discussion in Dana L. Cloud, "'To Veil the Threat of Terror': Afghan Women and the *Clash of Civilizations* in the Imagery of the U.S. War on Terror," *Quarterly Journal of Speech* (2004), 90(3): 285–306.

40. I see gender analysis as suggesting that the empirical results of the sex-equality peace are more complicated, both in terms of what the empirical research sees and how it is theorized.

41. The work in this section draws from, summarizes, and extends work that Jessica Peet and I have done on gender and nationalism as relates to the fighting of wars, including: "A(nother) Dark Side of the Protection Racket," *International Feminist Journal of Politics* (2011), 13(2): 163–182; and "Targeting Women in Wars," in *Feminism and International Relations: Conversations About the Past, Present, and Future*, ed. J. Ann Tickner and Laura Sjoberg (London: Routledge, 2011), 169–187.

42. For example, John Hoffman, *Gender and Sovereignty: Feminism, the State, and International Relations* (London: Palgrave, 2001); Cynthia Weber, *Simulating Sovereignty: Intervention, the State, and Symbolic Exchange* (Cambridge: Cambridge University Press, 1995); Cynthia Weber, "Performative States," *Millennium—Journal of International Studies* (1998), 27(1): 77–95.

43. For example, Yuval-Davis, *Gender and Nation*.

44. For example, Sjoberg, "Gender, the State, and War Redux."

45. For example, Tickner, *Gender in International Relations*; Peterson, *Gendered States*; Jan Jindy Pettman, *Worlding Women: A Feminist International Politics* (New York: Psychology Press, 1996).

46. R. W. Connell, *Masculinities* (Berkeley: University of California Press, 1995).

47. See discussion on gendered organizations in chapter 3.

48. Peterson, "Sexing Political Identities/Nationalism as Heterosexism," *International Feminist Journal of Politics* (1999), 1(1): 34–65, 38.

49. Connell, *Masculinities*, 73.

50. Sarah Brown, "Feminism, International Theory, and the International Relations of Gender Inequality," *Millennium: Journal of International Studies* (1988), 17(3): 461–475, 470.

51. Connell, *Masculinities*; Joan Acker, "Hierarchies, Jobs, Bodies: A Theory of Gendered Organizations," *Gender & Society* (1990), 4(2): 129–158. Cynthia Enloe talks about the real-world implications of these distributions in *Nimo's War, Emma's War: Making Feminist Sense of the Iraq War* (Berkeley: University of California Press, 2010).

52. This usage was introduced in Cynthia Enloe, "Womenandchilden: Making Feminist Sense of the Persian Gulf Crisis," *Village Voice* (September 25, 1990), arguing that "womenandchildren" are often grouped as helpless and in need of defense in war, feminizing children and infantilizing women.

53. Eric M. Blanchard, "Gender, International Relations, and the Development of Feminist Security Theory," *Signs: Journal of Women in Culture and Society* (2003), 28(4): 1289–1311.

54. Nancy Hirschmann, "Freedom, Recognition, and Obligation: A Feminist Approach to Political Theory," *American Political Science Review* (1989), 83(4): 1227–1244; 1228; see also Martha Nussbaum, "Capabilities as Fundamental Entitlements: Sen and Social Justice," *Feminist Economics* (2003), 9(2/3): 33–59.

55. R. W. Connell, "The State, Gender, and Sexual Politics: Theory and Appraisal," *Theory and Society* (1990), 41: 507–544; Rosemary Pringle and Sophie Watson, "Women's Interests in the Post-Structuralist State," in *Destabilizing Theory*, ed. Michele Barret (London: Polity, 1992); Jill Steans, *Gender and International Relations: An Introduction* (Rutgers, NJ: Rutgers University Press, 1998).

56. This is not meant to argue that states have one culture and/or one strategic culture, but instead to make the argument that states' production of strategic cultures that are outwardly presented are the result of internal and external gendered hierarchies of state identities and values.

57. See, for example, Sandra Whitworth, *Men, Militarism, and UN Peacekeeping: A Gendered Analysis* (Boulder: Lynne Rienner, 2004); Jennifer Turpin and L. A. Lorentzen, *The Gendered New World Order: Militarism, Development, and the Environment* (New York: Routledge, 1996); Cynthia Enloe, *Bananas, Beaches, and Bases: Making Feminist Sense of International Relations* (Berkeley: University of California Press, 1990).

58. Chris Cuomo, "War Is Not Just an Event: Reflections on the Significance of Everyday Violence," *Hypatia* (1996), 11(4): 32.

59. Ibid., 43.

60. In the United States, there are military bases in our towns and militarism in our culture, from a can of soup to commercials on *The Apprentice* (see, for a theoretical exploration, Enloe, *Bananas, Beaches, and Bases*).

61. Enloe, *Bananas, Beaches, and Bases*, 204.

62. Enloe, *Nimo's War, Emma's War*, chapter 8.

63. Ibid.

64. Ibid.

65. Ibid.

66. Militaries rely on masculine values to sustain their institutional existence. Still, individual men do not benefit from the triumph of masculine values in militarism. Men die in the wars that masculine militarism inspires and sustains. The sovereign state militarizes and genders both personal lives and political relations (J. Ann Tickner, *Gendering World Politics* [New York: Columbia University Press, 2001], 51).

State sovereignty, by giving states license to militarize their institutional cultures, encourages the gendering of human interaction.

67. Amy Allen, "Rethinking Power," *Hypatia* (1998), 13(1): 21–40.

68. Laura Sjoberg, *Gender, Justice, and the Wars in Iraq* (New York: Lexington, 2006), 97.

69. Judith Gardam, "Gender and Non-Combatant Immunity," *Transnational Law and Contemporary Problems* (1993), 3: 345–370, 348.

70. Steans, *Gender and International Relations*, 81.

71. Charlotte Hooper, *Manly States: Masculinities, International Relations, and Gender Politics* (New York: Columbia University Press, 2001).

72. Charlotte Hooper, "Masculinist Practices and Gender Politics: The Operation of Multiple Masculinities in IR," in *The "Man" Question*, ed. Marysia Zalewski and Jane Parpart, 34.

73. Hooper, "Masculinist Practices," 34.

74. John Tosh, "Hegemonic Masculinity and Gender History," in *Masculinities in Politics and War: Gendering Modern History*, ed. Stefan Dudink, Karen Hagemann, and John Tosh (Manchester: Manchester University Press, 2004), 41–60, 55.

75. Decision makers *as men.*

76. Laura Sjoberg, "The Gendered Realities of the Immunity Principle: Why Gender Analysis Needs Feminism," *International Studies Quarterly* (2006), 50(4): 889–910, 895.

77. Jean Elshtain, ed., *Just War Theory* (New York: Basic, 1992)

78. Ibid.; Lucinda Peach, "An Alternative to Pacifism? Feminism and Just-War Theory," *Hypatia* (1994), 9: 152–171, 152.

79. For example, Sjoberg, *Gender, Justice, and the Wars in Iraq*; Sjoberg and Peet, "A(nother) Dark Side of the Protection Racket."

80. Jan Jindy Pettman, *Worlding Women: A Feminist International Politics* (London: Routledge, 1995), 187.

81. Nira Yuval-Davis, *Gender & Nation* (London: Sage, 1997), 39.

82. Nira Yuval-Davis and Floya Anthias, *Women, Nation, State* (New York: MacMillan, 1989).

83. Anne McClintock ("Family Feuds, Gender, Nationalism, and the Family," *Feminist Review* [1993] 44: 61–80, 61) argues that "despite nationalisms' ideological investment in popular *unity*, nations have historically amounted to the sanctioned institutionalization of gender difference."

84. Ibid.

85. Pettman, *Worlding Women*, 193. Since women are central to national reproduction, their bodies often become the "second front" of the conflict (Ruth Seifert, "The Second Front: The Logic of Sexual Violence in Wars," *Women's Studies International Forum* [1996], 19[1/2]: 35–43).

86. Peterson, "Sexing Political Identities/Nationalism as Heterosexism," 48.

87. As discussed in more depth in Sjoberg and Peet, "A(nother) Dark Side of the Protection Racket," 168–169.

88. Discussed in more detail in chapter 7, but the idea is that if a belligerent fights to protect *its own* feminized others, killing them also kills the belligerent's reason to fight.

89. Pettman, *Worlding Women*, 192.

90. Yuval-Davis, *Gender & Nation*, 40.

91. Ken Booth, *Strategy and Ethnocentrism* (London: Croom Helm, 1979), 121; see also Alastair Johnston, *Cultural Realism: Strategic Culture and Grand Strategy in Chinese History* (Princeton: Princeton University Press, 1995).

92. Peter Katzenstein, ed., *Cultures of National Security* (New York: Columbia University Press, 1996).

93. Colin Gray, "Strategic Culture as Context: The First Generation of Theory Strikes Back," *Review of International Studies* (1999), 25(1): 49–69, 50.

94. Ibid.

95. For example, Gray, "Strategic Culture as Context"; Johnston, *Cultural Realism*.

96. Gray, "Strategic Culture as Context," 49.

97. Johnston, *Cultural Realism*, 5.

98. Jack Snyder, *The Soviet Strategic Culture: Implications for Limited Nuclear Operations* (Santa Monica, CA: Rand, 1977)

99. Johnston, *Cultural Realism*, 17; See also Colin Gray, *War, Peace, and Victory: Strategy and Statecraft for the Next Century* (New York: Simon & Schuster, 1990); Emmanuel Adler, "The Emergence of Cooperation: National Epistemic Communities and the International Evolution of the Idea of Nuclear Arms Control," *International Organization* 46(1), (1992): 101–145; Anatol Rappoport, "Changing Concepts of War in the United States," in *American Thinking About Peace and War*, Ken Book and Moorehead Wright, eds. (New York: Harvester, 1978).

100. See Bradley Klein, "Hegemony and Strategic Culture: American Power Projection and Alliance Defence Politics," *Review of International Studies* (1988), 14: 133–148, 139; Timothy Luke, "What's Wrong with Deterrence? A Semiotic Interpretation of National Security Policy," in *International/Intertextual Relations: Post Modern Readings in World Politics*, ed. James Der Derian and Michael J. Shapiro (Lexington, MA: Lexington, 1989); David Campbell, *Writing Security: United States Foreign Policy and the Politics of Identity* (Minneapolis: University of Minnesota Press, 1992).

101. Johnston, *Cultural Realism*, 21. There has been a debate between Johnston and Colin Gray about the separability of ideas and behaviors in the empirical study of strategic culture(s). See Gray, "Strategic Culture as Context."

102. There is a good literature review on this topic in Johnston's *Cultural Realism*.

103. See the brief discussion in Laura Sjoberg, "Gendering Power Transition Theory," in *Gender and International Security: Feminist Perspectives*, ed. Laura Sjoberg (London: Routledge, 2010), 83–102.

104. Gray, "Strategic Culture as Context," 54.

105. Ibid., 55.

106. Ibid., 56.

107. Johnston, *Cultural Realism*.

108. Joseph Nye and Sean Lynn-Jones, "International Security Studies: A Report of a Conference on the State of the Field," *International Security* (1988), 12(4): 5–27.

109. Cynthia Enloe, *Does Khaki Become You? The Militarization of Women's Lives* (Berkeley: University of California Press, 1989); Enloe, *Bananas, Beaches, and Bases*; Cynthia Enloe, *The Morning After: Sexual Politics at the End of the Cold War* (Berkeley: University of California Press, 1993); Cynthia Enloe, *Maneuvers: The International Politics of Militarizing Women's Lives* (Berkeley: University of California Press, 2000).

110. As Catherine MacKinnon, *Only Worlds* (Cambridge: Harvard University Press, 1993) has explained, "feminization is something that can happen to anyone. It is only that we assume it is natural to happen to people identified as women." See also, V. Spike Peterson, "Informalization, Inequalities, and Global Insecurities," *International Studies Review* (2010), 12(2): 244–270; and Peterson and Runyan, *Global Gender Issues*, 3rd ed. See other discussions in this book, including chapter 2 (bottom of 108), chapter 3 (188–89), and chapter 4 (230).

111. Peterson, "Informalization, Inequalities, and Global Insecurities."

112. Hooper, "Masculinities in Transition: The Case of Globalization," 70.

113. Gray, "Strategic Culture as Context," 57.

114. Ibid, emphasis in original.

115. Jane Parpart, "Masculinity/ies, Gender, and Violence in the Struggle for Zimbabwe," in Zalewski and Parpart, eds., *Rethinking the Man Question*, 181–203.

116. Enloe, *The Morning After*, 20, 120.

117. Parpart, "Masculinity/ies, Gender, and Violence in the Struggle for Zimbabwe," 182.

118. Ibid., 187.

119. Ibid., 189.

120. Ibid., 190.

121. Ibid., 196.

122. Dibeysh Anand, "'Porno-nationalism' and the Male Subject," in Zalewski and Parpart, eds., *Rethinking the Man Question*, 163–180.

123. Ibid.

124. Ibid., 164.

125. Ibid., 167.

126. Ibid., 170.

127. Ibid., 171.

128. Ibid., 174.

129. Sandra Whitworth, "Militarized Masculinities and the Politics of Peacekeeping: The Canadian Case," in *Critical Security Studies in World Politics*, ed. Ken Booth (Boulder: Lynne Rienner, 2005), 89–106.

130. Daniel Francis, *National Dreams: Myth, Memory, and Canadian History* (Vancouver: Arsenal Pulp, 1997), 10.

131. Benedict Anderson, *Imagined Communities*, rev. ed. (London: Verso, 1991), 6.

132. Whitworth, "Militarized Masculinities and the Politics of Peacekeeping," 89.

133. Ibid., 92.

134. Ibid., 94. There is some irony, as Whitworth notes, in that Canadian military training uses an aggressive, killer-training masculinity to train men for the military service/duty associated with tough-but-tender, protector, peacekeeper masculinity.

135. Ibid., 100.

136. Gray, "Strategic Culture as Context," 57.

137. This is from George W. Bush's 2002 speech at the West Point Military Academy graduation foreshadowing the war in Iraq georgewbush-whitehouse.archives. gov/news/releases/2002/06/20020601-3.html, accessed 1 May 2012.

138. Even when just war theorizing is not strictly used as a guide for war-making, world leaders often make just war claims, and those judging their choices often measure them by just war standards (Francis Beer and Robert Hariman, "Post-Realism, Just War, and the Gulf War Debate," in *Politically Speaking: A Worldwide Examination of Language Us in the Public Sphere*, ed. Ofer Feldman and Christ'l de Landsteer [Westport, CT: Praeger, 1998], 10). Even when members of the international community break the rules of just war, they do so under the guise of complying with those rules and claiming that those rules are of ultimate importance (Michael Walzer, "Justice and Injustice in the Gulf War," in *But Was it Just? Reflections on the Morality of the Persian Gulf War*, ed. David Decrosse [New York: Doubleday, 1992], 171).

139. Jean Elshtain, *Women and War* (New York: New York University Press Brighton, MA: Harvester, 1987).

140. Jean Elshtain, *Just War Theory* (New York: New York University Press, 1992).

141. Cynthia Enloe, The *Morning After*, 174. The integration of women into the U.S. military is adding women to the forces, but the process has paid little attention to the discursive and performative elements of gender dichotomies. The result has been the preservation of the discursive structures of gender subordination even in a gender-integrated military. For a more general discussion, see chapter 2, 125–126.

142. Joni Lovenduski, ed., *State Feminism and Political Representation* (Cambridge: Cambridge University Press, 2005).

143. Joyce Outshoon and Johanna Kantola, eds., *Challenging State Feminism: Women's Policy Agencies Confronting Shifting Institutional Terrain* (London: Palgrave, 2007).

144. Dorothy M. Stetson and Amy Mazur, *Comparative State Feminism* (London: Sage, 1995); Amy Mazur, *State Feminism, Women's Movements, and Job Training* (London: Routledge, 2001).

145. Catherine MacKinnon, *Toward a Feminist Theory of the State* (Cambridge: Harvard University Press, 1989), 170.

146. Ibid., 170.

147. Ibid., 238.

148. Michaele Ferguson, "'W' Stands for Women: Feminism and Security Rhetoric in the Post 9/11 Bush Administration," *Politics and Gender* (2005), 2(1): 10–40.

149. Ibid., 10. Liza Featherstone expresses a similar apprehension about the U.S. policy toward Iraq: "Bush has feebly attempted to justify the invasion [of Iraq], fantasizing that a 'democratic' Iraq would show 'that honest government, and respect for women, and the great Islamic tradition of learning can triumph in the Middle East and beyond.' But feminists aren't buying it; few see reason to hope war will relieve the miserable condition of the Iraqi people, women included." (Liza Featherstone, "Mighty in Pink," *The Nation*, 3 March 2003).

150. Sjoberg, *Gender, Justice, and the Wars in Iraq*.

151. Other analysis has suggested similar situations in Egypt and Tunisia, as discussed in Laura Sjoberg and Jonathon Whooley, "The Arab Spring for Women? Gender, Signification, and Middle East Politics in 2011." Paper presented at the 2012 Annual Meeting of the International Studies Association, 29 March to 3 April 2012, in San Diego, CA.

152. Consider, for example, the U.S. passage of the 1964 Civil Rights Act, in which proponents argued as much for combating communist claims as they did for giving women and minorities legal protection (Derrick Bell, *Silent Covenants: Brown v. Board of Education and the Unfinished Hopes for Racial Reform* [Oxford: Oxford University Press, 2004]).

153. MacKinnon, *Are Women Human?* In such an understanding, norm-based advocacy for gender equality functions like any other norm-based advocacy, in which "moral authority and influence" are "in no small measure due to" the appeal of norms that "advocate for the powerless." Martha Finnemore and Michael Barnett, *Rules for the World: International Organizations in Global Politics* (Ithaca, NY: Cornell University Press, 2004), 79.

154. Derrick Bell, a critical race theorist, provides a model for thinking about the fortuitous use of emancipatory policy rhetoric to appeal to states' sense of identity while at the same time holding onto existing power structures. Bell contends that (apparently) race-emancipatory policies in the United States are adopted for reasons of strategic interest to whites rather than to emancipate African Americans (*Silent Covenants*, 71). Because these policies are not originally intended to be primarily for the benefit of African Americans, Bell argues, their enforcement, when it occurs at all, will stop at the point where the policy would affect the relative power of whites (139). This theoretical framework can potentially be translated into understanding instrumental feminism in the international arena.

155. Ibid. Bell's analogy from race relations shows some of the reasons why the dominant might benefit from appearing to protect the weak.

156. At first glance, it does not seem to make sense to argue that power and strategic interests are at the core of global policies with explicit goals to protect the human rights of those most disempowered in global politics. On the contrary, international policies that protect those who are not "in power" in global politics are understood as transgressions against realism; symbols that the realist paradigm is falling apart. Policies such as the Landmines Treaty and United Nations Security

Council Resolution 1325 have been touted as the victory of true concern for those marginalized in global politics over the strategic interests of states.

157. Margaret Keck and Kathryn Sikkink, *Activists Beyond Borders: Advocacy Networks in International Politics* (Ithaca, NY: Cornell University Press, 1998), 16. The authors identify gender activism as one of the effective tools of transnational social movememnts

158. Stuart Kaufman, *Modern Hatreds: The Symbolic Politics of Ethnic War* (Ithaca, NY: Cornell University Press, 2001).

159. Peterson and Runyan, *Global Gender Issues*, 3rd ed., 116–117.

160. Brown, "Feminism, International Theory, and International Relations of Gender Inequality," 470.

161. Evidence for this hypothesis might be found in the large volume of gender-related treaties and agreements in global politics, matched with very few that have enforcement mechanisms and even fewer that are actually enforced. In other words, many gender-emancipatory international policies are *only* symbolic— there is no mechanism to bind their signatories to their contents. Other gender-emancipatory policies, such as the Convention on the Elimination of All Forms of Discrimination Against Women, have so many exceptions and exemptions that it is difficult to discern any remaining universal content. Perhaps the gulf between statements of support for gender equity and enforcement of redress of gender subordination shows that international actors do have an interest in *appearing* to emancipate women, but have a less urgent (or even nonexistent) interest in *actually* emancipating women.

6. PEOPLE, CHOICES, AND WAR(S)

1. This may or may not be true of Rwanda, where the lower house is 58.2 percent women, and the population is likely less than 58 percent women. Even if Rwanda is a place where women are not underrepresented numerically, it would be the only place in the world. For a deeper discussion of the Rwandan case, see Laura Sjoberg, "Reconstructing Womanhood in Post-Conflict Rwanda," in *Women, War, and Violence: Personal Perspectives and Global Activism*, ed. Robin Chandler, Lihua Wang, and Linda Fuller (London: Palgrave Macmillan, 2010), 165–180.

2. Genderstats, The World Bank Group Database of Gender Statistics, 2002; http://datatopics.worldbank.org/gender (accessed 15 December 2012).

3. See www.ipu.org/umn-e/classif.htm (accessed 13 February 2012). The highest representations of women in legislative bodies in the world are in Rwanda (56.3 percent), Andorra (50 percent), Sweden (45 percent), South Africa (44.5 percent), Seychelles (43.8 percent), Cuba (43.2 percent), Iceland (42.9 percent), Finland (42.5 percent), and Nicaragua (40.2 percent). Myanmar, Haiti, Samoa, Mongolia, Nigeria,

Tongo, Lebanon, Comoros, Iran, Vanuatu, Oman, Papua New Guinea, Yemen, Belize, Nauru, Qatar, Palau, Saudi Arabia, and Solomon Islands have less than 5 percent representation of women in parliaments.

4. See, e.g., J. Ann Tickner, *Gender in International Relations* (New York: Columbia University Press, 1992).

5. See, for example, Walter Lippmann's *Public Opinion,* new edition with an introduction by Michael Curtis (New York: Transaction, 1997); Rousseau's *Discourse on Political Economy* (London: Kessinger, 2004); Machiavelli's *The Prince,* trans. Rufus Goodwin (London: Braden, 2003); Dewey's *German Philosophy and Politics* (New York: Henry Holt, 1915); Vinod Singh's, *Leadership in the Indian Army* (London: Sage, 2005), Bennis' *On Becoming a Leader,* 4th ed. (New York: Basic, 2009).

6. See discussion in Laura Sjoberg, "Feminism and Styles of Political Leadership," in *The Ashgate Companion to Political Leadership,* ed. Joseph Masciulli, Mikhail Molchanov, and W. Andy Knight (Aldershot, UK: Ashgate, 2009), 149–176, 153. Emphasis in original.

7. For example, J. Ann Tickner, "Hans Morgenthau's Principles of Political Realism: A Feminist Reformulation," *Millennium: Journal of International Studies* (1988), 17(3): 429–440.

8. Daniel Byman and Kenneth Pollack, "Let Us Now Praise Great Men: Bringing the Statesman Back In," *International Security* (2001), 25(4): 107–146. See also Margaret Hermann, "How Decision Units Shape Foreign Policy: A Theoretical Framework," *International Studies Review* (2001), 31(2): 47–81; Ole Holsti, "Cognitive Dynamics and Images of the Enemy," in *Image and Reality in World Politics,* ed. John Farrell and Asa Smith (New York: Columbia University Press, 1967); Amos Tversky and Daniel Kahneman, "Judgment Under Uncertainty: Heuristics and Biases," *Science, New Series,* (1974), 185(4157): 1124–1131; Robert Jervis, "Perceiving and Coping with Threat," in *Psychology and Deterrence,* Robert Jervis, Richard Lebow, and Janice Stein, eds. (Baltimore, MD: Johns Hopkins University Press, 1985).

9. See chapter 1, note 187.

10. See the introduction, note 62.

11. The analytical relationship between sex and gender is difficult to parse here, but assumptions about masculinity and femininity are often inappropriately mapped onto men and women.

12. For examples of work that ignores that political leaders are sexed male or female, see Giacomo Chiozza and Ajin Choi, "Guess Who Did What: Political Leaders and the Management of Territorial Disputes, 1950–1990," *Journal of Conflict Resolution* (2003), 47(3):251–278; or Stephen Benedict Dyson and Thomas Preston, "Individual Characteristics of Political Leaders and the Use of Analogy in Foreign Policy Decision Making, *Political Psychology* (2006), 27(2):265–288. For examples of work that essentializes women leaders, see Nancy J. Adler, "Global Leadership: Women Leaders," *Management International Review* (1997/1): 171–196, which assumes women carry feminine traits; or Sidney Verba, Nancy Burns, and Kay Lehman Scholzman, "Knowing and Caring about Politics: Gender and Political Engagement," *The Journal*

of Politics (1997), 59(4):1051–1072, which suggests that women are less politically engaged generally and therefore less represented in leadership.

13. Sjoberg, "Feminism and Styles of Political Leadership."

14. Tickner, *Gender in International Relations.*

15. Ibid. For example, there is gendering evident in the labeling of Queen Elizabeth I as the "virgin queen," a nickname that would never have been given to a king, even were there some social perception about his virginity (for a discussion of this, see David Grant Moss, "A Queen for Whose Time? Elizabeth I as Icon for the Twentieth Century," *Journal of Popular Culture* [2006], 39[5]: 796–816).

16. For example, Fred Greenstein ("The Benevolent Leader Revisited: Children's Images of Political Leaders in Three Democracies," *American Political Science Review* [1975], 69[4]: 1371–1398) argues that good leadership is based in perception of benevolence, while Kanungo (R. N. Kanugo, "Looseness of the Loose-Tight Leadership Model," *Applied Psychology* [1997], 46[4]: 419–422) argues that tightness and apparent disinterest is the appropriate model.

17. Warren Bennis (in "The Leadership Advantage," *Leader to Leader* [1999], 12: 18–23, 18) describes the characteristics of a good leader as: "technical competence, a facility for abstract or strategic thought, a history of achieving results . . . judgment and character."

18. Deborah Best and John Williams, *Sex and the Psyche: Gender and Self Viewed Cross-Culturally* (London: Sage, 1990).

19. Leonie Huddy and Nayda Turkildsen, "The Consequences of Gender Stereotypes for Women Candidates at Different Levels and Types of Office," *Political Research Quarterly* (1993), 46(3): 503–525.

20. See Cynthia Enloe, *Maneuvers: The International Politics of Militarizing Women's Lives* (Berkeley: University of California Press, 2000).

21. For example, Margaret Thatcher, Condoleeza Rice, Madeline Albright, Golda Meir. For an analysis of these issues, see Peter Beckman and Francine D'Amico, *Women, Gender, and World Politics* (Westport, CT: ABC-CLIO, 1994). These women have often displayed characteristics of masculinity in leadership and have been recognized as such.

22. See discussion in Sjoberg, "Feminisms and Styles of Political Leadership," 157.

23. Francine D'Amico and Peter Beckman, *Women in World Politics: An Introduction* (Westport, CT: Bergin and Garvey, 1995). For these reasons, women candidates have "adopted parallel combative policy stances to fight voters' gender stereotypes" (Huddy and Terkildsen, "Consequences of Gender Stereotypes for Women Candidates," 504).

24. Sjoberg, "Feminism and Styles of Political Leadership," 158.

25. As D'Amico and Beckman (in *Women and World Politics*) pointed out, there is actually a higher burden of proof of masculinity on *women leaders* than there is on male leaders.

26. The rational actor model privileges self-interest, identifying selfishness as necessary and successful. Feminists, who see scholarship as theory and praxis

intertwined, critique this individualistic assumption (see, e.g. Marysia Zalewski, "All these Theories yet the Bodies Keep Piling Up: Theorists, Theories, and Theorizing," in *International Relations: Positivism and Beyond*, Steve Smith, Ken Booth, and Marysia Zalewski, eds. (Cambridge: Cambridge University Press, 1996. 340–353). It also assumes stable and fixed interests on the parts of leaders and states. V. Spike Peterson ("Sexing National Identities/Nationalism as Heterosexism," *International Feminist Journal of Politics* [1999], 1[1]: 34–65) argues that this assumption is unrepresentative and dangerous. Finally, rational actor models assume traits associated with masculinity, where "the workings of masculinity within modernity have remained invisible as dominant men have learned to speak in the impartial voice of reason. . . . a man's voice assumes a pitch of objectivity and impartiality as it becomes an *impersonalized* voice, a voice that has 'authority' because it belongs to no one in particular while claiming at the same time to respect all" (Victor Seidler, *Recovering the Self: Morality and Social Theory* [London: Routledge, 1994], 109).

27. For example, a study of the "foreign policy beliefs of women in leadership positions" asked whether having women in political leadership will change the nature of politics or not (Ole Holsti and James Rosenau, "The Foreign Policy Beliefs of Women in Leadership Positions," *Journal of Politics* [1981], 43[2]: 326–347). There are two major problems with such an approach. First, "the discussion of women qua women implies that all women hold the same views and that is it possible to view women as a single force in politics and policy" (Marian Palley, "Women's Policy Leadership in the United States," *PS: Political Science and Politics* [2001], 34[2]: 247–250, 247). Second, women are still being compared to men's concept of leadership in these studies (Estela Bensimon, "A Feminist Reinterpretation of Presidents' Definitions of Leadership," *Peabody Journal of Education* [1989], 66[3]: 143–156, 149).

28. R. W. Connell, *Masculinities* (Berkeley: University of California Press, 1995), 73.

29. Ibid.

30. Sjoberg, "Feminist Approaches to Political Leadership," 165, citing Bensimon, "A Feminist Reinterpretation of Presidents' Definitions of Leadership," 149.

31. See, e.g., William J. McGuire, "The Poly-Psy Relationship: Three Phases of a Long Affair," in *Explorations in Political Psychology*, ed. Shanto Iyengar and William J. McGuire (Durham, NC: Duke University Press, 1993).

32. Virginia Sapiro, "Theorizing Gender in Political Psychology Research," in *The Oxford Handbook of Political Psychology*, ed. David Sears, Leonie Huddie, and Robert Jervis (New York: Oxford University Press, 2003).

33. Jennifer Heeg Maruska, "When Are States Hypermasculine?" in *Gender and International Security: Feminist Perspectives*, ed. Laura Sjoberg (New York: Routledge, 2010), 235–255.

34. Ibid., 247.

35. Cheryl Schonhardt-Bailey, "Measuring Ideas More Effectively: An Analysis of Bush and Kerry's National Security Speeches," *Political Science and Politics* (2005), 38(4): 701–711.

36. Heeg Maruska, "When Are States Hypermasculine?", 247, citing Anna Cornelia Fahey, "French and Feminine: Hegemonic Masculinity and the Emasculation of John Kerry in the 2004 Presidential Race," *Critical Studies in Media Communication* (2007), 24(2): 132–150.

37. Cynthia Enloe, *Bananas, Beaches, and Bases: Making Feminist Sense of International Politics* (Berkeley: University of California Press, 1990), 196.

38. Ibid., 195; Charlotte Hooper, *Manly States: Masculinities, International Relations, and Gender Politics* (New York: Columbia University Press, 2001), 93. This builds on the "personal is political" phrase that has been a staple of the feminist movement for decades, discussed first in Carol Hanish's "The Personal Is Political," in *Notes from the Second Year: Women's Liberation* (1970), but widely believed to have been frequent parlance among activists before then.

39. Enloe, *Bananas, Beaches, and Bases*. Gillian Youngs concludes that feminisms need "multi-locational perspectives on patriarchal forces in terms of state and market, to recognize that the public/private social and spatial constructions are, in certain senses, mobilized and reconfigured in this globalizing world" (Gillian Youngs, "Breaking Patriarchal Bonds: Demythologizing the Public/Private," in *Gender and Global Restructuring: Sightings, Sites, and Resistances*, ed. Marianne Marchand and Anne Sisson Runyan [London and New York: Routledge, 2000], 56).

40. Joshua Goldstein, *War and Gender: How Gender Shapes the War System and Vice Versa* (Cambridge: Cambridge University Press, 2001), 53.

41. See discussion in chapter 6 of Laura Sjoberg and Caron Gentry, *Mothers, Monsters, Whores: Women's Violence in Global Politics* (London: Zed, 2007).

42. Katharine Moon, *Sex Among Allies: Military Prostitution in U.S.-Korea Relations* (New York: Columbia University Press, 1997).

43. Christine Chin, *In Service and Servitude: Foreign Female Domestic Workers and the Malaysian "Modernity" Project* (New York: Columbia University Press, 1998).

44. See, e.g., Dara Kay Cohen and Amelia Hoover Green, "Dueling Incentives: Sexual Violence in the Liberian Civil War and the Politics of Human Rights," *Journal of Peace Research,* (2012), 49(4): 445-58; Dara Kay Cohen, "Female Combatants and the Perpetration of Violence: The Case of Wartime Rape in Sierra Leone" *World Politics* (2013), 65(3); Megan MacKenzie, *Female Soldiers in Sierra Leone: Sex, Security, and Post-Conflict Development* (New York: New York University Press, 2012); Megan MacKenzie, "Securitization and Desecuritization: Female Soldiers and the Reconstruction of Post-Conflict Sierra Leone," *Security Studies* (2009), 18(2): 241–261.

45. Sjoberg and Gentry, *Mothers, Monsters, Whores*, 200.

46. A significant amount of feminist work has investigated the international *as personal*, including Sjoberg and Gentry, *Mothers, Monsters, Whores*; Enloe, *Bananas, Beaches, and Bases*; Brigit Locher and Elisabeth Prugl, "Feminism and Constructivism: Worlds Apart or Sharing the Middle Ground," *International Studies* Quarterly (2001), 45(1): 111–129; V. Spike Peterson, "Feminism and IR," *Gender and History* (1998), 10(3): 581–589; Laura J. Shepherd, "Gender, Violence, and Global Politics," *Political Studies Review* (2009), 7(2): 208–219.

47. Barry Buzan, *People, States, and Fear: An Agenda for International Security Studies in the Post-Cold War Era* (Boulder: Lynne Rienner, 1991); J. Ann Tickner, *Gendering World Politics: Issues and Approaches in the Post-Cold War Era* (New York: Columbia University Press, 2001).

48. Moon, *Sex Among Allies*, 2.

49. Ibid.

50. Ibid., 10.

51. Ibid., 11; Cynthia Enloe, *Bananas, Beaches, and Bases.*

52. Moon, *Sex Among Allies*, 12.

53. Alicia Appleman-Jurman, *Alicia: My Story* (London: Bantam, 1989).

54. Ibid.

55. Ibid.

56. Ibid.

57. Ibid.

58. Ibid.

59. Ibid.

60. A significant amount of feminist work has thought about the personal *as international*; e.g., Kimberly Hutchings, "The Personal Is International: Feminist Epistemology and the Case of International Relations," in *Knowing the Difference: Feminist Perspectives on Epistemology*, ed. Kathleen Lennon and Margaret Whitford (New York: Psychology Press, 1994), 149–163.

61. See, e.g., Jonathan S. Burgess, *The Tradition of the Trojan War in Homer and the Epic Cycle* (Baltimore, MD: Johns Hopkins University Press, 2001).

62. See, e.g., Retha M. Warnicke, *The Rise and Fall of Anne Boleyn: Family Politics at the Court of Henry VIII* (Cambridge: Cambridge University Press, 1992).

63. See, e.g., Krishna Dharma, *Ramayana: India's Immortal Tale of Adventure, Love, and Wisdom* (New Delhi: Torchlight, 2004).

64. Sjoberg and Gentry, *Mothers, Monsters, Whores*, 203.

65. Moon, *Sex Among Allies*, 52.

66. See, e.g., Golda Meir, *My Life* (New York: Putnam, 1975); Richard Amdur, *Golda Meir: A Leader in Peace and War* (New York: Fawcett Columbine, 1990); Jean F. Blashfield, *Golda Meir* (London: Marshall Cavendish, 2010).

67. See, e.g., Carol Dommermuth-Costa, *Indira Gandhi: Daughter of India* (New York: 21st Century, 2001); Varalaskhmi Jnapathy, *Indira Gandhi: Woman of India's Destiny* (New Delhi: Gyan).

68. See, e.g., Judith Warner, *Hillary Clinton: The Inside Story* (London: Signet, 1999). See discussion, particularly, of the conflict in Libya, e.g., Laura Sjoberg, "'Manning Up' and Making (the Libyan) War," *Duck of Minerva* 23 March 2011; http://duckofminerva.blogspot.com/2011/03/manning-up-and-making-libyan-war.html; (accessed 1 May 2012); R. Charli Carpenter, "Libya and Feminist Peace Theory," *Duck of Minerva* 21 March 2012; http://duckofminerva.blogspot.com/2011/03/libya-and-feminist-peace-theory.html (accessed 1 May 2012).

69. See, e.g., John Prendergast and Don Cheadle, *The Enough Moment: Fighting to End Africa's Worst Human Rights Crimes* (New York: Random House, 2010); Ellen

Johnson Sirleaf, *This Child Will Be Great: Memoir of the Remarkable Life of Africa's First Woman President* (New York: HarperCollins, 2010); Gwynn Thomas and Melinda Adams, "Breaking the Final Glass Ceiling: The Influence of Gender in the Elections of Ellen Johnson Sirleaf and Michelle Bachelet," *Journal of Women, Politics, and Policy* (2010), 31(2): 105–131.

70. Jacqui True, "Feminism," in *Theories of International Relations*, ed. Scott Burchill and Andrew Linklater (London: MacMillan, 1996), 227.

71. Sjoberg and Gentry, *Mothers, Monsters, Whores.*

72. Maureen Dowd, "Fight of the Valkyries," *New York Times* 22 March 2011; http://www.nytimes.com/2011/03/23/opinion/23dowd.html?_r=3&hp (accessed 1 May 2012). See discussion in Sjoberg, "'Manning Up' and Making (the Libyan) War."

73. Moon, *Sex Among Allies*, 56.

74. Ibid. See also Cynthia Enloe, *Nimo's War, Emma's War: Making Feminist Sense of the Iraq War* (Berkeley: University of California Press, 2010).

75. For example, Ben O'Loughlin ("Gender, Violence, and Digital Emergence," *Global Policy Journal Blog* June 18, 2012 accessed 15 December 2012 at http://globalpolicyjournal.com/blog/18/6/2012/gender-violence-and-digital-emergence) relates the ways that two women's deaths were related in a way contrary to representing their lives and lived experiences.

76. Moon, *Sex Among Allies.*

77. Ibid., 11; Cynthia Enloe, *The Morning After: Sexual Politics at the End of the Cold War* (Berkeley: University of California Press, 1993).

78. Alexander Wendt, *A Social Theory of International Politics* (Cambridge: Cambridge University Press, 1999), 169.

79. Ibid.

80. Nancy Hirschmann, *The Subject of Liberty: Towards a Feminist Theory of Freedom* (Princeton: Princeton University Press, 2004), 11.

81. V. Spike Peterson and Anne Sisson Runyan, *Global Gender Issues*, 2nd ed. (Boulder: Westview, 1999).

82. Sjoberg and Gentry, *Mothers, Monsters, Whores*, 218, propositions 1–6.

83. For example, the individual violence on 11 September 2001 in the attacks on the World Trade Center in New York; self-martyrdom; assassinations.

84. For example, the "war on terror," intervention responses to dictators' oppression(s), etc.

85. For example, Nobel Prize winners Ellen Johnson Sirleaf, Leymah Gbowee, and Tawakkol Karman, "for their non-violent struggle for the safety of women and for women's rights to full participation in peace-building work" (http://www.nobelprize.org/nobel_prizes/peace/laureates/2011/, accessed 15 December 2012); Barack Obama "for his extraordinary efforts to strengthen international diplomacy and cooperation between peoples" (http://www.nobelprize.org/nobel_prizes/peace/laureates/2009/, accessed 15 December 2012); Martti Ahtisaari, "for his important efforts, on several continents and over more than three decades, to resolve international conflicts" (http://www.nobelprize.org/nobel_prizes/peace/laureates/2008/, accessed 15 December 2012).

86. For example, Wafa Idris' suicide attack changed the meaning of martyr in the context of the Palestinian resistance movement. See discussion in Frances Hasso, "Discursive and Political Deployments by/of the 2002 Palestinian Women Suicide Bombers/Martyrs," *Feminist Review* (2005), 81(1): 23–51.

87. *Glocal* is a combination of *global* and *local*, with the idea that there is some combination of broad-scale globalization and resource-efficient localization, such that the equivalent of "think globally, act locally" is enacted. For in-depth discussion, see Victor Roudometof, "Translationism, Cosmopolitanism, and Glolocalization," *Current Research in Sociology* (2005), (1): 113–135. For its applications to international relations, see Neil Brenner, "Global Cities, Glocal States: Global City Formation and State Territorial Restructuring in Contemporary Europe," *Review of International Political Economy* (1998), 5(1): 1–37; Philip G. Cerny, "Globalization and Other Stories: The Search for a New Paradigm for International Relations," *International Journal* (1995–1996), 51: 617–637.

88. See discussion of gender and states in chapter 5.

89. True, "Feminism," 235.

90. Byman and Pollack, "Let Us Now Praise Great Men."

91. Amy Allen, "Rethinking Power," *Hypatia* (1998), 13(1): 21–40.

92. Sjoberg and Gentry, *Mothers, Monsters, Whores*, 220.

93. For example, it is alleged that Henry Kissinger once answered a question about who was the twentieth-century's most important political leader with his own name. Certainly, he told a story of leadership (from the perspective or a leader) as the business of elite men. See, e.g., Henry Kissinger, *Years of Upheaval* (New York: Little, Brown, 1982).

94. Stylizing images of the other is key to empire-building (see Zillah Eisenstein, *Against Empire: Feminisms, Racisms, and the West* [London: Zed, 2004]).

95. See discussion of gendered militarism in chapter 5 for further theorization, and discussion of gendered experiences of war in chapter 9 for empirical exploration.

96. Militaries, then, expect men to behave as men like they expect women to behave like women, as discussed both in chapter 5 and later in this chapter.

97. Melissa T. Brown, *Enlisting Masculinity: The Construction of Gender in U.S. Military Recruiting Advertising During the All-Volunteer Force* (New York: Oxford University Press, 2012), 21.

98. See chapter 5, notes 57–59.

99. Brown, *Enlisting Masculinity*, 20.

100. Ibid., 40.

101. Denise Horn, "Boots and Bedsheets: Constructing the Military Support System in a Time of War," in *Gender, War, and Militarism: Feminist Perspectives*, ed. Laura Sjoberg and Sandra Via (Santa Barbara, CA: Praeger Security International, 2010), 57–68. See discussion of Kim Gorski in chapter 5, from Cynthia Enloe's *Nimo's War, Emma's War: Making Feminist Sense of the Iraq War* (Berkeley: University of California Press, 2010).

102. Enloe, *Nimo's War, Emma's War*, 63.

103. Ibid., 64–65.

104. As concerns veterans' affairs, health care has been specifically highlighted. See, e.g., Bonnie Coyle, Diana Wolan, and Andrea van Horn, "The Prevalence of Physical and Sexual Abuse in Women Veterans Seeking Care at a Veterans Affairs Medical Center," *Military Medicine* (1996), 161(10), 588–593; Donna Washington, Susan Kleimann, Ann Michelini, Kristin Kleimann, and Mark Canning, "Women Veterans' Perceptions and Decision-Making about Veterans Affairs Health Care," *Military Medicine* (2007), 172(8): 812–817.

105. See chapter 1, notes 267–318.

106. J. Ann Tickner, "You Just Don't Understand: Troubled Engagements Between Feminists and IR Theorists," *International Studies Quarterly* (1997), 41(4): 611–632.

107. J. Ann Tickner and Laura Sjoberg, "Feminism," in *International Relations Theories: Discipline and Diversity*, 2nd ed., ed. Tim Dunne, Milja Kurki, and Steve Smith (Oxford: Oxford University Press, 2010), 195–212; 200.

108. Ibid., 201.

109. See V. Spike Peterson, "Transgressing Boundaries: Theories of Knowledge, Gender, and International Relations," *Millennium: Journal of International Studies* (1992), 21(2): 183–206; Jill Steans, "Engaging from the Margins: Feminist Encounters with the 'Mainstream' of International Relations," *British Journal of Politics and International Relations* (2003), 5(3): 424–453.

110. Tickner and Sjoberg, "Feminism," 201. For example, as Christine Sylvester notes, the Critical Approaches to Security in Europe (CASE) manifesto published in *Security Dialogue* gives only a token recognition of gender in a footnote along with "other" postmodern approaches (Christine Sylvester, "Anatomy of a Footnote," *Security Dialogue* [December 2007], 38[4]: 547–558, citing CASE Collective, "Critical Approaches to Security in Europe: A Networked Manifesto," *Security Dialogue* [December 2006], 37[4]: 443–487).

111. For example, early work including Jef Huysmans, "Security! What Do You Mean? From Concept to Signifer," *European Journal of International Relations* (1998), 4(2): 226–255; Simon Dalby, "Security, Modernity, Ecology: The Dilemmas of Post-War Security Discourse," *Alternatives* (1992), 17(1): 95–134; James Der Derian, *Antidiplomacy. Spies, Terror, Speed, and War* (Oxford: Blackwell, 1992); more recent work like James Der Derian, *Critical Practices of International Theory: Selected Essays* (London and New York: Routledge, 2009); Brad Evans, "Foucault's Legacy: Security, War and Violence in the 21st Century," *Security Dialogue* (2010), 41(4): 413–433.

112. For example, see Christopher S. Browning and Matt McDonald, "The Future of Critical Security Studies: Ethics and Politics of Security," *European Journal of International Relations* published online before print October 27, 2011 at 10.1177/1354066111419538; Joao Nunes, "Reclaiming the Political: Emancipation and Critique in Security Studies," *Security Dialogue* (2012), 43(4): 345–361; Ken Booth, *Theory of World Security* (Cambridge: Cambridge University Press, 2007).

113. Runa Das, "Strategic Culture, Identity, and Nuclear (In)security in Indian Politics: Reflections from Critical Constructivist Lenses," *International Politics* (2010),

47(4): 472–96; Amitav Acharya, *Constructing a Security Community in Southeast Asia: ASEAN and the Problem of Regional Order* (London: Routledge, 2nd ed., 2009); Theo Farrell, "Constructivist Security Studies: Portrait of a Research Program," *International Studies Review* (2002), 4(1): 49–72.

114. As Tickner (in *Gendering World Politics* [New York: Columbia University Press, 2001], 48) has observed, feminism and human security share "'bottom-up' modes of analysis . . . crucial for understanding security issues and . . . emancipatory visions of security must get beyond statist frameworks."

115. For example, Charlotte Bunch, "A Feminist Human Rights Lens," *Peace Review* (2004), 16(1): 29–34; Heidi Hudson, "'Doing' Security as Though Humans Matter: A Feminist Perspective on Gender and the Politics of Human Security," *Security Dialogue* (2005), 36(2): 155–174; Linda Basch, "Human Security, Globalization, and Feminist Vision," *Peace Review* (2004), 16(1): 5–12; Gunhild Hoogenson and Kirsti Stuvoy, "Gender, Resistance, and Human Security," *Security Dialogue* (2006), 37(2): 207–228.

116. Tickner, *Gendering World Politics*.

117. Thanh-Dam Truong, Saskia Wieringa, and Amrita Chhachhi, eds. *Engendering Human Security* (London: Zed, 2006), xii.

118. Tickner, "Hans Morgenthau's Principles"; Christine Sylvester, *Feminist International Relations in a Postmodern Era* (Cambridge: Cambridge University Press, 1994).

119. Truong et al., *Engendering Human Security*, xxi; Gunhild Hoogensen and Svein Rottem, "Gender Identity and the Subject of Security," *Security Dialogue* (June 2004), 35(2): 155–171; Gunhild Hoogensen and Kirsti Stuvoy, "Gender, Resistance, and Human Security," *Security Dialogue* (2006), 37(2): 207-228.

120. Barry Buzan, "What Is Human Security? A Reductionist, Idealistic Notion that Adds Little Analytical Value," *Security Dialogue* (September 2004), 35(3): 369–370.

121. Roland Paris, "Human Security: Paradigm Shift or Hot Air?," *International Security* (Fall 2001), 26(2): 87–102.

122. Truong et al., *Engendering Human Security*, xxv.

123. Laura Sjoberg, "Introduction to *Security Studies*: Feminist Contributions," *Security Studies* (2009), 18(2): 183–213.

124. Including work like Ken Booth, "Security and Emancipation," *Review of International Studies* (1991), 17(3): 313–326; Ken Booth, *Theory of World Security* (Cambridge: Cambridge University Press, 2007); Ken Booth, ed., *Critical Security Studies and World Politics* (Boulder: Lynne Rienner); Nick Vaughan-Williams and Columba Peoples, *Critical Security Studies: An Introduction* (London: Taylor and Francis, 2010); Stuart Croft and Terry Terriff, eds. *Critical Reflections on Security and Change* (London: Taylor and Francis, 2000).

125. Soumita Basu, "Security as Emancipation: A Feminist Perspective," in *Feminist International Relations, Conversations About the Past, Present, and Future*, ed. J. Ann Tickner and Laura Sjoberg (New York: Routledge, 2011), 98–114, 109–111.

126. See discussion of relationships in chapter 4.

127. Laura Sjoberg, "Emancipation and the Feminist Security Studies Project," in Tickner and Sjoberg, eds., *Feminist International Relations*, 115–122, 119.

128. Marysia Zalewski, "Do We Understand Each Other Yet? Troubling Feminist Encounters With(in) International Relations," *British Journal of Politics and International Relations* (2007), 9(3): 302–312; Sarah Brown, "Feminism, International Theory, and the International Relations of Gender Inequality," *Millennium: Journal of International Studies* (1988), 17(3): 461–75.

129. Sjoberg, "Emancipation and the Feminist Security Studies Project."

130. For definitional discussion, see Bill McSweeney, "Identity and Security: Buzan and the Copenhagen School," *Review of International Studies* (January 1996), 22(1): 86–93; as well as discussion in chapter 1 of this book.

131. Barry Buzan, *People, States, and Fear: The National Security Problem in International Relations* (Chapel Hill, NC: University of North Carolina Press, 1983), 1, 2.

132. Barry Buzan, Ole Waever, and Jaap de Wilde, *Security: A New Framework for Analysis* (Boulder: Lynne Rienner, 1998), 5; Michael C. Williams, "Words, Images, Enemies: Securitization and International Politics," *International Studies Quarterly* (December 2003), 47(4): 511–531.

133. See, e.g., Anna M. Agathangelou and L. H. M. Ling, "The House of IR: From Family Power Politics to the *Poisies* of Worldism," *International Studies Review* (December 2004), 6(4): 21–50.

134. See Lene Hansen, "The Little Mermaid's Silent Security Dilemma and the Absence of Gender in the Copenhagen School," *Millennium: Journal of International Studies* (June 2000), 29(2): 285–306; Lene Hansen, "Gender, Nation, Rape: Bosnia and the Construction of Security," *International Feminist Journal of Politics* (2000), 3(1): 55-75; Hoogensen and Rottem, "Gender, Identity, and Security."

135. Sjoberg, "Introduction to *Security Studies*: Feminist Contributions."

136. Hansen, "The Little Mermaid's Silent Security Dilemma," 285.

137. See discussion in chapter 9 for further implications of this difference.

138. See, e.g., Karin L. Tamerius, "Sex, Gender, and Leadership in the Representation of Women," in *Women, Gender, and Politics*, ed. Mona Lena Krook and Sara Childs (Oxford: Oxford University Press, 2010), 243–249; Ronald Inglehart and Pippa Norris, "The Developmental Theory of the Gender Gap: Women's and Men's Voting Behavior in Global Perspective," in Krook and Childs, *Women, Gender, and Politics*, 127–133.

139. Debra Friedman and Doug McAdam, "Collective Identity and Activism: Networks, Choices, and the Life of a Social Movement," in *Frontiers in Social Movement Theory*, ed. Aldon D. Morris and Carol McClurg Mueller (New Haven: Yale University Press, 1992), 159. Because individuals do not have unlimited time, energy, or resources, they will have to choose between those goals (159).

140. Stephen Walt, "Rigor or Rigor Mortis? Rational Choice and Security Studies," *International Security* (1999), 23(4): 5–48.

141. One reason it might be appealing is because it purportedly considers all individuals as political actors capable of making and acting on calculated decisions based on expected utility. The model is not the catch-all solution to the gendered nature of theories of war decision-making that it appears to be, however. Looking through gender lenses reveals it as partial.

142. According to Hooper, rational choice theory is "physically disembodied and socially disembedded" from the gendered "rational/emotional, mind/body, and reason/madness dichotomies of Western thought" (Hooper, *Manly States*, 99).

143. Tickner, *Gendering World Politics*, 52–53.

144. Freud, founder of the psychoanalytic tradition, argued that men "are not gentle creatures," they are "creatures among whose instinctual endowments is to be reckoned a powerful share of aggressiveness" (Sigmund Freud, *Civilization and Its Discontents*, ed. and trans. James Strachey [New York: W. W. Norton, 1961], 58). According to Freud, men are instinctively violent creatures whose violence stems from the id, the unconscious part of humans" psychological makeup and the one responsible for instincts or "drives" (59).

145. Ibid., 65–66. Freud's approach to this is repeated elsewhere in psychoanalytic theory as well, e.g., Konrad Lorenz, the "father of ethnology," agreed with Freud (Leonard Berkowitz, "Biological Roots: Are Humans Inherently Violent?" in *Psychological Dimensions of War*, ed. Betty Glad [Newbury Park, CA: Sage, 1991], 25).

146. Nancy J. Chodorow, *Femininities, Masculinities, Sexualities: Freud and Beyond* (Lexington: University of Kentucky Press, 1994), 1.

147. Walter Mischel, *Personality and Assessment* (New York: Wiley, 1968), 153.

148. Jody Miller, *One of the Guys: Girls, Gangs, and Gender* (New York: Oxford University Press, 2001), 219.

149. Ibid., 220.

150. Sjoberg and Gentry, *Mothers, Monsters, Whores*.

151. I am referring to the so-called the agent-structure debate, e.g., Colin Wight, *Agents and Structures* (Cambridge: Cambridge University Press, 2006); David Dessler, "What's at Stake in the Agent-Structure Debate?" *International Organization* (1989), 43(2): 441–473; Andreas Bieler and Adam David Morton, "The Gordian Knot of Agency-Structure in International Relations: A Neo-Gramscian Perspective," *European Journal of International Relations* (2001), 7(1): 5–35; J. Samuel Barkin, *Realist Constructivism* (Cambridge: Cambridge University Press, 2010), chap. 7.

152. Perhaps a bolder way to state this is that our interest lies primarily in the question of how much of an individual's decision to participate in proscribed violence is his/her own, and what influences that part that is not his/her own?

153. Nancy Hirschmann, "Freedom, Recognition, and Obligations: A Feminist Approach to Political Theory," *American Political Science Review* (1989), 83(4): 1217–1244, 1228.

154. Laura Sjoberg, *Gender, Justice, and the Wars in Iraq: A Feminist Reformulation of Just War Theory* (New York: Lexington Books, 2006), 124.; see also Catherine MacKinnon, *Sex Equality* (New York: Foundation Press, 2001) for a full exposition.

155. Hirschmann, "Freedom, Recognition, and Obligations," 1228–1229.

156. Ibid., 1233; Tickner, *Gendering World Politics*.

157. Hirschmann, *The Subject of Liberty*, 204. These limitations differ based on social group membership; oppressed social groups have less access to powers and freedoms (and thus to agency).

158. Hirschmann, "Freedom, Recognition, and Obligations," 1239.

159. Hirschmann, The Subject of Liberty, ix. When confronted with two bad options, most would pick "neither," given the ideal situation actually was not one of the available choices. Still, the suboptimal choice is a *choice*, and a preference between suboptimal options still exists. While such a choice is partly constrained and not completely free, it is also not fully constrained. Partially constrained choices are an indicator of relational autonomy.

160. Ibid., ix.

161. Christine Sylvester, Feminist International Relations: An Unfinished Journey (Cambridge: Cambridge University Press, 1992).

162. By relational, I mean reliant on relationships (both in the active and passive sense) with others.

163. Hirschmann, "Freedom, Recognition, and Obligation"; Sjoberg, Gender, Justice, and the Wars in Iraq; Catriona MacKenzie and Natalie Stoljar, Relational Autonomy: Feminist Perspectives on Autonomy, Agency, and the Social Self (New York: Oxford University Press, 2000); Sylvester, Feminist International Relations; Christine Sylvester, Feminist Theory in a Postmodern Era (Cambridge: Cambridge University Press, 1994); Christine Sylvester, "Feminists and Realists on Autonomy and Obligation in International Relations," in Gendered States, ed. V. Spike Peterson (Boulder: Westview, 1992), 155–178.

164. Sjoberg, Gender, Justice, and the Wars in Iraq.

165. Hirschmann, The Subject of Liberty, x.

166. Sjoberg, Gender, Justice, and the Wars in Iraq.

167. Allen, "Rethinking Power."

168. Jean Elshtain, "Reflections on War and Political Discourse: Realism, Just War, and Feminism in a Nuclear Age," Political Theory (1985), 13(1): 39–57, 51.

169. Allen, "Rethinking Power," 33; Peterson and Runyan, Global Gender Issues, 69.

170. Peterson and Runyan, Global Gender Issues, 213.

171. Allen, "Rethinking Power," 34.

172. John Hoffman, Gender and Sovereignty: Feminism, the State, and International Relations (London: Palgrave, 2001), 151.

173. Hannah Marlene Dahl, "A Perceptive or Reflective State?" European Journal of Women's Studies (2000), 7(4): 475–494.

174. See the introduction, last footnote (now 22).

175. Annica Kronsell, "Methods for Studying Silences: Gender Analysis in Institutions of Hegemonic Masculinity," in Feminism Methodologies for International Relations, ed. Brooke A. Ackerly, Maria Stern, and Jacqui True (Cambridge: Cambridge University Press, 2006), 108-128, 109; V. Spike Peterson and Jacqui True, "New Times and New Conversations," in Zalewski and Parpart, eds., The Man Question, 21.

176. Hilary Charlesworth, "Feminist Methods in International Law," American Journal of International Law (1999), 93(2): 379–394.

177. Tickner's Gender and International Relations has been presented as a good example of such deconstruction—it reveals what she considers to be the gendered underpinnings of the field.

178. These feminists believe that "the production of knowledge is deeply embedded in the gendered power structures of society and has excluded large segments of society from participating in the articulation of experiences as knowledge" (Kronsell, "Methods for Studying Silences," 121).

179. Charlesworth, "Feminist Methods in International Law," 381.

180. Tickner, *Gender in International Relations*, 129.

181. A question Cynthia Enloe is well-known for asking; she discusses it in some detail in *The Curious Feminist: Searching for Women in a New Age of Empire* (Berkeley: University of California Press, 2004).

182. Sylvester, *Feminism and International Relations in the Postmodern Era.*

183. This idea is discussed in more detail in chapter 7.

184. MacKinnon, in *Sex Equality*, presents a model of the time when the U.S. Congress will become sex-equal if the integration of women continues at its current exponential rate, and finds that it will be sometime in the twenty-sixth century. Rather than asking "Would the world be different if women ran it?"—a question I find to be counterproductive because it implies an inherent difference between women and men, it seems prudent to think about it temporally. Would the world be different "if women ran it" tomorrow? If there were somehow a peaceful sex "flip," and tomorrow the world's leadership was 80 percent women and 20 percent men? The answer to that question is definitely yes, because women and men live and perform different gender roles in this particular moment in "gender history" (Cynthia Enloe's words in the preface to *Nimo's War, Emma's War*) tied to women's relative exclusion from politics. So, if the women who are excluded from politics on the basis of association with femininity were suddenly included in politics, politics would be different. Contrast this, perhaps, with the question of whether the world will be different if sex integration happens "naturally"—culminating, for the United States, in the twenty-sixth century. That "process," happens, it seems to me, as a result of socializing women into the norms of masculinity that are expectations we have of political leaders (a socialization as fake as but not more fake than current socializations into femininity). That world, I doubt, would be any different. As such, perhaps the appropriate question is whether the world would be any different were femininity empowered in it—the answer to which seems almost indisputably *yes.*

7. GENDERED STRATEGY

1. See profile at: http://ourmilitaryheroes.defense.gov/profiles/chontoshB.html (accessed 4 May 2012).

2. Ibid.

3. Ibid.

4. Ibid.

5. Ibid.

6. Ibid.

7. Dan Reiter and Curtis Meek, "Determinants of Military Strategy, 1903–1994: A Quantitative Empirical Test," *International Studies Quarterly* (1999), 43(2): 363–387, 363.

8. See, e.g., Eric Blanchard, "Gender, International Relations, and the Development of Feminist Security Theory," *Signs: Journal of Women in Culture and Society* (2003), 28(4): 1289–1313, 1291.

9. See discussion in chapter 1.

10. Richard Betts, "Is Strategy an Illusion?" *International Security* (2000), 25(2): 5–50, 6.

11. Alan Stephens and Nicola Baker, *Making Sense of War* (Cambridge: Cambridge University Press, 2006), 3.

12. Betts, "Is Strategy an Illusion?" 13.

13. Stephens and Baker, *Making Sense of War*, 13. Using rationality, theorists from Clausewitz to the present have argued that "strategy can turn uncertainty to advantage" and help belligerents alter the direction of the war (Colin S. Gray, *War, Peace, and Victory: Strategy and Statecraft for the Next Century* [New York: Simon & Schuster, 1990], 113).

14. Williamson Murray and Mark Grimsley, "On Strategy," in *The Making of Strategy: Rulers, States, and War*, ed. Williamson Murray, Macgregor Knox, and Alvin Bernstein (Cambridge: Cambridge University Press, 1994), 1–24, 20; Reiter and Meek, "Determinants of Military Strategy," 370.

15. J. Ann Tickner, *Gendering World Politics* (New York: Columbia University Press, 2001), 48, 49.

16. Raia Prokhovnik, *Rational Woman: A Feminist Critique of Dichotomy* (Manchester, UK: Manchester University Press, 2012).

17. Carol Cohn, "Sex and Death in the Rational World of Defense Intellectuals," *Signs: Journal of Women in Culture and Society* (1987), 12(4): 687–718.

18. Ibid.

19. Julie Nelson, "The Study of Choice or the Study of Provisioning," in *Beyond Economic MAN: Feminist Theory and Economics*, ed. Julie Nelson and Marianne Farber (London: Routledge, 1996), 23–36, 27.

20. Anthony Leibter, "Deliberate Wartime Environmental Damage: New Challenges for International Law," *California Western Law Review* (1992–1993), 23: 67–138; Michael N. Schmitt, "Green War: An Assessment of Environmental Law of International Armed Conflict," *Yale Law Journal* (1997), 22: 1–110.

21. See R. Charli Carpenter, ed., *Born of War: Protecting Children of Sexual Violence Survivors in Conflict Zones* (San Francisco, CA: Kumarian, 2007).

22. Cynthia Enloe, *Nimo's War, Emma's War: Making Feminist Sense of the Iraq War* (Berkeley: University of California Press, 2010).

23. See discussion of relational autonomy in chapter 2.

24. Nelson, "Study of Choice."

25. Hanne Marlene Dahl, "A Perceptive or Reflective State?" *European Journal of Women's Studies* (2000), 7(4): 475–494.

26. Ibid., 488.

27. Arne Johan Vetlesen, *Perception, Empathy, and Judgment* (University Park, PA: Pennsylvania State University Press, 1994), 13.

28. Dahl, "A Perceptive or Reflective State?" 488.

29. Christine Sylvester, *Feminist Theory and International Relations in a Postmodern Era* (Cambridge: Cambridge University Press, 1994), 95; Jill M. Bystudzieski, *Women Transforming Politics: Worldwide Strategies for Empowerment* (Bloomington: Indiana University Press, 1992).

30. Kathleen B. Jones, *Compassionate Authority* (New York: Routledge, 1993).

31. Dahl, "A Perceptive or Reflective State?" 488, 489; Jones, *Compassionate Authority*, 21–22.

32. June Lennie, "Deconstructing Gendered Power Relations in Participatory Planning: Towards an Empowering Feminist Framework of Participation and Action," *Women's Studies International Forum* (1999), 22(1), 107.

33. Fiona Robinson, *Globalizing Care: Ethics, Feminist Theory, and International Relations* (Boulder: Westview, 1999), 31, 23.

34. "Dynamic objectivity" is Evelyn Fox Keller's term, in *Reflection on Gender and Science*, 10th anniversary ed. (New Haven: Yale University Press, 1996); "strong objectivity" is conceptualized in Sandra Harding, *Is Science Multicultural? Postcolonialisms, Feminisms, and Epistemologies* (Bloomington: Indiana University Press, 1998).

35. Keller, *Reflections on Gender and Science*.

36. Harding, *Is Science Multicultural?*, 19, 132.

37. Rebecca M. Blank, "What Should Mainstream Economists Learn from Feminist Theory?", in Nelson and Farber, eds., *Beyond Economic MAN*, 135.

38. Keller, *Reflections on Gender and Science*.

39. This is because the starkness of the levels-of-analysis system obscures the domestic/international and masculine/feminine dichotomies in perceptions of the structure of the international arena. For further discussion, see Sjoberg, "Feminist Approaches to Political Leadership, citing Jacqui True, "Feminism," in *Theories of International Relations*, ed. Scott Burchill and Andrew Linklater (London: Palgrave, 1996), 227.

40. Christine Sylvester, *Feminist International Relations: An Unfinished Journey* (Cambridge: Cambridge University Press, 2002), 119–120.

41. Much of this section builds on my work with Jessica Peet, including Sjoberg and Peet, "A(nother) Dark Side of the Protection Racket," *International Feminist Journal of Politics* (2011), 13(2): 163–1382. and Sjoberg and Peet, "Targeting Women in War(s) in J. Ann Tickner and Laura Sjoberg, eds. *Feminism and International Relations: Conversations About the Past, Present, and Future* (London: Routledge, 2011): 169–187.

42. Ujala Sehgal, "New Reports of Qaddafi Forces Using Rape as a Weapon of War," *The Atlantic Wire* 29 May 2011; http://www.theatlanticwire.com/global/2011/05/survey-libyan-trauma-reveals-hundreds-rapes-qaddafi-forces/38273/ (accessed 4 May 2012).

43. Ibid.

44. Ibid.

45. Michelle Faul, "Hundreds of Women Raped by Gaddafi Militia," *The Independent* 29 May 2011; http://www.independent.co.uk/news/world/africa/hundreds-of-women-raped-by-gaddafi-militia-2290609.html (accessed 4 May 2012).

46. Sjoberg and Peet, "A(nother) Dark Side of the Protection Racket: Sjoberg and Peet, "Targeting Womem in Wars."

47. See discussion in chapter 5 about the role of gendered narratives in justifying the making of wars.

48. Carl von Clausewitz, *On War*, ed. and trans. Michael Howard and Peter Paret (Princeton: Princeton University Press, [1832] 1976). See reference chapter 3, note 183.

49. Alexander Downes, *Targeting Civilians in War* (Ithaca, NY: Cornell University Press, 2008), 44.

50. Ibid.

51. Benjamin Valentino, Paul Huth, and Sarah Croco, "Covenants without the Sword: International Law and the Protections of Civilians in War," *World Politics* (2006), 58(3): 339–377.

52. See chapter 1, note 232.

53. Mark Salter, *Barbarians and Civilization in International Relations* (London: Pluto, 2002).

54. See chapter 1, note 234.

55. See chapter 1, note 236.

56. Downes, *Targeting Civilians in Wars*.

57. Ibid., 44.

58. Personal conversation with some of the authors in this research program.

59. This is discussed in more detail in chapter 8.

60. This was a review by an anonymous reviewer at *International Studies Quarterly* about quantitative work done to support the theoretical discussion in this chapter.

61. War rape largely targets civilians. See discussions in Claudia Card, "Rape as a Weapon of War," Hypatia (1996), 11(4): 5–18; Paul Kirby, "How Is Rape a Weapon of War? Feminist International Relations, Modes of Critical Explanation, and the Study of Wartime Sexual Violence," *European Journal of International Relations* (2012), DOI: 10.1177/1354066111427614. For a discussion of war rape as it targets and affects soldiers, see, e.g., Sheila Jeffreys, "Double Jeopardy: Women, the US Military, and the War in Iraq," *Women's Studies International Forum* (2007), 30(1): 16–25.

62. For a discussion of the relationship between war rape and death, see, e.g., Catherine MacKinnon, "Rape, Genocide, and Women's Human Rights," *Harvard Women's Law Journal* (1994), 17: 5–16; Catherine N. Niarchos, "Women, War, and Rape: Challenges Facing the International Tribunal for the Former Yugoslavia," *Human Rights Quarterly* (1995), 17: 649–690.

63. For discussion of territorial war and desperation, see Downes, *Targeting Civilians in War*; for a discussion of organizational culture, see Jeffrey W. Legro, *Cooperation*

Under Fire: Anglo-German Restraint During World War II (Ithaca, NY: Cornell University Press, 1995); Colin Kahl, "How We Fight," *Foreign Affairs* (2006), 85(6): 83–101; Isabel Hull, *Absolute Destruction: Military Culture and the Practices of War in Imperial Germany* (Ithaca, NY: Cornell University Press, 2005).

64. Sjoberg and Peet, "A(nother) Dark Side of the Protection Racket"; Sjoberg and Peet, "Targeting Civilians in War: Feminist Approaches."

65. This is not meant to conflate state and nation.

66. Laura Sjoberg, "The Gendered Realities of the Immunity Principle: Why Gender Analysis Needs Feminism," *International Studies Quarterly* (2006), 50(4): 889–910, 895.

67. Jean Elshtain, ed., *Just War Theory* (New York: Basic, 1992). See also discussion in Chapter 5.

68. Jean Elsthain, *Women and War* (Brighton, MA: Harvester, 1987); Lucinda Peach, "An Alternative to Pacifism? Feminism and Just-War Theory"; Helen Kinsella, "Securing the Civilian: Sex and Genders in the Laws of War," in *Power in Global Governance*, ed. Michael Barnett and Raymond Duvall (Cambridge: Cambridge University Press, 2004); Laura Sjoberg, *Gender, Justice, and the Wars in Iraq* (New York: Lexington, 2006).

69. Judith Gardam, "Gender and Non-Combatant Immunity," *Transnational Law and Contemporary Problems* (1993), 3: 345–370, 352.

70. See Anne Sisson Runyan, "Gender Relations and the Politics of Protection," *Peace Review* (1990), 2(4): 28–31; Pieter Spierenburg, *Masculinity, Violence, and Honor: An Introduction* (Columbus, OH: Ohio State University Press, 1998).

71. See, e.g., Laura Sjoberg and Caron Gentry, *Mothers, Monsters, Whores: Women's Violence in Global Politics* (London: Zed, 2007) for a discussion of the presumed innocence of women who are perpetrators of war and proscribed violence in global politics.

72. Susan Rae Peterson, "Coercion and Rape: The State as a Male Protection Racket," in Feminism and Philosophy, ed. Mary Vetterling-Braggin, Fredrick Elliston, and Jane English (Totowa, NJ: Littlefield, Adams, 1977).

73. Ibid.; Iris Young, "The Logic of Masculinist Protection: Reflections on the Current Security State," *Signs: Journal of Women in Culture and Society* (2003) 29(1): 1–25.

74. Lauren Wilcox, *The Practices of Violence: Theorizing Embodied Subjects in International Relations* (unpublished book manuscript).

75. See, e.g., George W. Bush, 2002 State of the Union Address (http://www.americanrhetoric.com/speeches/stateoftheunion2002.htm, accessed 15 December 2012), on the "war on terror." In this way, protecting "their women" provides legitimacy and justification for men's (and masculine states') making wars (Young, "The Logic of Masculinist Protection," 4).

76. Sjoberg and Peet, "A(nother) Dark Side of the Protection Racket," 167, citing Nancy Huston, "Tales of War and Tears of Women," in *Women and Men's Wars*, ed. Judith Stiehm (Oxford: Pergamon Press, 1983), 279. Emphasis in original.

77. Sjoberg and Peet, "A(nother) Dark Side of the Protection Racket"

78. R. W. Connell, *Masculinities* (Berkeley: University of California Press, 1995), 214.

79. Women's need for protection justifies wars, but it also justifies the social dominance of masculinity, a requirement of war-fighting. Defining women as innocent and in need of protection, then, is not only productive of gender subordination but also of war itself, which it justifies and makes noble.

80. Concerning Iraq, see Sjoberg, *Gender, Justice, and the Wars in Iraq*; concerning Afghanistan, see Miriam Cooke, "Gender and September 11: A Roundtable: Saving Brown Women," *Signs: Journal of Women in Culture and Society* (2002), 28(1): 468–470; Kevin Ayotte and Mary Hussain, "Securing Afghan Women: Neocolonialism, Epistemic Violence, and the Rhetoric of the Veil," *National Women's Studies Association Journal* (2005), 17(3): 112–133.; Mary Ann Franks, "Obscene Undersides: Women and Evil Between the Taliban and the United States," *Hypatia* (2003), 18(1): 135–156.

81. As well as (as I argued in chapter 5) a key part of how and why states fight and mobilize their citizens to commit wartime violence.

82. Sjoberg and Peet, "A(nother) Dark Side of the Protection Racket," citing Clausewitz, *On War*.

83. Antulio Joseph Echevarria, *Clausewitz's Center of Gravity: Changing Our Warfighting Doctrine—Again!* (Washington, DC: Strategic Studies Institute, 2002), 12.

84. Clausewitz, *On War*, 595–596. Italics added.

85. Stephens and Baker, Making Sense of War, 29.

86. Echevarria, *Clausewitz's Center of Gravity*, 12.

87. Ibid., 7; Clausewitz, *On War*, 486.

88. Sjoberg and Peet, "A(nother) Dark Side of the Protection Racket," 171.

89. Ibid.

90. Julie Mertus, "'Woman' in the Service of National Identity," *Hastings Women's Law Journal* (1994), 5(1): 5–23, 18.

91. Sjoberg and Peet, "A(nother) Dark Side of the Protection Racket."

92. Sjoberg and Peet, "Targeting Women in War(s)."

93. Tested using a lagged scalar variable of the second derivative of sex-disaggregated population functions controlling for military deaths.

94. Assuming there is such a thing as incidental or collateral civilian deaths in war. Bivariate *t*-tests confirm this finding.

95. With the addition of the "sexual violence" indicator, the pseudo R^2 of Downes' model 1 went from .60 to .73. Other models saw a similar change in the pseudo R^2.

96. With the addition of the "sex ratio" indicator, the pseudo R^2 of Downes' model 1 went from .60 to .71. Other models saw a similar change in the pseudo R^2.

97. Calculating marginal effects, when the gender-based variables are considered, a one-unit change in sexual violence in war leads to a 2.4 percent change in the likelihood that states attack civilians; since the sexual violence scale is an 11-point scale, accounting for 27 percent of the variation, making it the third most influential variable after territorial annexation (68 percent more likely to attack civilians) and attrition (27 percent more likely to attack civilians), but also including regime type (where democracy made states 11 percent more likely to attack civilians).

98. High representation of women in civilian deaths predicts 12 percent of the variation in civilian victimization.

99. See, e.g., Maria B. Olujic, "Embodiment of Terror: Gendered Violence in Peacetime and Wartime in Croatia and Bosnia-Herzegovina," *Medical Anthropology Quarterly* 12(1) (1988), 12(1): 31–50.

100. Hugo Slim, *Killing Civilians in War* (New York: Columbia University Press, 1998).

101. Stjepan Gabriel Metrovic, *The Balkanization of the West: The Confluence of Postmodernism and Postcommunism* (London and New York: Routledge, 1999), xi.

102. Ibid., 60.

103. Lene Hansen, "Gender, Nation, Rape: Bosnia and the Construction of Security," *International Feminist Journal of Politics* (2000), 3(1): 55–75, 59.

104. Ibid., 60.

105. Metrovic, *The Balkanization of the West.*

106. Ronnie Landau, *The Nazi Holocaust* (London: IB Tauris, 2006); Zoe Waxman, *Writing the Holocaust: Identity, Testimony, and Representation* (Oxford: Oxford University Press, 2006).

107. Elisabeth Jean Wood, "Variation in Sexual Violence During War," *Politics and Society* (2006), 34(3): 307–342.

108. James W. Messerschmidt, "The Forgotten Victims of World War II: Masculinities and Rape in Berlin, 1945," *Violence Against Women* (2006), 12(7): 706–712, 707.

109. Ibid., 710.

110. Atina Grossman, "A Question of Silence: The Rape of German Women by Occupation Soldiers," *October* (1995) 72: 42–63; Patricia Albanese, "Nationalism, War, and Archaization of Gender Relations in the Balkans," *Violence Against Women* (2001), 7(9): 999–1023; Anonymous, *A Woman in Berlin: Eight Weeks in A Conquered City* (New York: Henry Holt, 2005); Anthony Beevor, *Berlin: The Downfall 1945* (London: Penguin, 2002).

111. Beevor, *Berlin: The Downfall 1945.*

112. Wood, "Variation in Sexual Violence During War."

113. Andrew Roberts, "Stalin's Army of Rapists," *The Mail Online* 24 October 2008; http://www.dailymail.co.uk/news/article-1080493/Stalins-army-rapists-The-brutal-war-crime-Russia-Germany-tried-ignore.html (accessed 5 May 2010).

114. Chris Bellamy, *Absolute War: Soviet Russia in the Second World War* (New York: Knopf, 2007).

115. A number of competing explanations exist. The Germans argued that it was a signifier of Russian/Soviet/Mongol barbarism, and some history books have characterized it as a Soviet tactic of revenge (Grossman, "A Question of Silence"). Neither explanation, however, is satisfactory: the Soviet "barbarians" were not as "barbaric" at many places in Eastern Europe or as they pushed German troops back through the Soviet Union, and we could not find a single Soviet statement linking outrage about German rapes of Soviet women to Soviet rapes of German women.

116. Ruth Seifert, "War and Rape: A Preliminary Analysis," in *Mass Rape: The War Against Women in Bosnia-Herzegovina*, ed. Alexandra Stiglmayer and Marion Farber (Lincoln, NE: University of Nebraska Press, 1994).

117. Grossman, "A Question of Silence," 48; H. Fehrenbach, *Cinema in Democratizing Germany: Reconstructing National Identity After Hitler* (Chapel Hill, NC: University of North Carolina Press, 1995); Norman M. Naimark, *The Russians in Germany: A History of the Soviet Zone of Occupation, 1945–1949* (Cambridge: Harvard University Press, 1995).

118. As quoted in Danny S. Parker, *To Win the Winter Sky* (London: Da Capo, 1998).

119. Grossman, "A Question of Silence," 50.

120. Another example we have explored (Sjoberg and Peet, "Targeting Women in War(s)") is the British naval blockade in World War I.

121. Ibid.

122. Sjoberg, *Gender, Justice, and the Wars in Iraq*.

123. Peter W. Singer, *Corporate Warriors: The Rise of the Privatized Military Industry* (Ithaca, NY: Cornell University Press, 2003); Doug Brooks, "Messiahs or Mercenaries? The Future of International Private Military Services," *International Peacekeeping* (2000), 7(4): 129–144; Christopher Kinsey, *Corporate Soldiers and International Security: The Rise of Private Military Companies* (London: Taylor and Francis, 2006); Anna Leander, *Eroding State Authority? Private Military Companies and the Legitimate Use of Force* (Turin, Italy: Rubbettino Editore, 2006).

124. J. K. Gibson-Graham, *The End of Capitalism (As We Knew It): A Feminist Critique of Political Economy*, 2nd ed. (Minneapolis: University of Minnesota Press, 2006); for a discussion of market penetration of PMSCs specifically, see Les Johnston, "Transnational Private Policing: The Impact of Global Commercial Security," in *Issues in Transnational Policing*, ed. J. W. E. Sheptycki (New York: Psychology Press, 2000), 21–42; Tim Evans, "Conservative Economics and Globalization," *Political Quarterly* (2004), 75(4): 383–385.

125. For debate, see Jared F. Layer, "Military Effectiveness and Economic Efficiency in Peacekeeping: Public Versus Private," *Oxford Development Studies* (2005), 33(1): 99–106; Eike Krahmann, "Security Governance and the Private Military Industry in Europe and North America," *Conflict, Security, and Development* (2005), 5(2): 247–268; Jurgen Brauer, "An Economic Perspective on Mercenaries, Military Companies, and the Privatisation of Force," *Cambridge Review of International Affairs* (1999), 13(1): 130–146.

126. Scott Fitzsimmons, "Dogs of Peace: A Potential Role for Private Military Companies in Peace Implementation," *Journal of Military and Strategic Studies* (2005), 8(1): 1–26; Simon Chesterman and Angelina Fisher, *Private Security, Public Order: The Outsourcing of Public Services and Its Limits* (Oxford: Oxford University Press, 2009).

127. The *New Zealand Herald* contends that private military companies are becoming the fastest growing industry in the global economy, noting that the

sector is worth around $120 billion (in U.S. dollars) annually (Leonard Doyle and Daniel Howden, "Private Guards Now a $161b Global Industry," *New Zealand Herald* 25 September 2007; http://www.nzherald.co.nz/world/news/article.cfm?c_id=2&objectid=10465687 (accessed 5 May 2012).

128. For a discussion of the (intentionally apparent) apolitical performance of PMSCs, see Christian Olson, "The Politics of the Apolitical: Private Military Companies, Humanitarians, and the Quest for (Anti-)politics in Post-Intervention Environments," *Journal of International Relations and Development* (2007), 10(4): 332–361. Tina Garmon (in "Domesticating International Corporate Responsibility: Holding Private Military Firms Accountable under the Alien Tort Claims Act," *Tulane Journal of International and Comparative Law* [2003], 11: 325–354) argues that this apparent apolitical performance serves two masters: the private-sphere invisibility of PMSC service (discussed below) and the evasion of domestic prosecution (discussed in more detail in her article).

129. For broad discussions on the international implications of the public/private dichotomy, see Celina Romany, "Women as Aliens: A Feminist Critique of the Public/Private Distinction in International Human Rights Law," *Harvard Human Rights Journal* (1993), 6: 87–126; Raia Prokhovnik, "Public and Private Citizenship: From Gender Invisibility to Feminist Inclusiveness," *Feminist Review* (1988), 60: 84–104; Hilary Charlesworth, "Feminist Methods in International Law," *American Journal of International Law* (1999), 93(2): 379–394.

130. For discussion, see, e.g., Catherine MacKinnon, *Are Women Human?* (Cambridge, MA: Harvard University Press, 2006); Susan Moeller Okin, "Feminism, Women's Human Rights, and Cultural Differences," *Hypatia* (1998), 13(2): 32–52.

131. Documentation and discussion can be found in articles such as: Heather Carney, "Prosecuting the Lawless: Human Rights Abuses and Private Military Firms," *George Washington Law Review* (2005–2006), 74: 317–344; Nathaniel Stinnett, "Regulating the Privatization of War: How to Stop Private Military Firms from Committing Human Rights Abuses," *Boston College International and Comparative Law Review* (2005), 28: 212–224; J. T. Mlinarcik, "Private Military Contractors & Justice: A Look at the Industry, Blackwater, and the Fallujah Incident," *Regent Journal of Internaitonal Law* (2006), 4: 129–148; Michael H. Hoffman, "Emerging Combatants, War Crimes, and the Future of Humanitarian Law," *Crime, Law, and Social Change* (2000), 34(1): 99–110.

132. For example, the sources listed in note 128. See also Ian Kierpaul, "Mad Scramble of Congress, Lawyers, and Law Students after Abu Ghraib: the Rush to Bring Private Military Contractors to Justice," *Toledo Law Review* (2007–2008), 39: 406–443; Cedric Ryngaert, "Litigating Abuses Committed by Private Military Companies," *European Journal of International Law* (2008), 19(5): 1035–1053.

133. For example, Saad Gul, "Secretary Will Deny All Knowledge of Your Actions: The Use of Private Military Contractors and the Implications for State and Political Accountability," *Lewis and Clark Law Review* (2006), 10: 287–312; Fabien Mathieu and Nick Dearden, "Corporate Mercenaries: The Threat of Private

Military & Security Companies," *Review of African Political Economy* (2007), 34(114): 744–755; Deborah Avant, "Mercenaries," *Foreign Policy* (2004), 143: 20–29; Robert Mandel, "The Privatization of Security," *Armed Forces and Society* (2001), 28(1): 129–151.

134. Other feminist work on PMSCs so far has talked largely about the (hyper-masculine) culture of PMSCs and/or their place in the gendered political economy of military globalization. See, e.g., Sandra Via, "Gender, Militarism, and Globalization: Soldiers for Hire and Hegemonic Masculinity," in *Gender, War, and Militarism: Feminist Perspectives*, ed. Laura Sjoberg and Sandra Via (Santa Barbara, CA: Praeger Security International, 2010), 42–55; Paul Higate, "Drinking Vodka from the Butt-Crack': Men, Masculinities and the Private Militarised Security Company," *International Feminist Journal of Politics* (2012), 14(4): 450–469. Wilcox, *Practices of Violence*. My goal is neither to replicate or replace that work, nor to make a comprehensive statement. Instead, I look to understand the mapping of the public/private divide onto PMSCs. On this point, I have been heavily influenced by a project Maya Eichler is working on concerning gender and PMSCs.

135. See discussions, for example, in Carsten Hoppe, "Passing the Buck: State Responsibility for Private Military Companies," *European Journal of International Law* (2008), 19(5): 989–1014; Francesco Francioni, "Private Military Contractors and International Law: An Introduction," *European Journal of International Law* (2008), 19(5): 961–964; Shawn Engbrecht, *America's Covert Warriors: Inside the World of Private Military Contractors* (New York: Potomac, 2010); Simon Chesterman, "'We Can't Spy . . . If We Can't Buy!': The Privatization of Intelligence and the Limits of Outsourcing 'Inherently Governmental Functions," *European Journal of International Law* (2008), 19(5): 1055–1074.

136. e.g., Olsson, "The Politics of the Apolitical."

137. Which I identified (following Steve Niva) in chapter 5 as "tough but tender." See Steve Niva, "Tough but Tender: New World Order Masculinity and the Gulf War," in *The Man Question*, ed. Marysia Zalewski and Jane Parpart, (Boulder: Westview, 1998), 109–128.

138. Discussion on roundtable, "Feminist Security Studies: State of the Field," at the 2011 Annual Meeting of the International Studies Association, Montreal, Canada, March 26–29, 2011. This discussion was a follow-up from a (more productive) discussion at a meeting of the Gender and Security Working Group at the 2010 annual meeting on the International Studies Association, New Orleans, LA, February 16–19, 2010. Part of that discussion was published as a *Politics and Gender* Critical Perspectives section called "The State of Feminist Security Studies: A Conversation" (ed. Laura Sjoberg and Jennifer Lobasz, *Politics and Gender* [2011], 7[4]: 573–604. Other participants in the conversation, and some critics, respond in a forthcoming forum in *International Studies Perspectives*.

139. A fairly significant literature exists, evaluating a variety of factors, e.g., muscle and bone susceptibility (T. J. Beck, C. B. Ruff, R. A. Shaffer, K. Betsinger, D. W. Trobe, and S. K. Brodine, "Stress Fracture in Military Recruits: Gender Differences

in Muscle and Bone Susceptibility Factors," *Bone* [2000], 27[3]: 437–444; Michael Feuerstein, Steven Berkowiz, and Charles Peck, "Musculoskeletal-Related Disability in US Army Personnel: Prevalence, Gender, and Military Occupational Specialties," *Journal of Occupational and Environmental Medicine* [1997], 39[1]: 68–78); ability to jump out of a plane (Evangelos Papps, Ali Sheikhzadeh, Marshall Hagins, and Margareta Nordin, "The Effect of Gender and Fatigue on the Biomechanics of Bilateral Landings from Jump: Peak Values," *Journal of Sports Science and Medicine* [2007], 6[1]: 77–84); load carriage (Renee Attwells and Robin Hooper, "Gender Differences in Military Load Carriage," in *Contemporary Ergonomics 2005*, ed. Philip D. Bust and P. T. McCabe [London: Taylor and Francis, 2005]; Lei Ren, Richard K. Jones, and David Howard, "Dynamic Analysis of Load Carriage Biomechanics During Level Walking," *Journal of Biomechanics* [2005], 38[4]: 853–863); and boot suitability (G. D. Oliver, A. J. Stone, J. M. Booker, and H. A. Plummer, "A Kinematic and Kinetic Analysis of Drop Landings in Military Boots," *Journal of the Army Medical Corps* [2011], 157[3]: 218–221).

140. For example, Peter V. Karpovich and R. R. Ronkin, "Oxygen Consumption for Men of Various Sizes in the Simulated Piloting of a Plane," *American Journal of Physiology* (1946), 146(3): 394–398.

141. For example, Kenneth W. Kennedy, "International Anthropometric Variability and Its Effects on Aircraft Cockpit Design," Airforce Aerospace Medical Research Lab, Wright-Patterson Air Force Base, Ohio, July 1976; http://www.dtic.mil/cgi-bin/GetTRDoc?Location=U2&doc=GetTRDoc.pdf&AD=ADA027801 (accessed 4 May 2012); Terence J. Lyons, "Women in the Military Cockpit," Armstrong Lab, Brooks Air Force Base, Texas, June 1991; http://www.dtic.mil/cgi-bin/GetTRDoc?Location=U2&doc=GetTRDoc.pdf&AD=ADA238808 (accessed 4 May 2012); Kathrine Waterman and James C. Miller, "Women in Military Aviation," Air Force Academy, Colorado Springs, Colorado; http://www.dtic.mil/cgi-bin/GetTRDoc?Location=U2&doc=GetTRDoc.pdf&AD=ADA381795 (accessed 4 May 2012).

142. See discussion in Stephanie Gutmann, *The Kinder, Gentler Military: Can America's Gender-Neutral Fighting Force Still Win Wars?* (New York: Simon & Schuster, 2000).

143. Rachel N. Weber, "Manufacturing Gender in Commercial and Military Cockpit Design," *Science, Technology, and Human Values* (1997), 22(2): 235–253.

144. For example, Kathryn Abrams, "Gender in the Military: Androcentrism and Institutional Reform," *Law and Contemporary Problems* (1993), 56: 217–243; Orna Sasson-Levy, "Feminism and Military Gender Practices, Israeli Women Soldiers in 'Masculine' Roles," *Sociological Inquiry* (2003), 73(3): 440–465; Francine D'Amico, "Appendix," in *Wives and Warriors: Women and the Military in the United States and Canada*, ed. Laurie Lee Weinstein and Christie C. White (Boulder: Greenwood, 1997); R. Claire Snyder, "The Citizen-Soldier Tradition and Gender Integration of the US Military," *Armed Forces and Society* (2003), 29(2): 185–204.

145. Weber, "Manufacturing Gender in Commercial and Military Cockpit Design."

146. Peter W. Singer, *Wired for War: The Robotics Revolution and Conflict in the Twenty-First Century* (New York: Penguin, 2009). For a discussion of the implications of the turn to "unmanned" warfare, see, e.g., Tyler Wall and Torin Monahan, "Surveillance and Violence from Afar: The Politics of Drones and Liminal Security-Scapes," *Theoretical Criminology* (2011), 15(3): 239–254.

147. Peter W. Singer, "Ethical Implications of Military Robotics." The 2009 William C. Stutt Ethics Lecture, 25 March 2009, at the U.S. Naval Academy, Annapolis, Maryland; http://www.au.af.mil/au/awc/awcgate/navy/usna_singer_robot_ethics.pdf (accessed 4 May 2012).

148. Ibid.

149. Ibid.

150. Ibid. Apparently, rather than being sent to a mother, that letter was sent to the iRobot factory outside Boston that had produced the PackBot "who" had "died."

151. Wilcox, *Practices of Violence.*

152. Lauren Wilcox, "Gendering the Cult of the Offensive," *Security Studies* (2009), 18(2): 214–240, citing V. Spike Peterson, "Sexing Political Identities/Nationalism as Heterosexism," *International Feminist Journal of Politics* (1999), 1(1): 34–65.

153. Connell, *Masculinities,* explains the idea of a hegemonic masculinity and subordinated masculinities operating in political and social spaces. Jennifer Heeg Maruska ("When Are States Hypermasculine? The War on Terror in Historical Perspective," in *Gender and International Relations: Feminist Perspectives,* ed. Laura Sjoberg [London: Routledge, 2009], 235–255) argues that the policy-making realm of a state is dominated by the hegemonic masculinity in that place and time.

154. Heeg Maruska, "When Are States Hypermasculine?" describes in detail changes in the hegemonic masculinity in U.S. foreign policy-making.

155. Ibid.

156. Meghana Nayak, "Orientalism and 'Saving' U.S. State Identity after 9/11," *International Feminist Journal of Politics* (March 2007), 8(1): 42–61.

157. Heeg, "When Are States Hypermasculine?"

158. For example, Cynthia Weber, *Faking It: U.S. Hegemony in a "Post-Phallic" Era* (Minneapolis: University of Minnesota Press, 1999), where she discusses the United States' gendered perception of Cuba as influencing the strategy the United States adopts toward Cuba; Cynthia Weber, "'Flying Planes Can Be Dangerous'," *Millennium: Journal of International Studies* (2002), 31(2): 129–147, in which she compares gendered perceptions of Japan in World War II and al Qaeda in the "war on terror."

159. Weber, "'Flying Planes Can Be Dangerous'," 136, 141.

160. Ibid., 143.

161. Ibid., 146.

162. Weber "'Flying Planes Can Be Dangerous'" (138) talks specifically about the mixed messages of dropping bombs and food on Afghanistan in the same areas around the same time.

408 • 8. GENDERED TACTICS

8. GENDERED TACTICS

1. Womenforwomen.org, "Lucienne's Story," *Stories from Women: Democratic Republic of Congo*, accessed 4 May 2012 at http://www.womenforwomen.org/global-initiatives-helping-women/stories-women-congo.php#Lucienne.

2. The gender dimensions of each will be discussed later in this chapter. For a historical account of the British blockade of Germany, see Eric W. Osborne, *Britain's Economic Blockade of Germany, 1914–1919* (New York: Psychology Press, 2004). For a historical account of the Srebrenica massacre, see David Rohde, *Endgame: The Betrayal and Fall of Srebrenica, Europe's Worst Massacre since World War II* (Boulder: Westview, 1998).

3. See discussion in Alison Des Forges, *Leave None to Tell the Story: Genocide in Rwanda* (New York: Human Rights Watch, 1999).

4. See, e.g., Lisa Sharlach, "Rape as Genocide: Bangladesh, the Former Yugoslavia, and Rwanda," *New Political Science* (2000), 22(1): 89–102; Sherrie L. Russell-Brown, "Rape as an Act of Genocide," *Berkeley Law Review* (2003), 21: 350–374; Des Forges, *Leave None to Tell the Story*.

5. For example, Diana Milillo, "Rape as a Tactic of War: Social and Psychological Perspectives," *Affilia* (2006), 21(2): 196–205; Carolyn Nordstrom, "Rape: Politics and Theory in War and Peace," *Australian Feminist Studies* (1996), 11(23): 147–162; Tamara L. Tompkins, "Prosecuting Rape as a War Crime: Speaking the Unspeakable," *Notre Dame Law Review* (1994–1995), 70: 845–891; Catherine MacKinnon, "Rape, Genocide, and Women's Human Rights," *Harvard Women's Law Journal* (1994), 17: 5–17.

6. For example, UN Women's work on wartime rape (as reported on by Gabriella Casanas, "UN: Wartime Rape No More Inevitable, Acceptable than Mass Murder," CNN News 10 August 2010; http://articles.cnn.com/2010–08–12/world/un.wartime.rape_1_sexual-violence-war-crime-congo?_s=PM:WORLD (accessed 4 May 2012).

7. For example, Amnesty International, which has war rape as one of the key tenets of its "Women's Rights Are Human Rights" campaign (http://www.amnestyusa.org/our-work/issues/women-s-rights [accessed 4 May 2012]); Human Rights Watch, which has a zero tolerance advocacy for war rape (as reported in Marianne Mollman, "Rape in War: No More Excuses," *Chicago Tribune* 22 July 2011; http://www.hrw.org/news/2011/07/22/rape-war-no-more-excuses [accessed 4 May 2012]).

8. Elisabeth Jean Wood, "Variation in Sexual Violence During War," *Politics & Society* (2006), 34(3): 307–342; Inger Skjaelsbaek, "Sexual Violence and War: Mapping Out a Complex Relationship," *European Journal of International Relations* (2001), 7(2): 211–237.

9. See discussion in Madeline Morris, "By Force of Arms: Rape, War, and Military Culture," *Duke Law Journal* (1995–1996), 45: 651–782.

10. For example, Lee Marin, Robert H. Stretch, Leora N. Rosen, Kathryn H. Knudson, and Doris Briley Durand, "Prevalence and Timing of Sexual Assaults in a Sample of Male and Female U.S. Army Soldiers," *Military Medicine* (1998), 164(3): 213–216.

11. For a critical history, see Bulent Diken and Carsten Bagge Laustsen, "Becoming Abject: Rape as a Weapon of War," *Body & Society* (2005), 11(1): 111–128.

12. See, e.g., Hansen, "Gender, Nation, Rape"; Andrea Stiglmayer and Marion Faber, *Mass Rape: The War Against Women in Bosnia-Herzgovina* (Lincoln: University of Nebraska Press, 1994); Todd A. Salzman, "Rape Camps as a Means of Ethnic Cleansing: Religious, Cultural, and Ethical Response to Rape Victims in the Former Yugoslavia," *Human Rights Quarterly* (1998), 20(2): 348–378.

13. For example, Sondra Hale, "Rape as a Marker and Eraser of Difference: Darfur and the Nuba Mountains (Sudan)," in *Gender, War, and Militarism: Feminist Perspectives*, ed. Laura Sjoberg and Sandra Via (Santa Barbara, CA: Praeger Security International, 2010), 105–113.

14. See discussions of the Rape of Nanking in Joshua S. Goldstein, *War and Gender: How Gender Shapes the War System and Vice Versa* (Cambridge: Cambridge University Press, 2001), 367; Takahasi Yoshida, *The Making of the "Rape of Nanking": History and Memory in Japan, China, and the United States* (New York: Oxford University Press, 2006), 267.

15. Atina Grossman, "A Question of Silence: The Rape of German Women by Occupation Soldiers," *October* (1995), 72: 42–63.

16. For example, Molly Hennessy-Fiske and Nagham Osman, "Woman Denies Military's Claims about 'Virginity Test'" *Los Angeles Times* 2 June 2011 (http://latimesblogs.latimes.com/babylonbeyond/2011/06/egypt-victim-details-virginity-test-denies-military-claims.html [accessed 4 May 2012]; Xan Rice, "Egyptians Protest over 'Virginity Tests' on Tahrir Square Women," *The Guardian* 31 May 2011 (http://www.guardian.co.uk/world/2011/may/31/egypt-online-protest-virginity-tests [accessed 4 May 2012]).

17. For example, Aljazeera.net, "Rape of Women in DR Congo 'tops 1000 a day'" 12 May 2011 (http://english.aljazeera.net/news/africa/2011/05/2011511231649539962.html [accessed 4 May 2012]); Thomas Hubert, "DR Congo Army Commander 'Led Mass Rape' in Fizi," BBC News 19 January 2011 (http://www.bbc.co.uk/news/world-africa-12205969 [accessed 4 May 2012]); Jeffrey Gettleman, "Rape Epidemic Raises Trauma of Congo War," *New York Times* 7 October 2007 (http://www.nytimes.com/2007/10/07/world/africa/07congo.html [accessed 4 May 2012]).

18. For example, Karen Leigh, "Rape in Libya: The Crime that Dare Not Speak its Name," *Time* 9 June 2011 (http://www.time.com/time/world/article/0,8599,2076775,00.html [accessed 4 May 2012]); Stephanie Nebehay, "Rape Used as a Weapon of War in Libya and Elsewhere," *Reuters* 10 June 2011 (http://www.reuters.com/article/2011/06/10/us-un-rape-idUSTRE75945020110610 [accessed 4 May 2012]); BBC News, "Rape Is Used as a Weapon of War," evening broadcast, 8 June 2011 (http://www.bbc.co.uk/news/world-africa-13707445 [accessed 4 May 2012]).

19. For example, IRIN News, "Cote d'Ivoire: Rape a Daily Menace for Rural Women," 30 March 2009 (http://www.irinnews.org/report.aspx?ReportId=83707 [accessed 4 May 2012]); Human Rights Watch, "Cote d'Ivoire: Ouattara Forces Kill, Rape Civilians

During Offensive," 9 April 2011 (http://www.hrw.org/en/news/2011/04/09/c-te-d-ivo-ire-ouattara-forces-kill-rape-civilians-during-offensive [accessed 4 May 2012]); Selah Hennessy, "UN Reports on Murder and Rape in Ivory Coast," Voice of America News 10 June 2011(http://www.voanews.com/english/news/UN-Human-Rights-Violations-Were-Committed-In-Ivory-Coast-Conflict-123622149.html [accessed 4 May 2012]).

20. For example, Krystyna Kurczab-Redlich, "Torture and Rape Stalk the Streets of Chechnya," *The Observer* 27 October 2002 (http://www.guardian.co.uk/world/2002/oct/27/chechnya.russia2 [accessed 4 May 2012]); W. Andy Knight and Tanya Naro-zhna, "Rape and Other War Crimes in Chechnya: Is There a Role for the International Criminal Court?" *Spaces of Identity* (2005), 5(1): 89–100; Patrick Cockburn, "Russia's Filtration Camp Policy Is 'to Cripple Chechens for Life'," *The Independent* 17 February 2000 (http://www.independent.co.uk/news/world/europe/russias-filtration-camp-policy—-is-to-cripple-chechens-for-life-724924.html [accessed 4 May 2012]).

21. For example, Mian Ridge, "Kashmir: Rape and Murder Cases Touch off Anti-India Anger," *Christian Science Monitor* 24 June 2009 (http://www.csmonitor.com/World/Asia-Pacific/2009/0624/p06s14-woahtml [accessed 4 May 2012]); Zachary R. Dowdy, "Groups Say India Forces Use Rape in War," *Boston Globe* 9 May 1993 (http://pqasb.pqarchiver.com/boston/access/61773926.html?FMT=ABS&FMTS=ABS:FT&type=current&date=May+09%2C+1993&author=Zachary+R.+Dowdy%2C+Contributing+Reporter&pub=Boston+Globe+(pre1997+Fulltext)&desc=Groups+say+India+forces+use+rape+in+war&pqatl=google [accessed 4 May 2012]; *Los Angeles Times*, "Kashmiris Growing Weary of Brutal War Against India," 12 June 1999 (http://nl.newsbank.com/nlsearch/we/Archives?p_product=DM&p_theme=dm&p_action=search&p_maxdocs=200&p_topdoc=1&p_text_direct-0=0ED3DB9A13EA55FF&p_field_direct-0=document_id&p_perpage=10&p_sort=YMD_date:D&s_trackval=GooglePM [accessed 4 May 2012]).

22. See, e.g., Catherine MacKinnon, "Rape, Genocide, and Women's Human Rights"; Lisa Sharlach, "Rape as Genocide: Bangladesh, the Former Yugoslavia, and Rwanda," *New Political Science* (2000), 22(1): 89–102; Lene Hansen, "Gender, Nation, Rape: Bosnia and the Construction of Security," *International Feminist Journal of Politics* (2001), 3(1): 55–75.

23. Mary Kaldor, *New and Old Wars: Organized Violence in a Global Era* (Palo Alto, CA: Stanford University Press, 1999); Edward Newman, "The 'New Wars' Debate: A Historical Perspective Is Needed," *Security Dialogue* (2004), 35(2): 173–189; Dietrich Jung, ed., *Shadow Globalization, Ethnic Conflicts, and New Wars* (New York: Psychology Press, 2003).

24. A discussion of the advantages and disadvantages of the legal recognition of rape as a weapon of war from a feminist perspective can be found in Doris E. Buss, "Rethinking 'Rape as a Weapon of War'," *Feminist Legal Studies* (2009), 17(2): 145–163.

25. Christoph Schlessi, "An Element of Genocide: Rape, Total War, and International Law in the Twentieth Century," *Journal of Genocide Research* (2002), 4(2): 197–210.

26. Claudia Card, "Genocide and Social Death," *Hypatia* (2003), 18(1): 63–79.

27. Sherrie L. Russell-Brown, "Rape as an Act of Genocide," *Berkeley Journal of International Law* (2003) 21: 350–374. See discussion in Kelly Askin, "Prosecuting Wartime Rape and Other Gender-Related Crimes Under International Law: Extraordinary Advances, Enduring Obstacles," *Berkeley Journal of International Law* (2003), 21: 288–349. See also Catherine MacKinnon, *Sex Equality* (New York: Foundation, 2001), 897, who suggests that courts have also recently begun to recognize that *rape* and *genocidal rape* are different war crimes, wherein rape is a crime against its victim and women generally, and genocidal rape is such a crime used as a weapon against an ethnic or national group, attacking racial purity, national pride, or both (*Kadic v. Karadzic*, 70 F.3d 232 [2nd Cir 1995]; *Prosecutor v. Akayesu*, Case No. ICTR 96 4 T [1998], 694).

28. For example, Margareth Etienne, "Addressing Gender-Based Violence in an International Context," *Harvard Women's Law Journal* (1995), 18: 139–170; Carol Harrington, "Embodiment, Authority, and the International Criminalization of Sexual Violence Against Women," *Wagude* (2012), 10: 32–54. For discussion of advocacy, see, e.g., discussion in Charlotte Bunch, "Women's Rights as Human Rights: Toward a Re-Vision of Human Rights," *Human Rights Quarterly* (1990), 12(4): 486–498; Sally Engle Merry, *Human Rights and Gender Violence: Translating International Law into Local Justice* (Chicago: University of Chicago Press, 2006); Jutta Joachim, "Shaping the Human Rights Agenda: The Case of Violence Against Women," in *Gender Politics in Global Governance*, ed. Mary Meyer and Elisabeth Prugl (New York: Rowman and Littlefield, 1999), 142–160.

29. Francis Pilch, "Rape as Genocide: The Legal Response to Sexual Violence," Working Paper, Center for Global Security and Democracy, Rutgers University (2002, www.ciaonet.org/wps/pif01/pif01.pdf, accessed December 15, 2012), 4.

30. See discussion in Christine Chinkin, "Rape and Sexual Abuse of Women in International Law," *European Journal of International Law* (1996), 5: 326–341.

31. For example, United Nations Security Council Resolution 1325 (S/Res/2001/1325); United Nations Security Council Resolution 1820 (S/Res/2008/1820); United Nations Security Council Resolution 1888 (S/Res/2009/1888); United Nations Security Council Resolution 1889 (S/Res/2009/1889); United Nations Security Council Resolution 1960 (S/Res/2010/1960).

32. As discussed in the preface of Cynthia Enloe, *Nimo's War, Emma's War: Making Feminist Sense of the Iraq War* (Berkeley: University of California Press, 2010).

33. See discussion later in this chapter.

34. Lauren Wilcox, "Gendering the Cult of the Offensive," *Security Studies* (2009), 18(2): 214–240, 233.

35. See discussion of intentional civilian victimization in chapter 7 for the logic of this argument.

36. Cindy S. Snyder, Wesley J. Gabbard, J. Dean May, and Nihada Zulcic, "On the Battleground of Women's Bodies: Mass Rape in Bosnia-Herzegovina," *Affilia* (2006), 21(2): 184–195.

37. Ibid.

38. Maja Korac, "Understanding Ethnic-National Identity and Its Meaning: Questions from Women's Experience," *Women's Studies International Forum* (1996), 19(1–2): 133–143.

39. Ibid; Jan Jindy Pettman, *Worlding Women: A Feminist International Politics* (New York: Psychology Press, 1996), 191.

40. Inger Skjelsbaek, "Sexual Violence and War: Mapping out a Complex Relationship," *European Journal of International Relations* (2001), 7(2): 211–237, 225.

41. Jeanne Vickers, *Women and War* (London: Zed, 1993).

42. Pettman, *Worlding Women*, 190.

43. V. Spike Peterson, "Sexing Political Identities/Nationalism as Heterosexism," *International Feminist Journal of Politics* (1999), 1(1): 34–65, 34.

44. Siobhan Fisher, "Occupation of the Womb: Forced Impregnation as Genocide," *Duke Law Journal* (1996), 46(1): 91–133.

45. Kelly Askin, "The Quest for Post-Conflict Gender Justice," *Columbia Journal of Transnational Law* 41: 509–521 (2003).

46. See discussions of the role of gendered narratives in nationalism in chapter 5.

47. See Judith Gardam, "Gender and Non-Combatant Immunity," *Transnational Law and Contemporary Problems* (1993), 3: 345–370, 358–359; Claudia Card, "Rape as A Weapon of War," *Hypatia* (1996), 11(4): 5–17. See also discussion in Marianne H. Marchand and Anne Sisson Runyan, eds., *Gender and Global Restructuring: Sightings, Sites, and Resistances* (London: Taylor and Francis, 2011).

48. Gardam, "Gender and Non-Combatant Immunity."

49. Hansen, "Gender, Nation, Rape," 59.

50. Gardam, "Gender and Non-Combatant Immunity," 363–364.

51. See discussion in Laura Sjoberg and Jessica Peet, "A(nother) Dark Side of the Protection Racket: Targeting Women in Wars," *International Feminist Journal of Politics* (2011), 13(2): 163–182.

52. For example, discussion in Nicola Henry, "The Impossibility of Bearing Witness; Wartime Rape and the Promise of Justice," *Violence Against Women* (2010), 16(10): 1098–1119.

53. Jacqueline E. Lawson, "'She's a Pretty Woman . . . for a Gook': The Misogyny of the Vietnam War," *Journal of American Culture* (1989), 12(3): 55–65, citing David Howard Bain, *Aftershocks: The Tale of Two Victims* (London: Methuen, 1980).

54. Ibid.

55. Ibid.

56. See, e.g., considerations in Sheldon G. Levy, "Some Thoughts on Basic Concepts and Future Directions in the Study of Inter-Group Conflict," *Conflict Management and Peace Science* (1993), 13(1): 1–27.

57. For an exception, see, e.g., Vanessa A. Farr, Wendy Cukier, Hon. Zoe Bakojo Bakoru, Jane Sanyu Mpagi, Amani El Jack, Ruth Ojambo Ochieng, Olvie C. Kubusingye, and Kiflemariam Gebre-Wold, "Gender Perspectives on Small Arms and Light Weapons," Brief 24, Bonn International Center for Conversion, 2002; http://www.bicc.de/publications/briefs/brief-24.html (accessed 4 May 2012).

58. Thomas Mahnken, "Strategic Theory," in *Strategy in a Contemporary World*, 2nd ed., ed. John Baylis, James J. Wirtz, Eliot A. Cohen, and Colin S. Gray (Oxford: Oxford University Press, 2010), 66–81.

59. Elliot Cohen, "Technology and Warfare," in Baylis et al., eds., *Strategy in a Contemporary World*, 141–160; C. Dale Walton and Colin S. Gray, "The Second Nuclear Age: Nuclear Weapons in the Twenty-First Century," in Baylis et al., eds., *Strategy in a Contemporary World*, 209–227.

60. Carol Cohn, "Slick'ems, Glick'ems, Christmas Trees, and Cookie Cutters: Nuclear Language and How We Learned to Pat the Bomb," *Bulletin of the Atomic Scientists* (June 1987), 43: 17–24, 16, 17.

61. Ibid., 19.

62. Ibid.

63. Ibid., 22.

64. Carol Cohn, "Sex and Death in the World of Rational Defense Intellectuals," *Signs: Journal of Women in Culture and Society* (1987), 12(3): 687–718, 711.

65. Ibid., 717.

66. For example, Wilcox, "Gendering the Cult of the Offensive."

67. For example, John Matsumura, Randall Steeb, Thomas Herbert, Mark Lees, and Scot Eisenhard, *Analytic Support to the Defense Sciences Board: Tactics and Technology for 21st Century Military Superiority* (Santa Monica, CA: Rand, 1997); http://www.dtic.mil/cgi-bin/GetTRDoc?Location=U2&doc=GetTRDoc.pdf&AD=ADA323925 (accessed 4 May 2012).

68. Wilcox, "Gendering the Cult of the Offensive."

69. See discussion of this relationship in Stuart W. Leslie, *The Cold War and American Science: The Military-Industrial-Academic Complex at MIT and Stanford* (New York: Columbia University Press, 1993).

70. Wilcox, "Gendering the Cult of the Offensive."

71. Ibid. See also Eric Blanchard, "The Technoscience Question in Feminist International Relations: Unmanning the U.S. War on Terror," in *Feminism and International Relations: Conversations about the Past, Present, and Future*, ed. J. Ann Tickner and Laura Sjoberg (London and New York: Routledge, 2011), 146–164.

72. See, e.g., Jonathan Karl, "Is the U.S. Preparing to Bomb Iran?", ABCNews 6 October 2009 (http://abcnews.go.com/Politics/us-preparing-bomb-iran/story?id=8765343 [accessed 4 May 2012]); Mladen Rudman, "Penetrator Bomb Slides Under Radar," *Free Republic* 6 May 2006 (http://www.freerepublic.com/focus/f-news/1627902/posts [accessed 4 May 2012]).

73. Anthony Cordesman, *Israeli and US Strikes on Iran: A Speculative Analysis* (Washington, DC: CSIS, 2007).

74. Cohn, "Slick'ems, Glick'ems, Christmas Trees, and Cookie Cutters."

75. Wilcox, "Gendering the Cult of the Offensive," citing Max Boot, *War Made New: Technology, Warfare, and the Course of History, 1500 to Today* (New York: Gotham, 2006), 22, 59, 88.

76. See discussion in Wilcox, "Gendering the Cult of the Offensive."

77. Peter W. Singer, *Wired for War: The Robotics Revolution and Conflict in the 21st Century* (New York: Penguin, 2009); Brian Glyn Williams, "The CIA's Covert Predator Drone War in Pakistan, 2004–2010: The History of an Assassination Campaign," *Studies in Conflict and Terrorism* (2010), 33(10): 871–892; Malcom Nance, "How (Not) to Spot a Terrorist," *Foreign Policy* (2008), 166: 74–76; Leon Panetta, "AFPAK Drone Strikes Are Only Game in Town," *New Perspectives Quarterly* (2009), 26(3): 33–39.

78. This is how Peter W. Singer opened his talk, "Wired for War" at the 2010 Annual Meeting of the International Studies Association, 24 September 2010, in West, Los Angeles, CA, where I was in attendance.

79. Jason Horowitz, "Loose Lips Sank Afghan War Chief," *Washington Post* 28 June 2010; www.post-gazette.com/pg/10179/1067868.85.stm (accessed 15 December 2012).

80. Thomas C. Wingfield, "Chivalry in the Use of Force," *University of Toledo Law Review* (2000), 32: 111–136.

81. Auguste Beernaert, quoted in James Brown Scott, *The Proceedings of the Hague Peace Conference* (New York: Oxford University Press, 1920), 288.

82. Wilcox, "Gendering the Cult of the Offensive."

83. See Linda Robertson, *The Dream of Civilized Warfare: World War I Flying Aces and the American Imagination* (Minneapolis, MN: University of Minnesota Press, 2003), 324–326.

84. Wingfield, "Chivalry in the Use of Force," 125.

85. Wilcox, "Gendering the Cult of the Offensive."

86. Wingfield, "Chivalry in the Use of Force," 136.

87. Cohn, "Sex and Death in the World of Rational Defense Intellectuals."

88. Ibid.

89. Ibid., 692.

90. Except biological weapons, which are often themselves alive. For a recent discussion, see Judith Miller, William J. Broad, and Stephen Engelberg, *Germs: Biological Weapons and America's Secret War* (New York: Simon & Schuster, 2010).

91. See critical discussion in Karen Engle, "Female Subjects of Public International Law: Human Rights and the Exotic Other Female," *New England Law Review* (1991–1992), 26: 1509–1527.

92. For a recent use of the association of femininity and nonviolence, see Swannee Hunt and Cristina Posa, *Foreign Policy* (May–June 2001), 124: 38–47.

93. Laura Sjoberg and Caron Gentry, *Mothers, Monsters, Whores: Women's Violence in Global Politics* (London: Zed, 2007), 2.

94. Ibid., 14.

95. Helena Kennedy, *Eve Was Framed: Women and British Justice* (Vintage: London, 1992), 240.

96. The use of the word *terror* or *terrorist* here or elsewhere in the book is not meant to endorse its deployment in either military/strategic policy-making or academic policy analysis. This is because "the discourse is first and foremost founded on the deployment of a series of core labels . . . . organized into a series of dramatic binaries, such as West versus Islamic world" that obscures the political complexity

necessarily surrounding terrorism' (Richard Jackson, "Constructing Enemies: 'Islamic Terrorism' in Political and Academic Discourse," *Government and Opposition* [2007], 42[3]: 394–426). This constructs "a paradigm of security in the name of a state of emergency" that becomes a self-engaging cycle (Diane Enns, "Bare Life and the Occupied Body," *Theory and Event* [2004], 7[3]: 2–15). Not only are fears that this creates a self-fulfilling prophecy of terrorism (e.g., Jackson, "Constructing Enemies") legitimate, it also justifies endless violence against perceived terrorists (e.g., Edward Said, "Punishment by Detail," *Counterpunch* 13 August 2002 (http://www.counterpunch.org/said0813.html [accessed 4 May 2012]). The application of a neo-Orientalist gaze (e.g., Dag Taustad, "Neo-Orientalism and the New Barbarism Thesis: Aspects of Symbolic Violence in Middle East Conflict(s)," *Third World Quarterly* [2003], 24[4]: 591–599) and the cementing of a good–evil dichotomy (e.g., Kevin Coe, David Domke, Erica Graham, Sue Lockett John, and Victor W. Pickard, "No Shades of Gray: The Binary Discourse of George W. Bush and an Echoing Press," *Journal of Communication* [2004], 54[4]: 234–52) produced by the continued deployment of the term *terrorist* is problematic enough, and feminists have consistently found gendered elements of these discourses as well (e.g., Laura Shepherd, "Veiled References: Constructions of Gender in the Bush Administration Discourse on the Attacks on Afghanistan Post-9/11," *International Feminist Journal of Politics* [2006], 8[1]: 19–41). Here, the term is used to signify relationship with relevant literature, but my own disagreement with the initial deployment of the term meant it was also necessary to include the critique of its popularity in the literature this section engages.

97. For example, Mia Bloom, *Bombshell: The Many Faces of Women Terrorists* (Toronto: Penguin, 2011); Maura Conway and Lisa McInerney, "What's Love Got to Do with It? Framing 'Jihad Jane' in the US Press," *Media, War, & Conflict* (2012), 5(1): 6–21; Jessica Auchter, "Gendering Terror: Discourses of Terrorism and Writing Woman-as-Agent," *International Feminist Journal of Politics* (2012), 14(1): 121–139; Sjoberg and Gentry, *Mothers, Monsters, Whores*; Laura Sjoberg and Caron Gentry, eds., *Women, Gender, and Terrorism* (Athens, GA: University of Georgia Press, 2011); Karla Cunningham, "Cross-Regional Trends in Female Terrorism," *Studies in Conflict & Terrorism* (2003), 26(3): 171–195. There is older work on women terrorists (e.g., Luisella de Cataldo Neuburger and Tiziana Valentini, *Women and Terrorism* [London: Palgrave MacMillan, 1996]; Robin Morgan, *Demon Lover: On the Roots of Terrorism* [New York: Norton, 1989]), but it received little attention before the recent trend of work in this area began.

98. See discussion in Caron Gentry and Laura Sjoberg, "Gendering Women's Terrorism," in Sjoberg and Gentry, eds., *Women, Gender, and Terrorism*, 57–81, for details and citations for each case.

99. For an in-depth discussion, see Gentry and Sjoberg, "Gendering Women's Terrorism."

100. Theodore Feldman and Phillip Johnson (in "Aircraft Hijacking in the United States," in *Lethal Violence: A Sourcebook on Fatal Domestic, Acquaintance, and Stranger Violence*, ed. Harold V. Hall [New York: CRC, 1999], 403–440) estimate that 8.6 percent of hijackers who have committed crimes in the United States were female. While

I could find no such data elsewhere, Caron Gentry interviewed Leila Khaled (published in "The Committed Revolutionary: Reflections on a Conversation with Leila Khaled," in Sjoberg and Gentry, *Women, Gender, and Terrorism,* 120–130), who had been involved in hijackings for the People's Liberation Front of Palestine.

101. See discussion in Sjoberg and Gentry, *Women, Gender, and Terrorism.* Rajiv Gandhi is also a case study in Robert Pape, *Dying to Win: The Strategic Logic of Suicide Terrorism* (New York: Random House, 2005). For more detail on what happened, see D. R. Kaarthikenyan and Radhavinod Raju, *The Rajiv Gandhi Assassination: The Investigation* (New Delhi: Sterling, 2008).

102. See discussion in Gentry and Sjoberg, "Gendering Women's Terrorism," of organizations like the Shining Path (Peru), the FARC (Colombia), and the Liberation Tamil Tigers of Elam (LTTE, Sri Lanka).

103. Sjoberg and Gentry, *Mothers, Monsters, Whores;* Linda Ahall, "Motherhood, Myth, and Gendered Agency in Political Violence," *International Feminist Journal of Politics* (2012), 14(1): 103–120; Auchter, "Gendering Terror."

104. Laura Sjoberg, Grace D. Cooke, and Stacy Reiter Neal, "Introduction," in Sjoberg and Gentry, eds., *Women, Gender, and Terrorism,* 1–25, 5.

105. Sjoberg and Gentry, *Mothers, Monsters, Whores,* chapters 6 and 7.

106. For example, Libby Copeland, "Female Suicide Bombers: The New Factor in the Mideast's Deadly Equation," *Washington Post* 27 April 2002; http://www.discharges.org/s/Female%20Suicide%20Bombers_%20The%20New%20Factor%20in%20Mideast's%20Deadly%20Equation.pdf (accessed 4 May 2012).

107. See discussion of this opinion in Paige Whaley Eager, *From Freedom Fighters to Terrorists: Women and Political Violence* (Aldershot, UK: Ashgate, 2008).

108. I have discussed this at some length in Laura Sjoberg, "Women Fighters and the 'Beautiful Soul' Narrative," *International Review of the Red Cross* (2010), 877: 53–68. See broad overview in Teena Apeles, *Women Warriors: Adventures from History's Greatest Female Fighters* (London: Seal, 2003), and cites below for specific cases.

109. See, among others: Carol L. Myers, *Discovering Eve: Ancient Israelite Women in Context* (New York: Oxford University Press, 1991); Sue Blundell, *Women in Ancient Greece* (Cambridge: Harvard University Press, 1995); Gay Robins, *Women in Ancient Egypt* (Cambridge: Harvard University Press, 1993); R. A. Bauman, *Women and the Politics of Ancient Rome* (New York: Psychology Press, 1992); Xiaolin Li, "Chinese Women Soldiers: A History of 5,000 Years," *Social Education* (1994), 58(2): 67–71; Linda Grant De Pauw, *Battle Cries and Lullabies: Women in War from Prehistory to Present* (Norman, OK: University of Oklahoma Press, 2000).

110. See description in Rosalind Miles, *The Women's History of the World,* repr. ed. (London: Paladin, 1990), 94.

111. See, e.g., Patrick Howarth, *Attila, King of the Huns: Man and Myth* (New York: Barnes and Noble, 1994).

112. Hugh N. Kennedy, *The Early Abbasid Caliphate: A Political History* (London: Croom Helm, 1981), 188; Huseyin Abiva and Noura Durkee, *History of Muslim Civilization,* vol. 1 (New York: IQRA International Education Foundation, 2003).

113. Pandurang Bhimarao Desai, *Jainism in South India and some Jaina Epigraphs* (Delhi: Gulabchand Hirachand Doshi [for] Jaina Sarnskrti Samrakshaka Sangha, 1957); *Proceedings of the Indian History Congress*, vol. 64 (n.p., 2004).

114. See, e.g., Judith Jesch, *Women in the Viking Age* (London: Boydell and Brewer, 1991).

115. See Reina Pennington and Robin D. S. Higham, *Amazons to Fighter Pilots: A Biographical Dictionary of Military Women*, vol. 1 (New York: Greenwood, 2003); Susan M. Johns, *Noblewomen, Aristocracy, and Power in the Twelfth-Century Anglo-Norman Realm* (Manchester, UK: Manchester University Press, 2003), 14.

116. Clara Wing-chung Ho, *Windows on the Chinese World: Reflections by Five Historians* (New York: Lexington, 2009); Lingzhen Wang, *Personal Matters: Women's Autobiographical Practices in Twentieth-Century China* (Palo Alto, CA: Stanford University Press, 2004).

117. The American Revolution (Elizabeth Ellet, *The Women of the American Revolution*, vol. 3 [New York: Abe, 1856]), the American Civil War (DeAnne Blanton and Lauren Cook, *They Fought like Demons: Women Soldiers in the America Civil War* [Baton Rouge, LA: Louisiana State University Press, 2002]), the Mexican Revolution (Tabea Alexa Linhard Linhard, *Fearless Women in the Mexican Revolution and the Spanish Civil War* [St. Louis, MO: University of Missouri Press, 2005]), World War I (Kimberly Jensen, *Mobilizing Minerva: American Women in the First World War* [Urbana, IL: University of Illinois Press, 2008]), the Russian Civil War (Bruce Lincoln, *Red Victory: A History of the Russian Civil War, 1918–1921* [New York: De Capo, 1999]), the Spanish Civil War (Linhard, *Fearless Women in the Mexican Revolution and the Spanish Civil War*), World War II (Emily Yellin, *Our Mother's War: American Women at Home and at the Front During WWII* [New York: Free Press, 2004]), the Korean War (Lester Brune and Robin Higham, *The Korean War: Handbook of the Literature and Research* [Westport, CT: Greenwood, 1996]), the Vietnam War (Judith Stiehm, *Arms and the Enlisted Woman* [Philadelphia, PA: Temple University Press, 1989]), the Afghan Civil War (Elaheh Rostami-Povey, *Afghan Women: Identity and Invasion* [London: Zed, 2007]), the Iran–Iraq War (Valentine Moghadam, *Modernizing Women: Gender and Social Change in the Middle East* [Boulder: Lynne Rienner, 2003]), the Rwandan genocide (Sjoberg and Gentry, *Mothers, Monsters, Whores*; Sara E. Brown, "Female Perpetrators of the Rwandan Genocide," *International Feminist Journal of Politics* (2013), forthcoming, http://dx.doi.org/10.108 0/14616742.2013.788806), the civil war in Sierra Leone (Megan MacKenzie, "Securitization and Desecuritization: Female Soldiers and the Reconstruction of Women in Post-Conflict Sierra Leone," *Security Studies* [2009], 18[2]: 241–261), and many others.

118. Sjoberg and Gentry, *Mothers, Monsters, Whores*; Laura Sjoberg and Caron Gentry, "Profiling Terror: Gendering *The Strategic Logic of Suicide Terror* and Other Narratives," *Austrian Journal of Political Science* (2008), 2: 181–196.

119. Cynthia Cockburn, *In the Way of Women: Men's Resistance to Sex Equality in Organizations* (London: Zed, 1991); Cynthia Cockburn and Dubravka Zarkov, eds., *The Post-War Moment: Militaries, Masculinities, and International Peacekeeping* (London: Zed, 2002).

120. See Judith Stiehm, *Its Our Military Too! Women and the United States Military* (Philadelphia, PA: Temple University Press, 1996); Francine D'Amico and Laurie Weinstein, eds., *Gender Camouflage: Women and the U.S. Military* (New York: New York University Press, 1999).

121. "Gender mainstreaming" in these terms means considering the gender implications of each policy decision when the decision is made. For a discussion of gender mainstreaming in the policy world, see, e.g., Jacqui True and Michael Mintrom, "Transnational Networks and Policy Diffusion: The Case of Gender Mainstreaming," *International Studies Quarterly* (2001), 45(1): 27–57.

122. See, e.g., Judith Wagner Decew, "The Combat Exclusion and the Role of Women in the Military," in *The Employment Context*, ed. Karen J. Maschke (London: Taylor and Francis, 1997), 298–326.

123. For example, Barbara Palmer and Dennis Michael Simon, *Breaking the Political Glass Ceiling* (New York: Psychology Press, 2008).

124. Laura Sjoberg, "Agency, Militarized Femininity and Enemy Others: Observations from the War in Iraq," *International Feminist Journal of Politics* (2007), 9(1): 82–101.

125. Ibid. See also Cynthia Enloe, *Maneuvers: The International Politics of Militarizing Women's Lives* (Berkeley: University of California Press, 2000), 184.

126. Staff Sgt. Jason Epperson, "Female Soldiers Help Bridge Afghanistan Culture Gap," www.army.mil, 7 February 2012; www.army.mil/article./73301/female_soldiers_help_bridge_afghanistan_culture_gap/ (accessed 10 March 2012).

127. Ibid.

128. Sergeant Christopher McCullough, "Female Engagement Teams: Who They Are and Why They Do It," www.army.mil, (accessed 2 October 2012) http://www.army.mil/article/88366/, (accessed 15 December 2012).

129. For example, Jean Elshtain, *Just War Against Terror: The Burden of American Power in a Violent World* (New York: Basic, 2003); also, cf. discussion on this in Kelly Oliver's book *Women as Weapons of War: Iraq, Sex, and the Media* (New York: Columbia University Press, 2007).

130. Sjoberg and Gentry, *Mothers, Monsters, Whores*.

131. Kelly Oliver, "Interview with Kelly Oliver, Author of *Women as Weapons of War*," Columbia University Press website; http://cup.columbia.edu/static/kelly-oliver-interview (accessed 4 May 2012).

132. Jayne Lyn Stahl, "Women as Weapons of War," *Alternet* 6 March 2008; http://www.alternet.org/reproductivejustice/78776/ (accessed 4 May 2012).

133. Ibid.

134. See Oliver, *Women as Weapons of War*; see also Oliver, "Interview with Kelly Oliver."

135. Carol D. Leonnig and Dana Priest, "Detainees Accuse Female Interrogators: Pentagon Inquiry Is Said to Confirm Muslims' Accounts of Sexual Tactics at Guantanamo," *Washington Post* 10 February 2005; http://www.washingtonpost.com/wp-dyn/articles/A12431–2005Feb9.html (accessed 15 September 2012).

136. Oliver, as quoted in Stahl, "Women as Weapons of War."

137. See Jennie Stone and Katherine Pattillo, "Al-Qaeda's Use of Female Suicide Bombers in Iraq: A Case Study," in Sjoberg and Gentry, eds., *Women, Gender, and Terrorism*, 159–175.

138. See Katherine E. Brown, "Blinded by the Explosion? Security and Resistance in Muslim Women's Suicide Terrorism," in Sjoberg and Gentry, eds., *Women, Gender, and Terrorism*, 194–226; Farhana Qazi, "The *Mujahidaat*: Tracing the Early Female Warriors of Islam," in Sjoberg and Gentry, eds., *Women, Gender, and Terrorism*, 29–56.

139. See, e.g., Walter Laqueur, *Guerilla Warfare: A Historical and Critical Study* (London: Transaction, 1976).

140. See Gentry, "The Committed Revolutionary."

141. Marina Warner, *Joan of Arc: The Image of Female Heroism* (Berkeley: University of California Press, 1999)

142. Oliver, *Women as Weapons of War*.

143. Elshtain, *Just War Against Terror*.

144. Sjoberg and Gentry, *Mothers, Monsters, Whores*; Sjoberg, "Women Fighters and the 'Beautiful Soul' Narrative."

145. Discussing Jessica Lynch and militarized femininity, see e.g., John W. Howard III and Laura Prividera, "Rescuing Patriarchy or Saving 'Jessica Lynch': The Rhetorical Construction of the American Woman Soldier," *Women and Language* (2004), 27(2): 89–97; Veronique Pin-Fat and Maria Stern, "The Scripting of Jessica Lynch: Biopolitics, Gender, and the 'Feminization' of the U.S. Military," *Alternatives: Global, Local, Political* (2005), : 25–53; Jennifer Lobasz, "The Woman in Peril and the Ruined Woman: Representations of Female Soldiers in the Iraq War," *Journal of Women, Politics, and Policy* (2008), 29(3): 305–334; Sjoberg, "Agency, Militarized Femininity, and Enemy Others." While fewer discussions of the phenomenon of female engagement teams (FETs) have been published (yet), an analysis analogous to the ones above can be found in Sahana Dharmapuri, "Just Add Women and Stir?", *Parameters: Journal of the United States Army War College* (Spring 2011), 41(4): 54–70.

146. Sjoberg and Gentry, *Mothers, Monsters, Whores*.

147. See chapter 5, note 110.

148. R. W. Connell, *Masculinities: Knowledge, Power, and Social Change* (Berkeley: University of California Press, 1995).

149. Tim Kaufman-Osborn, "Gender Relations in an Age of Neoliberal Empire: Interrogating Gender Equality Models." Paper presented at the 2005 Annual Meeting of the Western Political Science Association, 5 March 2005, in Oakland, California, 5; cited in Mary Hawkesworth, "Feminists v. Feminization: Confronting the War Logics of the Bush Administration, *Comunicacion e Cidandania* (2006), 1(2): 117–142.

150. Hawkesworth, "Feminists v. Feminization," 132.

151. Ibid.

152. Laura Sjoberg, *Gender, Justice, and the Wars in Iraq* (New York: Lexington Books, 2006), citing Steve Niva, "Tough and Tender: New World Order Masculinity and the Gulf War," in *The Man Question in International Relations*, ed. Marysia Zalewski and Jane Parpart, (Boulder: Westview, 1998), 119.

153. Andy Sullivan, "FACTBOX-Previous US Comments about Kim Jong-Il," *Reuters U.S. Edition* 6 December 2007; www.reuters.com/article/2007/12/06/idusn06198902 (accessed 4 May 2012).

154. Hamish MacDonald, "Bush Gets a Spray from Pyongyang," *Sydney Morning Herald* 2 May 2005; http://www.smh.com.au/news/World/Bush-gets-a-spray-from-Pyongyang/2005/05/01/1114886252228.html (accessed 4 May 2012).

155. James Brooke, "North Korea, Eyeing Election, Issues a Stream of Insults at Bush," *New York Times* 24 August 2004; http://www.nytimes.com/2004/08/24/world/north-korea-eyeing-election-issues-stream-of-insults-at-bush.html (accessed 4 May 2012).

156. For example, V. Spike Peterson, "Gendered Identities, Ideologies, and Practices in the Context of War and Militarism," in *Gender, War, and Militarism*, ed. Sjoberg and Via, 17–30; Joshua Goldstein, *War and Gender* (Cambridge: Cambridge University Press, 2000); Veronique Pin-Fat and Maria Stern, "The Scripting of Private Jessica Lynch: Biopolitics, Gender, and the 'Feminization' of the U.S. Military," *Alternatives: Global, Local, Political* (2005), 30(1): 25–53; Michael Davidson, *Guys Like Us: Citing Masculinity in Cold War Politics* (Chicago: University of Chicago Press, 2003).

157. Brooke, "North Korea."

158. Sjoberg, "Agency, Militarized Femininity, and Enemy Others."

159. Ibid.; Lobasz, "The Woman in Peril and the Ruined Woman." For a broader discussion of this phenomenon, see V. Spike Peterson, "Gendered Identities, Ideologies, and Practices in the Context of War and Militarism," in Sjoberg and Via, *Gender, War, and Militarism*, 17–29.

160. Hilary Charlesworth, "Feminist Methods in International Law," *American Journal of International Law* (1999), 93(2): 379–394, lays out the method of searching for silences through gender lenses, which is discussed in detail in Brooke Ackerly, Maria Stern, and Jacqui True, *Feminist Methods in International Relations* (Cambridge: Cambridge University Press, 2006).

161. See discussion in Mary Ann Tetreault, "The Sexual Politics of Abu Ghraib: Hegemony, Spectacle, and the Global War on Terror," *NWSA Journal* (2006), 18(3): 33–50.

162. Elisabeth Prugl, "Gender and War: Causes, Constructions, and Critiques," *Perspectives on Politics* (2003), 1(2): 335–342.

163. Jack Cheng and Marian Feldman, *Ancient Near Eastern Art in Context* (New York: Brill, 2007), 384.

164. Sidney Donnell, *Feminizing the Enemy: Imperial Spain, Transvestite Drama, and the Crisis of Masculinity* (Lewisburg, PA: Bucknell University Press, 2003).

165. Nalia Ceribasic, "Gender Roles During the War: Representations in Croatian and Serbian Popular Music, 1991–1992," *Collegium Anthropologicum* (1995), 19: 91–101.

166. Goldstein, *War and Gender*, 356.

167. Ibid., 356.

168. Zillah Eisenstein, *Against Empire* (London: Zed, 2004).

169. Nancy Ehrenreich, "Disguising Empire: Racialized Masculinity and the 'Civilizing' of Iraq," *Cleveland State Law Review* (2004–2005), 52: 131–138, 138.

170. This is actually taken from a history in the form of game advice for those who would like to "play" the Hundred Years' War (http://www.hyw.com/books/history/Logistic.htm [accessed 4 May 2012]). For a detailed history of (the gendered paths of) logistics, see John Albert Lynn, *Feeding Mars: Logistics in Western Warfare from the Middle Ages to the Present* (Boulder: Westview, 1993).

171. See discussion in John F. Haldon, ed., *General Issues in the Study of Medieval Logistics* (Amsterdam: Brill, 2005).

172. For example, discussions in Susan Edgington and Sarah Lambert, *Gendering the Crusades* (New York: Columbia University Press, 2001); Jonathan Riley, "Logistics and Supply in Renaissance Armies," *Arms & Armour* (2011), 8(2): 139–151; Donald W. Engles, *Alexander the Great and the Logistics of the Macedonian Army* (Berkeley: University of California Press, 1978).

173. This is documented as late as World War I. See discussion in Tammy M. Proctor, *Civilians at War, 1914–1918* (New York: New York University Press, 2010).

174. Goldstein, *War and Gender*.

175. Enloe, *Nimo's War, Emma's War*.

176. See discussion of this phenomena in New Zealand in World War II in Deborah Montgomerie, *The Women's War: New Zealand Women 1939–45* (Auckland: Auckland University Press, 2001). A similar discussion about the United States in World War I can be found in Maurine Weiner Greenwald, *Women, War, and Work: The Impact of World War I on Women Workers in the United States* (Ithaca, NY: Cornell University Press, 1990). These discussions theorize a phenomenon identified in popular images like the United States' Rosie the Riveter (packaged for a young audience in Penny Colman, *Rosie the Riveter: Women Working on the Home Front in World War II* [New York: Paw Prints, 2008]) and problematized in Sherna Berger Gluck, *Rosie the Riveter Revisited: Women, War, and Social Change* (New York: Penguin, 1988).

177. Meghan K. Winchell, "'To Make the Boys Feel at Home': USO Senior Hostesses and Gendered Citizenship," *Frontiers: A Journal of Women's Studies* (2004), 25(1): 190–211; Laurie L. Weinstein, *Gender Camouflage: Women and the U.S. Military* (New York: New York University Press, 1999).

178. See, e.g., a critical discussion in Drew Gilpin Faust, "Altars of Sacrifice: Confederate Women and the Narratives of War," *Journal of American History* (1990), 76(4): 1200–1228.

179. See general discussion in Mady Wechsler Segal, "Women's Military Roles Cross-Nationally," *Gender and Society* (1995), 9(6): 757–775.

180. See explicit discussion of "sexual service" in Francine D'Amico, "Feminist Perspectives on Women Warriors," *Peace Review: A Journal of Social Justice* (1996), 8(3): 379–384.

181. See discussion in Enloe, *Nimo's War, Emma's War*.

182. See Ellen Messer, "Conflict as a Cause of Hunger," in *Who's Hungry? And How Do We Know? Food Shortage, Poverty, and Deprivation*, ed. Laurie Fields DeRose, Ellen Messer, and Sara Millman (New York: United Nations University Press, 1998), 164–180.

183. For a general discussion of base economies, see Mark A. Hooker and Michael M. Knetter, "Measuring the Economic Effects of Military Base Closures," *Economic Inquiry* (2001), 39(4): 583–598.

184. V. Spike Peterson and Anne Runyan, *Global Gender Issues in a New Millennium,* 3rd ed. (Boulder: Westview, 2010), 168.

185. See broad discussion in Sheila Jeffreys, "Globalizing Sexual Exploitation: Sex Tourism and the Traffick in Women," *Leisure Studies* (1999), 18(3): 179–196.

186. Prostitution (Katherine Moon, *Sex Among Allies: Military Prostitution in U.S.-Korea Relations* [New York, Columbia University Press, 1997]; bush "wifehood" (Chris Coulter, *Bush Wives and Girl Soldiers: Women's Lives through War and Peace in Sierra Leone* [Ithaca, NY: Cornell University Press, 2009]); forced sex (Card, "Rape as a Weapon of War"); unwanted children born out of wartime sexual abuse (R. Charli Carpenter, *Forgetting Children Born of War: Setting the Human Rights Agenda* [New York: Columbia University Press, 2010]; R. Charli Carpenter, ed. *Born of War: Protecting Children of Sexual Violence Survivors in Conflict Zones* [Seattle, WA: Kumarian, 2007]); breakouts of sexually transmitted diseases (discussed in Stefan Elbe, "HIV/AIDS and the Changing Landscape of War in Africa," *International Security* [2002], 27[2]: 159–177); and trafficking and migration crises (Jennifer Lobasz, "Beyond Border Security: Feminist Approaches to Human Trafficking," *Security Studies* [2009], 18[2]: 319–344).

187. Cynthia Enloe, *Does Khaki Become You? The Militarisation of Women's Lives* (Boston: South End Press, 1983).

188. Moon, *Sex Among Allies.*

189. Chris Coulter, *Bush Wives and Girl Soldiers: Women's Lives through War and Peace in Sierra Leone* (Ithaca, NY: Cornell University Press, 2009); Megan H. MacKenzie, *Female Soldiers in Sierra Leone: Sex, Security, and Post-Conflict Development* (New York: New York University Press, 2012).

9. LIVING GENDERED WAR(S)

1. Sarah Brown, "Feminism, International Theory, and the International Relations of Gender Inequality," *Millennium: Journal of International Studies* (1988), 17(3): 461–475.

2. Hedy Epstein, "About Hedy" (http://www.hedyepstein.com/abouthedy/ [accessed 4 May 2012]); Daniel Siegal, "Israel, Gaza: Holocaust Survival Explains Why She Became Palestinian Rights Activist," *Los Angeles Times* 6 January 2010 (http://latimesblogs. latimes.com/babylonbeyond/2010/01/israel-gaza-holocaust-survivor-hedy-epstein-explains-why-she-became-palestinian-rights-activist.html [accessed 4 May 2012]).

3. Deborah Haynes, "'Female Suicide Bomb Recruiter' Samira Ahmed Jassim Captured," *The Times Online* 3 February 2009; http://www.timesonline.co.uk/tol/news/world/iraq/article5653088.ece (accessed 4 May 2012).

4. Ibid.

5. Ibid. A reviewer for this project asked why this story was included if the reports of the most significant violence that Samira Ahmed Jassim was accused of committing were widely discredited. First, reports that Jassim ran a training camp for women terrorists have not been discredited, Second, the assumption that Jassim had to be monstrous in order to run such a training camp is an example of a widely held belief that while men's (criminal and terrorist) violence can be understood as normal, there needs to be something wrong with women for them to commit similar violence (see discussion in Laura Sjoberg and Caron Gentry, *Mothers, Monsters, Whores: Women's Violence in Global Politics* [London: Zed, 2007]).

6. *Suhal Najim Abdullah Al Shimari v. Timothy Dugan*, CACI International, CACI Premier Technology, and L-3 Services; http://ccrjustice.org/files/Al%20Shimari%20Complaint.pdf (accessed 4 May 2012).

7. Ibid.

8. James O'Donnell Bennett, "Kate Bartholomae Fitting Example of 'Sisters' who Mother Kaiser's Men," *Chicago Tribune* 13 November 1914; http://pqasb.pqarchiver.com/chicagotribune/access/383449321.html?dids=383449321: 383449321&FMT=AB S&FMTS=ABS:AI&type=historic&date=Nov+13%2C+1914&author=&pub=Chicago+Tribune&desc=WAR+NURSE+FOR+GERMAN+ARMY+TIRELESS+BEING&pqatl=google (accessed 4 May 2012).

9. Associated Press, "General Defends Tough Pregnancy Rules," 23 December 2009; http://www.adelaidenow.com.au/news/breaking-news/general-defends-tough-pregnancy-rules/story-e6frea73–1225812985697.

10. Joe Gould, "Commander Softens Punishment for Pregnancy," *Army Times* 3 January 2010; http://www.armytimes.com/news/2010/01/army_cucolo_010310w/ (accessed 4 May 2012).

11. "Pregnant Girls Can Be Dropped from Air Force," *Milwaukee Sentinel* 17 November 1971; http://news.google.com/newspapers?id=NSEsAAAAIBAJ&sjid=2p0FAAAAIBAJ&pg=4086,3086254&dq=a-compelling-public-interest-in-not-having+pregnant&hl=en (accessed 4 May 2012).

12. Elaine Engeler, "UN: Ugandan Rebel Attacks May Have Been War Crimes," Associated Press 21 December 2009; http://www.journal-news.com/news/nation-world-news/un-ugandan-rebel-attacks-may-have-been-war-crimes-457986.html (accessed 4 May 2012).

13. Sean Sutton, "Photo Gallery: Cambodian Women Clear Mines," *Reuters Alertnet.org* 19 December 2003. Archive has since been removed from its original URL, but is available at http://www.landmine.de/archiv/oeffentlichkeitsarbeit/news/news-detailseite/article/photo-gallery-cambodian-women-clear-mines.html (accessed 4 May 2012).

14. Ibid.

15. Sara Helman and Tamar Rapoport, "Women in Black: Challenging Israel's Gender and Socio-Political Orders," *British Journal of Sociology* (1997), 48(4): 681–700; Erella Shadmi, "Between Resistance and Compliance, Feminism and Nationalism: Women in Black in Israel," *Women's Studies International Forum* (2000), 23(1): 23–34.

16. Gertrude Bussey and Margaret Tims, *Women's International League for Peace and Freedom, 1915–1965: A Record of Fifty Years' Work* (New York: Allen and Unwin, 1965); Catia Confortini, *Intelligent Compassion: The Women's International League for Peace and Freedom and Feminist Peace* (Oxford: Oxford University Press, 2012).

17. Linda Milazzo, "Code Pink: The 21st Century Mothers of Invention," *Development* (2005), 48(1): 100–104; Kristin A. Goss and Michael T. Heaney, "Organizing Women *as Women:* Hybridity and Grassroots Collective Action in the 21st Century," *Perspectives on Politics* (2010), 8(1): 27–52.

18. Beth Junor and Katrina Howse, *Greenham Common Women's Peace Camp: A History of Non-Violent Resistance* (New York: Working Press, 1995); Barbara Harford and Sarah Hopkins, *Greenham Common: Women at the Wire* (London: Women's Press, 1984).

19. Penny Colman, *Rosie the Riveter: Women Working on the Home Front in World War II* (New York: Crown, 1998). See chapter 8, note 169 for further discussion.

20. Cynthia Enloe, *Nimo's War, Emma's War: Making Feminist Sense of the Iraq War* (Berkeley: University of California Press, 2010).

21. See chapter 8, note 177.

22. Clara Barton, *The Red Cross in Peace and War* (Washington, DC: Historical Press, 1898); Henriette Donner, "Under the Cross: Why V.A.D.s Performed the Filthiest Task in the Dirtiest War: Red Cross Women Volunteers, 1914–1918," *Journal of Social History* (1997), 30(3): 687–704.

23. See, e.g., Elisabeth Addis, Valeria Russo, and Loranza Sebesta, *Women Soldiers: Images and Realities* (New York: St. Martin's, 1994); Orna Sasson-Levy, "Feminism and Military Gender Practices: Israeli Women Soldiers in 'Masculine' Roles," *Sociological Inquiry* (2003), 73(3): 440–465.

24. See, e.g., Ilja Luciak, *After the Revolution* (Baltimore, MD: Johns Hopkins University Press, 2001).

25. See, e.g., Sjoberg and Gentry, *Mothers, Monsters, Whores*; Laura Sjoberg and Caron Gentry, eds., *Women, Gender, and Terrorism* (Athens, GA: University of Georgia Press, 2011).

26. Cristina Masters, "Femina Sacra: The 'War on/of Terror,' Women, and the Feminine," *Security Dialogue* (2009), 40(1): 29–49.

27. Ibid., citing Ronit Lentin, "*Femina Sacra:* Gendered Memory and Political Violence," *Women's Studies International Forum* (2006), (29)(4): 463–473, 465.

28. Chris Cuomo, "War Is Not Just an Event: Reflections on the Significance of Everyday Violence," *Hypatia* (1996), 11(4): 30–45.

29. Christine Sylvester, "Experiencing War: An Introduction," in *Experiencing War (War, Politics, and Experience)*, ed. Christine Sylvester (London: Routledge, 2011), 1.

30. Ibid., 1.

31. Ibid., 3.

32. Christine Sylvester, "War, Sense, and Security," in *Gender and International Security: Feminist Perspectives,* ed. Laura Sjoberg (London: Routledge, 2010), 24–37, 24.

33. Judith Butler, *Frames of War: When Is Life Grievable?* (London: Verso, 2009).

34. Many of wars' unseen impacts are not "important" enough to make appearances in war theorizing, but not only interrupt but structure people's daily lives. War

changes available jobs, commuting conditions, and living options, to name a few major needs of individual and family life/lives. Inspiration for thinking about these issues was drawn from Angela Raven Roberts, "Women and the Political Economy of War," in *Women and Wars*, ed. Carol Cohn (London: Polity, 2012), 36–54.

35. This is all the more true for families that operate in their daily lives on pooling resources among different families within a community, since one family breaking down has consequences for the other families that rely on them for resources.

36. Often, households that have temporary needs for support (due to illness or unemployment) rely on social networks around them in stable communities (neighborhoods, churches, etc.) to provide that support. In times of war, these networks often break down, given both that everyone has a time of need at the same time and that war displaces people and breaks up family structures.

37. See discussion in Peter H. Gleick, "Water and Conflict: Fresh Water Resources and International Security," *International Security* (1993), 18(1): 79–112.

38. See discussions in Hazem Adam Ghobarah, Paul Huth, and Bruce Russett, "The Post-War Public Health Effects of Civil Conflict," *Social Science and Medicine* (2004), 59(4): 869–884; Lawrence A. Palinkas, Sheila M. Pickwell, Kendra Brandstein, Terry J. Clark, Linda L. Hill, Robert J. Moser, and Abdikadir Osman, "The Journey to Wellness: Stages of Refugee Health Promotion and Disease Prevention," *Journal of Immigrant Health* (2003), 5(1): 19–28.

39. Michael J. Toole and Ronald J. Waldman, "Refugees and Displaced Persons: War, Hunger, and Public Health," *Journal of the American Medical Association* (1993), 270(5): 600–605.

40. Cynthia Enloe, *Maneuvers: The International Politics of Militarizing Women's Lives* (Berkeley: University of California Press, 2000).

41. Ronni Alexander, "Popoki's Peace Project: Creating New Spaces for Peace," *Journal of International Cooperation Studies* (2007), 14(3): 17–23.

42. See, e.g., Julie Cupples, "Counter-revolutionary Women: Gender and Reconciliation in Post-War Nicaragua," *Gender & Development* (2004), 12(3): 8–18.

43. For example, agricultural economies are organized on sexual divisions of labor—see Gary S. Becker, "Human Capital, Effort, and the Sexual Division of Labor," *Journal of Labor Economics* (1985), 3(1): S33-S58.

44. Ibid. See also Michael L. Burton and Douglas R. White, "Sexual Division of Labor in Agriculture," *American Anthropologist* (1984), 86(3): 568–583.

45. Cynthia Enloe, *Does Khaki Become You? The Militarization of Women's Lives* (Boston: South End Press, 1983).

46. David A. Hodge and Cynthia A. Lietz, "The International Sexual Trafficking of Women and Children: A Review of the Literature," *Affilia* (2007), 22(2): 163–174.

47. Stephen Castles, "Towards a Sociology of Forced Migration and Social Transformation," *Sociology* (2003), 37(1): 13–34.

48. Peter Andreas, "Symbiosis between Peace Operations and Illicit Business in Bosnia," *International Peacekeeping* (2009), 16(1): 33–46; William Reno, "Illicit Markets, Violence, Warlords, and Governance: West African Cases," *Crime, Law, and*

Social Change (2009), 52(3): 313–322; Michael Charles Pugh, Neil Cooper, and Jonathan Goodhand, *War Economies in a Regional Context: Challenges of Transformation* (Boulder: Lynne Rienner, 2004).

49. Vanda Felbab-Brown, "Peacekeepers Among Peoples: Afghanistan, Illicit Economies, and Intervention," *International Peacekeeping* (2009), 16(1): 100–114.

50. Heiko Nitzchke and Kaysie Studdard, "The Legacies of War Economies: Challenges and Options for Peacekeeping and Peacebuilding," *International Peacekeeping* (2005), 12(2): 222–239.

51. Anna Agathangelou and L. H. M. Ling, "Desire Industries: Sex Trafficking, UN Peacekeeping, and the Neo-Liberal World Order," *Brown Journal of World Affairs* (2003–2004), 10: 133–146.

52. Stefan Elbe, "HIV/AIDS and the Changing Landscape of War in Africa," *International Security* (2002), 27(2): 159–177; V. Spike Peterson, "'New Wars' and Gendered Economies," *Feminist Review* (2008), 88: 7–20.

53. Peterson, "'New Wars' and Gendered Economies."

54. Agathangelou and Ling, "Desire Industries"; Paul Higate, "Peacekeepers, Masculinities, and Sexual Exploitation," *Men and Masculinities* (2007), 10(1): 99–119; Keith J. Allred, "Peacekeepers and Prostitutes: How Deployed Forces Fuel the Demand for Trafficked Women and New Hope for Stopping It," *Armed Forces and Society* (2006), 33(1): 5–23.

55. For example, Sarah Elizabeth Mendelson, *Barracks and Brothels: Peacekeepers and Human Trafficking in the Balkans* (Washington, DC: Center for Strategic and International Studies, 2005); Kevin Bales, "What Predicts Human Trafficking?" *International Journal of Comparative and Applied Criminal Justice* (2007), 31(2): 269–279.

56. For example, discussion in Caroline Moser and Fiona Clark, *Victims, Perpetrators, or Actors? Gender, Armed Conflict, and Political Violence* (London: Palgrave MacMillan, 2001).

57. For example, J. K. Gibson-Graham, *The End of Capitalism (As We Knew It): A Feminist Critique of Political Economy*, 2nd ed. (Minneapolis: University of Minnesota Press, 2006); V. Spike Peterson, *A Critical Rewriting of Global Political Economy: Integrating Reproductive, Productive, and Virtual Economies* (New York: Psychology Press, 2003).

58. Mohammed Jamjoom, "War Forces Iraqi Mom into Prostitution," CNN News 14 November 2009; http://edition.cnn.com/2009/WORLD/meast/11/02/iraq.prostitute/ (accessed 4 May 2012).

59. Debra McNutt, "Military Prostitution and the Iraq Occupation: Privatizing Women," *Counterpunch* 11 July 2007; http://www.counterpunch.org/mcnutt07112007.html (accessed 4 May 2012).

60. Ibid.

61. Enloe, *Nimo's War, Emma's War.*

62. H. Patricia Hynes, "On the Battlefield of Women's Bodies: An Overview of the Harm of War to Women," *Women's Studies International Forum* (2004), 27(5–6): 431–455.

63. Ibid.

64. Paul W. Ewald, *Evolution of Infectious Disease* (New York: Oxford University Press, 1994).

65. Paul B. Spiegel, "HIV/AIDS Among Conflict-Affected Displaced Populations," *Disasters* (2004), 28(3): 322–339.

66. Roger Zetter and Camillo Boanom, "Gendering Space for Forcibly Displaced Women and Children: Concepts, Policies, and Guidelines," in *Women, Migration, and Conflict*, edited by S. F. Martin and J. Tirman (New York: Springer, 2009), 201–227.

67. Lynn L. Amowitz, Chen Reis, Kristina Hare Lyons, Beth Vann, Cinta Masaray, Adyinka M. Akisulure-Smith, Louise Taylor, and Vincent Iacopino, "Prevalence of War-Related Sexual Violence and Other Human Rights Abuses Among Internally Displaced Persons in Sierra Leone," *Journal of the American Medical Association* (2002), 287(4): 513–521.

68. See discussion in Joshua Goldstein, *War and Gender* (Cambridge: Cambridge University Press, 2001).

69. Michelle Hynes and Barbara Lopes Cardozo, *Journal of Women's Health and Gender-Based Medicine* (2000), 9(8): 819–823.

70. Enloe, *Nimo's War, Emma's War*.

71. Vigdis Broch-Due, *Violence and Belonging: The Quest for Identity in Post-Colonial Africa* (Abingdon, UK: Routledge, 2005), x, 261.

72. Nicola York, "Battling for Gender Equality in the Congo," *The Guardian* 29 June 2011; http://www.guardian.co.uk/journalismcompetition/battling-for-gender-equality-in-the-congo (accessed 4 May 2012).

73. Ibid.

74. Honorata Kizende, "Honorata's Story"; http://www.womenforwomen.org/global-initiatives-helping-women/stories-women-congo.ph (accessed 4 May 2012).

75. John Blake, "One Congolese Woman's 'Silent Scream' is Heard," CNN 7 March 2008; http://articles.cnn.com/2008-03-07/us/congo.woman_1_zainab-salbi-congolese-congo-war?_s=PM:US (accessed 4 May 2012).

76. Ibid.

77. Kizende, "Honorata's Story."

78. See, e.g., discussion in Kristen Boon, "Rape and Forced Pregnancy Under the ICC Statute: Human Dignity, Autonomy, and Consent," *Columbia Human Rights Review* (2000–2001), 32: 625–676.

79. Even in a world where it is possible to think about the "common" hardships of pregnancy born of rape.

80. Laura Sjoberg, *Gender, Justice and the Wars in Iraq* (New York: Lexington Books year), citing V. Spike Peterson, "Political Identities: Nationalism as Heterosexism," *International Feminist Journal of Politics* (1999), 1(1): 34–65, 44–52.

81. See, e.g., discussion in R. Charli Carpenter, *Forgetting Children Born of War: Setting the Human Rights Agenda* (New York: Columbia University Press, 2010); R. Charli Carpenter, ed. *Born of War: Protecting Children of Sexual Violence Survivors in Conflict Zones* (Seattle, WA: Kumarian, 2007).

82. This is a term largely used in the policy world. See, e.g., Geraldine Terry, *Gender-Based Violence* (New York: Oxfam, 2007).

83. Michele Ernsting, "Forced Marriage in Sierra Leone," Radio Netherlands Worldwide, 7 March 2008; http://www.essex.ac.uk/armedcon/story_id/000754.html (accessed 4 May 2012).

84. Ibid.

85. Ibid.

86. Ibid.

87. For the U.S. Civil War, see Jennifer Anne Hart, "Women of ILL Fame—Sex and Prostitution During the Civil War," Yahoo Associated Content 18 November 2006; http://www.associatedcontent.com/article/86310/women_of_ill_famesex_and_prostitution.html?cat=37 (accessed 4 May 2012). For Afghanistan, see Michael A. Bush, "Afghanistan and the Sex Trade," in *Sex Trafficking: A Global Perspective*, ed. Kimberly A. McCabe and Sabita Manian (New York: Lexington, 2010), 111–118. For Israel–Palestine, see discussion in Valentine M. Moghadam, "Peacebuilding and Reconstruction with Women: Reflections on Afghanistan, Iraq, and Palestine," *Development* (2005), 48(1): 63–72.

88. Like the Liberation Tamil Tigers of Elam (LTTE, Sri Lanka), the Shining Path (Peru), and the FARC (Colombia). For a discussion of the LTTE, see Miranda Alison, *Women and Political Violence: Female Combatants and Ethno-National Conflict* (London: Routledge, 2009); Miranda Alison, "'In the War Front We Never Think That We Are Women': Women, Gender, and the Liberation Tamil Tigers of Eelam," in Sjoberg and Gentry, eds., *Women, Gender, and Terrorism*, 131–155. For a discussion of the Shining Path and the FARC, see Caron Gentry and Laura Sjoberg, "Gendering Women's Terrorism," in the same volume, 57–80.

89. See, e.g., discussion in Melissa T. Brown, *Enlisting Masculinity: The Construction of Gender in US Military Recruiting Advertising During the All-Volunteer Force* (Oxford: Oxford University Press, 2012).

90. Marysia Zalewski and Jane Parpart, eds., *The "Man" Question in International Relations* (Boulder: Westview Press, 1998); Charlotte Hooper, "Masculinist Practices and Gender Politics," in Zalewski and Parpart, eds., *The "Man" Question*, 28–53; Charlotte Hooper, *Manly States: Masculinities, International Relations, and Gender Politics* (New York: Columbia University Press, 2001); Joshua Goldstein, *War and Gender*.

91. See, e.g., Paul Higate, "Drinking Vodka from the 'Butt Crack': Men, Masculinities, and Fratriarchy in the Private Militarized Security Company," *International Feminist Journal of Politics* (2012), 14(4): 450–469, where Higate suggests that norm-bound, homoerotic practices seal the complexities of militarized masculinities to make war *for men* embodied, contradictory, sexualized, and racialized. See also Aaron Belkin, *Bring Men Men: Militarized Masculinity and the Benign Façade of American Empire, 1898–2001* (New York: Columbia University Press, 2011), discussing the use of homosocial behavior to define straight, hegemonically masculine militarism.

92. Raewyn Connell, "Preface," in *Rethinking the Man Question: Sex, Gender, and Violence in International Relations*, ed. Marysia Zalewski and Jane L. Parpart (London: Zed, 2008), viii–xv, xii.

93. Zalewski and Parpart, eds., *The "Man" Question*, 2.

94. Ibid., 3, citing Mona Lloyd, *Judith Butler* (Cambridge: Polity, 2007), 8. See, for example, Maria O'Relly, "Muscular Interventionism: Gender, Power, and Liberal Peacebuilding in Post-Conflict Bosnia-Herzegovina," *International Feminist Journal of Politics* (2012), 14(4): 529–548. O'Reilly shows that gendered portrayals of Paddy Ashdown's masculinities are implicated in the salience of discources of the responsibility to protect (R2P), which constitute and are constituted by the OHR (the Office of the High Representative), one of the key post-conflict institutions in structuring and imposing liberal norms. There, sex and gender are implicated in one another—and both are implicated in the political shape of post-conflict Bosnia–Herzgovina.

95. See, e.g., the discusssion of the tensions between expecations of masculinity in military service and the policy needs of the communty being served in Marianne Bevan and Megan MacKenzie, "'Cowboy' Policing Versus 'the Softer Stuff': Masculinities and Peacekeeping," *International Feminist Journal of Politics* (2012), 14(4): 508–528. Bevan and MacKenzie study the New Zealand Community Policing Program in East Timor, observing that militarized masculinities persist despire the situational inappropriateness. The authors also observe that expectations of men in conflicts (and therefore militarized masculinities) are not singular, but multiple, complex, and miltidimensional, empirically and normatively.

96. Hooper, *Manly States*, 230–231.

97. Cynthia Enloe, *The Morning After: Sexual Politics at the End of the Cold War* (Berkeley: University of California Press, 1993), 25.

98. Ibid., 56.

99. Ibid., 73. See, for example, Ruth Streicher (in "Fashioning the Gentlemanly State: The Curious Charm of the Miltiary Uniform in Southern Thailand," *International Feminist Journal of Politics* [2012], 14[4]: 470–488), arguing that the performative function of the military uniform is to demarcate civilized (and therefore acceptable) violence in Southern Thailand, making militarized masculinity a function of the gentlemanly state, mediated by dress and appearance.

100. Goldstein, *War and Gender*.

101. Terrell Carver suggests that, in this way, militarized masculinity produces and makes palatable "a sanitized representation of legitimated (and sometimes illegitimated) violence" (Aaron Belkin in Conversation with Terrell Carver, "Militarized Masculinities and the Erasure of Violence," *International Feminist Journal of Politics* [2012], 14[4]: 558–567, 559). Carver argues that "the stereotypical version of militarized maxulinities 'approved for release' either erases real violence altogether or tames and sanitizes it through symbolism" (561).

102. Judith Gardam, *Non-Combatant Immunity as a Norm of International Humanitarian Law* (Amsterdam: Martinus Nijhoff, 1993), 348.

103. Craig Murphy, "Six Masculine Roles in International Relations and Their Interconnection: A Personal Investigation," in Zalewski and Parpart, *The Man Question*, 95–99; Hooper, "Masculinist Practices and Gender Politics."

104. Jill Steans, *Gender and International Relations: An Introduction* (New Brunswick, NJ: Rutgers University Press, 1998), 81. Luisa Maria Dietrich Ortega suggests (in "Looking Beyond Violent Militarized Masculinities: Guerilla Gender Regimes in Latin America," *International Feminist Journal of Politics* (2012), 14(4): 489–507) that, rather than a violent, virile version of militarized masculinity, a number of different gender tropes pervade insurgent groups in Peru, Colombia, and El Salvador, where gender relations are reflected on and carefully managed. I agree that militarized masculinities are multiple (a point also made by Bevan and MacKenzie in "'Cowboy' Policing"), and that the essence of the relationship between gender and militarism is in the control of gender relations and gender roles. I also see, however, that the dominant method of the control of gender roles in state militaries remains the link Steans discusses between masculinity, virility, and violence.

105. Ibid., 81.

106. Judith Stiehm, ed., *Women and Men's Wars* (Oxford: Pergamon, 1983), 367. See also O'Reilly, "Muscular Interventionism."

107. R. W. Connell, *Masculinities* (Berkeley: University of California Press, 1995), 214.

108. Goldstein, *War and Gender*, 64.

109. Judith Halberstam, *Female Masculinity* (Durham and London: Duke University Press, 1998), 2.

110. Goldstein, *War and Gender*, 272.

111. For example, Belkin (in *Bring Me Men*) suggests that one of the major constraints is a very internally contradictory set of governing rules about sexuality in militarized masculinities.

112. Connell, *Masculinities*. See also Melissa T. Brown, *Enlisting Masculinity: The Construction of Gender in US Military Recruiting in an All-Volunteer Force* (New York: Oxford University Press. Brown suggests that gender expectations about male (and female) recruits can be read through military recruitment materials.

113. As Maya Eichler (in *Militarizing Men: Gender, Conscription, and War in Post-Soviet Russia* [Palo Alto: Stanford University Press, 2012]) suggests, these expecations get even more complicated when the wars men are asked to fight in are unpopular or even losing, where even brave veterans can be emasculated based on popular derogatory war narratives.

114. Sandra Whitworth, "Militarized Masculinity and Post Traumatic Stress Disorder," in Zalewski and Parpart, eds., *Rethinking the Man Question*, 109–126.

115. Ibid.

116. Barbara Ehrenreich, *Blood Rites: Origins and History of the Passions of War* (New York: Henry Holt, 1997), 10.

117. Whitworth, "Militarized Masculinity and Post Traumatic Stress Disorder."

118. See, for example, Lesley Gill, "Creating Citizens, Making Men: The Military and Masculinity in Bolivia," *Cultural Anthropology* (1997), 12(4): 527–550.

119. Whitworth, "Militarized Masculinity and Post Traumatic Stress Disorder.

120. See, e.g., Goldstein, *War and Gender.*

121. For example, Enloe, *Nimo's War, Emma's War.*

122. Sylvester, "War, Sense, and Security"; Sylvester, ed., *Experiencing War*; Enloe, *Nimo's War, Emma's War.*

123. Enloe, *Nimo's War, Emma's War,* ix.

124. Hanne Marlene Dahl, "A Perceptive and Reflective State?" *European Journal of Women's Studies* (2000), 7(4): 475–494, 477.

125. Fiona Robinson, *Globalizing Care: Ethics, Feminist Theory, and International Relations* (Boulder: Westview, 1999), 31.

126. An idea that comes from Joan C. Tronto, *Moral Boundaries: A Political Argument for an Ethic of Care* (New York: Psychology Press, 1993).

127. June Lennie, "Deconstructing Gendered Power Relations in Participatory Planning: Towards an Empowering Feminist Framework of Participation and Action," *Women's Studies International Forum* (1999), 22(1), 107.

128. Christine Sylvester, *Feminist Theory and International Relations in a Postmodern Era* (Cambridge: Cambridge University Press, 1994), 96; Jill Bystudzienski, ed., *Women Transforming Politics: Worldwide Strategies for Empowerment* (Bloomington, IN: Indiana University Press, 1992).

129. Sylvester, *Feminist Theory and International Relations in a Postmodern Era.*

130. Sara Ruddick, *Maternal Thinking: Towards a Politics of Peace* (New York: Houghton-Mifflin, 1989), 239; Hannah Arendt, *On Violence* (New York: Harvest, 1970).

131. Beth Hartung, Jane C. Ollenburger, Helen A. Moore, and Mary Jo Deegan, "Empowering a Feminist Ethic for Social Science Research: The Nebraska Sociological Feminist Collective," in *A Feminist Ethic for Social Science Research*, Nebraska Sociological Feminist Collective (Lewiston, ME: Edwin Mellen, 1988).

132. J. Ann Tickner, *Gender in International Relations: Feminist Perspectives on Achieving Global Security* (New York: Columbia University Press, 1992).

133. J. Ann Tickner, *Gendering World Politics* (New York: Columbia University Press, 2001).

134. Jack Levy and William Thompson, *Causes of War* (Oxford: Wiley, 2010), 10, 5, 7, 8.

135. Laura Sjoberg, "Introduction to *Security Studies:* Feminist Contributions," *Security Studies* (2009), 18(2): 183–213.

136. Jill Steans, *Gender and International Relations*, 128–129.

137. Tickner, *Gendering World Politics.*

138. Julie Stone Peters and Andrea Wolper, eds., *Women's Rights, Human Rights: International Feminist Perspectives* (New York: Psychology Press, 1995).

139. Tickner, *Gendering World Politics*; Eric M. Blanchard, "Gender, International Relations, and the Development of Feminist Security Theory," *Signs: Journal of Women in Culture and Society* (2003), 28(4): 1289–1310. For a broader view on structural violence through gender lenses, see Mary K. Anglin, "Feminist Perspectives on Structural Violence," *Identities: Global Studies in Culture and Power* (1998), 5(2): 145–151.

140. Tickner, *Gender in International Relations*; Tickner, *Gendering World Politics*.

141. For example, discussion in Erhard Berner, "Opportunities and Insecurities: Globalisation, Localities, and the Struggle for Urban Land in Manila," *European Journal of Development Research* (1997), 9(1): 167–182, though my use of this example comes from my experience with the (now-defunct) Coalition to Protect Public Housing in Chicago, IL, in 2000–2001.

142. See discussion in Cynthia Enloe, *Maneuvers: The International Politics of Militarizing Women's Lives* (Berkeley: University of California Press, 2000).

143. See discussion in Michele Chwastiak, "Rendering Death and Destruction Invisible: Counting the Costs of War," *Critical Perspectives on Accounting* (2008), 19(5): 573–590.

144. Chris Cuomo, "War Is Not Just an Event," 31; Betty Reardon, *Sexism and the War System* (New York: Teachers College Press, 1985).

145. Barry Buzan, *People, States, and Fear: The National Security Problem in International Relations* (New York: Wheatsheaf, 1983). See also chapter 2, notes 285, 295, and 296. It is important to note that the choice to securitize these issues is itself both political and controversial.

146. Cuomo, "War Is Not Just an Event."

147. Ibid., 31.

148. Ibid., 30.

149. For example, Sam F. Ghattas, "U. N. Identifies 5 Pro-Syrian Suspects in Lebanese Leader's Assassination," *Milwaukee Journal-Sentinel* 31 August 2005; http://news.google.com/newspapers?id=20UuAAAAIBAJ&sjid=x44EAAAAIBAJ&pg=6677,9334169&dq=leader+assassination&hl=en (accessed 4 May 2012).

150. For example, Christine Hauser and Anahad O'Connor, "Virginia Tech Shooting Leaves 33 Dead," *New York Times* 16 April 2007; http://www.nytimes.com/2007/04/16/us/16cnd-shooting.html (accessed 4 May 2012).

151. For example, discussion of the Israeli reaction to Palestinian flotillas, for example, Edmund Sanders, "Netanyahu Ignores Calls for Investigation of Raid," *Los Angeles Times* 3 June 2010; http://articles.latimes.com/2010/jun/03/world/la-fg-israel-raid-20100603 (accessed 4 May 2012).

152. Betty Reardon, *Sexism and the War System*. This claim is not to be read as a claim that all violence on the continuum is *equally bad*, but only as a claim that *there are no clear delineating points between events of violence* because violence is a continuum, not a series of unrelated, discrete events.

153. Stories in this and the last paragraph are intentionally not descriptive of any particular individual and therefore not attributed.

154. Cuomo, "War Is Not Just an Event," 34.

155. Reardon, *Sexism and the War System*.

156. A number of conflicts have been described by historians in these terms, e.g., the Russian Revolution (Peter Holquist, *Making War: Forging Revolution: Russia's Continuum of Crisis, 1914–1929* [Cambridge: Harvard University Press, 2002]); the two world wars (E. H. Carr, *The Twenty Years' Crisis, 1919–1939*, new edition with introduction by Michael Cox [New York: Palgrave MacMillan, (1939) 2001]).

157. Hooper, "Masculinist Practices and Gender Politics."

158. For example, Peterson, "Nationalism as Heterosexism"; Meghana Nayak "Orientalism and 'Saving' US State Identity after 9/11," *International Feminist Journal of Politics* (2005), 8(1): 42–61; Melanie Richter-Montpetit, "Empire, Desire, and Violence: A Queer Transnational Feminist Reading of the Prisoner 'Abuse' in Abu Ghraib and the Question of 'Gender Equality,'" *International Feminist Journal of Politics* (2007), 9(1): 38–59.

159. Enloe, *Does Khaki Become You?*

160. Cuomo, "War Is Not Just an Event," 31.

161. Carol Cohn and Sara Ruddick, "A Feminist Ethical Perspective on Weapons of Mass Destruction," in *Ethics and Weapons of Mass Destruction: Religious and Secular Perspectives*, ed. Sohail H. Hashmi and Steven P. Lee (Cambridge: Cambridge University Press, 2004), 405–435.

162. Ibid., 410.

163. Carol Cohn, "Introduction," *Women and Wars*, ed. Carol Cohn (London: Polity, 2012).

164. Ibid.

165. Ibid., citing Cynthia Cockburn, *The Space Between Us: Negotiating Gender and National Identities in Conflict* (London: Zed, 1998), 8.

166. Ibid. In Cohn and Ruddick's words (in "A Feminist Ethical Perspective on Weapons of Mass Destruction," 411): "Practically, feminists see war as neither beginning with the first gunfire, nor ending when the treaties are signed. Before the first gunfire is the research, development and deployment of weapons; the maintaining of standing armies; the cultural glorification of the power of armed force; and the social construction of masculinities and femininities which support a militarized state."

CONCLUSION

1. Anne Sisson Runyan ("Resisting the Inside Job: Rethinking Feminist IR Divisions of Labor." Presented at the 2012 Annual Meeting of the International Studies Association, 30 March 2012, in San Diego, California) argues that the distinction between feminist security studies (FSS) and work in political economy, while it served a purpose, is in the end counterproductive because it makes the security and economic spheres appear separable when they really overlap significantly. Though it does not go so far as to use the marriage of biopolitics and necropolitics, this effort at feminist war theorizing has attempted to do just that, by recognizing the political economy dimensions and implications of war(s).

2. As argued in the introduction.

3. I use the term *research program* differently than Robert Keohane did when (in "International Institutions: Two Approaches," *International Studies Quarterly* [1988], 32[4]: 379–396, and "International Relations Theory: Contributions of a Feminist

Standpoint," *Millennium: Journal of International Studies* [1989], 18[3]: 245–253) he equated having a research program with hypothesis-testing. Instead, in the spirit that I have used it throughout this book in concluding each chapter (and in the spirit that J. Ann Tickner used it in "What Is Your Research Program? Some Feminist Answers to International Relations Methodological Questions," *International Studies Quarterly* [2005], 49[1]: 1–22), to mean research program broadly, encompassing causal, constitutive, and significatory analysis.

4. See concerns of J. Ann Tickner (most recently in "You May Never Understand: Prospects for Feminist Futures in International Relations," *Australian Feminist Law Journal* [2010], 23: 9–20) and Sarah Brown ("Feminism, International Theory, and the International Relations of Gender Inequality," *Millennium: Journal of International Studies* 17[3]: 461–475).

5. Mary Caprioli, "Feminist IR Theory and Quantitative Methodology: A Critical Analysis," *International Studies Review* (2004), 6(2): 253–269.

6. Caprioli, "Feminist IR Theory and Quantitative Methodology," citing Fred Halliday, "Hidden from International Relations: Women and the International Arena," *Millennium: Journal of International Studies* (1988), 17(3): 419–428.

7. Halliday, "Hidden from International Relations," 426, 427.

8. Craig Murphy, "Seeing Women, Recognizing Gender, Recasting International Relations," *International Organization* (1996), 50(3): 513–538, 536.

9. Brown, "Feminism, International Theory, and International Relations of Gender Inequality."

10. Ibid.

11. Christine Sylvester, "Empathic Cooperation: A Feminist Method for IR," *Millennium: Journal of International Studies* (1994), 23(2): 315–334, 316.

12. Marysia Zalewski, "Do We Understand Each Other Yet? Troubling Feminist Encounters With(In) International Relations," *British Journal of Politics and International Relations* (2007), 9: 302–312, 302.

13. Emily S. Rosenberg, "Gender," *Journal of American History* (1990), 116–124, cited in J. Ann Tickner, "You Just Don't Understand: Troubled Engagements Between Feminists and IR Theorists," *International Studies Quarterly* (1997), 41: 611–632, 620.

14. Annick Wibben, *Feminist Security Studies: A Narrative Approach* (London: Routledge, 2011), 113.

15. Ibid., 113–114.

16. Ibid., 114.

17. Ibid., 112.

18. Ibid., 113.

19. The question of "subfield of what," of course, matters. See Carol Cohn, "'Feminist Security Studies': Toward a Reflective Practice," *Politics and Gender* (2011), 7(4): 581–586, part of "Feminist Security Studies: State of the Art," a Critical Perspectives Section, ed. Laura Sjoberg and Jennifer Lobasz, *Politics and Gender* (2011), 7(4): 573–604.

20. Ibid.

21. There has been some talk about "occupying," as in IR theory, both as a substantive critique (e.g., http://occupyirtheory.info/) and as method "trying to broaden the political debate and discussion, . . . to create incongruity in the predominant understandings of society . . . [and] introduce a more complex set of issues into our political debate" (David Cisneros, "Occupy Wall Street: Considering Some of the Criticisms," 14 October 2011 (http://www.thepermutation.com/home/22-blog-post/50-occupy-wall-street-considering-some-of-the-criticisms [accessed 4 November 2012]). Christian Chessman and I consider this as method for International Relations theorizing in a recent paper, "The Biopower of Occupation: Insights for 'Knowledge Exchange' in (Gender and) IR," presented at the "Critical Reflections on the Researcher-Practitioner Relationship" conference on the Gender and Global Governance Net-work, November 17–19, 2012.

22. Wibben, *Feminist Security Studies*, 65–66.

23. Ibid., 106.

24. Betty Reardon, *Sexism and the War System* (New York: Teacher's College).

25. I have found chapter 2 of Laura Shepherd's *Gender, Violence, and Security* (London: Zed, 2008) very informative on this point, as it puts forward six critiques of the study of national security and six critiques of the study of international security.

26. Jeanne Vickers, *Women and War* (London: Zed, 1993).

27. Laura Sjoberg, "Gender, the State, and War Redux: Feminist International Relations Across the 'Levels of Analysis'," *International Relations* (2011), 25(1): 108–134.

28. J. Ann Tickner, *Gender in International Relations* (New York: Columbia University Press, 1992), 45.

29. Ibid.

30. Rebecca Grant, "Sources of Gender Bias in International Relations Theory," in *Gender and International Relations*, ed. Rebecca Geant and Kathleen Newland (Bloomington, IN: Indiana University Press, 1991), 8–26, 17.

31. Tickner, *Gender in International Relations*, 57.

32. Christine Sylvester, *Feminist International Relations in the Postmodern Era* (Cambridge: Cambridge University Press, 1994), 113.

33. Jacqui True, "Feminism," in *Theories of International Relations*, ed. Scott Burchill and Andrew Linklater (London: MacMillan, 1996), 227.

34. Kenneth Waltz, *Man, the State, and War* (New York: Columbia University Press, 1959).

35. True, "Feminism," 229.

36. Jill Steans, *Gender and International Relations: An Introduction* (New Brunswick, NJ: Rutgers University Press, 1998) 6.

37. Francine D'Amico and Peter Beckman, *Women in World Politics* (Westport, CT: Bergin and Garvey, 1994), 5.

38. Cynthia Enloe, *The Curious Feminist* (Berkeley: University of California Press, 2004) 6.

39. Kenneth Waltz, *Theory of International Politics* (New York: Columbia University Press, 1979), 89.

40. Joan Acker, "Hierarchies, Jobs, Bodies: A Theory of Gendered Organizations," *Gender and Society* (1990), (4)2: 146–147.

41. For example, Valerie M. Hudson, Mary Caprioli, Bonnie Ballif-Spanvill, Rose McDermott, and Chad F. Emmett, "The Heart of the Matter: The Security of Women and the Security of States," *International Security* (2009), 33(3): 7–45.

42. R. W. Connell, *Masculinities* (Berkeley: University of California Press, 1995), 73.

43. Sylvester, *Feminist International Relations in a Postmodern Era*, 34.

44. For example, V. Spike Peterson, ed. *Gendered States: Feminist (Re)Visions of International Relations Theory* (Boulder: Westview, 1992).

45. Carole Pateman, *The Sexual Contract* (Palo Alto, CA: Stanford University Press, 1988).

46. J. Ann Tickner, "Feminism Meets International Relations: Some Methodological Issues," in *Feminist Methodologies for International Relations*, ed. Brooke Ackerly, Maria Stern, and Jacqui True (Cambridge: Cambridge University Press, 2006), 19–41, 39–40.

47. Spike Peterson and Anne Sisson Runyan, *Global Gender Issues* (Boulder: Westview, 1993), 258.

48. Cynthia Enloe, *The Morning After: Sexual Politics at the End of the Cold War* (Berkeley: University of California Press, 1993). Instead, Enloe argued that "militarization occurs because some people's fears are allowed to be heard, while other people's fears are trivialized and silenced" (246). See also Peterson and Runyan, *Global Gender Issues*, 118.

49. J. Ann Tickner, *Gendering World Politics* (New York: Columbia University Press, 2001), 57; Joshua Goldstein (in *War and Gender: How Gender Shapes the War System and Vice Versa* [Cambridge: Cambridge University Press, 2001]); for elaborations, see Meghana Nayak and Jennier Suchland, "Gender Violence and Hegemonic Projects," *International Feminist Journal of Politics* (2006), 8(4): 467–485; J. Ann Tickner, "Feminist Responses to International Security Studies," *Peace Review* (2004), 16(1): 43–48; Cynthia Enloe, *Does Khaki Become You? The Militarization of Women's Lives* (London: Pandora, 1989).

50. Cynthia Enloe, *Bananas, Beaches, and Bases* (Berkeley: University of California Press, 2000) 204.

51. Laura Sjoberg, *Gender, Justice, and the Wars in Iraq* (New York: Lexington, 2006); Enloe, *Does Khaki Become You?*. Goldstein (in *War and Gender*) points out that this system is oppressive of *both* sexes; men need to be convinced of the need to protect women to compel them to fight and risk death, and women are subordinated as passive potential victims in need of protection.

52. Lauren Wilcox, "Gendering the Cult of the Offensive," *Security Studies* (2009), 18(2): 214–240, 233.

53. Anne McClintock, "Family Feuds, Gender, Nationalism, and the Family," *Feminist Review* (1993), 44: 61–80, 62.

54. Carol A. Stabile and Deepa Kumar, "Unveiling Imperialism: Media, Gender, and War in Afghanistan," *Media, Culture, and Society* (2005), 27(5): 765–782; Krista

Hunt, "The Strategic Co-optation of Women's Rights: Discourse in the 'War on Terrorism,'" *International Feminist Journal of Politics* (2002), 4(1): 116–121.

55. Laura Sjoberg and Caron Gentry, *Mothers, Monsters, Whores: Women's Violence in Global Politics* (London: Zed, 2007).

56. Marysia Zalewski, "Well, What Is the Feminist Perspective on Bosnia?" *International Affairs* (1995), 71(2): 339–356.

57. Ibid.; Tickner, *Gender in International Relations*.

58. Enloe, *The Morning After*.

59. Jean Elshtain, *Women and War* (Brighton, MA: Harvester, 1987), 6.

60. Nira Yuval-Davis, *Gender and Nation* (London: Sage, 1997).

61. Nancy Huston, "Tales of War and Tears of Women," *Women's Studies International Forum* (1982), 5(3/4): 271–282.

62. Tickner, *Gendering World Politics*; Laura Sjoberg, "Why Just War Needs Feminism Now More than Ever," *International Politics* (2008), 45(1): 1–18; Helen Kinsella, "Securing the Civilian: Sex and Gender in the Laws of War," in *Power in Global Governance*, ed. Michael Barnett and Raymond Duvall (Cambridge: Cambridge University Press, 2005), 249–272.

63. Tickner, *Gender in International Relations*, 42.

64. Ibid.

65. See, e.g., Richard K. Ashley, "Untying the Sovereign State: A Double Reading of the Anarchy Problematique," *Millennium: Journal of International Studies* (1988), 17(2): 227–262; Thomas Biersteker and Cynthia Weber, *State Sovereignty as a Social Construct* (Cambridge: Cambridge University Press, 1996). See also Tickner, *Gendering World Politics*, 21.

66. Sjoberg, *Gender, Justice, and the Wars in Iraq*, 65–66.

67. Eric Blanchard, "Gender, International Relations, and the Development of Feminist Security Theory," *Signs: Journal of Women in Culture and Society* (2003), 28(3): 1289–1313.

68. See, e.g., Vickers, *Women and War*; the particulars of this argument can be found in many other feminist works, but are left out here for reasons of space. Others have argued that states' war victories come at the expense of their lower classes or racial minorities as well.

69. For a feminist critique, see, e.g., Louise M. Antony and Charlotte Witt, *A Mind of One's Own: Feminist Essays on Reason and Objectivity*, 2nd ed. (Boulder: Westview, 2001).

70. See, e.g., Linda Basch, "Human Security, Globalization, and Feminist Visions," *Peace Review* (2004), 16(1) : 5–12; Heidi Hudson, "'Doing' Security as though Humans Matter: A Feminist Perspective on Gender and the Politics of Human Security," *Security Dialogue* (2005), 36(2): 155–174; Georgina Waylen, "Gender, Feminism, and Political Economy," *New Political Economy* (1997), 2(2): 205–220.

71. See J. Ann Tickner, "Hans Morgenthau's Principles of Political Realism: A Feminist Reformulation," *Millennium: Journal of International Studies* (1988), 17(3): 429–440.

72. See Sjoberg and Gentry, *Mothers, Monsters, Whores*.

73. See Cynthia Enloe, *Maneuvers: The International Politics of Militarizing Women's Lives* (Berkeley: University of California Press, 2000).

74. Tickner, "Hans Morgenthau's Principles of Political Realism," 67.

75. Tickner, *Gender in International Relations*, 37. Christine Sylvester (in *Feminist Theory and International Relations in a Postmodern Era*, 81), argued that gendered views of human nature can be found in the philosophical foundations of modern IR theory as well, whether it be in Hobbes' assignment of state of nature roles on the basis of gender or Machiavelli's writings on women ruining polities.

76. Brown, "Feminism, International Theory, and International Relations of Gender Inequality," 462.

77. Tickner, *Gender in International Relations*, 43.

78. This argument was best articulated by Daniel Byman and Kenneth Pollack, in "Let Us Now Praise Great Men: Bring the Statesman Back In," *International Security* (2000), 25(4): 107–146.

79. Sjoberg and Gentry, *Mothers, Monsters, Whores*, 199–200.

80. Tickner, *Gender in International Relations*.

81. Katharine Moon, *Sex Among Allies: Military Prostitution in US-Korea Relations* (New York: Columbia University Press, 1997).

82. Enloe, *Does Khaki Become You?*, 196.

83. R. W. Connell, "The State, Gender, and Sexual Politics: Theory and Appraisal," *Theory and Society* (1990), 41: 507–544; Tickner, *Gendering World Politics*, 54.

84. Ackerly, Stern, and True, eds. *Feminist Methods For International Relations*

85. Wibben, *Feminist Security Studies*, 113.

86. For example, Ackerly, Stern, and True, eds. *Feminist Methods For International Relations*; Tickner, "So What Is Your Research Program?"

87. Hayward Alker, *Rediscoveries and Reformulations: Humanistic Methodologies for International Studies* (Cambridge: Cambridge University Press, 1996).

88. Stephen White, *Sustaining Affirmation: The Strength of Weak Ontology in Political Theory* (Princeton: Princeton University Press, 2001).

89. White, *Sustaining Affirmation*, 30.

90. Sjoberg, *Gender, Justice, and the Wars in Iraq*, 104.

91. Robin May Schott, "Just War and the Problem of Evil, *Hypatia* (2008), 28(2), 122–140, 133.

92. Ibid.

93. Schott, "Just War"

Index

209–210, 216, 221, 222, 223, 224, 230, 233, 235–238, 246, 247, 258, 259, 260, 262, 281, 379n85; *see also* prostitution; rape
Booth, Ken, 36, 37, 330n268, 331n276, 331n277, 332n289, 392n124
Bosnia, 64, 203–204, 219, 429n94
Bougainville Crisis, 96, 97
boundaries, 126; among the levels of analysis, 302n9; national, 145; public/private, 288; self/other, 180, 370n148; of war theorizing, 130, 184, 279; *see also* liminality; public/private divide
Boyer, Mark, 306n30, 361n14, 373n10
Bremer, Stuart, 317n89, 360n10
Britain. *see* United Kingdom
Brock-Utne, Brigit, 62
Brown, Melissa, 171, 375n24
Brown, Sarah, 57, 281
Brown, Wendy, 350n53
Bueno de Mesquita, Bruce, 319n116, 320n128
Bush, G. W., 150, 151, 152, 163, 240, 371n174, 381n137
Bush, G. H. W., 86
Bush, Laura, 139
Butler, Judith, 253, 307n43, 350n53, 367n197, 370n159
Buzan, Barry, 302n9, 318n102, 332n295
Byman, Daniel, 28–29, 170, 438n77

Cambodia, 251, 423n13; *see also* Khmer Rouge
Canada 86, 149, 381n134
capitalism: capitalist states, 23, 26; as a cause of war, 26; and gender emancipation, 50, 338n48; and gender subordination, 338n48, 357n170; and gendered militarization, 143; as harmful, 363n39; shared, 9; and war economies, 262; *see also* capitalist peace; Marxism, trade

capitalist peace, 23, 107, 112, 317n93, 318n100, 262n39
Caprioli, Mary, 280, 281, 282, 304n17, 306n30, 336n19, 342n95, 347n164, 353n90, 361n14, 363n41, 373n10, 436n40
Card, Claudia, 400n61, 422n186
care, 95, 111, 215, 269; among states, 132; care ethic, 108, 132, 269; care labor, 171, 190, 230, 273; feminized, 171; global, 132; in policy-making, 108; as strategy, 191, 192; *see also* empathy; health; labor; solidarity; work
Carpenter, R. Charli,304n18, 335n6, 336n18, 336n24, 397n21, 422n186, 427n81
Carr, E. H., 18
Carter, Jimmy, 101
Carver, Terrell, 429n101
causal analysis, 36, 38, 41, 65, 66, 130–131, 168, 169, 170, 186, 195, 205, 214, 216, 252, 286, 295, 305n20, 308n38, 310n4, 351n66, 434n3; of sex inequality and war, 135, 138–139; *see also* constitutive analysis; correlation; epistemology; method
Cederman, Lars-Erik 24, 320n120
center of gravity, 200, 202, 215, 218, 221
Charlesworth, Hilary, 181, 350n50, 420n160
Chechnya, 92, 97, 220, 292, 342n100, 356n142, 410n20
Cheng, Jack, 241
China, 92, 219, 234, 312n34, 356n142
chivalry, 82, 87, 88, 89, 90, 101, 264, 354n121; as a motive for war, 101; and the immunity principle, 198; leaders' 158; and tactics, 229; *see also* "beautiful soul"; "just warrior"; masculinity
Chontosh, Brian, 185–186

military (*continued*)
leadership 34, 35, 161, 226, 228, 233, 322n154; movement 11, 35, 110, 244, 296; power 20, 23, 93; recruiting 172; security 36, 37, 111, 132, 268, 311n11; United States 90, 168, 185, 208, 228, 235, 240, 250; U.S. Air Force 227, 250–251; U.S. Army 7, 250, 257; U.S. Navy 106; use of force 18, 32, 36, 146, 188, 270, 273; women in 171, 210, 211, 233, 235, 236, 262, 263;*see also* arms races, logistics; power; private military and security companies; soldiering; strategy; tactics; technology
militarism, 12, 65, 96, 134, 145, 146, 150, 155, 171, 188, 191, 207, 237, 255, 264, 265, 271, 274; cultures of, 23; gendered, 63, 66, 142–145, 147, 149, 199, 241, 275, 291, 292
militarization, 64, 96, 97, 148, 151, 159, 161, 167, 171–172, 197, 212, 238, 245, 255, 257, 258, 269, 311n10; news stories 6; *see also* military; soldiering; strategic culture
Militarized Interstate Disputes (MID) Dataset, 317n84, 359n197, 374n18
Millet, Kate, 307n40
Missiles, 120, 227
Mongolia, 384n3
Monism, 339n65; *see also* dualism; epistemology; method
Moon, Katherine, 165, 168, 361n21, 422n186
Morgenthau, Hans, 18, 305n20
motherhood, 166, 230, 249, 266, 273; of bombs, 227; in feminisms, 342n97; motherland, 145, 153; and peace, 61, 62, 343n111; of robots, 211, 407n150; soldiers', 211, 250; of states, 113, 114; *see also* preganancy
Mumford, Lewis, 1
Myanmar, 384n3

Narizny, Kevin, 309n62, 323n160
narratives, 12, 41, 50, 127, 145, 149, 167, 198, 230, 266; feminist, 55, 340n70; foreign policy, 124, 150, 165; gendered, 104, 115, 119, 120, 121, 130, 138, 139, 140, 150, 151, 153, 154, 155, 168, 173, 197, 198, 238, 248, 266, 399n47, 412n46; metanarratives, 39; as method, 66, 339n63; rape of Belgium, 87–88; research, 300; security, 104, 144, 285; universalist, 53; of wars, 55, 57, 65, 115, 119, 120, 132, 138, 139, 140, 141, 145, 151, 155, 168, 169, 170, 173, 182, 197, 198, 199, 200, 238, 253, 277, 284, 292, 295, 367n98, 399n47, 430n113; *see also* argument; disidentification; method; signification
nationalism, 86, 135, 139, 155, 166, 197, 304n15; Canadian, 86; in constructivist International Relations, 2; in domestic politics accounts of war, 26; gendered ,9, 11, 77, 86, 88, 89, 138, 139, 140, 142–150, 154, 155, 163, 171, 186, 198, 205, 209, 212, 215, 222, 223, 242, 285, 291, 292, 296, 376n41, 378n83; hypermasculine, 100; *see also* militarism; strategic culture
Nauru, 384n3
Nayak, Meghana, 213, 433n158, 436n48
Nelson, Julie, 190, 366n78
networks, social, 206, 256, 425n36
"new wars", 17, 311n17
New Zealand, 404n127, 421n176, 429n95
Nicaragua, 384n3, 425n42
Nigeria, 384n3
Nobel Peace Prize, 389n85
Norris, Pippa, 336n19, 353n90, 373n10, 373n14
Nussbaum, Martha, 37